the **complete** book of
# fishing

# the **complete** book of
# *fishing*

**TACKLE**
**TECHNIQUES**
**SPECIES**
**BAIT**

John **Wilson**

Arthur **Oglesby**

Trevor **Housby**

Mike **Millman**

Peter **Gathercole**

**hamlyn**

First published in Great Britain in 1987 by Hamlyn an
imprint of Reed Consumer Books Limited Michelin
House, 81 Fulham Road, London SW3 6RB and
Auckland, Melbourne, Singapore and Toronto

Reprinted 1989, 1990, 1993, 1995
Revised and updated 1997

Copyright © Bookbourne Limited 1997
The Old Farmhouse
Newton
Sleaford
Lincs NG34 OD1

ISBN 0 600 59210 3

Produced by Mandarin Offset

Printed in China

# FOREWORD

It has been estimated that published fishing books outnumber the total printed on all other sports combined. This I can certainly believe. I have read literally thousands of books on fishing and written no less than eighteen myself. A few decades ago it was possible in any given year for me to fish in half-a-dozen countries (some of which no longer exist!), write a monthly fishing column for *Field & Stream* magazine, write all or most of a new fishing book, and still find time to read almost everything on the subject published in English.

Those days are gone forever. The exponential curve of population growth has produced a geometric progression of fishing authors. Nowadays, to keep up would require a speed-read addict functioning in a haze of amphetamines, as few volumes cover every discipline of angling.

To what source, then, can the beginner turn if he wants to learn about modern angling techniques as they are practised today? Somewhere within *The Complete Book of Fishing* almost every reader will find those words or pictures that will set him on the right path, whether it is in the aesthetically elegant practice of fly fishing, or the physically demanding sport of big-game fishing. In these pages even most veteran anglers will learn than there are new ramifications of the art that they have not yet explored. To the extent that any body of knowledge can ever be 'complete', this volume is indeed the ultimate modern work of reference, worthy of every angler's bookshelf.

A. J. McCLANE

# CONTENTS

# INTRODUCTION

One picture is *not* worth a thousand words: a bad picture is worthless and a thousand ill-chosen words are stupefying. With *The Complete Book of Fishing* you hold in your hands an outstanding example of state-of-the-craft communication for pedagogical means, the very latest in teaching techniques. Its function is to present in vivid and succinct form the way Anglo-Saxons fish for sport. Other breeds with other laws may be absolutely whiz-bang at skiing, scuba-diving, kick-fighting and hockey, but all the world follows the English-speaking folk when angling.

Logically, an English-derived behavioural set should be irrelevant to Japanese, but they are dedicated fly-fishermen, or to Spanish-speaking peoples, though they have made a cult of wingshooting. But logic has little to do with it. Perhaps cultural acquisitions are controlled by the pineal glands of men and women. The pineal is the ductless gland that sits in your brain (presumably for a reason) and performs functions utterly unknown to our sciences. If this book fails to make your ductless glands oozy, perhaps you should try billiards.

Permit me, as one who has been there, to tell you how to read the five sections of the text that follows.

## TACKLE

*Homo ludens*, the player, must be preceded by *Homo faber*, the maker. Every sport needs its tools, and TACKLE is the tools of fishing. There are 22 chapters specific to every aspect of this nice stuff. Since this is a reference work, devoted to scope rather than detail, you can follow up any element of TACKLE that intrigues you. Whole books for instance, and quite a few of them, have been devoted to hooks, the very essence of angling. Read or scan through this chapter, then go back and dwell on whatever has twigged your fancy, which will change with time, because *you* do.

## BAIT

The efficacy of baiting your angle with something that smells like animal protein is indisputable, yet artificial lures are a growth industry which attracts Harvard MBA's and London School of Economics graduates. Some manufacturers in this field rarely fish, on the same grounds that criminal lawyers seldom commit crimes: their interest in the subject is largely satisfied by making money off those who do. The Wisdom of the Ages is to begin fishing BAIT to learn the ways of fishes, move on to artificial lures such as spoons and spinners and plugs, and then attempt fly-fishing (but only if you have a true vocation, and aren't some sort of nasty little *arriviste* given to puttin' on airs).

## FISH SPECIES

In this section you will find 26 chapters covering more than 60 popular sport fishes, fresh- and saltwater, on both sides of the North Atlantic Ocean. The coverage is zoological: the physiological eccentricities of each SPECIES, their behaviour, habitats, distribution and favourite foods. You are also advised which tackle and techniques to use for them. Note that some of these fish would cost a fortune on the menus of posh restaurants, while others would be unacceptable to a judicious dung-fly. Some are extremely wary and fascinating to beguile, then on the hook are almost devoid of wriggle. Others will gobble any bait, then make you sweat to boat them, and thank you for doing so by trying to take your leg off (at times they succeed!).

## TECHNIQUES

These are simply how you go about manipulating TACKLE. Read about the TECHNIQUES and TACKLE appropriate to the fish you are likely to have first crack at, if you are a neophyte, or next crack if you are not. Remember that on the tennis court you are using the same ball, racquet, net and strokes as the latest winner at Wimbledon or Forest Hills. TECHNIQUES are the Art of fishing.

## READING THE WATER

Everyone is susceptible to the charms of Conan Doyle's marvellous Victorian thinking-machine, Sherlock Holmes, the biological supercomputer. The particular type of thinking at which he excelled is called induction, or deduction; its practitioners see the obvious, and infer the hidden. The reflective/refractive indices of the meniscus, the top of the water column, dictate that human vision, even with polarizing aids, will see mere glimpses of what takes place below. Thus we have READING THE WATER, which is to infer from superficial telltales the underlying reality. If you think that Holmes, from calluses on a man's hand, could deduce the work that caused them only in fiction, then think again, angler. Successful physicians, psychiatrists and politicians have built careers on evidence less obvious than that. I can think of four different reasons for one tiny bubble of gas to rise to the surface: two animal, one vegetable and one mineral. That is an essentially stillwater inference made by an angler who much prefers to fish in torrents, where bubbles are numbered in the billions!

Consider that a stream trout, with one eye, can fix his position in the current by looking at a subsurface rock, while another fovea of that same eye focuses on a bankside tree behind which you are hiding. At the same time, with the two foveae of his other eye, he can sharply see both a near sunken and a distant floating insect. You are behind the tree because the rock he is taking a bearing from creates a pressure wave that very slightly bumps the surface a few feet downcurrent from its position in the stream-bed. You think that if he is anywhere, he is there. Read the nine chapters of READING THE WATER, slowly, then do it again.

Fish were (and are) the world's first vertebrates, and therefore precede mammals in the chain of life. We fish for our ancestors, whose capabilities and traits are embodied within us, either implicitly or obviously. Fish can be categorized on many bases, one of which is the tripartite organization of their pineal glands. Some fish are positively phototactic and have a clear spot in their cranial roof that allows electromagnetic radiation to freely strike the gland. Some, such as the salmonids, can vary their reaction to light through the movement of chromatophores that permit or restrict the entrance of radiation. A third category of fish are negatively phototactic. They have opaque skulls that admit no light to the gland.

Some questions should be posed. Did (and do) pineal glands struck by electro-magnetic radiation see visible light, or some other portion(s) of the spectrum? Have they become partly vestigial, and useless as organs of radiation perception, because that capability has been superseded by the hard, focused light from the eyes? Or was the development of opaque skulls evolutionarily retrograde, one of those curses that can bring ruin to entire classes, such as Class Dinosauria? Why are the ductless, or endocrine, glands so mysterious? What is pineal vision? Who is hiding something from us?

When it is a long time between bites, and a fisherman's wits have been dulled by bucolic scenery, and by quiet sylvan noises at the edge of perception (such as a million insects chewing a million blades of grass) and you have lost the hard focus that comes only from civilization, then your mind may blither off into vagrant speculations like these, asking unanswerable questions, wasting time, making a fool of yourself — but thank God it is in private, in silence, where no one else can know what you are really like and make fun of you!

KEITH GARDNER

# TACKLE

Over the past couple of decades, the fishing tackle industry has consistently been among the first to make widespread use of new materials, first glass fibre and then other composites, most successfully those based on carbon fibre. These light, strong materials now form the basis of many rods, reels and other items. The performance of tackle made from them is often so good that some people are tempted to claim that there is now little scope for any further worthwhile improvement. But to make such a claim would be foolish; technology generally is developing at a steadily increasing rate, and there is no reason to believe that its progress won't continue to have an impact on angling.

The tackle industry is now more international than ever before. Japanese manufacturers, perhaps predictably, are now a major force in the market, and European and American companies are not just exporting products designed originally for their domestic markets, they're also producing items intended specifically for export. For instance, American firms are making rods, such as carp and other specialist rods, for the European market, while European companies produce reels and other items designed primarily for sale in the USA.

The most obvious differences between North American and European angling practices are found in freshwater fishing. Baitcasting and spinning, with artificial lures, constitute by far the largest part of American freshwater sport, perhaps 90 percent of it; in Europe, the situation is almost completely the opposite. For example, probably less than 10 percent of British freshwater anglers regularly fish with artificial lures.

This state of affairs gives anglers on both sides of the Atlantic plenty of scope for trying out techniques which are new to them. For instance, the sheer delight of flipping out a lure with an American baitcasting outfit is an experience sadly unknown to the vast majority of British anglers, who have yet to appreciate the pleasure of fishing with these short, light rods and tiny multiplying reels.

The situation is changing, although so far only slowly, as more and more British anglers, especially pike fishermen, are getting into the American lure scene. Conversely, some British methods, such as static deadbaiting for pike, and ledgering with electronic bite alarms for bottom-feeding species, are catching on in the USA. As increasing numbers of anglers are crossing the Atlantic for fishing holidays, and trying the local techniques, these trends are likely to continue.

Another American technique that could be used to great advantage on many British waters is downrigger trolling. This method, used in conjunction with fish-locating sonar, would transform the angling scene on large, deep British lakes, lochs and reservoirs.

Some of the more recent developments in angling tackle (and techniques) have come about because of changing attitudes more than through technical progress alone – anglers have become more conservation-minded. Modern attitudes to conservation originated largely in America, but soon gained ground in Europe as well. Anglers began to understand that the need to preserve fish stocks would not, in the long term, be met by simply imposing a close season while fish are spawning, or by artificial restocking. In America, the catch-and-release approach is steadily gaining ground, while in countries such as Britain, where the pressure on fish stocks is much greater, a new breed of specialized tackle items has been developed.

For instance, large, lightweight landing nets, made from soft, knotless netting, are replacing the gaff as the means of landing fish. Increasingly, it's only large fish designed for the table, such as salmon and various sea fish, which are gaffed. The others are caught and returned with as little injury as possible.

For freshwater anglers who want to retain their fish for a short time, to allow for photographing or weighing them, soft nylon keep sacks were introduced. Fish will lie perfectly still in these black sacks, which are also ideal for keeping species like pike and carp quiet prior to release. There are also unhooking mats, a great idea, which protect large fish from injury such as lost scales as they flap about while they're being unhooked.

This chapter describes the main types of tackle, such as rods and reels, that are used in freshwater and saltwater angling. The individual makes and models illustrated are but a very small sample of the vast range available; further information on these products can be obtained from the manufacturers and distributors listed at the back of the book.

# BIG GAME TACKLE

To stand up to the rigours of the rough, tough sport of big game fishing, the tackle has to be of the best available design and quality – inferior or untested tackle isn't trustworthy and often breaks down under hard usage.

All big game fishing is done with multiplying reels, either star drag or lever drag types. The star drag system, which has a control knob that's turned by hand to increase or decrease the drag, may look old-fashioned but it works well and these reels are the basic workhorses of the sport.

There once were a number of American manufacturers producing star drag reels, but now only one – Penn – still does. These Penn Senator reels range in size from 4/0 up to the massive 16/0, the commonest being the 10/0, 12/0 and 14/0 models.

The lever drag reels, as their name implies, are operated by a smooth-acting lever that is pushed forwards to increase the drag or pulled backwards to decrease it. These reels, which are widely used in big game tournament fishing, are produced by a number of companies around the world. The top of the market includes the

Hardy Zane Grey range (UK) and the Fin-Nor range from Tycoon Tackle (USA), which are highly sophisticated and correspondingly expensive. Also very good, but less costly, are the Penn Internationals and the lever drag reels from Everol (Italy) and Triton and Daiwa (Japan).

The reason for the popularity of the lever drag over the older star drag lies in its greater sensitivity. With lever drag, you can increase the drag tension slowly and accurately, whereas with the star drag it's easy to apply just a fraction too much drag, which can result in a broken line. Lever drag reels are seldom cheap, although the Everol range cost little more than the Senator star drag reels, and they offer extremely good value for money.

Big game rods come in many styles and sizes, but when fishing for truly big game you need a rod in the IGFA 50-, 80- or 130-pound classes, or occasionally in the unlimited class. The line should be in the same class as the rod; unlimited class rods, for instance, are those which should be used with lines of over 130 pounds test. The IGFA is the International Game

Fishing Association, based in Fort Lauderdale, Florida, which sets all the rules for the sport, including general tackle specifications.

Any rod bearing an IGFA class number will conform to the IGFA regulations – for instance, the rod tip must be at least 40 inches long, and the butt length mustn't exceed 27 inches. If the rod has a curved butt, the length is measured across the curve, rather than around it.

Big game rods are designed for hard work, and so most are fitted with a full set of roller rings, AFTCO and Fin-Nor being the most popular types. Japanese manufacturers are now producing non-roller 'turbo' rings, which are lined with hard, low-friction materials such as silicon carbide or titanium, providing a good, lightweight alternative to bulky roller rings.

Reel seats should always be of the heavy-duty, hooded type, and the rod butt of anodized aluminium, but whether you have a

straight or curved rod butt depends entirely on your own personal preference.

Nylon monofilament lines are the most popular type for big game fishing. Tough enough to withstand scuffing and even minor nicks, monofilament has only one real disadvantage: stretch. Its inherent elasticity means that it acts as a great shock absorber, but it often stops the hook from being set solidly.

For shark and tuna, which normally gulp the bait back, this isn't too much of a disadvantage, but with billfish the elasticity of the nylon often absorbs the strength of the strike and so the hook doesn't set in the bony jaw plates. This occurs mostly during fast water trolling with artificial lures.

The alternative to nylon mono is Dacron, a polyester fibre that is prestretched during manufacture. Dacron sets hooks solidly, but the slightest damage to the line will

## CHOOSING A ROD

| USE | LENGTH | IGFA |
|---|---|---|
| Light rods with roller tip and roller or conventional guides. Good for the smaller species like snook, blackfin tuna, snappers and pollack. | 7–7ft 6ins | 15–30lbs |
| Medium rods can handle bigger fish such as wahoo, tarpon, barracuda, king mackerel and sailfish. | 6–7ft | 30–50lbs |
| Heavy duty rods are for the big ones, including marlin, bluefin tuna, large sharks and cobia. | 5ft 6ins–6ft 6ins | 80–130lbs |

**BIG GAME REEL**
This reel has a smooth, sensitive lever drag mechanism.

one piece spool
harness attachment points
drag lever
cage
foot
handle
torpedo grip

**BIG GAME ROD**

screw winch reel fitting
curved butt extention
deck end fitting
locking collar
hyperlon grip
butt ring

cause it to snap instantly when tension is applied. The same thing happens if the line gets dragged across the back of another fish

*Big game fishing is a tough sport that calls for robust, well made tackle.*

while tensioned. Because of this, Dacron lines are now used by only a few, highly experienced, big game anglers.

Whichever line you use, it should always be one that has an IGFA rating. The most popular nylon lines are Ande and Berkley

Trilene. Berkley also make a range of rated Dacron lines.

Traces for big game fishing are almost always made from either heavy longliner's nylon or from braided or single-strand stainless steel wire. The normal strength of a big game trace is 300 to 500

pounds test, far heavier than the actual reel line. This is to soak up damage and severe punishment during the battle, and to allow a beaten fish to be pulled to within gaffing range. Under IGFA rules, the leader must not exceed 30 feet in length.

one piece blank for strength

heavy duty roller rings

tip ring

# CENTREPINS AND MULTIPLIERS

The centrepin is one of the simplest of all reels, but also one of the most difficult to use. Casting with the centrepin takes skill, especially over long distances, which is one of the main reasons for its dramatic decline in popularity after the easy-casting fixed spool reel was introduced to the mass market in the 1940s. Centrepins are still used by some anglers in the UK and Europe, but they are virtually unknown in the US and scarcely used in Canada.

The centrepin consists of a flanged drum that carries the line and revolves freely on a steel axle. Most have a ratchet mechanism and some also have a drag system, but it's the reel's free-running action and the way that it can be controlled simply by thumb pressure that are its main advantages.

Because the line winds directly onto the spool, instead of first passing over a bale arm, the centrepin gives extremely sensitive control over float tackle that is being allowed to drift smoothly downstream with the current. The line can be retrieved rapidly by giving the drum a series of sharp taps with the fingertips to spin it, or it can be wound in by using a handle fixed to the outer flange of the drum.

The amount of line retrieved for each turn of the handle depends on the drum diameter: the larger the drum, the more line it will wind on with each revolution. Most centrepins have a drum diameter of three to six inches.

Most multipliers, on the other hand, have small-diameter drums that don't take up much line per revolution, but rapid retrieval is possible because the handle drives the drum via a gear mechanism. This gearing makes the drum turn more than once for each turn of the handle, which is why the reels are called multipliers. The gear ratio varies from one model to another, but it's usually between 2:1 and 4¹/₂:1.

Many multipliers, especially the smaller ones, are fitted with level wind mechanisms. These track the line from side to side across the drum as the handle is turned, so that the line is wound on neatly and evenly. Another feature of most small multipliers is a magnetic braking system, which avoids the risk of overruns when casting. This allows the angler to make a long, powerful cast without having to worry about the drum continuing to spin and spew out line after the terminal tackle has hit the water. Once the weight of the tackle is no longer pulling line from the spool, the magnetic brake brings it smoothly to a stop.

To minimize the possibility of line breakage when a fish is being played hard, multipliers have a slipping clutch or drag mechanism. This is adjusted, by means of a star-shaped knob or lever, so that the reel will turn and give line only when the line is pulled strongly, but not so strongly as to break it. When the drag is set correctly, the angler can confidently put maximum pressure on the fish.

Among the smallest of the multipliers are the little teardrop-shaped baitcasters. These fit snugly into the hand, allowing you to fish with two or three fingers in

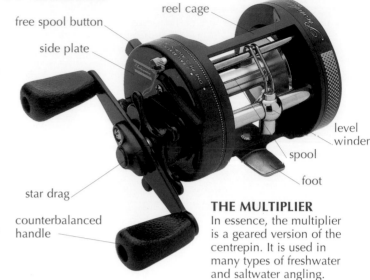

**THE MULTIPLIER**
In essence, the multiplier is a geared version of the centrepin. It is used in many types of freshwater and saltwater angling.

free spool button
reel cage
side plate
level winder
spool
foot
star drag
counterbalanced handle

## THE CENTREPIN
Centrepin reels are difficult to use and once seemed doomed to extinction, but they have been making a comeback in recent years.

foot
casing
handle
spindle cover

front of the rod trigger. This makes for comfortable all-day casting, to which reel makers have further contributed by designing a smooth endplate without protruding buttons and bearing caps.

Another good feature of most of these little reels is the thumb bar, which disengages the spool for easy casting.

These baby multipliers can hold from 100 to 150 yards of

spool

cage

spool end
float adjuster

side plate

free
spool
release
bar

star drag

counterbalanced
handle

## THE BAITCASTER

Baitcasters are compact, teardrop-shaped multiplier reels, small enough to fit into the hand and designed for fishing with lightweight baitcasting rods and artificial lures.

useful for heavy baitcasting, light surfcasting and estuary fishing. These have the same sort of features as the little baitcasters, such as the magnetic cast control which is so beneficial to the long-distance beachcaster.

A much more rugged reel with a greater line capacity is needed for uptide fishing, light sea trolling or trolling large lakes with a downrigger. The reel should hold 250 to 300 yards of line of 15- to 18-pound test or heavier.

A level wind is useful but not essential, but the spool must be strong, crushproof and corrosion-resistant, preferably diecast aluminium. The handle should be a sensibly-sized torpedo shape, and instead of a thumb bar a positive-actioned gear lever that cannot be engaged accidentally is a must, as is a click or ratchet for when the reel needs to be left in free spool. A handy feature of some models is a

lever drag control, which is a faster and more sensitive system than the star drag when you're controlling the run of a big fish.

Even larger reels are needed for offshore boat and wreck fishing when you're after the smaller pelagic species or big bottom feeders like rays, groupers, white sea bass or conger. These reels, up to around size 4/0 (the small end of the big game range), need both strength and durability to cope with the hard work of pirking, wrecking or trolling. The spool should be of brass or stainless steel to withstand the constriction of heavy nylon or wire lines, and the body reinforced with strong, chromed endplates.

A level wind isn't necessary, but a large line capacity is, if only to give a faster retrieve when the reel is full. Between 300 and 400 yards of 30- to 40-pound line should cope with most situations.

10- to 12-pound test line, which means they can be used for catching fish as large as a pike or bass.

Larger multipliers, with a capacity of between 200 and 300 yards of 14- or 15-pound line, are

**Above** *The multiplier reel is mounted on top of the rod.*

**Right** *A baitcaster loaded with 12 pound line can be used to catch large fish such as pike.*

# FIXED SPOOL REELS

The fixed spool or spinning reel opened up a whole new chapter in casting performance when it became widely available in the 1940s. It was said then that 'anyone can cast a long way with a fixed spool reel', and that statement still holds true today.

There are several different types of fixed spool reel, but they all work on the same basic principle. On the retrieve, the line is wound around the spool of the reel by a rotating bale arm. The spool doesn't revolve, but it does move up and down along the line of the rod to facilitate even line lay. The spool needs to be almost full

of line for best casting: line should fill the spool to just below the rim and be wound on firmly. Many anglers fail to appreciate this, and their casting deteriorates as the level of line on the spool drops due to wear.

Although the spool doesn't turn when the line is being retrieved, it does revolve to give line to a running fish. The spool turns under the control of a drag or slipping clutch, which can be adjusted so that the spool turns and gives line before the breaking point of the line is reached. An antireverse mechanism (some are silent, some audible) prevents the handle from

turning backwards when the spool is rotating.

Fixed spool reels are available in a variety of retrieve rates. A ratio of about 4:1, which will retrieve around 20 inches of line for each turn of the handle, is suitable for most purposes. However, many anglers prefer a 3:1 ratio (about 15 inches per turn) for spinning when they want to work the lure at a slow, steady rate, or a 6:1 ratio (30 inches per turn) for cranking in lures at high speed when after pelagic species in clear water.

The closed face reel is a type of fixed spool reel that doesn't have an exposed bale arm. The line

*The fixed spool reel is ideal for spinning in both fresh and saltwater, and for float fishing and ledgering.*

passes through a hole in the completely enclosed front face of the reel, and is wound round the spool by a rotating steel bale pin. During casting, this bale pin is disengaged from the line by finger pressure on the front face of the reel, or on some models by pressing a button at the rear.

Depending on the make, the drag control is mounted either on the handle shaft or at the rear. Most reels will allow the spool to

should be hard wearing and free running, with a wide, deep spool for easy, long casting.

The largest fixed spool reels are those designed for surfcasting and estuary fishing. These should be corrosion-resistant for regular use in saltwater (many aren't), and have wide, smooth-lipped spools capable of holding somewhere between 200 and 250 yards of 15- to 25-pound test line.

More so than for any other type of fishing, beach reels need to be very smooth-running, so look for those whose spools turn effortlessly on ball or roller bearings.

A sensibly-sized, torpedo-shaped handle is essential for a good grip, and a sensitive, progressive drag (either front or rear) is a must for playing fast, hard-fighting fish. Spools with conical-shaped inners are preferable for long-distance casting, as are small, manually operated bale arms that won't accidentally snap closed during a powerful cast.

## THE CLOSED FACE REEL

On a closed face reel, the line emerges from a hole in the face of the reel. The spool is fixed during the retrieve, and the line is wound onto it by a rotating steel pin called the bale pin. Closed face reels are designed for use with light lines and can be used for jigging, float fishing or ledgering for small species such as perch.

reel foot · leg · antireverse button · handle · line release button · paddle grip · body · bell housing

## THE FIXED SPOOL REEL

The fixed spool is one of the most popular types of reel. As the name suggests, the spool of the reel doesn't revolve during the retrieve, and the line is wound onto it by a rotating bale arm. During casting, the line peels freely from the spool and this allows the terminal tackle to be cast a long way.

reel foot · leg · antireverse lever · spool release button · spool · bale arm · spool skirt · body · handle · rear drag adjuster knob · grip

rotate and give line only when the antireverse is on, but a few allow line to be given by back-winding.

Closed face reels are very efficient for light line fishing, but their use with lines in excess of 4 or 5 pound test is not recommended. Far too much torque would be transmitted to such a sensitive machine when playing a heavy fish on such lines.

All the closed face reels and the smallest fixed spools will hold around 100 yards of 2- to 4-pound test line, and are ideal for jigging and lightweight float fishing and ledgering for species such as perch, the smaller cyprinids and crappies.

For anything heavier, the medium sized fixed spool reels should be used. One reel and two interchangeable spools should cover all your needs: one spool with 100 to 150 yards of 5 or 6 pound test, plus a deeper one holding 150 to 200 yards of 8 to 12 pound test. The deeper spool should be crush-proof, as the constriction of the line can be considerable when you're playing larger species such as carp, catfish, pike, salmon or big bass.

Lightweight graphite bodies, disengaging spools and rear drag levers are all useful on this type of reel, but most importantly the reel

# FLOAT RODS

The modern float rod, made of composite materials based on glass fibre or graphite (carbon fibre), is a very powerful and versatile tool despite its fragile looks – a good 13-foot graphite rod can weigh as little as 6 ounces.

When you're choosing a float rod, it's important to pick one with the right sort of action for the type of fishing you do. For instance, a soft, highly flexible rod will be next to useless if much of your fishing demands hitting quick bites.

To assess the action of a rod, hold it horizontally as you would when fishing, with your forearm along the handle, then lower the tip to about 12 inches from the floor. Try a smart upward strike, keeping your eye on the tip; if it dips and touches the floor, the action is too sloppy for float fishing and the rod should be rejected. With a stiff, fast-actioned rod, the tip shouldn't touch down on a strike when it's held only 6 inches from the floor.

If the rod passes this test, have the tackle dealer hold the top ring at waist height while you slowly lift the rod upwards into a nice bend. You will then be able to see if the action is more or less confined to just the tip, the top section or the middle, or if it's completely all-through, which is preferable.

Other points to watch for when you're selecting a float rod include the number, height and type of rings, and the length and diameter of the handle. Rings of hard chrome stainless steel are very popular and usually stand a couple of seasons of hard use before starting to groove, but lined rings provide a significant reduction in friction and subsequent grooving and line wear.

Float rod rings should stand high off the blank to keep the line clear of the rod and minimize line slap and eliminate line stick during wet weather, and there should be one ring for every foot of overall rod length (although they will, of course, be placed at varying intervals, not simply every 12 inches).

The handle size is a more important part of float rod design than many anglers realize. Too many handles are too thick or too long, or both: a diameter of one inch is ideal for a firm grip, while a length of 22 to 24 inches is quite sufficient. There's little point in investing in an expensive 14-foot rod if its handle is so long that a foot of it sticks out behind your elbow when you're fishing; this

## CHOOSING A ROD

| USE | LENGTH |
|---|---|
| For small rivers, canals and stillwaters. Hollow tip for wagglers. Spliced tip for sticks. | 12ft |
| Standard waggler rod for river or lake, for short and long distance float fishing. Look for about 16 rings to allow ease of casting. | 13ft |
| Few waggler rods are designed at this length, but can be useful when extra casting distance is required, or for doubling as a stick float rod.<br><br>A spliced tip rod is perfect for fishing a stick float in deep water, or when an extra degree of control is needed to run the float along a river. | 14ft |
| For Bolognese fishing, which basically involves fishing a pole float on a running line. A rod of this length has little application for general use. | 16ft plus |

BUTT SECTION

double legged lined butt ring

sliding reel fitting

MID SECTION

TIP SECTION

*Made of composite materials, float rods are light but strong.*

reduces its effective length to 13 feet. As for the handle material, whether you choose cork or a synthetic material depends entirely upon your personal preference.

At the bottom end of the price range, 10 to 12-foot hollow glass rods are well-suited to general float fishing for roach, bream, tench and other species. Being thicker in wall section and heavier than graphite rods, they are ideal for youngsters and beginners because the action is more progressive than superfast, which makes them easier to use.

Rods in the 12- to 15-foot range are now mostly made of graphite, often mixed with boron, silicon carbide or Kevlar. In general, the higher the proportion of graphite in the rod, the better it will perform. Flexing the rod in a mock strike is a good way to get an idea of how much graphite the rod contains. A sloppy rod that doesn't return quickly won't have a very high percentage of graphite in its structure. Look for a rod with a snappy return and the sort of action that will best suit your requirements.

Pick a delicate tip action if you intend fishing for small species, and one that will bend right through to the middle and bottom sections if you're going to be angling for fish that weigh pounds, rather than ounces.

Overall, a rod of around 13 feet will generally suffice, but 14- and 15-foot float rods are very useful for fishing into exceptionally deep lakes and pits.

Whatever length of rod you choose, if it's a graphite rod don't fish near overhead power lines, or when there's lightning about. Graphite is an excellent conductor of electricity, and if your rod touches a power line you'll get a serious, even fatal, shock.

cork handle

ferrule

single legged stand-off intermediate rings

lined tip ring

**THE FLOAT ROD**
The typical modern float rod is made of glass fibre or graphite, with a cork handle and a sliding reel fitting that allows the reel position to be varied.

# FLOATS

The float is one of the most sensitive and versatile bite indicators an angler could wish to use, and it not only gives excellent bite indication, it also allows the bait to be presented in a natural way.

Plastics, such as polycarbonates, dominate float production these days. Early floats were made from porcupine quills or the quills of bird feathers, with bodies of cork, elder pith or balsa if extra buoyancy was needed.

Of these materials, balsa is still used quite extensively, and for the 'waggler' type of floats a better material than peacock quills has yet to be found. There is, as yet, no synthetic material to match it for its combination of strength, lightness and buoyancy, although synthetics can always beat quill on price and availability.

Sarkansas reed, which has a buoyancy similar to that of peacock quill, is another natural material still used for making float stems, along with cane and balsa. To make a waggler float, a small metal eye is inserted into the bottom of the stem. For partially-weighted wagglers, a small brass or steel rod, with one end formed into an eye, is fitted into the stem.

In use, the reel line is passed through the eye of the waggler and the float is locked in position with a split shot or shots on the line at each side of the eye. Other types of float are fixed to the line by silicone rubber float bands at the top and bottom of the float. Despite the hundreds of different shapes and sizes of float available, most of them fall into just one of two general groups: those fixed to the line at the bottom end only, usually through an eye, and those fixed at both the top and bottom ends by rubber bands.

The most popular of all the top and bottom fixed floats are the wire-stemmed balsa or cane stick-type floats. Used only in rivers, these floats allow you to drift the bait slowly downstream. You can hold back hard on the float so that it travels slower than the current, and the bait (usually maggots or casters) will swing forwards ahead

**Above** *On running water, a stick float can be allowed to drift with the current to carry the bait downstream.*

**Left** *Floats for pike fishing are large and very buoyant.*

of the float. These floats work most effectively at quite close range, certainly no farther out than about 1¹/₂ rod lengths.

Thicker versions, balsa floats carrying more weight, are good in medium to fast water where the lighter ones are less effective.

Two other useful top and bottom fixed floats are the Avon and the loafer (or chub trotter). The Avon has all its buoyancy concentrated in a balsa body immediately below the tip (also balsa). This allows it to ride evenly through turbulent water such as weir pools, and it can be held back to swing the bait upwards without being dragged off course.

Loafers are made from solid balsa or clear, hollow plastic. They are, in effect, shorter, squatter versions of the balsa float, being much thicker and carrying more weight so that they hold steady in fast currents. Their thick tips are easily visible even when they're fished a long way downstream, and they're ideal for grayling or chub fishing in fast rivers.

The most versatile of all floats are the peacock quill wagglers, which are fixed bottom end only. A handful of peacock wagglers of various sizes would easily meet threequarters of all float fishing requirements, either in still or running water. They are locked on the line with split shot either side of the eye, and in running water they're always fished preceding the bait. If all the weight is concentrated around the float, very slow-moving swims can be fished well over depth so that the bait trundles along the bottom very slowly, with just a couple of tiny shots down the line.

A peacock waggler works equally well with all the shots close

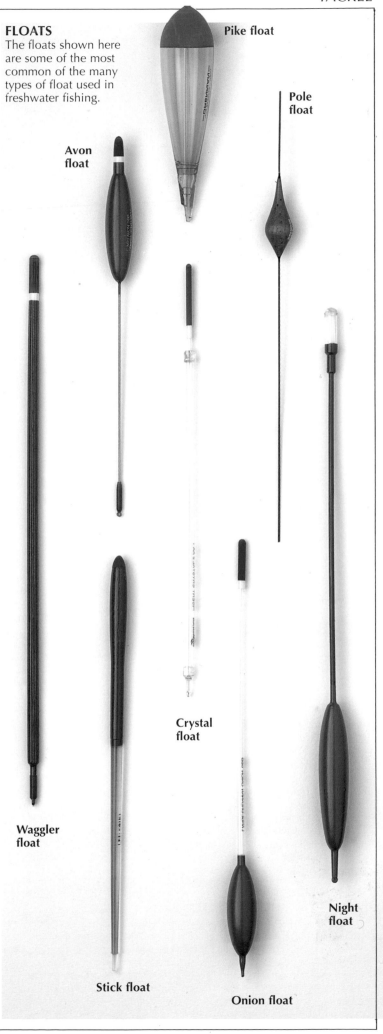

## FLOATS

The floats shown here are some of the most common of the many types of float used in freshwater fishing.

**Pike float**

**Pole float**

**Avon float**

**Crystal float**

**Waggler float**

**Night float**

**Stick float**

**Onion float**

to the hook, for fishing with the lift method. With all the shots down at the hook, the float is fixed to the line with a rubber float band.

The bodied peacock waggler allows you to cast farther than with the waggler, because the extra buoyancy provided by its polystyrene body allows more shot to be used. As well as being useful for fishing distant swims, these floats are good in windy weather, but remember to sink the line well to avoid surface drift.

To facilitate quick, easy changing of all waggler style floats, use a rubber or plastic float attachment. This threads onto the line just like the bottom of a float, and the float is simply pushed into it.

Darts are tiny, bulbous-bottomed floats with extra-fine tips, designed to indicate the tiniest of bites. They are good for fishing close-in in still water. Pole floats are also very small, sometimes with super-fine 'bristle' tips. They may be fixed bottom end only or top and bottom, and they work in just

the same way as other floats. They are, however, much easier to control. This is because of their small size and because the pole tip is positioned directly above, with as little line as possible between tip and float.

For float fishing at night, you can use luminous elements which are glued to the float or attached to it by a length of tubing. Alternatively, battery-powered floats (which are more or less the same shape as a bodied waggler) are available.

Most floats used for live- or deadbaiting for predators are cigar-shaped slider floats. The line either passes through an eye at the bottom of the float, or, if it's a tubed float, through a hole running right through the float from end to end.

Drift floats, which have little vanes or sails that catch the wind to take them and the bait (live or dead) out beyond casting distance, are useful for predator fishing from the bank on large waters.

# FLY REELS

Anyone who says that a fly reel is used merely to hold the line has probably never hooked a big rainbow trout or a wily specimen brown trout that spends most of the fight powering toward the nearest snag. Anyone who has will know that to use the light lines so often needed to fool big 'educated' trout, you need a reel that will give line smoothly with no jerks and jars that can snap that line.

One of the most important developments in the modern fly reel is its drag system. Where once a simple check mechanism was considered good enough, today, even average-priced reels come with a sophisticated drag. The most popular and efficient of these is the disc drag, which is both smooth in operation, completely variable, and hard wearing.

Whether using light tippets for ultra-selective trout, tackling big saltwater species that can run hundreds of yards at breakneck speeds, or simply in the hope of hooking a good fish, it is imperative that the reel is able to give line as the fish runs. Smoothness is the key: a drag mechanism that gives with an initial jerk is likely to break the line as a fish bolts, especially at short range, while for big, brawling tuna and sailfish, a drag that locks up as the fish powers off is an absolute disaster.

Fly reels are now made from a variety of materials. Wood and brass were once the standard, but developments in modern lightweight materials means that we now have models made of graphite (carbon fibre), magnesium alloy, polycarbonate and aluminium, the latter being preferred for most fly reels.

Depending on the price and specification, aluminium reels can be made either from cast aluminium or from a solid bar that has been machined to shape. Being stronger weight-for-weight than cast aluminium, aluminium bar stock allows reels to be made lighter and is normally used on the higher priced models.

With lightness one of the main requirements of a fly reel, many have perforated spools or cages. This reduces the amount of metal used and therefore the weight. The fly line and backing are wound around a cental pillar or arbor in the spool.

In many models of fly reel the spool can be removed by depressing a central catch, allowing it to be replaced by another spool carrying a different density of fly line. This enables the angler to switch

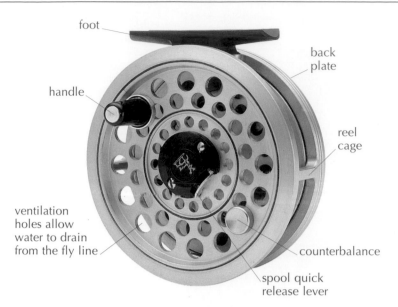

foot

handle

back plate

reel cage

counterbalance

spool quick release lever

ventilation holes allow water to drain from the fly line

## THE FLY REEL
Most fly reels are made of lightweight materials, cast with holes and slots to lighten them and give good ventilation to the line. Some are made from light metal alloys, while there are a few ultralight graphite (carbon fibre) models. A good check mechanism is essential, and when set properly it should offer more resistance to the line when it is going out than when being wound in.

lines rapidly and without the need to carry many different reels.

Most fly reels are single action, that is, each turn of the handle produces one turn of the spool. The advantage of this system is that the angler remains in direct contact with the give and take of line as a fish is played. This produces a better feel, and allows the angler to exert extra control by palming the rim of the reel, with the hand providing additional braking. To this end, some reels are designed with exposed spool rims that overlap the cage so that pressure can be easily applied.

The disadvantage of the single action system is that rewinding the line can be a slow process. With a small reel, this can mean that each turn of the handle will retrieve only a few inches of line. This is a particular problem when a lot of line has been taken, as it can be difficult to wind fast enough to keep tension on the fish if it runs quickly toward the angler.

Multiplying reels, which produce 1.5–2 revolutions of the spool for every turn of the handle, solve this problem – to a degree. They retrieve line more quickly but their disadvantage is that a multiplying reel of corresponding size and line capacity is heavier, and does not have the direct feel of the single action when playing a fish. Rewinding the line can also be more difficult as each turn of the handle must be made through a series of gears.

Another option for rapid line retrieval is the automatic reel. The early models of this type were very heavy and used a large spring that was wound up as the line was

*The fly reel is always mounted below the rod and usually very close to the end of the cork handle.*

pulled from the reel. Depressing a lever caused the spring to unwind, revolving the spool and rewinding the line.

Modern versions are much lighter and usually rely on a semi-automatic mechanism in which the line is retrieved by repeatedly squeezing a lever. This activates the reel's high-speed rewind action, which can retrieve a full fly line a just a few seconds. Due to their small size and line capacity, semi-automatic fly reels, such as the Vivarelli from Italy, are best suited to fishing for small river trout and to light stillwater use.

Selecting the right size of fly reel depends on the type of rod and fly line being used. For a light, 8-foot singlehanded fly rod rated for a 5-weight line, the reel need only be 3 inches in diameter – enough to hold the fly line plus 50 yards of 16 pound backing. Unless you are using this type of light tackle specifically for very big fish, this set-up is more than ample to handle the average-sized trout.

However, if you are using heavier tackle, such as that needed for reservoir trout or for salmon in a fast-flowing river, the reel will need to be larger. To hold an 11-weight line, which is normally used with a 15-foot two-handed salmon rod, a 4-inch diameter reel will be required to accommodate the fly line along with 125 yards of 25 pound backing.

Most single action and multiplying fly reels are direct drive. This means that the reel handle revolves both when line is being retrieved and when it is being pulled off the spool. When tackling large, fast-running species, the handle of a direct drive reel will often spin to a blur as the fish careers toward the horizon.

Any fingers that come in to contact with the handle at such a time can easily be badly hurt, if not broken. To solve this problem, a number of models, such as the Billy Pate and Abel series, are now produced with an antireverse mechanism where the handle will only revolve when the line is being rewound.

The antireverse mechanism is part of the drag system, and its tension should be set a little below the breaking strain of the tippet being used. This means that as the fish tires, line can be retrieved without the risk of breakage, as it can run even if you are still winding line in.

This development obviously makes for a more expensive reel but it is a tremendous advantage when fishing for big salmon, or for saltwater species such as billfish and tuna, which can run at tremendous speeds.

# FLY RODS

**F**ly rods, excluding salmon rods, range in length from the little 6¹/₂-foot brook rods up to 11¹/₂-foot models that give superb water command over still waters and large rivers. Apart from length, there are other factors to take into account when you're choosing a rod. For instance, will you want a stiff-actioned rod for long-distance casting on lakes or reservoirs, or a softer-actioned one for delicate wet-fly fishing on small streams?

In general, there are three basic types of fly rod: those with a soft action to cover water successfully with shorter casts, and where you don't have to play very large fish; those with a stiff action, but which are not so long as to be too cumbersome for singlehanded use yet have enough power to double-haul a long line and to command big fish in play; and those rods of the maximum length for singlehanded use, and which have some ease of action for comfortable use but can still command a fish in play.

Although split cane was the great rod-making material of bygone days, it's now rarely seen. Even the glass fibre rods so popular until recently tend to be regarded now as too heavy for prolonged use. Nowadays, there is nothing to beat graphite (carbon fibre), and there has been a steady swing to this material since the mid Seventies. The snag with all tubular rods, however, even those made from graphite (and one that manufacturers have been reluctant to admit), is that when stressed to extremes, the tube assumes an oval shape and there's a sudden and dramatic loss of power and an increased risk of breakage.

One way of avoiding this problem is that used for the Bruce and Walker Hexagraph series. These have six graphite cores cemented together to form a solid section without being too heavy.

The longer the rod, the greater the area of water you will be able to command or cover, but don't forget that the advantages of extra length might be offset by drawbacks such as increased weight.

For instance, you can get a superb 11-foot rod that is very powerful and may even be used for salmon fishing. It might be the most useful rod for up to 15 minutes at a stretch, but to fish with it all day, making frequent casts, might make you feel as though your arm's falling off. A delicate little rod, on the other hand, might be a joy to use but not give you the water command you need or deal adequately with very big fish.

Of course, it all boils down to the fact that, just as a golfer needs differing clubs, you will need a set of different rod actions and lengths to meet all your needs. For fishing on a small stream of little more than 25 feet wide, you would easily cope with a 7- to 8¹/₂-foot rod and still have more distance casting power than you're ever likely to need.

A river 45 feet wide, however, might well call for a rod of between 8¹/₂ and 10 feet. But if you want to limit yourself to only one rod for all types of fly fishing, including salmon, sea trout and trout, you should choose a medium-action 10-footer.

If you want to fish on still waters, you have to decide whether

you will spend the bulk of the time fishing from a boat or wading along the shore line: boat rods can be slightly less substantial than bank ones.

Ideally, you should have access to a more powerful 9¹/₂- or 10-foot rod for bank fishing, but you should avoid those over-stiff devices that need the strength of a gorilla to flex them properly. They may be fine for the tournament caster who wants to throw a line into the next county, and who will only use it for a five-minute session anyway, but they are not nice for prolonged fishing. Also bear in mind that the stronger and stiffer the rod, the songer your leader will have to be to avoid breakage on the strike.

*Fishing a river for brown trout. Trout rods range from the little 6¹/₂-foot brook rods up to the 11¹/₂-foot models for fishing still waters and large rivers.*

With all singlehanded rods it's preferable to have the reel fittings near the butt. Various fitments are available, and those that are the lightest are usually the best. Screw fittings offer greater security than those with a friction hold, although you're unlikely to have a reel fall off whichever type you choose.

Despite the great variety of rod actions to suit different fishing situations, to some extent there is room for personal preference. It is usually said that a slightly stiffer-actioned rod is better for dry-fly

## THE FLY ROD
With the traditional cork handle fly rods can come in two to six sections, and range from six to twelve foot.

reel fitting

**Two piece fly rod**

tip ring

traditional cork handle

single leg, lined guides

fishing, and a soft-actioned rod is better for wet flies. But beware of any rod that is truly limp; these might be able to handle very light lines in calm conditions, but they often lack the stamina to cope with contrary winds and longer-than-average casts. Even though a fly rod shouldn't have too soft an action, when it's flexed it should have a good all-through action down into the butt. Tip-actioned rods with stiff butt sections have little use in fly fishing.

If you can afford it, get a rod in graphite by one of the more reputable manufacturers. There is much dumping of foreign overproduction and these rods, while exceptionally cheap, may not represent very good value.

## CHOOSING A ROD

| USE | LENGTH | AFTM |
|---|---|---|
| Short rods for small stream work where the ultra-light lines give the delicacy needed. Ideal for light nymph and dry fly fishing. | 6–7ft 6ins | 1–4 |
| Medium rods for larger rivers and stillwaters, especially when longer casts are needed. Will cast large dry flies and weighted nymphs but are fine enough to handle light tippets. | 8–9ft | 5–7 |
| Rods of this size are good for larger fish in big lakes and powerful rivers. For fast sinking lines or casting big flies and lures. | 9ft 6ins–10ft | 6–9 |
| Long rods range from high powered models for casting heavy weight forward and shooting head lines to softer, through-action. | 10ft 6ins–11ft 6ins | 6–9 |

# FRESHWATER HOOKS

**A**lthough they're often taken for granted, hooks are not only the essential point of angling tackle but also, in many ways, one of the most complicated. There is a hook, or a choice of hooks, for every angling need.

Hooks are made of carbon steel or stainless steel, and usually bronzed, blued, japanned or plated with nickel or cadmium. Until the 1980s, hooks were all about equal in terms of sharpness. Then a new process – called chemical etching – was introduced, first by Kamatsu and then by other manufacturers.

This method of sharpening the hook produces a point which is much sharper than that which can be obtained by any other process. This means that chemically-sharpened hooks will penetrate extremely easily, but it has been suggested that they're sometimes too sharp for soft-mouthed fish because they will actually cut their way out quicker than conventionally-sharpened hooks.

For freshwater fishing, double and treble hooks are used mostly on artificial lures, such as spinners and plugs, and for rigging live or dead fishbaits when fishing for predators such as pike.

The smallest sizes of single hook usually have flattened, spade-shaped ends, rather than eyed ends. For delicate presentation of baits to small fish, the spade end is superior to the eyed hook in the sizes from 12 down to 26, because it hangs well on the line and may be tied direct to a finer hook length. All sizes of spade end hook are available pre-tied to a short hook length which is easily knotted to the reel line. This saves you the trouble of whipping the hook to the line.

For presenting single tiny bloodworms or maggots, use a very fine wire hook of from size 16 to size 26, with a long, slightly reversed shank, a crystal bend and a chemically-sharpened point with a micro barb. Larger maggots or worms, or pairs of them, call for a hook with a thicker wire and a shorter shank. Sizes 12 to 20 should be strong enough for most fish up to about 3 pounds in weight. For a single maggot intended for a larger, more powerful species, or for presenting larger baits such as sweetcorn or small pieces of bread flake, a forged hook is needed.

Forged hooks have a flattened cross-section, as opposed to the round cross-section of the ordinary unforged wire hook, and size-for-size are much stronger.

Forged, eyed hooks of size 2 to size 12, with short shanks, round bends and small barbs, are ideal for general freshwater fishing with baits large and small. Hooks with medium-sized wires are suitable for most purposes, but where large fish are expected, or for fishing close to snags, use stronger hooks made from a heavier wire with a reversed, medium-length shank.

With heavy lines and for powerful fish such as carp and catfish, go for a black, forged hook with a long shank, a crystal bend and a whisker barb; sizes 1/0 down to 10 are most useful. For hooking small livebaits, or large bean or peanut baits, use a size 2 to 8 forged, bronzed hook with a long, reversed shank and a round bend.

Weedless hooks are worth using if you're fishing among thick weed. The incurving point of a weedless hook is shielded by a sprung wire guard which is fixed just below the eye. This guard prevents the hook from snagging on weeds, but when a fish bites, the guard wire is pushed towards the shank and the point and barb are exposed.

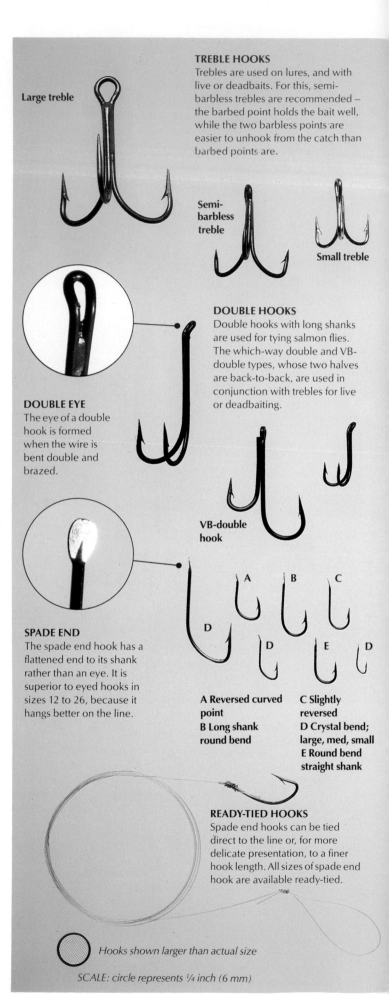

### TREBLE HOOKS
Trebles are used on lures, and with live or deadbaits. For this, semi-barbless trebles are recommended – the barbed point holds the bait well, while the two barbless points are easier to unhook from the catch than barbed points are.

**Large treble**

**Semi-barbless treble**

**Small treble**

### DOUBLE HOOKS
Double hooks with long shanks are used for tying salmon flies. The which-way double and VB-double types, whose two halves are back-to-back, are used in conjunction with trebles for live or deadbaiting.

**VB-double hook**

### DOUBLE EYE
The eye of a double hook is formed when the wire is bent double and brazed.

### SPADE END
The spade end hook has a flattened end to its shank rather than an eye. It is superior to eyed hooks in sizes 12 to 26, because it hangs better on the line.

**A** Reversed curved point
**B** Long shank round bend
**C** Slightly reversed
**D** Crystal bend; large, med, small
**E** Round bend straight shank

### READY-TIED HOOKS
Spade end hooks can be tied direct to the line or, for more delicate presentation, to a finer hook length. All sizes of spade end hook are available ready-tied.

*Hooks shown larger than actual size*

*SCALE: circle represents ¼ inch (6 mm)*

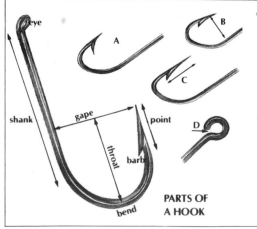

**PARTS OF A HOOK**

eye
shank
gape
point
throat
barb
bend

## COMMON HOOK FAULTS
**A.** Barb cut too deep — the hook might snap.
**B.** Gape too small.
**C.** Over-long, weak point.
**D.** Wide eye gap allows hook to slip off the line.

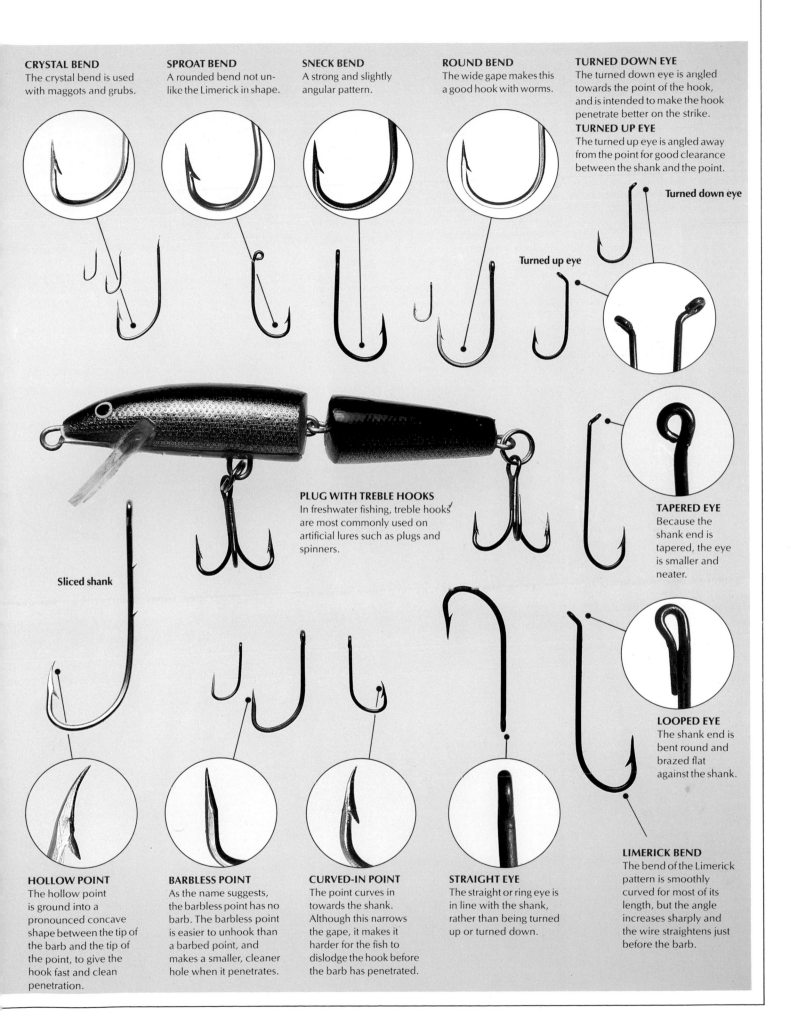

**CRYSTAL BEND**
The crystal bend is used with maggots and grubs.

**SPROAT BEND**
A rounded bend not unlike the Limerick in shape.

**SNECK BEND**
A strong and slightly angular pattern.

**ROUND BEND**
The wide gape makes this a good hook with worms.

**TURNED DOWN EYE**
The turned down eye is angled towards the point of the hook, and is intended to make the hook penetrate better on the strike.

**TURNED UP EYE**
The turned up eye is angled away from the point for good clearance between the shank and the point.

**Turned down eye**

**Turned up eye**

**PLUG WITH TREBLE HOOKS**
In freshwater fishing, treble hooks are most commonly used on artificial lures such as plugs and spinners.

**TAPERED EYE**
Because the shank end is tapered, the eye is smaller and neater.

**Sliced shank**

**LOOPED EYE**
The shank end is bent round and brazed flat against the shank.

**HOLLOW POINT**
The hollow point is ground into a pronounced concave shape between the tip of the barb and the tip of the point, to give the hook fast and clean penetration.

**BARBLESS POINT**
As the name suggests, the barbless point has no barb. The barbless point is easier to unhook than a barbed point, and makes a smaller, cleaner hole when it penetrates.

**CURVED-IN POINT**
The point curves in towards the shank. Although this narrows the gape, it makes it harder for the fish to dislodge the hook before the barb has penetrated.

**STRAIGHT EYE**
The straight or ring eye is in line with the shank, rather than being turned up or turned down.

**LIMERICK BEND**
The bend of the Limerick pattern is smoothly curved for most of its length, but the angle increases sharply and the wire straightens just before the barb.

# FRESHWATER WEIGHTS

**W**eights are an integral part of fishing, and range from the split shot needed to cock a float to the heavy 'bomb' weights used to anchor baits firmly on the bottom of the lake or river.

Split shot is the most common type of freshwater fishing weight. It is split to allow it to be pinched gently onto the line, where its weight pulls the float down to the required position in the water and also adds casting weight.

Standard shot is graded in ten different sizes, from number 8 up to the biggest, SSG (swan shot, so called because it's the size of shot – 15 to the ounce – that was once used for shooting swans for food). There are also smaller shot, known as microshot, which are most often used for the delicate weighting of tiny pole floats.

Once all shot was made of lead, but in the United Kingdom only number 8 and smaller is now formed from lead. The rest must be made out of a non-toxic material, and tungsten is a popular substitute for lead.

But split shot apart, there are many other freshwater fishing weights used on their own in order to fish baits on the bottom. This style of fishing is generally known as ledgering. Ledger weights come in a variety of shapes and sizes, and some are incorporated into small plastic containers that can be filled with bait. These are called swimfeeders.

Most ledger weights are attached to the line via a small half-swivel fixed into the top. They can be left free-running or fixed firmly. Other methods of attachment include threading the line through a central hole, as is the case with in-line carp weights and the round drilled 'bullet' weights.

The size and shape of the ledger weight used is largely dependent on where the angler is fishing and how far he needs to cast. For example, the weight needed to keep a bait anchored firmly on the bottom of a fast-flowing river will be greater than that required in a still water.

A flattened ledger weight will hold bottom better in a strong flow than a rounder weight that offers more resistance to the current. Sometimes, of course, a round weight, which does get pushed along the bottom, may be exactly

*Swimfeeders, such as the amber-coloured blockend feeder seen here near the tail of the fish, are a very popular form of ledger weight.*

what the angler requires. Flat ledger weights can be purchased commercially, or made at home by flattening rounded weights with a hammer or in a vice.

Round weights known as drilled bullets are used to trundle a bait, such as luncheon meat, along a riverbed. The flow pushes the bullet along, pulling the bait with it. The advantage of this is that sometimes fish are less suspicious of a bait that is moving slowly along than one that is firmly anchored on the bottom.

Ledgering works well for a number of reasons. Firstly, it allows the angler to place an anchored bait in fast-flowing water where a float will struggle to perform adequately. It also gets the bait down to the bottom quickly, perhaps avoiding small 'nuisance' fish that are feeding in the upper layers. Bigger, bottom-feeding

species, such as barbel, bream and tench, can often be targeted better by ledgering than by float fishing. The extra weight also allows a larger hookbait to be used, which is another great way to avoid those unwanted little species. It's little wonder, really, that ledgering is the number one method for those anglers who like to catch big fish.

A simple 'bomb' is the easiest ledger weight to use. It comes in a variety of sizes and is so called because of its slightly pear-shaped and bomb-like appearance. On still water, when bream or roach are the target, there's little need to put a bomb of more than half an ounce on the line, unless a long casting distance is required.

Carp anglers, too, make use of bombs (although even in still water these tend to be heavier than for ledgering) so that they can maintain an ultra-tight line between

weight and reel. This allows for the use of electronic bite alarms, which work by detecting the movement of line across a sensor.

Some carp weights have a hollow centre through which the line can be passed. This keeps them directly in line with the rod tip, which aids bite sensitivity and makes the rig more streamlined when a fish is being played.

Swimfeeders are a very popular form of ledger weight. Until they were invented, anglers had to rely on loose feed to get free offerings close to their ledgered hookbaits. Most swimfeeders are made of plastic, with a lead strip worked into the design to add the necessary casting and holding weight. There are also swimfeeders made from wire, which are called cage feeders.

Swimfeeders come in either open-end form, which means they

have no end caps and can be filled with stiff groundbait mixes or bread, or they have end caps, which means they can be filled with loose baits such as maggots. These days, most standard feeders have clip-on weights, so their weight can be adjusted to make them just right to cast to the distance required or to sit firmly on the bottom of the flowing river.

Salmon anglers also have cause to use weights when they want to send light spinners deeper into the river. They generally use one of two types of weight, the Wye and the Jardine. Both are fixed in line with the spinner, so as not to affect its action unduly.

The Wye is tied to the end of the main line, with a trace linking its base to the spinner. The Jardine is fixed by wrapping the line around a spiralled groove on the body of the weight and around a small spiral of wire at each end. These weights are also used by pike anglers.

One other form of weight is the plummet. This isn't used for presenting a hookbait, but rather for assessing the depth when float fishing. Most have a small block of cork in the base into which the hook is stuck. The float rig is cast out so that the plummet sinks straight to the bottom. If the float sinks out of sight, you add depth by sliding the float up the line. If the float does not cock properly, you reduce depth by sliding the float down the line. When you have found the right depth, with the plummet on the bottom and the float properly cocked, you can adjust the float to work the bait at the depth you require, remove the plummet, and begin fishing.

There are also weights designed specifically for use when pole fishing. These are called olivettes and provide a streamlined and relatively tangle-free bulk of weight on a pole rig. Most are attached to the line simply by threading the line through a narrow central bore.

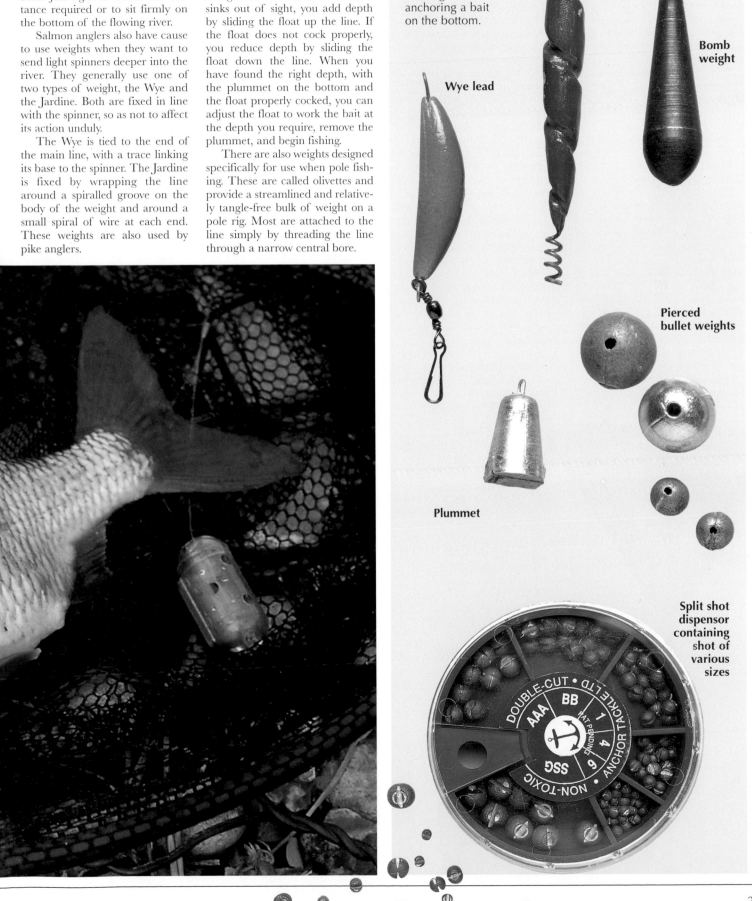

### WEIGHTS
There is a great variety of weights on the market, each designed to perform a specific function such as cocking a float or anchoring a bait on the bottom.

**Jardine or Spiral lead**

**Bomb weight**

**Wye lead**

**Pierced bullet weights**

**Plummet**

**Split shot dispensor containing shot of various sizes**

# LANDING TACKLE

There is little point going to all the effort of hooking and playing a fish if it is to be lost at the end of the fight because it can't be landed safely. The culmination of hours of anticipation and determination should never be left to chance, and a few minutes considering the right equipment to land your quarry, be it a net, tailer or gaff, is time well spent.

The most popular means of landing a fish is with a specially designed landing net. These come in various forms to suit the size and species of fish being sought.

In freshwater specimen hunting where carp, pike or catfish are the quarry, a large triangular net, with sprung glass fibre arms, is the most efficient type because it is able to scoop up fish of 30 pounds or more. Even for fish of this size a net with 36-inch-long arms is quite adequate, although some specialist anglers use nets with arms as long as 50 inches – just to make sure. If the fish is to be returned unharmed, as little damage as possible must be inflicted and so nets with soft, knotless nylon mesh are now used. These nets have bags up to 3 feet deep, to prevent a large, powerful fish from injuring itself.

For most coarse fishing, flat-bottomed pan nets are the most popular type, but their size and construction means they are not ideal for very large fish or for species such as trout or salmon, which are apt to jump. Pan nets allow the angler to remove the fish quickly and easily without having to search through folds of mesh, making them a great favourite with competition anglers who fish with ultralight tackle. A pan net has a round or a triangular frame and is attached to the end of a long, telescopic pole so the fish can be netted well away from the angler.

For trout fishing, nets with extendable handles, and which can be carried either strapped to the angler's back or attached to a belt, are the most commonly used type. Many also fold, with the head hinged so that it collapses back along the handle when not in use. This makes the net easier to carry and minimizes the risk of it catching on bushes and barbed wire fences while the angler is walking. When a fish is hooked, the head of the net is simply flipped into place with a flick of the wrist, and a mechanism at the fork of the frame locks it into position.

For salmon fishing, a large, rigid-framed net such as the Gye Net, which has a strong alloy frame and handle, is the perfect choice. This type of net is usually held by a strap to the angler's back, the extendable handle sliding through the frame prior to landing a fish. Because of the strong fast flow typically found in salmon rivers, the landing net should have a wide, open mesh to reduce water resistance and make it as manoeuvrable as possible.

When wading or float-tubing for trout, some anglers prefer a light tennis-racket style of net, although these are only of any use when the angler can get very close to the hooked fish. These nets have a wooden or alloy frame similar in shape to a tennis racket head, and a deep, soft mesh. This type of net is light and easily carried either clipped to the angler's waistcoat or attached to it by an elastic cord. Tennis racket nets come in a range of sizes and are capable of landing large fish, but using this type of net properly requires experience.

With a mind to conserving stocks, more and more sea anglers

### LANDING NETS
Landing nets range from the shallow pan nets on long, telescopic handles, which are little more than scoops for lifting out small fish, to the large specimen nets with rim diameters of 36 to 42 inches or more which are designed to engulf the largest carp or pike.

### KEEPNETS
A keepnet is a long net in which fish can be kept after capture until the end of the fishing session, when they can be weighed, measured and released. The open end of the net is anchored to the bank and the rest of it is submerged in the water to keep the fish alive.

are netting their fish. Bass and sea bream, which are often returned, are regularly netted rather than being gaffed, while non-edible species such as tope are either netted or tailed by hand. From boats, rigid-framed nets with large, open mesh are the most often used, though from piers and high rocks a drop net often makes the difference between landing a fish and losing it.

This latter type of net has a circular frame up to 36 inches in diameter, and rather than having a handle it is dropped into the water on the end of a thin, strong rope. The base of the mesh is weighted so that it sinks quickly, the technique being for the angler to steer the hooked fish over the mouth of the net before the netsman hauls it up by the rope.

Although salmon may be netted, some anglers prefer to use a tailer. This device consists of a metal loop, fixed to a rigid handle, which slips over the salmon's tail.

### THE GAFF

A gaff is a large metal hook that is impaled in the body of a hooked fish to drag it from the water. Gaffs are used mainly for landing large seafish.

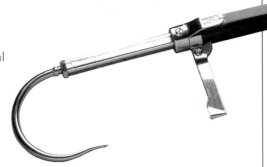

When the loop is in position, it is quickly but gently pulled tight. It takes an experienced eye to use the tailer efficiently, but where carrying a large net is a problem or where beaching or tailing by handing is impossible, a mechanical tailer is a safe and effective method of landing a salmon.

The fact that a salmon has a 'wrist', a rigid step between the base of its tail and its body, means that this implement is extremely secure, but can cause damage to the tail and it should not be used if the fish is going to be returned.

Some anglers still use a gaff, which is a large metal hook, on a handle, which is thrust into the fish's body. Now rarely used for salmon, pike or trout, the gaff is still a common method for landing large seafish such as cod, ling and conger eels plus big game fish such as shark, tuna and marlin.

With big game fish, which can weigh hundreds of pounds, a special gaff with a detachable head is used. This type of gaff is particularly important with fish such as shark, which are inclined to roll when gaffed. The breakaway or flying gaff, as it is known, is attached securely to a rope, the handle pulling free once the gaff head has been deployed. The gaffed fish is then pulled to the side of the boat with the rope. However, IGFA rules do not permit the use of a flying gaff, and therefore a world record claim cannot be made for a fish secured in this manner.

With conservation in angling becoming increasingly important, many anglers are forsaking the gaff – which seriously damages or even kills the fish – in favour of netting, tailing or beaching. With these methods, the fish can be landed and released unharmed.

Even big, powerful species such as marlin are now no longer always gaffed, many being unhooked before being measured, tagged and released.

*Using a landing net is the best way to remove a hooked fish from the water.*

# LEDGER AND SPECIALIST RODS

Ledger rods suitable for all-round freshwater bait fishing come in two basic formats, the standard type with a screw-threaded tip ring to take either a swing tip or a quiver tip, and those with a tapered quiver tip spliced directly into the tip.

Standard ledger rods have actions varying from fairly stiff to sloppy. With the stiffer-actioned rods, the rod tip will usually provide adequate bite indication when you're fishing in fast water, but when more sensitive indication is needed you should use a quiver tip screwed into the threaded tip ring. A threaded tip ring can be fitted to any ledger rod that hasn't already got one.

The floppy or easy-actioned rod works well with a swing tip bite indicator and, unlike the stiff-actioned rod, it won't cause the swing tip to wrap around the rod tip on the strike, which should be an easy pull-and-follow-through wrist action. Standard ledger rods are usually 9 to 10 feet long, and such rods will handle a wide range of fishing situations in both still and running water.

Two-piece ledger rods, 10 to 12 feet long with built-in quiver tips, are another extremely versatile type of rod. Although they're generally used for river fishing, the quiver tip also provides good indication of shy bites in still waters. The graphite (carbon fibre) rods are lighter than glass fibre models and can be held comfortably for long periods, an important advantage when you're ledgering for fast-biting fish and you have to hold the rod rather than put it into rod rests.

The best of these rods remain quite rigid when fishing fast-flowing water, with only the flexible quiver tip moving to the pull of the current or of a biting fish. The rod handle should be short – only 20 inches or so – to maximize the length of rod through which the action is developed, and the rings, especially if you're going to be playing large fish, should have hardened or lined centres.

Most specialist rods, for pike, carp or whatever, are classified according to their test curves as well as their lengths. The test curve is the amount of pull, measured on a spring balance, that is needed to bend the tip of the rod round into a quarter-circle. The resulting figure gives an indication of the range of line strengths that the rod will handle best. Lighter or heavier lines may be used, but the optimum strength of line for a particular rod can be calculated by multiplying the test curve, in pounds, by five or six. So a rod with a test curve of, say, 1 pound, will work best with a line of 5 or 6 pounds test, while a rod of 2 pounds test curve should be used with lines of 10 to 12 pounds test.

The higher the test curve, the more powerful the rod and the wider its range of uses. A 3-pound test curve rod, capable of handling lines of between 15 and 18 pounds, would be a very powerful freshwater rod indeed, really suitable only for fishing large, wild waters where snaggy or rocky conditions or exceptionally large fish, or both, are expected.

Avon style rods of 11 or 12 feet and 1 1/4 pounds test curve (with a 6- to 7-pound line) are perhaps the most versatile of all ledger rods. Those made of graphite have the ability to pick up line even when using a swimfeeder to present bait at distances of 50 to 60 yards, but they are still soft enough for close-range fishing.

These rods were first developed for hooking and playing powerful fish on fast-flowing rivers, but they are also useful for light carp fishing both on the bottom or at the surface, as well as for float fishing for

ALTERNATIVE TOP SECTION WITH QUIVER TIP

STANDARD TOP SECTION

threaded tip ring for quiver or swing tip attachment

BUTT SECTION

single leg intermediate rings

twin leg intermediate rings

sliding ring reel fitting

mixed cork and hyperlon handle

## CHOOSING A ROD

| USE | LENGTH |
| --- | --- |
| A short, ultralight rod, ideal for fishing a straight bomb at short range for small species such as roach and perch. Use on rivers, lakes and canals. | 10ft |
| As above , with extra length to fish feeders on stillwaters and slow moving rivers. | 11ft |
| A stronger rod enabling feeder fishing at distance on stillwaters or fast rivers. Will cast feeders up to 2 1/2 oz. | 12ft |
| A strong, robust rod, capable of casting feeders of 3 oz into big, fast-flowing waters | 12ft 6in |

*Ledger rods are used for fishing baits on the bottom in both still and running water.*

tench, plug fishing for chub, livebaiting for perch and all types of zander fishing.

Specialist rods with a test curve of 1½ pounds and over are suitable for carp and pike fishing, and also for taking large eels and catfish. You should choose a rod that

has enough power to handle the type and size of fish you expect to catch, and the conditions in which you expect you are going to fish for it. A 1¾-pound test curve rod will cope with most pike and carp fishing, but the rod action should be chosen carefully.

For instance, a powerful rod with a soft, all-through action would be useless for fishing at long range, say 70 yards or more. Here,

a fast-taper, tip-action rod that can pick up this length of line is essential. On the other hand, using such a rod for large carp or pike only a few yards out from the bank would be asking for trouble. The only real elasticity in the outfit would be the line, and once that was exhausted, line breakage would be inevitable.

Most specialist pike and carp rods are available in lengths of 11 or 12 feet. Overall, the longer

models of specialist rod are more versatile, but if most of your fishing is close-in, or from locations with overhanging trees, the shorter ones are advisable.

Always fix the rod together firmly by twisting the joints to ensure that the two halves are fully home, or the ferrule might split under heavy pressure. If the two sections are not properly fitted together, damage could result.

# LINES AND LEADERS

For the majority of fishing, nylon monofilament (mono) is still the most popular line. The fact that it is produced in a vast range of diameters and breaking strains, and that it is relatively cheap, makes nylon mono extremely versatile. It is used for most types of fishing from the ultralight styles of float fishing to all kinds of bait fishing in fresh and saltwater, spinning, and even fly fishing, where a short length is added to the front of the fly line to give a delicate presentation of the fly.

Mono is produced in breaking strains as light as 4 ounces, which are used by specialist coarse anglers, right up to IGFA 130 pound rating, which is used for big game fish such as shark and marlin. Though there is nylon line heavier than this, it is used mainly for big game traces rather than for main lines.

Having inherent stretch, nylon monofilament offers a good deal of shock absorption, which is a real advantage when a fish is close to the angler and almost played out. If the fish makes a final bolt, this stretch can be enough to cushion the impact and prevent the line breaking. But at long range, this stretch is a disadvantage because it makes striking and hooking the fish more difficult.

Dacron lines, made by weaving a polyester fibre around a central core, are ideal for fishing in deep water beacuse their lack of stretch allows the angler to keep in touch with the bait, making bite detection and hooking more positive. This makes them popular with sea anglers fishing in deep water.

Unfortunately, being woven, Dacron is not as robust as nylon, and chafing on a wreck or reef can easily damage it and reduce its breaking strain, although some of the hard-braided makes such as Gudebrod and Berkley are more robust than the softer weaves.

Being limp, Dacron is also used by carp anglers for hair rigs. The lack of stiffness that Dacron exhibits means that the bait moves in a natural enough way to fool wily carp.

For spinning and baitcasting, a new generation of braided polyethylene lines is becoming popular. The main advantage of these polyethylene lines over nylon mono is that they are much finer for the same breaking strain, being approximately half the diameter of mono of a similar strength.

They are limp, and as they have little stretch, bite detection and hooking are much more positive, especially at long range. The main disadvantage is that they are much more expensive than mono.

Like Dacron, metal wire line has little or no stretch, making it ideal for bite detection and hooking at extreme range. Because of their stiffness and tendency to kink, wire lines are used only for trolling or for deep sea fishing where they are simply paid off a multiplying reel rather than cast.

In saltwater angling, a wire line is ideal for bottom fishing in deep water and very fast tides, where wire is the only practical way to get terminal tackle down to the bottom. Wire line does, however, have its own tackle demands and in-use disciplines.

The rod should have a soft action and carry a full set of roller rings or guides lined with a very hard material, such as aluminium oxide, to resist the wire's cutting effect. Wire line must be fished from a narrow, metal-spool multiplier, and it must be under constant control and allowed to run to the bottom under tension. Failure to observe this basic rule will result in a hopeless tangle.

Unlike most types of line, which need the addition of weight to enable them to be cast, fly lines have the weight as an integral part of their profiles. Fly lines come in a wide range of weights and densities in accordance with an international system called the AFTM (Association of Fishing Tackle Manufacturers) rating, which gives a specific weight for the first 30 feet of the line's belly.

Each weight of line is given a number, from 1, the lightest, up to the 13 or greater used for saltwater fly fishing. A number 5, 6 or 7 line is the usual weight for most types of fly fishing for trout. The rating of the line should always be matched to that of the rod – all fly rods carry their AFTM rating on the butt section, and this will tell you which rating of line is best for that particular rod. For instance, a rod with an AFTM rating of 6/7 will cast most efficiently with a number 6 or number 7 line.

Fly lines are produced in three profiles: double taper (DT), weight-forward (WF) and shooting head. With the double taper, the line has a symmetrical profile tapering equally at either end, with the thickest and heaviest part of the line in the middle. Where accuracy and delicacy are more important than distance, such as on small clear rivers, the double taper is the most efficient.

With the weight-forward, the heavy belly, approximately 35 feet long, is at the front of the line and is backed by a thinner running line. The technique with this type of line is to aerialize the belly, so that when it is cast, the thinner running line shoots easily through the rings. This enables the weight-forward to be cast farther than a double taper but with less delicacy. To aid presentation, models of weight-forward line are now available with a longer belly than standard. Long bellies offer the delicacy of the double taper at short to medium range, but can be cast longer distances.

The shooting head takes the weight-forward profile one step further by using a short, heavy belly of fly line 10 to 12 yards long, which is backed by ultra-slick monofilament shooting line that

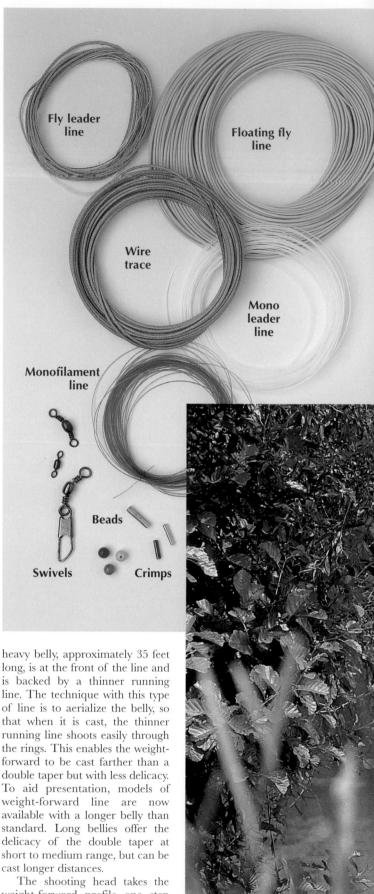

*Fly lines are made in three profiles and a wide range of densities and colours.*

**Fly leader line**

**Floating fly line**

**Wire trace**

**Mono leader line**

**Monofilament line**

**Beads**

**Swivels**

**Crimps**

passes easily through the rings. Accuracy and delicacy are drastically reduced with the shooting head, but the long distances it can be cast allow the angler to cover fish otherwise out of range.

The density of the line governs its sink rate. The lightest of all fly lines are those designed to float. Floating fly lines are used for many styles of fly fishing where the fly itself is intended to float or fish close to the surface. By using a weighted fly, a floating line may even be used to reach trout lying deep. However, for consistent depth control it is more efficient to use a sinking line. These vary in density from intermediate lines, which sink very slowly, to medium- and fast-sinking lines. Fast- sinking lines are designed to present a fly in either very deep lakes or fast moving rivers.

If your quarry includes pike, zander or indeed any freshwater fish with sharp teeth, it is essential to use a metal trace between the reel line and bait or lure to prevent being bitten-off. For spinning, a trace of 12 inches of 10 to 20 pounds test braided wire is fine, with a swivel at one end to attach it to the reel line and a snap link at the other to clip onto the spinner or plug.

For using live or dead baits, the same type of braided wire can be used but it should be longer, about 20 inches, with a swivel at one end and a treble hook attached to the other. A second treble should be allowed to slide freely along the trace, being locked in position, when mounting a bait, by wrapping the wire trace around it three or four times.

Traces are used more often for sea fishing than in freshwater. Where fish have either very small or no teeth, nylon traces are quite adequate. These should be from 8 to 10 pounds test for medium-sized species up to 25 pounds or so for larger species such as bass and cod. The main exception to this is when fly fishing, where a leader made up of tapered or straight nylon monofilament is used to provide a delicate step-down from the thick fly line to the fly itself.

For larger sea fish, such as skate and halibut, a leader of 100 pounds test is perfect, but for species such as conger or grouper, which are caught over rocky ground or from wrecks, 150 pounds test nylon will resist the chafing such fishing brings.

Big game species such as tuna and marlin are best tackled with 300 to 600 pounds test nylon, which will stand the punishment that fish of this size and power can dish out. Nylon up to 100 pounds test can be knotted, but the heavier nylons must be crimped or even double crimped at each end to pre-vent them slipping. For shark, which have teeth and even scales that can cut through the strongest nylon, it is imperative to use a trace of heavy braided wire.

These can be either of plain galvanized wire or plastic coated. There are differing opinions as to the merits of each, though plastic coated wires can trap moisture leading to rust and eventual failure – usually when the fish of a life-time has been hooked.

All metal traces must be crimped and those used for shark, which are prone to spinning and kinking the line, should be made in two parts and joined with a large, free-moving swivel. The type of swivel depends on the strength and thickness of the trace, but for shark and marlin the sizes 6/0 to 8/0 made by Berkley or Sampo are ideal. For smaller, lighter traces, the size of swivel should be scaled down accordingly.

# POLES

Although poles have been in use for many years, they are generally regarded by anglers as a product of the modern era. This is because there is a fundamental difference between the old type of pole and its modern version, and that difference lies in the materials used to construct them. Where once bamboo was the main component of the pole, resulting in a 'saggy' and heavy tool, it was replaced first by glass fibre and then by graphite (carbon fibre). Graphite now reigns supreme, and it has revolutionized pole fishing.

Most modern poles are of the take-apart type and consist of sections (lengths) of graphite tubing, each formed so that it fits over or into the next, resulting in a continuous length of tubing that tapers smoothly from butt to tip. Some poles, mainly the relatively short, slim models known as whips, are telescopic with sections that retract into the butt.

Today, pole fishing is so popular the world over that there are literally hundreds of different styles of pole. They all look basically the same – thick at one end and thin at the other – but there can be many important differences.

Price is the most obvious one. A pole can be bought quite cheaply, but a top quality pole may cost as much as a small car. An expensive pole should be offering the angler many advantages.

Length is vital. A pole has the major benefit of being able to present a bait as

## POLES

Most poles are made of graphite and range in length from less than 6 metres (20 ft) to 16 metres (52 feet) or more. The shortest models are often telescopic, but most poles are of the take-apart type.

butt section - doubles as case for other sections

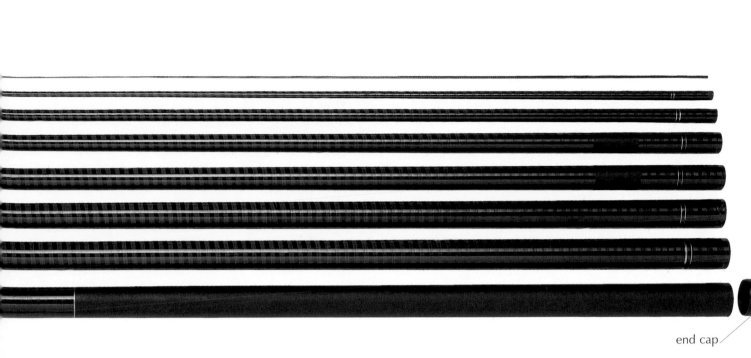

end cap

*Despite its length, a pole is relatively easy to control because of its light weight.*

delicately as possible and an angler wants to be able to do this at maximum range. A good quality pole will be manageable at 12 to 14 metres (39 to 46 feet), and may even extend to beyond 16 metres (52 ft). A cheap pole may sometimes offer up to 14 metres in length, but it will usually be too heavy and 'floppy' in the middle part to fish correctly and efficiently. A good pole will remain rigid, even when fished at its maximum length, making it far easier for the angler to control.

Strength is extremely important. When a pole is designed, there is always a compromise between length and strength. It is feasible for manufacturers to make a super-long pole, but to make it light enough for anglers to handle at beyond 20 metres (66 ft) would mean a reduction in the strength of the graphite being used. The pole would simply be too fragile to risk using.

Only a few years ago, poles were considered to be suitable only for small fish and for venues like canals. But these days the pole is regarded as a more versatile tool and there are few venues, or for that matter fish, that aren't right for the pole. Everywhere you go, from small stream to wide river, you're likely to see poles being used,and the fish you can catch on them range from tiny roach and bleak up to large chub, barbel and even carp.

Carbon fibre plays its part in this versatility by creating poles strong enough to handle relatively big and powerful fish, but also important is the use of elastic. A length of elastic is anchored inside the end few sections of the pole and the line is attached to its free end. The stretchiness of the elastic absorbs the shocks of fighting a large fish. When a fish is hooked, the elastic helps to tire it out so that it can eventually be netted. Elastics are graded from fine to ultra-thick and should be balanced with the pole and the size of fish you are aiming for. This way, even carp weighing 10 lb or more can be landed using a pole.

Until elastic became widely used, many poles relied on a slim and solid but flexible length of graphite, known as a flick tip, as the final section of the pole, and the line was attached to this. Although still used today for catching small fish, the flick tip is not as versatile as elastic, and is mainly used with the pole's slimmer, telescopic cousin, the whip.

Many anglers with poles will keep two, three, or even four spare sets of top sections, all neatly fitted out with different strengths of elastic, so that exactly the right gear for the occasion can be used. Top sections can be switched in seconds, if it appears the elastic being used is either too fine or too thick for the fish on offer.

Fishing with a pole brings many specific benefits to the angler. Finer and more delicate terminal tackle can be used, making it easier to fool the fish, and absolute accuracy can be obtained because the rig is being dropped precisely in place by the pole, rather than cast out using rod and line. For example, when canal fishing it is possible to position your rig and hook right against the side of a boat or beneath a bush or some similar feature, accurately and time and time again.

It is also possible to use the pole to hold back your float against any water movement, in a way that is impossible with any running-line set-up, even the stick float. This works the bait in a manner that can be extremely attractive to the fish you're trying to catch.

There are, however, a few disadvantages to pole fishing. For example, the pole has a relatively limited range, and although large fish can be landed, there is also every possibility that some will be lost, especially those 'bonus' fish that are hooked when small fish are the target.

But on the whole, the many advantages of using a pole outweigh the disadvantages. Just look at the world championships over the last few years: the majority of the top-class competitors will have been using a pole for some, if not all, of the time. In fact, there can be few, if any, match anglers who don't include a pole of some sort in their armoury.

There can be little doubt that graphite poles have changed the face of coarse fishing, and as manufacturers strive to produce ever more advanced poles, the outlook for anglers can only be good.

Please note that you should never use a pole anywhere near overhead power lines or during a thunderstorm. Graphite is highly conductive, and damp glass fibre can conduct electricity through the surface moisture.

# ROD RESTS AND BITE INDICATORS

**W**hen you are using more than one rod, or when the rod must be left static for long periods, a rod rest is an extremely useful piece of equipment. It allows you to perform other tasks, such as baiting up, tying rigs or taking a drink, without having to keep constant hold of the rod. Indeed, for certain types of fishing, such as ledgering, where the rod needs to be kept perfectly still, a rod rest is an absolute necessity.

Most rod rests are in two parts: the rod rest head itself, and the light alloy pole that supports it and which is fixed into the ground. Rod rest heads can vary from the simple V-shaped or cup-shaped versions to wide, plastic-covered frames into which the rod can be dropped quickly but safely without the need for careful positioning.

When some types of bite indicator are used, such as those that work close to the butt, the front rod rest must have a groove to allow the line to run through freely as a fish pulls away. Without this, the line will be trapped and any bites may remain undetected.

The most commonly used support for a rod rest is a bank stick, typically 2 to 4 feet long, which can be fixed or telescopic, the latter using a twist-and-lock

### ELECTRONIC INDICATORS

An electronic bite indicator gives an audible alarm when a fish takes the bait and pulls line from the reel.

collar or a thumb screw to lock the sections into place at the desired length. A point at the end allows the bank stick to be pushed into the mud or sand, or even pebbles, but on rock a self-supporting tripod is the most effective. Bank sticks have a female screw thread that accepts most rod rest heads, allowing the angler to keep a variety of heads for varying conditions without having to carry too many heavy metal sticks.

For anglers who use extremely long graphite (carbon fibre) poles, which can be over 15 metres (49 feet) long, there are also double-headed pole rests, which often form part of a seat system. These support the longer poles, which are too difficult and heavy to hold unsupported for long periods. Pole rollers are also popular as rests for pole fishing, and they allow the pole to be fed back quickly when breaking down the sections without risk of damage.

For sea fishing from the beach, a monopod pushed into the sand or shingle is extremely useful. Better still, though, is a tripod with two rest heads. This allows two rods to be used, which is the norm when surfcasting for species such as cod and bass, while the tripod itself is more stable than the monopod. It can even be used on pebble beaches or rocky areas, which are difficult if not impossible to penetrate with a monopod.

When you are using multiple rod set-ups, it is often preferable to use a multiple rod rest or Rod Pod. This comprises a self-supporting frame which has two or three uprights at either end, with threaded connections. The connections allow either rod rest heads or bite alarms to be screwed in to support up to three rods.

For many types of ledgering, bite detection can entail simply watching the rod top or holding the line and feeling for a bite. The rod top is a clumsy indicator, while holding the line on a winter's day can be an uncomfortable experience, so many anglers use simple but highly efficient swingtips and quivertips for bite indication.

The swing tip detects a bite by swinging upward when a fish pulls on the line, or falling back when a slack-line bite occurs. Swingtips come in various lengths, from around 10 inches up to 20 inches. The deeper the water and the stronger the current, the longer the swingtip needs to be.

Quivertips are lengths of glass fibre or graphite, which taper to a very fine point and are either made as integral parts of a quivertip rod or can be screwed into the tip of a standard ledger rod. Either way, the bite is detected by movement of the quivertip.

As an additional aid to bite detection when using either a swingtip or a quivertip, a target board is often set up in front of the tip. This board is marked with lines that show the position of the tip. This makes any movement of the tip easier to see, which allows delicate bites to be seen even when the water is rough. The board also protects the tip itself from being blown about by the wind and possibly registering false bites.

There are also a number of sophisticated electronic bite alarms on the market, such as the ever-popular Optonic and the high-tech Fox Micron. These are used mainly in carp and pike fishing where two or three rods are

*A rod rest is useful in ledgering, when the rod may not be not moved for long periods.*

used. The line passes over a sensor in the alarm, and when a fish picks up the bait, a sounder bleeps and a light flashes, giving both an audible and a visual sign of a bite.

To detect drop-back bites, many specialist anglers use a drop-back bobbin or 'monkey climber', which is positioned close to the rod between the reel and the butt ring. A monkey, as it is often known, is a light plastic sleeve that runs freely along a metal rod set vertically in the ground. The line is fixed into a clip just above the reel and looped over the monkey, then tensioned so that if a bite occurs, the monkey will lift. If, however, it is a drop-back bite, the monkey will fall. Monkey climbers are usually made of highly visible white plastic or painted in fluorescent colours.

For pike fishing, where bites usually take the form of a line-

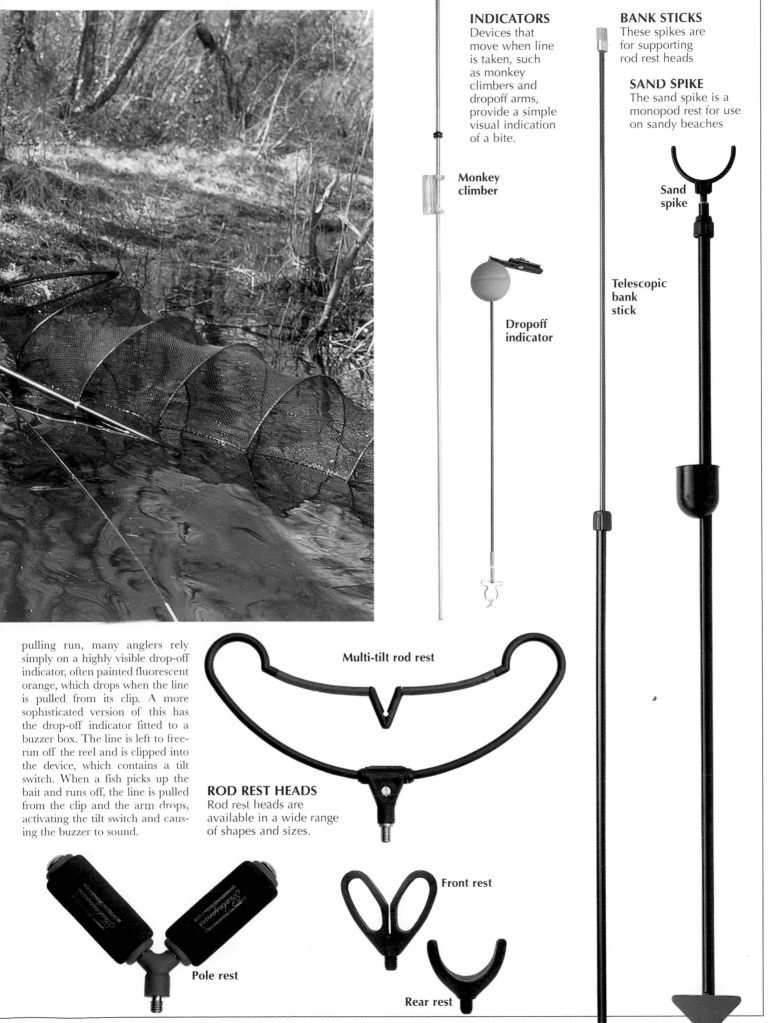

## INDICATORS
Devices that move when line is taken, such as monkey climbers and dropoff arms, provide a simple visual indication of a bite.

**Monkey climber**

**Dropoff indicator**

## BANK STICKS
These spikes are for supporting rod rest heads

## SAND SPIKE
The sand spike is a monopod rest for use on sandy beaches

**Sand spike**

**Telescopic bank stick**

**Multi-tilt rod rest**

pulling run, many anglers rely simply on a highly visible drop-off indicator, often painted fluorescent orange, which drops when the line is pulled from its clip. A more sophisticated version of this has the drop-off indicator fitted to a buzzer box. The line is left to free-run off the reel and is clipped into the device, which contains a tilt switch. When a fish picks up the bait and runs off, the line is pulled from the clip and the arm drops, activating the tilt switch and causing the buzzer to sound.

## ROD REST HEADS
Rod rest heads are available in a wide range of shapes and sizes.

**Pole rest**

**Front rest**

**Rear rest**

# SALMON RODS

Salmon fishing in the UK and Europe differs from trout fishing in that you may need to spend part of the season with spinning tackle, rather than using fly tackle throughout as you would for Atlantic salmon angling in North America. The all-round salmon angler, then, may well opt for one or two spinning outfits and a similar number of fly outfits. A lot will depend on where and when you are going to fish: big rivers in early spring are very different to small spate rivers in summer, or any lake or impoundment you might want to fish from a boat.

Initially, you might be content to start off salmon fishing by concentrating on spinning, although it's not always the most productive method. For fishing small rivers, there's little to beat a 7$^1$/$_2$- or 8-foot graphite (carbon fibre) spinning rod with a medium-sized fixed spool reel and 8-pound test monofilament line.

Most rods of this length are singlehanded and don't need much effort when casting. They prove ideal for casting into little crannies in a small river, and the bait can be brought quickly under control and into action in the most likely-looking water. You might have to cast more accurately than you would with a longer, double-handed rod on a big river, but spinning on small rivers is tremendous sport and a very effective way of catching a few fish.

For spinning on bigger rivers, two double-handed outfits worth considering are a 9$^1$/$_2$-foot rod with a fixed spool reel and 12-pound test line, which would be ideal for medium-sized rivers; and a stout 10-footer with a multiplying reel and 15- to 25-pound line for heavier baits of up to an ounce on large rivers.

The great advantage of the multiplying reel is that it gives good control over the heavier baits – but use it with baits that are too light and you'll get frequent overruns and loss of casting distance. With the fixed spool reel, though,

## THE SALMON ROD

DOUBLE-HANDED ROD GRIP

fore grip

button    butt grip    fixed position graphite reel fitting    traditional cork handle

*Fly fishing for salmon in a fast-flowing river. Salmon are caught mostly on flies, but they are also taken on lures and prawns.*

you'll get good casting distances with lighter baits, and perhaps a little more accuracy.

Screw reel fittings are ideal for all spinning rods, and it's important to have a large butt ring and good open bridge rings out to the tip. The large butt ring proves very useful with a fixed spool reel, where there may be a build up of friction as the line comes off the reel in wide spirals.

For fly fishing on small to medium-sized rivers you can use a singlehanded rod of 9$^{1}/_{2}$ or 10 feet and a number 7 line. On larger waters, a 12$^{1}/_{2}$- or 13-foot, double-handed model with a number 9 line makes an ideal all-round salmon fly rod. But for the really heavy work, when you're fishing with large flies and lines of size 10 and upwards, you need a double-handed rod of 14 to 18 feet.

In mid season, where the water's low and clear, you can often use a good, medium-action 10-foot trout rod. This, with a number 7 weight-forward floating line, will handle the smaller sizes of salmon fly (8s, 10s and 12s) very admirably.

It's important to remember that the longer and more powerful fly rods will need stronger terminal tackle to cope with the stress of playing a big fish. For early spring and late autumn you should rarely use leaders of less than 14 pounds test, and go to 20 pounds or more when using the large and heavy tube flies in the colder months. During the low water of summer, when fishing with shorter, single-handed rods, there's little need to

go stronger than 8 pounds test. This also frequently proves more than adequate when casting from a boat on still waters.

For much stillwater boat fishing it pays to use as long a rod as you can comfortably manage. A single-handed, 11$^{1}/_{2}$-foot graphite rod, for instance, will enable you to trip the fly over the waves and to bring it close into the boat before making your next cast. Very often, a salmon will take the fly just as you are about to retrieve for the next cast. This behaviour is unlike that of sea trout, which are more likely to take your fly only following a long cast and a quick retrieve.

If you can afford it, for all-round salmon fishing you should go for at least two spinning outfits and two for the fly. For spinning, you should be able to handle most situations with a singlehanded 8-foot rod and a fixed spool reel, and a double-handed 10-foot rod capable of being used both with a medium-sized fixed spool reel and with a multiplier.

For fly fishing, a good choice is a 15-foot, double-handed graphite rod with a number 11 line, and a singlehanded 10-foot rod carrying a number 7 line. As with trout rods, there is a variety of rod actions available. Avoid tip-actioned rods like the plague, and consider only those with a steely through-action down to the butt and the ability to put great pressure on a strong fish. Remember, the rod has to serve two principal functions: it has to act as a spring when you're casting and as a lever when you're playing a fish.

## CHOOSING A ROD

| USE | LENGTH | AFTM |
| --- | --- | --- |
| Singlehanded rod for summer rivers when flow rates are reduced. Will handle light tippets and small flies. | 10–10ft 6ins | 6–8 |
| Light double-handed rod gives ideal coverage for medium to large rivers, when summer fishing with floating or intermediate lines. | 11ft 3ins – 12ft 6ins | 7–10 |
| Heavy double-handed rod will Spey and overhead cast even large weighted tube flies. Ideal when river is in flood or at spring or autumn level, with power to fish heavy lines. | 14–16ft | 9–11 |

BUTT SECTION

MID SECTION

lined butt / stripping ring

TIP SECTION

# SALTWATER HOOKS

With so many sizes and patterns of hooks on the market, it's essential to choose a selection of hooks that are properly suited to the type of fishing you intend to do.

For example, if you go fishing for flatfish, which have small, rather distorted mouths, you should use long-shanked, narrow-gape hooks. These are readily available, but like most hooks they need attention before use. With the exception of the chemically-sharpened hooks, you should regard every hook you buy as blunt. Before use, sharpen each hook on an oilstone or, if it's a big one, use a file first then finish off with a stone.

For larger shore-caught fish such as bass and cod, chemically-sharpened hooks such as the Kamatsu range are ideal. Available in sizes up to 4-0, these hooks are strong enough in the wire to resist bending or breaking under hard stress, and the round bend and short point makes them a near-perfect overall hook design. The same hooks can be used for rock fishing for medium-sized species, but when you're fishing in rocky waters you should check the fine hook point regularly for damage.

The fine-wire Kamatsu type of hook is good for fish of up to 10 or 15 pounds, but for larger species such as conger, tope or big cod, a more substantial hook is essential. One of the best and strongest readily-available patterns is the 4-0/6-0 O'Shaughnessy bronzed or stainless steel hook, a flat-forged, straight-eyed, no-nonsense iron which will retain its shape even during brutal usage. Again, these hooks should be carefully sharpened before and during use.

The O'Shaughnessy hooks are also ideal for most inshore boat fishing. Available in sizes up to 10-0, the most useful boat fishing sizes are 6-0 and 8-0, which can be used with whole or cut fish or squid baits. The beauty of these hooks is their strength; many sea hooks snap or distort in use, but the O'Shaughnessy is unlikely to.

Inexperienced anglers make the mistake of buying expensive rods, reels and lines, then using cheap, poor quality hooks. The best equipment in the world won't be much use if the hook lets you down. The worst sort of sea hooks are those with a point which is too long, fragile and curved, because such a point is likely to be too brittle to withstand hard use.

Careful choice of hook is even more important when you're fishing for really large fish. Even a small shark is a big fish which calls for a strong, well-shaped hook. Hook sizes suitable for shark and other large fish range from 8-0 to 16-0, the most widely-used sizes being 10-0, 12-0 and 14-0.

The best sort of hook for shark is a heavy, forged pattern with a straight eye and an offset point. Shark hooks with flat points lack the excellent penetration of the offset point. The beauty of the offset pattern is that when a fish is struck, the point of the hook is actually clear of the bait. With the flat style of hook, the bait often masks the hook point to such an extent that it doesn't always engage on impact.

Eye shape is also important. For shark fishing, a round eye is better than a needle eye because it allows the hook to swing freely on the trace loop so that the taking shark feels no unnatural stiffness as it mouths the dangling bait. Shark, like most big fish, can be cautious feeders, quick to reject any bait that arouses their suspicions.

Although they're not particularly good for shark fishing, flat, needle-eyed hooks are perfect for use with trolling lures such as Kona Heads. The offset hook is useless for this purpose because it causes the lure to twist in use, wrapping the skirt of the lure tightly around the shank and bend of the hook. Even when trolling a mounted natural bait the offset hook will tend to spin it, a movement that soon destroys the trace.

The flat-pointed hook is also excellent for fishing for big blue marlin, using a Kona head type of lure mounted on a two-hook rig with a stiff bar to hold the two hooks rigid.

Hooks are made of high-carbon steel or stainless steel wire. The wire is cut to length, the point is ground and the eye formed, and the barb is cut by a chisel. After this, the bend is formed and the eye is turned up or down (if required) and sometimes brazed to close the gap in it and make it stronger. The shaped hook is hardened and tempered, then cleaned. Finally, it may be blued, japanned or lacquered, or plated with bronze, nickel or cadmium, to protect it from corrosion. For added strength, the hook bend is often forged before tempering.

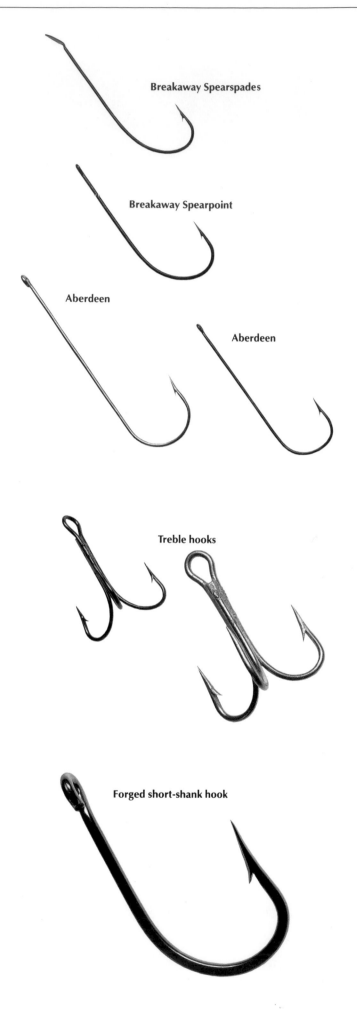

Breakaway Spearspades

Breakaway Spearpoint

Aberdeen

Aberdeen

Treble hooks

Forged short-shank hook

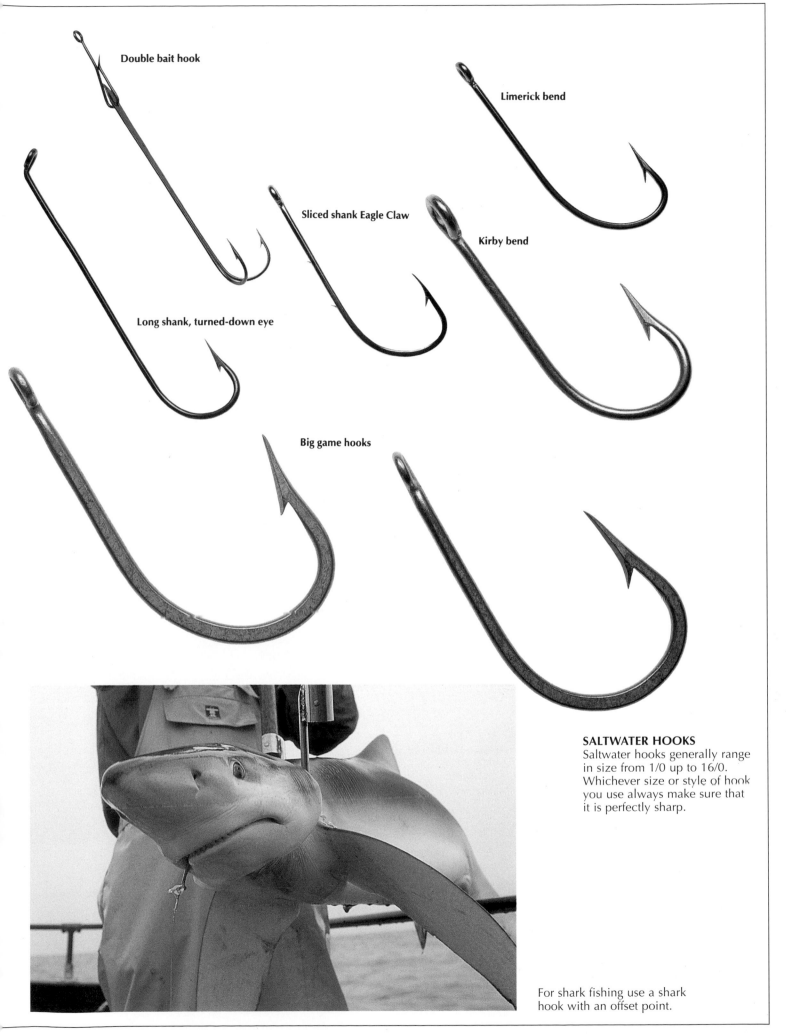

Double bait hook

Limerick bend

Sliced shank Eagle Claw

Kirby bend

Long shank, turned-down eye

Big game hooks

**SALTWATER HOOKS**
Saltwater hooks generally range in size from 1/0 up to 16/0. Whichever size or style of hook you use always make sure that it is perfectly sharp.

For shark fishing use a shark hook with an offset point.

# SALTWATER RODS

The majority of saltwater rods are designed for boat fishing. Some are straightforward fishing sticks, some are custom-built, but most are IGFA-rated in the 6, 12, 20 and 30-pound classes and should be used with lines of the same rating.

Boat rods are made of solid or hollow glass fibre or a combination of glass fibre and graphite (carbon fibre). Solid glass fibre rods first appeared a half century ago and are still produced. They are generally less expensive than hollow rods, but the blank is virtually indestructible, and they are often found on charter boats where gear is hired out. The American company Penn produces high-quality solid glass rods in a range of line classes, and Shakespeare offers solid glass rods for light, medium and heavy classes.

Hollow glass fibre rods were developed in the 1960s. Glass fibre construction gave the opportunity for saltwater rods of immense strength but of very thin profile and outstanding action, and these could be designed for specific types of fishing and species.

Rods made mainly of graphite don't usually perform well as boat rods, and pure graphite rods have a tendency to split or shatter. The glass/graphite mixture, however, combines the best features of both materials and is ideal for this type of fishing. Glass fibre and graphite in combination, however, produces a rod blank of immense strength

and action. A unique process known as Howald, developed in the United States for the Shakespeare Company, produces the famed Ugly Stik range of rods. Basically, the blank has an inner spiral of graphite covered by an outer layer of glass fibre.

This technology paved the way for multiclass rods called Stand Up Stiks. These are short, one-piece rods with a minimum length of 5 feet and a maximum of 6¹/₂ feet. They have caused a revolution in deepwater wreck fishing, particularly for conger. The principle of the Stand Up multiclass rod, usually rated 30–80 pounds and used in association with a special butt pad worn low, is a soft top section that in effect folds down under pressure, reducing the lever action working against the angler.

Its lifting power is awesome, which is exactly the what is needed to get a big conger quickly away from the hazardous nature of a wreck or a rock canyon. These rods feature roller rings and a roller tip that reduces line friction as a heavy fish is pumped up.

For general downtide bottom fishing, 20 and 30 pound rods of 7 or 7¹/₂ feet are suitable for most species. 12 and 20 pound class rods of 7¹/₂ feet are perfect for taking pollack from an anchored or drifting boat. If you are targeting potentially heavy fish such as conger, ling or skate, use a rod with a rating of at least 30 pounds, and for deepwater wreck fishing you

should step up to a 50 pound rod or a Stand Up Stik. Blue shark, being a running fish, can be taken with a 30 pound rod, but the much larger porbeagle is a very different proposition and you should use 50 or 80 pound tackle.

The technique of uptiding is very effective in shallow water where the bottom is free of hazards. It requires a rod of 8 to 10 feet, capable of casting 4 to 8 ounces of terminal tackle, and can bring fine catches of cod, bass and ray species. Uptide rods are avail-

able in a range of casting weights, for example 2–6 ounces and 2–10 ounces. The heavier rods are necessary in very strong tidal flows, while the lighter rods, by virtue of their length, also make excellent trolling rods for bass and pollack over reefs and open ground.

In uptiding, the boat is at anchor and the terminal gear is cast away uptide. A lead with grip wires is used if the end rig, which is usually a running ledger, is to remain in one place. The instant the lead hits the water, the reel

## CHOOSING A ROD

| USE | LENGTH | IGFA |
|---|---|---|
| Light rods for reef and open ground fishing. Use a lever or star drag multiplier. Casts 2–6oz weight. | 7–7ft 6ins | 12–20lbs |
| Medium rods for wreck as well as reef and open ground work. Use a multiplier reel without level line mechanism. Casts 2–10oz weight. | 6ft 6ins– 7ft 6ins | 30–50lbs |
| Heavy rods for wreck and open ground fishing. Use with multiplier. Ideal for conger and smaller sharks. | 6ft 6ins– 7ft 6ins | 50–80lbs |

### DETACHABLE BUTT SECTION

screw winch reel fitting

rubber but end  hyperlon butt grip

gimbel fitting  hyperlon fore grip

double roller butt ring

one piece blank for strength

locking collar

spool is braked to stop backlash. A few seconds later, pressure is released to allow extra line to pay off the reel. Once the terminal rig is on the bottom, the slack line is wound in and the grip lead is anchored firmly into the mud, sand or shingle.

An alternative to the running ledger, the rolling ledger, allows a great deal more ground to be searched and differs only in that a

*Fishing at sea calls for tough, well made tackle.*

conventional bomb type lead replaces the grip weight.

For shore fishing, an 11 to 12 foot surfcasting rod with a medium-fast action and rated for 6 ounces of lead is capable of casting a good distance and will meet the needs of most anglers. It is also ideal for fishing rocky areas, as it has the lift and power characteristics necessary for such species as conger, bull huss and big wrasse. A heavy duty, double-handed 10 foot spinning rod can also be used with success for most species in this cat-

egory of shore fishing, but it is a touch light for conger.

Boat uptide rods are quite useful for rough-ground shore fishing, particularly when fishing from sea ledges where the backing cliff limits casting space, while 7 to 11 foot spinning rods can be used as float rods for such fish as mullet, bass, mackerel and pollack. A 12 foot freshwater carp rod with a $1^{1}/_{2}$ to 2 pound test curve is also suitable for taking grey mullet, which have soft mouths very prone to tearing. The rod tip's gentle

action prevents the hook from pulling out.

Saltwater fly fishing calls for long, accurate casting. Reservoir trout rods are well suited to this sort of work, particularly 10 foot graphite rods capable of throwing a number 9 weight-forward line. You can use shorter rods, but these generally lack the casting ability and stopping power of a 10-footer. The reel should be a corrosion-resistant graphite or anodized aluminium model, large enough to take the line plus ample backing.

## SALTWATER RODS

Rods for boat fishing are built to IGFA test curve ratings from 6 pounds upwards, and the most widely used are those rated at 20 and 30 pounds.

lined intermediate rings with low bridge for extra strength

double roller tip guide

# SALTWATER WEIGHTS AND BOOMS

The great variety of weights for use in saltwater fishing is necessary because every fishing area requires a lead that will suit its particular run of tide and seabed formation. In some areas, though, over wrecks or where the bed is composed of jagged rock or jumbled boulders, using a conventional weight is pointless.

Weights are not cheap, so to lose one on each cast can be a costly business. In such circumstances it's much better to use an expendable weight: old spark plugs are ideal, and a visit to your local service station should get you enough old plugs for many days of hard fishing.

Wrecks present a great hazard to terminal tackle, and weights for wreck fishing should be rigged with a 'rotten bottom' or break-out line. Attach the weight to the terminal tackle with a short length of light monofilament. Then if a hangup should occur (the weight being the usual culprit), tugging breaks the light line allowing the terminal gear, to be retrieved, minus the weight but quite often with a large fish attached. Without the break-out line it would have been lost. The same trick is also effective for bottom fishing in rough-ground areas, where weight hangups are just as likely.

Inshore boat fishing can be divided into three categories: uptiding, bottom ledgering and trolling. Uptiding requires leads with four wire spikes, each 3 to 10 inches long, that dig into the bottom, holding the terminal tackle in the desired position, but pull out when a fish picks up the bait. Similar leads, with shorter spikes, are useful for beachcasting on stony or heavily tidal beaches.

When ledgering on a bottom of soft mud, flat weights with a thin profile are best, but bottom ledgering over firm sand demands more robust leads such as the cone-shaped Capta and the six-pointed star. The circular watch-type grip, although useful for flatfishing from shallow, slack-tide beaches, is useless for boat fishing because it tends to spin in the tide and tangle the terminal tackle.

Trolling, which is towing a bait or lure behind a moving boat for such fish as bass, pollack, and mackerel, demands a straight Jardine or preferably a curved model weighing 2 to 8 ounces. The Jardine is fixed by wrapping the line around a spiralled groove on its body and around a small spiral of wire at each end.

The ball weight, also known as the pierced bullet, runs freely on the line and is used, for example, to weight a long trace for bass when fishing from an anchored or drifting boat. Split shot can be employed for this purpose where there is little tide or when the trace is not required to sink more than a few inches below the surface. Ball weights can also be used on fixed

## WEIGHTS
These three common weights can all be used with the lifter, which will raise them clear of any snags on the retrieve.

**Uptide sinker**

**Breakaway lead**

**Torpedo**

**Weight Lifter**

*Terminal tackle incorporating a bomb-shaped weight.*

or sliding float rigs. For example, a small ball can be used to weight a float rig carrying a bait, such as a sandeel or prawn, along on the tide. This is a technique that takes many bass, and it is particularly useful for drifting a bait into areas of rough ground where it would be dangerous or even impossible for even a small boat to venture. Coffin and barrel weights should not be used for float rigs because they cause the trace to twist around the reel line.

Bomb-shaped leads come in sizes from one ounce upwards. The smaller sizes are perfect for casting over sand or into rocky gullies, while the larger ones, from 8 ounces up to 2 pounds or more, are designed for boat fishing. To eliminate line twists, the small versions have built-in swivels and the larger ones an inset wire loop.

Terminal bottom tackle in tidal sand and mud estuaries is usually weighted with small bombs, but flat-sided torpedoes or watch-type grip weights can also be used. The bomb weight is also much the best for fishing hazardous ground, but it should be used with a 'rotten bottom' attachment to assist terminal tackle breakout if it becomes hopelessly jammed.

Bombs with folding wire grips, and spiked torpedo weights, hold well to sand and can be cast almost as far as a plain bomb. Off-the-bottom wreck and reef techniques, such as the 'flying collar' used to take pollack, coalfish and cod, call for bombs of 6 to 16 ounces.

For spinning, the ideal type of weight is the banana-shaped Wye lead, which has a centre of gravity below the level of the line. It has an eye at each end to carry the swivels that prevent line twist.

A sea boom is a device for holding the weight or the bait away from the reel line, to prevent tangling or to present the bait in a more natural manner. For example, the plastic tube boom, which has an angled bend at one end, is available in 4, 6, 8 and 10 inch lengths and is widely used on long trace rigs fished above the bottom. The reel line is passed through the boom and then through a bead, and tied to a swivel that connects it to the trace. A weight clip positioned at the bend carries the desired amount of lead. The boom successfully fishes a trace of up to 18 feet long, which flows out in the tide and gives the bait a very natural appearance.

By holding the trace clear of the reel line, the tube boom keeps the two from tangling when they are lowered from a boat, which can be done at some speed if the tide is running fairly fast. A wire French boom can be a successful alternative, but it must be kitted out with a weight carrier and with split rings and swivels at the points that connect reel line and trace.

Booms of wire and plastic that fasten to the body of a paternoster are used as snood standoffs, but ballpoint pen tubes do the job just as well. Spreader booms, shaped like curved coathangers, are swivelled and weighted at the centre point and have swivels at each end. These are effective for fishing two short traces of equal length for plaice, dabs and flounder, and it's customary to position a number of small, brightly coloured beads behind the fine wire hooks. This type of flattie rig has been around for well over 150 years.

Sliding Kilmore and Clements booms, made of stiff wire, have long been used as weight carriers for bottom ledgering, principally for conger and big skate.

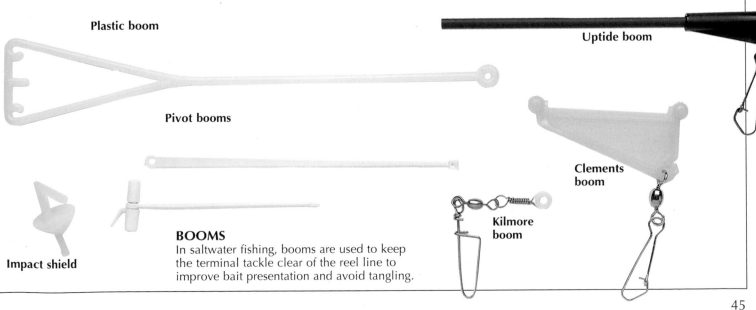

**Plastic boom**

**Uptide boom**

**Pivot booms**

**Clements boom**

**Impact shield**

**Kilmore boom**

## BOOMS
In saltwater fishing, booms are used to keep the terminal tackle clear of the reel line to improve bait presentation and avoid tangling.

# SPINNING AND BAITCASTING RODS

With some exceptions, spinning and baitcasting rods are principally used for fishing with artificial lures. The spinning rods are used with fixed spool reels, and baitcasters with multipliers or any other reel designed to be used on top of the reel, facing the angler, rather than below it.

Modern rods are made from graphite (carbon fibre) composites or a mix of glass fibre and graphite. In general, the lightness and strength of a rod with a high graphite content is an advantage for most spinning or baitcasting, simply because of the number of times it will probably be cast during a day's fishing.

However, a somewhat cheaper glass/graphite mix is worth considering if it's to be used by youngsters or beginners, and also for the rough usage of creek and estuary fishing over rocky shore-lines. A good glass/graphite mix is also a perfectly acceptable alternative to graphite for trolling, where the rod is only held while the fish is being played.

Most graphite rods have the fibres laid at angles around the tube, but 100 percent linear carbon rods, pioneered by Berkely, have the fibres running in just one direction, along the line of the rod from the butt to the tip. This type of construction produces a significantly lighter tube that is said to provide greater sensitivity.

Some of the most versatile rods, though, are those wrapped in a mesh of Kevlar fibres. This construction combines good shock resistance with tremendous strength and rigidity, but allows the tube to bend progressively to give an easy action when the fish is being played.

Good rod rings are essential on any rod intended for use with artificial lures because of the amount of wear they have to withstand – a lure fisherman may well make up to 2000 casts in a day. Aluminium oxide-centred rings, such as the Fuji range, are well proven, while those lined with heat-dissipating, diamond-polished silicon carbide offer minimal friction and thus minimal line and ring wear. The lightweight Dynaflo rings, with either polished stainless steel or titanium centres, also give superbly smooth casting and retrieval with minimal friction.

Whatever type of rings your rod is fitted with, if you can hear the line passing through them then there is excessive friction between the line and the rings. When that happens, line damage and ring

## CHOOSING A ROD

| USE | LENGTH | ACTION |
|---|---|---|
| Marries with baby fixed spool reel and light line to work tiny lures and jigs. | 5½–6ft | Ultralight |
| Obtaining maximum action in small rivers, canals and ponds. | 6–7ft | Light tip action |
| Rivers and small to medium sized stillwaters. | 7½–8½ft | Medium tip action |
| Powerful rod for lures and bait in river, lake and reservoir fishing. Use with fixed spool or multiplier reels. | 9–10ft | Fast tip action |
| For working lure or bait rigs in deep, fast flowing rivers and stillwaters. Use with fixed spool or multiplier reels. | 10 - 11ft | Powerful all-through action |

butt cap

hyperlon or cork handle

**SPINNING RODS**
The lighter a spinning rod is, the easier it will be to use for repeated casting.

fixed position screw lock reel fitting

female ferrule

*Because spinning with lures involves repeated casting, a spinning rod must be light and easy to handle.*

grooving are likely, so the rings should be replaced.

Next to the diminutive ice hole sticks, the smallest baitcasting rods ($4^1/_2$ to 6 feet long) are the shortest of all fishing rods. All baitcasters up to 6 feet long have the short, hand-sized pistol grip with forefinger trigger that's so desirable for a secure grip of both reel and rod throughout a day's fishing.

The blank itself is usually inserted into the preformed handle via a ferrule, and glued, but some handles, such as the Fuji range, have ferrule adapters that enable various different tips to be used with the same handle.

For greater sensitivity, the handle on some modern rods is simply a wider, shaped extension of the blank itself, while on others the blank runs right through the preformed pistol grip to the very end of the rod.

Rod lengths start at around the ultralight $4^1/_2$ feet, but for serious bass fishing you need one about $5^1/_2$ feet long and weighing between 5 and 7 ounces. Short baitcasting rods, that is, those less than 6 feet long, are ideal for short, low-trajectory casting beneath overhanging trees when you're working shorelines from a boat. They're also much less tiring than longer rods for continual one-handed casting.

Short rods come in a variety of different actions, from a slow all-through to a super-stiff fast taper. Slow-action rods are usually more forgiving when casting and playing, but they lack the power of the stiffer, fast-taper rods for slinging heavy lures and setting hooks.

For general fishing, a medium tip or compromise action is recommended – a rod that bends enough through the tip and middle section for effortless casting, but has a reserve of power just above the handle for subduing large fish.

For working surface lures, however, there is no compromise.

BUTT SECTION

butt ring TIP SECTION

intermediate ring tip ring

# SPINNING AND BAITCASTING RODS -2

**Single handed baitcaster**

pistol
grip

## BAITCASTING RODS

The shorter baitcasting rods are among the smallest of all fishing rods,
and have short, pistol-grip handles for comfortable one-handed use.

Action cannot be imparted with anything other than a stiffish, fast-tapered rod. Plastic worms are also worked more effectively with such a rod.

Rods in the somewhat more versatile 6½- to 7½-foot range differ considerably from the short rods in both power and handle construction. To counteract the greater leverage that comes with a longer rod, the handle length below the trigger is increased so that the handle can be braced against the forearm. There is also a hand grip above the reel fitting for two-handed fishing.

Rods of over 7 feet in length are either of two-piece construction, or telescopic with several sections that collapse into the handle. Only use a telescopic rod if a two-piece is inconvenient for you to transport, because every joint in the telescopic rod is a potential weak spot.

Choose the action that suits your requirements best, remembering that for general lure work with species such as bass, zander and pike, a medium-fast tip will handle most situations. For cranking big-lipped diving plugs, though, a rod with a faster, more powerful action and a reserve of power in the butt is the one to choose, while for working very light lures the rod should have a soft middle and tip section.

Within the range of 8- to 11-foot baitcasters, there are rods for just about every form of lure fishing. Some have trigger grips at the reel fitting, although on rods of 9 feet or more this feature isn't really necessary.

An 8- to 9-foot rod with a medium tip action is ideal for bass, zander and pike, while salmon anglers often use a 10- or even 11-foot rod with a similar action for systematically covering wide, deep, fast-flowing rivers. These rods can easily handle lines of 10 to 14 pounds test.

For much heavier work, such as trolling on large lakes or on salt water, and for putting large plugs or surface poppers around mangrove swamps for battlers such as tarpon, the action needs to be stepped up considerably. More power is needed through the middle to the butt section, so use a fast-taper, tip-action rod that is capable of handling lines of 15 to 20 pounds test.

Rods for trolling should also have enough good-quality rod rings to support the line and keep it away from the blank whatever the curvature, and long handles that fit snugly into the rod holders.

For estuary and heavy shore lure work, the rod needs a powerful but more progressive action, with lightweight fittings so that it can be worked comfortably all day. The handle should be no longer than necessary – even for two-handed casting, a distance of about 22 inches between reel and butt cap is quite sufficient. Anything longer can make it difficult to swap hands after casting.

In many categories, the spinning rod differs from the baitcaster only in the choice of reel fitting (spinning rods don't need triggers) and the fact that the reel is positioned slightly nearer the butt end on the spinning rod, as well as being used beneath the rod instead of on top.

Spinning rods also usually have rings two sizes larger than those on baitcasters, because of the way the line pulls off in coils from the fixed spool reel. Many rod makers use the same blanks, with different fittings, for each type of reel.

To start a youngster on the road to becoming a lure fishing enthusiast, there's no better outfit than a short spinning rod/fixed spool combination, whether in hollow glass, a glass/graphite mix, or top quality graphite. In the shorter rod lengths (5½ to 7 feet), the differences in weight between the various materials are not significant, and the simple cork or synthetic handles weigh far less than the preformed pistol grip of a baitcaster. As a result, these short spinning rods weigh little more than short fly rods.

As with baitcasters, there is a range of actions available to suit all techniques, from jigging for crappies and other small panfish on 4-pound lines, to popping large, double-jointed surface plugs for big bass, pike and muskies.

*Baitcasting rods are used with the little baitcasting reels or with small closed face reels.*

The longer spinning rods, from about 8 to 11 feet long, are perhaps even more versatile than the long baitcasters. A 9-foot, medium-action spinning rod, fitted with a fixed spool reel loaded with 15-pound line, is one of the most useful fishing outfits in the world.

With such an outfit, you could plug and spin for steelheads and salmon in fast rivers; fish for pike and muskie in reservoirs and lakes; toss plugs to big estuary jumpers such as snook and tarpon; or go bait fishing for huge stillwater carp. You could also use it for downrigger trolling for giant lake trout; deadbaiting at night for catfish and eels; casting into the surf with bait or lures for bass and mackerel; and even for tackling the legendary masheer in the fast-flowing rivers of India, with plugs, bait or large spoons. If you had to

## CHOOSING A ROD

tip ring

| USE | LENGTH | ACTION |
| --- | --- | --- |
| Short rod ideal for singlehanded lure fishing in small rivers, ponds, and overgrown lakes. | 5½–6ft | Single handed |
| Longer more powerful rod for casting farther. Good for bigger fish using top water lures and jerk baits. | 6–7ft | Double handed |

choose just one outfit for a round-the-world fishing trip, you couldn't choose better than this one.

An 8-foot spinning rod is also a versatile tool, and one that always feels comfortable to fish with. A light, middle-to-tip action is ideal for trout, zander, bass, and even general pike and muskie fishing. For catching big fish in snaggy conditions, where heavy lines of over 15 pounds test are needed, a rod with a stiffer, fast tip action is advisable.

The 10- to 11-foot spinning rods usually have a more progressive taper. For playing salmon in deep, fast rivers, they need to bend well or else the hooks will be ripped out.

However, even an 11-footer can be used for pike and steelheads, and is especially useful for presenting livebaits (shiners) to bass where 40 to 60 yards of line needs to be picked up on the strike. Long, easy-action spinning rods are also great for presenting soft crab and fish baits to species such as sea bass over rocky ground.

# SURFCASTING RODS

Years ago, before inshore waters were depleted of fish stocks by longliners, trawlers, factory ships and other commercial fishing, the need for long casting from the shore was nowhere near as important as it is today.

As a result, the early thick and heavy cane rods, with their brass ferrules and huge, porcelain-centred rings, were perfectly adequate. These beautiful rods would be of little use today, but the development of new rod-building materials and methods has kept pace with the shore angler's need for greater casting distances.

The first glass fibre rods were solid, and even heavier than the cane which they were intended to replace, but the arrival of hollow glass revolutionized the design of surfcasting rods.

The revolution began with the 'reverse taper' rod designed by Leslie Moncrieff. This rod, like all surf rods of its day, had two joints connected by brass ferrules, but from the reel fitting downwards the butt became progressively thinner instead of widening. The inherent spring of the reverse taper butt enabled surf fishermen to cast consistently over distances of 100 yards or more with bait, something quite unknown before.

The reverse taper reigned supreme for over a decade, but by the 1970s it was being steadily supplanted by the fast-tip rods that had been pioneered by Abu of Sweden with their Atlantic 484 beach rods. These rods had rigid, Duralumin-cored butts and fast-action, hollow-glass tips. The same high-tensile Duralumin is still used to produce butt rigidity in most contemporary surfcasters, well-covered in a plastic shrink tube to protect it from corrosion. The rigidity allows the full power of the blank to be used in casting, instead of being partly absorbed by the butt. Graphite (carbon fibre) butts are also produced today, and are popular for tournament casting.

Modern surf rod blanks are of hollow glass, a glass/graphite mix

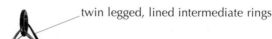

male push fit

twin legged, lined intermediate rings

## SURFCASTING RODS
Surfcasting rods are strong, two-piece outfits designed for use with either fixed spool reels or multipliers.

screw collar · fixed ring

hyperlon or rubber butt grip · fore grip · sliding ring · fore grip

*Surfcasting rods are designed for casting the terminal tackle out to where the fish are.*

(considered by many to be the ideal) or a material containing a very high proportion of graphite. Some are lighter than others, and some are rather faster in the tip, but all are designed to work best with a particular range of weights, such as 1 to 3 ounces, 4 to 6 ounces, or 6 to 8 ounces, and they all have the power to subdue most species, provided there's enough line on the reel.

Most surf rods have very similar diameters, the most obvious differences between one model and another being in the number of rod rings, the type of reel fitting and the overall length. The most popular lengths, whether the rods are designed for fixed spool or for multiplier reels, are from 11½ to 11¾ feet, made up of two joints of equal length with individually-rolled internal spigots. Others have a shorter, 4-foot butt and a tip of 7½ feet or so; these are usually more efficient for casting, but they can be more difficult to transport.

Rods for multipliers usually have a finger trigger at the reel fitting, and eight smallish, graduated rings, including the tip ring. For use with fixed spool reels, rods have just four large rings including the tip ring, starting with a 50 mm butt ring set high up the rod to reduce the coils of line as they peel from the large diameter of the fixed spool.

Rings with hard-wearing, non-grooving, heat-dissipating centres are imperative. Well-proven makes include Fuji, which have centres of aluminium oxide or silicon carbide, and the polished stainless steel Dynaflo rings.

Most production surfcasters are now fitted with the robust yet lightweight tubular (Fuji-type) screw reel fitting, but the actual positioning of the reel fitting varies tremendously from manufacturer to manufacturer.

Ideally, the distance between the butt grip and the reel should be enough to give good leverage on the cast, but not so long that you can't follow through with the rod tip, pointing it at the lead until it hits the water. A distance of around 28 to 30 inches from the butt cap to the middle of the reel fitting will suit most anglers. Some rods are fitted with adjustable reel fittings, so that you can position the reel where it suits you best.

When it comes to choosing a surfcasting rod, look for one that's suited to the type of fishing you intend to do. Selecting a powerful rod that can cast heavy sinkers and subdue large fish in fast tides is rather pointless, and an unnecessary expense, if you're going after little flatfish in a placid estuary or a quiet bay.

## CHOOSING A ROD

| USE | LENGTH | ACTION |
| --- | --- | --- |
| For beach, pier or harbour wall, casting weights of 4–8ozs. Use with fixed spool (20–30lb line) or multiplier (20lb line) fixed with coster clips or winch fitting. Suitable for most fish from cod to rays. | 12ft | medium/stiff |
| For rock fishing, casting 4–8ozs, with fixed spool or multiplier (15–20lb line). Suitable for most fish including conger and wrasse. | 12ft | stiff |

heavy duty whipping

tip ring

butt ring

# BAIT

52

The purpose of any bait – lure, fly or hookbait – is to fool the fish into taking the hook. Lures and flies are, in general, designed to imitate the natural food of the fish they're intended to catch, while hookbaits are either whole or cut natural fish foods or other edible items such as sweetcorn or pieces of bread.

Many fly fishermen tie their own flies, while others prefer to buy them ready-tied. The range of fly patterns is almost endless, as is the variety of lures on sale, but very often the difference between one lure or fly and another is in its appeal to the angler rather than to the fish.

Some hookbaits can be bought from tackle dealers (or, in the case of baits like bread or canned meats, from supermarkets), which is convenient, but there are many effective baits which can be gathered from the shore or from the water you're going to fish. The angler adept at seeking out natural baits on location will usually be guaranteed a good catch.

In addition to gathering worms from the lawn at night, after heavy rain, in the warmer months the freshwater angler can find a host of good baits, such as caterpillars, snails (crush the shells to remove the flesh), slugs and grasshoppers at the waterside. The freshwater predator hunter can collect a supply of baitfish by using a small net in the shallows. Bullheads, loach and small lampreys make great baits, and in clean streams and rivers you can find crayfish, the freshwater bait *par excellence* for numerous species.

In both running and still waters, the caddis grub – the larva of the sedge fly – can be found in its mobile home, clinging to rocks and sunken branches where it feeds on algae. The size of the caddis varies according to its species, but most are roughly the size of a maggot, and they are a first-class natural bait. To remove the caddis from its case, gently squeeze the closed (tail) end until the grub's legs and head appear at the other. Then carefully pull it out, using just the nails of your thumb and index finger.

Freshwater mussels are another great natural bait,

and in just a few minutes you can dig up enough for a day's fishing from the mud and silt in the shallows. There is enough diversity in natural baits to make them effective for almost every freshwater fish, and all they cost is the time it takes to collect them. As a bonus, while gathering them you get to know a lot about the ecology of the water and its banks.

The saltwater angler also has plenty of natural baits to choose from, whether bought or collected from the sea or the shore. Shellfish can be gathered from the beach at low tide, along with small fish, prawns, shrimps and crabs from the rock pools, and baitfish such as sandeels and mackerel abound in the sea.

If you want to use crabs as bait, it's well worth searching specifically for 'peelers'. These are crabs which have shed their shells in order to grow, and whose new shells have yet to harden. During the few days between shells, the crabs are soft and rubbery and are a favourite food of many species which feed in the shallows along the beaches and up the estuaries.

Some of the natural baits found in the sea are as effective for many freshwater species as they are for marine fish. The oily-fleshed mackerel, for instance, is an excellent bait for many species such as shark, swordfish and marlin, but presented either whole or halved it is also one of the best deadbaits for catching large pike.

Another such bait is the humble prawn. It's an unbeatable bait for the smaller saltwater and brackish-water species, while in fresh water the mounted prawn is the most deadly bait for salmon. Peeled prawns are also worth using when you're after other large freshwater species, including catfish and carp. Trouble is, if you take a pot of fresh, peeled prawns with you for bait, you tend to eat most of them yourself.

In this chapter, we look at the various types of natural and artificial baits, including flies, used in freshwater and saltwater angling, and tell you how they're used and the sort of fish you can expect to catch on them.

# ARTIFICIAL FLIES

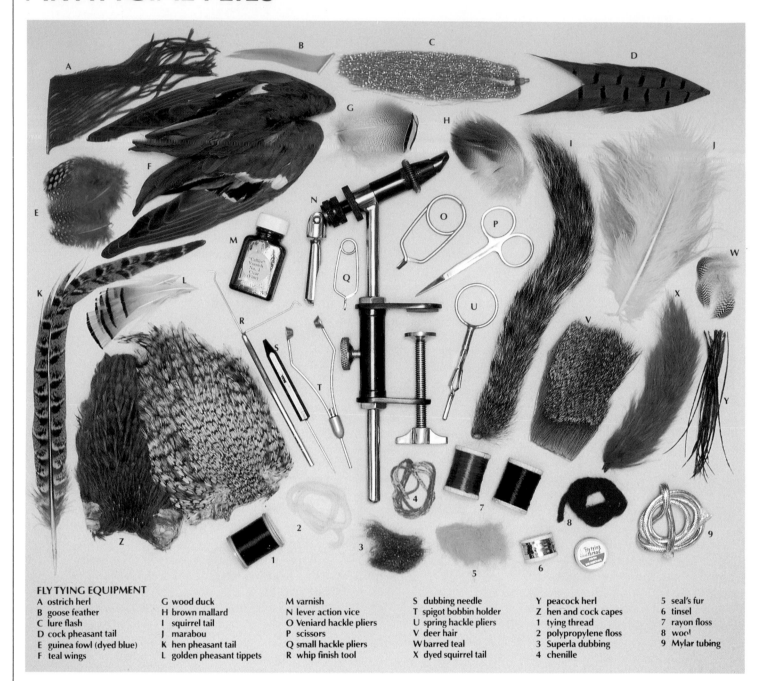

**FLY TYING EQUIPMENT**

| | | | | | |
|---|---|---|---|---|---|
| A ostrich herl | G wood duck | M varnish | S dubbing needle | Y peacock herl | 5 seal's fur |
| B goose feather | H brown mallard | N lever action vice | T spigot bobbin holder | Z hen and cock capes | 6 tinsel |
| C lure flash | I squirrel tail | O Veniard hackle pliers | U spring hackle pliers | 1 tying thread | 7 rayon floss |
| D cock pheasant tail | J marabou | P scissors | V deer hair | 2 polypropylene floss | 8 wool |
| E guinea fowl (dyed blue) | K hen pheasant tail | Q small hackle pliers | W barred teal | 3 Superla dubbing | 9 Mylar tubing |
| F teal wings | L golden pheasant tippets | R whip finish tool | X dyed squirrel tail | 4 chenille | |

Early anglers, with foreheads villanous low, nevertheless noticed those lengthy periods in spring and summer when trout feed greedily on abundant hatches of aquatic insects, and they soon began trying to catch fish on artificial imitations of the natural bugs.

Thus began the primeval fly fishing of the Stone Age. Tackle then was more a limiting factor than the artificial flies themselves. These used hooks carved from antler and bone, or made of soft-boiled thorns bent to shape and then dried. Fleshed out with underfur from an animal and legged with a neck feather plucked from a bird, these flies were delicate, subtle and devious.

But before the reel, and before oiled silk lines made fly casting possible, presentation was limited to dangling a fly over fish, using a long pole with plaited line of horse mane and tail lashed to the tip. This type of outfit was still in use in the nineteenth century.

It wasn't until the mid 1800s that fly fishing, as we know it today, really bloomed into one of the more challenging angling pursuits. Frederic M Halford did much to create the cult of dry fly fishing in Britain, while his contemporary in North America, Theodore Gordon, was doing much the same thing there. Then around the turn of the century, G E M Skues broadened the horizons of fly fishing with his strong support of fishing for trout with a sunken imitation nymph.

For many anglers, those years at the turn of the century represented the golden age of fly fishing. Halford had already started the 'exact imitation' tradition, whereby it was almost a mortal sin to cast a fly to a fish unless it was an identical replica of the fly on which the fish were seen to be feeding at that time. Frankly, the whole scene became a little farcical by present-day standards. But between them, Halford, Skues and Gordon brought some semblance of order to fly dressing in that some firm commitment was at least made to 'match the hatch'.

Salmon flies evolved from the trout patterns, long before it was discovered that salmon don't actually feed during their journey

upriver to their spawning grounds. In the early part of this century, salmon fly dressers paid more attention to colour and shape than to size and presentation, but their flies were nonetheless very successful, perhaps because salmon were more plentiful then.

Of the natural materials which emerged as essential for fly tying, there is little doubt that silk thread and chicken or bantam neck feathers ranked high. The silk was used for tying and as a body material, while the hackle from a chicken's neck could be wound round the hook shank to form a hackle or wing and so give a rough resemblance to a natural fly.

Feathers from the wings of

## BASIC FLY TYING

The art of decorating a hook with feathers, tinsel and fur to imitate a natural insect is one which any angler can acquire. Artificial flies consist mainly of a tail, a body, and where appropriate, a wing. All you need is a few simple tools and neat, precise fingers.

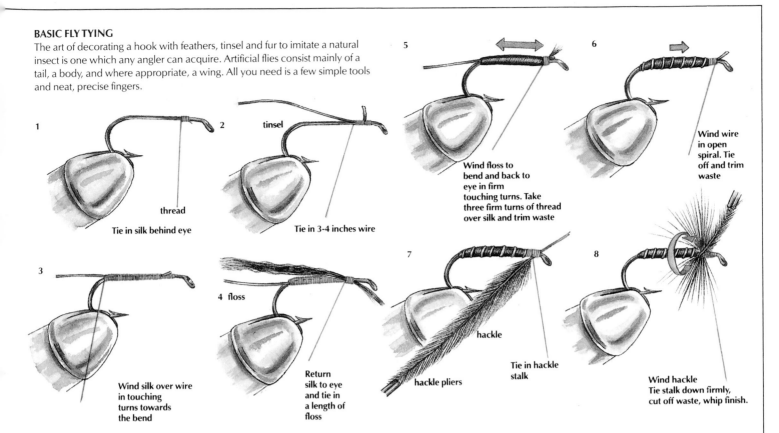

**1** thread
Tie in silk behind eye

**2** tinsel
Tie in 3-4 inches wire

**3** Wind silk over wire in touching turns towards the bend

**4** floss
Return silk to eye and tie in a length of floss

**5** Wind floss to bend and back to eye in firm touching turns. Take three firm turns of thread over silk and trim waste

**6** Wind wire in open spiral. Tie off and trim waste

**7** hackle pliers    hackle    Tie in hackle stalk

**8** Wind hackle
Tie stalk down firmly, cut off waste, whip finish.

other species of bird, such as teal or mallard, were used for dry flies and salmon flies, while the construction of nymphs relied heavily on copper wire to get the necessary weight. By the time of those golden years between the wars, the sport of fly fishing was flourishing; silken lines could be greased to float, and the fragile horsehair casts were being replaced by silkworm gut.

Silk thread and chicken feathers are still used, but they're now supplemented by an abundance of natural and synthetic materials. As a result, fly dressers can now create so many different fly patterns that things have tended to get a bit out of hand.

While the exact-imitation school of fly dressing is still with us to some extent, hatches of only one specific species of fly at a time are not so common as they once were, and the need for exact imitation has diminished. In addition to all the insect and non-imitative patterns, there are now also many flies which represent the freshwater shrimp, small fry and fish upon which trout feed.

The popularity of fly dressing as a hobby has grown steadily over the years, even among non-anglers. There are many good books on the subject, and there aren't many communities these days, even small ones, where fly tying tuition isn't available.

If you're going to tie your own flies, a vice for holding the hook is essential. This leaves both hands free to manipulate the silk thread and all the other materials which are to be spun in. Frequently, a silk body will be overlaid with tinsel, peacock herl or fur before the final hackle or wings are added and the fly completed.

Dry flies are often winged or tied with stiff cockerel hackles, while wet flies tend to be made with softer hackles so that they sink more readily. Fancy flies such as lures and streamers may be made from synthetic fibres, while hooks may be singles of a suitable size, or mounted in tandem with single, double or treble hooks.

There are times and conditions when the use of one type of fly or lure is likely to bring more success than another. The early season, for example, when trout are just recovering from spawning and hatching insects are not so frequent, may be a time when a deeply fished lure will attract the fish. Most times, though, lures are more generally used in still waters, either in cold weather when the fish are laid low, or in the very warm weather when they again go down deep to keep cool.

The smaller wet fly patterns may be best used on rivers and streams as spring warms into early summer and there is a portion of the day when flies are hatching. Searching all the likely water will often get a fish or two until a good hatch of fly comes along.

## THE WHIP FINISH

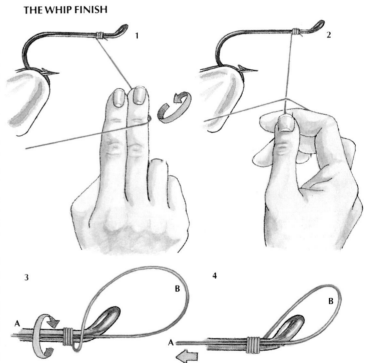

Before tying a fly you must learn to whip finish. Practice on a bare hook; the steps for a right-handed tier are as follows. Wind a few turns of thread onto the shank, trapping loose end. Swing bobbin up towards you. Pass the backs of first and second fingers (of right hand) behind, then over, thread, forming a loop in an inverted figure 4. Lay thread A along near side of shank trapping it with thread B. Maintain tension between fingers and lay the bobbin over the rear out of the way. Transfer thread B to left hand. Pass thread B around shank five times, trapping thread A. Insert a needle into loop, using it to maintain tension while drawing thread A towards rear of hook. As loop tightens, slip it out. Finally, trim thread A and varnish.

# ARTIFICIAL FLIES — DRY

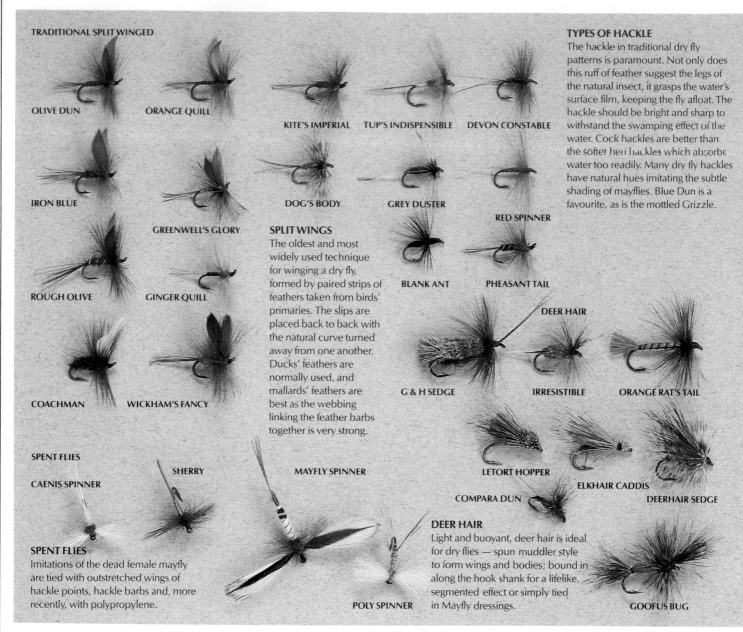

**TRADITIONAL SPLIT WINGED**

OLIVE DUN

ORANGE QUILL

KITE'S IMPERIAL

TUP'S INDISPENSIBLE

DEVON CONSTABLE

IRON BLUE

GREENWELL'S GLORY

DOG'S BODY

GREY DUSTER

RED SPINNER

ROUGH OLIVE

GINGER QUILL

## SPLIT WINGS
The oldest and most widely used technique for winging a dry fly, formed by paired strips of feathers taken from birds' primaries. The slips are placed back to back with the natural curve turned away from one another. Ducks' feathers are normally used, and mallards' feathers are best as the webbing linking the feather barbs together is very strong.

BLANK ANT

PHEASANT TAIL

COACHMAN

WICKHAM'S FANCY

**SPENT FLIES**

SHERRY

MAYFLY SPINNER

CAENIS SPINNER

G & H SEDGE

DEER HAIR

IRRESISTIBLE

ORANGE RAT'S TAIL

LETORT HOPPER

ELKHAIR CADDIS

COMPARA DUN

DEERHAIR SEDGE

## SPENT FLIES
Imitations of the dead female mayfly are tied with outstretched wings of hackle points, hackle barbs and, more recently, with polypropylene.

POLY SPINNER

## DEER HAIR
Light and buoyant, deer hair is ideal for dry flies — spun muddler style to form wings and bodies; bound in along the hook shank for a lifelike, segmented effect or simply tied in Mayfly dressings.

GOOFUS BUG

## TYPES OF HACKLE
The hackle in traditional dry fly patterns is paramount. Not only does this ruff of feather suggest the legs of the natural insect, it grasps the water's surface film, keeping the fly afloat. The hackle should be bright and sharp to withstand the swamping effect of the water. Cock hackles are better than the softer hen hackles which absorbs water too readily. Many dry fly hackles have natural hues imitating the subtle shading of mayflies. Blue Dun is a favourite, as is the mottled Grizzle.

Dry fly fishing is primarily used for taking the various species of trout and salmon. In North America, especially on the rivers of the east coast of Canada, the dry fly is frequently used for the capture of Atlantic salmon during June, July and August. In Europe, though, particularly in the United Kingdom, summer water temperatures are lower and so there is rarely an opportunity to attempt serious dry fly fishing for salmon.

Many of the fly patterns which find favour with Canadian salmon anglers are big, bushy creations, such as the Grey Wulff, which rarely represent known insects other than the large land-bred flies (terrestrials) or the stone flies. For most other dry fly fishing, especially for trout, the fly is usually a representation of the winged stage of many ephemerid species (mayflies) or of various terrestrials.

Anglers and fly dressers keen to imitate the various stages of the life cycle of the mayfly start with representations of the nymph. This is fished like many other nymphs, but the dry fly angler is more interested in the second phase, when the duns or sub-imago flies shed their nymphal cases and take to the wing.

Upon leaving the water, the newly hatched flies frequently get blown in among trees and bushes. Here they get shelter from rain and wind, and undergo a slow process of moulting or ecdysis, when the outer skin is shed and the fly then emerges as an imago or 'spinner'. The spinner is the adult fly, and it is only as a spinner than it can breed.

Shortly after the spinners emerge the mayfly dance begins, when swarms of males rise with a rise-and-fall motion to attract the females. Mating takes place in the air, and soon afterwards the female flies off to deposit her fertilized eggs on the surface of the water. Having laid her eggs, the female drifts off downstream in her final death throes.

By this time, of course, most trout are already gorged on the mayfly and they will become more difficul to catch. While looking very realistic to our eyes, many patterns of the spent spinner fail miserably when it comes to deceiving the fish. Because of this, the dun and early spinner stages are of more interest to the fly fisherman.

The large spring olive dun and the large dark olive dun play a very important role for the fly fisher during the early part of the season. There are many artificial patterns based on these, the better known ones being the Blue Dun, Blue Upright, Hare's Ear, Dark Olive Quill and the Rough Olive.

The March Brown is another popular fly, dressed to imitate a natural fly of the same name. It's a popular fly with anglers even on waters where the natural fly is unknown or comparatively rare, and it will take trout anywhere in the world.

The iron blue dun is an extremely common fly, particularly during the colder days of spring. Representations of this fly include the Dark Watchet and the Blue Bloa; the spinners of the iron blue, depending on their sex, may be known as the Jenny or Claret Spinner.

It is doubtful if there are many ephemerids more plentiful than the blue winged olive. This fly is

**WULFF PATTERNS**

**WHITE WULFF**

**GREY WULFF**

**ROYAL WULFF**

**PALMERS**

**BROWN BIVISIBLE**

**SHADOW MAYFLY**

**SPECIALS**

**BLACK SEDGE**

**SKATER**

**WHITE MOTH**

**HAWTHORN FLY**

**CRANE FLY**

**WULFF PATTERNS**
Available in a wide range of shades and sizes. With wings and tails of hair, they are robust and float well even in the roughest water. Dressed on a variety of hook sizes, they can suggest all but the smallest Mayfly, and are often used to tempt salmon.

With a dense hackle along the body, Palmers float well. Though many imitate adult caddis, the hackles allow the fly to be skated across the surface, copying the emerging natural.

**SPECIALS**
Both hawthorn and crane flies are land-born. Their long legs are imitated by feather or hair tied to suggest joints.

**Left** A natural olive dun, the inspiration for many popular and successful dry fly patterns such as the Rough Olive Dun.

**Above** Mayflies are an important part of the diet of trout, both in their larval stage and after they have hatched.

**Left** The caddis or sedge fly, like the mayflies, is a widely-imitated natural as well as an important food of the trout.

**NATURALS**

one of the easiest to recognize because close examination will reveal that it is the only olive to have three tails. Several imitations are offered, with the Orange Quill being one of the most popular. The Sherry Spinner is a popular choice when the spinner is on the water, and there are many anglers who rely on local patterns of olives in the hope that they will prove successful.

The pale water dun is yet another ephemerid worthy of note. The Blue Quill and the Little Marryat imitations of the dun are well known, as is the Amber Spinner for the imago stage.

Of the many other flies popular with the angler, the most important are the caddis or sedge flies and the stone flies. Caddis flies in flight resemble moths, and

may be sought by the fish during a late spring or summer evening just on dusk.

Stone flies, on the other hand, often appear during the late spring, and there are times when trout become so preoccupied feeding on these flies that they refuse to look at the hordes of ephemerids which might be hatching at the same time. The large stone fly, also known as the creeper, may be prolific on many rivers in late April and May.

For trout fishing, the North American fly fisherman has countless patterns to choose from, most of which are variations of only about eight basic types which between them provide flies suitable for most conditions.

When the trout are feeding on mayfly in good light and smooth water, it's best to use a fly which is a good representation of the

natural, because the fish are likely to be wary of taking anything that looks very different. In these conditions try a divided-wing type, such as a Light Cahill.

In poor light or broken water the fly needn't be such a close imitation of the natural mayfly, but it should be a robust pattern which can easily be seen. A hairwing type, such as a Grey Wulff or a Hairwing Royal Coachman, will often raise fish when visibility is poor.

When, as often happens, the trout are feeding on other insects, a mayfly imitation might have little success and other types of fly will get better results. The bivisibles, such as the Brown Bivisible, are good when the fish are taking a variety of different insects, but when the larger naturals such as dragonflies are being taken, a downwing type – a

dry Muddler Minnow, for example – is well worth trying. On the other hand, if the trout are feeding on tiny insects, and ignoring larger food, including mayflies, a midge type fly such as the little Black Midge is called for.

For making a really delicate presentation to trout in smooth, quiet waters the spider type, the Blue Dun Spider, for instance, hits the water gently and floats with minimum drag. Fast, turbulent waters demand a far tougher type of fly, a hair-bodied pattern with hair wings that floats well and isn't easily damaged, such as an Irresistible.

The last of the basic types of trout fly is the fanwing. Fanwings will take trout on most waters, but their wings are delicate, and repeated casting with them will twist and weaken the leader because they spin in flight.

# ARTIFICIAL FLIES — WET

The term 'wet fly' covers all those representations of insects which spend all or some of their lives underwater, including larval and nymph stages of the ephemerids whose winged stages are the inspiration for so many dry fly patterns. It also includes imitations of drowned terrestrial insects, not to mention the representation of the fry of various fish – even trout. Trout are usually the major predators in trout streams, and cannibalism is a large part of the diet of trout longer than 12 inches.

Many of the flies devised for fishing beneath the surface are fairly recognizable imitations of non-winged insects and small fish. Others, used especially on still waters, are simply attractor flies based on the fact that highly predatory fish are likely to attack anything that moves or remotely resembles food. As a result, stillwater fly patterns offer a myriad of choices.

It is principally on rivers that fly fishermen seek to imitate the larval and nymphal stages of ephemerids, relying heavily on tried and tested patterns which are known to be best for a specific area. It's not always obvious what some of these patterns are meant to represent. The Partridge and Orange is among these; it's actually based on one of the olive dun family, as is the Waterhen Bloa. But it's not difficult to see that the Snipe and Purple bears some resemblance to the iron blue dun, or that the Alexandra is designed to represent the fry of some fish species, or maybe a minnow.

Fish feeding on nymphs and larval flies will often accept a wide range of artificial patterns, so there's something to be said for getting the size and hue of the fly about right, and for knowing those times when sub-surface activity is likely to be at its highest. During the early season, you might rely heavily on the fact that fish are very hungry, and that their natural food supply is still very scarce. On that basis, it could be assumed that fish will take almost anything you might offer them, but it's not quite as simple as that.

Being cold-blooded creatures, all fish have a metabolic rate which is directly related to water temperature. Trout, for instance, show little inclination to feed in cold water, nor can they very easily or quickly digest any food they may take. In the cold water

conditions of early spring, their protein demand is well below what it might be in May or June, or when the water temperature gets to 19°C (66°F), the temperature at which trout are said to feed most voraciously.

Most times in cold water, they're content to rest in the deeper pools, and will only bother to feed avidly when some warming sun breaks through and a few nymphs begin to fidget on the bed of the river. Because of this, it's a good idea to confine early season attempts to short periods between, say, 11 am and 3 pm, although you'll often find that the fish seem to wait until you break for lunch before they start feeding actively. Never make the mistake of offering extra-large flies to early season trout, and do be careful to make your flies move as slowly and as deep as you can.

There are no hard and fast rules about which wet fly patterns to use and when to use them. For instance, Snipe and Purple, Partridge and Orange and Waterhen Bloa can be used throughout the season, but there are scores of alternatives from the whole range of non-specific patterns like the Claret and Mallard, Teal and Green, Grouse and Claret, Peter Ross, Royal Coachman and Bloody Butcher. All will take fish on their day, but they're probably better on still waters than those rivers with good stocks of natural ephemerids. Even then, it would be a clever fish that could tell the difference between, say, a Waterhen Bloa and a Dark Watchet, and a hungry fish wouldn't care to know anyway.

As for nymphs, good all-rounders include the Early Olive Nymph or the Hatching Olive Nymph, the March Brown, the stonefly nymph, the sedge pupa and, specifically for the chalk streams, a few imitations of the freshwater shrimp.

Much the same tactics are used when seeking fish on wet fly anywhere in the world. The trout of Montana, Chile or New Zealand, for instance, are little different in their basic habits. Even the natural subaquatic insects or fry upon which they feed don't vary much from one location to another, but it pays to make a study of the natural life on the bed of any stream you are going to fish. Turn over the stones or stir up the silt or gravel, and use a small butterfly net to see what you can collect.

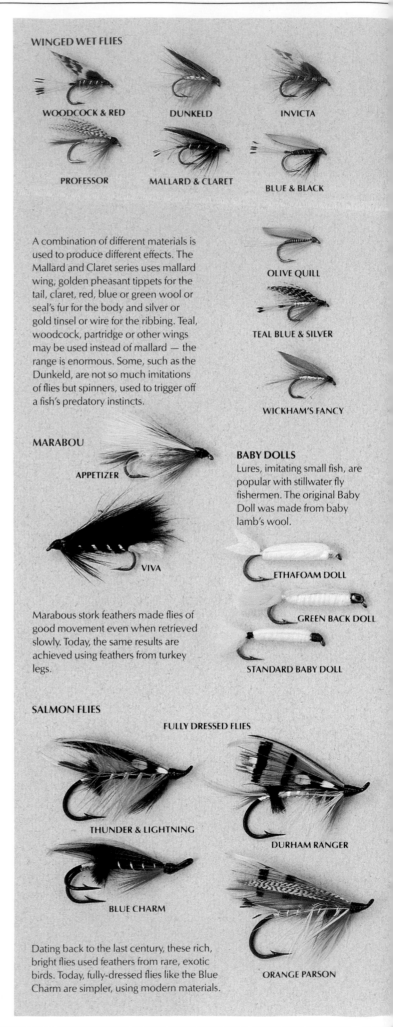

**WINGED WET FLIES**

WOODCOCK & RED  DUNKELD  INVICTA

PROFESSOR  MALLARD & CLARET  BLUE & BLACK

A combination of different materials is used to produce different effects. The Mallard and Claret series uses mallard wing, golden pheasant tippets for the tail, claret, red, blue or green wool or seal's fur for the body and silver or gold tinsel or wire for the ribbing. Teal, woodcock, partridge or other wings may be used instead of mallard — the range is enormous. Some, such as the Dunkeld, are not so much imitations of flies but spinners, used to trigger off a fish's predatory instincts.

OLIVE QUILL

TEAL BLUE & SILVER

WICKHAM'S FANCY

**MARABOU**

APPETIZER

VIVA

Marabous stork feathers made flies of good movement even when retrieved slowly. Today, the same results are achieved using feathers from turkey legs.

**BABY DOLLS**

Lures, imitating small fish, are popular with stillwater fly fishermen. The original Baby Doll was made from baby lamb's wool.

ETHAFOAM DOLL

GREEN BACK DOLL

STANDARD BABY DOLL

**SALMON FLIES**

FULLY DRESSED FLIES

THUNDER & LIGHTNING

BLUE CHARM

DURHAM RANGER

ORANGE PARSON

Dating back to the last century, these rich, bright flies used feathers from rare, exotic birds. Today, fully-dressed flies like the Blue Charm are simpler, using modern materials.

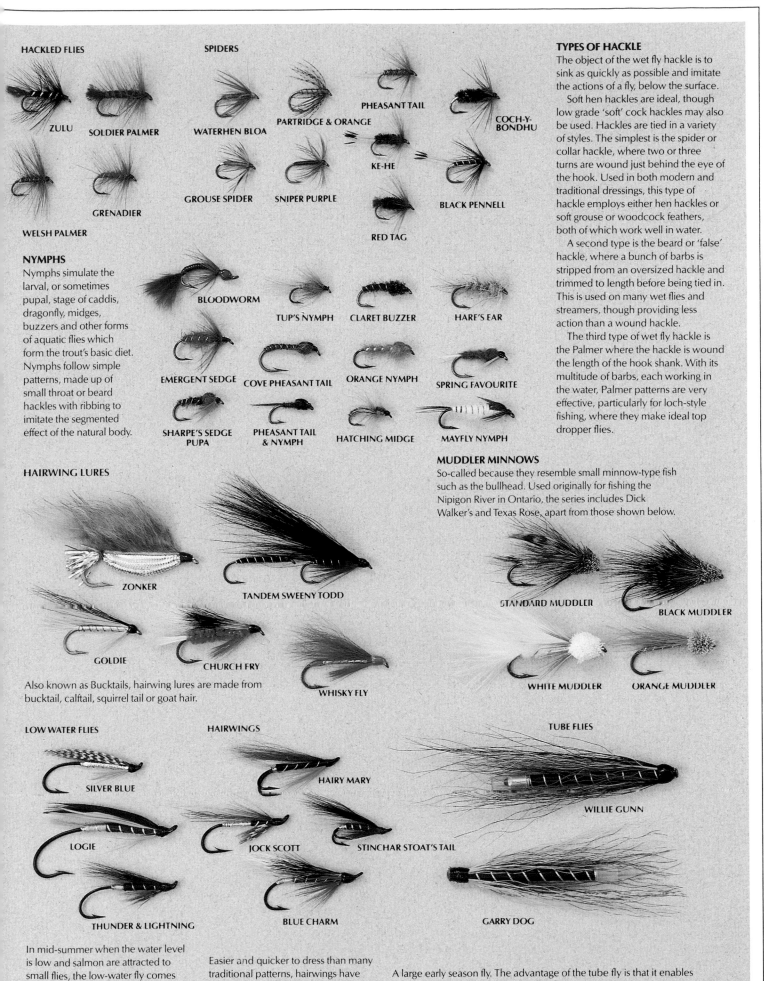

**HACKLED FLIES**

ZULU

SOLDIER PALMER

GRENADIER

WELSH PALMER

**SPIDERS**

WATERHEN BLOA

PARTRIDGE & ORANGE

PHEASANT TAIL

KE-HE

COCH-Y-BONDHU

GROUSE SPIDER

SNIPER PURPLE

BLACK PENNELL

RED TAG

## TYPES OF HACKLE

The object of the wet fly hackle is to sink as quickly as possible and imitate the actions of a fly, below the surface.

Soft hen hackles are ideal, though low grade 'soft' cock hackles may also be used. Hackles are tied in a variety of styles. The simplest is the spider or collar hackle, where two or three turns are wound just behind the eye of the hook. Used in both modern and traditional dressings, this type of hackle employs either hen hackles or soft grouse or woodcock feathers, both of which work well in water.

A second type is the beard or 'false' hackle, where a bunch of barbs is stripped from an oversized hackle and trimmed to length before being tied in. This is used on many wet flies and streamers, though providing less action than a wound hackle.

The third type of wet fly hackle is the Palmer where the hackle is wound the length of the hook shank. With its multitude of barbs, each working in the water, Palmer patterns are very effective, particularly for loch-style fishing, where they make ideal top dropper flies.

## NYMPHS

Nymphs simulate the larval, or sometimes pupal, stage of caddis, dragonfly, midges, buzzers and other forms of aquatic flies which form the trout's basic diet. Nymphs follow simple patterns, made up of small throat or beard hackles with ribbing to imitate the segmented effect of the natural body.

BLOODWORM

TUP'S NYMPH

CLARET BUZZER

HARE'S EAR

EMERGENT SEDGE

COVE PHEASANT TAIL

ORANGE NYMPH

SPRING FAVOURITE

SHARPE'S SEDGE PUPA

PHEASANT TAIL & NYMPH

HATCHING MIDGE

MAYFLY NYMPH

## MUDDLER MINNOWS

So-called because they resemble small minnow-type fish such as the bullhead. Used originally for fishing the Nipigon River in Ontario, the series includes Dick Walker's and Texas Rose, apart from those shown below.

## HAIRWING LURES

ZONKER

TANDEM SWEENY TODD

GOLDIE

CHURCH FRY

WHISKY FLY

Also known as Bucktails, hairwing lures are made from bucktail, calftail, squirrel tail or goat hair.

STANDARD MUDDLER

BLACK MUDDLER

WHITE MUDDLER

ORANGE MUDDLER

## LOW WATER FLIES

SILVER BLUE

LOGIE

THUNDER & LIGHTNING

## HAIRWINGS

HAIRY MARY

JOCK SCOTT

STINCHAR STOAT'S TAIL

BLUE CHARM

## TUBE FLIES

WILLIE GUNN

GARRY DOG

In mid-summer when the water level is low and salmon are attracted to small flies, the low-water fly comes into its own. Though small and dressed short, the hook is large.

Easier and quicker to dress than many traditional patterns, hairwings have become one of the most popular, and effective salmon flies in recent years.

A large early season fly. The advantage of the tube fly is that it enables an angler to use a treble hook, offering better hooking. Line is less likely to tangle and though weighty, they are streamlined.

# ARTIFICIAL LURES — FRESHWATER

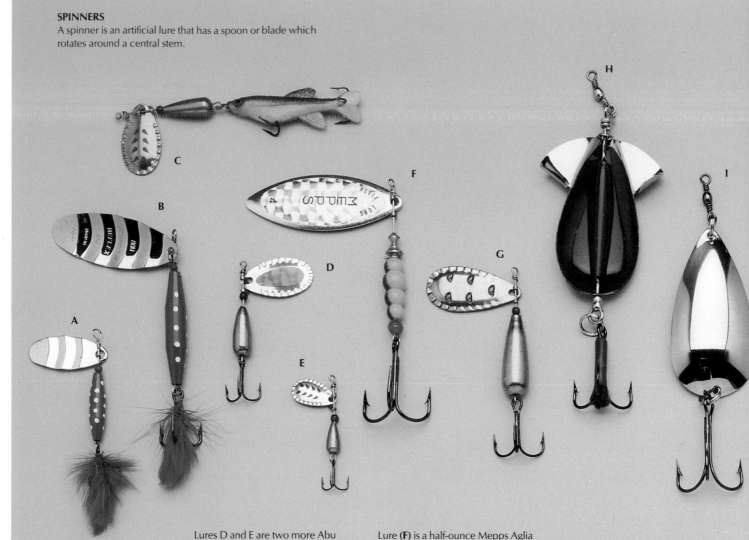

**SPINNERS**
A spinner is an artificial lure that has a spoon or blade which rotates around a central stem.

The Abu Reflex 7g (**lure A**) and the larger Reflex 18g (**B**) are designed to catch a variety of species including perch, pike, trout and salmon. The Abu Drop Fish 8g (**C**), one of Abu's Droppen range, has a realistic, plastic imitation fish attached to tempt predators.

Lures D and E are two more Abu Droppen spinners. The Drop Flex 6g (**D**) has a patch of reflective plastic on the blade to make it more visible in murky waters. The Droppen 2g (**E**), like the rest of the Droppen lures, has most of its weight concentrated at the rear of its body for good casting.

Lure (**F**) is a half-ounce Mepps Aglia Long. The weighted body casts well, and as with all spinners the rotating blade creates strong vibrations as it spins. The Abu Droppen Sono 18g (**G**) has perforated flanges on its blade to increase the sound produced by its rotation when it's retrieved.

The Taylor & Johnson 2½-inch Colorado spoon (**H**) and the Rapier 2½-inch kidney spoon (**I**) are both spinners despite being known as 'spoons'. The blade of the Colorado rotates around a central bar, to which it's attached at both ends. The kidney spoon is attached to a swivel so that it (and its treble hook) spins as it's pulled through the water.

A lure is any artificial device which, when pulled through the water, incites a predatory fish to grab it, either through territorial aggression, cussedness or hunger. A lure can be made of wood, plastic, rubber, metal, or other materials such as feathers or hair, and rigged with single or multiple treble hooks.

It can be buoyant, heavily weighted so that it sinks, or made to dive on the retrieve by means of a lipped vane built into its head. Its action, an important part of its attractiveness to fish, can be imparted by the angler or result from its body shape or from angled vanes attached to it, with

extra vibratory attraction coming from steel balls which rattle inside it. External spinning or vibrating blades also create sound waves, as do hinged arms which flap as floating plugs are wound across the surface.

One of the most straightforward types of lure is the spoon, made from chrome-plated steel, brass, aluminium or hammered copper, with a single treble at one end and a swivel at the other, both joined to the body by split rings.

The spoon has two great assets: its weight gives it good casting ability (particularly into the wind), and it can be counted down, in seconds, to the desired

depth before retrieving. It doesn't spin, but simply wiggles or wobbles from side to side and so it can be retrieved at almost any speed. As a general rule, a slow retrieve is best for coloured water, and a medium to fast pace for really clear water.

The spoon's shape is usually oval, some being more elongated than others, and the choice of both weight and size depends on the species you're fishing for. Spoons of from four to six inches long (even longer for trolling) are ideal for larger fish such as pike, while those of three inches or less will catch anything from crappies and trout upwards.

Large, 8 to 12-inch spoon blades (without hooks) called dodgers or flashers are often used as an attractor when trolling, rigged 3 feet ahead of the lure. They also help to give a natural movement to the lure, and to natural fishbaits when 'mooching' for salmon. The salmon homes in on the vibration and flash of the dodger, but grabs the fish bait.

There are also many excellent weedless spoons (a fine, sprung wire hook guard protects the point) from which to choose, which have a single hook joined to the body and a rubbery skirt to help mask the point. Unlike the

## SPOONS
Spoons are lures that wobble, rather than spin.

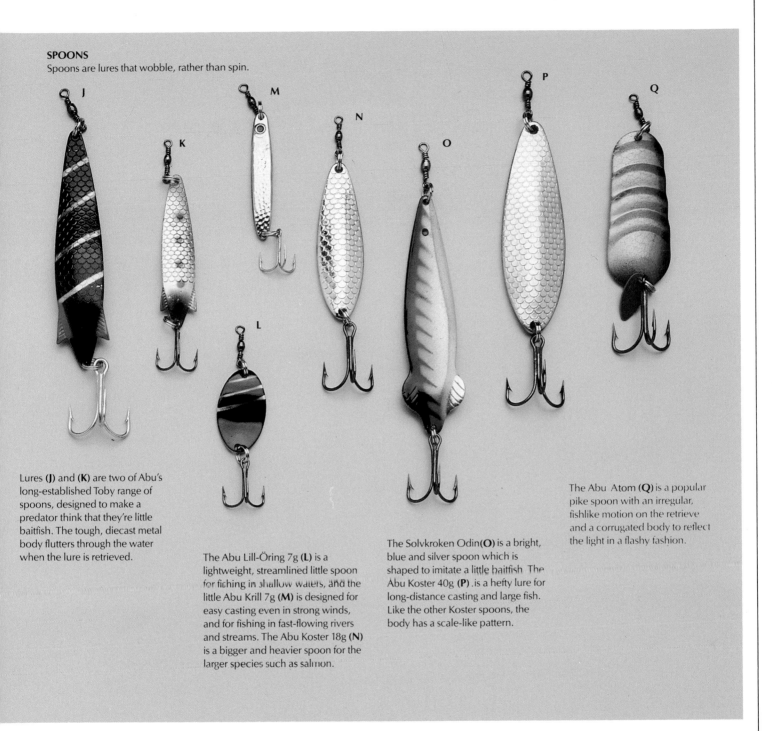

Lures (**J**) and (**K**) are two of Abu's long-established Toby range of spoons, designed to make a predator think that they're little baitfish. The tough, diecast metal body flutters through the water when the lure is retrieved.

The Abu Lill-Öring 7g (**L**) is a lightweight, streamlined little spoon for fishing in shallow waters, and the little Abu Krill 7g (**M**) is designed for easy casting even in strong winds, and for fishing in fast-flowing rivers and streams. The Abu Koster 18g (**N**) is a bigger and heavier spoon for the larger species such as salmon.

The Solvkroken Odin(**O**) is a bright, blue and silver spoon which is shaped to imitate a little baitfish. The Abu Koster 40g (**P**) .is a hefty lure for long-distance casting and large fish. Like the other Koster spoons, the body has a scale-like pattern.

The Abu Atom (**Q**) is a popular pike spoon with an irregular, fishlike motion on the retrieve and a corrugated body to reflect the light in a flashy fashion.

trailing trebles on basic spoons, these hooks won't snag, even in thick vegetation.

Many large spoons (and other lures) often come with treble hooks that are far too thick in the wire for general freshwater use. Simply replace them with a more suitable type, and always keep the points sharp. Gently flattening the barbs with pliers also aids hook penetration, particularly into the hard, bony jaws of species like pike and muskies.

A natural progression from spoon baits is the spinner, where the spoon or blade actually revolves around a weighted centre bar or stem. These come in a variety of blade colours and hook trimmings, from squirrel tail to red wool tassels or plastic worms and fish.

Colorado spoons and kidney spoons, which are actually spinners because they have revolving blades, have been popular for many years. Both have a red-painted, lead centre bar, and red wool tags around the treble which are reputed to be very good at inciting pike.

Devon minnows are a popular type of spinner, used mainly for trout but particularly for salmon. They either have metal bodies of various weights and colours, for fast, deep river work, or wooden bodies for shallow rivers or for fishing the lure above rocks.

With all types of lures that spin, you should guard against line twist and kinking by fitting a plastic anti-kink vane or a vaned swivel guard at the head of the trace.

Evolving from both spoons and spinners come the spinning baits, buzz baits and other lures which rely on a spinning or vibrating blade to create sound to attract the fish, but which also have a soft, tempting body for the fish to grab at. The body incorporates a large, single hook, the idea being that a fish will take the lower, body section or even attempt the entire lure, as do pike, for instance, although fish do sometimes hit the blade in preference to the body.

Some spinner baits have a single blade, others a pair of blades mounted tandem-style on a V-shaped, stainless steel shaft. The lure is leaded so that it always fishes with the blade or blades uppermost, and the body material usually consists of a rubber, squid-like skirt that folds back over the hook to mask it from weed on the retrieve.

Spinner baits can be retrieved either fast or slow, and at all depths, but are particularly effective (perhaps more than any

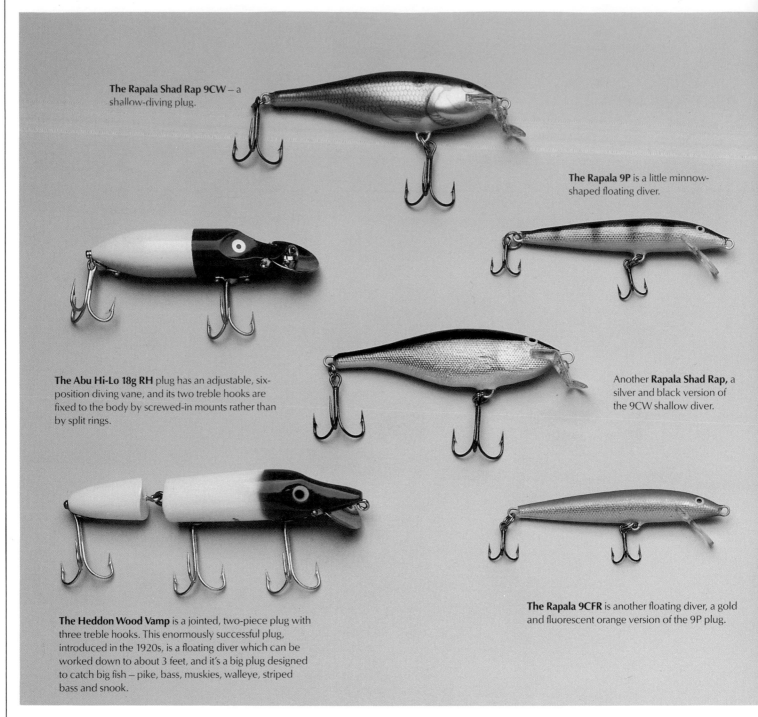

**The Rapala Shad Rap 9CW** – a shallow-diving plug.

**The Rapala 9P** is a little minnow-shaped floating diver.

**The Abu Hi-Lo 18g RH** plug has an adjustable, six-position diving vane, and its two treble hooks are fixed to the body by screwed-in mounts rather than by split rings.

Another **Rapala Shad Rap,** a silver and black version of the 9CW shallow diver.

**The Heddon Wood Vamp** is a jointed, two-piece plug with three treble hooks. This enormously successful plug, introduced in the 1920s, is a floating diver which can be worked down to about 3 feet, and it's a big plug designed to catch big fish – pike, bass, muskies, walleye, striped bass and snook.

**The Rapala 9CFR** is another floating diver, a gold and fluorescent orange version of the 9P plug.

other freshwater lure) in coloured water where visibility is low.

Buzz baits are similar in format, but are used as surface attractor lures, with the blade churning through the surface film to create vibrations.

In complete contrast to these noisy lures, lead-headed jigs work on the principle of the weighted head dropping downwards when winding stops or the rod tip is lowered, and quickly 'jigging' upwards on the retrieve or when the rod tip is raised.

The jig has a ball or wedge-shaped head made of painted lead moulded onto the hook shank. The shank is bent at right angles

some quarter of an inch from the eye, so that the eye always faces upwards in line with the hook point. This helps to make the jig relatively snag and weed free. Jigs will catch almost any freshwater fish, from crappies to salmon, and are best used on very light tackle.

Many jigs have bodies and tails, made from materials such as rubber, bucktail and marabou feathers, while others incorporate plastic worms, shrimps or various grub-like tails. Some tiny jigs may not even have a body or tail, simply a brightly painted head used bare or with a small livebait such as a maggot, worm, fish fry or grub on the hook.

Another type have tiny heads weighing only a fiftieth or even a hundredth of an ounce, and fluttering bodies of marabou. These are outstanding lures for trout and panfish, and can be used on a fly rod outfit, jigged gently beneath a float when ice fishing, or on ultralight tackle in the normal way.

Plastic worms come in a range of thicknesses and in lengths of from three to ten or more inches. As well as the plain, earthworm type, there are worms with twister tails, crawfish tails, fish tails and other patterns. Often, they're impregnated with special salts and pungent natural oils to make

them smell just like the real thing, or worse.

The colour range is astounding, but all the reds, purples, yellows and blacks work well, as do some of the fluorescent colours, pink and dark green in particular.

In addition to the basic synthetic worm, there are also soft, jelly-like imitations of creatures such as lizards, frogs and toads. These are all fished in the same way as the worms, either floating on the surface or taken down to the bottom by a bullet-headed worm weight, threaded on the line just in front of the lure. These weights vary from an eighth of an

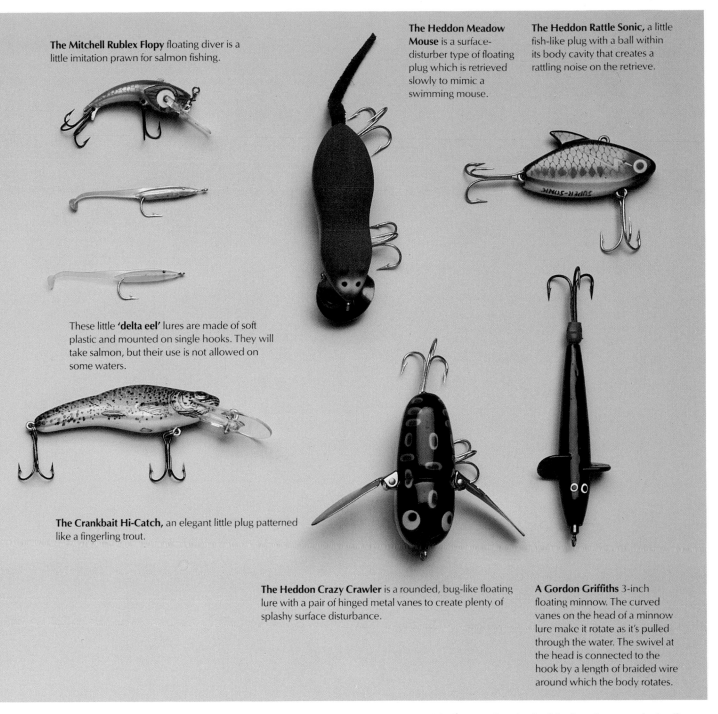

**The Mitchell Rublex Flopy** floating diver is a little imitation prawn for salmon fishing.

**The Heddon Meadow Mouse** is a surface-disturber type of floating plug which is retrieved slowly to mimic a swimming mouse.

**The Heddon Rattle Sonic,** a little fish-like plug with a ball within its body cavity that creates a rattling noise on the retrieve.

These little **'delta eel'** lures are made of soft plastic and mounted on single hooks. They will take salmon, but their use is not allowed on some waters.

**The Crankbait Hi-Catch,** an elegant little plug patterned like a fingerling trout.

**The Heddon Crazy Crawler** is a rounded, bug-like floating lure with a pair of hinged metal vanes to create plenty of splashy surface disturbance.

**A Gordon Griffiths** 3-inch floating minnow. The curved vanes on the head of a minnow lure make it rotate as it's pulled through the water. The swivel at the head is connected to the hook by a length of braided wire around which the body rotates.

ounce, to over half an ounce, and allow the lure to be fished in all waters, still or running.

The plastic worm is retrieved in a similar way to a jig, but in much longer pulls, and with longer pauses between them. During the pause, the worm can be left on the bottom for dead, or twitched on the surface.

Lastly, there's the large and very popular range of wooden or plastic lures known as plugs — floating plugs, floating divers and sinking plugs.

The floating plugs are surface attractor lures, and some have skirts, tassels, revolving blades or vibrating arms to help them create maximum disturbance on the surface. For casting into dense cover, weedless surface poppers will provide just what's needed: a splashy, floppy, non-hangup retrieve to bring the fish out of their cover and after the lure. Surface plugs are among the most exciting to use, because you not only anticipate the surface take, you also see it.

Floating divers, which float on the surface after being cast, begin to dive when they're retrieved; the faster the retrieve, the deeper they dive. If you pause during the retrieve, they'll pop back up to the surface again. By using a combination of fast and slow retrieve rates, with the occasional pause, you can create strikingly lifelike action in the lure.

Floating divers are the most versatile and probably the most widely used of all plugs. The diving action is created by an aluminium or plastic diving vane (or lip) set into the head of the plug. A good-sized vane will take the plug down to ten or fifteen feet on a fast retrieve.

The bodies of floating divers are often brightly coloured in fluorescent enamel or have an extremely effective, light-reflecting prism pattern. Some have a steel ball sealed within the body cavity, which rattles around inside the plug to make it vibrate, while others have jointed bodies.

Floating divers can be used for trolling as well as for casting, as can the sinking plugs. Designed for fishing deep waters where the lure has to sink some distance before it can be fished effectively, these plugs are heavy, strongly built and come in a variety of weights and colours. Most are up to about 4 or 5 inches long, but a few, intended for trolling rather than casting, are up to 10 inches in length. Sinking plugs often have rattles inside them, but few are fitted with a diving vane because their weight is enough to take them down to fishing depth.

# ARTIFICIAL LURES — SALTWATER

**Lure A** is the Tony Accetta PET 23, a large chromed steel spoon with a 7-ounce, 10-inch blade and a single hook, for trolling for big game fish such as wahoo and barracuda. **Lure B** is a plastic sandeel, a deadly lure for predators such as cod, ling and pollack. **Lures C** and **D** are also plastic — Shakespeare Wondershine imitation squid, 3 inches long, and one of the most successful types of lure for cod, ling and other predators.

**Lure E** is a 7-ounce Abu Sextett pirk, which has reflective sides to make it more visible.

The little Nils Master Invincible floating diver plug, **lure F,** is 3 inches long and weighs just over ¼ ounce. The body is made of balsa, and the hooks are attached to a stainless steel wire inside the plug. **Lure G**, at the top of this picture, is a large, soft plastic squid with a big single hook, a good lure for big game trolling for species such as bluefin tuna and broadbill swordfish.

**Lure H** is a Kona Head lure. The Kona Head, first developed in Hawaii, is one of the standard big game fishing lures, and it will take a large number of species including bonito, marlin, tuna and dorado.

The Ilander, from Tournament Tackle Inc, **lure I**, is a 9-inch, 2-ounce trolling lure designed to be used at speeds of between 4 and 10 knots, mounted on a wire or mono leader with an 8/0 to 10/0 hook.

The lures used in saltwater fishing range from tiny trout and salmon flies adapted to saltwater fly casting up to the huge Kona Head lures designed for fast big-game trolling.

Many standard freshwater fly patterns can be used to good effect for the smaller saltwater fish, one of the most successful patterns being the Dog Nobbler, a weighted fly which incorporates a long, flowing marabou tail. When this fly is retrieved, the tail undulates enticingly through the water to give the fly a natural-looking, swimming motion.

Streamer flies, which are also extremely good, range in size from little, inch-long patterns up to huge, six-inch creations designed to take small tuna, tarpon and sailfish. For bottom feeding fish such as bonefish or permit, a shrimp imitation fished with a slow retrieve can be a deadly bait.

Japanese feathers were originally designed as lures for commercial bonito and tuna fishing, but rod anglers soon discovered their potential and they have now become a standard trolling lure. Japanese feathers have a chromed lead head, which gives them weight, red glass eyes, and a bunch of mixed hackle feathers which form the tail, the most popular tail colours being red/white, green/yellow, all black and all dark blue.

These lures are available in weights of one to ten ounces, and they attract and catch many kinds of predatory fish. For example, the smaller lures are perfect for bonito, while the larger patterns will take big tuna.

Another good trolling lure is the wobbling spoon. As its name suggests, this is a one-piece, concave lure designed to wobble rather than spin through the water. Many of these lures originated in Sweden and Canada, where they were designed for deepwater trolling for giant lake trout, pike and muskellunge.

Their success in freshwater eventually led to their adoption by saltwater fishermen, and they are particularly useful as attractor spoons for cod or as barracuda lures. Wobbling spoons are now made in many sizes, colours and scale patterns, and some are designed specifically for casting; these are made from thicker metal to give them casting weight.

Spinners used in saltwater are also based on freshwater patterns, especially the Colorado and kidney spinners devised in the last century for pike fishing. Modern engineering and design have improved on these basic patterns to produce a wide range of revolving lures. Most of the available patterns are designed for ultralight spin fishing techniques for bass, mackerel, garfish, medium-weight barracuda and a host of small sporting fish such as flounders.

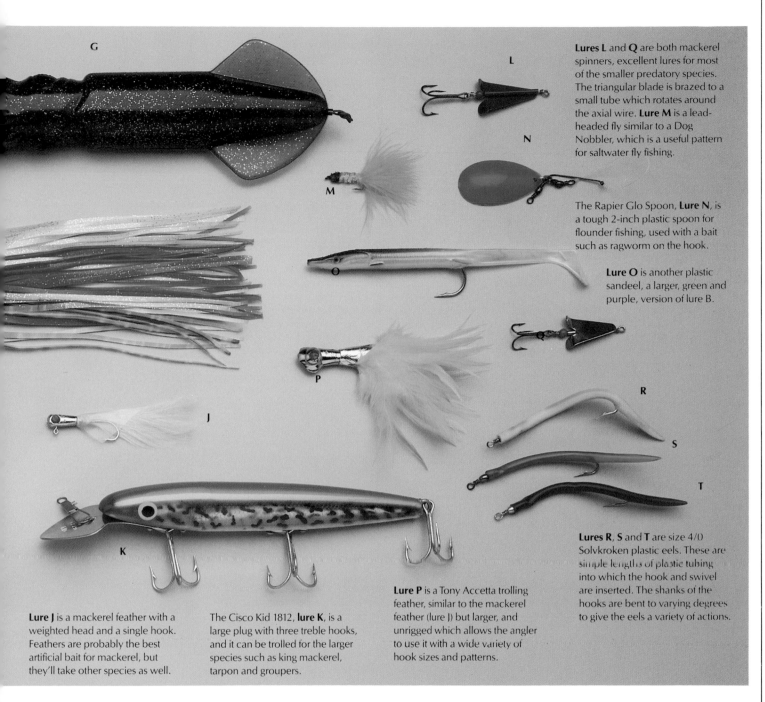

Lures **L** and **Q** are both mackerel spinners, excellent lures for most of the smaller predatory species. The triangular blade is brazed to a small tube which rotates around the axial wire. **Lure M** is a lead-headed fly similar to a Dog Nobbler, which is a useful pattern for saltwater fly fishing.

The Rapier Glo Spoon, **Lure N**, is a tough 2-inch plastic spoon for flounder fishing, used with a bait such as ragworm on the hook.

**Lure O** is another plastic sandeel, a larger, green and purple, version of lure B.

**Lures R**, **S** and **T** are size 4/0 Solvkroken plastic eels. These are simple lengths of plastic tubing into which the hook and swivel are inserted. The shanks of the hooks are bent to varying degrees to give the eels a variety of actions.

**Lure J** is a mackerel feather with a weighted head and a single hook. Feathers are probably the best artificial bait for mackerel, but they'll take other species as well.

The Cisco Kid 1812, **lure K**, is a large plug with three treble hooks, and it can be trolled for the larger species such as king mackerel, tarpon and groupers.

**Lure P** is a Tony Accetta trolling feather, similar to the mackerel feather (lure J) but larger, and unrigged which allows the angler to use it with a wide variety of hook sizes and patterns.

The saltwater plug bait is another lure which has its origins in freshwater fishing. Some of the deadliest patterns come from Finland, where they were once hand carved for pike and trout fishing. Other extremely good patterns started life in America, again being hand carved by anglers for their own personal use.

A few modern plugs are still made of wood, but most are made from moulded plastic. Floating plugs are designed to work in the surface layers, slow sinkers mainly in midwater, and fast sinkers for searching the bottom. Plug baits range from inch-long midgets up to the 12-inch giants designed for trolling for many species of open-ocean game fish.

Plugs are often hand finished, which makes them expensive, but very cheap plugs seldom have the good, inbuilt action of a top quality lure and are best avoided.

Some models have a diving vane which can be altered to several different positions, allowing the plug to be changed in seconds from deep diving to shallow running. Such lures can be very useful when fish come up or go down after bait fish shoals.

Like the early plugs, the original Kona Head lures were hand carved from hardwood, but they were then fitted with improvised skirts. These baits were found to be very effective for a host of game fish including blue and white marlin and tuna. So

great was their popularity, a whole industry has grown up around this style of big game lure, producing hundreds of variations on the original patterns.

The modern lure has a plastic head and a brightly coloured plastic skirt or skirts. Head styles include singles, double-jointed knuckled heads and triple action heads. Some are moulded in a single coloured plastic such as nylon, while others have translucent acrylic heads containing moulded plastic eyes that move and roll as the bait trolls through the water. The heads are either dished, scooped out, drilled or fluted to add movement, vibration and overall attraction to the lure.

Most big game anglers use two skirts of different colours on each lure, and the colour combinations are often intended to mimic a particular fish, for instance blue/white for bonito, and green/yellow for dorado.

Other combinations are just put together to create a flashy bait that will trigger off the attack reaction of predatory fish. An interesting variant of this is the 'bird', a modern version of an old Japanese fish attractor called a *shiva-shava*. The bird, which has short, stiff 'wings', splashes crazily over the surface like a crippled flyingfish trying to get airborne. This is a good lure for dorado, which feed extensively on flyingfishes.

# FRESHWATER BAIT — NATURALS

Although they're less convenient to use than artificial lures, natural baits have their advantages; they're usually part of the fish's natural diet, there's a wide choice, and you can get most of them for free.

The common earthworm, for instance (also called the lobworm or nightcrawler), will catch any freshwater fish from greedy little perch up to bass, barbel or salmon. You can dig them up, or simply collect them from the lawn at night, especially after prolonged rain.

Brandling worms, which are much thinner and shorter than earthworms, are usually found in manure heaps. These worms, distinctly ringed with white or yellow bands, emit a smelly, yellow fluid when they're hooked which is most attractive to bottom feeding fish. Another type of worm that appeals to most fish is the redworm, a dark red, slow-moving little worm found in compost heaps.

The humble maggot, which is seldom seen in the USA except for ice fishing, is by far the most widely used freshwater bait in Britain. The larva of the bluebottle fly, it's effective for all fish both large and small, except for the pike family. Some anglers prefer maggots dyed bronze, yellow or red to the natural white ones, because in certain water conditions the fish seem to show a liking for a particular colour.

Smaller maggots such as squats (housefly larvae) and pinkies (greenbottle fly larvae) are generally used as loose-feed groundbait, but they can be used on the hook for smaller fish. They are particularly effective when the water's very clear and the temperature low.

To hook a maggot without breaking the skin, squeeze it gently until a little 'tab' protrudes from the blunt end, then simply nick the hook point through. Always use a hook size to match that of the maggot, and loose feed sparingly for the smaller shoaling species. Little and often is the rule to follow.

The same goes for fishing with casters, which are pupated maggots. Initially, the caster is heavy and juicy and will sink, but as the grub changes slowly into a fly it becomes lighter and so it floats. Floating casters are great for surface feeding fish such as dace, rudd, chub and even carp, while the sinkers catch good roach, bream and chub.

Slugs are excellent chub bait, as are large, juicy caterpillars and grubs, which are also very good for catching trout.

You can find many subsurface naturals in shallow water during the summer months. One of the best of these is the caddis grub, the larva of the sedge fly, which builds its protective case with tiny stones and twigs. To get it out of its case, squeeze gently at the tail end and pull it out by its head. Also very effective, especially for trout, grayling and chub, are large mayfly and stonefly nymphs and small crustaceans such as freshwater shrimp and crayfish.

Predatory species, including trout, pike and perch, all love crayfish, the freshwater answer to lobster. It can only grow by periodically shedding its shell and then growing a new one, and during its soft or 'peeler' stage it hides under large stones while its shell hardens. Use a size 4 or 6 hook, put once through the last tail segment. Crayfish are equally effective on the retrieve or drifted downstream, and although the peeler stage is preferable, small hard-shelled ones will also work.

Freshwater mussels, particularly the large swan mussel, are another fine natural bait. Gather them from the muddy shallows, and open the shell by cutting through the strong hinges with a thin-bladed knife. Use the orange flesh on a number 4 hook, freelined on the bottom, for catfish, carp and eels, or cut into half-inch cubes for smaller species.

Seafood naturals, like shellfish, shrimps and prawns, work superbly for freshwater species. Unpeeled shrimps and prawns, raw or boiled, will take bass, crappies, barbel, carp, tench and chub, and if peeled just about everything loves them. Large prawns are, of course, one of the deadliest of salmon baits, float fished down with the flow or worked across the current on a weighted cast.

Any small, live freshwater fish, as long as it's presented properly, will catch predators. The size of the bait fish you use should be related to the size of fish you're after: up to three inches long for trout, zander, perch and chub, and four to six inches for larger fish such as bass, pike and catfish.

Any drifted, wobbled or static freshwater deadbait will catch predators effectively, but so too will many small sea fish. Smelt, herring, mackerel and sprat all make good deadbaits, and almost any readily-available small sea fish will catch pike. Pilchard, sardines and mullet in the five to seven inch range are all great pike baits; larger fish can be cut in half, and half baits catch just as many pike as whole baits do. What is important is that the bait lies static on the bottom, where the big old lazy pike prefer to spend much of their time.

Baby squid is another good pike bait, and the freshwater eel is even better – cut a twelve inch eel in half and use either end. Small eels, or just the tail ends, are also good for trolling and wobbling because they are tough and move in an enticing way.

Many soft-fleshed sea fish break up easily when continually cast, so for spinning or wobbling stick to small freshwater fish. Little trout are particularly tough, and can usually be bought quite cheaply from a trout farm.

**Right:** Some of the many natural baits used in freshwater fishing. Freelined slugs are one of the most deadly chub baits, and will also take barbel and tench, but they're nowhere near as versatile as worms, which will catch almost any freshwater species. Another bait which will take most species is the maggot, fished singly or in bunches. The caster, the pupated form of the maggot, is a useful bait for many of the smaller species of fish such as bream and roach. Shellfish, such as mussels, together with prawns and shrimps, make excellent bait, especially for the larger species, while whole or cut seafish such as mackerel and mullet are ideal baits for predators

### HOOKING NATURAL BAITS

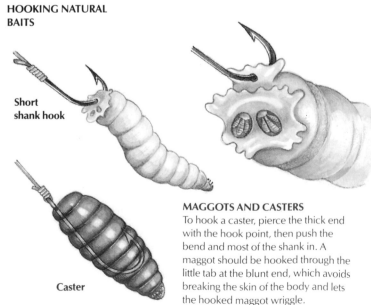

**Short shank hook**

**Caster**

### MAGGOTS AND CASTERS

To hook a caster, pierce the thick end with the hook point, then push the bend and most of the shank in. A maggot should be hooked through the little tab at the blunt end, which avoids breaking the skin of the body and lets the hooked maggot wriggle.

## WORMS

With a large worm the hook should pierce the body at least twice, to prevent it wriggling off. A small worm should be pushed round onto the bend and shank.

**Earthworm**

**Brandling worm**

## CRAYFISH

Crayfish should be hooked through the tail, with the point pushed in from below through the second or third segment. Remove the shell if it's hard.

**Crayfish**

## MUSSELS

To open a mussel, slide a sharp knife between the shell halves to sever the hinge. Thread the yellow flesh onto the hook shank, leaving the barb exposed.

**Mussel**

## EELS

To hook a freshwater eel tail, pass the leader through it leaving the point and barb exposed at the cut end.

**Eel tail**

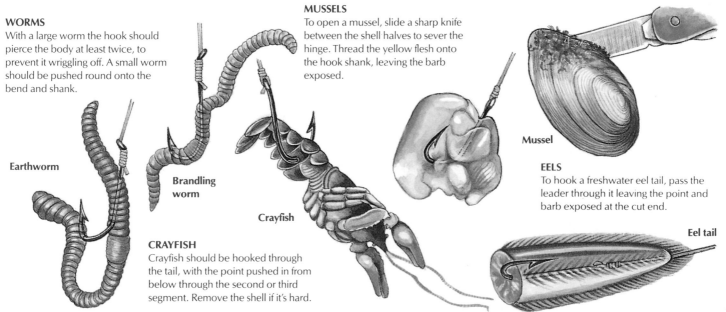

# FRESHWATER BAIT — PROCESSED

As well as all the natural freshwater baits, there's an almost endless choice of raw or cooked baits which, although very effective, are rarely part of the fish's natural food. Bread, cheese, sweetcorn, vegetables, nuts, seeds and canned meats are just a few of the possibilities.

Bread, in one form or another, is a bait much loved by most non-predatory species, especially the cyprinids. Cubes of crust can be trotted or ledgered on the bottom for roach and bream, or floated on the surface for carp and chub, while the soft inner crumb can be squeezed onto the hook shank as 'breadflake'. Always use a fresh, doughy loaf for breadflake, or it won't stay on the hook for more than a few seconds.

Stale bread is best used in the form of a paste. Soak the crumb, then squeeze it in a piece of cloth to remove excess water and form the paste. Use it on its own, or mix it with an equal amount of grated cheese or sausage meat. Mashed sardines or fish-based cat food also make great paste ingredients, especially for catfish bait.

For convenience, a chunk of canned tuna is a bait few catfish can resist, and luncheon meat cut into half-inch cubes is one of the finest instant carp and chub baits yet discovered. Equal to canned meat in convenience, as far as carp are concerned, are small dog or cat biscuits used as a floating bait. Some of the richer, spicier biscuits can be crushed, mixed with a binder such as beaten egg, and stiffened with maize meal to form a paste.

Many grains and seeds make excellent freshwater baits. Sweetcorn is one of the most deadly of all the grain baits, especially for carp and tench. Hard maize, its elder brother, is equally good but it has to be softened before use. You can do this by soaking it in water for a few hours, then giving it about twenty minutes in a pressure cooker. It will swell to about twice its size during cooking, so leave plenty of room in the pan for expansion.

Wheat and barley are useful baits if you prepare them properly. Tip the grain into a large, lidded bucket, then pour in enough boiling water to cover it by at least three or four inches. Stir it thoroughly with a stick, put the lid on, and leave it overnight to stew and absorb the water.

In the morning, strain off any excess water, and if you're not going to use it that day, pack it in freezer bags and freeze it. Preparing enough for several fishing sessions at a time and then freezing it will save you a lot of time. You can use the same method to prepare other normally-hard baits such as seedbaits, dried peas and beans, and peanuts.

Stewed hempseed is the most productive of the seedbaits, because it's highly attractive to all cyprinids. Use it on the hook, or as a loose feed with a maggot, caster, elderberry or tare seed on the hook. Tare seeds are almost as good, but they lack that special aroma of stewed hempseed so they should only be used as hookbait.

Peanuts, dried peas, chickpeas and haricot beans, when softened, can be used in rivers or still water, but you usually need to prebait the swim with them for a few successive nights before fishing so that the fish can acquire a taste for them.

Other vegetable baits worth trying are potatoes and carrots. The potatoes should be part-boiled to soften them slightly, and used sliced, cubed or, if they're small enough, whole. Prebait the water with small balls of mashed potato, or make the hookbait even more attractive by dipping it in honey or black treacle. Small, thin baby carrots can be used as a spinning bait instead of an artificial lure.

Macaroni and pasta shells, cooked until soft but not sloppy, will also take fish if the swim has been prebaited. They work better in rivers than in still waters, because then they twist and turn in the current and the movement attracts the attention of the fish.

A more convenient bait, which needs no preparation or pre-baiting, is cheese. Cheddar cheese, or similar, works well in summer but cold winter waters can turn it rock-hard, so processed cheese spread should be used then. Cheese will take most non-predators, and even perch and pike on occasions, and in running water the scent will drift downstream and attract fish from some distance away. For this reason, strong cheeses will often be more effective than mild ones.

High protein (HP) bait mixes are now a big part of the British and European carp fishing scene. These baits are derived from refined milk products, wheat-germ, animal proteins and eggs, and sold as ready-prepared pastes or balls, or as powders.

**Sweetcorn**

**Cheese**

**High Protein (HP) baits**

**Peas, beans and pasta**

Colourings and flavourings can also be added, and the bait is used either as a paste or in balls called 'boilies'. These are made by dropping small (1/4 to 3/4 inch) balls of the paste into boiling water for a couple of minutes. This gives them a thin, tough skin which makes it difficult for fish other than carp or tench to take them.

**Sweetcorn:** the most convenient form is the canned, ready-cooked corn. An excellent bait for most non-predatory fish.
**Cheese:** like sweetcorn, cheese will take most non-predatory species, but it will also, on occasion, take pike and perch.

Seeds and grains

Bread

Potato and carrot

Meats

**High protein (HP)** baits: these baits were formulated originally for carp fishing, but by varying the ingredients they can be made attractive to most species. On waters where the fish have never seen high protein bait, it may be necessary to prebait the swim to give them a taste for it.

**Peas, beans and pasta:** clean and convenient, these baits will take a good variety of non-predatory fish, but prebaiting may be needed. **Seeds and grains:** these must be softened before use, but not allowed to get so mushy as to be unusable. Good for most non-predators.

**Bread:** a cheap and versatile bait which can be prepared in a number of ways. Excellent for species such as carp, catfish, grayling, bream, chub, roach, rudd, tench and barbel. Bread paste can be made even more effective by mixing it with cheese, meat, fish or cat food.

**Potato and carrot:** these should be part-boiled to soften them before use. As with other vegetable baits, prebaiting is usually needed.
**Meats:** canned meats are effective and convenient baits for species such as carp, catfish, eels and chub and sometimes predators.

# FRESHWATER GROUNDBAIT

When you're fishing for coarse fish, one way to increase your success is by the careful use of groundbait. Unlike prebaiting – where you put bait into the swim hours, or even days, before you fish, so that the fish get used to the type of bait or to feeding at that spot – groundbaitng is done while you're actually fishing.

What confuses most anglers about groundbait is whether they should use it to feed the fish or to attract them – or, indeed, whether they should use it at all. Ultimately, the decision depends on the kind of fish you're after, how numerous they are, and the type of water they're living in.

Always remember the two basic functions of groundbaiting. The first is to attract fish into the area of your hookbait (if they're not already there). The second is to keep them feeding in the area long enough to notice and take the baited hook, without feeding them so much that they ignore it.

For instance, there's no way you will keep a large shoal of bream around with just three balls of groundbait, but the same amount thrown to a small group of wily old roach in a clear little stream would ruin any chance of a bite. So think carefully before using any groundbait other than a few loose feed fragments. Whether the water is running or still, groundbait scores best where fish have to compete strongly for food.

A good basis for groundbait mixtures is stale bread. You might be able to get stale, unsold bread from a local shop, but if not, save all the household bread scraps and soak them for a few hours in a bucket of water. Then drain off the water and squeeze the bread between your hands to make a mushy pulp. Mix in bran, maize meal or any other cereal meal to give it bulk and weight, plus fragments of the hookbait you're going to use (such as sweetcorn, maggots or chopped worm), and you'll have a good, heavy groundbait which will sink to the bottom of the swim before it breaks up.

If you need to throw or catapult it a long way, add two cupfuls of flaked maize or cornflakes to each half-bucket of groundbait and work it in until the mixture's stiff (add more if necessary). Then you can squeeze it into balls for throwing or catapulting. If you leave these to harden for a few hours before you use them, you'll be able to throw them much

further than when they're fresh.

This basic mixture can be made even more attractive by adding flavourings and colourings. Trial and error is probably the only reliable way to find the best mixture for a particular swim or type of fish, but some additives worth considering are honey, treacle, maple syrup, fish oil and aromatic oils such as aniseed to flavour it, and food dyes to colour it.

Another type of groundbait – cloudbait – can be made from breadcrumbs. This is used to attract fish in still or slow-moving waters by creating a cloud of fine particles which fish will explore, looking for something that's big enough to eat.

Cut stale bread into slices (or use stale sliced bread) and leave them to dry out, or heat them in an oven, until they're crisp. Then crush them down into fine crumbs and sieve them to remove any lumps. When you get to the water, dampen the crumbs and squeeze them into small balls. When you throw these into the swim, they'll break up as they sink and create a cloud of crumbs. You'll get an even better cloud if you mix dried milk powder in with the crumbs: a large spoonful for every two pounds of dry crumbs should be enough.

When you're ledgering, you can concentrate groundbait close to the hook by using a swimfeeder. This is a perforated plastic tube about two to three inches long and an inch in diameter, usually attached to the line about 15 inches from the hook.

The open-ended version is packed with hookbait particles and the ends are plugged with groundbait. When it hits bottom, the groundbait disintegrates and releases the hookbait particles.

The blockend feeder is closed at each end by plastic caps, one or both of which can be removed so that it can be filled with maggots. When it's on the bottom, the maggots escape through the holes in the side and attract fish to the area of the maggot hookbait.

When swimfeeders are packed with bait, they are comparatively heavy and so they can be accurately cast a considerable distance, usually much further than you could throw or catapult a ball of groundbait.

*Above right You can get good results by using a catapult to put groundbait into distant swims.*

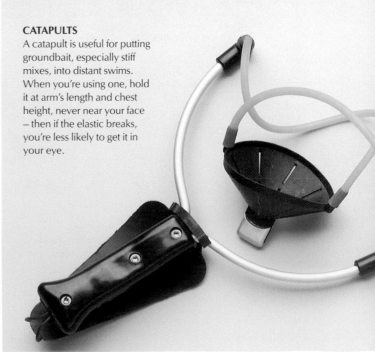

**CATAPULTS**
A catapult is useful for putting groundbait, especially stiff mixes, into distant swims. When you're using one, hold it at arm's length and chest height, never near your face – then if the elastic breaks, you're less likely to get it in your eye.

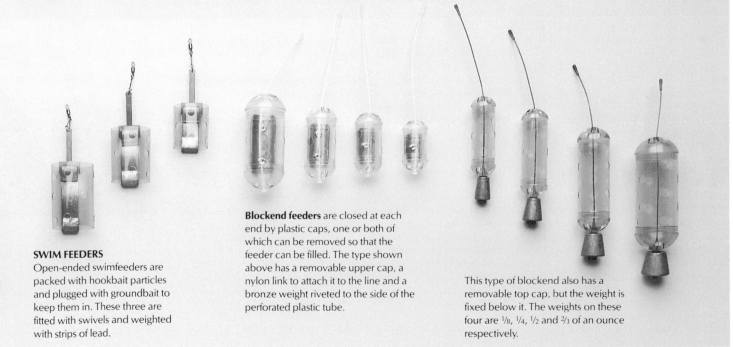

### SWIM FEEDERS
Open-ended swimfeeders are packed with hookbait particles and plugged with groundbait to keep them in. These three are fitted with swivels and weighted with strips of lead.

**Blockend feeders** are closed at each end by plastic caps, one or both of which can be removed so that the feeder can be filled. The type shown above has a removable upper cap, a nylon link to attach it to the line and a bronze weight riveted to the side of the perforated plastic tube.

This type of blockend also has a removable top cap, but the weight is fixed below it. The weights on these four are ⅛, ¼, ½ and ⅔ of an ounce respectively.

# SALTWATER BAIT

The choice of baits for saltwater fishing is enormous, ranging from worms up to cut or whole fish and octopus.

One of the most popular sea fishing baits is king ragworm, which is big, easy to get, and has instant fish appeal. A large king ragworm can be 15 to 20 inches long, and when broken will provide at least three good baits. King ragworm live in U-shaped tunnels and become increasingly common the closer you get to the low spring tide mark. Smaller ragworm can also be found in harbours. There are various other sorts of ragworm which can be used as bait, including one species which burrows into soft rock, and the white ragworm which is normally found sheltered away where the beach is of soft, yellow sand.

Lugworms are another common and very popular worm bait, the variety known as black lug being the best, and they can be used fresh or as a preserved and salted bait. Earthworms can make a good substitute for marine worm baits, and they're particularly good for rock fish and flounder.

Many kinds of fish eat crab, and while some will happily eat hardbacked shore crab, others prefer to take the crab when it's in the process of moulting its shell. In the various stages of moulting, crabs are called softbacks and peelers.

When moulting, crabs are extremely vulnerable to attack from passing fish, so to avoid this danger they hide up beneath weed-fringed rocks, sea walls or other solid structures which give them shelter. Crabs that are hidden away like this are often easy to catch in quantity, and they can be kept alive in a bucket half full of seaweed, or deep-frozen for later use.

Many bottom-living fish feed on shellfish of one sort or another, one of the most popular bait types being the slipper limpet; two or three limpet bodies make one good bait. For rock fishing, the conical limpet can provide a good standby, and because of its extremely tough flesh it will stay on the hook almost indefinitely.

Edible mussels also make excellent bait, especially for flatfish and cod, but one of the finest of all shellfish baits is the razorshell. It lives in a little tunnel which it digs for itself and it's never easy to gather in quantity, but it makes a bait which few fish can resist.

Another deadly bait for most predatory sea fish is the sandeel or lance. These eels can be caught either by hand or, better still, by a specially constructed sandeel seine net. The greater lance, which may measure 12 to 15 inches long, can also be taken on feathers.

Sandeel are best used as live bait, but unfortunately they are very difficult to keep alive, needing constant water aeration to keep them in perfect condition. Once dead, they lose much of their attraction, but they can still be useful as bottom fishing bait. Sandeel can be frozen, although when they're thawed out their flesh tends to be rather soft.

Fish such as mackerel, herring and pompano can be cut into strips or fillets for bait. The oilier the fish, the better the bait it makes. Balls of fish scraped clear of the skin can also be used for soft-mouthed fish like mullet. Any fish used as bait should be as fresh as possible, because fresh fish stays on the hook far better than stale fish.

Whole fish make an excellent bait for the larger predatory fish, and again a fresh bait will always outfish a stale one. Choice of bait is wide, but most fish have a natural preference for certain types of bait fish. Giant common skate and halibut, for example, will fall readily to a whole pollack, while conger prefer mackerel. Shark show a distinct preference for oily-fleshed fish, and bonito, Spanish mackerel and horse mackerel are the three best shark baits. Tuna take herring, mackerel and flyingfish, while billfish will take just about any food-sized fish they come across.

Livebaits seem to work better than deadbaits, except when the bait is being trolled, when a deadbait correctly mounted will catch as well as a live fish. A good trick when using dead fish for shark bait is to tip the point of the hook with a pair of pilchard or sardine, because the truly oily flesh of these fish will encourage the shark to take the whole bait.

All predatory fish will eat squid, octopus or cuttlefish. For the smaller fish these large baits can be cut into sections or strips. Californian squid is now exported to many parts of the world, and although it's intended for human consumption much of it ends up as bait. Large cod are particularly fond of it.

Large squid can be used for drift fishing for shark, or as a

Above *For both shore fishing and boat fishing, popular saltwater baits are razorshells, sandeels, marine worms such as ragworms, and squid, cuttlefish and mussels.*

deepwater bait for mighty broadbill swordfish. Cuttlefish, a near relative of the true squid, is normally used as a cut bait. Both squid and cuttlefish should be skinned before use. This skinning only takes a matter of seconds, but it definitely improves the attractiveness of the bait.

Octopus is another bait which works well in any part of the world. Most octopus are too large to be used whole, so each tentacle should be cut from the main body and chopped into bait-sized sections. You can usually get frozen octopus from Chinese supermarkets.

### HOOKING SALTWATER BAITS

**RAGWORMS**
Ragworms and other marine worms can be used whole or cut. They should be threaded onto the bend and shank of the hook, leaving the point exposed.

### MACKEREL
A piece of mackerel cut from the tail end is a good bait for smaller species. The bait is threaded onto the hook and tied to the shank near the eye.

### OCTOPUS
Small pieces of octopus tentacle should be threaded onto the hook and bound to the shank near the eye to hold them firmly in position.

### RAZORSHELL
Open the shell by cutting through the hinge, then remove the flesh and thread it onto the hook with the foot at the bottom, supporting the softer flesh.

### SANDEEL
Sandeel can be rigged for livebait by passing the hook through the lower lip and then hooking it into the belly.

# SALTWATER GROUNDBAIT

Many kinds of sea fish respond to the use of groundbait or chum, but groundbaiting methods can vary considerably from one locality to another, as much because of different local traditions as because of differences in the fish.

On rocky coastlines with deep tidal gullies, a low-tide prebaiting session can often attract a number of good fish into the gully area. The type of groundbait to use depends on the type of fish you hope to attract and catch. For instance, fish makes the best groundbait for bass or conger, but crushed crab is better for wrasses.

Place the groundbait in position when the tide is at its very lowest, stuffing mashed fish or crushed crab into every likely crevice between the low water and high water marks. If you do this correctly, the rising tide will wash out a continuous stream of bait particles that will attract the fish to the gully.

When you're bottom fishing from an anchored boat, a simple but useful method of groundbaiting is to tie a large mesh bag full of mashed fish to the anchor rope several feet above the anchor. It's important to make sure the bag isn't actually on the bottom, or it will quickly be ripped open aand emptied by crabs. Some fish can also destroy a bait bag, small shark being particularly good at chewing through a mesh to get at the fish inside.

The beauty of this style of groundbaiting is that all the smell and the bait particles pass under the boat to wash across the area covered by the baited lines. This method is good for conger, cod, tope and many kinds of rock fish.

Another way of groundbaiting the bottom is to use a custom-built bait dropper. This consists of a square box with its front loosely hinged at the bottom. A heavy wire runs through holes in the top and bottom of the box, near the front, with its top end shaped into a hook and a lead weight fixed to the end beneath the box.

You fill the box with mashed fish, crab, and/or worm, then close the hinged front and fasten it with the hooked end of the wire. Using a rope attached to the top of the box, lower it to the bottom. As the lead touches down, the wire is pushed up through the box so that its hooked top releases the front panel, which drops open allowing the bait to spill out onto the bottom.

A very effective way of attract-

**Above** *Lowering a bag of chum (or 'rubby dubby') over the side of a boat to create a trail of groundbait particles that can drift miles with the tide flow. This trail attracts cruising sharks and other fish, which follow it back to the boat.*
**Right** *Rubby dubby is a mixture of mashed fish, bran and fish blood or fish oil.*

**Left** *Groundbait for mullet can be made from meat, meat fat, fish blood and bran, or (as shown here), from a mixture of bread and pilchard oil. As with rubby dubby, these groundbaits are usually mixed in a bucket before use.*
**Right** *The mixture of bread and pilchard oil is put into a mesh bag and lowered into the sea.*

ing shark is to use rubby dubby, a noxious mixture of mashed stale fish, bran (or sawdust) and fish blood or fish oil. This mess is mixed in a bucket until it forms a thick paste, then it's put into a mesh bag or a perforated zinc container which is hung over the side of the boat so that it just touches the surface.

The natural rise and fall of the boat will continually slam the bag or container down on the surface. Each time this happens, particles of bait are released to drift away with the tide flow. Some boatmen prefer to use frozen blocks of rubby dubby, which are used in the same way but are easier to handle.

To be effective, the bag or container must be constantly replenished, but during a single day's drifting it's possible to lay a bait trail eight or ten miles long. This technique is primarily used to attract cruising shark, but it also incidentally attracts mackerel shoals and packs of surface-running bluefish.

Chumming is another method used mainly for shark fishing, although it can also be used for tuna. It can be used either as the sole method of groundbaiting or in conjunction with the rubby dubby bag. Cut fish and squid are the ingredients used in chumming, and to be effective it needs one man constantly chopping bait and dropping it into the water.

Stale mackerel, herring and horse mackerel are the main fish used for this type of groundbaiting. Each fish should be chopped into a number of small pieces so that each piece entering the water creates its own tiny scent lane.

If you're shore fishing for mullet, you can groundbait with a mixture called shirvy. This is very similar to rubby dubby in content, except that finely minced meat and meat fat is used as a substitute for the fish, and fish blood (but not fish oil) is used to blend the meat and fat with the bran.

Mullet are shoaling fish which, once attracted, will remain in an area for long periods. Experienced mullet fishermen distribute their shirvy with an old serving spoon on a little-but-often basis. Being a comparatively small fish, mullet will actually eat the meat and fat particles instead of just being attracted by the scent. If you throw in too much groundbait they will overeat and refuse the hookbait.

# FISH
## SPECIES

In this chapter, which gives brief descriptions of the major sporting fish of European and North American waters, the species (or groups of species) appear in alphabetical order under their most widely-used common names.

A species is an individual type or breed of fish, and in biological terms two or more closely-related species can be grouped together as a *genus*, and two or more related genuses (or genera) make up a family. The size of fish families and genera varies considerably. The wrasse family (the Labridae), for example, has some 450 members, while the bowfin, on the other hand, is the only living member of its genus, and its genus is the only one in its once-large family.

One of the most important of fish families, from an angling point of view, is the Salmonidae, which includes the salmons, trouts, chars, graylings, whitefishes and others. Within this family, the genus *Salmo*, for instance, includes the Atlantic salmon *(Salmo salar)* and the brown trout *(Salmo trutta)*, while the members of the genus *Oncorhynchus* include the chinook salmon *(Oncorhynchus tshawytsoha)* and the chum salmon *(Oncorhynchus keta)*. There are also subspecies, such as the brown trout subspecies the Caspian trout *(Salmo trutta caspius)* and the Black Sea trout *(Salmo trutta labrax)*.

In freshwater, the species of interest to anglers range in size from tiny dace and bullheads to the huge catfish which, apart from the rarely-hooked sturgeon which enters rivers to breed, are the largest freshwater fish an angler is likely to encounter. In North America, the biggest catfish are the blue and the flathead, both of which attain weights of over 100 pounds. The only catfish living in British waters is the wels or Danubian catfish, an introduced species which in its native Eastern European waters can grow to several hundred pounds.

All catfish are voracious predators, but even more voracious are the members of the pike family – the pike, the muskellunge and the pickerels. Few fish, either freshwater or saltwater, have as many teeth or can move as fast over short distances as these can. Pike are, in fact, one of the few species held in high esteem by anglers on both sides of the Atlantic.

In complete contrast, members of the carp family (the Cyprinidae) are not. While cyprinids form the mainstay of British freshwater fishing, they are mostly regarded as nuisance fish in North America. For the American freshwater angler, the most highly-prized species are probably the largemouth and smallmouth basses. These are members of the freshwater sunfish family (the Centrarchidae), a group of 30 species which collectively provide the bulk of American freshwater sports fishing. In addition to the basses, the sunfishes include popular panfish species such as the pumpkinseed and the bluegill.

Although most species spend all their lives in either fresh water or salt water, some migrate from one to the other to spawn. The *anadromous* fish, such as the sea trout and most of the salmons, are born in rivers but spend most of their lives in the sea, returning to their native rivers only to spawn. *Catadromous* fish – eels, for instance – do the opposite. The young fish travel from their saltwater birthplaces to mature in fresh water, and go back to the sea to spawn.

Some other species are nominally saltwater fish, but live in inshore waters and are often found quite far up estuaries into brackish waters. Mullet and flounder are typical of the sea fish that enter brackish waters, while the tarpon and snook are more truly *euryhaline*, that is, they can tolerate waters of greatly differing salinities.

Among the saltwater species are fish which offer some of the best sport an angler could wish for; even small species such as the saltwater basses and breams will put up a good fight. For sheer speed, power and stamina, though, the warm water pelagic species (fish which live near the surface, as opposed to the demersal species which stay near the bottom) like swordfish, sailfish, marlin and tuna are in a league of their own. Smaller warm water species such as barracuda, wahoo, amberjack, permit, bonefish and tarpon are also amazing fighters, and there is simply no comparison with freshwater fish of similar size.

Each of the entries in this chapter on fish species includes a brief guide to the tackle, techniques and bait that you can use when fishing for that particular species. The methods given are by no means the only ones you can use, but they are well worth trying; those for saltwater fish are tinted in blue, and those for freshwater species in green.

# ANATOMY

Although there are almost twenty-five thousand species of fish, they are biomorphically divided into two groups. The vast majority belong to the group known as the *bony* fish, that is, fish whose skeletons are made of bone. The others, including the sharks, rays and skates, are the *cartilaginous* fishes. These have skeletons of cartilage rather than bone.

Cartilaginous fishes also differ from most, though not all, bony fishes in that their eggs are fertilized within the bodies of the females, the eggs of most bony fishes being expressed into the water and then fertilized by milt from the males. After fertilization, the eggs of many cartilaginous species hatch within the mother and the young are born alive. Others, such as the skates, lay their fertilized eggs (each covered in a hard protective casing) to hatch in the sea.

Unlike the bony fishes, the cartilaginous fishes don't possess a gas or air bladder. This bladder allows a bony fish to control its buoyancy by regulating the amount of gas (usually oxygen, but sometimes nitrogen) in the bladder. This enables the fish to hover in the water at any depth it chooses, whereas the shark, for instance, must keep swimming or sink to the bottom.

The respiratory systems of both bony and cartilaginous fishes are similar, despite the fact that the former are equipped with gill *plates*, as opposed to the 4 to 7 gill *slits* of sharks. A fish breathes by taking water into its mouth and passing it out through its gills, extracting oxygen from the water as it moves through the gill filaments. The oxygen is absorbed into the blood vessels of the gill filaments, and carbon dioxide from the blood is released from the blood vessels into the water.

Being constantly immersed in water, fish have to be able to cope with the effects of osmosis. Osmosis is a process that occurs when a concentrated solution of salts (or sugars) is separated from a weak one (or plain water) by a thin membrane. The two solutions try to equalize their concentrations of salts; water from the weaker solution will pass through the membrane into the stronger one, which will lose salts through the membrane into the weaker one.

As a result, freshwater fish, whose bodies contain a greater concentration of salts than does the water in which they swim, have to be able to conserve their body salts and to get rid of the water which they absorb through the linings of their mouths, gills and intestines. Any body salts picked up by the absorbed water are removed by the fish's kidneys before it is excreted, and there are various glands whose function is to prevent salts being lost to the surrounding water.

Because of the absorbed water, freshwater fish don't need to drink as such, but saltwater fish do. Being surrounded by water that is saltier than they are, saltwater fish are continually losing water from their bodies – which they have to replace by drinking – and absorbing excess salt, which they have to excrete. Fish which migrate from fresh to salt water, or vice versa, are able to adapt to the changes in salinity.

The sensory systems of fish are more complex than most people realize. They are less aware of pain than are the higher vertebrates, but their senses of touch, sight, taste, smell and hearing are well developed, and in addition they have a line of sensory organs – the lateral line – along each side of the head and body. These sensory organs detect low-frequency sounds and vibrations, enabling the fish to sense movements or obstacles close to it, and they also sense changes in pressure and temperature and help the fish to maintain its balance.

Most fish swim by flexing their bodies from side to side in a wave-like motion, using their pectoral and pelvic fins as stabilizers, for braking, and for making small changes in position. Some fishes can produce enormous thrust from seemingly little actual body movement, relying instead on their powerful tails and the muscles around the tail root. Members of the tuna and marlin families, for example, have tails made of rigid bones and rays which propel their large, heavy bodies through the water at high speeds over enormous distances.

The bodies of most fish are covered with protective scales, but not all species have them. Many catfish, for instance, are completely scaleless, as is the leather carp. Usually, fish keep the same scales for life, and close examination of a scale reveals growth rings, like the annual growth rings of a tree. Should a scale be lost, a new one will grow in its place.

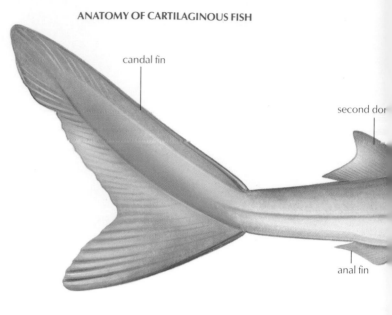

ANATOMY OF CARTILAGINOUS FISH

candal fin

second dor

anal fin

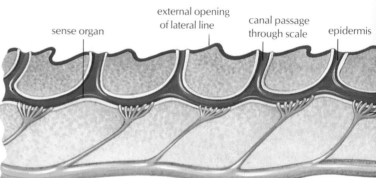

sense organ

external opening of lateral line

canal passage through scale

epidermis

**CROSS-SECTION OF THE LATERAL LINE**
The lateral line of a fish is a row of sensory organs on the mid side of the body and running from the gill cover to the caudal fin. These organs detect sound, vibrations and changes in temperature and pressure, and help the fish to keep its balance. This cross-section shows the sense organs and the nerves which connect them to the fish's central nervous system.

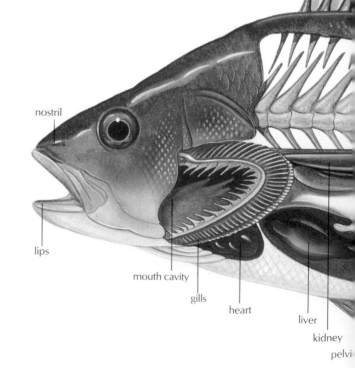

nostril

lips

mouth cavity

gills

heart

liver

kidney

pelvi

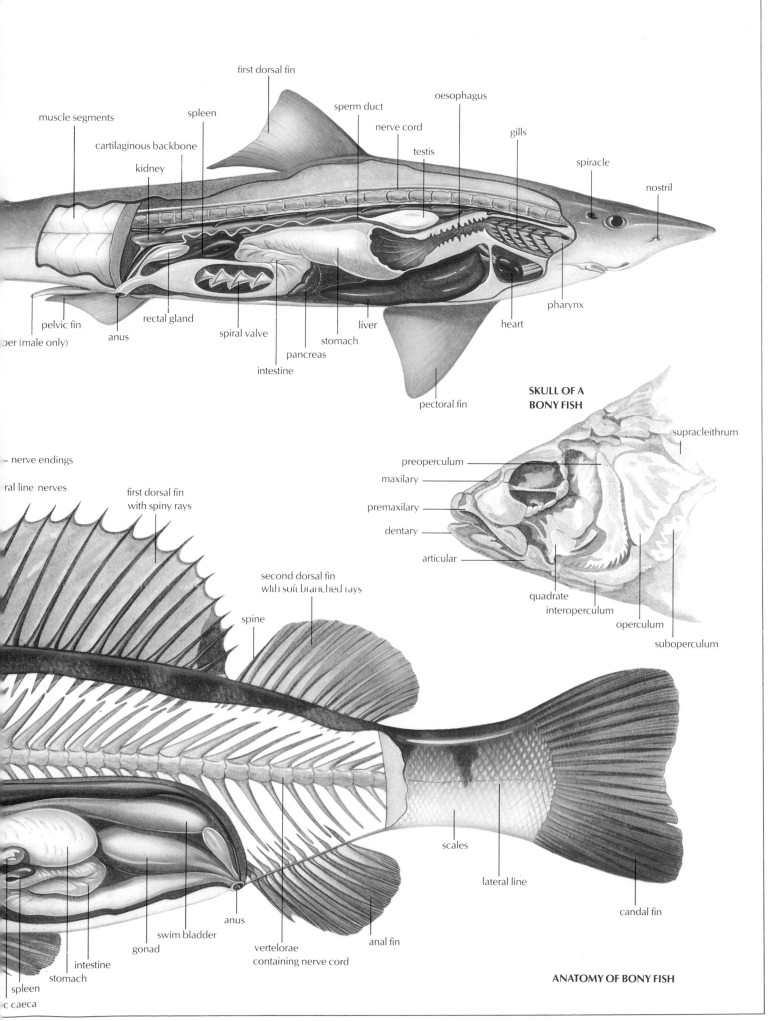

first dorsal fin

muscle segments

cartilaginous backbone

kidney

spleen

sperm duct

nerve cord

oesophagus

testis

gills

spiracle

nostril

pelvic fin

per (male only)

anus

rectal gland

spiral valve

intestine

pancreas

stomach

liver

heart

pharynx

pectoral fin

**SKULL OF A BONY FISH**

supracleithrum

preoperculum

maxilary

premaxilary

dentary

articular

quadrate

interoperculum

operculum

suboperculum

nerve endings

ral line nerves

first dorsal fin
with spiny rays

second dorsal fin
with soft branched rays

spine

scales

lateral line

candal fin

anus

swim bladder

gonad

vertelorae
containing nerve cord

anal fin

intestine

stomach

spleen

c caeca

**ANATOMY OF BONY FISH**

79

# AMBERJACKS

The amberjacks are a widely-distributed group of marine gamefish, the largest and most important of which are the greater amberjack (*Seriola dumerili*), which is found in the Atlantic, and the similar but smaller Pacific amberjack (*S. colburni*).

A big, powerful fish much sought after by sports fishermen, the greater amberjack can be caught in a variety of ways: trolling, freelining with live or dead fish or squid, and even on occasion by bottom fishing. Most amberjacks are hooked close to the surface, however, and only bottom-feed in really bad weather.

The greater amberjack commonly reaches weights of over 100 pounds, and it ranges from the western to the eastern Atlantic and into the Mediterranean. The lesser amberjack (*S. fasciata*) is a small and rare inhabitant of the western Atlantic.

The Pacific amberjack is found in the eastern Pacific from Ecuador up to the south of California, where its range overlaps the territory of the related California yellowtail (*S. dorsalis*). As well as its yellow tail, this fish has yellow fins and a broad yellow band separating the bright blue/green upper body from the silvery white lower.

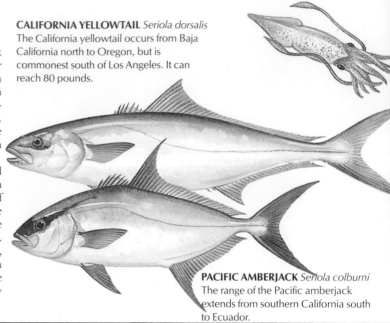

**CALIFORNIA YELLOWTAIL** *Seriola dorsalis*
The California yellowtail occurs from Baja California north to Oregon, but is commonest south of Los Angeles. It can reach 80 pounds.

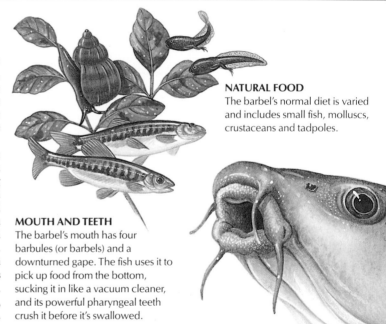

**PACIFIC AMBERJACK** *Seriola colburni*
The range of the Pacific amberjack extends from southern California south to Ecuador.

# BARBEL *Barbus barbus*

The barbel, a large European member of the carp family, is a long, wiry fish, with a body almost heart-shaped in cross-section and a decidedly flat belly which enables it to keep close to the bottom in fast water. Although occasionally found in sluggish rivers, the barbel prefers fast, clean, well-oxygenated water.

It breeds in the late spring among the weeds on gravelly shallows, and the translucent, yellowy eggs hatch in 12 to 15 days. The fry hide between the stones and in the weed, feeding at first on algae and then, as they mature, on nymphs, shrimps, snails and even tiny fish.

The adults are a greeny bronze on the back, fading downwards and along the flanks into a pale, yellowy bronze with a dull white belly and throat. The scales are small and set very close to the skin, which produces very little protective mucus.

The snout is long, with an underslung, protrusible mouth and thick, rubbery lips. Four long barbules on the upper lip are used for probing for food in the silt and gravel. The enormous mouth contains powerful pharyngeal teeth, set far back in the throat.

Barbel average 3 to 6 pounds in weight and a length of 30 inches or more, even in sluggish rivers. The maximum weight, in fast, clear rivers, is about 17 pounds.

**NATURAL FOOD**
The barbel's normal diet is varied and includes small fish, molluscs, crustaceans and tadpoles.

**MOUTH AND TEETH**
The barbel's mouth has four barbules (or barbels) and a downturned gape. The fish uses it to pick up food from the bottom, sucking it in like a vacuum cleaner, and its powerful pharyngeal teeth crush it before it's swallowed.

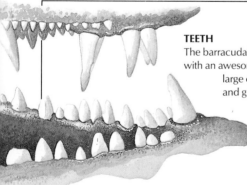

**TEETH**
The barracuda's mouth is equipped with an awesome set of teeth. The large ones are used to seize and grip the prey, then the smaller, dagger-edged teeth cut it to ribbons. They will attack humans, even in shallows.

**GREAT BARRACUDA** *Sphyraena barracuda*
The great barracuda can weigh over 100 pounds, but most are less than 50 pounds. Small fish are found in shallow water, but larger ones prefer the depths.

| TECHNIQUE | ROD | REEL | LINE | TERMINAL TACKLE | HOOK | WEIGHT | BAIT |
|---|---|---|---|---|---|---|---|
| **Greater barracuda:** trolling or spinning | 30-pound class boat rod or heavy spinning rod | Multiplier or large fixed spool | 30-pound nylon | Wire | 6/0 or 8/0 | Banana-shaped for trolling | Spinner, plug, dead/live fish |
| **Pacific barracuda:** trolling or spinning | 12-pound class boat rod or light spinning rod | 4/0 multiplier or fixed spool reel | 12-pound nylon | Wire | 4/0 or 6/0 | | Spinner, plug, dead/live fish |

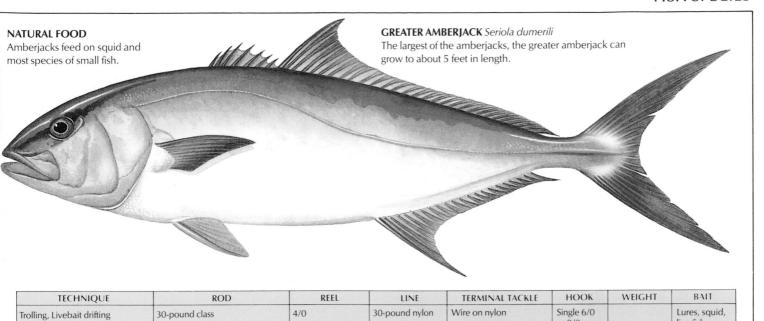

### NATURAL FOOD
Amberjacks feed on squid and most species of small fish.

### GREATER AMBERJACK *Seriola dumerili*
The largest of the amberjacks, the greater amberjack can grow to about 5 feet in length.

| TECHNIQUE | ROD | REEL | LINE | TERMINAL TACKLE | HOOK | WEIGHT | BAIT |
|---|---|---|---|---|---|---|---|
| Trolling, Livebait drifting | 30-pound class | 4/0 | 30-pound nylon | Wire on nylon | Single 6/0 or 8/0 | | Lures, squid, live fish |

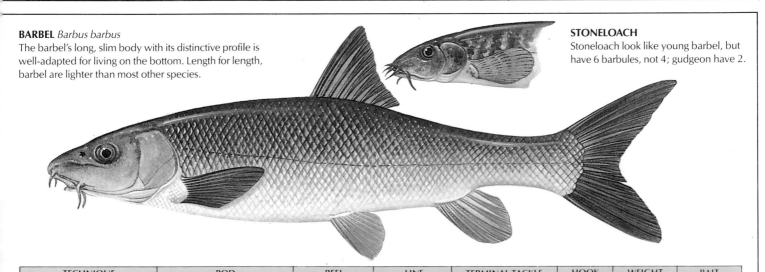

### BARBEL *Barbus barbus*
The barbel's long, slim body with its distinctive profile is well-adapted for living on the bottom. Length for length, barbel are lighter than most other species.

### STONELOACH
Stoneloach look like young barbel, but have 6 barbules, not 4; gudgeon have 2.

| TECHNIQUE | ROD | REEL | LINE | TERMINAL TACKLE | HOOK | WEIGHT | BAIT |
|---|---|---|---|---|---|---|---|
| Ledgering downstream or across the flow, with heavy blockend swimfeeder | 10-12-foot Avon action, 1¼-pound test curve with built-in quivertip | Fixed spool | 5-6 pounds test, or 7-8-pounds for swims | Fixed paternoster 8-inch feeder link 12-inch hook link | Sizes 12 to 8, eyed, tied direct | | Maggots, canned meat, tares |

# BARRACUDAS

The barracudas are fierce, sharply-toothed predators found in both Atlantic and Pacific waters. The largest member of the family is the great barracuda (*Sphyraena barracuda*), an Atlantic species whose range extends from Africa, through the Azores to the West Indies and Florida, and down to Brazil.

The guaguanche (*Sphyraena guachancho*) and the northern sennet (*Sphyraena borealis*) are two other members of the barracuda family found in the Atlantic, the guaguanche from Florida south to Brazil and the northern sennet from New England to Florida; south of Florida, the variety known as the southern sennet (*Sphyraena picudilla*) replaces the northern sennet.

The guaguanche, a little barracuda with an olive-grey back and a silver belly, averages about 20 inches in length when fully grown. Guaguanche normally form small schools and can be caught on lures, and livebait.

The northern sennet is closely related to the four barracudas found in the Pacific. The largest of these, the Pacific barracuda (*Sphyraena argentea*), occurs from Alaska down to Mexico. Of the others, the Gulf barracuda (*S. lucasana*) is found in the Gulf of California, *S. ensis* from Mexico to Panama, and *S. idiastes* from there south to Peru.

### NATURAL FOOD
Barracuda feed voraciously on almost any shoaling fish, especially silvery, flashy species.

# BASSES

The term 'bass' covers a number of different species of freshwater and saltwater fish. The freshwater basses include the six species and various subspecies of black bass, which are members of the sunfish family, plus the white bass and the related yellow bass. These last two are also related to the saltwater basses – the striped bass, which is also found in freshwater, the black sea bass and the European sea bass. Of the black basses, the most important are the largemouth bass *(Micropterus salmoides)* and the smallmouth bass *(M. dolomieui)*.

The largemouth bass is happiest in waters with plenty of vegetation, where it finds shelter and a good supply of the insects, crustaceans, fish, crayfish, waterdogs and even small waterfowl on which it feeds.

The largemouth differs from the other black basses in several respects, but the most reliable way of identifying it is to look for three key points. Firstly, the line of the upper jaw extends beyond the rear of the eye; secondly, the spiny part of the dorsal fin is almost separate from the soft rays; and thirdly, there are no scales on the base of the soft dorsal rays. These features are absent from the other black basses.

Largemouth bass, because of introduced stocks, are found all over the USA. The Northern largemouth, whose original range was the Great Lakes Basin and most states east of the Rockies, averages about 3 pounds and seldom tops 10 pounds, but a subspecies, the Florida largemouth *(Micropterus salmoides floridanus)*, grows to over twice these weights.

The smallmouth bass has also benefited from nationwide introduction from its original range in the Ohio River and Lake Ontario systems. Its average and maximum sizes are a pound or two higher than those of the Northern largemouth, although it's a somewhat slimmer fish.

This acrobatic bass, one of the most exciting of North American freshwater sports fish, feeds on much the same prey as the largemouth, but prefers a very different habitat. Clear waters, still or flowing, with rocky, uneven bottoms and little vegetation are where you're likely to find it. There is one subspecies, the now-rare Neosho smallmouth *(Micropterus dolomieui velox)* found in the Neosho River and other waters in Oklahoma, Missouri and Arkansas.

The other black bass species are the spotted, redeye, Suwanee and Guadalupe basses. The spotted bass *(Micropterus punctulatus)* is greenish in colour, with a white belly and a row of diamond-shaped dark patches along each flank. Found mainly in the Ohio and Mississippi drainage systems, has two subspecies – the Alabama and Wichita spotted basses.

The redeye bass *(M. coosae)* is similar in colouring to the smallmouth, except for its red eyes and fins. It can reach weights of over 6 pounds but the average is less than a pound. Found in Tennessee, Alabama and Georgia, the redeye occurs in two slightly different forms, the Apalachiola River form and the Alabama River form.

The Suwanee bass *(M. notius)* of Florida also resembles the smallmouth, but has bright blue-green underparts. The Guadalupe bass *(M. treculi)* is found in Texas. This fish is similar in appearance to the spotted bass, but is smaller and has more distinct markings.

Although it has a wide distribution in North America, the white bass *(Morone chrysops)* is most popular with anglers in the southern and southwestern states of the USA. A silvery-coloured fish with 8 to 10 thin, dark horizontal stripes, the white bass does attain weights of over 5 pounds, but most of those caught are only about 1½ pounds.

The smaller yellow bass *(Morone mississippiensis)*, a close relative of the white bass, has a dark olive-green back, bright yellow sides and a white belly, plus 6 or 7 dark horizontal stripes.

The striped bass *(Morone saxatilis)* is much bigger than its white and yellow cousins, often reaching a length of over 4 feet and weights of 60 pounds or more.

Unlike the striped bass, the black sea bass *(Centropristis striata)* of the northwest Atlantic never enters fresh water. Though small – averaging 14 to 18 inches and 1½ to 3 pounds – the bottom-feeding black sea bass is very popular with anglers and has tasty flesh.

The black sea bass is found inshore during the warmer months, but it moves offshore when winter comes. This pattern of behaviour is shared by the European sea bass *(Dicentrarchus (Morone) labrax)*, which is found from the coasts of southern England and northern France down to the Iberian Peninsula and into the Mediterranean.

**LARGEMOUTH BASS** *Micropterus salmoides*
The largemouth has been introduced into waters all over the USA, and to some lakes in Britain. It can grow to over 10 pounds.

**NATURAL FOODS – FRESHWATER BASSES**
Freshwater basses have a varied diet which includes insect larvae, tadpoles and fish, plus crustaceans, crayfish and waterdogs, and the larger species will even take small waterfowl.

**NATURAL FOOD – SEA BASSES**
The sea basses and the striped bass feed on fish, crabs, shellfish, shrimps, prawns, worms and squid.

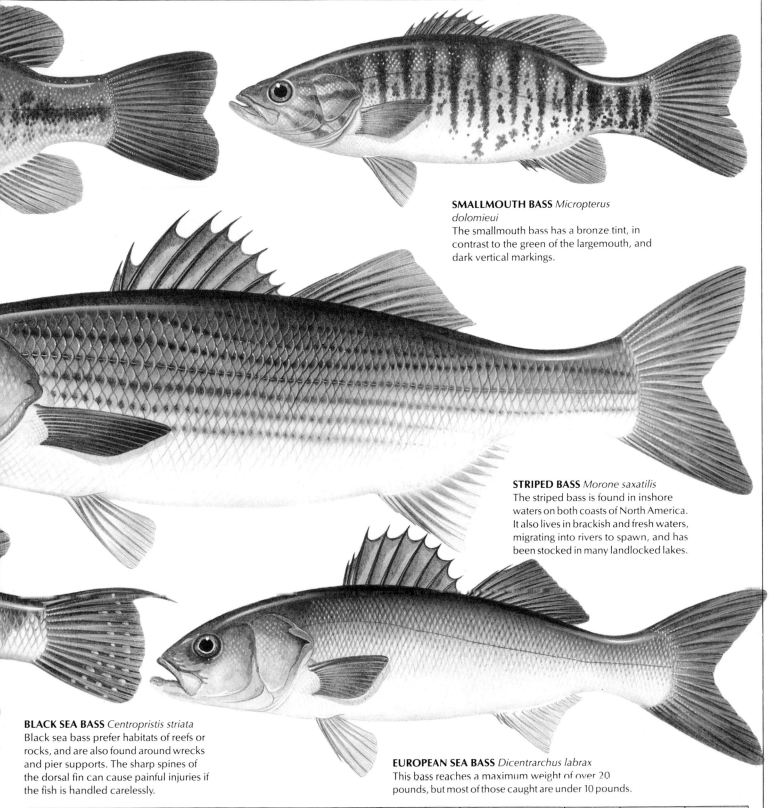

**SMALLMOUTH BASS** *Micropterus dolomieui*
The smallmouth bass has a bronze tint, in contrast to the green of the largemouth, and dark vertical markings.

**STRIPED BASS** *Morone saxatilis*
The striped bass is found in inshore waters on both coasts of North America. It also lives in brackish and fresh waters, migrating into rivers to spawn, and has been stocked in many landlocked lakes.

**BLACK SEA BASS** *Centropristis striata*
Black sea bass prefer habitats of reefs or rocks, and are also found around wrecks and pier supports. The sharp spines of the dorsal fin can cause painful injuries if the fish is handled carelessly.

**EUROPEAN SEA BASS** *Dicentrarchus labrax*
This bass reaches a maximum weight of over 20 pounds, but most of those caught are under 10 pounds.

| TECHNIQUE | ROD | REEL | LINE | TERMINAL TACKLE | HOOK | WEIGHT | BAIT |
|---|---|---|---|---|---|---|---|
| **Black bass:** lure fishing | 5½ to 7-foot snappy action bass spinning or baitcasting rod | Fixed spool or multiplier | 6 to 10-pound nylon | | | | Artificial lures |
| **Black bass:** fly rodding | 7 to 9-foot fast taper bass fly rod | Single action fly reel | Floating bass bug taper, sizes 7 to 9 | 6 to 8-foot leader, 6 to 10 pounds | | | bugs, jigs, bucktails |
| **Black bass:** trolling/drifting livebaits under float rig | 9 to 10-foot, stiff action 2¼-pounds test curve | Muliplier | 10 to 20-pound nylon | 3-foot swiveled nylon or Dacron | 2/0 to 5/0 | Keel weight or split shot | Minnows, shiners |
| **European sea bass:** surfcasting | 11 to 12-foot light surfcaster, 1 to 3-ounce range | Fixed spool or multiplier | 12 to 15-pound nylon | Running ledger or paternoster | 1/0 to 4/0 | 1 to 3-ounce | Peeler crab, worm, squid |
| **European sea bass:** anchored | 7 to 9-foot uptide rod, 12 to 20-pound class | Multiplier | 12 to 15-pound nylon | Running ledger | 1/0 to 3/0 | 24-ounce | Sandeel, worm, squid, sprats |
| **Striped bass:** surfcasting | 11 to 12-foot tip-action surfcaster | Multiplier or fixed spool | 20 to 25-pound nylon | 3-foot nylon, running sinker above swivel | 2/0 to 5/0 | 1 to 4-ounce | Menhaden, worm, squid |
| **Striped bass:** spinning | 8 to 9-foot powerful, medium to fast action spinning rod | Fixed spool or multiplier | 12 to 15-pound nylon | | | | Plugs or spinners |

# BLUEFISH *Pomatomus saltatrix*

Much sought after as a sport fish, the bluefish is a hard-hitting, savage predator capable of putting up a tremendous battle when hooked on lightish tackle.

The body of the bluefish is broad but streamlined. The mouth is large with extremely sharp, triangular teeth, the lower jaw projecting pugnaciously to give the fish a hard, aggressive appearance. The fish has two dorsal fins.

The lateral line angles smoothly above the pectoral fins, and the scales are smooth and small, covering both the head and the body. The body is blue/green above, fading to silvery white on the belly, and there's a dark patch at the base of each pectoral fin.

A voracious feeder, the bluefish swims in huge schools, destroying just about anything edible in its path. Once mad on the feed, bluefish have been known to invade bathing beaches, and numerous attacks on swimmers have been recorded.

Highly migratory, bluefish have a worldwide distribution. Anglers often locate bluefish shoals by literally sniffing them out: bluefish have a distinctive, cucumberish odour which is easy to detect. Bluefish can be caught on live or deadbaits, spinners or plugs, using mashed or minced fish to induce them to feed.

## NATURAL FOOD

The bluefish is a voracious predator which will take young fish of its own species but is usually found following shoals of menhaden, herring or anchovy. Bluefish eat whatever you put in front of them, including the fingers trying to unhook them. Old bluefishermen talk about their scars rather than their bait.

## YOUNG FISH

Non-breeding and younger bluegill have heavier vertical bars on their flanks than do the breeding adults.

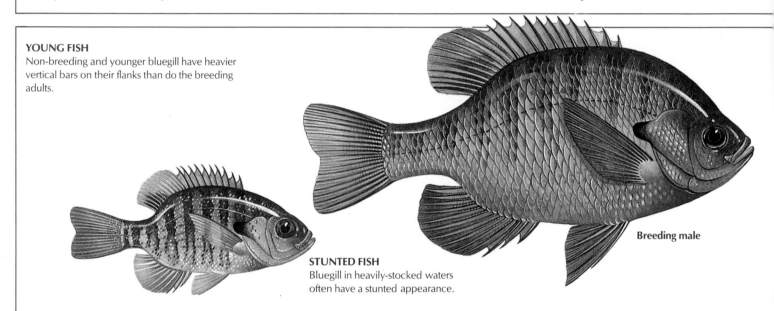

**STUNTED FISH**
Bluegill in heavily-stocked waters often have a stunted appearance.

**Breeding male**

| TECHNIQUE | ROD | REEL | LINE | TERMINAL TACKLE | HOOK | WEIGHT | BAIT |
|---|---|---|---|---|---|---|---|
| Jigging or float fishing | 6 to 7-foot ultralight Spinning rod | Fixed spool | 3-pound nylon | With or without small float | Sizes 10 to 14 | | Worms, tiny baited jigs |

## NATURAL FOOD

The food of the bonefish consists mainly of shrimps and small crabs, plus shellfish, worms, squid, sea urchins and small fish. It often feeds tail-up, digging in the bottom with its snout.

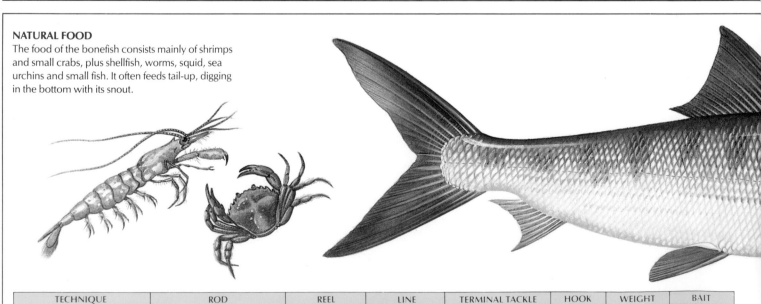

| TECHNIQUE | ROD | REEL | LINE | TERMINAL TACKLE | HOOK | WEIGHT | BAIT |
|---|---|---|---|---|---|---|---|
| Fly fishing | Fly rod | Fly reel | 8-pound fly line | Nylon leader | 1/0 or 2/0 | | Shrimp imitator |
| Bait fishing | Spinning rod | Fixed reel | 8-pound nylon | Nylon leader | 1/0 or 2/0 | | Shrimp |

**BLUEFISH** *Pomatomus saltatrix*
Bluefish weighing over 50 pounds have been caught by commercial fishermen, but most rod-caught specimens are less than half that weight.

| TECHNIQUE | ROD | REEL | LINE | TERMINAL TACKLE | HOOK | WEIGHT | BAIT |
|-----------|-----|------|------|-----------------|------|--------|------|
| Trolling | 20-pound class boat rod | 4/0 multiplier | 20-pound nylon or Dacron | Wire | 4/0 to 6/0 | Trolling weight | Plugs or live fish |

**BLUEGILL** *Lepomis macrochirus*
The bluegill is an attractive little panfish which prefers waters with plenty of weed in which it can hide and feed.

**NATURAL FOOD**
Bluegills eat the larvae, nymphs and adult forms of aquatic insects, plus snails, crustaceans, fish fry, fish eggs and water weed.

# BLUEGILL *Lepomis macrochirus*

The bluegill, sometimes called the bream or brim, is one of the largest of the thirty members of the sunfish family native to North America. Highly popular with anglers, the bluegill makes excellent eating.

In coloration, the bluegill is a dusky fish with a pronounced dark flap on the tip of each gill cover, which is normally (though not always) the blueish that gives the fish its name. There's another dark spot on the rear section of the soft dorsal fin, and there are also normally seven or eight dark, vertical bars on its sides. Large specimens have a dark orange/red tint to the breast and a purplish overall cast.

These beautiful fish can reach lengths of around 14 inches and weights of 3 to 4 pounds. Mostly, though, they are between 6 and 9 inches long, and 8 to 10 ounces in weight.

The bluegill is a common and widespread fish in the USA, its distribution having been widened by its introduction into waters across the country as a food for black bass. It can also be found in southern Ontario, Canada, and along with several other sunfishes is a popular aquarium fish in Britain and Europe.

In still waters it is normally found in the deeper parts, and in streams it prefers to keep strictly to the deep pools.

**BONEFISH** *Albula vulpes*
The eight or nine dark bars across the back of the bonefish are prominent when the fish is young but fade as it grows older, and when it's taken out of the water. Most bonefish caught weigh between 2 and 10 pounds.

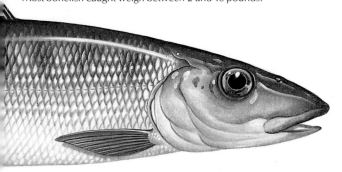

# BONEFISH *Albula vulpes*

The bonefish, which is found in most tropical and subtropical seas, is essentially a shallow-water, inshore species that feeds on shrimps, prawns, crabs, clams and sea urchins.

Early in its life, the bonefish looks more like an eel than a true fish, undergoing a larval stage during which it grows to a length of about 2½ inches. Once this point is reached, the eel-like larva undergoes a reversal of growth, shrinking to half its former size. Then it begins to grow fins, and after 10 to 12 days, a tiny, true bonefish appears, a little over an inch long, which then grows and matures in the normal way.

As the name suggests, bonefish have an abundance of bones, but despite this they make excellent eating. Sometimes referred to as 'ocean dynamite', the bonefish is one of the fastest fish in the sea. This fish has a long, slender body and a prominent, overhung snout; the lower jaw is small and unobtrusive and the teeth are tiny.

Often found in small schools, bonefish can be located by looking for projecting tails or for areas of stirred-up mud. They can be caught on natural prawn or conch flesh, or on small lead-headed jigs, and they also present a great challenge to the fly fisherman. Most are caught in depths of 6 inches to 6 feet.

# BONITOS

The bonitos are members of the mackerel family, the most important being the Atlantic bonito *(Sarda sarda)*, the Pacific bonito *(S. chiliensis)* and the striped bonito *(S. orientalis)*.

The Atlantic bonito has a distinctive steel blue or occasionally blue-green back, with silvery lower flanks and belly and prominent stripes running from just below the wavy lateral line back towards the dorsal fin. The body is covered in minute scales, and there are 20 to 26 large, conical teeth on each side of the lower jaw plus a few scattered teeth in the upper jaw and on the tongue.

The Atlantic bonito is found in the Mediterranean and the Black Sea, as well as in the Atlantic, and reaches weights of 12 pounds or more. The Pacific and striped bonitos are very similar in appearance to the Atlantic bonito, the main differences between the three being in the number of spines in the first dorsal fin, the number of gillrakers, and the size and weight.

The Pacific bonito, which grows to over 20 pounds, occurs from British Columbia south to Mexico, and from Peru down to Chile. The much smaller striped bonito (around 7 to 10 pounds) is found in between, from Mexico to Peru. Bonito are pelagic-feeding fish, feeding on squid and small fish taken just beneath the surface. They can be caught on live or deadbaits, or on trolled natural or artificial baits.

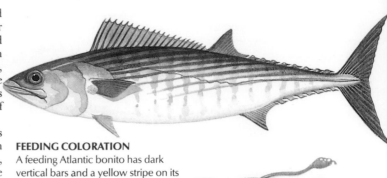

### FEEDING COLORATION
A feeding Atlantic bonito has dark vertical bars and a yellow stripe on its back. These fade when the fish is landed or stops feeding.

### NATURAL FOOD
Bonitos feed mainly on schooling fish such as mackerel, and on squid.

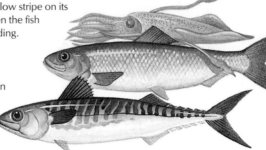

# BOWFIN *Amia calva*

The bowfin, a voracious predator found in shallow lakes and slow-flowing rivers, is the last surviving member of a once-large family whose fossil remains have been found in Europe and North America. Today, the bowfin occurs in eastern and southern states of the USA, feeding on small fish and crayfish and growing to about 3 feet in length and 20 pounds in weight.

The overall colour is a drab, mottled olive, with a noticeable dark spot high on the base of the powerful tail. In the males, this spot is ringed with orange, but in females this spot is either unringed or absent altogether. The body is thick-set and elongated,

and the head is rather squat. The mouth is large and the jaws are equipped with strong, sharp teeth, and beyond the throat is an air bladder which acts as a lung. This lung enables the bowfin to breathe air, which means that it can survive in poorly-oxygenated water.

The bowfin breeds in the spring, when one or more females spawn in a nest that a male has made by clearing a small patch from an area of thick weed. The eggs hatch in 8 to 10 days, guarded during incubation by the male. The newly-hatched larvae stay on the bottom of the nest for about 9 days, watched over by the male, until they start to swim.

### TAIL SPOT
The spot on the tail of the male bowfin is clearly marked in bright orange, but that of the female is dull and indistinct.

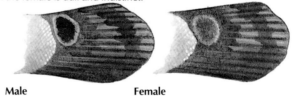

**Male**         **Female**

### BRONZE BREAM/ROACH HYBRID
Bronze bream/roach hybrids are usually infertile, but can grow to a good size because they don't use up protein by spawning.

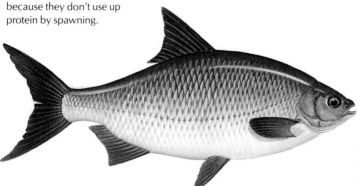

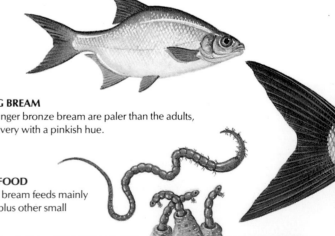

### YOUNG BREAM
The younger bronze bream are paler than the adults, being silvery with a pinkish hue.

### NATURAL FOOD
The bronze bream feeds mainly on worms, plus other small creatures.

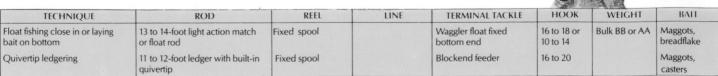

| TECHNIQUE | ROD | REEL | LINE | TERMINAL TACKLE | HOOK | WEIGHT | BAIT |
|---|---|---|---|---|---|---|---|
| Float fishing close in or laying bait on bottom | 13 to 14-foot light action match or float rod | Fixed spool | | Waggler float fixed bottom end | 16 to 18 or 10 to 14 | Bulk BB or AA | Maggots, breadflake |
| Quivertip ledgering | 11 to 12-foot ledger with built-in quivertip | Fixed spool | | Blockend feeder | 16 to 20 | | Maggots, casters |

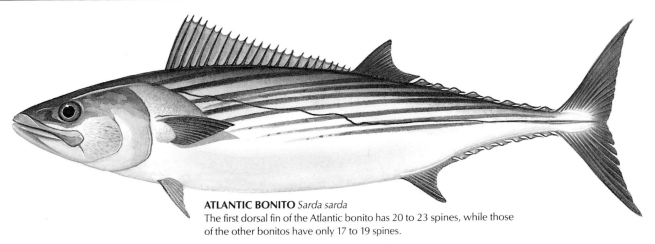

**ATLANTIC BONITO** *Sarda sarda*
The first dorsal fin of the Atlantic bonito has 20 to 23 spines, while those of the other bonitos have only 17 to 19 spines.

| TECHNIQUE | ROD | REEL | LINE | TERMINAL TACKLE | HOOK | WEIGHT | BAIT |
|---|---|---|---|---|---|---|---|
| Trolling | 12-pound class boat rod | 2/0 multiplier | 12-pound nylon | | 2/0 | | Plugs or spoons |
| Spinning | Light spinning rod | Fixed spool | 12-pound nylon | | 2/0 | | Plugs or spoons |

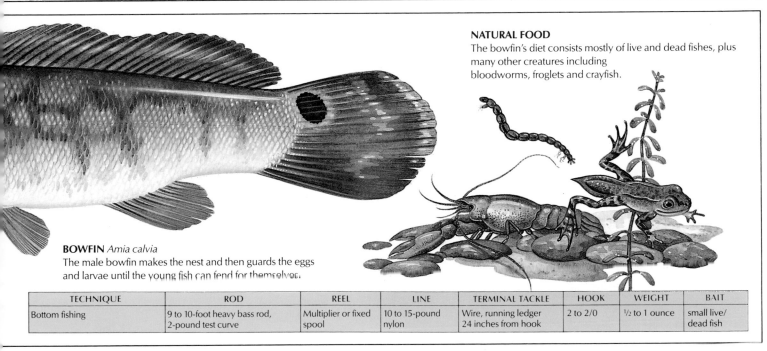

**NATURAL FOOD**
The bowfin's diet consists mostly of live and dead fishes, plus many other creatures including bloodworms, froglets and crayfish.

**BOWFIN** *Amia calvia*
The male bowfin makes the nest and then guards the eggs and larvae until the young fish can fend for themselves.

| TECHNIQUE | ROD | REEL | LINE | TERMINAL TACKLE | HOOK | WEIGHT | BAIT |
|---|---|---|---|---|---|---|---|
| Bottom fishing | 9 to 10-foot heavy bass rod, 2-pound test curve | Multiplier or fixed spool | 10 to 15-pound nylon | Wire, running ledger 24 inches from hook | 2 to 2/0 | ½ to 1 ounce | small live/dead fish |

# BREAMS

**BRONZE BREAM** *Abramis brama*
In crowded waters the average bream weighs about 4 pounds, but in better conditions they average 7 pounds and can reach 16 pounds.

Among the many species of bream, those of most interest to anglers are the freshwater bronze bream, the black sea bream and the red sea bream.

The bronze bream *(Abramis brama)* has the deepest and most laterally compressed body of all British and European freshwater species.

The body colour varies according to the environment. In clear waters, the back is a deep bronze colour, softening into golden bronze sides and a cream belly. In highly coloured waters, though, the back is dark grey and the colour lightens in shades of pale parchment along the sides to an off-grey belly.

The black sea bream *(Spondyliosoma cantharus)* has a deep, compressed body with long dorsal and anal fins, large eyes, and strong jaws with rows of sharp teeth. The back is dark, and there are 6 or 7 dark vertical bars along the silver-grey flanks. It prefers a rocky habitat where it feeds on fishes, worms and crabs, and it can reach over 7 pounds.

The black sea bream is common in north European waters, the Mediterranean and around the west coast of Africa, as is the red sea bream *(Pagellus bogaraveo)*. This fish is a pinky-red colour with silver sides and a dark 'thumbprint' just above the gill cover. It prefers very deep water, feeding on worms, crabs, fish and squid. It can grow to over 10 pounds.

# CARP *Cyprinus carpio*

The carp originated in Asia, where it was farmed for food as early as 400 BC. It slowly spread across Europe, both naturally and by introduction, and was brought to Britain in the middle of the fifteenth century. In 1876, the United States Fish Commission introduced the carp to North America. These fish, from Germany, were put into breeding ponds in Baltimore, Maryland, and for several years carp were distributed enthusiastically around the country. However, it was soon realized that the introduced carp were disrupting the natural balance of American waters and often displacing the native species, and the emphasis switched from propagation to eradication. Despite this, the carp remains well-established in the USA.

The original, fully-scaled wild carp is a slow-growing, long, wiry and incredibly strong fish which rarely exceeds a weight of 20 pounds. In general, the average weight is much less, being only 2 to 5 pounds in most environments.

From this wild carp, different strains were produced by selective breeding over the years in European countries such as

Hungary, Yugoslavia, Poland and Germany, resulting in a faster-growing, deeper-bodied fish known as the king carp. These larger, heavier carp now form the basis of carp fishing in Britain and Europe, although plenty of wild carp are still caught.

Like the wild carp, king carp breed in late spring or early summer. Each ripe female is often accompanied by several males, which chase her and sometimes even lift her out of the water in their eagerness to fertilize her eggs. The spawning can be a noisy business, with much splashing and shuddering as each group of fish crashes through weedbeds, reeds and the fibrous underwater roots of bankside trees. The eggs stick to the plants, and those which aren't eaten by small fish, or even by the carp themselves, hatch after 8 to 10 days.

King carp grow quickly, gaining 1 to 3 pounds a year to a maximum of about 10 pounds in poor environments, and 20 to 30 pounds in most rich waters if they're not overstocked. They can grow much larger than this; king carp of 50 to 70 pounds are regularly caught in France, and

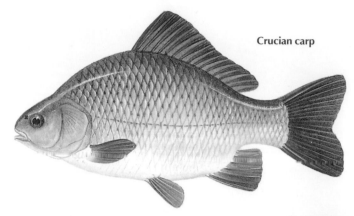

Crucian carp

**CRUCIAN CARP** *Carassius carassius*
The crucian carp is more closely related to the goldfish (*Carassius auratus*) than to the wild and king carps. The Prussian carp (*Carassius carassius gibelo*) is a subspecies of crucian.

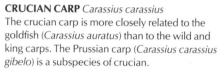

Common carp

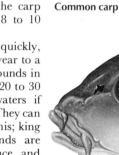

Wild carp

**WILD CARP** *Cyprinus carpio*
The wild carp is the species from which the various strains of king carp were produced by selective breeding on fish farms over hundreds of years.

**MUTANT CARP**
While selective breeding can and does produce good results, it can also result in mutants. In some waters, particularly lakes and canals where the genetic variety is limited, mutant carp may occur. These very deep-bodied, clumsy and somewhat grotesque fish can be almost spherical in shape.

| TECHNIQUE | ROD | REEL | LINE | TERMINAL TACKLE | HOOK | WEIGHT | BAIT |
|---|---|---|---|---|---|---|---|
| **Crucian carp:** float fishing, lift method | 12 to 13-foot light action float match rod | Centrepin, closed-face or fixed spool | 1½ to 2½-pounds | Small waggler or antennae float | 18 to 12 | 8 to BB split shot | Sweetcorn, breadflake |
| **Common, mirror carp:** float fishing, lift method | 11 to 12-foot 1¼-pound test curve | Centrepin/fixed spool | 6 pounds | Waggler float, one shot 3 to 6-inches from hook | Sizes 10-8 | AA to swan shot | Breadflake, sweetcorn |
| Freelining | 10 to 12-foot 1½ to 1¾-pound test curve | Fixed spool | 8-10 pound | Hook only | Sizes 8-4 | None | Worms, pastes |
| Float fishing for surface feeding carp | 11 to 12-foot 1 to 1½-pound. test curve | Fixed spool | 6 to 8-pounds well greased | self cocking controller float | Sizes 12-8 | None | Breadcrust |
| Sliding link ledgering | 11 to 12-foot 1½ to 2¼-pound test curve | Fixed spool | 8 to 11-pounds | 12 inch hook link with 1-inch fine Dacron hair tied to hook | Sizes 10-6 | ½ to 1½-ounce bombs | Boiled baits |
| Shock or bolt ledger rig | 11 to 12-foot 1¾ to 2¼-pounds test curve | Fixed spool | 11 to 12-pounds | Fixed or running bomb | Sizes 8-6 | 1½ to 2½-ounce bombs | Boiled baits |

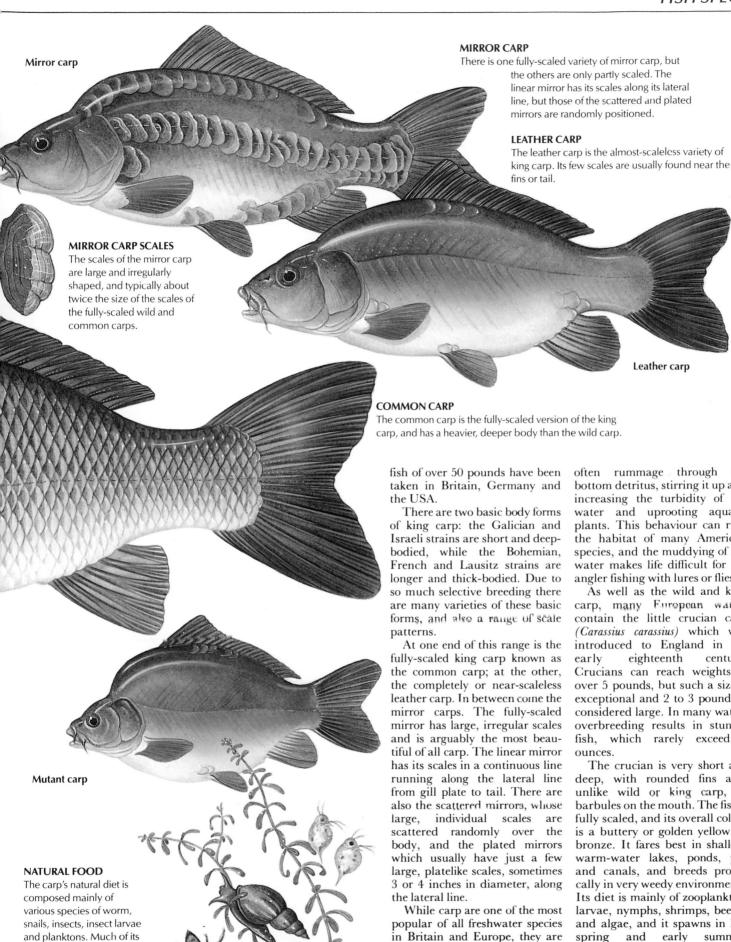

**Mirror carp**

**MIRROR CARP SCALES**
The scales of the mirror carp are large and irregularly shaped, and typically about twice the size of the scales of the fully-scaled wild and common carps.

**Mutant carp**

**NATURAL FOOD**
The carp's natural diet is composed mainly of various species of worm, snails, insects, insect larvae and planktons. Much of its food is found within the bottom detritus, and in searching for it the carp can muddy the water and uproot many types of aquatic plants.

**MIRROR CARP**
There is one fully-scaled variety of mirror carp, but the others are only partly scaled. The linear mirror has its scales along its lateral line, but those of the scattered and plated mirrors are randomly positioned.

**LEATHER CARP**
The leather carp is the almost-scaleless variety of king carp. Its few scales are usually found near the fins or tail.

**Leather carp**

**COMMON CARP**
The common carp is the fully-scaled version of the king carp, and has a heavier, deeper body than the wild carp.

fish of over 50 pounds have been taken in Britain, Germany and the USA.

There are two basic body forms of king carp: the Galician and Israeli strains are short and deep-bodied, while the Bohemian, French and Lausitz strains are longer and thick-bodied. Due to so much selective breeding there are many varieties of these basic forms, and also a range of scale patterns.

At one end of this range is the fully-scaled king carp known as the common carp; at the other, the completely or near-scaleless leather carp. In between come the mirror carps. The fully-scaled mirror has large, irregular scales and is arguably the most beautiful of all carp. The linear mirror has its scales in a continuous line running along the lateral line from gill plate to tail. There are also the scattered mirrors, whose large, individual scales are scattered randomly over the body, and the plated mirrors which usually have just a few large, platelike scales, sometimes 3 or 4 inches in diameter, along the lateral line.

While carp are one of the most popular of all freshwater species in Britain and Europe, they are generally far from welcome in North America. They feed on molluscs, beetles, shrimps, larvae and nymphs, plus various algae found within the bottom silt or mud. When they're feeding, they often rummage through the bottom detritus, stirring it up and increasing the turbidity of the water and uprooting aquatic plants. This behaviour can ruin the habitat of many American species, and the muddying of the water makes life difficult for the angler fishing with lures or flies.

As well as the wild and king carp, many European waters contain the little crucian carp *(Carassius carassius)* which was introduced to England in the early eighteenth century. Crucians can reach weights of over 5 pounds, but such a size is exceptional and 2 to 3 pounds is considered large. In many waters overbreeding results in stunted fish, which rarely exceed 8 ounces.

The crucian is very short and deep, with rounded fins and, unlike wild or king carp, no barbules on the mouth. The fish is fully scaled, and its overall colour is a buttery or golden yellow, or bronze. It fares best in shallow, warm-water lakes, ponds, pits and canals, and breeds prolifically in very weedy environments. Its diet is mainly of zooplankton, larvae, nymphs, shrimps, beetles and algae, and it spawns in late spring and early summer, sometimes hybridizing with wild carp where the two species are found together. The resulting hybrids are not so golden in colour as the crucian, nor so deep in the body.

# CATFISH AND BULLHEADS

There are at least 15 families of catfish around the world, both freshwater and sea, characterized by numerous barbules around the mouth and an absence of scales.

The largest is the wels or Danubian catfish *(Siluris glanis)*, native to the rivers of central and eastern Europe. The wels is the only catfish found in British waters, having been introduced over 100 years ago. It still has limited distribution, confined mainly to lakes and pits in Bedfordshire and Buckingham-shire, although it is spreading slowly to other parts.

The wels has a long, tapered body with a tiny, stunted tail and a huge, flattened head. The large, wide mouth has rubbery lips and many little teeth, with two long barbules on the upper lip and four smaller ones below the chin.

It feeds mainly on fish, but will eat almost anything, including frogs, rats and water birds. It usually feeds at night, but will occasionally go on a daylight feeding binge during hot or thundery weather. The British record is a little over 40 pounds, but in Europe 100 and 200 pound wels are quite common. In the large rivers of the USSR, such as the Dneiper, it can reach over 650 pounds and a length of 16 feet; such fish are probably around a hundred years old.

The largest North American catfish is the blue catfish *(Ictalurus furcatus)*, which can grow to over 100 pounds although 20 to 50 pounds is more typical. The blue catfish is silvery blue on the back, lightening down the sides to a silver or white belly. The tail is forked, and like all North American catfish the blue has two short barbules on the top of the snout, two large ones extending back from the jaw hinges and four more slender ones below the chin.

The fish thrives in large, clear, fast-flowing rivers, where it feeds on fish and crayfish, and is widely distributed through the midwest and south of the USA and in Mexico.

The channel catfish *(Ictalurus punctatus)* is reared commercially for its fine-tasting flesh, and also offers good sport for the angler. Found in large, clean lakes and rivers from the Great Lakes south to the Gulf of Mexico, the channel cat migrates to small streams to spawn. The younger fish have a relatively slender body, with a silvery blue or olive back, paler flanks and a silver-white belly, and varying numbers of black spots. Older fish are thicker in the body and much darker in colour. The channel catfish can grow to 60 pounds, but most rod-caught fish are less than 15 pounds.

The flathead catfish *(Pylodictis olivaris)* is a large, mottled brown fish with a noticeably flattened head, which lives in the larger rivers of the Mississippi Valley. It feeds mainly on fish, and although its maximum weight is about 100 pounds, most of those caught weigh only a few pounds.

The flathead catfish is popular for its tasty flesh, as is the little white catfish *(Ictalurus catus)* found in the coastal streams of the eastern and southern USA, and in western waters where it has been widely introduced. It grows to about 3 pounds, and its colour varies from a pale, silvery blue to a silvery beige or white, with a white belly.

The most important of the American saltwater catfishes are the sea catfish *(Arius felis)* and the gafftopsail catfish *(Bagre marinus)*. These are found from Cape Cod to the Gulf of Mexico, and there are several closely-related species in Pacific waters. The sea catfish has a maximum weight of about 3 pounds, around half that of the gafftopsail.

The bullheads are a group of small freshwater catfish which grow to weights of 1 to 3 pounds and are often caught for the pan. The brown bullhead *(Ictalurus nebulosus)* is a sleek, mottled brown fish found from the Great Lakes south to Florida and west to Mexico, living in weedy lakes and slow-flowing streams.

The black bullhead *(Ictalurus melas)* is green to black on the back, with paler sides and a white or yellow belly. Originally found from North Dakota south to Texas, and from there north east to New York, it has been introduced to many other parts of the country, and to some European waters where it has often multiplied to almost plague proportions, especially in France.

The natural range of the yellow bullhead *(Ictalurus natalis)* is from North Dakota to New York and Florida. This mottled yellow catfish prefers sluggish streams, ponds and lake shallows with muddy bottoms, and is often confused with the flat bullhead *(Ictalurus platycephalus)*. This fish, which occurs in the south eastern states, is best distinguished from the yellow bullhead by its flattened head, and a dark patch on the lower part of the dorsal fin.

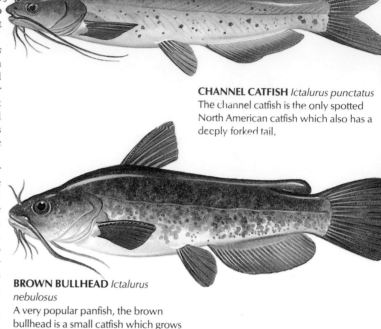

**CHANNEL CATFISH** *Ictalurus punctatus*
The channel catfish is the only spotted North American catfish which also has a deeply forked tail,

**BROWN BULLHEAD** *Ictalurus nebulosus*
A very popular panfish, the brown bullhead is a small catfish which grows to about 16 inches long.

**NATURAL FOOD**
Small freshwater catfish live on insects, larvae, molluscs and small fish, but the larger ones feed on any species of live or dead fish as well as seemingly unlikely prey such as ducklings.

**WHISKERS**
The 'whiskers' around the mouths of catfish are highly sensitive organs with which the fish can taste, smell and feel when they're searching for food. The wels and the sea catfish have 6 whiskers, the gafftopsail 4, and the North American freshwater catfishes have 8.

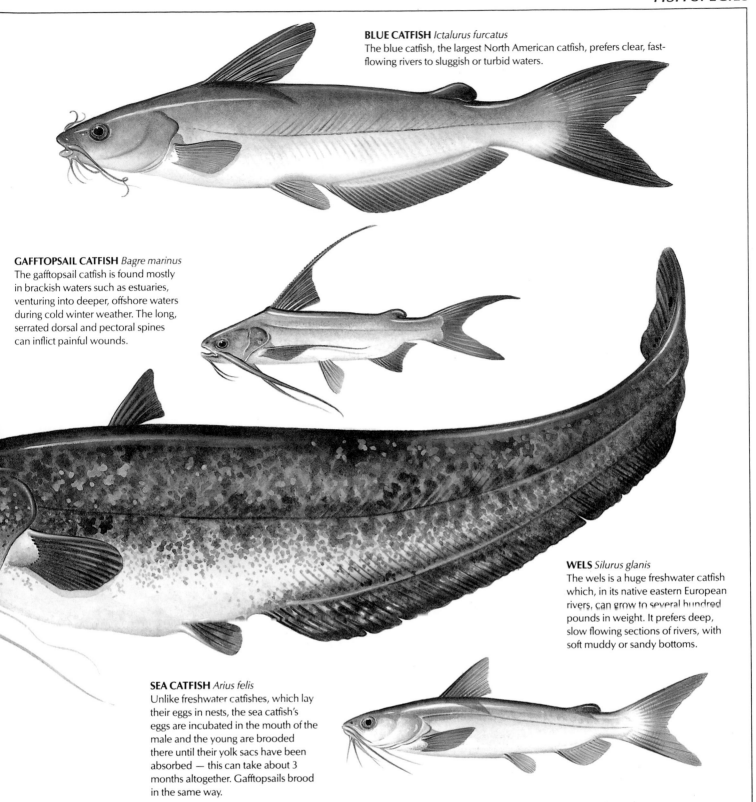

**BLUE CATFISH** *Ictalurus furcatus*
The blue catfish, the largest North American catfish, prefers clear, fast-flowing rivers to sluggish or turbid waters.

**GAFFTOPSAIL CATFISH** *Bagre marinus*
The gafftopsail catfish is found mostly in brackish waters such as estuaries, venturing into deeper, offshore waters during cold winter weather. The long, serrated dorsal and pectoral spines can inflict painful wounds.

**WELS** *Silurus glanis*
The wels is a huge freshwater catfish which, in its native eastern European rivers, can grow to several hundred pounds in weight. It prefers deep, slow flowing sections of rivers, with soft muddy or sandy bottoms.

**SEA CATFISH** *Arius felis*
Unlike freshwater catfishes, which lay their eggs in nests, the sea catfish's eggs are incubated in the mouth of the male and the young are brooded there until their yolk sacs have been absorbed — this can take about 3 months altogether. Gafftopsails brood in the same way.

| TECHNIQUE | ROD | REEL | LINE | TERMINAL TACKLE | HOOK | WEIGHT | BAIT |
|---|---|---|---|---|---|---|---|
| **Wels:** freeline short to medium range | 10 to 12-foot powerful all through action, 2 to 2½-pounds test curve | Fixed spool | 11 to 15-pounds | Hook only on 24-inch 15 to 20-pound Dacron swiveled hook length | Sizes 4 to 2/0 | None | Worms mussels |
| Ledgering, distance casting | 11 to 12-foot powerful all-through action, 2 to 2½-pound test curve | Fixed spool | 11 to 15-pounds | Dacron hook length, with running bomb, stopped by bead and swivel | Sizes 4-2/0 | 1-ounce bomb | Live baits, squid |
| Ledgering, running bomb | 9 to 10-foot heavy bass rod 1 pound test curve | Fixed spool | 6 to 12-pounds | 2-foot hook length with bead and swivel | Sizes 6-1/0 | ½ to 2-ounce bombs | Worms deadbaits |
| Float ledgering | 9 to 10-foot bass rod or long pole | Fixed spool | 6 to 8-pounds | Hook tied direct with shots 12-inches above | Sizes 6-2 | Split shot | Worms, grubs |

# CHAR *Salvelinus alpinus*

The char, or Arctic char, is widely distributed in the cold waters of the high latitudes of the Northern Hemisphere. In its migratory form, it's found in Alaska, northern Canada, Greenland, Iceland, northern Norway and the north of Siberia. The non-migratory, lake-dwelling form occurs further south, in Britain, Ireland, France, Germany, Scandinavia and the USSR.

Migratory char are mostly silver when they're at sea, with a steely blue-green back, pale pink spots on the sides and a pale orange-red tinge to the belly. When the fish enters the rivers to spawn the colours deepen, giving the fish a predominantly orange or red appearance. The non-migratory char are greeny-brown with an orange-red belly and reddish and white spots on the sides.

The non-migratory char spawn in late winter or early spring, just about the time when migratory char are leaving the fresh water for the sea. These fish spend the summer in the sea, returning to spawn in late summer.

A close relative of the Arctic char, the Dolly Varden or bulltrout *(Salvelinus malma)*, is found in the rivers and lakes of lands bordering the northern rim of the Pacific, from northern California round to Korea and Japan.

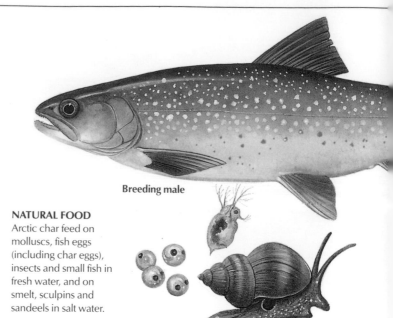

**Breeding male**

**NATURAL FOOD**
Arctic char feed on molluscs, fish eggs (including char eggs), insects and small fish in fresh water, and on smelt, sculpins and sandeels in salt water.

# CHUB *Leuciscus cephalus*

The European chub is primarily a river fish, although it has been successfully introduced into many still waters. It prefers a secluded river habitat, either between beds of thick weed or close in to the bank where the branches of willows and alder trees provide shelter.

The chub has a thick-set body, rounded yet streamlined, with a wide, blunt head and enormous mouth. The jaws are toothless, but the pharyngeal teeth are strong and sharp. The colouration along the back is slate grey to bronze, quickly lightening to pale gold on the large, even-patterned scales along the sides. The belly is a creamy white, and the pelvic and anal fins are tinted orange-red while the dorsal fin and the forked tail are steel grey.

Chub are found in most English river systems, some of the southern Scottish rivers, and much of Europe. Spawning takes place in late spring, when chub gather on fast, gravelly shallows to lay their eggs on streamer weed and the fibrous underwater roots of bankside trees.

Immature chub form scavenging shoals, often with other species such as dace or roach. The shoals break up when the fish mature, and the older fish lead more solitary lives. However, because of this mixed shoaling, hybridization is quite common.

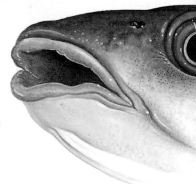

**NATURAL FOOD**
Chub are ominvorous, but particularly enjoy caddis larvae and small fishes.

**MOUTH**
The chub has a very large mouth and will gulp down almost anything that comes its way. Chub often wait under overhanging trees for falling berries and insects.

**COBIA** *Rachycentrum canadum*
The stripes along the sides of the cobia include a broad, black lateral band, which is prominent in young fish but often much less obvious in older ones.

| TECHNIQUE | ROD | REEL | LINE | TERMINAL TACKLE | HOOK | WEIGHT | BAIT |
|---|---|---|---|---|---|---|---|
| Livebaiting Light bottom fishing | Heavy duty spinning rod | Multiplier | 20-pound nylon | Fine line light ledger | Sizes 2/0-4/0 | Pear or bomb | Live fish, crab/prawn |

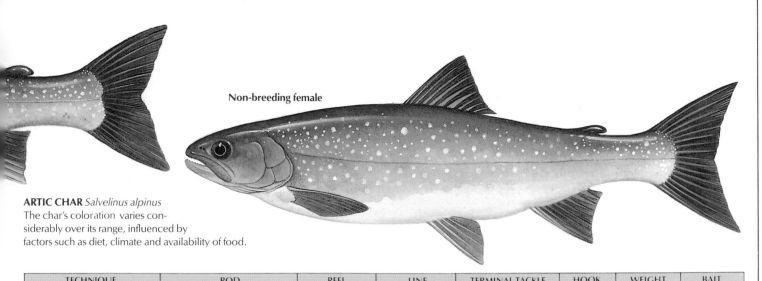

**Non-breeding female**

**ARTIC CHAR** *Salvelinus alpinus*
The char's coloration varies considerably over its range, influenced by factors such as diet, climate and availability of food.

| TECHNIQUE | ROD | REEL | LINE | TERMINAL TACKLE | HOOK | WEIGHT | BAIT |
|-----------|-----|------|------|-----------------|------|--------|------|
| Deep trolling | Spinning rod | Small multiplier | 7-pounds nylon | | Treble 8 | | Gold Spinner |
| Bait fishing | Spinning rod | Fixed spool | 4-pounds | | Treble 6 | Bomb lead | Worms |

**Dace**

**Chub**

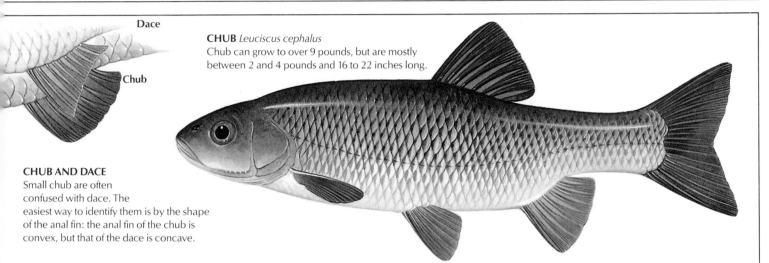

**CHUB** *Leuciscus cephalus*
Chub can grow to over 9 pounds, but are mostly between 2 and 4 pounds and 16 to 22 inches long.

**CHUB AND DACE**
Small chub are often confused with dace. The easiest way to identify them is by the shape of the anal fin: the anal fin of the chub is convex, but that of the dace is concave.

| TECHNIQUE | ROD | REEL | LINE | TERMINAL TACKLE | HOOK | WEIGHT | BAIT |
|-----------|-----|------|------|-----------------|------|--------|------|
| Ledgering | 11 to 12-foot ledger rod with built-in quivertip | Fixed spool | 4 to 5-pound | Fixed paternoster ledger or blockend feeder rig | Sizes 8-16 | 1/4-3/4-ounce bomb or swan shot link | Casters, maggots, cheesepaste |
| Long trotting in rivers | 12 or 13-foot match, float rod | Fixed spool | 2 to 2 1/2-pounds | Waggler float rig | Sizes 14-20 | | Maggots |

**NATURAL FOOD**
The cobia's varied diet includes most kinds of small fish, but it's especially fond of squid and crabs.

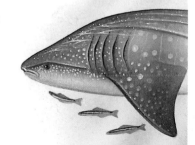

**COBIA AND SHARKS**
The cobia is not closely related to any other species, but its shape is similar to that of the sharksuckers (remoras) and it often swims alongside sharks such as this great white.

# COBIA *Rachycentrum canadum*

The cobia is a large, strong predatory fish which is found worldwide in warm and tropical waters. The body is elongated, and tapers from the middle to the strong, broad, rather flattened head and to the large, crescent-shaped tail. Along the back, 8 to 10 short dorsal spines precede a dorsal fin with one spine and 28 to 33 soft rays. Both the dorsal fin and the anal fin, which has one spine and 23 to 26 soft rays, are very long and noticeably peaked at the front end.

The cobia is distinctively coloured, with a chocolate-brown back and paler sides which carry horizontal stripes of brown and silver or bronze and white. The belly is yellowish-white.

The overall shape is not unlike that of the remora, and like the remora the cobia is often found in the company of cruising sharks. Cobia usually inhabit shallow, continental-shelf waters and are attracted to buoys, floating wreckage and other flotsam.

In really shallow waters, small schools of cobia often follow rays, picking up crabs and other crustaceans stirred out of the mud by the passing ray. In Australia, the cobia is nicknamed 'crabeater' because of its fondness for crab meat. Cobia can reach weights of over 100 pounds, but 30 to 50 pounds is more common. They can be caught by bottom fishing.

# CODS

The many species of the large cod family live mainly in the temperate and arctic waters of the Atlantic and Pacific Oceans. Many of them, such as the Atlantic cod *(Gadus morhua)*, are of considerable commercial importance as well as being of interest to anglers.

The Atlantic cod is a large, heavy fish with a single chin barbel, receding lower jaw, squared tail and arched lateral line. Like many other members of its family, it has three separate dorsal fins and two separate anal fins, and the tips of all these fins are rounded. The Pacific cod *(Gadus macrocephalus)* is very similar, but smaller and with pointed rather than rounded fins.

Cod are bottom feeders which show a liking for rough ground composed of sand and exposed rocks, and they also frequent wrecks. They feed on fish, squid, crabs, starfish and marine worms.

The pollack *(Pollachius pollachius)*, haddock *(Melanogrammus aeglefinus)* and pollack or coalfish *(Pollachius virens)* are all Atlantic members of the cod family. The burbot *(Lota lota)* is an unusual codfish in that it lives in fresh water. The cod family also includes the little Atlantic and Pacific tomcods *(Microgadus tomcod* and *M. proximus)*, but the hakes are now usually classified as a separate family, the Merlucciidae. These include the Atlantic or silver hake *(Merluccius bilinearis)* and the Pacific hake.

**BURBOT** *Lota lota*
Thought to be extinct in Britain but fortunately still widespread in northern Europe and North America, the burbot is the only freshwater cod species.

**NATURAL FOOD**
Cod sweep across the seabed feeding on whatever they can find, but prefer cuttlefish, squid, small flatfish, crabs, worms and various shellfish.

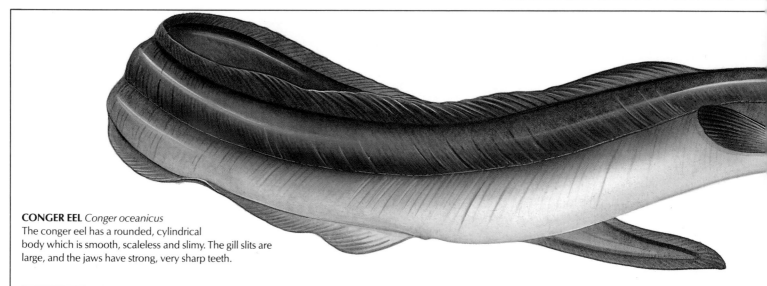

**CONGER EEL** *Conger oceanicus*
The conger eel has a rounded, cylindrical body which is smooth, scaleless and slimy. The gill slits are large, and the jaws have strong, very sharp teeth.

| TECHNIQUE | ROD | REEL | LINE | TERMINAL TACKLE | HOOK | WEIGHT | BAIT |
|---|---|---|---|---|---|---|---|
| Rock fishing | Heavy-duty surfcaster | 4/0 multiplier | 30 to 35-pounds | Running ledger wire | Size 6/0 | Pear/pyramid | Fish, squid |
| Boat fishing | 50-pound class boat rod | 8/0 multiplier | 50 to 60-pounds | Heavy nylon | Sizes 8/0 | Pear/pyramid | Cuttlefish |

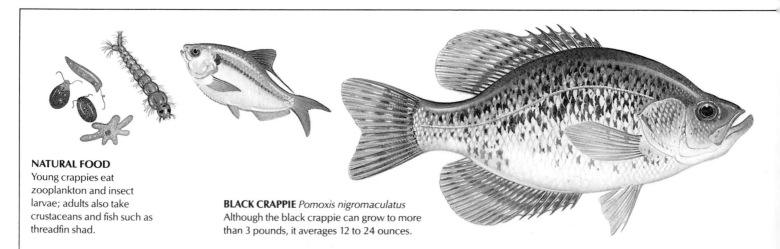

**NATURAL FOOD**
Young crappies eat zooplankton and insect larvae; adults also take crustaceans and fish such as threadfin shad.

**BLACK CRAPPIE** *Pomoxis nigromaculatus*
Although the black crappie can grow to more than 3 pounds, it averages 12 to 24 ounces.

| TECHNIQUE | ROD | REEL | LINE | TERMINAL TACKLE | HOOK | WEIGHT | BAIT |
|---|---|---|---|---|---|---|---|
| Jigging | 6 to 7-foot light tip action spinning rod | Fixed spool | 4 to 5-pounds | | | | Lead headed grub tails, marabou jigs |
| Dabbling from a boat | 10 to 14-foot cane pole | None. Line tied to end of pole | 6 to 15-pounds | Small float. Make hook knot so jig hangs level | | | |

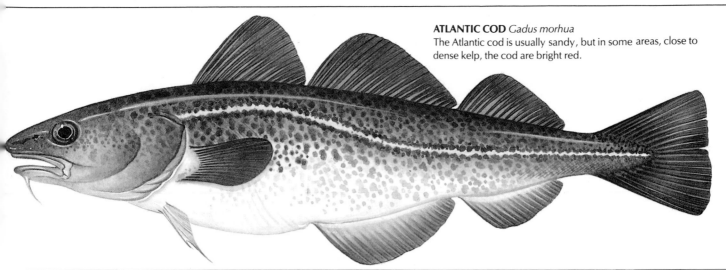

**ATLANTIC COD** *Gadus morhua*
The Atlantic cod is usually sandy, but in some areas, close to dense kelp, the cod are bright red.

| TECHNIQUE | ROD | REEL | LINE | TERMINAL TACKLE | HOOK | WEIGHT | BAIT |
|---|---|---|---|---|---|---|---|
| Bait fishing (boat), jigging, feathering, surfcasting | 30-pound class boat rod or 12-foot surfcaster | 4/0-6/0 multiplier, or beach size multiplier | 30-pound wire or nylon | Heavy nylon/wire tackle/running ledger | Sizes 2/0-8/0 | Bomb-shaped or grip lead | Squid, cuttle fish, feathers |

# CONGER EEL *Conger oceanicus*

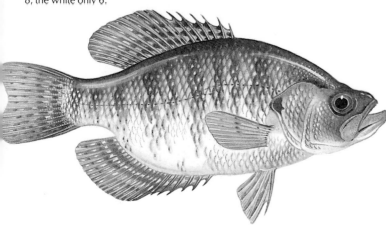

**NATURAL FOOD**
The conger eel has a varied diet which includes fish (especially members of the cod family), octopus, starfish, crabs and smaller conger.

Eight distinct species of conger are found in the Atlantic, but *Conger oceanicus* is the largest and commonest of the tribe. The biggest on record is a 250-pound monster caught by a commercial fishing boat; numerous other conger up to and over 150 pounds have been recorded.

The colour of the conger depends on the type of bottom it inhabits; on rocks, the back is charcoal grey and the underparts are pale, but over sand the back is a light grey-brown. The margins of the dorsal and anal fins are black.

The conger is a bottom feeder more than capable of catching live food. Crabs, squid, fish and smaller congers are all eaten avidly. In shallow waters the conger are mostly nocturnal feeders, but in depths of more than 60 feet they feed at any time.

Conger migrate to the subtropical Atlantic to breed, spawning at depths of 10,000 to 12,000 feet. The larvae are transparent and flattened, and drift at the surface for up to 2 years before reaching the shoreline. When they do, they change shape to become cylindrical; at this stage they are still transparent, and about 3 inches long. The full colouring doesn't appear until the eel is about 12 inches long.

# CRAPPIES

**WHITE CRAPPIE** *Pomoxis annularis*
The white crappie is generally larger than the black and paler overall, but it's sometimes difficult to distinguish between the two. The most accurate way is to count the spines on the dorsal fin: the black has 7 or 8, the white only 6.

The black crappie *(Pomoxis nigromaculatus)* and the white crappie *(P. annularis)* are two of the most popular North American panfish. Members of the sunfish family, the crappies are widely distributed in ponds, lakes and rivers, and the black crappie is even found in brackish water.

The black crappie has a deep, compressed body with silvery sides marked in dark blotches that form short, irregular horizontal lines. It has 6 spines at the front of the anal fin and 7 or 8 on the dorsal; the white crappie has 6 spines on each of these fins, and counting the spines is the most accurate way of telling the black crappie from the white.

The black crappie prefers rivers, lakes and reservoirs with clear water and rich vegetation, where it feeds on aquatic insects, crustaceans and small fish. It breeds in late spring.

The white crappie is lighter in overall colour than the black, with dusky vertical bars along the flanks, and the body is more elongated. It also grows larger than the black, but although weights of over 5 pounds have been recorded the average is about 16 to 24 ounces.

White crappies will tolerate more turbid water than the black will, and are usually found in larger concentrations. They are often found in deep water, although not on the bottom, or lurking among brush piles, reedbeds or sunken tree stumps.

# DACE *Leuciscus leuciscus*

The European dace is the smallest freshwater species to be taken seriously by British and European anglers. The maximum weight is under 1½ pounds, and a fish of 10 to 12 ounces and 11 inches long is a good specimen. Yet this diminutive shoal fish, which inhabits the well-oxygenated water of streams and rivers, remains popular with anglers because it can be readily caught on light float tackle.

The dace is a slim fish, almost round in cross-section, with a small, neat mouth and head. The colour is olive-grey along the back, lightening quickly to bright silver along the flanks and a white belly. The dorsal fin and tail are light grey, while the pectoral, anal and pelvic fins are usually tinted a warm pink. The anal fin is concave, unlike that of the chub (which is often mistaken for dace) which is convex, and the dace has a smaller mouth than the chub.

The dace is found throughout England and Wales, but not in Scotland and in only a few rivers in Ireland. It's also widespread in continental Europe and in Asia. It feeds on all the smaller crustaceans, plus the nymphs of most aquatic flies, caddis in particular. Often in spring and summer, dace can be seen rising freely to emerging flies, and taking the nymphs just below the surface.

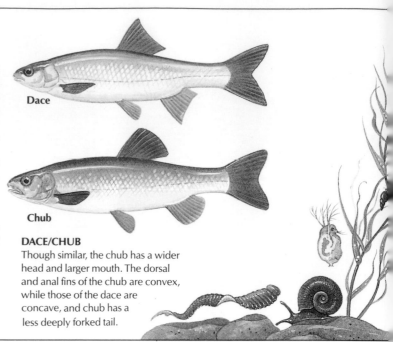

**DACE/CHUB**
Though similar, the chub has a wider head and larger mouth. The dorsal and anal fins of the chub are convex, while those of the dace are concave, and chub has a less deeply forked tail.

# DORADO *Coryphaena hippurus*

The dorado or dolphin is without question one of the most beautiful of all marine game fish. In the water, the colour of the dorado is iridescent blue-green on the back, with sides of speckled, burnished gold and silver-white underparts. Once out of the water, the colour fluctuates between blue, green and yellow, and when the fish dies it fades to grey, or at best golden grey.

The foreheads of large males are almost vertical, whereas those of the females are more rounded. There is just one dorsal fin, which rises steeply from its origin just above the eyes and then tapers down to the root of the tail, and has between 55 and 66 soft rays.

The anal fin, with 25 to 31 soft rays, starts midway along the belly and also tapers away towards the tail.

Dolphin are distributed worldwide in tropical and warm seas, feeding on flyingfish and squid. They reach weights of over 80 pounds, but most of those caught are only 5 to 15 pounds. They are a popular light-tackle fish, and can be taken on trolled naturals and lures or on spinning tackle.

The pompano dolphin (*C. equiselis*) is often confused with the dorado, but it can be identified by its dorsal fin, which starts further back, and its anal fin, which doesn't have an extended anterior lobe or such a concave outline.

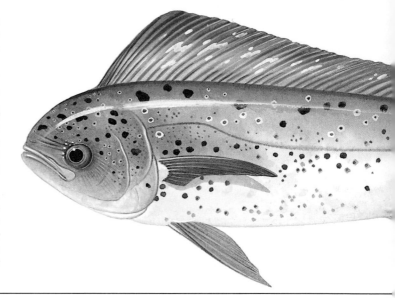

# DRUMS

The drums, or croakers, are a large family of American fish which consists of over thirty saltwater species and one freshwater. They get their name from the drumming sound which the males make by rapidly contracting a special muscle connected to the swim bladder.

The red drum (*Sciaenops ocellata*) is a great favourite with shore and small boat anglers along the Atlantic coast. This copper-coloured fish, which has a large black spot on the base of its tail, can weigh over 80 pounds, but most are in the 15 to 40-pound range.

The black drum (*Pogonias cromis*) is found in the same waters as the red, but is generally heavier with a deeper body and a more brassy colour. It lacks the black tail spot of the red drum, and unlike the red it has small barbules under the chin. The commonest Atlantic drum, the Atlantic croaker (*Micropogon undulatus*) is a small, silver to bronze fish which averages 2 to 4 pounds in weight.

The Pacific drums are found mainly along the Californian coast. The most important is the white seabass (*Cynoscion nobilis*), which is found as far north as Alaska.

The freshwater drum (*Aplodinotus grunniens*) is found in lakes and large rivers, in Canada from Manitoba to Quebec, and in the USA in most states to the east of the Missouri drainage.

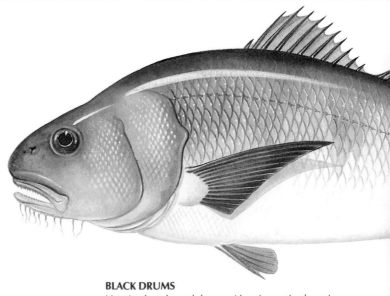

**BLACK DRUMS**
Heavier than the red drum, with a deeper body and more brassy. Up to 6 feet in length.

### DACE
Dace are more slender than roach, and have yellowish eyes with dark spots on the iris. There are 47-54 scales on the lateral line and two rows of pharyngeal teeth.

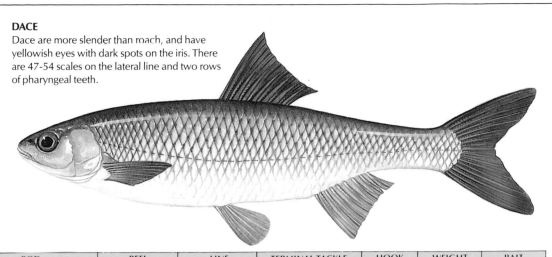

### NATURAL FOOD
Dace feed on surface insects, such as damselflies in summer, as well as snails, daphnia and leeches. In cold weather dace are restricted to bottom feeding.

| TECHNIQUE | ROD | REEL | LINE | TERMINAL TACKLE | HOOK | WEIGHT | BAIT |
|---|---|---|---|---|---|---|---|
| Long trotting – rivers, shallow glides, confluences, weir pools | 12 to 13-foot match or float, light tip action | Centrepin, closed face or fixed spool | 2-pound | Light float waggler or stick | 16 to 20 | 4 to BB | Casters, maggots |
| Dry fly fishing | 8½ to 9-foot light action DT6 | Single action fly | DT 6 floating | 10-foot tapered cast down to 2-pounds tippet | | | Black Gnat, Blue Olive Dun |

### DORADO
The body is elongated with very compressed sides, tapering sharply from the high, blunt forehead to the deeply forked tail.

### NATURAL FOOD
Dorado feed in shoals or groups on the surface, eating tiny animals floating on the sea, and squid and flyingfish.

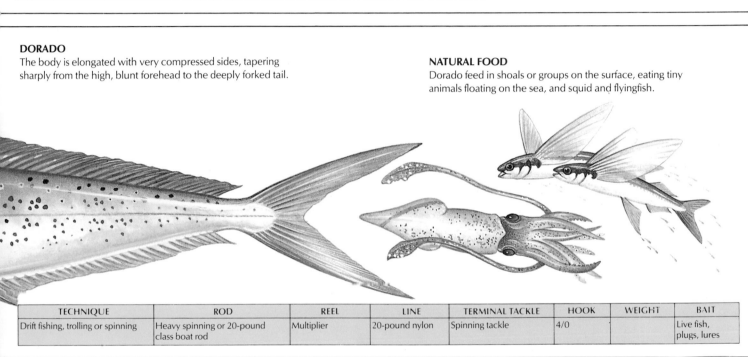

| TECHNIQUE | ROD | REEL | LINE | TERMINAL TACKLE | HOOK | WEIGHT | BAIT |
|---|---|---|---|---|---|---|---|
| Drift fishing, trolling or spinning | Heavy spinning or 20-pound class boat rod | Multiplier | 20-pound nylon | Spinning tackle | 4/0 | | Live fish, plugs, lures |

### RED DRUM
Much smaller than the black drum, the red drum is identified by a red spot on the origin of the caudal fin. At depth it changes from copper to brick red.

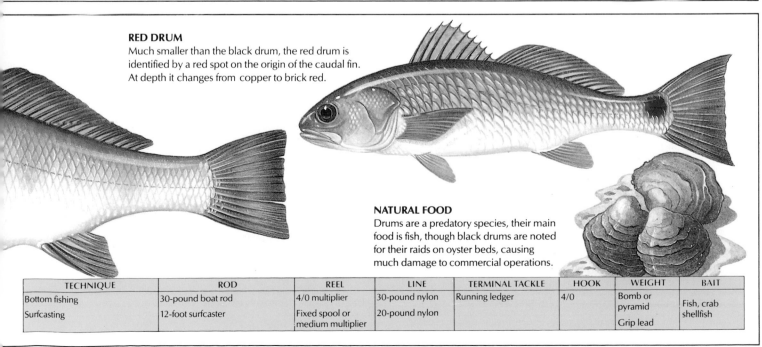

### NATURAL FOOD
Drums are a predatory species, their main food is fish, though black drums are noted for their raids on oyster beds, causing much damage to commercial operations.

| TECHNIQUE | ROD | REEL | LINE | TERMINAL TACKLE | HOOK | WEIGHT | BAIT |
|---|---|---|---|---|---|---|---|
| Bottom fishing | 30-pound boat rod | 4/0 multiplier | 30-pound nylon | Running ledger | 4/0 | Bomb or pyramid | Fish, crab shellfish |
| Surfcasting | 12-foot surfcaster | Fixed spool or medium multiplier | 20-pound nylon | | | Grip lead | |

# EELS

The European eel *(Anguilla anguilla)* and the closely-related American eel *(A. rostrata)* both spend most of their lives in fresh water, but to breed, they make a long and hazardous journey to the Sargasso Sea, from which they never return. The Sargasso Sea is a relatively calm area of the Atlantic Ocean, north east of the West Indies. After spawning, the adult eels die and the larvae which hatch from the eggs make their way to the rivers from whence their parents came.

The journey to the rivers takes about a year for the American eel larvae, but three years for the Europeans. By the time the larvae reach shore, they have changed into little elvers. Large numbers of these are netted as they run up estuaries. They travel by night, and many leave the water on damp, moonless nights to travel overland to ponds and lakes unconnected with the sea.

The elvers grow into yellow eels, which are yellow to brown in colour, darker on the back, and have a pair of small, rounded pectoral fins and long dorsal and anal fins which merge at the tail. Sexually mature eels take on a deep, silvery hue, and these silver eels set off in autumn for the sea and their ocean journey to the Sargasso. The females are larger than the males, and can grow to over 4 feet in length.

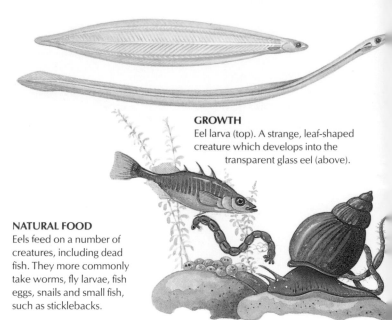

### GROWTH
Eel larva (top). A strange, leaf-shaped creature which develops into the transparent glass eel (above).

### NATURAL FOOD
Eels feed on a number of creatures, including dead fish. They more commonly take worms, fly larvae, fish eggs, snails and small fish, such as sticklebacks.

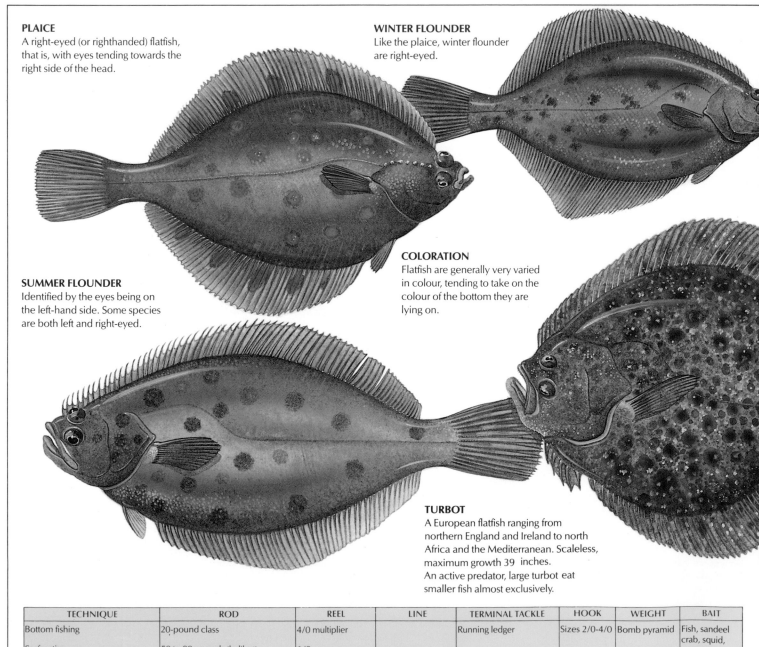

### PLAICE
A right-eyed (or righthanded) flatfish, that is, with eyes tending towards the right side of the head.

### WINTER FLOUNDER
Like the plaice, winter flounder are right-eyed.

### COLORATION
Flatfish are generally very varied in colour, tending to take on the colour of the bottom they are lying on.

### SUMMER FLOUNDER
Identified by the eyes being on the left-hand side. Some species are both left and right-eyed.

### TURBOT
A European flatfish ranging from northern England and Ireland to north Africa and the Mediterranean. Scaleless, maximum growth 39 inches. An active predator, large turbot eat smaller fish almost exclusively.

| TECHNIQUE | ROD | REEL | LINE | TERMINAL TACKLE | HOOK | WEIGHT | BAIT |
|---|---|---|---|---|---|---|---|
| Bottom fishing | 20-pound class | 4/0 multiplier | | Running ledger | Sizes 2/0-4/0 | Bomb pyramid | Fish, sandeel crab, squid, worm |
| Surfcasting | 50 to 80-pounds (halibut) | 6/0 | | | | | |
| Spinning | Spinning or beach rod | Fixed spool | | Flounder spoon rig | Long shank | Barrel lead | |

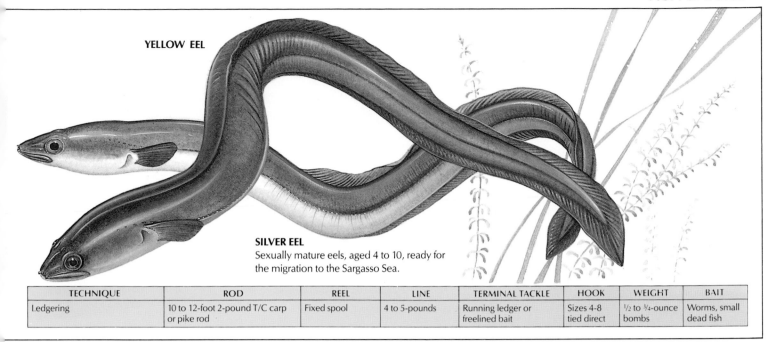

**YELLOW EEL**

**SILVER EEL**
Sexually mature eels, aged 4 to 10, ready for
the migration to the Sargasso Sea.

| TECHNIQUE | ROD | REEL | LINE | TERMINAL TACKLE | HOOK | WEIGHT | BAIT |
|---|---|---|---|---|---|---|---|
| Ledgering | 10 to 12-foot 2-pound T/C carp or pike rod | Fixed spool | 4 to 5-pounds | Running ledger or freelined bait | Sizes 4-8 tied direct | ½ to ¾-ounce bombs | Worms, small dead fish |

**EYE MIGRATION**
The illustration shows the
development of eye migration in
the plaice, seen head-on. As a
hatchling the plaice, in common
with other true flatfish species,
begins life as a round fish.
Gradually the eyes migrate to
one side of the head and the fish
lies flat on the bottom as an
adult. Plaice swim with their right
side uppermost.

**Poor cod,**
food of
the turbot

**NATURAL FOOD**
Smaller species of
flatfish feed on
mussels, razorshells
and lugworms, while
larger species, such
as turbot and halibut,
feed mainly on other
fish species.

# FLATFISH

Of the many species of flatfish
(a term which doesn't
include rays and skates), the
largest is the Atlantic halibut
(*Hippoglossus hippoglossus*), which
is also one of the largest bony fish
in the sea. The largest recorded
specimen was caught off the
Swedish coast and weighed 720
pounds.

Halibut of such a size are,
however, extremely rare, and
even fish of 300 pounds or so –
which measure about 8 feet long
and 4 feet wide – are seldom
found.

The Atlantic halibut is a
righteye (or righthanded) flatfish,
that is, it swims with its right
hand side uppermost, and during
its larval stage its left eye migrates
over its head towards the right
eye. The eye migration begins
when the larva is about an inch
long, and by the time the larva
has grown to about 1½ inches the
eye migration is complete and the
tiny fish begins to live on the
seabed, instead of drifting with
the current.

The immature fish live in
relatively shallow water, feeding
on crustaceans, sandeels and
small flatfish. As the fish mature,
they move into deep water,
preferring depths of from 200 to
3000 feet, where they feed on fish
such as cod, haddock, coalfish,
herring and even shark. They
hunt their prey in mid water as
well as on the bottom, and
supplement their basic diet of fish
with squid, octopus, cuttlefish,
lobster and crab.

Halibut can be caught on live
or dead baits fished on the bottom
or on the drift, or on baited pirk-
type lures. The Pacific halibut
(*Hippoglossus stenolepis*), which can
reach a weight of 500 pounds, can
be caught in the same way.

Another Pacific flatfish, the
California halibut (*Paralichthys
californicus*) which grows to over
60 pounds, is a lefteye flatfish. It
swims with its left side
uppermost, and during its larval
stage it is the right eye which
migrates. However, both lefteye
and righteye flatfish species
occasionally produce larvae
which show reversed eye
migration, and this trait is
especially common in the
California halibut.

Other lefteye flatfish include
the brill (*Scophthalmus rhombus*),
turbot (*S. maximus*), summer
flounder (*Paralichthys dentatus*),
Gulf flounder (*P. albigutta*) and
the megrim (*Lepidorhombus
whiffiagonis*), and a host of other
species.

The major examples of righteye
flatfish are the Atlantic and
Pacific halibuts, but there are
many others, including the plaice
(*Pleuronectes platessa*), the dab
(*Limanda limanda*), the sole (*Solea
solea*) and the winter flounder
(*Pseudopleuronectes americanus*).

The plaice is one of the most
popular of the flatfish in
European waters from the Baltic
to Biscay, and is taken both by
shore anglers and by boat
fishermen. On the American side
of the Atlantic, the winter
flounder and the summer
flounder (or fluke) provide shore
and small-boat anglers with
much of their sport.

# GARS

The freshwater gars are members of an ancient family of predatory fish. Of the nine species found in North American waters, only five are of interest to anglers. The largest is the alligator gar (*Lepisosteus spatula*), which is found from northeast Mexico to the Mississippi Valley, up to Missouri and Kentucky.

The alligator gar can reach a length of 10 feet, and a weight of 302 pounds has been recorded. It feeds on fish, and will also attack and eat ducks and other waterfowl. One 163-pound specimen was found to contain no less than 40 pounds of fish.

The other gars – including the longnose gar (*L. osseus*), shortnose gar (*L. platostomus*), spotted gar (*L. oculatus*) and Florida gar (*L. platyrhincus*) – are all much smaller. The longnose reaches about 50 pounds, the shortnose only 4½ pounds; the spotted grows to over 7 pounds, and the Florida to over 20 pounds.

The longnose is the commonest and most widely distributed of the gars, occurring from Montana east to Quebec and south through the Mississippi River system and into Mexico.

All the gars can survive in very poorly-oxygenated water, because their air bladders are supplied with blood vessels that enable them to be used as lungs. Their scales are so hard that pioneer farmers once used the skin and scales to cover their wooden ploughshares.

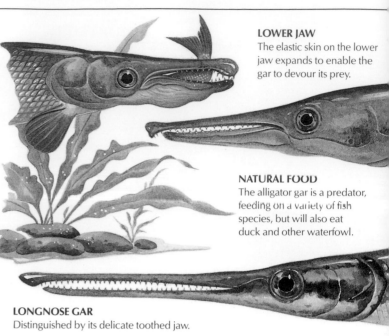

**LOWER JAW**
The elastic skin on the lower jaw expands to enable the gar to devour its prey.

**NATURAL FOOD**
The alligator gar is a predator, feeding on a variety of fish species, but will also eat duck and other waterfowl.

**LONGNOSE GAR**
Distinguished by its delicate toothed jaw.

# GRAYLING

The European grayling (*Thymallus thymallus*) and the closely-related American grayling (*Thymallus arcticus*) are beautiful freshwater members of the salmon family, living in swift, clean, gravel-bottomed rivers and pure, well-oxygenated lakes. The European grayling is found in most of Europe except Ireland, Spain, Portugal, southern France and the south of Italy. Most of the American grayling live in northern waters, from Alaska through to Saskatchewan, but small numbers are found in Montana, Wyoming and Utah.

The grayling is distinctive in appearance, with a long, slim body, a pointed snout, bony jaws and gill plates and hard scales. The adipose fin is tiny, but the dorsal is huge and sail-like and spotted and edged with red. The dorsal fin of the male is low at the front and rises towards the rear, whereas that of the female is high at the front and is either level or slopes to the rear; it's also smaller than the male's.

Grayling will not tolerate anything but the purest of waters, and they feed on shrimps, snails, nymphs and small fishes. They spawn in the spring, and the European grayling reaches weights of from just over 3 pounds in Britain to more than twice that in Scandinavia; American grayling grow to about 1½ pounds in their more southerly habitats, and reach over 5 pounds further north.

**STUNTED GROWTH**
Like other commercially bred species, a dwarf form occurs in stocked rivers.

**NATURAL FOOD**
As well as surface flying insects, grayling will eat aquatic insect larvae, fish fry, freshwater shrimps, snails, nymphs and small fishes.

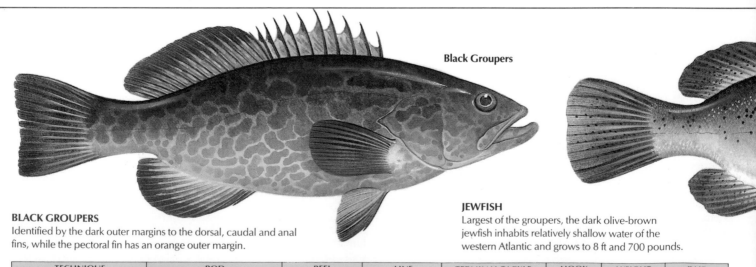

**Black Groupers**

**BLACK GROUPERS**
Identified by the dark outer margins to the dorsal, caudal and anal fins, while the pectoral fin has an orange outer margin.

**JEWFISH**
Largest of the groupers, the dark olive-brown jewfish inhabits relatively shallow water of the western Atlantic and grows to 8 ft and 700 pounds.

| TECHNIQUE | ROD | REEL | LINE | TERMINAL TACKLE | HOOK | WEIGHT | BAIT |
|---|---|---|---|---|---|---|---|
| Bottom fishing | 30-50-pound class boat rod | 4/0-6/0 multiplier | 35-pound nylon | Running ledger | 4/0-6/0 eyed | Pyramid egg, bomb | Live fish, cut squid, crab |
| Trolling | 80-pound class | 9/0 multiplier | 80-pound nylon | Heavy wire | 10/0 eyed | egg | Yellow Japanese feathers |

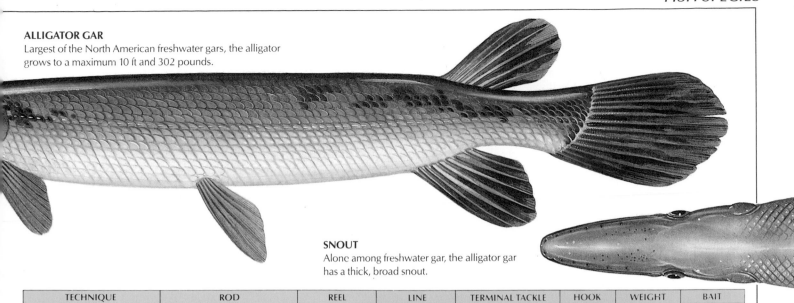

**ALLIGATOR GAR**
Largest of the North American freshwater gars, the alligator grows to a maximum 10 ft and 302 pounds.

**SNOUT**
Alone among freshwater gar, the alligator gar has a thick, broad snout.

| TECHNIQUE | ROD | REEL | LINE | TERMINAL TACKLE | HOOK | WEIGHT | BAIT |
|-----------|-----|------|------|-----------------|------|--------|------|
| Spinning | Medium 9-foot spinning rod | Fixed spool | 8-10-pound nylon | | 6, 4, 2 eyed | Barrel | Spinners, squid, crab, fish |

**SCALE**
The darker area only is visible in the living fish.

**EUROPEAN GRAYLING**
There is no visible difference between the European grayling and the American grayling.

| TECHNIQUE | ROD | REEL | LINE | TERMINAL TACKLE | HOOK | WEIGHT | BAIT |
|-----------|-----|------|------|-----------------|------|--------|------|
| Trotting | 11-13-foot float rod | Fixed spool | 2-3-pound | Chunky float with 4AA-4 swan shot | 10-16 | Bulk shot low down | Maggots bloodworms |
| Fly fishing | 8½-9-foot medium action, 6/7 | Single action fly reel | Dry line | Long cast | | | Leaded shrimp |

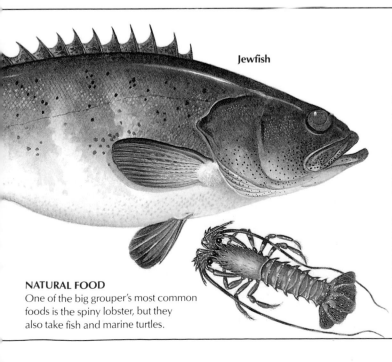

Jewfish

**NATURAL FOOD**
One of the big grouper's most common foods is the spiny lobster, but they also take fish and marine turtles.

# GROUPERS

Groupers, of which there are more than 400 known species, are large, predatory fish distributed worldwide in temperate to tropical freshwaters and seas. Groupers range in size from small to very large, but most are caught in similar ways and, being good table-fish, are commercially valuable.

Some of the commonest groupers are the red grouper (*Epinephalus morio*), the Nassau grouper (*E. striatus*), the black grouper (*Mycteroperca bonaci*), the yellowfin grouper (*M. venenosa*) and the jewfish (*E. itajara*).

The jewfish is the largest of the groupers, and can grow to 8 feet in length and a weight of over 700 pounds. Jewfish are found in the western Atlantic from Florida to Brazil, including the Gulf of Mexico, and the eastern Pacific from Costa Rica down to Peru.

The jewfish is brownish green or brownish yellow, mottled with dark brown spots and blotches and having 5 or more dark vertical bars on each side. Very large specimens tend to be darker, and may be uniformly olive-brown or even black.

Despite its size, the jewfish normally lives in comparatively shallow water close to the shore, rocks, reefs and ledges being its preferred habitat. It lives on fish and crustaceans, and has also been known to catch and eat turtles. There are even reliable reports of huge jewfish trying to swallow divers.

# JACKS

The jacks are a large family of marine fishes widely distributed in the warmer waters of the world. One of the jacks most popular with anglers is the crevalle or jack crevalle *(Caranx hippos)*. This is a superb fish to catch on light tackle, a hard-hitting predator that can be taken by spinning, trolling, jigging or surfcasting.

The body is deep and rather fat, with a deeply forked tail and long, elegant pectoral fins. The forehead is blunt and steep, and the metallic blue-green colour of the back gives way to silver or silvery yellow on the flanks and belly.

The crevalle is found in the western Atlantic, and an almost identical species *(C. caninus)* occurs in the eastern Pacific. It grows to at least 55 pounds, and although most are taken in coastal waters they also inhabit the deeper offshore areas.

The crevalle differs from other jacks in that its chest area is scaleless apart from a small, circular patch of scales. The other jacks, such as the Atlantic and Pacific horse-eye jacks *(C. latus* and *C. marginatus)* are fully scaled on the chest.

The jack family also includes the yellow jack *(C. bartholomaei)*, a pale silvery-blue Atlantic species with an overall yellowish tinge that is more prominent when the fish is dead, and the beautiful blue runners of the Atlantic *(C. crysos)* and Pacific *(C. caballus)*.

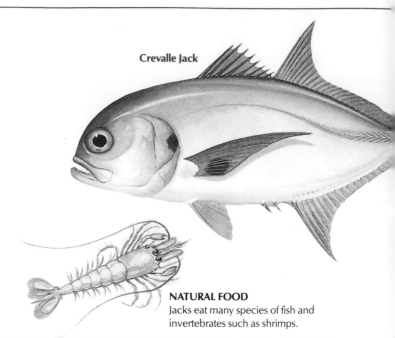

**Crevalle Jack**

**NATURAL FOOD**
Jacks eat many species of fish and invertebrates such as shrimps.

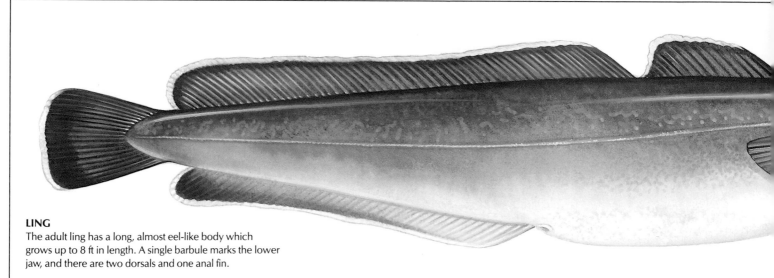

**LING**
The adult ling has a long, almost eel-like body which grows up to 8 ft in length. A single barbule marks the lower jaw, and there are two dorsals and one anal fin.

| TECHNIQUE | ROD | REEL | LINE | TERMINAL TACKLE | HOOK | WEIGHT | BAIT |
|---|---|---|---|---|---|---|---|
| Baited pirk | 50-pound class boat rod | 6/0 multiplier | 50-pound nylon | Pirk and wire trace | Size 8/0 | Pirk acts as weight | Fish, squid, cuttlefish |

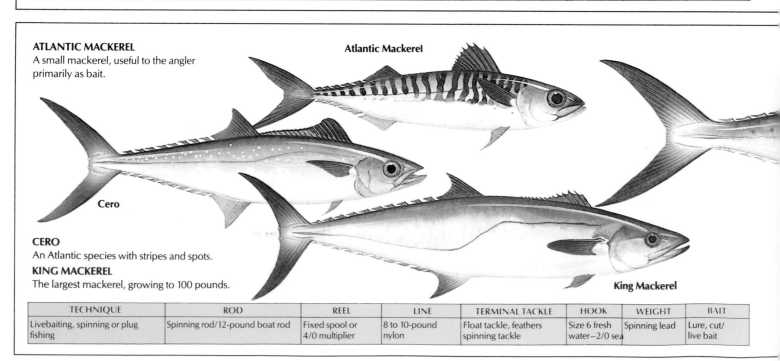

**ATLANTIC MACKEREL**
A small mackerel, useful to the angler primarily as bait.

**Atlantic Mackerel**

**Cero**

**CERO**
An Atlantic species with stripes and spots.

**KING MACKEREL**
The largest mackerel, growing to 100 pounds.

**King Mackerel**

| TECHNIQUE | ROD | REEL | LINE | TERMINAL TACKLE | HOOK | WEIGHT | BAIT |
|---|---|---|---|---|---|---|---|
| Livebaiting, spinning or plug fishing | Spinning rod/12-pound boat rod | Fixed spool or 4/0 multiplier | 8 to 10-pound nylon | Float tackle, feathers spinning tackle | Size 6 fresh water–2/0 sea | Spinning lead | Lure, cut/ live bait |

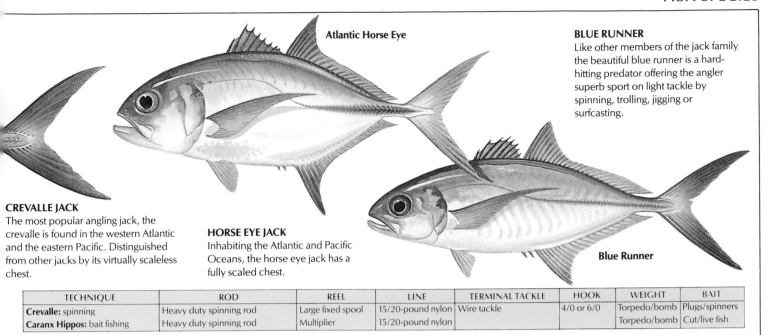

**Atlantic Horse Eye**

**BLUE RUNNER**
Like other members of the jack family, the beautiful blue runner is a hard-hitting predator offering the angler superb sport on light tackle by spinning, trolling, jigging or surfcasting.

**CREVALLE JACK**
The most popular angling jack, the crevalle is found in the western Atlantic and the eastern Pacific. Distinguished from other jacks by its virtually scaleless chest.

**HORSE EYE JACK**
Inhabiting the Atlantic and Pacific Oceans, the horse eye jack has a fully scaled chest.

**Blue Runner**

| TECHNIQUE | ROD | REEL | LINE | TERMINAL TACKLE | HOOK | WEIGHT | BAIT |
|---|---|---|---|---|---|---|---|
| **Crevalle:** spinning | Heavy duty spinning rod | Large fixed spool | 15/20-pound nylon | Wire tackle | 4/0 or 6/0 | Torpedo/bomb | Plugs/spinners |
| **Caranx Hippos:** bait fishing | Heavy duty spinning rod | Multiplier | 15/20-pound nylon | | | Torpedo/bomb | Cut/live fish |

# LING *Molva molva*

The ling is a large member of the cod family, widely distributed in the northeast Atlantic from the Arctic south to the Bay of Biscay. It lives mainly in deep waters from about 150 feet down to 1200 feet or more, preferring rocky or rough ground and wrecks.

Ling are active hunters, feeding on all kinds of small fish, crustaceans, squid and cuttlefish. They are normally caught on cut fish or squid baits, fished with heavy bottom tackle, and grow to over 6 feet long and 80 pounds.

Ling are dark brown-green on the back with white underparts, and the body is long and almost eel-like. There is a single barbule on the lower jaw, and there are two dorsal fins, the first short and rounded and the second long and even in height. The single anal fin is also long, although not as long as the second dorsal, and the rounded tail is small for the size of the fish. There is a dark blotch on the rear edge of the first dorsal fin, and the leading edges of the fins are tinged with blue.

Ling spawn between March and July, and a large female can produce up to 60 million eggs. The eggs, each about one millimeter in diameter, float on the surface until they hatch. The young ling live in shallow water for the first two or three years before moving to deeper waters.

**NATURAL FOOD**
Ling feed on bottom-dwelling fish such as flatfish, eels and squid.

# MACKERELS

Mackerels are an abundant and commercially-important group of fishes found in both the Atlantic and the Pacific. The small species are useful to the angler more as bait than sport, but the larger species are popular gamefish. The small Atlantic mackerels include the common or Atlantic mackerel *(Scomber scombrus)* and the chub mackerel *(S. colias)*. The small Pacific mackerel *(S. japonicus)* is very similar to the chub mackerel.

The giant of the mackerel tribe is the king mackerel *(Scomberomorus cavalla)* of the western Atlantic, which can grow to 100 pounds. A long, lean fish, the king mackerel has a pointed snout, two dorsal fins plus a row of eight or nine dorsal finlets, and an anal fin plus eight to ten anal finlets. Keenly sought by anglers off the coasts of Florida and the Gulf of Mexico, king mackerel are taken on trolled or drifted bait, and on spinners and plugs.

The Spanish mackerel *(Scomberomorus maculatus)* is another popular gamefish in these waters. Most weigh 6 to 10 pounds, and the maximum is about 20 pounds. The Spanish mackerel has spots on its sides and no stripes on its back, unlike the striped but spotless king mackerel and the striped and spotted cero mackerel *(S. regalis)*, another Atlantic species which grows to 35 pounds.

**SPANISH MACKEREL**
Found off the Florida coast and in the Gulf of Mexico, Spanish mackerel is a popular gamefish, averaging between 6 to 10 pounds, reaching a maximum of 20 pounds.

**NATURAL FOOD**
Mackerel are predators, feeding on shoaling species such as the easy pickings offered by anchovy.

# MARLINS

Most anglers would like to tangle at least once with one of the world's most sought-after gamefish – a marlin. Blue marlin *(Makaira nigricans)*, black marlin *(M. indicus)*, white marlin *(Tetrapturus albidus)* and striped marlin *(T. audax)* are all true big-game species.

The blue marlin is the most widely distributed, being found in warm and temperate waters all round the world. The white marlin is an Atlantic fish, and the striped occurs in the Indian and Pacific Oceans, as does the black marlin which is also found in the far southeastern corner of the Atlantic.

Like all marlins, the blue has an elongated upper jaw or 'bill', long, thin, thorn-like scales, ventral fins, and a huge, deeply-forked tail with a pair of keels at either side of its root. The dorsal fin is high and pointed, and the pectoral fins are never rigid as they are in the black marlin. The back is cobalt blue, while the belly and flanks are silvery white.

All marlin spawn in summer, and feed mainly on fish and squid. Cannibalism also occurs; a 448-pound marlin caught off Walker's Cay in the Bahamas was found to contain the partly-digested remains of another, 72 inches long. Blue marlin reach weights of over 1500 pounds, and black marlin slightly more; the maximum for striped marlin is around 480 pounds, about three times that of white marlin.

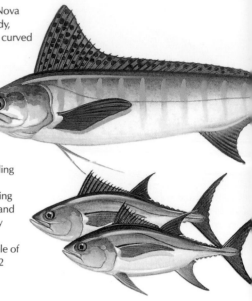

**WHITE MARLIN**
A sporting fish found from Nova Scotia to Brazil. Slender body, rounded lobe on dorsal fin, curved pectoral fin.

**NATURAL FOOD**
Marlin feed mainly on shoaling fish and squid, they are particularly fond of shadowing shoals of tuna. Their speed and power is such that their prey have no chance of escape. Marlin are cannibals, capable of devouring other marlin of 72 inches.

# MULLETS

All the mullet family are re-garded as tricky fish to catch. Soft-mouthed, shy and extremely strong when hooked on light tackle, mullet are a match for any angler's skill.

The thick-lipped mullet *(Crenimugil labrosus)*, thin-lipped mullet *(Liza ramada)*, golden grey mullet *(Liza Aurata)*, the striped or black mullet *(Mugil cephalus)* and the white mullet *(Mugil curema)* are all very similar in appearance.

The body is torpedo-shaped, with a broad, rather flattened head and two dorsal fins, the first having four heavy spines. The colour is grey-blue on the back, with silvery grey sides and white underparts; the golden grey variety has a conspicuous gold patch on the cheek and gill cover.

Mullet are found in all temperate and tropical seas. They are fond of brackish water, and in large estuaries they often penetrate well inland beyond the influence of salt water. They are mostly caught on ultralight float tackle, used with bread or tiny marine worms as bait. In some areas, they will also take tiny, worm-baited spinners, and this method works particularly well in estuaries.

Mullet can reach weights in excess of 10 pounds, although most rod-caught fish are only 3 to 5 pounds. They are an excellent food fish, and equally good as bait for big game fish, marlin in particular.

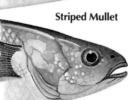

**Striped Mullet**

**Golden Mullet**

**Thin-Lipped Mullet**

**MULLET VARIATIONS**
Mullets have attractive heads with large, irregular shade patterns. Striped mullet have blunt heads and clear adipose eye-lids. Golden mullet have golden blotches on their cheeks and gill covers. Thin-lipped mullet are so-called because their top lip is less than half the diameter of their eye.

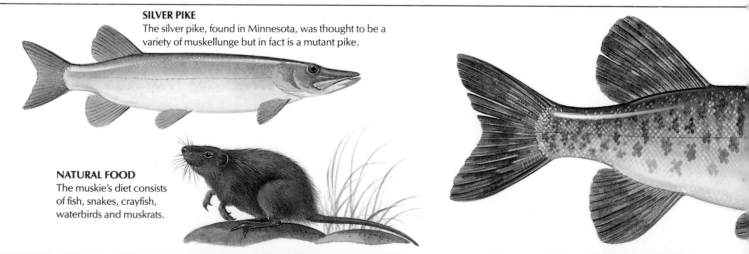

**SILVER PIKE**
The silver pike, found in Minnesota, was thought to be a variety of muskellunge but in fact is a mutant pike.

**NATURAL FOOD**
The muskie's diet consists of fish, snakes, crayfish, waterbirds and muskrats.

| TECHNIQUE | ROD | REEL | LINE | TERMINAL TACKLE | HOOK | WEIGHT | BAIT |
|---|---|---|---|---|---|---|---|
| Baitcasting, spinning | 6 to 8-foot heavy action baitcasting/spinning rod | Multiplier or fixed spool | 12 to 15-pounds | 12-foot strong wire trace, 20-pounds test | | | Plugs, spinner and buzz baits |
| Downrigger trolling | 6 to 7-foot fast taper action | Multiplier | 15 to 20-pounds | 12-foot strong wire trace, 25 pounds test | | | Large spoons plugs, minnows |

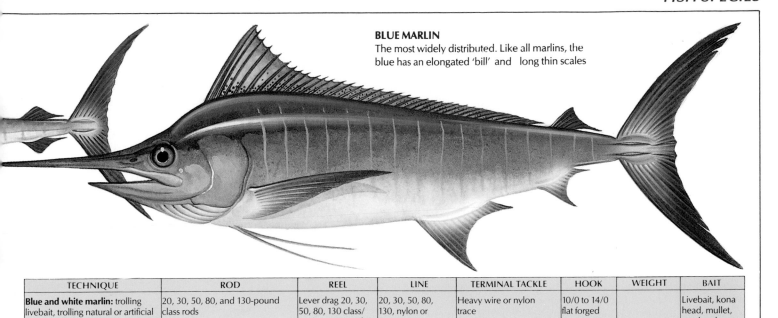

**BLUE MARLIN**
The most widely distributed. Like all marlins, the blue has an elongated 'bill' and long thin scales

| TECHNIQUE | ROD | REEL | LINE | TERMINAL TACKLE | HOOK | WEIGHT | BAIT |
|---|---|---|---|---|---|---|---|
| **Blue and white marlin:** trolling livebait, trolling natural or artificial lures | 20, 30, 50, 80, and 130-pound class rods | Lever drag 20, 30, 50, 80, 130 class/ 6/0,7, 14/0 star drag | 20, 30, 50, 80, 130, nylon or Dacron | Heavy wire or nylon trace | 10/0 to 14/0 flat forged | | Livebait, kona head, mullet, mackerel |

**THICK-LIPPED MULLET**
Most widely distributed of British mullet. The top lip is more than half the diameter of its eye.

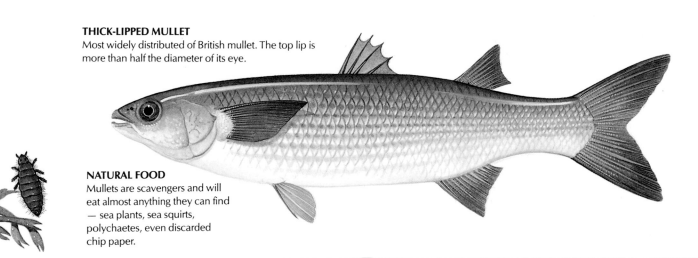

**NATURAL FOOD**
Mullets are scavengers and will eat almost anything they can find — sea plants, sea squirts, polychaetes, even discarded chip paper.

| TECHNIQUE | ROD | REEL | LINE | TERMINAL TACKLE | HOOK | WEIGHT | BAIT |
|---|---|---|---|---|---|---|---|
| Bait or baited line | 12-foot float or light spinning | Fixed spool | 5-pound nylon | Shotted float, bar spoons | 6-10 fresh water or 10 treble | Split shot | Worm, banana, macaroni, meat, sweetcorn |

**MUSKERLUNG**
Almost identical to the northern pike in appearance, the muskie is, however, bigger — up to 70 pounds and 5 feet.

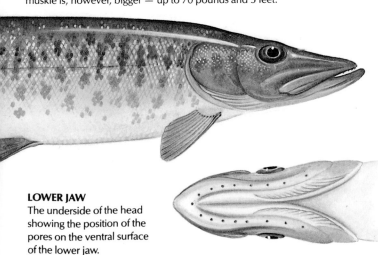

**LOWER JAW**
The underside of the head showing the position of the pores on the ventral surface of the lower jaw.

# MUSKELLUNGE *Esox masquinongy*

The muskellunge of North America is without doubt the king of the pike family. Although somewhat slimmer than its closest rival the northern (or Euopean) pike, the muskie grows to over 70 pounds and 20 to 30-pounders are not uncommon.

In build and fin structure the muskies are like all other pike, being long and sleek in the body with strong, tooth-filled jaws, and with the dorsal and anal fins set well back for short, controlled bursts of speed. The back is usually olive to bronze, with paler sides, but the markings vary considerably and usually differ from those of other pike.

Muskellunge most prefer clear streams, rivers and lakes with plenty of vegetation where they can wait for passing shoal fish.

Muskellunge are found in and around the Great Lakes, in eastern lakes such as Chautauqua Lake (NY) and down the Ohio drainage to Tennessee, and into North Carolina and Georgia. There are in fact three very similar varieties of muskellunge: the Great Lakes muskellunge *(Esox masquinongy masquinongy)*; the tiger or northern muskellunge *(Esox masquinongy immaculatus)* of Minnesota, Wisconsin and parts of Michigan; and the Chautauqua or Ohio muskellunge *(Esox masquinongy ohioensis)*.

# PADDLEFISH *Polyodon spathula*

The paddlefish is a large, almost scaleless freshwater fish with a huge, paddle-shaped snout. It has a large, shark-like tail, and like the sharks its skeleton is mostly of cartilage. The head and mouth are large, but the eye is tiny, and the fish feeds on plankton and insect larvae by straining them from the water through large and numerous gill rakers. To do this, it swims with its mouth wide open, like a basking shark.

The body is a dusky blue to dark grey on the back and dirty white below, and the gill cover extends backwards as a long, pointed flap. The paddlefish is large for a freshwater fish, and has been known to reach 200 pounds

and a length of 6 feet, but the average maximum is less than 100 pounds and most of those caught are less than 40 pounds.

The paddlefish's range is smaller than it was, but it's still quite widely distributed throughout the larger rivers and lakes of the Mississippi drainage. Spawning takes place in April and May, and as the eggs are laid on gravel beds in shallow, running water, lake-dwelling paddlefish often have to travel great distances to suitable streams in order to spawn. Paddlefish can be caught on small baits, but apart from the high quality of its flesh it isn't regarded as a particularly worthwhile catch.

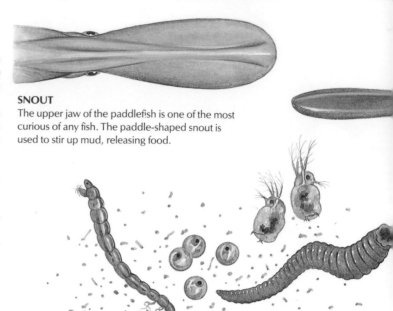

**SNOUT**
The upper jaw of the paddlefish is one of the most curious of any fish. The paddle-shaped snout is used to stir up mud, releasing food.

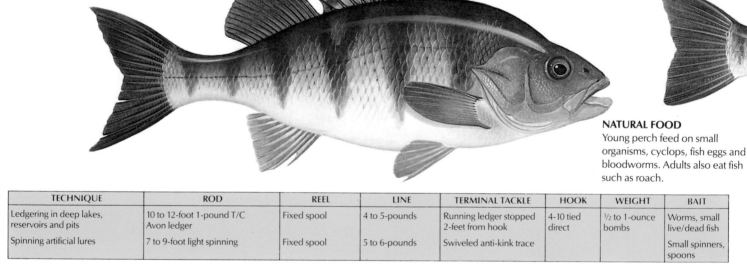

**EUROPEAN PERCH**
Identified by its pronounced striped pattern on body and divided dorsal fin.

**NATURAL FOOD**
Young perch feed on small organisms, cyclops, fish eggs and bloodworms. Adults also eat fish such as roach.

| TECHNIQUE | ROD | REEL | LINE | TERMINAL TACKLE | HOOK | WEIGHT | BAIT |
|---|---|---|---|---|---|---|---|
| Ledgering in deep lakes, reservoirs and pits | 10 to 12-foot 1-pound T/C Avon ledger | Fixed spool | 4 to 5-pounds | Running ledger stopped 2-feet from hook | 4-10 tied direct | ½ to 1-ounce bombs | Worms, small live/dead fish |
| Spinning artificial lures | 7 to 9-foot light spinning | Fixed spool | 5 to 6-pounds | Swiveled anti-kink trace | | | Small spinners, spoons |

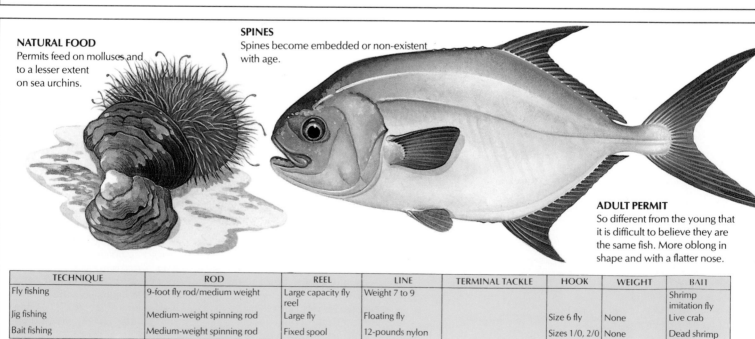

**NATURAL FOOD**
Permits feed on molluscs and to a lesser extent on sea urchins.

**SPINES**
Spines become embedded or non-existent with age.

**ADULT PERMIT**
So different from the young that it is difficult to believe they are the same fish. More oblong in shape and with a flatter nose.

| TECHNIQUE | ROD | REEL | LINE | TERMINAL TACKLE | HOOK | WEIGHT | BAIT |
|---|---|---|---|---|---|---|---|
| Fly fishing | 9-foot fly rod/medium weight | Large capacity fly reel | Weight 7 to 9 | | | | Shrimp imitation fly |
| Jig fishing | Medium-weight spinning rod | Large fly | Floating fly | | Size 6 fly | None | Live crab |
| Bait fishing | Medium-weight spinning rod | Fixed spool | 12-pounds nylon | | Sizes 1/0, 2/0 | None | Dead shrimp |

### PADDLEFISH
Large, scaleless, freshwater fish with strange, paddle-shaped snout. Known to reach 200 pounds.

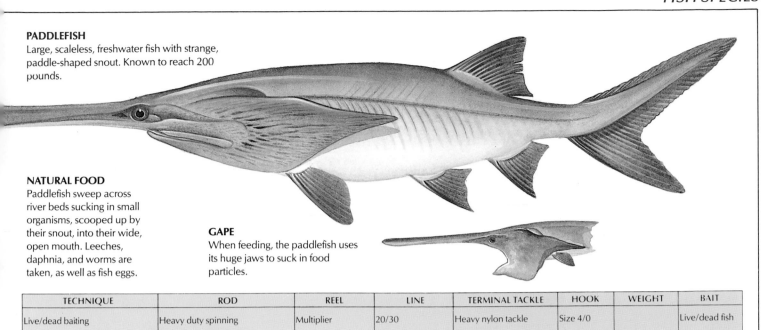

### NATURAL FOOD
Paddlefish sweep across river beds sucking in small organisms, scooped up by their snout, into their wide, open mouth. Leeches, daphnia, and worms are taken, as well as fish eggs.

### GAPE
When feeding, the paddlefish uses its huge jaws to suck in food particles.

| TECHNIQUE | ROD | REEL | LINE | TERMINAL TACKLE | HOOK | WEIGHT | BAIT |
|---|---|---|---|---|---|---|---|
| Live/dead baiting | Heavy duty spinning | Multiplier | 20/30 | Heavy nylon tackle | Size 4/0 | | Live/dead fish |

# PERCHES

### YELLOW PERCH
Closely related to the European perch, the yellow perch is regarded by some as a sub-species.

The European perch *(Perca fluviatilis)* is a freshwater shoalfish which is widely distributed throughout the British Isles and most of Europe and Asia, and is also found in southern Africa and in Australasia. The very similar, closely-related yellow perch *(Perca flavescens)* occurs in southern Canada and the central and eastern parts of the USA.

The body is oval in cross-section, and while young perch are quite elongated, they become chunkier and humpbacked as they get older. There are two separate dorsal fins, the first of which has strong spines, and the scales are very rough to the touch.

The colour is dark olive along the back, with golden flanks marked by a series of vertical dark bars, and a white belly.

The perch lives on a diet of snails, crayfish, insects and small fish, including small perch. Its preferred habitats are clean, slow rivers and ponds, pits, lakes and reservoirs. The European perch grows to about 6 pounds in the British Isles and to 10 pounds or more elsewhere.

The white perch *(morone americana)*, which is related to the striped bass, is another popular North American panfish. More silver in colour than the yellow perch, and without the vertical dark markings, it lives in salt, brackish and fresh waters along the eastern seaboard and inland to the Great Lakes.

### JUVENILE PERMIT
Young permit have a deep body and elongated dorsal, anal and caudal lobes.

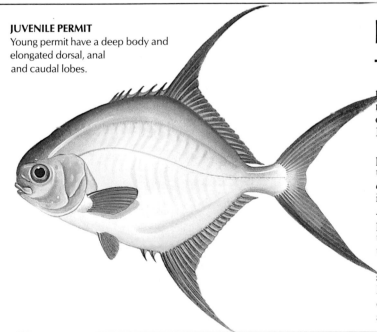

# PERMIT *Trachinotus falcatus*

The permit, one of the great light tackle species, is a fish of the western Atlantic. The largest numbers are found off the coasts of southern Florida and the Bahamas.

Often called the 'great pompano', the permit differs from the common pompano *(T. carolinus)* by having fewer soft rays in the dorsal and anal fins. Another difference is that the permit has very large second and third ribs, which can be easily felt through the side of the fish.

The adult permit is oblong in shape, with a small mouth and a high, blunt forehead. The overall colour is silvery with dusky fins, and some specimens have a touch of orange on the margin of the anal fin.

Permit are a shallow-water species, often travelling in schools over coral flats. They feed in much the same way as bonefish and in the same sort of waters, eating mostly shellfish, crabs, shrimps and sea urchins. Peak spawning time is May, and the major spawning grounds are believed to be about 200 miles from the Florida coast. The maximum weight is probably around 60 pounds, and most are taken on streamer flies or bonefish jigs. The mouth of the permit is as tough as leather, so to make sure of setting the hook it pays to make a series of strikes when a fish bites.

# PICKERELS

The pickerels are small American members of the pike family. In overall shape and body structure they are similar to other pikes, and just as well-equipped with strong, sharp teeth.

The largest is the chain pickerel (*Esox niger*), which grows to a top weight of around 9 pounds and a length of about 3 feet. As with other pikes, the body colours and markings provide excellent camouflage for a predator that likes to lurk in weedbeds to ambush its food as it passes.

The chain pickerel feeds on almost anything edible that comes its way, including fish, frogs, newts, crayfish and small rodents, and like all pikes the

pickerel is a cannibal. It breeds in early spring, among vegetation in the shallows, and the fry feed on small creatures such as zooplankton and shrimp until they're large enough to take small fish.

The chain pickerel is widely distributed in the eastern USA, particularly the Atlantic states, and in Georgia and Florida, being most plentiful in waters where it isn't competing with (or being eaten by) larger pike.

There are two other species of pickerel, the redfin pickerel (*Esox americanus americanus*) found in waters of the Atlantic drainage, and the grass pickerel (*E. a. vermiculatus*) of the Mississippi drainage and the Great Lakes. These little pike (10 to 15 inches long) provide excellent sport on ultralight tackle.

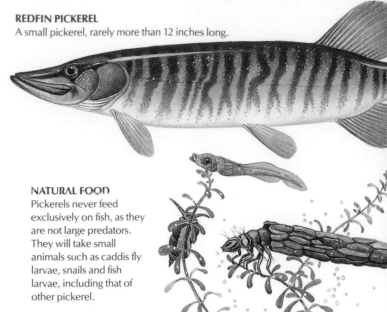

**REDFIN PICKEREL**
A small pickerel, rarely more than 12 inches long.

**NATURAL FOOD**
Pickerels never feed exclusively on fish, as they are not large predators. They will take small animals such as caddis fly larvae, snails and fish larvae, including that of other pickerel.

# PIKE *Esox lucius*

The pike is one of the most popular sports fish of Europe and North America, and in many areas it offers the anglers their best chance of catching a heavy fish. Pike can grow to over 4 feet long and 50 pounds, although fish of between 10 and 20 pounds are worthwhile catches.

In colour, the pike is bronze to olive green along the back, with flanks of light olive patterned with blotches and spots of cream which create a highly effective camouflage. The fins are large and red to yellow in colour, with dark markings, and the powerful forked tail gives the fish sudden and rapid acceleration when it ambushes its prey. The eyes are

set high in the flattened head, which has strong, bony jaws.

Pike are found in most types of water, from deep, clear-watered lakes to shallow streams and ponds and even tidal rivers. Pike are essentially lazy fish, preferring to scavenge on dead food or to lie in ambush for a passing meal, but they will hunt if they have to. Their staple diet is live shoal fish, which may be up to a third or even half their own length, but they will also take rats, voles, frogs, mice and waterfowl. Spawning is in early spring, when the female, accompanied by one or more (much smaller) males, deposits her eggs in weedy shallows or on reed stems.

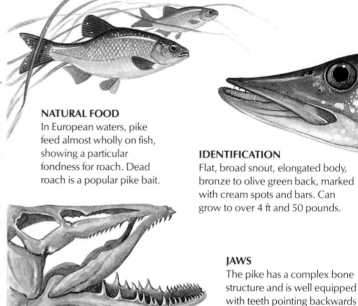

**NATURAL FOOD**
In European waters, pike feed almost wholly on fish, showing a particular fondness for roach. Dead roach is a popular pike bait.

**IDENTIFICATION**
Flat, broad snout, elongated body, bronze to olive green back, marked with cream spots and bars. Can grow to over 4 ft and 50 pounds.

**JAWS**
The pike has a complex bone structure and is well equipped with teeth pointing backwards for seizing and holding prey.

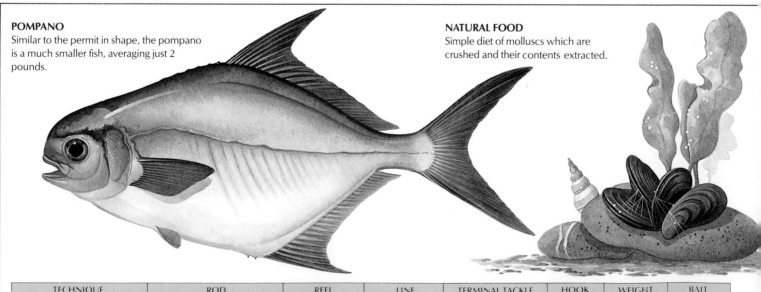

**POMPANO**
Similar to the permit in shape, the pompano is a much smaller fish, averaging just 2 pounds.

**NATURAL FOOD**
Simple diet of molluscs which are crushed and their contents extracted.

| TECHNIQUE | ROD | REEL | LINE | TERMINAL TACKLE | HOOK | WEIGHT | BAIT |
|---|---|---|---|---|---|---|---|
| Spinning | Medium spinning rod | Fixed spool | 10-pound nylon | Nylon trace | Size 8 treble | Light spinning/ bomb-shaped | Small spinner |
| Bait fishing | Medium spinning rod | Fixed spool | 10-pound nylon | Nylon trace | Size 2 eyed | | Fish strip |

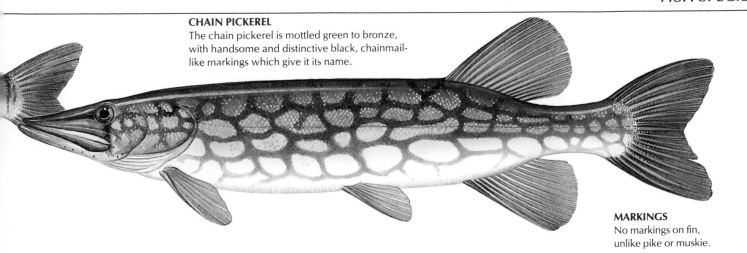

**CHAIN PICKEREL**
The chain pickerel is mottled green to bronze, with handsome and distinctive black, chainmail-like markings which give it its name.

**MARKINGS**
No markings on fin, unlike pike or muskie.

| TECHNIQUE | ROD | REEL | LINE | TERMINAL TACKLE | HOOK | WEIGHT | BAIT |
|---|---|---|---|---|---|---|---|
| Popping surface lures through weedbeds | 5½-foot baitcaster | Multiplier | 6 to 8-pounds | Short wire trace | | | Small spinners buzz baits |
| Casting beside reedy shorelines | 6 to 7-foot action spinning | Fixed spool | 6-pounds | Short wire trace | | | Bar spoons, etc |

| TECHNIQUE | ROD | REEL | LINE | TERMINAL TACKLE | HOOK | WEIGHT | BAIT |
|---|---|---|---|---|---|---|---|
| Livebaiting with small fish | 10 to 12-foot test curve pike or carp | Fixed spool | 10 to 12 | Sliding float below bead and stop knot | Two 8 trebles on 20-in wire trace | 2 to 3 swan shots | 4 to 6-inch roach, dace, etc |
| Lure fishing from boat or bank | 7 to 9-foot 2-pound test curve medium-fast action spinning rod | Fixed spool | 10 to 12-pounds | 12-inch wire trace with snaplock swivel | | | plugs, spoons |

# POMPANOS

**AFRICAN POMPANO**
A beautiful fish characterized by long wispy fin rays. The first seven dorsal rays and the first five anal rays are elongate.

From an angling point of view, the two most important species of pompano are the common pompano *(Trachinotus carolinus)* and the African pompano *(Alectis ciliaris)*. The common pompano, a fish of the western Atlantic, has a bluish-silvery back and silvery sides and is similar in shape to the permit *(Trachinotus falcatus)*. However, the pompano has more soft rays in its dorsal and anal fins, and lacks the prominent second and third ribs of the permit. It is also much smaller than the per-mit, averaging about 2 pounds with a maximum of around 8 pounds.

The African pompano is found in the warmer waters of both sides of the Atlantic. Its back is bluish green, fading to silver-white on the sides and belly. Juveniles, and some adults, have a series of dark, vertical bars on the flanks, and some also have a dark blotch on the gill plate and on the front of the dorsal and anal fins. Young fish have almost diamond-shaped bodies, and elongated, thread-like rays extending from the front of the dorsal fin. These rays can be three or four times the length of the immature fish, but as the fish matures the rays become shorter, while the body shape itself changes. The adult fish have very jack-like bodies and high, blunt foreheads, and grow to a maximum weight of over 40 pounds.

# PUMPKINSEED *Lepomis gibbosus*

Many consider the pumpkinseed to be the prettiest of all the North American panfish. This little fish, which grows to about 9 inches at most, is olive green overall with flecks and spots of yellow and blue, and bright blue lines running from the mouth to the edges of the gill plates. There's a red-tipped black spot on the upper corner of each gill plate, and the more brightly-coloured males have distinctly red breasts.

The pumpkinseed spawns from May to late July or early August, the eggs being laid in hollows scooped out of sand or gravel beds, and the male guards the nest until several days after the fry have hatched. The growth rate is slow, and most rod-caught fish are only a few inches long, but the pumpkinseed is very popular with young anglers.

It prefers shallow water with plenty of cover, so it's seldom found far from the bank, and although it's relatively easy to catch it puts up a good fight for a fish of its size. It can be caught on wet flies during spring, on grubs in summer, and on worms all year round.

The pumpkinseed, also known as the common sunfish, is found from the Dakotas and Iowa through to the eastern seaboard, where its range extends south to Georgia.

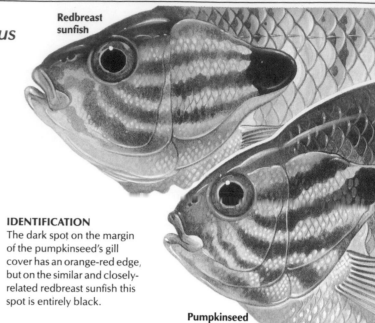

Redbreast sunfish

**IDENTIFICATION**
The dark spot on the margin of the pumpkinseed's gill cover has an orange-red edge, but on the similar and closely-related redbreast sunfish this spot is entirely black.

Pumpkinseed

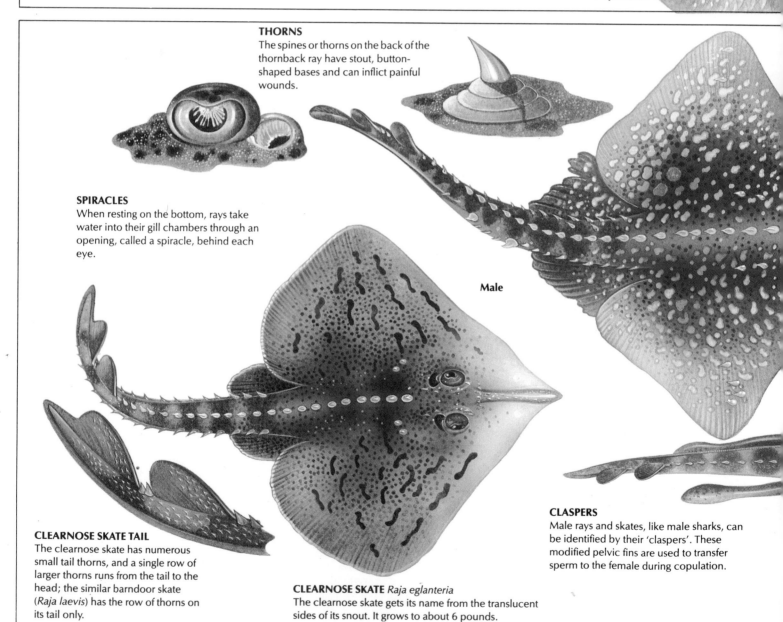

**THORNS**
The spines or thorns on the back of the thornback ray have stout, button-shaped bases and can inflict painful wounds.

**SPIRACLES**
When resting on the bottom, rays take water into their gill chambers through an opening, called a spiracle, behind each eye.

Male

**CLEARNOSE SKATE TAIL**
The clearnose skate has numerous small tail thorns, and a single row of larger thorns runs from the tail to the head; the similar barndoor skate (*Raja laevis*) has the row of thorns on its tail only.

**CLEARNOSE SKATE** *Raja eglanteria*
The clearnose skate gets its name from the translucent sides of its snout. It grows to about 6 pounds.

**CLASPERS**
Male rays and skates, like male sharks, can be identified by their 'claspers'. These modified pelvic fins are used to transfer sperm to the female during copulation.

| TECHNIQUE | ROD | REEL | LINE | TERMINAL TACKLE | HOOK | WEIGHT | BAIT |
|---|---|---|---|---|---|---|---|
| Bottom fishing | Heavy beachcaster; 30 to 50-pound class boat rod | Multiplier 4/0 to 6/0 | 25/50-pounds | Heavy nylon trace or running ledger | Size 4/0 8/0 | Bomb/pyramid | Whole or cut fish or squid |

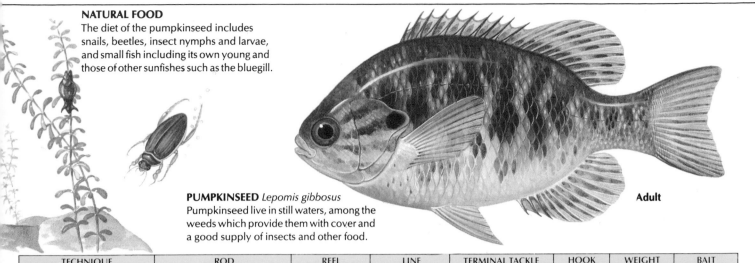

### NATURAL FOOD
The diet of the pumpkinseed includes snails, beetles, insect nymphs and larvae, and small fish including its own young and those of other sunfishes such as the bluegill.

**PUMPKINSEED** *Lepomis gibbosus*
Pumpkinseed live in still waters, among the weeds which provide them with cover and a good supply of insects and other food.

**Adult**

| TECHNIQUE | ROD | REEL | LINE | TERMINAL TACKLE | HOOK | WEIGHT | BAIT |
|-----------|-----|------|------|-----------------|------|--------|------|
| Float fishing along margins | 10-foot cane pole line tied direct | None | 2-pounds | small float | Sizes 10-14 | Shot 12-inch from hook | Worms, maggots |
| Jigging from boat, bridges, etc | 6-foot ultra light action spinning rod | Fixed spool | 2-pounds | Set well above jig | | | Tiny grub head jig |

### THORNBACK RAY *Raja clavata*
The thornback lives in depths of from 6 feet to 250 feet. Most of those caught weigh less than 15 pounds, but it can grow to over 40 pounds. Like all rays and skates, the thornback has powerful, flat teeth which grind up its food.

### EGG CASES
The eggs of skates and of the oviparous rays are each enclosed in a tough casing which is attached to rocks and weeds. The empty cases, known as 'mermaid's purses', are often washed up on beaches.

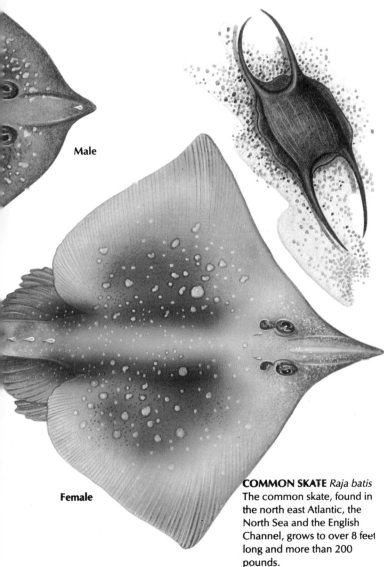

**Male**

**Female**

**COMMON SKATE** *Raja batis*
The common skate, found in the north east Atlantic, the North Sea and the English Channel, grows to over 8 feet long and more than 200 pounds.

# RAYS AND SKATES

The rays and skates are mostly bottom-dwelling fish species, although they do sometimes hunt in mid water. They are related to the sharks, and like them they have cartilaginous rather than bony skeletons. Their bodies are flattened, and the broad pectoral fins or 'wings' give them their characteristic diamond or circular shapes.

Their tails are long and thin, and while rays lack both caudal and anal fins, skates have small but noticeable caudal fins. Most rays, however, have at least one spine or barb near or at the base of the tail. These spines can inflict painful injuries, and in many species of ray they are also poisonous. Another general difference between skates and rays is that rays have smooth skins, while the skin of most skates carries small barbs or thorns.

As with sharks, the eggs of skates and rays are fertilized within the bodies of the females. All skates are oviparous, laying their eggs to hatch in the sea. Some rays, such as the thornback ray *(Raja clavata)* of the eastern Atlantic, are oviparous, but most are oviviparous, that is, the eggs develop and hatch within the mother and the young are born alive.

The thornback is the commonest ray in the shallow waters of the North Sea, the English Channel and the eastern Atlantic, and also occurs in the Mediterranean and the western Baltic. It gets its name from the rows of sharp spines on its back and tail – usually a long row running from the back of the head to the tip of the tail, with a smaller row on either side of it plus others on the tail and sometimes on the wings and snout. These spines are not poisonous, like those of the stingrays, but they are bacteria-ridden and so any wound they inflict on the unwary angler can become infected.

Most thornbacks are taken by boat anglers, usually in waters of less than 30 feet, but during the summer months many come close inshore and are taken by anglers fishing from the beach or rocks.

Rays and skates range in size from comparatively small fish such as the Atlantic guitarfish *(Rhinobatos lentiginosus)* and the clearnose skate *(Raja eglanteria)* which are normally under 2½ feet long and weigh only a few pounds, to the Atlantic common skate *(Raja (Dipturus) batis)* which can top 400 pounds and the manta *(Manta birostris)* of the tropical western Atlantic which grows to about 2 tons. These huge rays, over 20 feet long and almost as wide, feed and bask at or near the surface, and are strong enough to overturn a small boat with a flip of wing. The Pacific manta *(Manta hamiltoni)* is a few feet smaller and about half the weight.

Rays and skates feed mostly on molluscs, crustaceans, fish, squid and worms. Despite their ugly appearance and general lack of true fighting ability, they are popular with many anglers because they often feed when other fish are noticeable by their absence.

# ROACH *Rutilus rutilus*

The roach may only be modest in size, but it's the most commonly-sought of all British and European freshwater fish. Roach attain a maximum weight of 4 to 5 pounds and a length of about 18 inches, but anything over 2 pounds is considered a noteworthy catch.

In cross-section the roach is oval, the adult fish being particularly humpbacked and deep-bodied, but shape varies from one environment to another. Roach in small rivers tend to be more streamlined, while those living in deep, rich reservoirs are always very deep-bodied.

The colour along the back varies from grey to blue or green, with bright, silvery flanks and a clearly-defined lateral line. Winter roach have a bluish tint to their scales, while in summer they take on a more brassy look. The belly is always a creamy white.

Roach are abundant shoal fish, often shoaling in numbers of several hundred, and are found in every type of water from tiny streams to the tidal reaches of major rivers. They also thrive in still water, and are to be found in lakes, reservoirs and village ponds everywhere. They often shoal with other species, such as rudd and bream, and when they gather in late spring or early summer to spawn this often results in roach/rudd and roach/bream hybrids.

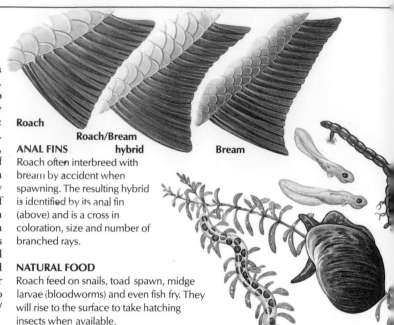

Roach

Roach/Bream

**ANAL FINS** hybrid

Bream

Roach often interbreed with bream by accident when spawning. The resulting hybrid is identified by its anal fin (above) and is a cross in coloration, size and number of branched rays.

**NATURAL FOOD**
Roach feed on snails, toad spawn, midge larvae (bloodworms) and even fish fry. They will rise to the surface to take hatching insects when available.

# RUDD *Scardinius erythrophthalmus*

The rudd is the prettiest of all British and European shoaling freshwater species. This gentle fish has a rather slim, oval cross-section and a small, neat head with a protruding jaw.

The back is medium olive, shading into beautifully-scaled flanks of bright, golden, buttery yellow with a sheen quite unlike that of any other freshwater species, and along the belly the colour changes to a more creamy yellow. The fins are rather pert and of a brilliant orange-red colour, and the tail is forked.

Rudd are sometimes confused with roach, with which they often hybridize. The points to look for are the richer colour and protruding lower jaw of the rudd, and the more rearward position of its dorsal fin. When the rudd's dorsal is folded flat along its back, it easily overlaps a point directly above the front edge of the anal fin, whereas the roach's does not.

Rudd feed on shrimps and nymphs in the bottom detritus or among weeds and reed stems, but in summer they can be seen at the surface, feeding on the rising pupae and the emerging flies.

Rudd are found mainly in still waters, but also thrive in slow-flowing rivers. They usually stay close to underwater vegetation, and they spawn in soft weeds or among rush or reed stems in warm shallows in late spring.

**NATURAL FOOD**
The rudd has a sharply upturned mouth, ideal for surface feeding. Rudd will take mayflies and damselflies from the surface as well as diving beetles and aquatic animals. In winter, or when insect activity is low, rudd feed on the bottom.

**OLD RUDD**
Old, large rudd are a rich bronze and become very deep-bodied.

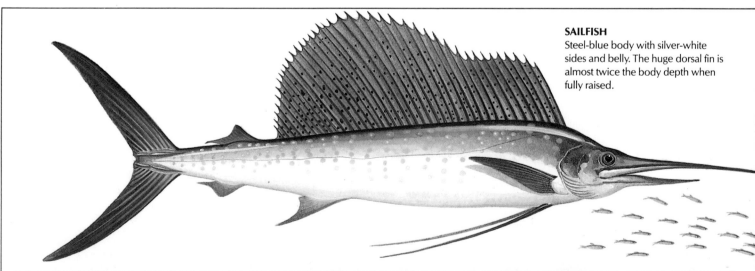

**SAILFISH**
Steel-blue body with silver-white sides and belly. The huge dorsal fin is almost twice the body depth when fully raised.

| TECHNIQUE | ROD | REEL | LINE | TERMINAL TACKLE | HOOK | WEIGHT | BAIT |
|---|---|---|---|---|---|---|---|
| Trolling | 20, 30, 50-pound class boat rod | 20, 30, 50 lever drag multiplier | 20, 30 50-pound nylon/Dacron | Heavy nylon/wire trace | 8/0 flat-forged eye | | Small Kona Head |
| Fly fishing | Heavy fly rod | salt water fly reel | Weight forward 10 | 20-pound fly leader | 2/0 | | Streamer fly |

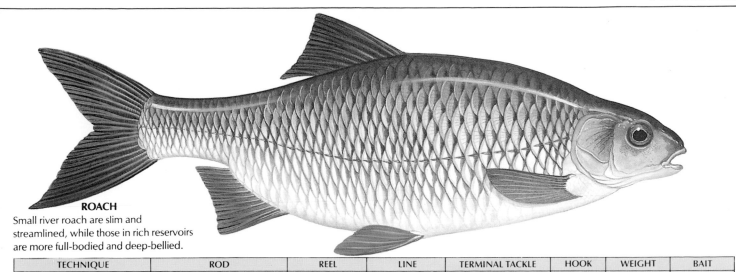

## ROACH

Small river roach are slim and
streamlined, while those in rich reservoirs
are more full-bodied and deep-bellied.

| TECHNIQUE | ROD | REEL | LINE | TERMINAL TACKLE | HOOK | WEIGHT | BAIT |
|---|---|---|---|---|---|---|---|
| Trotting in slow-flowing rivers with bait tripping bottom | 12 to 14-foot match/float light tip action | Centrepin, fixed spool, closed face | 2½-pound | Waggler/stick float | Sizes 14-20 | 4 no. 6 to 4BB | Casters, tares maggots |
| Quivertip ledgering in rivers watch tip for delicate bites | 10 to 11-foot ledger with screw in quiver to built in quivertip | Fixed spool | 2½-pounds | Fixed link or block end swimfeeder | Sizes 10-12 | Swan shot link | Casters, bread-flake, maggots |

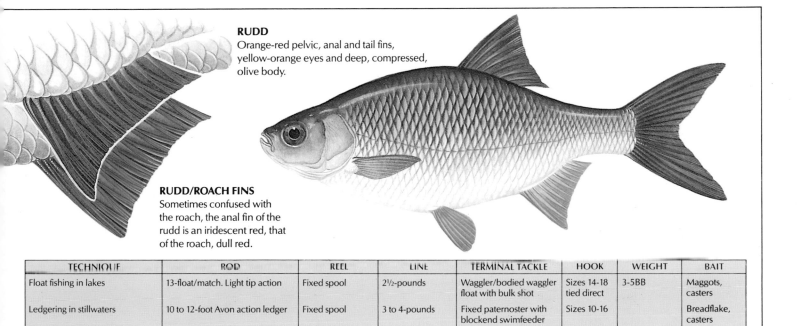

## RUDD

Orange-red pelvic, anal and tail fins,
yellow-orange eyes and deep, compressed,
olive body.

### RUDD/ROACH FINS

Sometimes confused with
the roach, the anal fin of the
rudd is an iridescent red, that
of the roach, dull red.

| TECHNIQUE | ROD | REEL | LINE | TERMINAL TACKLE | HOOK | WEIGHT | BAIT |
|---|---|---|---|---|---|---|---|
| Float fishing in lakes | 13-float/match. Light tip action | Fixed spool | 2½-pounds | Waggler/bodied waggler float with bulk shot | Sizes 14-18 tied direct | 3-5BB | Maggots, casters |
| Ledgering in stillwaters | 10 to 12-foot Avon action ledger | Fixed spool | 3 to 4-pounds | Fixed paternoster with blockend swimfeeder | Sizes 10-16 | | Breadflake, casters |

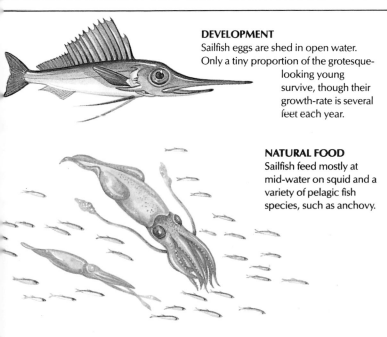

### DEVELOPMENT

Sailfish eggs are shed in open water.
Only a tiny proportion of the grotesque-
looking young
survive, though their
growth-rate is several
feet each year.

### NATURAL FOOD

Sailfish feed mostly at
mid-water on squid and a
variety of pelagic fish
species, such as anchovy.

# SAILFISH *Istiophorus platyperus*

Although both the Atlantic and the Pacific sailfishes are considered to be a single species, the Pacific sailfish grows to over twice the size of the Atlantic fish. As a result, the IGFA lists them separately for record purposes. Commercially-caught Pacific sailfish of 275 pounds have been recorded, but rod-caught fish are smaller.

The outstanding feature of the sailfish is its huge dorsal fin, which when fully raised may be more than twice the body depth of the fish. This fin is normally a beautiful cobalt blue, with a sprinkling of black spots, while the body is steel blue on the back with silver-white sides and belly.

There is usually a series of vertical rows of pale spots along the sides, which tend to fade after the fish dies. The upper jaw is elongated into a long, slender spear, and the tail is symmetrical and deeply forked; the pectoral fins are longer than those of any other billfish.

Sailfish tend to travel in small, loose schools, feeding on squid and a wide variety of fish. They feed mostly at mid water, but on occasions when the baitfish shoals move to the surface, a school of feeding sailfish is a spectacular sight. Once hooked, on live or dead fishbaits, sailfish put up a dramatic, acrobatic fight which makes them very popular with light tackle anglers.

# SALMON

The various species and subspecies of salmon are the most highly-regarded of all the fish that can be caught in fresh water, both for their angling value and for their flesh. The Atlantic salmon *(Salmo salar)*, for instance, can be guaranteed to put up a strong and often spectacular fight when hooked, and its flesh can be cooked or smoked to provide one of the finest of foods.

Although hatched in fresh water, the Atlantic salmon spends most of its life at sea, returning to fresh water only to spawn. In the sea, the salmon travel widely, and many make transatlantic migrations to feeding grounds off Greenland or in the Norwegian Sea.

Unfortunately, many of these isolated feeding grounds have been discovered and over-exploited by commercial fishing interests, and this has resulted in a marked decline in stocks throughout the known range of the Atlantic salmon.

Atlantic salmon normally return to their parent river after about 3 or 4 years at sea, although some return sooner. They often die after spawning, but many survive to make two or more spawning runs.

The Atlantic salmon spawn far upriver in November and January, the eggs being deposited in a redd, a nest scooped out in the gravel by the hen fish. Once buried in the gravel, the eggs remain in place until they hatch in late April or early May. The fry remain in the gravel for 3 to 5 weeks, until they're free of their egg sacs, and begin to feed actively as soon as they emerge.

At this stage, the small fish (or parr, as they are called) swim and feed in shoals, but as they grow they spread out along the length of the river. After some 3 to 5 years in the river, the parr, now about 6 inches long, lose their mottled colours and become silvery, ready for their journey to the sea.

In the sea, mature Atlantic salmon are normally green-blue on the back, with silvery white sides and underparts. This colouring changes as the fish approach the spawning stage, when they become brown or bronze with spots of red and black, and the fins darken. After spawning, many salmon die, but the few weak and emaciated survivors, known as kelts, slowly make their way downstream to the sea.

Although adult salmon are believed not to feed while they are in fresh water, they will nonetheless attack a fly, spinner, plug, prawn or bunch of earthworms, possibly out of bad temper.

The Pacific salmon *(Onchorhynchus* spp), unlike their Atlantic cousins, all die after spawning. However, apart from this rather tragic wipeout of the parent fish, the life cycle of most of the species is comparable to that of the Atlantic salmon.

There are six species of Pacific salmon, one of which – the cherry salmon *(Onchorhynchus masou)* – is found only in Asian waters. Of the others, the chum salmon *(O. keta)* is occasionally encountered by anglers but mostly caught by commercial netting. This fish is commonest off Alaksa.

The king salmon *(O. tshawytscha)*, also called the chinook, is the largest of the Pacific salmon. The biggest recorded – a commercially-caught fish – weighed in at a staggering 126 pounds, but most rod-caught chinook are less than 20 pounds.

The other Pacific salmon species are the coho salmon *(O. kisutch)*, the pink salmon *(O. gorbuscha)* and the sockeye salmon *(O. nerka)*. A small, landlocked form of sockeye, the kokanee, was once found only in lakes from Oregon to Alaska, but has been introduced into lakes and reservoirs in many parts of the USA.

There is also a landlocked form of Atlantic salmon, found originally in New England and the Maritime Provinces of Canada but since introduced into other areas, is known as the landlocked salmon in the USA and as the ouananiche in Canada.

In Europe, there is a landlocked relative of the Atlantic salmon known as the huchen *(Hucho hucho)*. The huchen, which originated in the Danube Basin, has been successfully introduced into rivers in eastern France. There was also an unsuccessful attempt to introduce it into the River Thames.

This huge fish, which is usually confined to the upper reaches of its resident river system, can attain a weight of over 45 pounds. The huchen has a greeny-blue back, silvery sides and white underparts, and the sides have a subtle pink sheen and delicate, X-shaped markings.

A voracious feeder, the predatory huchen is normally caught on spinners or wobbled deadbaits. Unfortunately, in many areas the huchen has been severely overfished, but efforts are being made to replenish stocks.

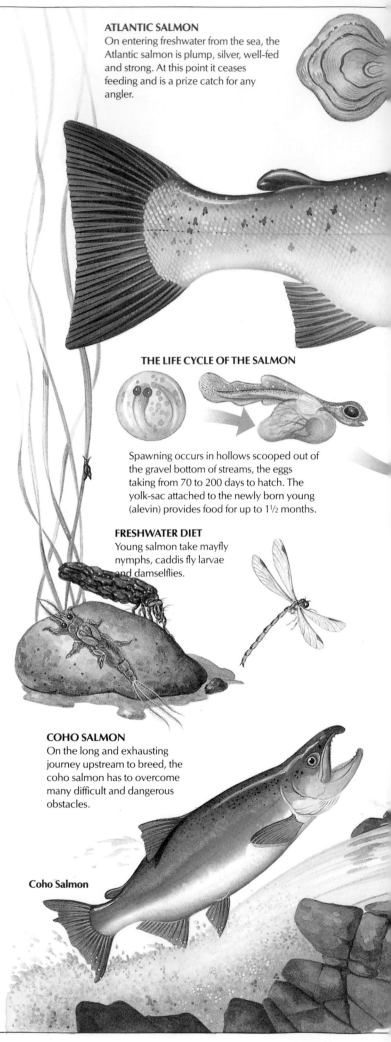

**ATLANTIC SALMON**
On entering freshwater from the sea, the Atlantic salmon is plump, silver, well-fed and strong. At this point it ceases feeding and is a prize catch for any angler.

**THE LIFE CYCLE OF THE SALMON**

Spawning occurs in hollows scooped out of the gravel bottom of streams, the eggs taking from 70 to 200 days to hatch. The yolk-sac attached to the newly born young (alevin) provides food for up to 1½ months.

**FRESHWATER DIET**
Young salmon take mayfly nymphs, caddis fly larvae and damselflies.

**COHO SALMON**
On the long and exhausting journey upstream to breed, the coho salmon has to overcome many difficult and dangerous obstacles.

Coho Salmon

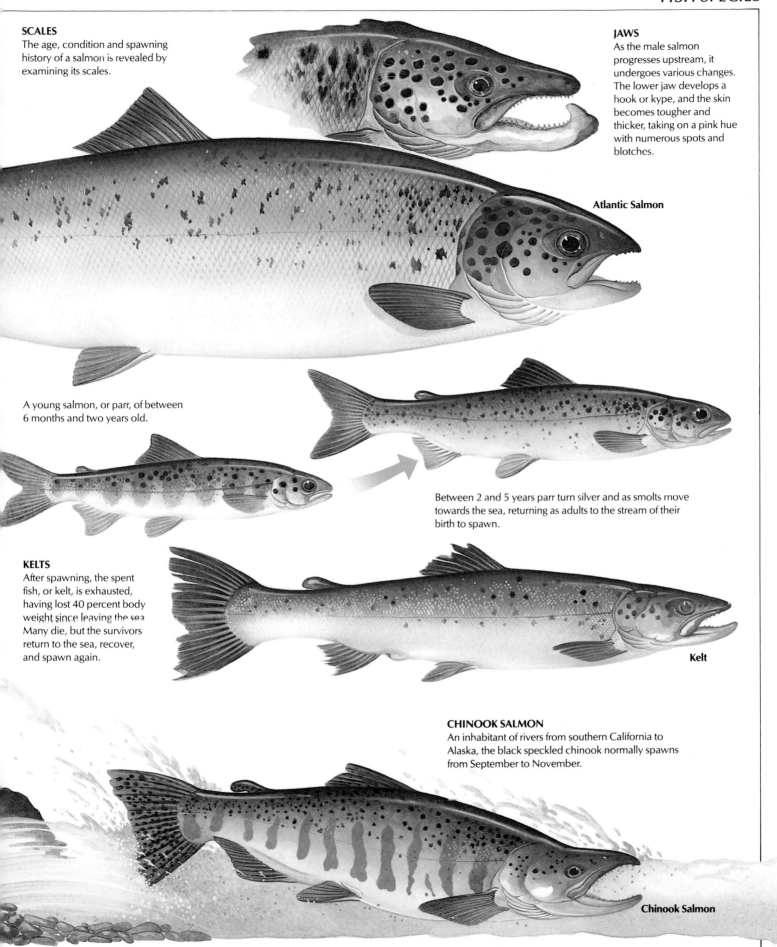

**SCALES**

The age, condition and spawning history of a salmon is revealed by examining its scales.

**JAWS**

As the male salmon progresses upstream, it undergoes various changes. The lower jaw develops a hook or kype, and the skin becomes tougher and thicker, taking on a pink hue with numerous spots and blotches.

**Atlantic Salmon**

A young salmon, or parr, of between 6 months and two years old.

Between 2 and 5 years parr turn silver and as smolts move towards the sea, returning as adults to the stream of their birth to spawn.

**KELTS**

After spawning, the spent fish, or kelt, is exhausted, having lost 40 percent body weight since leaving the sea. Many die, but the survivors return to the sea, recover, and spawn again.

**Kelt**

**CHINOOK SALMON**

An inhabitant of rivers from southern California to Alaska, the black speckled chinook normally spawns from September to November.

**Chinook Salmon**

| TECHNIQUE | ROD | REEL | LINE | TERMINAL TACKLE | HOOK | WEIGHT | BAIT |
|---|---|---|---|---|---|---|---|
| Fly fishing | 12 to 16-foot rod | Fly reel | Fly line Weight forward | Heavy fly cast | Single or double | None | Salmon flies |
| Spinning | 10-foot heavy spinning rod | Multiplier | 20-pound nylon | 15 to 20-pound nylon | Trebles | Wye lead | Plugs, Toby |
| Bait fishing | | multiplier | 20-pound nylon | 15 to 20-pound nylon | Size 1 eyed | Bullet lead | Worms |

# SHADS

The shads are a group of marine fishes, related to the herring, which migrate into rivers to spawn. In Europe, the numbers of the once-plentiful twaite shad *(Alosa fallax)* and allis shad *(Alosa alosa)* have been greatly reduced by pollution and the destruction of spawning grounds.

Shads have fared better in North American waters, where the American shad *(A. sapidissima)* and, to a lesser extent, the hickory shad *(A. mediocris)* and the skipjack herring *(A. chrysochloris)* are of interest to anglers.

The American shad was originally found only in Atlantic waters and associated rivers from the Gulf of St Lawrence to the Florida Keys, but in 1871 it was introduced, with great success, to the California coast. Since then, its range has extended as far north as Alaska. In Atlantic waters, the shad can attain a weight of about 12 pounds, and those in the Pacific tend to grow even larger.

Most shads are caught when they come into the rivers to spawn, normally in March and April. The males mature about 3 or 4 years after hatching, but females may take twice this time.

American shad are a popular sporting fish, taken by trolling or spinning with small spoons, spinners or jigs, or by fly fishing with streamer flies.

**EUROPEAN SHAD**
The twaite and allis shad are so closely matched that the only distinct feature separating the two species is that the twaite shad has six to eight blotches on the dorsal area, whereas the allis shad has just a single dark blotch.

**NATURAL FOOD**
In freshwater, younger shad feed on a simple diet of small organisms such as cyclops, water fleas and rotifers. At sea, opossum shrimps form part of their diet.

# SHARKS

The sharks, of which there are over 250 species, are an ancient group of fishes whose skeletons are composed of cartilage rather than bone. They do, how-ever, have bony teeth, and their tiny scales are formed from a similar material.

Sharks are commonly thought of as ruthless predators, and while many are – the white shark *(Carcharodon carcharias)*, for instance – others such as the 50-foot basking shark *(Cetorhinus maximus)* and the 70-foot whale shark *(Rhincodon typus)* are harmless plankton-eaters.

Like those of their relatives the rays and skates, the eggs of sharks are fertilized within the bodies of the females. Some species are oviparous, laying their eggs to hatch in the sea, but most are oviviparous – the eggs hatch within the mother, and the young are born alive.

One of the most commonly caught sharks is the blue shark *(Prionace glauca)*, which is distributed worldwide and can reach a weight of more than 450 pounds. The mako *(Isurus oxyrhincus)* is also a very popular game fish, and one which puts up a good fight when hooked. Other sporting sharks include the great hammerhead *(Sphyrna mokarran)*, the porbeagle *(Lamna nasus)*, the thresher *(Alopias vulpinas)*, the tiger shark *(Galeocerda cuvieri)*.

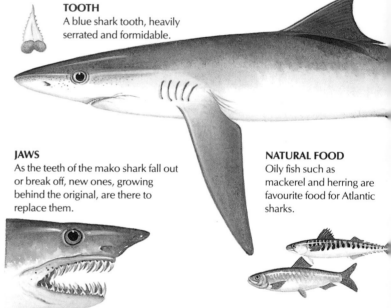

**TOOTH**
A blue shark tooth, heavily serrated and formidable.

**JAWS**
As the teeth of the mako shark fall out or break off, new ones, growing behind the original, are there to replace them.

**NATURAL FOOD**
Oily fish such as mackerel and herring are favourite food for Atlantic sharks.

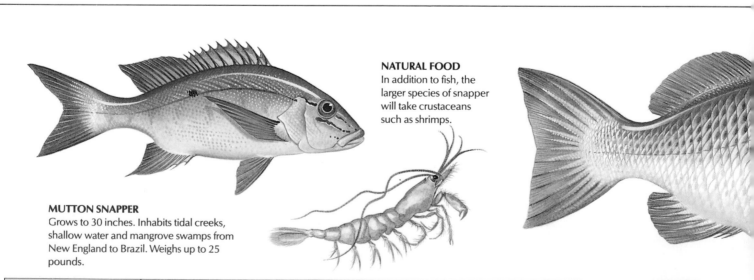

**NATURAL FOOD**
In addition to fish, the larger species of snapper will take crustaceans such as shrimps.

**MUTTON SNAPPER**
Grows to 30 inches. Inhabits tidal creeks, shallow water and mangrove swamps from New England to Brazil. Weighs up to 25 pounds.

| TECHNIQUE | ROD | REEL | LINE | TERMINAL TACKLE | HOOK | WEIGHT | BAIT |
|---|---|---|---|---|---|---|---|
| Plug fishing | Heavy duty spinning rod | Small multiplier | 15/20-pound nylon | Wire/heavy nylon trace | 2/0 treble | | Plugs |
| Bottom fishing | Heavy duty spinning rod | Medium fixed spool | 15/20-pound | Wire/heavy nylon trace | 2/0 eyed | Bomb/pyramid | Live/dead bait |

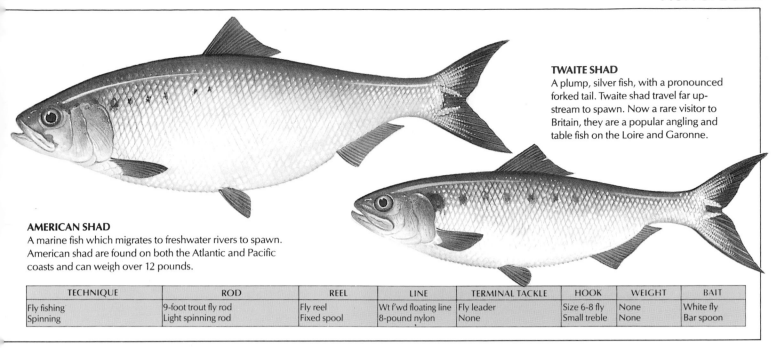

**TWAITE SHAD**
A plump, silver fish, with a pronounced forked tail. Twaite shad travel far upstream to spawn. Now a rare visitor to Britain, they are a popular angling and table fish on the Loire and Garonne.

**AMERICAN SHAD**
A marine fish which migrates to freshwater rivers to spawn. American shad are found on both the Atlantic and Pacific coasts and can weigh over 12 pounds.

| TECHNIQUE | ROD | REEL | LINE | TERMINAL TACKLE | HOOK | WEIGHT | BAIT |
|---|---|---|---|---|---|---|---|
| Fly fishing | 9-foot trout fly rod | Fly reel | Wt f'wd floating line | Fly leader | Size 6-8 fly | None | White fly |
| Spinning | Light spinning rod | Fixed spool | 8-pound nylon | None | Small treble | None | Bar spoon |

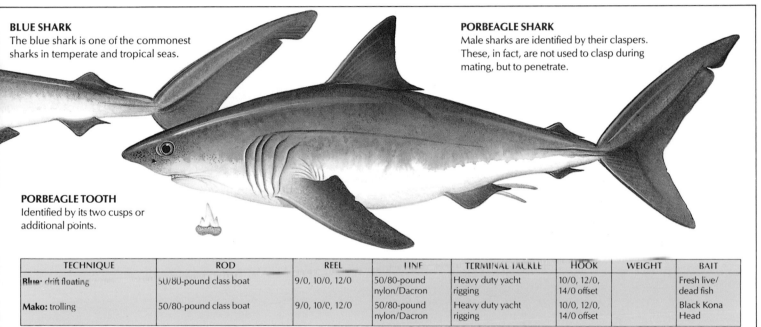

**BLUE SHARK**
The blue shark is one of the commonest sharks in temperate and tropical seas.

**PORBEAGLE SHARK**
Male sharks are identified by their claspers. These, in fact, are not used to clasp during mating, but to penetrate.

**PORBEAGLE TOOTH**
Identified by its two cusps or additional points.

| TECHNIQUE | ROD | REEL | LINE | TERMINAL TACKLE | HOOK | WEIGHT | BAIT |
|---|---|---|---|---|---|---|---|
| **Blue:** drift floating | 50/80-pound class boat | 9/0, 10/0, 12/0 | 50/80-pound nylon/Dacron | Heavy duty yacht rigging | 10/0, 12/0, 14/0 offset | | Fresh live/ dead fish |
| **Mako:** trolling | 50/80-pound class boat | 9/0, 10/0, 12/0 | 50/80-pound nylon/Dacron | Heavy duty yacht rigging | 10/0, 12/0, 14/0 offset | | Black Kona Head |

# SNAPPERS

The snapper family includes such fish as the mutton snapper *(Lutjanus analis)*, red snapper *(L. blackfordi)*, dog snapper *(L. jocu)*, gray snapper *(L. griseus)*, lane snapper *(L. synagris)*, blackfin snapper *(L. buccanella)*, mahogany snapper *(L. mahogani)*, the yellowtail snapper *(Ocyurus chrysurus)* and the cubera snapper *(L. cyanopterus)*, which is the largest of them all.

The cubera snapper can reach a weight of over 100 pounds, and like most snappers it occurs in the tropical western Atlantic. In colour, the cubera snapper is green to grey, with dark red eyes and sometimes a reddish tinge to the flanks. The cubera is a shallow-water species found close to submerged reefs and rock ledges at depths of from a few feet to a maximum of about 120 feet, and small specimens are also to be found in estuaries and salt lakes.

The cubera is a good sports fish which readily takes live or dead natural baits and will also attack artificial lures, in particular plug baits trolled close to the bottom.

Small cubera snappers have tasty flesh, but they aren't as commercially important as the gray snapper and the very popular red snapper. Gray snapper can be taken on a light tackle with live shrimp bait, but red snapper are usually taken with deadbaits on heavier tackle.

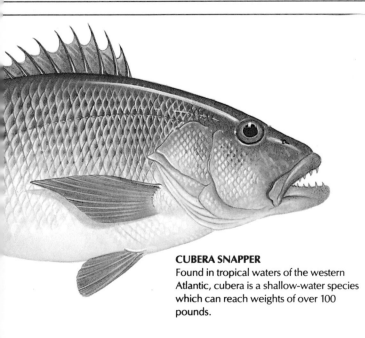

**CUBERA SNAPPER**
Found in tropical waters of the western Atlantic, cubera is a shallow-water species which can reach weights of over 100 pounds.

# SNOOK *Centropomus undecimalis*

The snook is a popular salt-water game fish found along the coasts of Florida and Texas and throughout the West Indies, and in the tropical Pacific. Its most noticeable feature is the thick, black lateral line which runs from behind the shoulder to the very end of the tail, quite unlike that of any other fish.

The back is goldish brown to brown or dark grey, lightening quickly to silvery sides and a white belly. The head is very flat with a strongly-protruding lower jaw, and the snook has no teeth as such, just strong, sharp bristles along the jaw rims and on the tongue; the edges of the gill covers are very sharp.

The snook spends most of its time in shallow coastal waters, often venturing into estuaries, creeks, lagoons and mangrove swamps, and sometimes travelling well inland along rivers or canals into almost completely fresh water, a habit it shares with the tarpon.

The snook's diet consists of shrimp, small crabs and fish. It can be taken on artificial lures, but live bait, especially mullet, is one of the best ways to tempt a large snook; it should be set to fish shallow beneath a float. Most rod-caught snook are of 5 to 8 pounds, rising to 12 to 25 pounds in some areas, and the top weight is around 50 pounds.

## NATURAL FOOD
Snook are a predatory species feeding on many types of fish, and they also take shrimps and small crabs, which make up an important part of their diet.

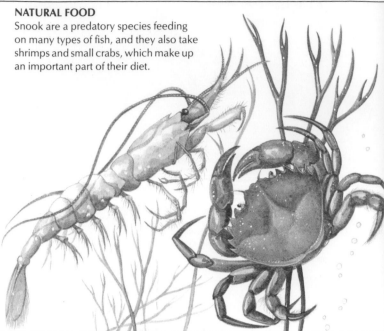

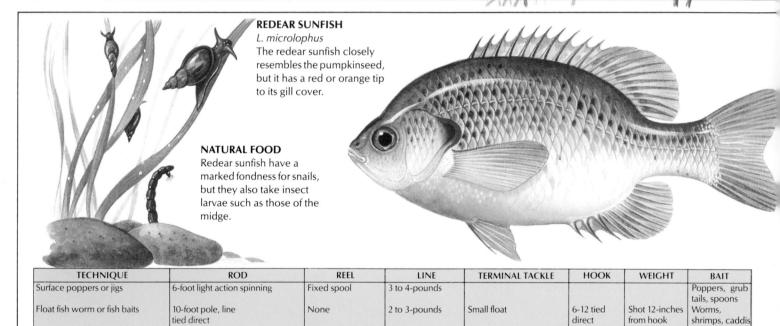

## REDEAR SUNFISH
*L. microlophus*
The redear sunfish closely resembles the pumpkinseed, but it has a red or orange tip to its gill cover.

## NATURAL FOOD
Redear sunfish have a marked fondness for snails, but they also take insect larvae such as those of the midge.

| TECHNIQUE | ROD | REEL | LINE | TERMINAL TACKLE | HOOK | WEIGHT | BAIT |
|---|---|---|---|---|---|---|---|
| Surface poppers or jigs | 6-foot light action spinning | Fixed spool | 3 to 4-pounds | | | | Poppers, grub tails, spoons |
| Float fish worm or fish baits | 10-foot pole, line tied direct | None | 2 to 3-pounds | Small float | 6-12 tied direct | Shot 12-inches from hook | Worms, shrimps, caddis grubs |

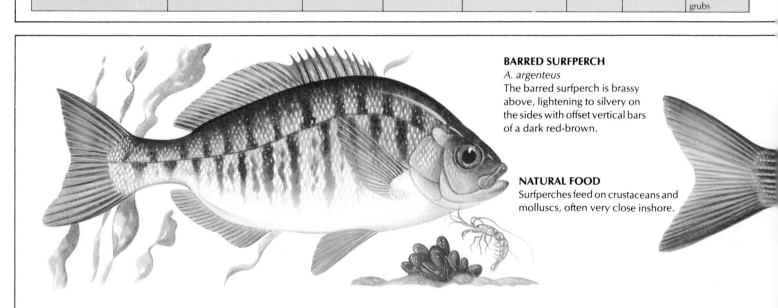

## BARRED SURFPERCH
*A. argenteus*
The barred surfperch is brassy above, lightening to silvery on the sides with offset vertical bars of a dark red-brown.

## NATURAL FOOD
Surfperches feed on crustaceans and molluscs, often very close inshore.

| TECHNIQUE | ROD | REEL | LINE | TERMINAL TACKLE | HOOK | WEIGHT | BAIT |
|---|---|---|---|---|---|---|---|
| Light surf fishing | Surfcasting rod | Small multiplier | 10 to 15-pound | Short nylon trace | 1/0 eyed | Grip or bomb | Cut fish, crab |
| Bottom fishing | Spinning or 12-pound class boat | Small multiplier | 10 to 15-pound | Short nylon trace | 1/0 eyed | Grip or bomb | Cut fish, crab |

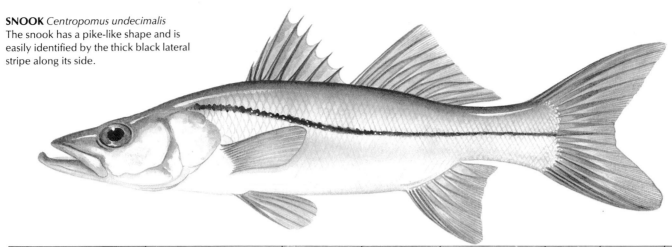

**SNOOK** *Centropomus undecimalis*
The snook has a pike-like shape and is easily identified by the thick black lateral stripe along its side.

| TECHNIQUE | ROD | REEL | LINE | TERMINAL TACKLE | HOOK | WEIGHT | BAIT |
|---|---|---|---|---|---|---|---|
| Lure fishing | 6-foot surfcaster | Multiplier/fixed spool | 10 to 12-pounds | | | | Plugs, spoons |
| Fly fishing | 9-foot fast tip action fly WF 8-9 | Single action fly | Bass taper floating | 12-pound cast | | | Streamers jigs |

**GREEN SUNFISH** *L. cyanellus*
Many species of sunfish are very similar in appearance. One of the distinguishing features of the green sunfish is its large mouth, which extends back to below the mid point of the eye, unlike the mouths of, say, the redear sunfish and the redbreast sunfish (*L. auritis*).

# SUNFISH

The sunfish are a family of over thirty North American freshwater species, including many of the fish most popular with American anglers such as bluegill, crappies, pumpkinseed and the highly-prized largemouth and smallmouth basses. Other commonly caught sunfish are the green, redbreast and redear sunfishes and the rock bass.

The green sunfish (*Lepomis cyanellus*) averages 5 to 7 inches long, with a maximum of about 9 inches. An inhabitant of streams, rivers and lakes, its main range is from the Mississippi valley east to the Alleghanies, west to Colorado and New Mexico and north to the Great Lakes.

The redbreast sunfish (*Lepomis auritis*) is a handsome, red-breasted fish which reaches a length of about 12 inches, although most are between 6 and 8 inches, and is found in the rivers, and sometimes ponds and lakes, of the Atlantic drainage. The redear sunfish (*Lepomis microlophus*) is larger, and can grow to over 4 pounds.

The rock bass (*Ambloplites rupestris*) is a sturdy, olive-green fish which is found mainly in waters from Manitoba to New England and south to Texas, and reaches a maximum of about 12 inches long and a pound in weight.

# SURFPERCHES

**STRIPED SEAPERCH** *E. lateralis*
The striped seaperch is one of the most beautiful of the surfperches. It grows to a length of about 15 inches, and is found from California to Alaska.

Most of the 23 species of surfperch are found in shallow water along the Pacific coast of North America. The exceptions are the pink seaperch (*Zalembius rosaceus*) which lives in deep waters of about 100 to 300 feet, and the tule perch (*Hysterocarpus traski*), is a freshwater fish found in rivers and one lake (Clear Lake) in central California.

Many surfperches are commercially important, and also provide shore anglers with some of their sport in California and elsewhere along the Pacific coast. The most important species for anglers is the barred surfperch (*Amphistichus argenteus*), which reaches a maximum of over 4 pounds; as with all surfperches, the females give birth to live young.

Other surfperches of angling interest include the black perch (*Embiotoca jacksoni*), calico surfperch (*Amphistichus koelzi*), pile perch (*Rhacochilus vacca*), rainbow seaperch (*Hypsurus caryi*), redtail surfperch (*Amphistichus rhodoterus*), rubberlip seaperch (*Rhacochilus toxotes*), shiner perch (*Cymatogaster aggregata*), silver surfperch (*Hyperprosopon ellipticum*), spotfin surfperch (*Hyperprosopon anale*), striped seaperch (*Embiotica lateralis*), walleye surfperch (*Hyperprosopon argenteum*) and the white seaperch (*Phanerodon furcatus*).

# SWORDFISH *Xiphias gladius*

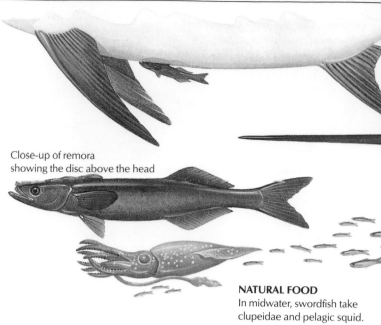

Close-up of remora
showing the disc above the head

The swordfish or broadbill rates as the ultimate challenge to big game anglers, and this great, leathery, prehistoric-looking fish can be one of the most difficult of all the mighty ocean predators to tempt into taking a bait.

A totally unmistakable fish, the swordfish has a smooth, flattened bill, longer and wider than that of any other billfish. It also has a high, non-retractable dorsal fin and a large single keel on each side of the base of the big, crescent-shaped tail. Adult swordfish lack scales, and their colouring varies a good deal. The back can be dark brown, bronze, grey-purple, blue or even black, but the belly and sides are usually a dirty white and the fins are dark. The eyes are large and dark blue.

Swordfish are distributed worldwide in temperate and warm waters, and are probably more common than many people realize. They are, however, rather solitary fish and are rarely seen in pairs, and are often found at extreme depths.

The swordfish has a very soft mouth, and many hooked fish are lost when the hooks tear out, but once hooked it puts up a strong, savage fight. Swordfish can be taken on slowly-trolled fish or squid bait, and fishing at night using squid in conjunction with a chemical light stick can be very successful.

**NATURAL FOOD**
In midwater, swordfish take clupeidae and pelagic squid.

# TARPON *Megalops atlantica*

**FIGHTING TARPON**
A ferocious fighter, the tarpon will leap clear of the water when hooked, making repeated attempts at escape.

The tarpon is thought by anyone fortunate enough to have landed one to be one of the most exciting sports fish in the world. They fight ferociously when hooked, hurling themselves as much as ten feet out of the water in an attempt to get free.

The distribution of tarpon covers many tropical and sub-tropical waters around the world, with the largest concentrations being in and around the Gulf of Mexico, the Florida Keys and Everglades, Surinam, Costa Rica and many of the Caribbean islands.

The tarpon is a deep-bodied fish, with compressed flanks and huge, tough scales. The back is a dark grey, often with a blue or green tinge, quickly turning to burnished silver along the flanks, and the belly is milky white. The fins are large and powerful, and the last ray of the dorsal is distinctively elongated.

Although tarpon are occasionally caught by offshore trolling, they are essentially a fish of estuaries and tidal creeks and channels. They love to explore mangrove swamps, lagoons and shallow rivers, which is where they spawn in the spring.

Tarpon can reach lengths of over 8 feet and weights of over 300 pounds, though most of those taken by anglers are in the 20 to 80 pound range.

**TENCH**
Deep-bodied, smoothly rounded fins, bronze-green back and golden-green sides.

**Adult male**

**GOLDEN TENCH**
An ornamental variety, found in private ponds and park lakes. More banana than gold, with a few black spots.

| TECHNIQUE | ROD | REEL | | LINE | TERMINAL TACKLE | HOOK | WEIGHT | BAIT |
|---|---|---|---|---|---|---|---|---|
| Float fishing, lift method | 12 to 13-foot medium action | Centrepin, fixed 2½ to 4-pounds spool | Peacock quill float fixed bottom end | | | | 1 AA shot | Breadflake, sweetcorn |
| Ledgering | 10 to 12-foot Avon 1¼-pounds test curve ledger | Fixed spool | | 6-pounds | Fixed paternoster with open-ended feeder | 10-14 on 4-pound link | Only on feeder | Maggots casters |

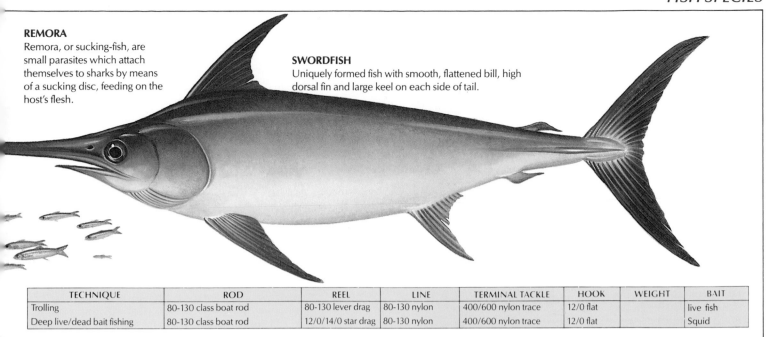

**REMORA**
Remora, or sucking-fish, are small parasites which attach themselves to sharks by means of a sucking disc, feeding on the host's flesh.

**SWORDFISH**
Uniquely formed fish with smooth, flattened bill, high dorsal fin and large keel on each side of tail.

| TECHNIQUE | ROD | REEL | LINE | TERMINAL TACKLE | HOOK | WEIGHT | BAIT |
|---|---|---|---|---|---|---|---|
| Trolling | 80-130 class boat rod | 80-130 lever drag | 80-130 nylon | 400/600 nylon trace | 12/0 flat | | live fish |
| Deep live/dead bait fishing | 80-130 class boat rod | 12/0/14/0 star drag | 80-130 nylon | 400/600 nylon trace | 12/0 flat | | Squid |

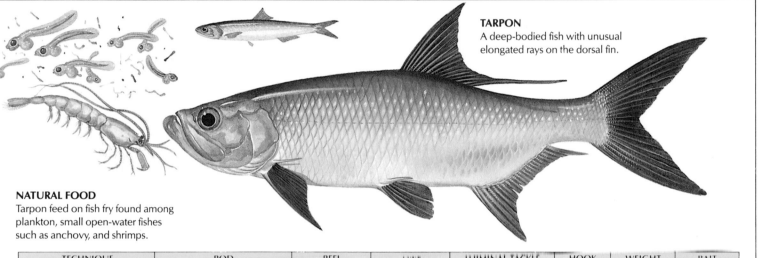

**TARPON**
A deep-bodied fish with unusual elongated rays on the dorsal fin.

**NATURAL FOOD**
Tarpon feed on fish fry found among plankton, small open-water fishes such as anchovy, and shrimps.

| TECHNIQUE | ROD | REEL | LINE | TERMINAL TACKLE | HOOK | WEIGHT | BAIT |
|---|---|---|---|---|---|---|---|
| Float fished live bait | 9 to 10-foot powerful spinning, 2½-pounds test curve | Fixed spool/ multiplier | 15/18-pounds | 20-inch wire trace slider float. Fish bait midwater | Single size 1/0 treble | Swan shot | 5-7-inch fish, crab |
| Fly casting | 9 to 10-foot powerful fast taper reservoir fly 9/10 | Large fly holding 200 yds | Bass taper floating size 9-10 | 12-inches 70-pounds mono | | | Bucktail streamer |

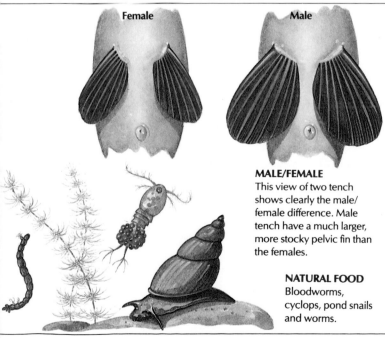

**Female**    **Male**

**MALE/FEMALE**
This view of two tench shows clearly the male/ female difference. Male tench have a much larger, more stocky pelvic fin than the females.

**NATURAL FOOD**
Bloodworms, cyclops, pond snails and worms.

# TENCH *Tinca tinca*

The tench is a popular European cyprinid, most commonly found browsing through thick vegetation in lakes, pits, reservoirs and lowland rivers. It has a thick-set body, bronze-green along the back and golden-green on the sides, sometimes more gold than green. There is even a rare variety called the golden tench, which is distinctly banana-coloured with a few black specks, and rather pointed, pink-tinted fins instead of the rounded, brown-grey fins of the common tench, with which it is unlikely to be confused.

The scales of the tench are tiny and set flat against the body, and covered in a thick layer of protective slime. The eyes are tiny and orange-red, and the mouth, which is semiprotrusible, has a tiny barbule at each corner and thick, rubbery lips.

The tench is found in Britain, Europe and much of Asia, and was introduced into many Irish waters in 1958. In Europe and Asia it's valued as a food fish, and commercially fished for and farmed. Its natural diet consists of bloodworms, annelid worms, crustaceans, small molluscs and algae, and it loves burying its snout in thick silt and weedbeds to feed. The tench can attain a length of 26 inches and a weight of over 12 pounds, but most good rod-caught fish weigh only 2½ to 6 pounds and growth rate is slow.

# TROUT

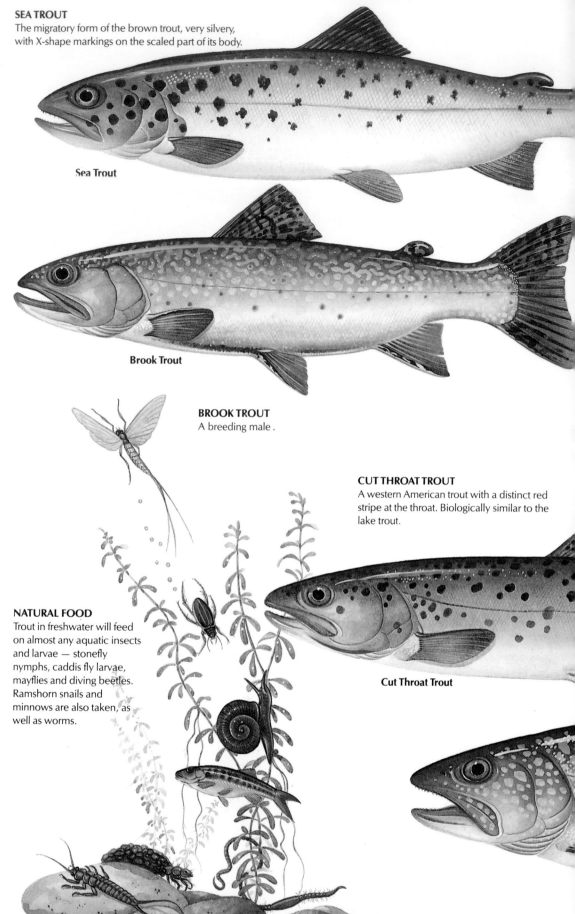

**O**f the many species of trout, the brown trout *(Salmo trutta)* and the rainbow trout *(Salmo gairdneri)* are probably the most widely known.

In shape, the brown trout is an elongated fish. The wrist of the tail is deep, and the upper and lower tail fin rays seem to flow into the outline of the body. The tail itself is broad and normally square-cut, although younger fish occasionally have a slightly concave tail outline which usually vanishes when the fish reaches maturity.

The colour of the brown trout varies considerably from one locality to another. In tiny, often acid, streams, they are mostly brownish in colour with a sprinkling of black and rust red spots. Fish from rich chalk waters are much brighter, having a golden brown back and buttercup yellow sides, and only rarely have red spots.

Brown trout that live in large lakes and reservoirs are different again, normally having an overall silver appearance and minimal spotting. The exception to this are the huge brown trout that live a cannibal existence in deep, peat-water lochs. These giants are dark gold in colour and the spots are very pronounced.

Brown trout spawn in winter, normally between October and January, the eggs being deposited in gravel redds dug by the females. The eggs hatch after 6 to 8 weeks, depending on the water temperature, and the fry remain in the gravel for a further 4 to 6 weeks before beginning to feed.

Like all trout, brown trout feed on insects and crustaceans, but the larger the fish grows the more predatory it becomes, until eventually it feeds almost exclusively on fish; cannibalism is common. Under the right circumstances, brown trout can reach a weight of over 30 pounds.

The sea trout is a migratory form of brown trout which leaves its parent river to spend much of its life in salt water, but returns to it to spawn. Sea trout normally grow faster than their non-migratory brethren, and when fresh-run they have a decidedly silver appearance.

The brown trout, a native European fish, was introduced

**SEA TROUT**
The migratory form of the brown trout, very silvery, with X-shape markings on the scaled part of its body.

Sea Trout

Brook Trout

**BROOK TROUT**
A breeding male .

**CUT THROAT TROUT**
A western American trout with a distinct red stripe at the throat. Biologically similar to the lake trout.

Cut Throat Trout

**NATURAL FOOD**
Trout in freshwater will feed on almost any aquatic insects and larvae — stonefly nymphs, caddis fly larvae, mayflies and diving beetles. Ramshorn snails and minnows are also taken, as well as worms.

| TECHNIQUE | ROD | REEL | LINE | TERMINAL TACKLE | HOOK | WEIGHT | BAIT |
|---|---|---|---|---|---|---|---|
| Fly fishing | 8, 9, 10, 11-foot fly | Fly reel | Floating/sinking fly | Fly leader | Fly hooks | | Wet/dry flies |
| Spinning | 9-foot medium spinning | Fixed spool | Floating/sinking fly | Fly leader | Trebles | | Spinners |
| Trolling/bait fishing | 9-foot medium spinning | Fixed spool | 10/15-pound nylon | Nylon tackle | Trebles 10-2 f/water | Split shot | Live/dead fish |

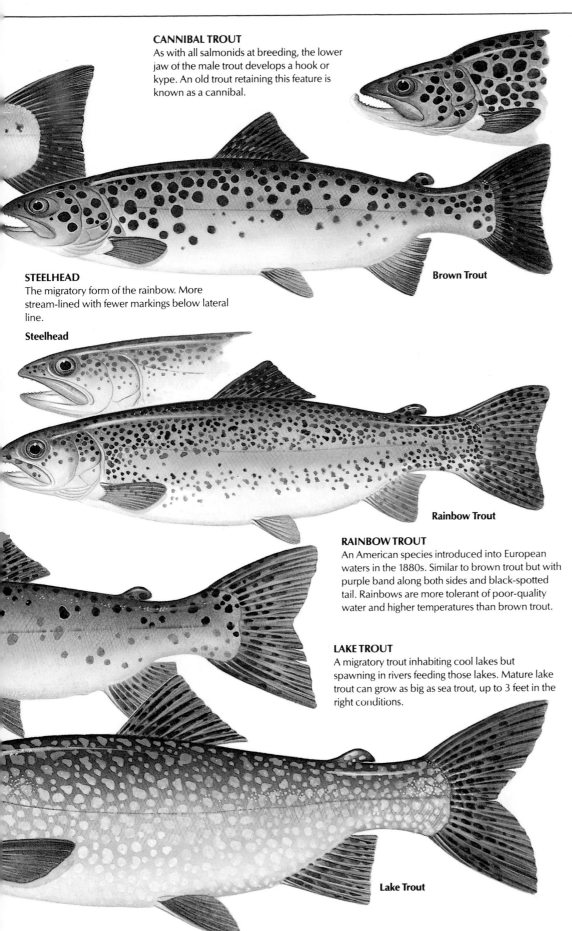

### CANNIBAL TROUT
As with all salmonids at breeding, the lower jaw of the male trout develops a hook or kype. An old trout retaining this feature is known as a cannibal.

**Brown Trout**

### STEELHEAD
The migratory form of the rainbow. More stream-lined with fewer markings below lateral line.

**Steelhead**

**Rainbow Trout**

### RAINBOW TROUT
An American species introduced into European waters in the 1880s. Similar to brown trout but with purple band along both sides and black-spotted tail. Rainbows are more tolerant of poor-quality water and higher temperatures than brown trout.

### LAKE TROUT
A migratory trout inhabiting cool lakes but spawning in rivers feeding those lakes. Mature lake trout can grow as big as sea trout, up to 3 feet in the right conditions.

**Lake Trout**

into North American waters in 1883; the following year saw the beginning of the introduction of rainbow trout to European and other waters from its original range in western North America.

The rainbow trout is slightly more hardy than the brown trout, and can withstand higher water temperatures and poorer water quality. The growth rate of the rainbow is extremely rapid when adequate food is available, one reason why it's now probably the most widely farmed fish in the world. On trout farms, rainbows can reach 20 to 30 pounds in just 4 or 5 years.

Interbreeding with other species and subspecies of trout, plus selective breeding on trout farms, has led to a wide range of colour variations in rainbow trout. The most common colouring, though, is blue-brown on the back, silvery white on the underside and iridescent magenta on the sides. Some varieties are heavily spotted, while others show few or no spots and are an overall silver colour. Like the brown trout, the rainbow has a migratory form which spends most of its time in the sea. This migratory rainbow is known as the steelhead trout.

The brook trout (*Salvelinus fontinalis*) was originally a native of the northeastern part of North America, but like the rainbow it has been introduced into waters throughout the USA and Canada and in Europe. Although the brook trout has the typical trout shape, it is actually closely related to the char.

Like most of the trout types, the colouring of the brook trout is exremely variable, but a typical pattern is olive to brown on the back, silvery white below, with light green sides dappled with creamy spots and tiny magenta blotches.

Fish farmers have successfully crossed male brook trout with female brown trout to produce a hybrid known as the tiger trout. Tigers are often highly coloured, voracious fish that hit a fly or lure like an express train.

Trout can be caught on fly, bait and spinners, but fly fishing is generally regarded as the most sporting and most satisfying technique. When hooked, most trout put up a tremendous fight, sometimes jumping repeatedly in an attempt to shake the hook free.

# TUNAS

The tunas, which are members of the mackerel family, are of great importance to commercial fishermen as well as to anglers. The largest, the bluefin tuna (*Thunnus thynnus*) is also one of the largest bony fishes in the sea, growing to over 1500 pounds. The bluefin is distributed worldwide and is highly migratory, travelling in huge schools over great distances; tagged fish have been recorded as travelling 5000 miles in just 50 days.

The bluefin is dark blue-black on the back, paling to silvery white on the lower flanks and belly. Its pectoral fins are rather short, especially when compared to those of the albacore (*Thunnus alalunga*). This fish, which is dark steel blue with yellowish blue sides and a white belly, has elongated, sickle-shaped pectoral fins and is also known as the longfin tuna as a result.

Other tunas include the blackfin tuna (*Thunnus atlanticus*), yellowtail tuna (*Thunnus albacares*), bigeye tuna (*Thunnus obesus*), little tuna (*Euthynnus alleteratus*), the little tunnies (*Euthynnus lineatus* and *E. affinis*) and the skipjack tuna (*Katsuwonus pelamis*). All tunas are predatory, and can be caught by drift fishing with live or dead baits (live mackerel or dead herring), or by trolling with rigged natural or artificial baits.

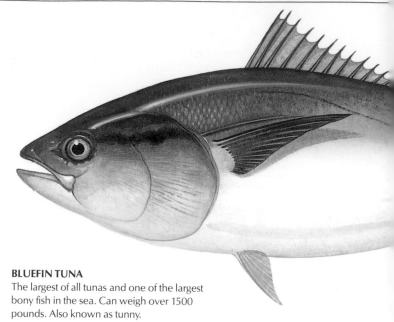

**BLUEFIN TUNA**
The largest of all tunas and one of the largest bony fish in the sea. Can weigh over 1500 pounds. Also known as tunny.

# WAHOO *Acanthocybium solandri*

One of the world's great game fish, the wahoo puts up an explosive fight and is a challenge to any angler on light to medium tackle. The wahoo is a member of the mackerel family, and is found worldwide in subtropical and tropical waters. Although it can grow to over 150 pounds, anything over 60 pounds can be regarded as a fine catch.

The body is long and slim, and the long head has a pointed, cylindrical snout and large, strong teeth. The first dorsal fin is long, with 21 to 27 spines, and it folds down into a groove along the fish's back. The second dorsal and the anal fin are very small, and behind the second dorsal a row of finlets leads to a strong, tuna-like tail.

The colour of the back is a deep, almost electric blue, the sides are bluish grey and marked with vertical, dark blue bands, and the underparts are white.

Wahoo normally travel in small groups, eating just about any baitfish or squid that crosses their path. They are commonly taken on trolled deadbaits, such as mullet, and on feathers and other artificial lures. Livebait, fished from a drifting boat, is also effective.

Wahoo are very susceptible to infestation by a trematode parasite, numbers of which are usually present in their stomachs.

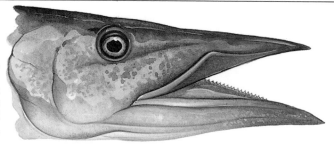

**TEETH**
Typical of predatory species, the wahoo has a large mouth with numerous razor-sharp teeth.

**NATURAL FOOD**
Wahoo feed on shoaling fishes such as members of the herring family.

**FIRST DORSAL FIN**
The pattern of the walleye is smudged and vague, that of the zander regular. The walleye also has a black spot, not present on the zander.

**WALLEYE**
Similar to the zander, but the lower lobe of the caudal fin is pale or white.

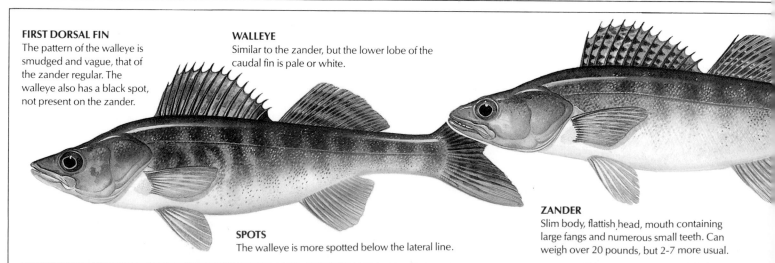

**SPOTS**
The walleye is more spotted below the lateral line.

**ZANDER**
Slim body, flattish head, mouth containing large fangs and numerous small teeth. Can weigh over 20 pounds, but 2-7 more usual.

| TECHNIQUE | ROD | REEL | LINE | TERMINAL TACKLE | HOOK | WEIGHT | BAIT |
|---|---|---|---|---|---|---|---|
| Spinning | 8-foot medium action spinning | Fixed spool | 6-8-pounds | Short fine-wire trace | | | Bucktail lead heads |
| Ledgering live or deadbait | 10 to 11-foot medium action ledger, 1¼-ounce test curve | Fixed spool | 6-8-pounds | 20-inch wire trace with running bomb | Two size 10 trebles | 1-ounce bomb | Small live/dead fish |

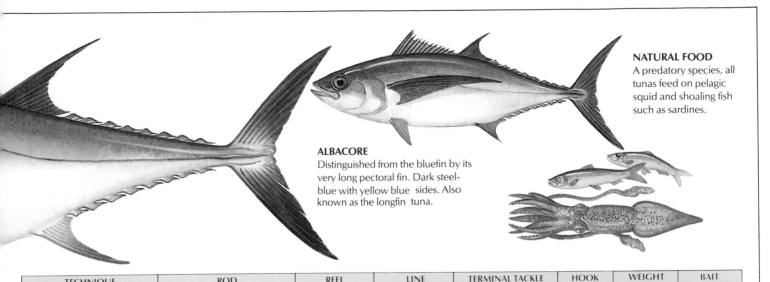

### ALBACORE
Distinguished from the bluefin by its very long pectoral fin. Dark steel-blue with yellow blue sides. Also known as the longfin tuna.

### NATURAL FOOD
A predatory species, all tunas feed on pelagic squid and shoaling fish such as sardines.

| TECHNIQUE | ROD | REEL | LINE | TERMINAL TACKLE | HOOK | WEIGHT | BAIT |
|---|---|---|---|---|---|---|---|
| Trolling | 80-130 class, full roller rings | Lever drag multiplier | 80-130 class nylon | 400-600-pound nylon | 10/0-12/0 flat | | Kona Head |
| Live/dead baiting | 80-130 class, full roller rings | | 80-130 class nylon | 400-600-pound nylon | 10/0-12/0 offset | | Live mackerel dead hearing |

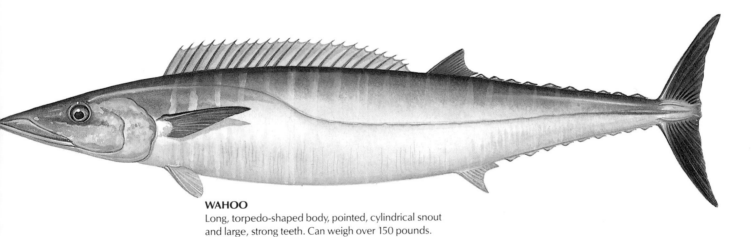

### WAHOO
Long, torpedo-shaped body, pointed, cylindrical snout and large, strong teeth. Can weigh over 150 pounds.

| TECHNIQUE | ROD | REEL | LINE | TERMINAL TACKLE | HOOK | WEIGHT | BAIT |
|---|---|---|---|---|---|---|---|
| Trolling | 30 to 50-pound class | 6/0 star drag or 30-50 class multiplier | 30-50-pound nylon | Heavy wire tackle | Sizes 8/0-10/0 flat | | Kona Head Natural bait mounted for trolling |

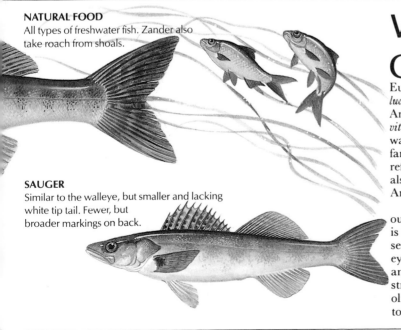

### NATURAL FOOD
All types of freshwater fish. Zander also take roach from shoals.

### SAUGER
Similar to the walleye, but smaller and lacking white tip tail. Fewer, but broader markings on back.

# WALLEYE, ZANDER AND SAUGER

Only very slight genetic differences separate the European zander (*Stizostedion lucioperca*) from the North American walleye (*S. vitreum vitreum*). The zander and the walleye are members of the perch family, and both are often referred to as 'pikeperch', a term also applied to the North American sauger (*S. canadense*).

The zander and walleye are outwardly very similar. The body is elongated and round in cross-section, with a flattish head. The eye is large, and the powerful jaws and the roof of the mouth carry strong, sharp teeth. The colour is olive on the back and sides, fading to metallic white on the belly, and the back and sides are marked by darker bands. The fins are large, and the tail of the walleye has a white tip, absent in the zander, on its lower fork. Both fish can reach weights of over 20 pounds, but 2 to 7 pounds is more usual and anything over 10 pounds is noteworthy.

Sauger are smaller, only 1 to 3 pounds in most waters, although Missouri fish can reach 8 pounds.

All the pikeperches live in rivers, lakes and reservoirs (although the sauger are found in only the very biggest), staying close to the bottom where they hunt in packs for small shoalfish, feeding mostly from dusk till dawn.

# WEAKFISHES

The weakfishes are members of the corvina family, most of which live in the Pacific off the coasts of Central and South America. The weakfish (*Cynoscion regalis*) itself, however, is a very popular gamefish of the eastern Atlantic, occurring in inshore waters from Massachusetts to Florida but commonest from Chesapeake Bay to New York. A slim, well-shaped fish, it gets its name from its delicate mouth, which tears easily when hooked.

In appearance, the weakfish is similar to its relative the spotted seatrout (*C. nebulosus*) which is found in the same waters. Both fish average about 4 pounds in weight, although the weakfish can top 19 pounds and the spotted seatrout 16 pounds. Two other seatrout, the sand seatrout (*C. arenarius*) and the silver seatrout (*C. nothus*), which occur further south, are much smaller and generally weigh well under a pound.

In contrast, the white seabass (*C. nobilis*), another relative of the weakfish and not a true sea bass, can reach weights of over 80 pounds, although most are only 15 to 30 pounds. The white seabass is a Pacific species, found from Alaska south to Chile.

All these fishes are good table fish, and the spotted seatrout and the white seabass both have commercial importance.

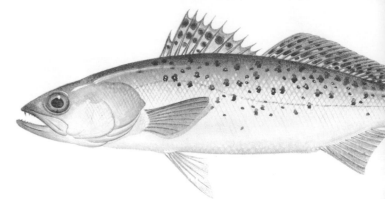

**NATURAL FOOD**
Weakfish are predators feeding on shoaling, silvery fishes and molluscs. Noted for their taking flashing, artificial baits.

# WHITEFISHES

The whitefishes of Canada and the northern USA are a group of freshwater species related to the trout and salmon. For anglers, the most important of them are the lake whitefish (*Coregonus clupeaformis*), mountain whitefish (*Prosopium williamsoni*), inconnu (*Stenopus leucichthys*), round whitefish (*Prosopium cylindraceum*) and the eight species of ciscoes (*Coregonus* spp).

The lake whitefish, which also enters rivers, is a popular gamefish which averages about 4 pounds but can reach over 20 pounds. The mountain whitefish is smaller, most being around 2 pounds with a maximum of 5 pounds or so, and is usually sought in the winter months when its flesh is at its most tasty. Round whitefish are even smaller, rarely exceeding 2 pounds, but the inconnu is to reach 50 pounds.

The ciscoes, found in New England and the Great Lakes Basin, are also popular with anglers and mostly reach about 2 pounds in weight. Like the lake, mountain and round whitefish, the ciscoes feed mainly on insects and crustaceans, and provide good sport for fly fishermen during the summer mayfly hatches. Inconnu can also be taken on flies, but as they are a predatory species, fishing for them with spinners or spoons is more likely to bring results.

**MOUTH SHAPE**
The many species of whitefish are so similar that fin ray counting is sometimes the only means of identification. With the lake and mountain whitefish, however, there are obvious differences in mouth shape and head size.

**Lake Whitefish**

**Mountain Whitefish**

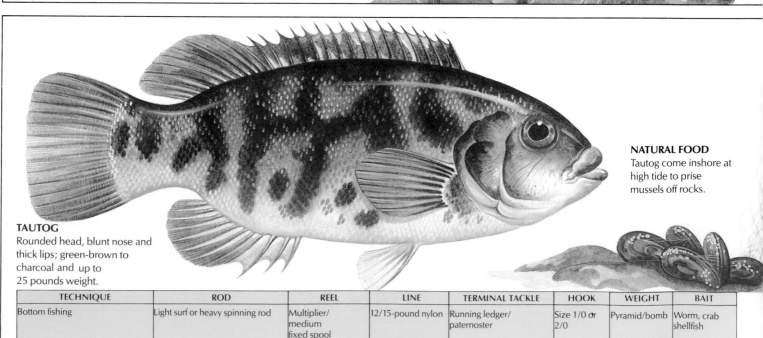

**TAUTOG**
Rounded head, blunt nose and thick lips; green-brown to charcoal and up to 25 pounds weight.

**NATURAL FOOD**
Tautog come inshore at high tide to prise mussels off rocks.

| TECHNIQUE | ROD | REEL | LINE | TERMINAL TACKLE | HOOK | WEIGHT | BAIT |
|---|---|---|---|---|---|---|---|
| Bottom fishing | Light surf or heavy spinning rod | Multiplier/ medium fixed spool | 12/15-pound nylon | Running ledger/ paternoster | Size 1/0 or 2/0 | Pyramid/bomb | Worm, crab shellfish |

## SPOTTED SEATROUT

Not a trout at all but with markings and the torpedo-shaped body similar to the sea trout.

## WEAKFISH

A slim, well-shaped marine fish. Its name derives from its delicate mouth which tears easily when hooked. A popular gamefish.

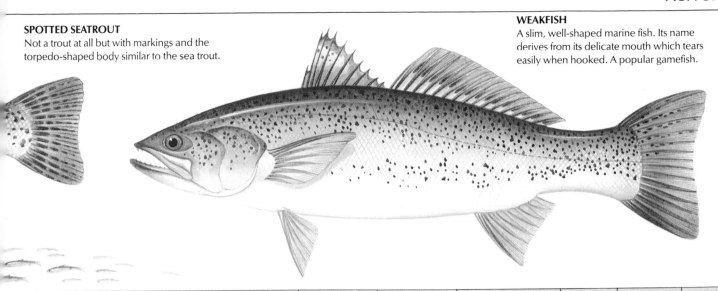

| TECHNIQUE | ROD | REEL | LINE | TERMINAL TACKLE | HOOK | WEIGHT | BAIT |
|---|---|---|---|---|---|---|---|
| Bottom fishing | Medium weight | Fixed spool 6/0 | 15/20-pound nylon | | 1/0 eyed | Pyramid, spiked grip | Bar spoon |
| Spinning | 8/9-foot spinning | | 15-20-pound nylon | Single hook ledger | 1/0 eyed | | Fish shrimp |

## WHITEFISH SPECIES

The most important angling whitefishes are the lake, mountain, inconnu and round whitefish, together with the eight species of ciscoes.

## LAKE WHITEFISH

A popular freshwater gamefish, which despite its name is also found in rivers. Averages about 4 pounds, but capable of reaching over 20.

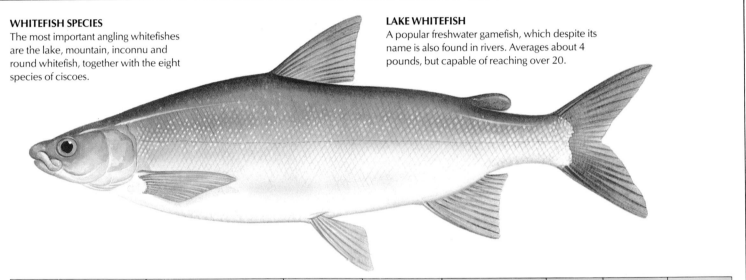

| TECHNIQUE | ROD | REEL | LINE | TERMINAL TACKLE | HOOK | WEIGHT | BAIT |
|---|---|---|---|---|---|---|---|
| Fly fishing | 8-foot fly rod | Single action fly reel | Floating or sinking 5/6 | Tapered leader | | | Small wet or dry flies |

## PHARYNGEAL TEETH

Ballan wrasse have a set of secondary, pharyngeal or throat teeth, used to crush food against the bony palate.

## BALLAN WRASSE

When the mouth of the ballan wrasse is open and the lips extended for feeding, the blunt and crushing teeth are exposed. These are ideal for crunching molluscs and crustaceans.

# WRASSES

Although the wrasse family of saltwater fishes includes some 450 species, the majority of them are tropical and comparatively few species are found in temperate waters. In the Pacific, the temperate wrasses include the California sheephead (*Pimelometopon pulchrum*) and the señorita (*Oxyjulis californica*). The principal temperate Atlantic wrasses are the tautog (*Tautoga onitis*) and cunner (*Tautogolabrus adspersus*) of the north west, and the ballan wrasse (*Labrus bergylta*) and cuckoo wrasse (*Labrus mixtus*) of the north east.

The tautog is commonest from Nova Scotia to South Carolina, and has a rounded back, blunt nose and thick lips. In colour, tautog range from green-brown to charcoal grey, but like all wrasses they can alter their colour to match their surroundings, The ballan wrasse ranges in colour from yellow to green or red, and like the tautog feeds mainly on molluscs and crabs. Unlike most saltwater fish, the ballan wrasse lay their eggs in nests, which they build by jamming pieces of seaweed and debris into rock crevices.

The ballan wrasse can grow to a weight of over 8 pounds, and the tautog up to 25 pounds, although weights of around 3 pounds are more usual for rod-caught tautog. Other wrasses of the north east Atlantic include the rainbow wrasse (*Coris julis*) and the corkwing (*Crenilabrus melops*).

# TECHNIQUES

One of angling's great strengths is that the basic techniques are easily learnt, which makes the sport more accessible, to more people, than most others are. Another is that once the basics have been mastered, there are so many subtleties involved in fishing that the dedicated angler never stops learning about it, and gaining increasing pleasure from it.

Unfortunately, because there is so much that can be learnt, many anglers tend to concentrate on one particular type of angling, and rarely try their hand at anything very different from their chosen method. This is a pity, because every kind of fishing has much to commend it and can offer great enjoyment to those who practise it.

Fly fishing, for example, is generally accepted to be the most refined and artistic form of angling, and because of this it's often regarded by lure and bait fishermen as rather mysterious and far from easy. In fact, the vast majority of anglers who try it find that they can soon master the basic techniques of casting and retrieving a fly, and are surprised at just how quickly they can learn to catch fish on it; to become an expert, though, takes a little longer.

Fly fishing – using the submerged wet fly or the dry fly which floats on the surface – is primarily a freshwater technique. However, saltwater fly fishing is growing in popularity as a method of catching shallow-water species such as pollack and bonefish. For this, you need a basic knowledge of fly casting, corrosion-resistant tackle, and a good understanding of the feeding habits of the fish you're after and how to work the fly to attract their attention. Saltwater fly fishing can even be used to catch small shark that come close inshore, if the fly is attached to a short wire leader and cast to within a few inches of the snout of the essentially short-sighted fish.

The more usual methods of fishing from the shore, though, are surfcasting, using long, two-piece rods with multiplier or fixed spool reels, and saltwater spinning, which employs lighter rods and fixed spool reels. Most other saltwater fishing is done from boats – from dinghies close inshore, and from larger boats (usually chartered) further out in deep water. Charter boats, generally purpose-built, are also used for big game fishing, hunting ocean giants like billfish and tuna.

Trolling, one of the basic big game fishing techniques, can be used to good effect when fishing for smaller saltwater species such as sea bass and pollack, and on fresh waters it's a very good way to get at fish living in the depths of large lakes and reservoirs. Downrigger trolling from motorboats, using heavy weights to keep the terminal tackle down where the fish are, is often the only way to take species such as lake trout in really big waters, but in shallower waters lines can simply be trailed behind a rowed boat or a canoe.

Most freshwater angling methods can be used from a boat, but the majority of freshwater fishing is done from the shore or bank or by wading in shallow water. The techniques can be divided into three main categories: fly fishing, lure fishing and fishing with hookbaits.

Fly fishing, one of the oldest forms of sports fishing, is popular all over the world, but there are distinct regional preferences for either lure fishing or bait fishing. This is partly due to local traditions, but mainly to the types of fish predominant in the region. In North America, because so many of the popular sports fishes – such as the basses — are predatory, the majority of anglers fish with artificial lures. In Europe, on the other hand, there are comparatively few predatory species – mostly trout, pike and perch – and so most of the fishing is with hookbaits for fish such as carp, tench and roach.

As a result, the major American freshwater techniques are spinning and baitcasting, using spinners, spoons, plugs, jigs and other artificial lures. These neat, effective methods, using light and relatively uncomplicated tackle, are as yet sadly underrated in Europe. Conversely, there is much scope for the wider use of European-style ledgering and float fishing techniques in North America. They're all described in this chapter, so why not try them?

# BAITCASTING

Baitcasting was originally a technique which used natural baits (hence its name) and fixed spool reels, and although this method is still used, most anglers today use the term to refer to the art of throwing an artificial lure, using a baitcasting (revolving spool or multiplier) reel. And an art it certainly is. Making a lure land exactly where you want it to, cast after cast, takes considerable skill and good quality, well-balanced tackle.

Whether you're using a single or a double handed rod, it should fit your hand like a comfortable old glove. With the shorter, single handed rod, for instance, your index finger should hook comfortably around the trigger, with your thumb snugly yet firmly over the spool.

The reel should be full of monofilament line wound on under firm tension, line which is not old, kinked or abraded. If your line's in good condition you'll lose fewer big fish on the strike, and you'll also cast more fluently.

Before you start casting, set the star drag and the cast control of your reel to suit the lure you're using. The star drag should be set so that the spool will only give line to the firm pull of a good fish. To set the cast control, put the reel in free spool and adjust the control so that the lure will drop slowly to the ground under its own weight. This will give you an approximate starting setting: when you start casting, you might find that you need to tighten the control some more for wind resistant plugs, or loosen it off quite a bit for denser models.

The weight of the lure will also determine your casting drop, the distance from the lure to the rod tip before you start your cast. For a ½ to ¾ ounce plug, a drop of about 6 inches should be enough.

## BASIC OVERHEAD CAST

plug pulls on rod tip

reel in free spool

1

stop rod at 11 o'clock position

rod flexes

### THE BAITCASTING REEL
As with other reels, the secret of successful casting with the baitcasting (or multiplying) reel is careful preparation. You may consider the effort a chore, but the rewards will be trouble-free performance and improved casting.

**THE BOW-AND-ARROW CAST**
This short-distance cast is very useful in a confined space with no room for a conventional cast. A fixed spool reel, because of its low line friction, is ideal.

Hold the bait's tail treble carefully between thumb and index finger and with the reel in free spool, stopped by thumb pressure, flex the rod aiming the bait above the target. Release the hooks and spool pressure simultaneously. Complete the cast pointing the rod tip at the target.

Heavier plugs might need slightly less than this, but lightweights such as spinner baits, plastic worms, weedless spoons or jigs and bucktails, will need from 10 to 30 inches.

There are other occasions when casting with a longer drop is advisable, for example to avoid snap up when you're using ultralight tackle, or when you're fishing with soft naturals such as worms, crayfish, small fish and strip baits. Sharp, short casting would only throw them off.

When you're using a single handed rod, the easiest cast is probably the simple overhead flick cast. Pick the spot you want the plug to land at, then with the reel in free spool and your thumb on the spool, rotate your wrist so the reel handles are pointing up and bring the rod smartly back until you feel the weight of the plug flexing the rod.

Now in one positive, fluid movement, flick the rod forwards as though you're hitting a nail with a hammer, and ease your thumb pressure off the spool when you feel the plug pull. With your thumb pressure completely off the spool, and the plug racing towards its target, gentle thumbing of the spool will stop it overshooting the mark. As soon as the plug hits the water, clamp your thumb down firmly, then swap the rod to your other hand and put the reel into gear by winding.

Keep the rod tip pointing at the plug during the retrieve to maximize the chances of setting the hooks when a fish hits, and lift the rod high into the strike. Working the plug, particularly if it's a surface lure, does of course take the rod tip a little to either side as you twitch, freeze, twitch again, bob, or jerk the lure to give it

lifelike movement. So be careful not to allow an acute angle between the rod and the plug, or the fish will be lost simply because the hooks never went fully home on the strike.

Over-the-shoulder and side casting use the same basic routine, but although good methods for cutting through strong winds, they lack the accuracy of standard overhead casting.

For flipping plugs into awkward spots such as beneath low, overhanging branches or under piers, a flip-type cast works best. Stand sideways-on to the target spot, holding the rod out in front of you with the tip a little lower than the butt. Now whip the rod tip quickly round in a circle (like stirring paint).

When the plug's moved through about 2/3 of the circle, take your thumb off the spool so

that the plug flies off towards the target, and gently follow through with the rod tip.

Another useful technique for getting to awkward spots, or for casting when you're surrounded by dense vegetation, is the 'bow and arrow' or 'catapult' cast.

Start with the plug on a drop of about 2/3 the length of the rod. With your left hand, hold the last hook tightly by the bend with your thumb and index finger (be careful here), with the reel in free spool and held by your right thumb. Pull back on the plug to bend the rod like a bow, aim the plug at the target, then let it fly. At the same time, release the spool and follow through to point the rod tip at the target.

With longer, double handed rods, the casting techniques are basically the same, but with the left hand gripping the butt of the rod at around chest height.

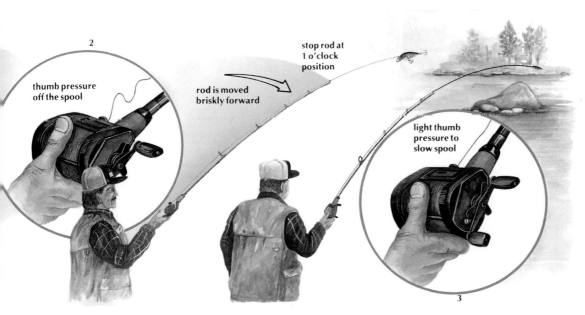

thumb pressure off the spool

rod is moved briskly forward

stop rod at 1 o'clock position

light thumb pressure to slow spool

**THE OVERHEAD CAST**
**1.** With the reel correctly adjusted, the lure on the correct drop for its weight and the thumb locking the spool, start the cast by bringing the rod briskly back and stopping it at about the 11 o'clock position.

**2.** When you feel the pull of the lure on the rod tip, flick the rod forwards as if you're hammering a nail. Stop the rod at the 1 o'clock position and remove your thumb pressure as the lure pulls line out.

**3.** As the lure drops towards the water apply thumb pressure to brake the spool. As the lure hits the water clamp your thumb firmly on the spool to prevent overrun and the resulting tangle of line.

# BIG GAME FISHING — DRIFTING

**B**ig game fishing takes many forms, ranging from simple drift fishing for shark up to complex trolling techniques developed for species such as billfish and tuna.

Drift fishing consists of fishing a natural live or dead fishbait from a boat which drifts with the wind and tide flow. This technique was developed primarily for shark fishing, but it's been effectively adapted for catching broadbill swordfish as well.

For shark, the boat is taken out to an area known to hold them, the most usual species for deepwater sport fishing being mako, porbeagle, blue and hammerhead. Once the shark grounds are reached, the engines are cut and the boat begins to drift.

The first job now is to create a 'smell lane' through the water to attract hungry shark to the baits. This is known as chumming or rubby-dubbying, and the easiest way to do it is to hang a mesh bag full of minced fresh, frozen or rotting fish over the side of the boat. Each time the boat rises and falls on a swell the bag pumps up and down in the water and releases additional bait particles into the water. To make the trail more attractive, the minced fish can be 'hotted up' with fish oil or blood.

If you know the shark are feeding close to the surface, hang the bag over the side on which the rods are to be placed. If the sharks are down deep, you should hang the bag on the opposite side to the rods, so that the released bait particles drift under the boat and are deflected downwards by the keel, laying a deep trail to attract shark up from the depths.

Drift fishing tackle is always kept as simple as possible: a rod, reel, line, leader (trace) and bait. For anglers who like to watch a float, a partially inflated balloon can be used both as a bait support and as a bite indicator. It should be allowed to slide on the reel line until stopped at the required depth by a rubber band half-hitched to the line.

Most shark drifting boats use four rods fished at staggered distances and depths. Baits are normally fished at about 25, 30, 60 and 70 feet; whichever bait it taken first indicates the feeding level of that particular species of shark on that particular day. However, even when a deep set bait is taken, you should still keep one bait working close to the

surface. An individual shark will often come in close to the surface intent on attacking the chumming bag, and will usually stop to pick up any bait in its path.

The choice of bait is wide, as almost any fish can be used as shark bait, but oily fish such as mackerel, sardine or bonito are probably the best. The method of hooking the bait depends a great deal on its size. Small fish like sardine are best fished in

bunches, each fish being threaded on the hook via its eye sockets.

Mackerel, unless large, are best fished in pairs, tandem fashion, to create the illusion of a big bait. Bonito are large enough to be fished singly, but as shark are highly adept at chopping big baits in half, pass the wire trace through the body of the bait so the hook protrudes through the gill slit.

Although shark are often

regarded as greedy, rather stupid creatures, there are occasions (and species, such as mako and great white) when they show a distinct cunning. Because of this, take great care not to alarm the fish during the initial stages of the take or strike. At the first indication of a bite, pick the rod up and hold it so that the tip

**Below** *Boating a shark with a flying (breakaway) gaff.*

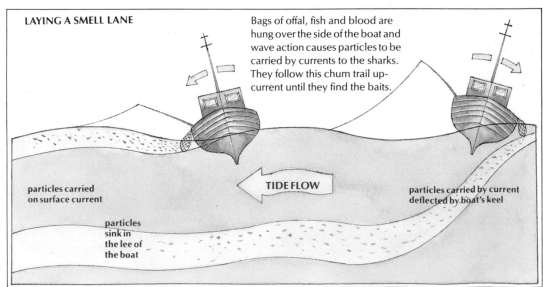

**LAYING A SMELL LANE**

Bags of offal, fish and blood are hung over the side of the boat and wave action causes particles to be carried by currents to the sharks. They follow this chum trail up-current until they find the baits.

particles carried on surface current

TIDE FLOW

particles carried by current deflected by boat's keel

particles sink in the lee of the boat

points directly down the line into the sea. At the same time, put the reel into free spool and control it by thumb pressure only. This allows the shark to take line freely without feeling any suspicious drag.

Normally, the fish will take the bait and run out a few yards of line, then stop and begin to

**Below** *Casting to a small school of tarpon from a drifting boat.*

swallow the bait before moving away again. As this second run begins, put the reel into gear so that you can strike the moment the line goes tight, and then play the fish out in the normal way.

The basic technique for broadbill swordfish is similar to that for sharks, except that swordfish are normally fished for at night with the bait exceeding 1000 feet. The two major baits for swordfish are livebaits and squid,

although there are many local variations. In Portugal, for example, the bait is normally a live Ray's bream hooked once through the back. Elsewhere, the technique is to fish a whole dead squid in conjunction with a chemical light stick, which is either pushed into the mantle of the squid or attached to the leader directly above the bait.

The light stick is simply a light plastic tube containing two

separate chemicals, and it's activated by bending the tube so that the chemicals mix. The mixed chemicals react and give off a steady, greenish light for up to twelve hours.

When the stick is inserted into a natural squid, it makes the bait glow with a natural-looking phosphorescence that broadbill swordfish find highly appealing. Broadbill normally take a fish bait savagely.

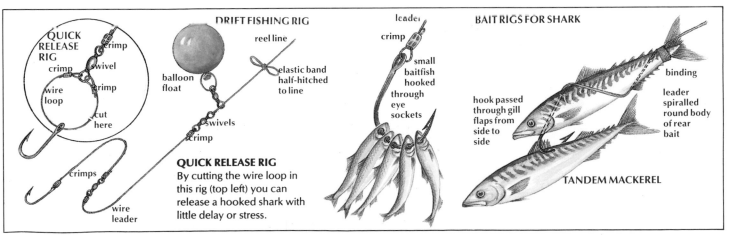

**QUICK RELEASE RIG**
By cutting the wire loop in this rig (top left) you can release a hooked shark with little delay or stress.

QUICK RELEASE RIG — crimp, swivel, crimp, wire loop, crimp, cut here, crimps, wire leader

DRIFT FISHING RIG — balloon float, reel line, elastic band half-hitched to line, swivels, crimp

leader, crimp, small baitfish hooked through eye sockets

BAIT RIGS FOR SHARK — hook passed through gill flaps from side to side, binding, leader spiralled round body of rear bait

TANDEM MACKEREL

# BIG GAME FISHING — TROLLING

Although shark and other fish are regularly caught on bait presented from a drifting boat, other species are better taken on moving baits. The more active ocean predators like marlin, sailfish, wahoo and tuna show little interest in static baits, but they're likely to strike at a moving bait. Because of this, these species are fished for by trailing baits behind a moving boat, so that the baits resemble the living food on which the big game fish prey.

This trailing, or 'trolling' as it's known, is a highly selective way of showing baits to fish over a wide area. Most big game boats fish four rods at a time, with two directly over the stern and two on specially designed outriggers that keep their lines away from the sides of the boat. These are called 'rigger lines', while the central rods, whose baits are fished closest to the boat, are known as 'flatlines'.

Normally, all lines are staggered to present baits over a wide area, and to create the illusion of a small shoal of frantically swimming bait fish. Strangely enough, the baits fished closest to the boat often produce the most strikes. This is particularly true of solitary fish like marlin, which seem to be atracted by the wake of the boat itself.

The choice of bait for trolling is up to the individual angler and the boat captain. Most anglers prefer to leave the decision to the captain, whose experience is usually far greater than theirs. Traditionally, bait choice would be specially mounted or rigged natural baits, mackerel, balao (ballyhoo), mullet or ladyfish being the most favoured bait

species. In more recent years, many boat captains have switched bait preferences from naturals to artificial lures, in particular the Kona Head type which originated in Hawaii.

Initially, these baits were hand carved from hardwood and wrapped with an improvised skirt. Nowadays, many companies specialize in producing a wide range of head shapes and plastic skirts in a host of colour combinations. These lures are all known as Kona Heads, but are often marketed under various trade names.

Most baits are fitted with two differently coloured skirts, usually to simulate a specific fish colour: blue on white for mackerel and tuna, for example, or yellow and green for dorado, and pink and red for shrimp.

In operation, each bait is mounted on a wire or preferably heavy nylon trace fitted with one or two flat forged hooks. Hooks with offset points are useless for lure fishing, because they have a tendency to spin and wrap up the tail of the bait's plastic skirt. A bait tangled in this fashion catches nothing.

Normally, the strike drag on the reel is set before fishing begins. With both the lever drag and star drag types of multiplier it's usually set on the quayside, using a spring balance to check the poundage. When a fish strikes a bait, the initial power of the rod and the setting of the drag should be enough to set the hooks. The drag setting depends on the weight class of the rod and the breaking strain of the line. For instance, for an 80 pound class outfit the drag would be set at 28 pounds.

As a technique, trolling is a highly efficient way of catching fish. Unfortunately, though, many strikes fail to produce hooked fish. This is particularly true when trolling for billfish with artificial baits. The hardness of the fish's mouth, and the rapidity with which artificial baits are tasted and rejected, lead to a high incidence of lost fish – one marlin hooked for every three strikes could be regarded as the norm. Frustrating as this may seem, the beauty of the Kona Head style lure is that under most circumstances it raises more billfish than do natural lures.

With tuna, missed strikes are a rarity. The tuna's mouth is very different from that of the marlin, and tuna also have a tendency to gulp a bait straight down. More tuna are lost through tackle breakage than pulled hooks. The

drawback to tuna is that they invariably school, and when one bait is taken the chances are that the other lines will produce strikes within seconds.

Some fish, like wahoo and sailfish, seem to prefer natural baits to artificial lures, wahoo being particularly good at cutting a bait in half on the strike.

As a method, trolling – especially with artificial lures – has much to recommend it. It's clean, the baits are easy to rig, and it catches many big fish.

**Right** *Trolling is the best way to fish for species such as marlin, tuna and sailfish, using either natural baits or artificial lures.*
**Below** *Shark are usually caught by drifting, but they can also be taken on slowly-trolled strip or whole fishbaits. This one is a 186-pound whitetip shark.*

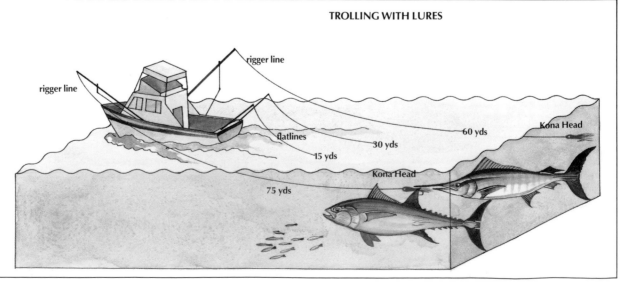

**BIG GAME TROLLING**
Trolling is a very effective method, but with marlin the ratio of strikes to hooked fish is only 3:1. Marlin often hit the lures nearest the boat, perhaps attracted by the wake. The tuna's way of hitting a lure means that it is rarely missed. Tuna strikes on all lures at once are common.

**TROLLING WITH LURES**

rigger line

rigger line

flatlines

15 yds

30 yds

60 yds

Kona Head

75 yds

Kona Head

# BOAT FISHING

Boat fishing at sea falls into two main categories: inshore dinghy or small boat fishing and offshore big boat fishing. Dinghy fishing is an inexpensive way to get out to marks that are beyond the reach of the shore caster but inside the grounds worked by larger boats. Often, dinghy anglers can get to saltwater creeks, estuaries and reefs that are rarely, if ever, fished.

One of the best techniques to use for this small boat fishing is the rolling ledger, which works well in waters of up to 30 feet, from an anchored boat. For this style of angling an 8 to 10 foot rod and a fixed spool reel should be used, and the trace and weight or lead are critical factors.

The trace should never be less than 3 feet long, and it could be longer depending on the type of bottom you're fishing over, the shorter trace being ideal for fishing over rocks or other solid snags. Over a flat sand or mud bottom, use a longer trace to allow the bait to swirl around in the tide flow.

A nylon trace is best, made up with a single size 1-0 or 2-0 hook and a swivel. Slide the lead, which should be bomb shaped, directly over the reel line, then knot the reel line to the trace swivel. This lets the lead slide easily on the main line, and the swivel acts as a stop to keep the lead from sliding down to the hook. For bait, use worm, fish, squid or crab.

Cast the tackle uptide and well away from the boat. The lead should be just heavy enough to take the bait to the bottom but not heavy enough to anchor it in one position; you rarely need to use a lead of more than one ounce. The idea is that the bait should travel slowly down the tide until it reaches a position directly astern of the dinghy.

Hold the rod at all times, as bites may occur anywhere along the search path of the bait, and once the bait comes to rest astern of the boat, retrieve the tackle and recast it. By changing your casting distances you can thoroughly search out the sea on either side of the anchored boat.

Offshore fishing in deep water is different. The boat is anchored over a known mark but the fishing takes a very different form, the light inshore tackle being changed for a heavier boat outfit, such as a 30 or 50 pound class rod and a 4-0 or 6-0 size multiplying reel.

Make up the terminal tackle as before, but with a wire or heavy nylon trace and a 6-0 or 8-0 hook. The lead size depends on the strength of the tide flow, but you may need anything from 6 ounces up to 2 pounds or more; it should be just heavy enough to hold bottom. The trace length depends on the type of fish you're after: for cod or conger a 3 foot trace is ideal; for tope, turbot or bass you need a 6 or even 8 foot trace.

The technique is simple. With the reel out of gear but braked gently with your right thumb, drop the terminal tackle down until you feel the lead touch bottom. At this stage the reel is still in free spool but clamped firmly by your thumb. After the lead has been in position for a moment or two, raise the rod tip to lift the lead, and release a yard or two of line. This has the effect of trotting the line back a yard or so with the tide flow. Each time the lead comes to rest, leave it there for a few moments and then repeat the process if no bites are registered. When you feel a bite, give the fish a yard or so of slack line and then put the reel in gear ready for the strike.

Fishing over wrecks is usually carried out from a drifting boat, the boat skipper setting up the drift so that the boat passes directly over the wreck. This technique calls for little finesse but a great deal of muscle. Most wrecks are fished with either an artificial or a natural bait, the most popular artificial being a rubber eel of the red gill type fished on a long trace.

Once the boat's drifting, you

*Fishing from a boat, whether close inshore or further out, will usually provide good sport.*

lower the terminal tackle until the lead touches the wreck. The moment this happens, crank the reel handle at high speed to get the tackle clear of the wreck and activate the bait or rubber eel. Strikes on this sort of rig, mostly from pollack, coalfish and the occasional cod, are extremely savage.

When you're fishing a natural bait, keep the trace short – about 2 feet being ideal. Again, lower the tackle until the lead touches the wreck, then crank the reel handle two or three times to lift the bait above the wreckage. Bites are normally indicated by a slow pull on the rod tip. This method often produces large catches of big fish such as ling, cod, conger and very occasionally a big turbot or halibut.

After each drift the boat is re-positioned, and this allows a brief breathing space to repair or totally replace your terminal tackle. On a good day you might lose a dozen sets of tackle; on a bad day, losses can be astro-nomical. Despite this, wrecking is great fun.

### UPTIDE ROLLING LEDGER
The seabed beyond the range of the shore angler but inshore of the charter boat grounds is a lightly-fished area which the dinghy fisherman is ideally situated to explore. The uptide rolling ledger enables the fisherman to search a large area of the bottom to either side of his boat. Casts are made uptide and the ledger allowed to swing round until it's dead astern. Repeat casts at different distances give thorough coverage.

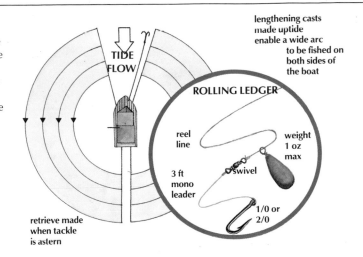

### OFFSHORE FISHING

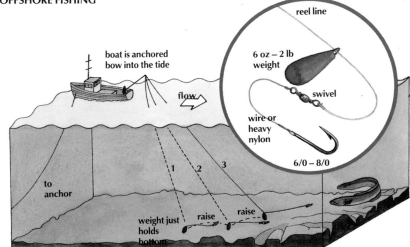

### OFFSHORE RIG
This rig is similar to that used for uptide fishing, but scaled up for the rougher ground and potentially much larger fish you can expect to catch over deep water marks.

This form of fishing is done at anchor over the chosen mark, using tackle similar to the uptide rolling ledger rig, but much stronger. With the reel out of gear, feed out line until the weight touches bottom. Brake the spool with your thumb, raise the rod and let out a yard or two of line as the weight drops back on the tide. Repeat until you get a strike, then give some slack, put the reel in gear, and hit the fish hard.

### SIMPLE DRIFT RIG
Rigs for drift fishing over wrecks or reefs are best kept fairly simple. This minimizes the inevitable tangles and lost tackle, and the subsequent frayed tempers.

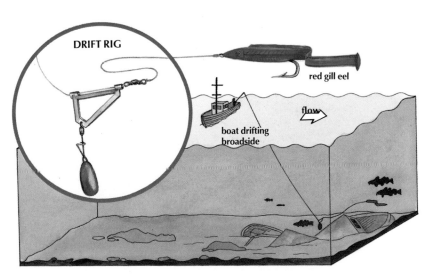

### DRIFT FISHING OVER WRECKS
Using a rig similar to that illustrated above, offshore wrecks can be fished 'on the drift', with the boat drifting with the current directly over the mark, rather than at anchor. All rods fish from the downtide side to reduce the risk of lines tangling or chafing on the keel.

The tackle is lowered until the weight touches the wreck, then it is cranked at high speed to activate the lure. Strikes are savage. When the drift is completed, the boat is taken back uptide on the motor and repositioned for another drift down the current and over the wreck.

# FEATHERING AND PIRKING

Many sea fish are totally predatory, and such fish fall readily to artificial lures. Some lures are highly sophisticated, but others, like feathers and pirks, are more basic.

Feathers – hackle feathers pulled from the neck of a domestic cockerel – are one of the simplest of all lures. They can be used in the natural state or dyed in various colours, and are simply lashed to the shank of a flat forged, tinned sea hook. The origins of feather-ing lie in the traditions of commercial fishing, where they are used to catch cod, pollack, coalfish and mackerel in quantity.

Feathers are fished from boats and used in long strings, traces carrying six or a dozen separate hooks being normal. The idea is to give the impression of a shoal of small, brightly coloured fish or sand eels. Feathers (and pirks) can be worked up and down as well as across or through a tide flow.

The technique is simple, the string of feathers being worked above a bomb shaped lead. You just lower the lead to any position between the seabed and the surface, and animate the feathers by raising and lowering the rod

**Above** *Fishing with a strin of feathers will get you good catches of shoaling mackerel, and also of other predators such as cod.*

top at regular intervals.

Every angler will develop an individual feathering routine, and almost any routine will catch fish, with the possible exception of really rapid rod movements.

Feathering is particularly

useful when mackerel are shoaling in vast numbers. Bites often come as the feathers are lowered; often the line will appear to go slack, a sure indication that a quantity of mackerel have taken the feathers. The apparent slackness is created by the fish taking the feathers and swimming upwards, dragging the weight behind them.

Such a bite normally indicates a full string or 'full house' of prime mackerel, and since you can find yourself with a number of fish on the line at the same time, you should use a 30 to 50 pound rod. When fish are less abundant, most bites will be signified by a light rattling pull on the rod tip.

Larger fish such as cod and pollack normally take the feathers savagely, firmly hooking themselves in the process. If you're expecting to catch these bigger fish you should cut back on the number of feathers on the trace, three being the maximum it's safe to use.

Commercial fishermen will never use blue coloured nylon for making up feathered traces, as they believe that blue line drives fish away from the feathers.

A variant on the feathers is a short length of brightly coloured electrical sleeving slid over the bend of the hook. These plastic 'feathers' may seem to hold little fish appeal, but in use the plastic has proved deadly with shoaling mackerel. The beauty of the plastic is that it's very durable; feathers, being soft, are often totally destroyed by the fish.

The pirk is an equally basic lure which can be extremely good for cod and pollack, and when baited for ling and halibut. Pirk baits are an updated version of the scraped lead lures used by Grand Banks cod fishermen, though most commercially made pirk style baits now originate in Scandinavia.

The pirk is basically a single piece of chromed metal fitted with a large treble hook. The shape of the pirk varies from one manufacturer to another, but all incorporate the same wicked style of hook. Commercial fishermen call the bait a 'ripper' or 'iron murderer', apt names considering how many fish are foul hooked in the head or belly on one or more prongs of the huge treble. Sporting anglers normally replace the treble with a large, well sharpened single hook.

Pirk baits are worked in the same way as feathers, but without a lead as the weight of the lure is enough to take it down to the bottom. Fish obviously mistake the pirk for a natural food, perhaps a herring, as bites are heavy and decisive.

When you're fishing for ling or halibut, you can enhance the attraction of the pirk by baiting the large single hook with a fillet of fish or a chunk of squid or cuttlefish. A pirk baited in this way can be extremely deadly, and wreck fishermen make spectacular ling catches on baited pirks. For big fish, mount the pirk on a heavy wire or nylon trace. Line of normal breaking strain will be cut through instantly by a ling's sharp teeth.

Pirks come in a variety of sizes and weights, ranging from tiny lures for catching live bait up to huge metallic slabs weighing in at over 2 pounds. The small lures are for use in shallow or tide-free water, the largest for deep, tide-ripped water. These large lures can be extremely expensive, and to cut costs many anglers prefer to make their own. You can save a good deal of money by making pirks at home, particularly if you go wreck fishing.

Sometimes, anglers and manufacturers go to extreme lengths to bend and shape pirk baits in the hope of making them move more in use. The truth of the matter is that a hungry fish feeding in deep water doesn't have the time to be picky about the way its lunch moves. Food is food, and a straight pirk will be taken as savagely as the most carefully bent 'tuned up' lure.

## FEATHER RIGS

Whether it's to be used as a quick method of collecting baitfish such as mackerel for shark or other predator fishing, or as a fishing technique in its own right, the feather string is easily made.

1 hook size to suit species sought

tie in two suitably bright spade hackles

2

pull both ends of line tight and trim

3

Feathering and pirking is often done over rough ground, which means that large amounts of tackle can be lost. Luckily, these simple lures are easily made from readily obtainable materials, and instead of using lead weights you can use scrap metal attached to the line by weak links of light line or even thread ('rotten bottom'). Then if the weight snags, you won't lose your lures as well.

swivel — reel line

feathers tied either to loop links or stand-off loops

**THE PATERNOSTER LOOP LINK**

swivel

lead weight or scrap metal

## PIRK

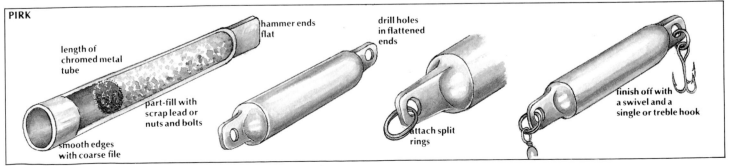

length of chromed metal tube

part-fill with scrap lead or nuts and bolts

smooth edges with coarse file

hammer ends flat

drill holes in flattened ends

attach split rings

finish off with a swivel and a single or treble hook

# FLOAT FISHING — 1

Fishing with a float is the most widely used angling method in the UK and Europe. Almost any freshwater fish can be caught by float fishing, and the float is the most sensitive type of bite indicator yet invented.

Despite the vast range of shapes and sizes of floats, they all fall into one or other of just two distinct functional categories: those which are attached to the line at the bottom end only, and those attached at both top and bottom.

Fishing with a float attached bottom end only allows some or all of the line between the rod tip

and the float to be sunk beneath the surface, so that the float (and consequently the bait presentation) is hardly affected by wind or surface drift.

With a float (usually a stick type) attached top and bottom to the line by silicone rubber float bands, you can trundle the bait along close to the bottom, even in deep water. The bait will travel at the same speed as the flow, which is nowhere near as fast as the surface currents.

For accurate casting at close range, use a one-handed underarm or sideways flick, and feather the line to a standstill

(with your forefinger against the rim of the spool) so that the tackle doesn't land abruptly. Always aim for a spot several feet beyond your swim, and quickly dip the rod tip a few inches below the surface once the float touches down. Then wind in a few rapid turns to sink all the line and draw the float to the position you want it before lifting the rod tip.

The overhead cast is best for long range work of twenty yards or more. Grip the rod butt firmly in your left hand with your right hand firmly over the tip of the reel seat. With the bale arm open, hook the line around your index

**Above** *Playing a fish caught on float tackle, rigged with the float fixed to the line at both the top and bottom ends.*

finger so that it's taking the weight of the terminal tackle.

Start with the rod pointing upwards directly in front of you, and then tilt it backwards over your right shoulder so that the tip flicks the float tackle out behind you. Now, in one smooth stroke, punch forward with your right arm and pull in with your left, keeping the rod in a straight, forward line. As before, aim for a spot beyond your swim. When the

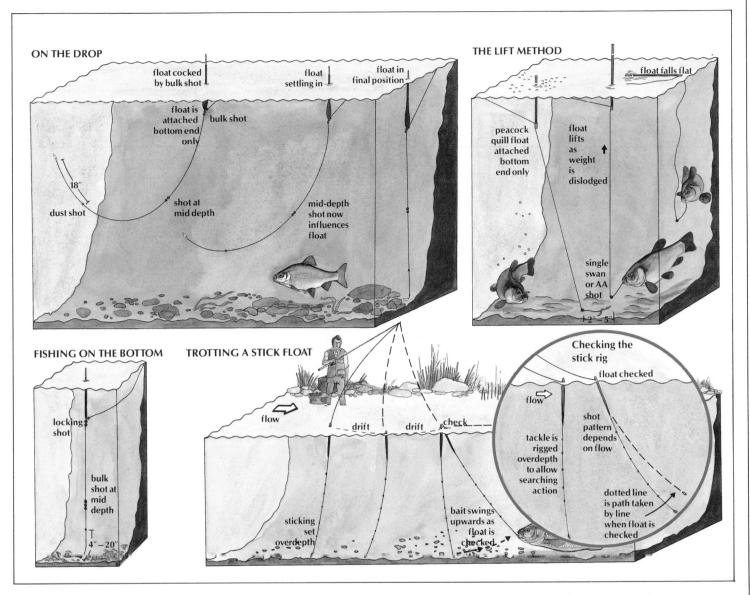

**ON THE DROP**

float cocked by bulk shot

float settling in

float in final position

float is attached bottom end only

bulk shot

18″

dust shot

shot at mid depth

mid-depth shot now influences float

**THE LIFT METHOD**

float falls flat

peacock quill float attached bottom end only

float lifts as weight is dislodged

single swan or AA shot

1 2″–5 4′

**FISHING ON THE BOTTOM**

locking shot

bulk shot at mid depth

4″–20″

**TROTTING A STICK FLOAT**

flow

drift

drift

check

sticking set overdepth

bait swings upwards as float is checked

**Checking the stick rig**

float checked

flow

tackle is rigged overdepth to allow searching action

shot pattern depends on flow

dotted line is path taken by line when float is checked

tackle lands, close the bale arm, sink the rod tip and get the line sunk quickly.

For most stillwater float fishing, the float is attached bottom end only by passing the line through the eye and locking it into position at the required depth (distance from float to hook) with one or more shots an inch or so either side of the eye.

To present a falling bait ('on the drop'), group most of the shots on both sides of the float's bottom eye, leaving a tiny shot fixed at around mid-depth and another (a dust shot) 18 inches from the hook. After casting, let the bulk shot cock the float and then count how many seconds afterwards first the middle shot and then the dust shot take to sink the float tip to its final position.

A few practice casts and count-downs will soon show you how long it's taking for the float to settle. Then if a fish takes the bait while it's dropping, the tip won't

settle when it should, and that's when you should strike. Once the bait has reached the end of its fall and hangs in the water, bites will register with the float going under.

To present the bait just on the bottom (use a plummet to find the exact depth) when bites aren't expected on the drop or at higher levels – such as when the water temperature is low – get the bait down quickly by regrouping some of the bulk (locking) shots at mid-depth. Try the bottom shot at various positions between four and twenty inches from the hook until bites come.

To fish on the bottom with large baits like breadflake, pastes and corn, for species such as bream, tench and carp which tilt nose-downwards to suck up the bait, use a lift method rig. A very buoyant peacock quill float is ideal for this, fixed bottom end only with a float band, rather than locking shots, because this

rig works best with just a single large shot (a swan or AA shot) fixed two to five inches from the hook.

Set the float several inches deeper than the swim so that it lies flat on the surface, then gently wind in line until it cocks. The instant a fish sucks up the bait and dislodges the shot, the float will lift or pop out of the water and lie flat. Strike as soon as the float starts to lift.

Depending on the type of circumstances, river fishing demands either waggler floats, attached bottom end only, or stick type floats attached top and bottom. Shotting patterns can vary from just a couple of tiny shots down the line for fishing a slow flow, to bulk shot fixed within three feet of the hook for deep, fast rivers.

The technique is simply an extension of stillwater control, except that the float moves ahead of the bait and line is given from

the spool, with the bale arm open, as the float 'trots' downstream.

Cast the float a little downstream of you rather than directly opposite, and start the trot through by allowing line to pull from the spool under gentle pressure from your forefinger. After each coil goes, return finger pressure to the spool rim so that when you get a bite, you can strike and hold the line tight until the bale arm comes round to gather it as you wind. Bottom end only floats should be adjusted to present the bait just off, or actually dragging , the bottom.

Set stick type floats a little deeper than the swim, and cast with an underarm swing, controlling the float gently as it settles and is pulled downriver by the current. Apart from slightly overshotting the float, the secret of trotting with stick type floats is in holding back hard on the float every so often, encouraging the bait to swim enticingly upwards.

# FLOAT FISHING — 2

In still water, float ledgering is useful for presenting a bait at long distances where a light tackle rig can't be cast, or at best might drag and pull the bait into weed. Use a long peacock quill waggler, attached bottom end only with a float band. All the casting weight should be concentrated in either a running bomb or a swan shot link ledger, and stopped some six to twelve inches from the hook by a BB shot. In depths greater than the length of the rod, use the slider float style with a stopknot.

If set too shallow, the ledger should easily sink the float, so in effect the rig becomes its own depth gauge. Set the float so that it lies half cocked or flat on the water. Sink the line after casting, and put the rod on two rests with the tip above the surface. Then gently wind the reel until an easily visible amount of the float tip is showing, and wait for the fish to bite.

Float ledgering in running water (often called stret pegging) is more difficult because of current pressure against the line,

so you can't fish directly out as in still water. Sit or stand facing downstream and place the bait only a few yards out.

Make up a rig similar to that for still water, but fix the float top and bottom. Set it at least three feet overdepth, allowing current pressure to bow the extra line to reduce water resistance, and cast directly downriver to the desired spot.

Once the ledger has settled, put the rod horizontally into rests and gently take up the slack. The float is more sensitive when it's pushed well up the line so that it lies flat on the surface. Bites will register as gentle twitches of the float, quickly followed by its disappearance beneath the surface at a steep angle.

Slider float fishing is a versatile technique, its uses ranging from casting light float rigs with small baits into deep, far-off swims, to presenting live or dead fishbaits at prearranged depths. You can also use it to offer baits on or just below the surface for species like carp.

To rig up a bodied waggler or antenna float for fishing deep water, thread the line through the eye of the float so that it can slide. Then tie the hook on, and make a sliding stopknot.

Form a loop with 12 inches of reel line, leavng one end twice as long as the other. Hold the loop tightly against the line at the required depth, and wind the short end five times around both the reel line and the long end, then feed it through the loop. Remember to wet the line before tying the knot, and when you're moving it to a new position, or the line might break through frictional heat.

Pull the knot tight, and cut off both ends to 1½ inches long so that they will easily fold through the rod rings for casting or playing a fish. Rig the bulk shot no more than five or six feet from the hook, so that the float slides down and rests against them for casting regardless of preset knot depth, and pops up to the surface against the stopknot when it's in the water.

*Returning a good-sized pike – caught on a deadbait float rig – safely to the water.*

Sink the line to minimize drag, and remember to leave the bale arm open for a few seconds so the line can feed through the eye of the float as the bait drops downwards. Then carefully wind in the slack and expect the same kind of bites as with fixed floats.

Bottom end sliders can be set to offer a livebait well away from the bottom and over weedbeds at any prearranged depth fished static, or fished with or across the wind on the drift. Even deadbaits, mounted horizontally and suspended beneath a slider, can be made to 'come alive' by casting well across the wind and encouraging a belly of line to zoom them along with the waves.

To anchor deadbait on the bottom beneath a slider in still water, with the line between float and rod sunk, simply pinch on enough swan shots to cock the float immediately above the wire trace, and set the float slightly overdepth. This will prevent the float from shooting under every few seconds in rough conditions and giving false bite indications.

To present a livebait in this way, rig up a running paternoster with the bomb link set however many feet above the bottom you wish to fish. The main benefit from a slider in these situations is that regardless of depth, the strike is very much more direct than with a large fixed float.

Close-range livebaiting in calm conditions, in both still and running water, can be most effectively presented with tubed sliders and a greased line. A good example of this is fishing for pike in still water, with a deadbait on the bottom in lee of the bank or boat. Set the float to at least twice swim depth so that when it comes to rest against the stopknot it will lie completely flat on the surface. When a pike sucks up the bait it will feel no resistance, because the float won't go under but simply follow the fish across the surface of the water.

A similar rig can be used in running water, but with the bait anchored down on the bottom by a bomb running above the trace. Cast directly downstream, and the float won't be pulled under by even the strongest flow, provided it's been set far enough over swim depth.

Small, self-cocking controller sliders are great for presenting surface baits. Whether you're using floating crust for carp, or casters for roach or rudd, the (greased) line runs straight through the eye, providing wonderfully visual bite indications. You simply watch the line near the float or close to the rod, or just keep an eye on the bait itself. Baits fished on the drop work well too.

To rig a controller, fix up a link about three feet long with a swivel on one end and the hook on the other. Then tie the reel line to the swivel, after first threading on the float followed by a tiny bead to stop the float eye jamming over the swivel. The controller simply slides up and down the line as you play a fish, and it can be made heavy enough to be cast to most far-out spots.

The float ledger rig for still water is useful for presenting baits at long distances. The rig for stret pegging has the float set at least 3 feet overdepth to allow for the effect of the current.

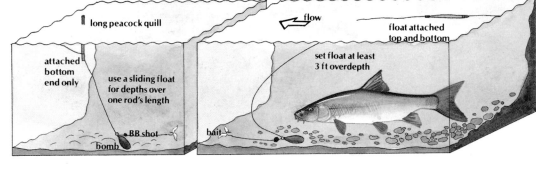

**FLOAT LEDGER RIG FOR STILL WATER**

long peacock quill

attached bottom end only

use a sliding float for depths over one rod's length

BB shot

bomb

**RUNNING WATER — STRET PEGGING**

flow

float attached top and bottom

set float at least 3 ft overdepth

bait

For deepwater fishing with a sliding float, use a bodied waggler or an antenna float. A good way to present deadbaits in still water, for fish such as pike, is to use a bottom end sliding float rig.

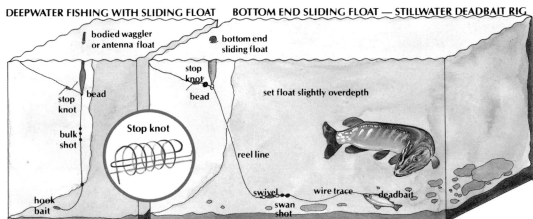

**DEEPWATER FISHING WITH SLIDING FLOAT**

bodied waggler or antenna float

stop knot

bead

bulk shot

Stop knot

hook bait

**BOTTOM END SLIDING FLOAT — STILLWATER DEADBAIT RIG**

bottom end sliding float

stop knot

bead

set float slightly overdepth

reel line

swivel

wire trace

deadbait

swan shot

An alternative to the bottom end sliding float rig for stillwater deadbaiting is the tubed sliding float rig. The float is set at double the swim depth so that it lies flat on the surface.

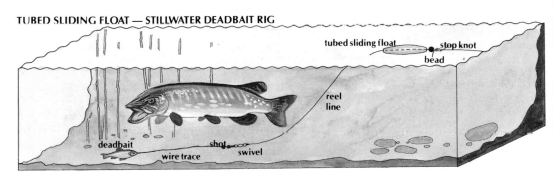

**TUBED SLIDING FLOAT — STILLWATER DEADBAIT RIG**

tubed sliding float

stop knot

bead

reel line

deadbait

wire trace

shot

swivel

Sliding controller float rigs are ideal for presenting surface baits such as floating breadcrust, and can also be used for baits fished on the drop.

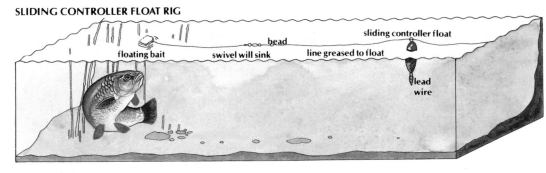

**SLIDING CONTROLLER FLOAT RIG**

sliding controller float

bead

floating bait

swivel will sink

line greased to float

lead wire

# FLY CASTING

In many fly fishing situations, especially for trout, it only needs one good cast to catch one. It therefore pays to develop all the skill and dexterity with your tackle that you can muster. Even if you don't catch anything, you will get a great deal of satisfaction and pleasure from just casting well and being by the water.

In the early stages of learning to cast it's essential to master the basics. All good casting is done with a combination of wrist and forearm movement. Some novices develop too much wrist action while others think that sheer, brute strength will enable them to wave the rod about to good effect, using only body power.

For most of us, the hammer-and-nail analogy has proved to be the best way of visualizing the way to handle a single handed fly rod. If you're using a hammer to knock in a large nail, you don't use it with a totally stiff wrist. Nor do you use wrist action only with no forearm movement. Instead, you bring the hammer back with forearm movement and return it in much the same way. But just before the hammer hits the nail you flick your wrist forwards to add extra impetus to the forearm power stroke. You should use the same sort of action when casting with a single handed fly rod.

In overhead casting, all good forward casts begin with a good back cast. This is essential to load the 'spring' of the rod, so that when it's driven forward there will be a release of that spring to drive the line and fly towards the target.

When you're learning to cast, the first thing to do is to practise this wrist/arm action. It may help to sit on a small stool, with the rod in your right hand. Place your right elbow on your right knee, and keep it there while flicking the line back and forth to get the right rhythm.

The rod should be raised and flicked with your thumb coming up alongside your right eye. But if you find that you're tending to bring the rod too far back, angle your arm slightly to the left, so that when you raise the rod your thumb comes up to your nose. Then, if you're doing it all wrong, the rod will bang you on the forehead at the precise moment that it should be stopped anyway.

Following some practice, casting a modest length of line becomes easy. But beware of trying to cast too much line, for this is when faults start to creep in. You may let the rod go too far back and have the line catch the ground behind. Alternatively, you may develop a tendency to push during the final forward cast. This push will do nothing to give more power (and thus greater distance), as it merely kills the spring of the rod.

Greater distances are best achieved by what is termed 'shooting a line'. This is best done by holding spare coils of line in your left hand and releasing them at the precise moment of the application of power in the forward cast. With practice, some remarkable lengths of line may be shot in this fashion; but it's not a technique you can master in the first five minutes.

Once you've gained some experience you'll want to try some other types of casting. The roll cast, for instance, is most useful for laying out a line under trees or for merely recasting in the same direction without bringing the line and fly behind you in a back cast.

Instead of lifting the line off the water in a back cast, just bring it feathering back slowly until the rod is just past the vertical behind you and the line is sagging down from it at your side. Then, with a powerful flick forwards and upwards (you should exert enough power to try to break your rod), send the line rolling out like a large 'O' and follow through by bringing the rod tip down to almost water level.

Modifications of this cast are most useful when you're fishing under trees or in places where a back cast is impracticable or impossible. Known to salmon anglers as the Spey casts, they are easily achieved with the longer single handed rods and involve something akin to a roll cast with a change of direction.

The type of Spey cast you should use will depend on which bank you're fishing from. The single Spey cast, for instance, is best done from the left bank (looking downstream), while the double Spey cast is most used on the right bank. Both entail an initial positioning of the line in front of or slightly upstream of where you're standing before the final roll out.

Whenever you're making overhead casts, however, it's important to be able to place the line and fly accurately at the required distance to cover a fish. Differing techniques will be needed for dry fly and wet fly fishing, and there is also a most useful distance cast known as the double-haul cast.

Casting in a wind poses many problems, but it can sometimes be made easier by casting with the rod held horizontally and down near the water. Most times a headwind will cause the leader and fly to curl back and thus upset your plans. The late application of power in the forward cast will sometimes ensure that the line and leader just unfurl in time to alight on the water before the wind can do its damage; but sometimes it's better to find a more sheltered spot or move to a position where the wind is more helpful.

**Right** *Being able to cast well and to present your fly accurately is one of the joys of fly fishing.*

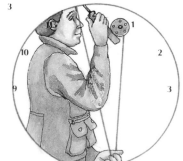

**THE BACK CAST**

3

rod flexes under
pull of line
straightening behind

**THE BASIC OVERHEAD CAST**
This is best approached
in two stages: the back
cast and the forward
cast, both shown here
in two colours

**THE BACK CAST**
It is impossible to make a good cast forward without first making a good basic back cast.
With the rod in the 2 o'clock position (1) and the wrist cocked downwards, the line is held firmly in the free hand. The rod is accelerated briskly to the 12 o'clock position (2). Now flick the wrist backwards taking care not to allow the rod to drift beyond 11 o'clock (3).

## THE FORWARD CAST

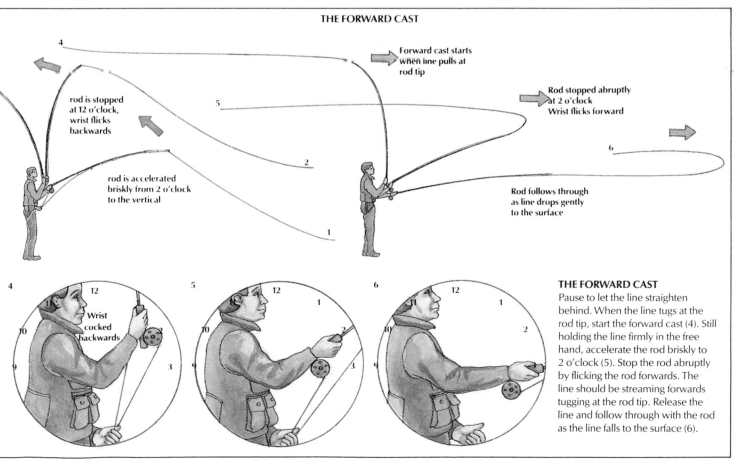

rod is stopped at 12 o'clock, wrist flicks backwards

rod is accelerated briskly from 2 o'clock to the vertical

Forward cast starts when line pulls at rod tip

Rod stopped abruptly at 2 o'clock Wrist flicks forward

Rod follows through as line drops gently to the surface

Wrist cocked backwards

### THE FORWARD CAST
Pause to let the line straighten behind. When the line tugs at the rod tip, start the forward cast (4). Still holding the line firmly in the free hand, accelerate the rod briskly to 2 o'clock (5). Stop the rod abruptly by flicking the rod forwards. The line should be streaming forwards tugging at the rod tip. Release the line and follow through with the rod as the line falls to the surface (6).

# FLY FISHING — DRY FLIES

**M**uch mystique has been built up about dry fly fishing over the years, but hatches of fly are less likely to be dominated by just one species than they were a hundred years ago, and the fish (thanks to hatchery breeding) are more catholic in their diet anyway. However, there is still a lot to be said for the challenge of pursuing trout with a dry fly which has been carefully chosen to match the hatching flies, although it can be argued that skilful, accurate presentation counts for more than precise fly selection.

There are many factors which can affect your chances of a catch. For instance, most of the bigger fish in the water didn't get that way by being easily hoodwinked by anglers' flies; it always pays to have an eye for colour and size and to know the times of the season, or the day, when a specific species of fly might hatch. Also remember that fish will sometimes feed more greedily on one species of fly than another. Other factors to take into account include the direction and quality of the light and its effect on fish vision, and the more subtle effects of drag, often undetected by you but not by the fish you hope to delude.

Most times on running water you should try to cast upstream to the rising fish. This will ease your problem of remaining unobserved and of placing your fly over the fish without instant drag being induced to scare it away.

It often pays not to cast too far upstream of the fish, for the simple reason that there is then more time for drag to be induced before the fly gets into the taking zone. When fish prove very difficult it's sometimes a good plan to cast into the receding ripples from a previous rise. This requires great accuracy and dexterity, but it will often get you a fish which is now taking on impulse, before it's had time to give the fly or its movement some critical examination.

This style will often work wonders when there is more than one fish in the same taking

**Above right** *A brown trout taken on a dry fly tied to imitate an adult cranefly or daddy-longlegs.*
*Dry flies, designed and tied so that they float on the surface, are used mainly on streams and rivers, but are also useful on still waters. On running waters, it's usually best to cast them upstream.*

### THE TROUT'S VISION (WINDOW)

A trout's view of the world beyond the water depends on the laws of refraction. Light rays passing vertically into the water are not bent, but the amount of refraction increases as the angle from the vertical increases, until at about 10° from the horizontal they are bent to about 48.5° to the vertical. 10° is the lowest angle at which useful light penetrates to the trout. This gives the trout a field of view (or 'window') of about 160° (180°−20°). The area of surface through which it cannot see is called the 'mirror'. A simple calculation shows that the trout's window diameter is proportional to its depth in the ratio of 9:4, and so the deeper the trout is lying, the larger its window.

**DRY FLY PRESENTATION**

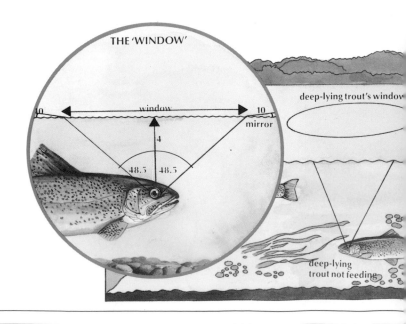

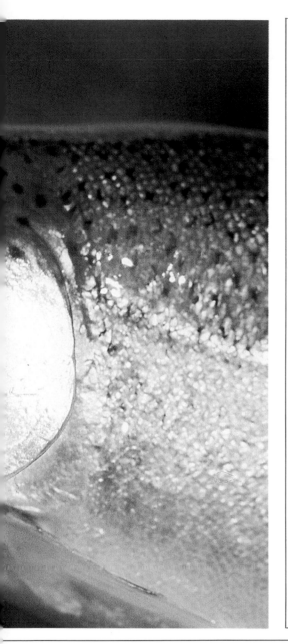

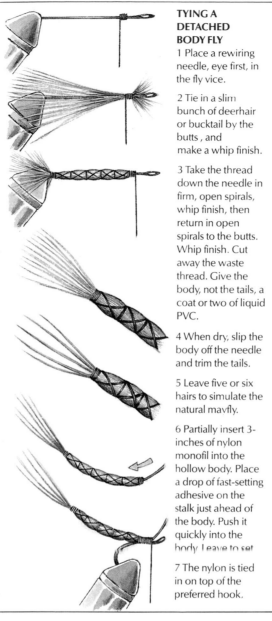

### TYING A DETACHED BODY FLY

1 Place a rewiring needle, eye first, in the fly vice.

2 Tie in a slim bunch of deerhair or bucktail by the butts, and make a whip finish.

3 Take the thread down the needle in firm, open spirals, whip finish, then return in open spirals to the butts. Whip finish. Cut away the waste thread. Give the body, not the tails, a coat or two of liquid PVC.

4 When dry, slip the body off the needle and trim the tails.

5 Leave five or six hairs to simulate the natural mayfly.

6 Partially insert 3-inches of nylon monofil into the hollow body. Place a drop of fast-setting adhesive on the stalk just ahead of the body. Push it quickly into the body. Leave to set.

7 The nylon is tied in on top of the preferred hook.

angler kneels for concealment

loose line cast upstream to delay drag. cast to nearside of fish allowing fly and as little as possible of the leader to enter window

flow

surface-feeding trout's window

alert trout 'on the fin' surface feeding

trout rooting for nymphs

weedbeds

gravel pockets

position. This is when greed comes first, and in a mad dash to get the fly first, the fish will often throw all caution to the winds.

Most times, of course, a large trout in a stream will occupy its own well-defended territory and will seek to drive off other small fry or fish which try to intrude. Trout born and accustomed to life in the wild are essentially very territorial creatures. Those with hatchery origins, which spent a lengthy period being pampered with artificial feeding, tend to form into schools at first rather than establish territories, and it may be some time after their release into the wild before they abandon this habit.

In the clear chalk streams, a territorial trout can easily be identified as it cruises up and down its pitch sipping in the hatching duns. Chalk streams, because of their origins, are much more alkaline than rain-fed rivers. As a result, they have abundant weed growth which harbours a large number of natural insects, and for this reason the chalk stream trout are invariably larger than other river trout and much easier to see.

Trout which have got used to the plentiful supply of food in a chalk stream can be very selective in their feeding habits, but so, too, can fish in other waters. So being able to recognise the natural flies and choose an artificial to match them is a skill worth learning.

Although it's usually best to catch a dry fly upstream when fishing running water, there's nothing to stop you casting it across or downstream if you prefer. However, if you do this, there's more chance of your being seen, and of imparting drag to the fly before the fish has time to intercept it. If you do cast downstream, try to cast a slack line which may, for a few seconds, present your fly well without any drag. It will also stop the fish being covered with your leader.

Dry fly fishing is practised mostly on flowing water, but it may also be used to good effect on still waters. Here the technique is merely to cast the fly out and wait hopefully for a cruising fish to come and take it, sometimes giving the fly an occasional twitch to attract the fish's attention. But the use of the dry fly is essentially a tactic for the chalk streams or those rivers with only a modest rate of flow, where it provides one of the most exciting of all forms of trout fishing.

# FLY FISHING — WET FLIES

The dry fly technique is one of the more interesting ways of catching fish, but many anglers will argue that successful wet fly fishing demands greater expertise and so provides greater satisfaction. However, both methods have their own type of challenge, and both may be very easy at times or test the patience of a saint at others.

Unlike the dry fly, which is fished floating on the surface, the wet fly or nymph is used below the surface. In general, sparsely dressed wet flies are preferable to the bulkier patterns.

Nowadays, a lot of wet-fly anglers fish with an imitation nymph cast upstream and then manipulated so that it drifts close to a fish which has been seen taking nymphs. At other times, perhaps when the fish may not be seen so easily, you can cast across and downstream and let your fly swing round in the current until you feel the pull of a taking fish. However, it's usually better to work the fly a bit to make it more attractive.

This is especially true if you're fishing with more than one fly on the leader, for instance with three flies, each separated by about twenty inches of leader monofilament and mounted on what are known as droppers. This team of flies can be trailed behind a moving boat, but when cast across and downstream they will merely dangle in the current, tethered by the line, with no natural-looking movement.

To work a team of flies in a lively way you should cast with a slack line and let the flies sink well down. Then, as the current takes them downstream, lift the line slightly just before the full drag of the stream takes effect. The tail fly will obviously swim at a greater depth than the top one, and it will be largely a question of a fish's mood at that moment whether it's more interested in the tail fly or the top or middle one.

During the cold water of the early season, for example, it's often the tail fly which attracts most trout. But it only needs a bright spell around lunchtime and a spasmodic surface hatch of natural flies for the fish to be more interested in taking the top fly or even a dry fly.

One very successful method of fishing with wet flies is to stand at the head of a pool or run, cast the flies out and across, and pay off as much line from your reel as is needed for the flies to reach the tail of the pool. Then slowly handline the flies back towards you and through the deeper water. This is a good way of enticing deep-lying trout in cold water and, depending on current strength, may be practised with either a sinking or a floating line.

On shallow rivers you might find it helpful to use a full, white floating line for the simple reason that it can be seen better than a sunken green one. Quite frequently, the first indication that a fish has intercepted your fly will come as a brief hesitation at the end of the floating line before you feel a pull. Constant alertness to what's happening to the end of your line will often get you more fish than if you just wait for a good pull. You may only detect a subtle hesitation or twitch at the end of the line, but when you do you should strike instantly.

In very deep water, though, it often pays to fish with either a full sinking line or one with a sinking tip. It's also wise to use patterns of fly which have been tied to sink well down, rather than those with more buoyancy which are intended for low water conditions.

For nymph fishing, where you want to get your fly down to a trout's level in the shortest possible time, use those with a piece of lead wire tied to the hook shank before the nymph is dressed. Known as leaded or weighted nymphs, these are ideal for chalk streams as well as for many of the large rain-fed rivers with deep runs and pools.

The real advantages of wet fly fishing are to be realized at those times preceding a surface hatch or when all surface activity has ceased. There will also be specific times of the season when surface activity will be minimal but when the fish are feeding hectically on or near the bottom of the river.

If you're fishing in still water you can use the same sort of techniques as for rivers, but you'll need to work the fly more to take account of the lack of current to make it move. When you're after rainbow trout rather than browns you'll often need to replace the small, sparsely dressed flies with larger, often bolder patterns. But there will be occasions when small flies will win the day.

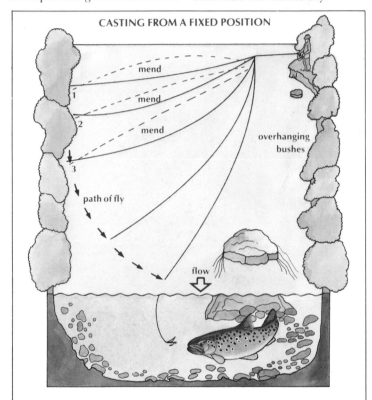

**CASTING FROM A FIXED POSITION**

mend
1
mend
2
mend
3
path of fly
overhanging bushes
flow

When you're unable to move downstream, judicious use of the mend or upstream bow can get your fly to where you want it.

**THE UPSTREAM NYMPH**

lightly greased leader

dipping point

leaded nymph sinks to trout's level

THE INDUCED TAKE

dipping points

1
2
3 lift nymph now
4

angler kneeling for concealment

flow

**THE INDUCED TAKE**

This nymph fishing ploy, developed by the famous keeper Frank Sawyer on England's Hampshire Avon, is intended to trigger a response from a trout which has previously declined the drifting nymph. As the nymph reaches the trout it is made to dive sharply by lifting the rod or drawing in line by hand, often inducing the fish to take involuntarily hence the term 'induced take'.

Above *Wet flies and nymphs are fished below the surface of the water, and are more sparsely dressed than the floating dry fly patterns.*

# FLY FISHING—SALTWATER

Fly casting for saltwater fish is not like casting for trout or even salmon. The tackle and casting techniques are broadly the same, but the type of fly or lure used is very different. Most trout flies, for instance, are tied to 'match the hatch', in other words the fly tier has gone to a great deal of trouble to reproduce an insect pattern to match the existing fly life of the water to be fished.

By comparison with this selective approach, saltwater fly fishing is a rough and ready style of angling. Saltwater fish are opportunists, and their food comes in many forms and many shapes and sizes. The angler's problem is not in finding a fly that exactly reproduces a shrimp or sandeel, but in finding one that will trigger an aggressive feeding response in whatever species of fish is sought.

Many species of fish can be induced to strike at a fly, up to and including large game fish such as sailfish. Mostly, though, it's the smaller inshore species that respond to fly-style lures. Bass, bluefish, bonefish, mackerel, pollack, permit, tarpon and a host of other species fall readily to fly gear, the trick to saltwater casting being to fully understand your tackle and the movement and preferred habitat of the fish you're after.

Choice of tackle is of vital importance. Most experienced saltwater fly fishermen prefer long rods, the ideal weapon being a 10 foot, two piece boron or carbon rod capable of throwing weight-forward lines in the 9 to 10 class rating. The reel should be a specially constructed, fully anodized saltwater fly reel. Failing this, you can use a good-sized salmon fly reel, but whichever reel you use it must be capable of taking a minimum of 200 yards of 20 pound backing line as well as the bulky fly line.

Tapered leaders of the type tied and used for trout fishing have little practical advantage for saltwater use. Sunken rocks, coral beds or sharp-edged shellfish have little respect for a fly leader. The trick is to cut costs by purchasing individual spools of nylon line of various breaking strains, and cutting off a 9 or 10 foot length whenever you need a new leader.

By cutting costs in this way, you might even catch more fish. If a leader costs very little, you don't have to worry about losing it and you can happily fish amongst the really rough stuff where most fish are found. Fear of losing costly tackle cuts many anglers' success rates to a dismal minimum.

If you can use a fly rod well enough to cast 60 feet or more in an accurate line, the only difficulty you're likely to encounter lies in the choice of fly and the way you work it through the water. For shallow water or surface feeding fish you should use a floating fly line, but for depths of over 6 feet a slow sinking line is preferable.

Flies (except surface bugs) remain the same irrespec-tive of the type of fly line you use, but the choice of fly depends a great deal on the species of fish, the time of day and the water conditions.

Take evening fishing for pollack, for example. During most of the daylight hours pollack live and feed close to the bottom. Then, as the light intensity begins to fade, the fish come up to feed close to the surface. Under these circumstances, any fly working through the surface layers is seen by the fish as a dark, moving silhouette. For this reason, black/brown or dark coloured flies seem most effective.

The movement of the fly is often as critical as its colour. With flies working on or just under the surface the trick is to create the illusion of a terrified and totally isolated bait fish. A natural fish finding itself in such a vulnerable situation panics and heads at speed for the nearest cover.

To imitate the movement of a bait fish you can retrieve the fly in two ways. A long pull of line at medium speed will make the fly shoot forwards at an even speed. To a hunting predator this will look like a natural fish heading for safety. Effective though this style of retrieve is, an even better technique is to retrieve line with a very fast, very short chopping stroke of the hand, each pull taking in no more than six inches of line. This odd but high speed retrieve will give the fly a sort of panicked motion that few predatory species can resist.

For bottom fish such as bone-fish or permit, both shallow water feeders, use a very slow style of retrieve. Both these species are browsers, living on shrimp and crab which they pick up directly from the sea bed. Most of their food is located by the little cloud

**Right** *Fly fishing in saltwater is an interesting alternative to surfcasting or saltwater spinning.*

### KNOTS

### THE NEEDLE KNOT

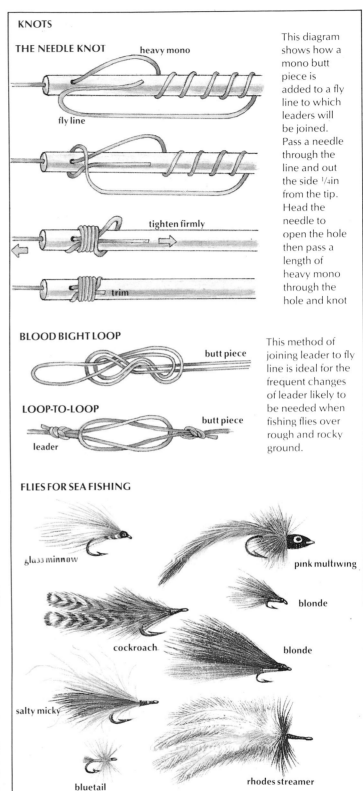

heavy mono

fly line

tighten firmly

trim

This diagram shows how a mono butt piece is added to a fly line to which leaders will be joined. Pass a needle through the line and out the side ¼in from the tip. Head the needle to open the hole then pass a length of heavy mono through the hole and knot

### BLOOD BIGHT LOOP

butt piece

### LOOP-TO-LOOP

leader

butt piece

This method of joining leader to fly line is ideal for the frequent changes of leader likely to be needed when fishing flies over rough and rocky ground.

### FLIES FOR SEA FISHING

glass minnow

pink multiwing

blonde

cockroach

blonde

salty micky

bluetail

rhodes streamer

of sand or mud which is stirred up as the shrimp or crab crawls over the bottom.

A fly tied over a lightly weighted body can be inched back over the bottom to simulate this movement. The weighted body of the fly helps it to dig into and stir up the sand or silt, and is essential to this type of fishing.

For large fish like tarpon or sail-fish, the fly should be tied in streamer fashion to imitate a reasonable-sized bait fish. Flies tied from fine hair material give a bulky appearance without being too heavy to cast. This sort of fly should be worked at speed through the surface layers, and most big game fly casters wait until a fish has been sighted before attempting a cast.

# KNOTS

Whenever you're fishing with mono or Dacron line, you'll have at least two knots on your line – the knot tying the line to the reel spool, and another fixing the hook to the line. It's very likely that you'll have other knots as well, such as fly dropper knots, or knots attaching swivels or leaders to the reel line.

Because each knot is a potential weak point in the line, it's advisable to keep the number of knots to a minimum, use a suitable knot for the job, and tie it carefully. Even the best of knots will have only around 90 percent of the strength of the line it's tied in, a point worth remembering, especially when you're joining two lines of different strengths. In practice, the knot might well have as little as 80 percent of the strength of the weaker line.

When you're learning to tie a knot, it's best to start by trying it out on a piece of string, which is easier to handle than nylon line and, being thicker, makes it easier for you to follow the formation of the loops, turns and tucks involved in making the knot.

To reduce the risk of damaging the line when you're tying a knot, wet it well to minimize friction before pulling it tight. Use a firm, steady pull when you tighten it, and trim off any loose ends so that they won't catch in the rod rings or create an unwanted disturbance in the water.

•

The knots illustrated here include knots for joining terminal tackle, such as hooks, swivels and lures, to the line; knots for joining line to line and line to leader; and knots for forming loops in lines or leaders. All of them are easy to tie, and are reliable and well-proven. They can be used with either nylon monofilament or Dacron, for freshwater or saltwater use.

The blood knot and the clinch knot can be used for attaching eyed hooks or swivels, and the spade end whip is for tying spade-end hooks to lines. The Domhof knot is for snelling eyed hooks, the Palomar is for attaching hooks, swivels or lures, and the spool knot is for tying line to spool.

For joining line to line or line to leader, the knots shown are the full blood knot, the water knot (or surgeon's knot), and a knot for tying a shock leader to a line. Finally, the knots for forming loops in lines or leaders are the double overhand loop (or the surgeon's end loop) and the blood bight.

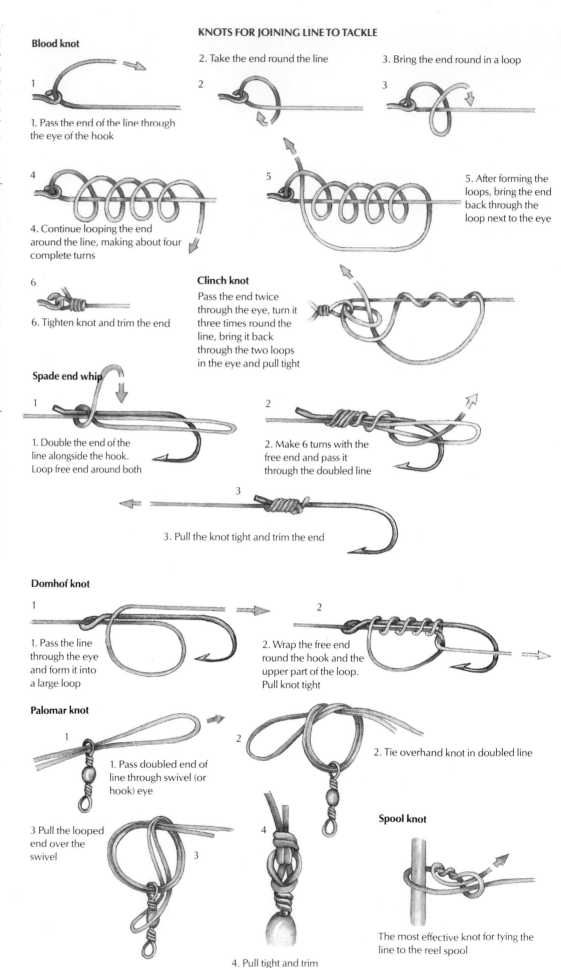

**Blood knot**

1. Pass the end of the line through the eye of the hook

**KNOTS FOR JOINING LINE TO TACKLE**

2. Take the end round the line

3. Bring the end round in a loop

4. Continue looping the end around the line, making about four complete turns

5. After forming the loops, bring the end back through the loop next to the eye

6. Tighten knot and trim the end

**Clinch knot**

Pass the end twice through the eye, turn it three times round the line, bring it back through the two loops in the eye and pull tight

**Spade end whip**

1. Double the end of the line alongside the hook. Loop free end around both

2. Make 6 turns with the free end and pass it through the doubled line

3. Pull the knot tight and trim the end

**Domhof knot**

1. Pass the line through the eye and form it into a large loop

2. Wrap the free end round the hook and the upper part of the loop. Pull knot tight

**Palomar knot**

1. Pass doubled end of line through swivel (or hook) eye

2. Tie overhand knot in doubled line

3 Pull the looped end over the swivel

4. Pull tight and trim

**Spool knot**

The most effective knot for tying the line to the reel spool

**KNOTS FOR JOINING LINES**

## Full blood knot

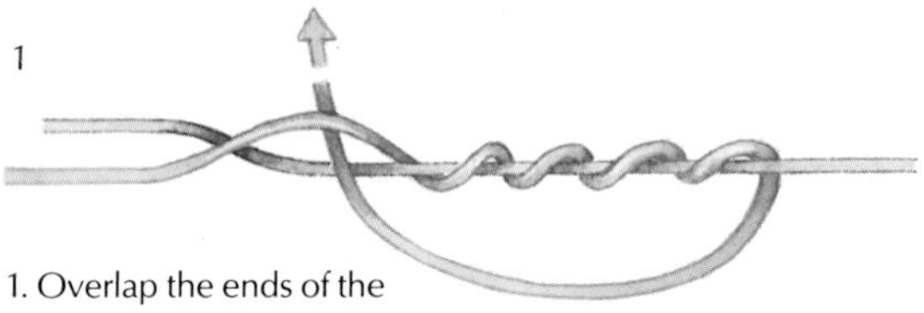

1

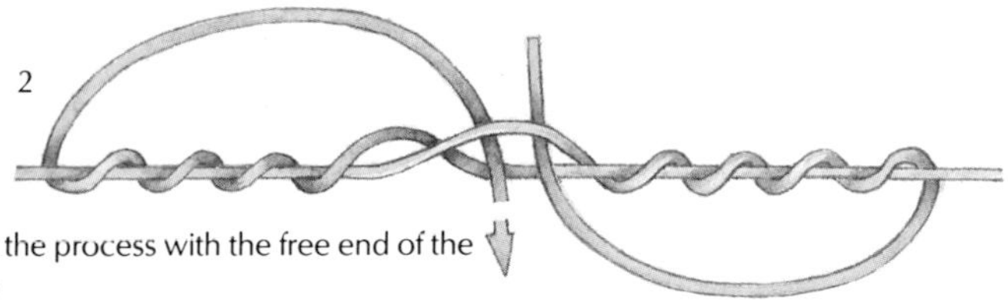

2. Repeat the process with the free end of the other line

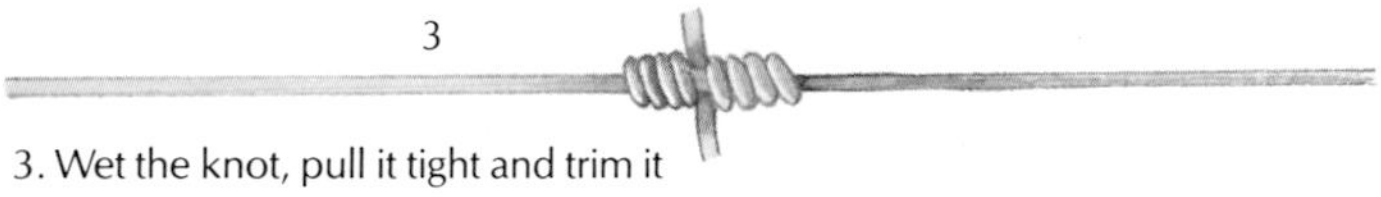

3

3. Wet the knot, pull it tight and trim it

1. Overlap the ends of the two lines. Take one end and wind it around the opposing line. Bring it back through the first loop.

## Water knot (surgeon's knot)

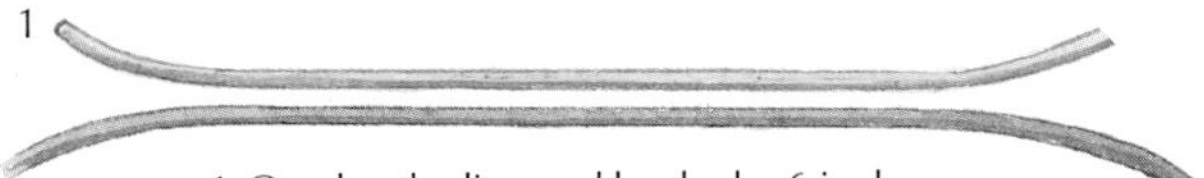

1

1. Overlap the line and leader by 6 inches

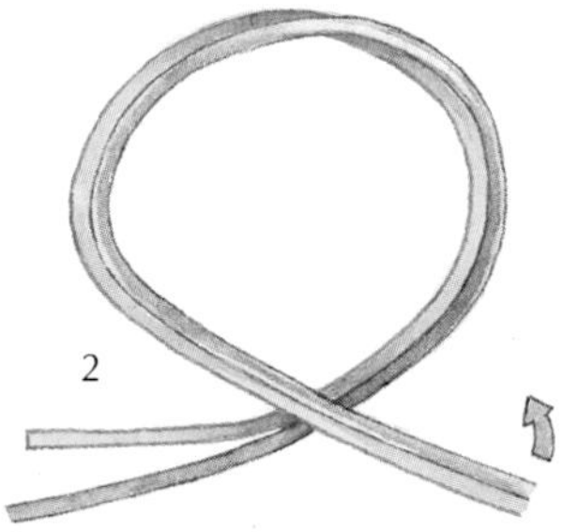

4

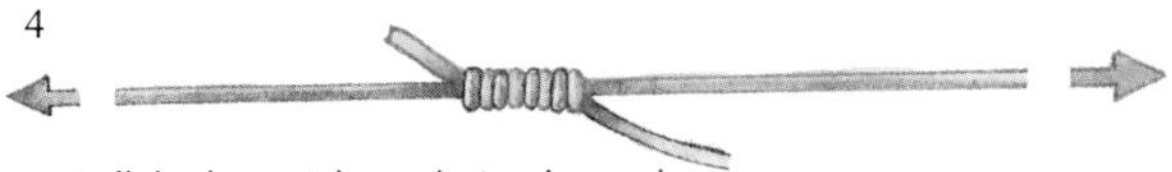

4. Pull the knot tight and trim the ends

2

2. Form a loop, treating the line and leader as a single line

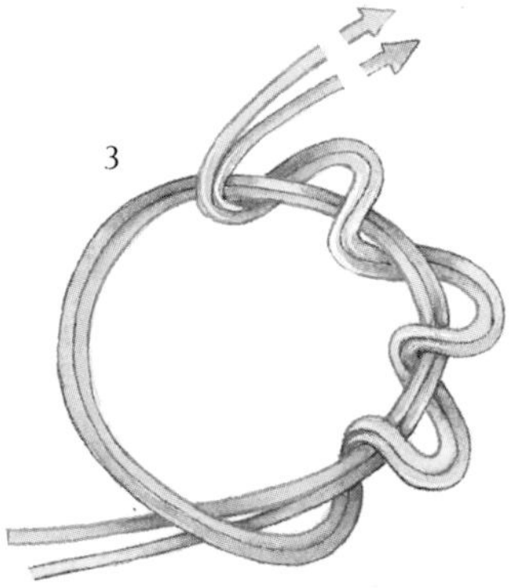

3

3. Make an overhand knot, pulling entire leader through the loop. Repeat 4 times

## Shock leader knot

1

1. Double the ends of the leader and the line back six inches, and pass the line loop through the leader

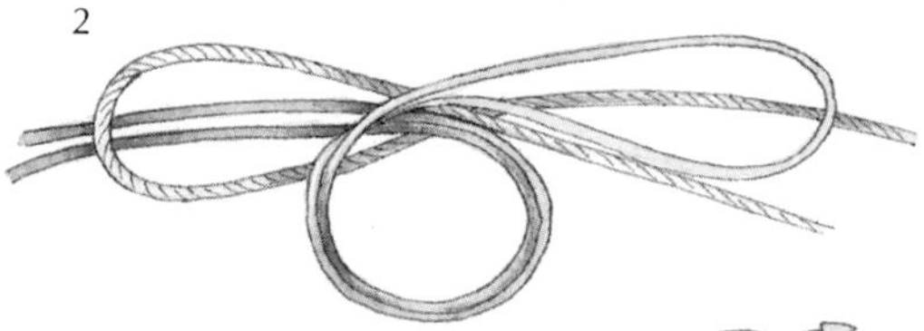

2

2. Form the doubled line into a loop

3

3. Pass the end of the doubled line around both strands of the leader and through its loop

4

4. Repeat three more times

5

5. Holding the looped end, pull the line and its tag end

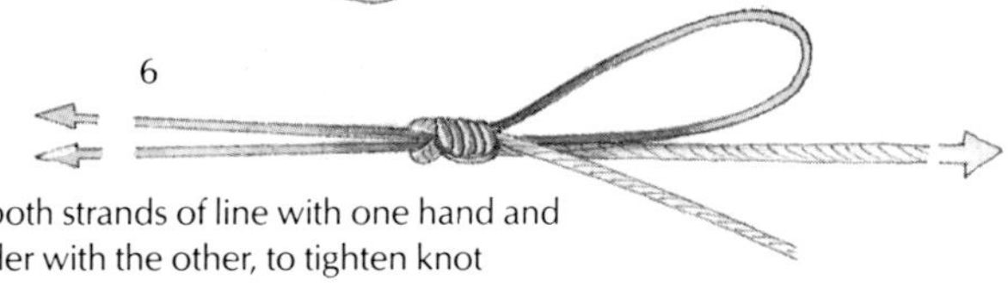

6

6. Pull both strands of line with one hand and the leader with the other, to tighten knot

**KNOTS FOR FORMING LOOPS**

## Double overhand loop (surgeon's end loop)

1

1. Double the end back along the line

2

2. Tie an overhand knot

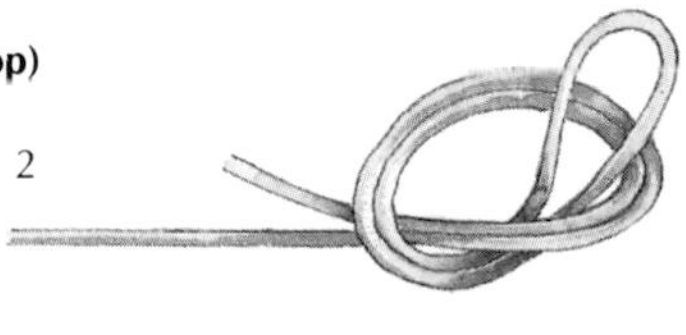

3

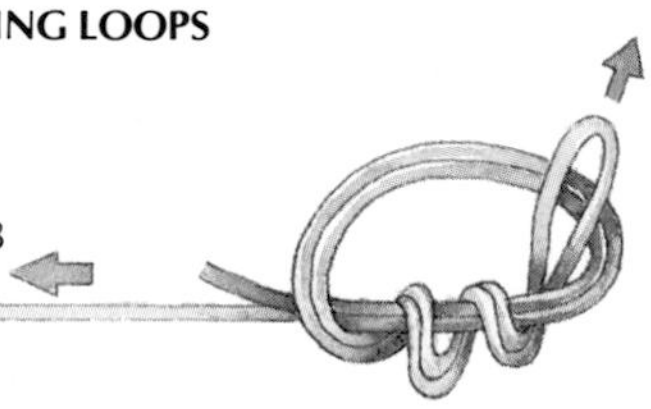

3. Repeat the overhand knot

4

4. Pull tight

## Blood bight

1

1. Double the end back along the line

2

2. Turn double end around the line

3

3. Pass looped end through the turn

4

4. Pull tight

# LEDGERING

It is a popular misconception among anglers that ledgering is the lazy way to catch fish. This is simply not true. Ledgering, which involves presenting a bait on the bottom by means of an anchoring weight, may not be as sensitive as float fishing but it is an effective and demanding technique.

Ledgering in running water requires a slightly different approach to ledgering in still water, because the flow of the river or stream affects what happens to your terminal tackle. However, there are a number of points that must be considered wherever you decide to ledger.

Use a rod that is specifically designed for ledgering, such as a quivertip rod with three or more different tips that can be pushed into the end of the blank. You must match the tip you choose with the weight you wish to cast and, most importantly, any flow you may encounter. On a lake, a soft glass quivertip is generally the best option. It gives a very sensitive bite indication, and this sensitivity is important because you are relying on the movement (quiver) of the tip of the rod to tell you that a fish has picked up your bait.

When there is flow to cope with, and consequently you need a heavier weight to hold bottom, you need a stiffer (usually carbon) tip. Anything lighter will simply be constantly pulled round by the current and you will never know if you are getting bites or not.

Casting accuracy is something you need whether fishing in still water or in a river. Remember, you don't have a float to give you a focus on where you've cast each time, but you must try to drop your ledger and bait in the same area each time so that you can feed and attract the fish into one zone.

Pick a stationary feature on the far bank, such as a bush or a tree, and use it as a marker; try to keep in line with it every time you cast. (Don't choose objects that move, such as people or cows.)

If you are fishing for species that don't fight too hard, such as roach or bream, you can decide on the distance you want to cast, then after casting you can slip the line around the clip on your reel, so that the ledger is actually stopped at the same point on every subsequent cast. But with bigger species, such as carp, barbel or chub, you may find a line clip leads to a snapped line as the fish runs away, and so you are better off relying on your own judgement where distance is concerned.

The position of your rod is also of critical importance when quivertipping. On a still water, the rod should be at an angle of roughly 45 degrees to the side of where the ledger is sitting, with the tip pointing down so it sits just above the surface of the water. Like this, you are able to see every indication on the quivertip. The front of the rod should be placed across a rod rest, with the butt sitting over your knee as you sit on your seat box. This way, you are ready to react at a second's notice to any bite.

When fishing in medium to fast flowing water, set the rod with the tip angled upward instead of pointing down to the surface of the water. This helps to hold much of the line up and out of the current, which helps to prevent the ledger weight from being dragged round out of position. By allowing some extra line off the reel's spool, a bow can be formed that also does its bit to hold the ledger in place.

This way you will be able to use a lighter ledger than you would otherwise, meaning everything is better balanced and bites are more obvious. When you get this system right, bites will often be indicated by the tip going slack. This is known as a drop-back bite, and is caused by the fish picking up the bait and shifting the ledger.

Terminal rigs for ledgering are many and varied, but a good basic rig for both still and running water is the fixed paternoster, in which the ledger weight is attached to the end of the reel line by a swivel and the hook link is tied to the reel-line eye of the swivel. This system keeps the hook away from the ledger, avoids tangles, and allows for any length of hook link.

Other rigs for both still and running water include the running ledger and the sliding link ledger.

## RUNNING LEDGER

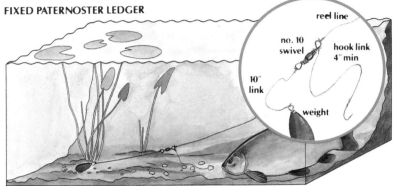

reel line

BB shot

nylon loop carries swan shot

shot to hook 12"

The running ledger can be weighted with up to 4 swan shots, mounted on a nylon loop and stopped about twelve inches from the hook by a BB shot or a plastic ledger stop.

## FIXED PATERNOSTER LEDGER

reel line

no. 10 swivel

hook link 4" min

10" link

weight

The fixed paternoster ledger consists of a size 10 swivel with the reel line and hook link tied to one eye, and the link carrying the weight attached to the other.

## SLIDING LINK LEDGER

bead

swivels

weight link

weight

The sliding link ledger has the reel line and hook link joined by a swivel, with the weight link fixed to a swivel sliding along the reel line.

## BOLT LEDGER

6" from backstop to swivel

swivel

2 oz bomb

backstop

The bolt ledger has a 2-ounce weight sliding on the 6 to 10 inches of line between the backstop and the swivel joining the hook link to the reel line.

**Above** *An angler holding the line between his fingertips so that he can detect any bites.*

In the running ledger, the weight is provided by up to four swan shot carried on a nylon loop, which is free to slide on the reel line but stopped about 12 inches from the hook by a BB shot.

In the sliding link ledger, the hook link is joined to the reel line by a swivel. The weight is carried on a short link tied to a swivel that is free to slide along the reel line.

A fourth type of ledger rig, the shock or bolt ledger, was devel-oped primarily for carp fishing in still water but can be effective for other species such as tench. It works on the principle of making the fish bolt at the shock of sud-denly feeling the weight of a heavy lead when it picks up the bait. The fish instinctively closes its mouth and flees, hooking itself as it goes. Once the fish is on the move and the line is going steadily out (use a minimum of 12 pounds test), pick the rod up and strike.

The bolt rig consists of a 2 ounce bomb stopped at around 10 inches from the hook by a swivel, with a ledger stop (the backstop) on the reel side of the bomb about 6 inches from the swivel. The backstop makes the fish pick up the heavy bomb by stopping the line from running freely through it.

Another point to remember when ledgering is that your main line must be of sufficient strength to cope with the strain of casting a heavy weight out into the lake or river. But note that that the heavier the line you use, the more air resis-tance it causes and the more your casting distance is reduced.

Where extreme distance is needed, a shock leader of a heav-ier monofilament can be attached between the lighter main line and the terminal rig. This allows extra force to be exerted in the cast with-out fear of the ledger weight cracking off in midair.

# PLAYING AND LANDING — FRESHWATER

Playing a fish, especially on light, well-balanced tackle, is one of the most enjoyable parts of freshwater angling, and there's far more subtlety involved than even experienced anglers give themselves credit for. Consistent success can only come through practice and experience.

First of all, though, you need to appreciate just what your tackle is capable of, for instance how much the line can be stretched before it breaks, and what sort of curve your rod will take. Dacron line, for example, has next to no inherent stretch, while the stretch in monofilament nylon might be as much as 25 percent. It's important to use well-balanced tackle, that is, with the breaking strain and elasticity of the line matched to the power and action of the rod, and a good, smooth-acting reel.

Before you make your first cast at the beginning of a fishing session, check the adjustment of the reel's slipping clutch. If you're using a fixed spool reel put the antireverse on, or put the reel in gear if it's a multiplier (baitcaster). Then adjust the drag until it's just possible to pull line from the spool by hand.

With the drag properly set you'll be able to put maximum pressure on the fish, knowing that the clutch will slip and give line before the strain on the line reaches breaking point. Remember to check the clutch setting every so often while you're fishing, because temperature changes and prolonged use can greatly affect it.

Each time the fish runs allow both line stretch and the rod tip to absorb the lunges together. When the fish starts to slow down, lower the rod tip so that you can wind and gain line. Then pump the rod back up again into a nice full curve and wait for the fish's next move, either another run or an opportunity for you to gain still more line by pumping again.

There will be occasions when a fish powers towards snags and you have to forget the clutch, clamp down and just hang on, throwing caution to the wind. It's only when this sort of make-or-break situation crops up that you find out exactly what you, and more importantly your tackle, are capable of.

Rods will sometimes bend into the kind of curve no tackle dealer would wish to let you try out in the shop, while the elasticity of monofilament line allows it to cope with some seemingly impossible loads. So don't be afraid to really work your tackle, and play the fish with a controlled, firm hand whatever the outcome.

The time will come, however, when you hook into something so large that playing it seems immediately to be a hopeless task. Yet no matter how light your outfit, if it's well balanced and you have plenty of clear water in which to play the fish, success will be yours.

One of the best ways to control a powerful fish and make it change course is to use sidestrain. From an upright bend, you lower the rod tip down to or even below the surface and towards the direction in which the fish is headed.

Now, if you apply powerful sideways pressure in the opposite direction, the fish will eventually have no choice but to kite towards the line of strain. A strong fish, once pulled off course, will then try another run in the opposite direction. When it does this, repeat the sidestrain from the new angle. Go on doing this until the fish tires and can be coaxed towards you.

More fish, especially big ones, are lost during landing than at any other stage of the ganme, usually because the fish isn't fully played to a standstill. The angler tries to grab hold with the fish held on a short line, but the fish fights back, the hook flies out or the line breaks, and the fish is free.

So the first rule to remember, whether you intend netting your catch or picking it out by hand, is to wait until it's completely beaten and not still thrashing. Then you won't suffer from hooks in your fingers, blood spurting from bite wounds, or hurt pride.

When catching really large fish, or small to medium sized fish on extra light tackle, a landing net is always the best way to get them out of the water. Wait until the fish is beaten, then draw it over the net, already sunk beneath the surface. If the fish is heavy, don't lift the rod by the handle because the rim could bend; draw the net towards you and grab the mesh itself for hauling out.

Where the water is very shallow in the margins the fish may be beached. This is often better than netting for fish caught on plugs or snap tackle, where flying hooks are bound to get entangled in the mesh of the net. Simply ease the fish up into the shallows and onto its side in one long, positive movement.

Taking the fish from the water by handing out will, now and again, cost you a lost fish. Nevertheless, it's an easy operation which allows you to unhook the fish and return it to the water in the shortest possible time. You can even unhook the fish while it's still in the water.

Draw the fish alongside the boat or bank, and reach down slowly. For pike, use a gloved left hand and slip your fingers into its left gill casing. Then clamp down firmly with your thumb, and lift. Be particularly careful of any loose hooks if the fish tries to twist or flap, which they usually do.

To pick out a bass or other less toothy fish, get a firm thumb and forefinger grip on its lower lip, if protruding, or simply pincer your hand around its neck immediately behind the gill case and lift it out.

Alternatively, if you aren't going to keep the fish or photograph it, reach down and flip the hooks out with long-nosed artery forceps while it's still in the water.

Above *It's vital to play the fish to a standstill before you try to land it, otherwise you'll risk losing it at the last minute.*

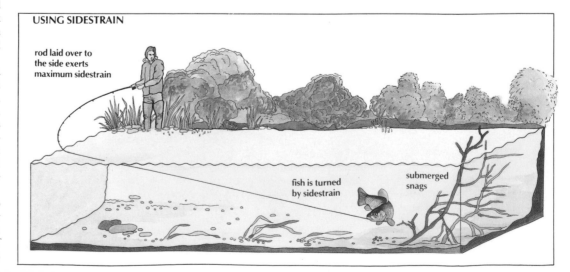

USING SIDESTRAIN

rod laid over to the side exerts maximum sidestrain

fish is turned by sidestrain

submerged snags

## LANDING TECHNIQUES

Never try to land a fish which is full of fight by making wild lunges with the net. Wait until the fish is completely played out and on its side, then draw it steadily over the net.

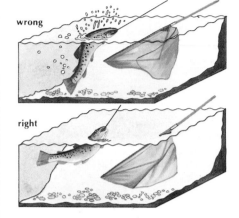

wrong

right

tailing

lipping

The salmon angler need not be encumbered with gaff or net as nature has provided the salmon with a perfect landing aid – a 'wristed' tail.

This method enables you to unhook without taking the fish from the water or damaging its natural protective mucus with a landing net.

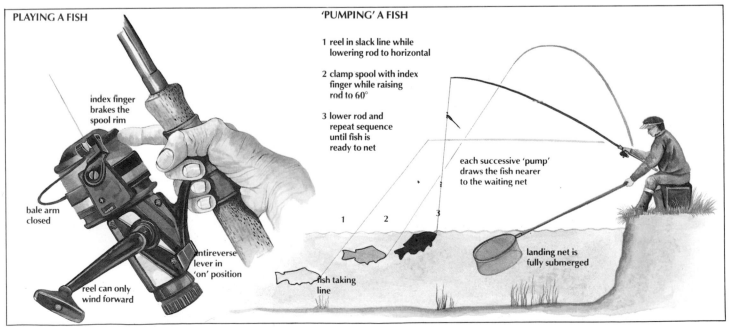

### PLAYING A FISH

index finger brakes the spool rim

bale arm closed

antireverse lever in 'on' position

reel can only wind forward

### 'PUMPING' A FISH

1 reel in slack line while lowering rod to horizontal

2 clamp spool with index finger while raising rod to 60°

3 lower rod and repeat sequence until fish is ready to net

each successive 'pump' draws the fish nearer to the waiting net

landing net is fully submerged

1   2   3

fish taking line

# PLAYING AND LANDING — SALTWATER

When you're playing a fish from the shore, the general tactics – pump-and-wind and the use of the reel drag and sidestrain – are similar to those used in freshwater fishing. If the water's calm and flat, you can play the fish to a standstill and draw it in to beach it. But when waves are running, you should bring the fish in on a good wave rather than try to pull it in against the undertow.

If you're boat fishing for small to medium-sized fish, the tactics are again the same, but for large fish such as shark, tuna or billfish a very definite playing technique is needed. These fish usually make a long initial run for freedom the second they feel the hook and the restricting rod pressure. During this first run you should make no attempt to turn the fish, because that usually results in a broken line and a lost fish.

The technique for these big game fish is to keep the rod up to absorb sudden shocks and let the reel drag work in the normal way, to slow the fish down. Even the largest of fish will only take 200 to 300 yards of line before slowing down and starting to circle.

Once this point is reached, you should begin to pump the fish hard to regain as much line as possible; at this stage the boat should be backing down on the fish to allow you to gain line more easily. The real battle begins when the fish goes deep. That's when you'll have to use your back, arm and leg muscles to try to raise the fish by applying maximum rod pressure.

Watch your rod tip at all times; as the fish lifts, the tip will come up, and when it reaches the 12 o'clock position drop it back down, at the same time winding in the slack. This pump-and-wind action often has to be repeated hundreds of times, depending on the size and type of fish on the hook, so always use a shoulder harness, clipped to the lugs on the reel rim, to take some of the strain off your arms.

At all times keep your left hand solidly on the foregrip of the rod. This is important, for should the line part under continuous pressure, your left arm will act as a brake to stop the rod from flying back in your face. Once the fish is finished and the double line swivel is against the rod tip, you should wait until the mate and skipper have 'wired' the fish. At this stage the drag system should

be wound back a fraction, so that should the fish make a sudden dive the reel will be free enough to give line without breakage occurring.

Landing or boating a fish takes skill and a variety of specialized tools. Most very big fish, from cod, ling and conger up to shark and billfish, are gaffed, the size and style of gaff depending on the size and type of fish. For fish of up to 100 pounds, a fixed head gaff – one which has been securely lashed to a strong handle – is best.

Never use screw-threaded gaffs, because they have an unpleasant tendency to unscrew themselves in use, and this can lead to lost fish. Fish like shark, conger or moray eels, which often twist at high speed when they're pulled out of the water, soon show up any weak-ness in a gaff.

For fish of over 100 pounds a flying or breakaway gaff is essential. This works on the harpoon principle, in as much as the gaff head detaches from the handle, leaving the angler or

boatman attached to the fish by rope and wire. The reason for using a breakaway gaff is to avoid accidents: big fish often go into a final frenzy when first gaffed, and a flailing gaff handle could easily break a man's arm or head.

When you're surf fishing for striped bass or other large fish you can use a fixed gaff. But when you're fishing from piers or harbour walls, landing fish can be something of a problem because of the drop between where you're standing and the water surface.

## THE FLYING GAFF

The flying gaff is used for large fish such as sharks and conger eels which, if gaffed on a fixed head, are powerful enough to break the arm of an unwary deckhand with their violent contortions as they are brought aboard.

## THE DROP NET

A drop net is the only feasible method of landing a fish from such places as steep rocks, sea walls or piers. Lower the net into the water and bring the played-out fish over it. Then lift the net, and with the fish enmeshed lay the rod to one side and haul up the fish.

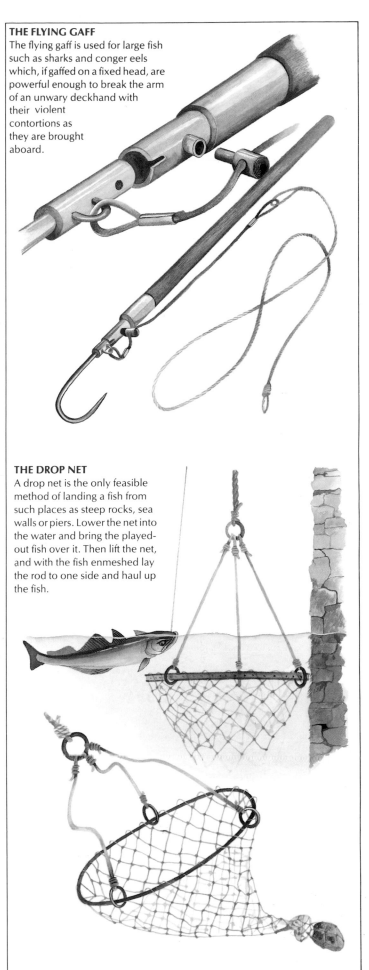

In these situations you need a drop net.

This consists of a large, round frame to which a heavy net bag is fixed. Four cords tied to the rim of the net are centrally secured to a suitable length of heavy cordage, which allows the net to the dropped down and held just below the surface. You guide the fish over the net frame, then raise the net to get the fish into the bag. Once the fish is safely inside the net you can pull it up.

For boat fishing where it's easy

**Above** *Large fish need the gaff, but smaller ones can be safely boated with a good-sized net.*

to reach down into the water, you can use a normal landing net. Where possible it should be sunk in position before the fish is actually ready to be netted. The sight or sound of a net being pushed into the water is often enough to send a big fish into a final bid for freedom. By positioning the net beforehand this can often be avoided.

# POLE FISHING

**W**ithout doubt, the pole is one of the most effective items of fishing tackle available to the coarse angler. First impressions suggest that using a pole is simplicity itself; after all, there is no fiddly reel to contend with. But while the pole is not difficult to use, the truth is that there is more to mastering it than is instantly apparent.

For instance, holding a pole is different to holding a rod. Instead of a length of around 4 metres (13 ft) you have upwards of 11 metres (36 ft) to contend with. The way you strike, play a hooked fish, and 'cast' are completely different.

Let's assume that the end two sections of your pole have been fitted with a standard elastic set-up – that is, anchoring bung, elastic, a small plastic bush fitted into the cut-back graphite (carbon fibre) tip, and finally a connector to join elastic to pole rig. The pole rig, consisting of float, line, shotting weight and hook, is attached to the connector via a loop over the connector's hook, and held in place by a small sliding sleeve.

The length of rig to use depends on a number of factors, but mainly on the depth of water you are fishing. For example, if the swim is three feet deep, add another two feet to give you some line between float and pole tip and you have a rig of five feet.

The exact length should be matched to a point on the pole where a section can be broken apart. The reason for this is as follows. If you are using, for example, an 11 metre pole at its complete length, with a rig matched to just three sections, you have a logistic problem to overcome when a fish is hooked. What you have to do is carefully feed the the pole back behind you, ensuring the elastic system is controlling the fish. Don't rush or you may risk losing the fish. (Many anglers use a pole roller to support the pole as they feed it back, to help keep this process as smooth as possible.)

When you reach the section that the rig length has been matched to, you can break it apart, ready to bring the fish to your net. However, it's worth remembering that elastic stretches and a larger fish may well require you to break apart at the next section down to allow the for the extra length of the stretched elastic.

There are a number of important points to remember when fishing with a pole. Firstly, you must do it from an even, stable position. This may not be easy when you are sitting on an uneven

bankside, but you can avoid this problem by using a seat box with levelling legs or placing it on an adjustable platform.

When a pole is fully extended, the best way to hold it from your seated position is with the butt across your knees. If you are right-handed, your right hand should be at the back of the pole while your left hand grips it just in front of your knees. If you are left-handed, reverse these positions. When holding your pole like this it is possible to lift it, push it forward, ship it back and hold it steady with relative ease.

Feeding bait with a catapult is one of the hardest things to do while holding a pole, but it can be done. One option is to place the butt of the pole between your legs and grip it with your knees. This leaves both hands free to fire the catapult. But it also means that if a bite occurs, you can do nothing about it. It is better to sit with the pole positioned across your knees, holding the pouch of the catapult with your rearmost hand as it maintains a grip on the butt of the pole. The pole is now balanced across your knees and your other hand is free to hold the stem of the catapult. Now push the catapult forward and, when ready, release the pouch.

When a bite occurs, strike by making a steady and sharp lifting of the pole tip. An over-zealous strike can result in a fish being bumped, or worse still, a break in the line. When playing a fish, although the elastic works for you, it's still important to watch what the fish is doing. If it is fighting hard, you may have to feed your pole out to keep it under control, and then, as you feel it beginning to run out of energy, begin to bring it back. The elastic itself should be lubricated regularly to ensure it runs smoothly, and the cut-back pole tip must be wide enough to allow it to run through without hindrance.

Strictly speaking, you don't 'cast' with a pole, as you do with running line. Instead, you ship out to the fishing point and then lay your rig down across the water in a neat fashion. If you simply get to the fishing point, lift your pole, and allow the rig to drop down onto the water in a heap, you will end up with a tangle.

*If the line is long enough, small fish can simply be swung into the hand once the hook is firmly set. For larger fish you need a landing net.*

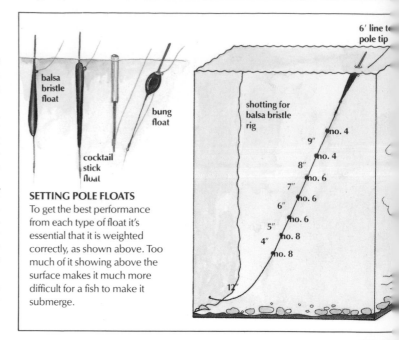

## SETTING POLE FLOATS
To get the best performance from each type of float it's essential that it is weighted correctly, as shown above. Too much of it showing above the surface makes it much more difficult for a fish to make it submerge.

## BALSA BRISTLE RIG – RUNNING WATER

It is worth taking trouble to space out the shotting pattern accurately, using progressively smaller shot towards the hook. This allows perfect control of the float, which can be held back hard, thus allowing the bait to precede it. Always use the minimum length of line between pole tip and float, and follow through smoothly as the float is drawn downstream by the flow. The float to choose for running water has its buoyancy towards the tip for stability and sensitivity.

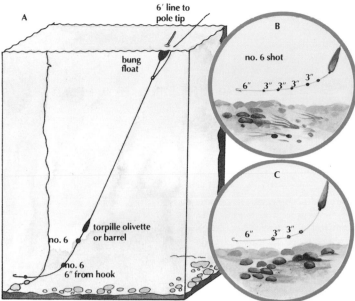

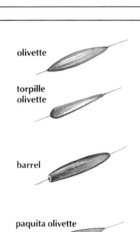

## BUNG FLOAT RIG – RUNNING WATER

This rig, employing the German 'bung' float, is for running water when the balsa bristle pattern is unsuitable. Whichever of the three patterns you use, the olivette must never be fished more than 6 inches from the bottom. The 6 feet from float to pole tip gives maximum trotting distance in the swim. This float must be held back hard and inched along the swim if it is to fish correctly. Try position A first; this arrangement is the most efficient. With the float cocked so that only its antenna shows above the water, hold back with the pole as you inch it down the swim. Stop for one or two minutes, and if a bite doesn't result, repeat the pattern to the end of the swim. If this is unsuccessful, try pattern B, then C.

## BALSA BRISTLE RIG – SHORT LINE, STILLWATER METHOD

This rig, sometimes described as the classic pole tackle, is designed for bottom fishing still waters at a range of about 15 feet, with a flick tip and a short line. As an example, for a water depth of 6 feet at a range of 15 feet, the length of main line from pole tip to hook length should be about 9 feet – 2 feet from float to pole tip, 6 feet for the depth of the swim, plus the hook length on the bottom. The rig should be set up before fishing, so that you can check the balance of shot and float; only the bristle and the white collar of the float should be above the surface. In this example the stop shot is a number 6, and the number 8 is the unsuspended 'tell-tale' shot which registers the bite.

## LONG LINE RIG FOR STILL WATER

Longlining means fishing with the float beyond the pole tip, as opposed to directly below it as in shortlining. For an average depth of, say, 6 feet, at a range of 15 feet, fishing with a 15-foot pole enables you to fish 24 feet out, where fish should take more boldly. This rig has other merits: set up this way it will take fish at all depths 'on the drop' from the surface to the bottom, and its self-cocking quality allied to quiet water entry is less likely to scare fish near the surface. Strike horizontally to avoid breakoffs with these fish, as they usually make off directly with the bait.

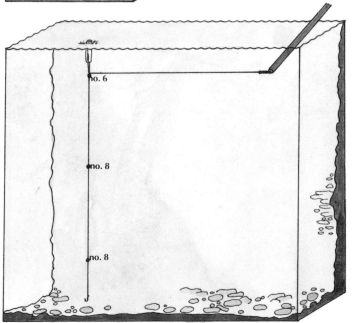

# SPINNING—1

Just as the looose term 'baitcast-ing' is used to describe casting artificial lures with a revolving spool (multiplier) reel, the term 'spinning' refers generally to all forms of artificial lure fishing with a fixed spool (spinning) reel, and not simply to fishing with revolving blade spinners.

The fixed spool reel is easy to cast with compared to the revolving spool, which demands a higher level of skill. For most situations, the simple underarm and over-the-shoulder casts (as used in float fishing) are fine for spinning.

The beauty of the fixed spool reel is that, unlike the revolving spool, it can be used on almost any rod except the trigger-type baitcaster. Short rods are favoured for tossing artificials short to medium range, say up to 35 yards, with longer rods being good for casting up to 70 yards or more. Long, supple-actioned rods are also useful for flipping little jigs or worms into or over tall reeds for perch or crappies.

Choosing a rod is seldom easy, but while the keen angler may own a couple or three different rods to use with a wide range of lures, a medium-fast action rod of between six and nine feet will be good enough for most purposes.

For the constant casting which spinning involves, always choose the smoothest reel you can afford. It should have a large diameter, smooth-lipped spool for long effortless casts, a silent antireverse, and be capable of holding 200 yards of, say, 8, 12 or 15 pounds test line, depending on the size of fish you're after.

The slipping clutch should be smooth and there should be a non-grooving roller on the bale arm. For ultralight spinning the choice should be a small model holding 4 to 5 pounds test line.

One of the most important factors in fishing with a lure is the depth at which you work it. It's no good retrieving a lure two feet below the surface if the fish are ten feet down in thick weed, or hugging the bottom in even deeper water because the temperature's very low.

So think in terms of horizontal 'layers' of water when presenting artificials. At various times of the season, fish will live at different levels according to the temperature and/or where the bait fish shoals are gathered.

The spoon, due to its weight and shape, is one of the best lures for finding the right level because it can be 'counted down'. On your first cast, leave the bale arm open during the time it takes the spoon to flutter down to hit bottom and the line to fall slack.

As the line slips through the rings, count the spoon down in seconds, one foot per second being on average a reasonable descent rate to assume. This will give you a rough idea of how deep the water is at that point, and on your following casts you can count the spoon down to whatever depth you want before you start the retrieve.

The retrieve should be slow at first, using the spoon's inherent vibrations to attract a fish, but if there's no response to this then it's time to work the lure more. Always imagine that a fish is

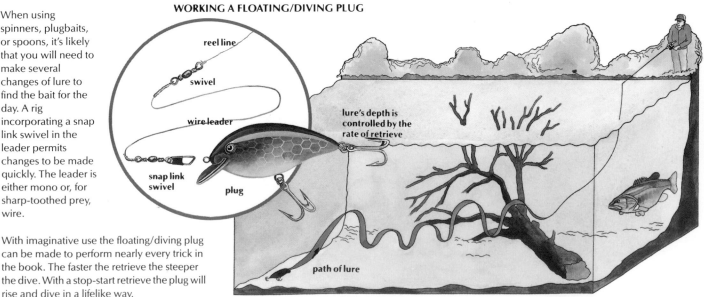

When using spinners, plugbaits, or spoons, it's likely that you will need to make several changes of lure to find the bait for the day. A rig incorporating a snap link swivel in the leader permits changes to be made quickly. The leader is either mono or, for sharp-toothed prey, wire.

**WORKING A FLOATING/DIVING PLUG**

reel line

swivel

wire leader

snap link swivel

plug

lure's depth is controlled by the rate of retrieve

path of lure

With imaginative use the floating/diving plug can be made to perform nearly every trick in the book. The faster the retrieve the steeper the dive. With a stop-start retrieve the plug will rise and dive in a lifelike way.

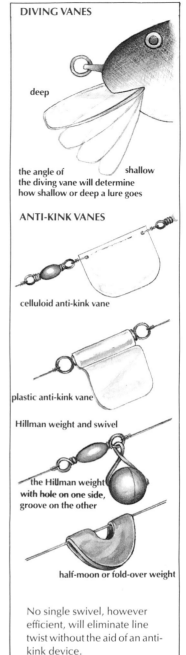

**DIVING VANES**

deep

the angle of      shallow
the diving vane will determine
how shallow or deep a lure goes

**ANTI-KINK VANES**

celluloid anti-kink vane

plastic anti-kink vane

Hillman weight and swivel

the Hillman weight
with hole on one side,
groove on the other

half-moon or fold-over weight

No single swivel, however
efficient, will eliminate line
twist without the aid of an anti-
kink device.

**Above** *Spinning with artificial lures is an ideal way to fish for predators such as pike, which will also readily take a properly mounted deadbait fished on a spinning outfit.*

following the lure, then you can visualize how it will be reacting to the movements of the lure.

Try suddenly speeding up the retrieve for a few turns of the handle, then give the lure a sharp twitch and stop winding altogether. Now the spoon will be fluttering downwards, and if it's being followed the fish will probably go down after it; pike especially respond to this. Now suddenly zoom it upwards again, and that's when the fish is most likely to strike.

Always keep the rod pointing towards the lure during the retrieve, with only a slight sideways deviation for twitching and jerking, otherwise the hooks may not be driven home on the strike.

Some fish, such as large trout, hit a lure hard and swim off all in one movement, which really hooks them well. Others, though, particularly bass, zander, pike and perch, open their mouths, grab the lure and stop swimming. These really do have to be hit with a heavy upwards strike to force the hooks in. Then, throughout the early stages of the fight, keep the rod well bent with as much torque on as you dare.

Much of the general technique of presenting spoons also applies to sinking plugs, which can also be counted down to the desired depth. But unlike spoons, which are always angled upwards from

the first turn of the handle, plugs with deep diving vanes will stay deep and fish more or less at the same level throughout the retrieve.

Many plugs, particularly the throbbers and rattlers, have such good built-in action and vibration due to body shape and vane angle that little jerking or twitching is required from the rod tip. The rate of retrieve is, again, most of the secret.

When clipping on a new lure (use a wire trace if you're after toothed predators) always make a few trial pulls through the water close to the boat or bank to familiarize yourself with its action. Unless you know just what a lure can do, you'll never really use it to its full advantage.

Fishing with surface plugs such as crazy crawlers, jitterbugs or

concave-headed poppers, is probably the single most exciting part of all artificial throwing because you can actually see the strike.

But unlike deep divers with their inbuilt action, these lures have to be made to move in a lifelike way and so soft-tipped rods, which absorb all the action you're trying to create, are out. Movement can really only be given to these surface lures with a stiffish rod.

From the moment the lure touches the surface, the retrieve should be as varied and unusual as you can make it. Twitch it, leave it static for a few seconds, then twitch it again. Make it gurgle by slamming the rod tip down to the surface, jerk it, pause, gurgle again and so on. Anything that will give action to the lure

# SPINNING—2

should be tried, because the way a fish will respond to a particular movement cannot be forseen. The time of day, changes in subsurface visibility, the availability of bait fish shoals and the presence of other predators are all influential factors.

Surface lures invariably work best close to natural features or snags because that's where fish are hiding up, either waiting for predators or prey to pass by, others just holed up for a rest. So never consider a spot unworthy of a throw or two just because of vegetation or because the chances of extracting a hooked fish seem remote. Slam the hooks home first, and then worry about landing the fish. As likely as not,

by the time a fish has caught up with the lure it will have had to leave its hideaway to give chase anyway. Even so, it's always wise to use weedless lures where the vegetation's likely to cause problems.

A stiff, snappy rod is also the tool for plastic worms in heavily reeded waters on fish such as bass. With the worm weedfree rigged and the hook point buried so that it slips easily through the vegetation, the stiff rod helps strike the hook home through the rubbery worm and into the fish's hard mouth.

To present artificials such as plastic worms, newts or twisters in deep water, use a weighted head directly in front of the lure.

Then it can be counted down like a spoon. Worms seem to produce more interest when retrieved in a twitching and darting movement along the bottom, over boulders or through weed.

Large, live worms can prove a deadly bait for many species. In shallow, still water, hook the worm once only through the middle and simply freeline it to the bottom. Leave it there for a few seconds, then retrieve it in a series of short, sharp jerks, with a long pause between each so it starts to flutter down again. Expect a hit at any time during

the retrieve.

In flowing water, pinch a swan shot or two 18 inches from the worm and fish it in the same way, allowing it to bounce across the current as it drifts downstream. For very fast water, rig up a fixed link ledger and use a bomb to either hold bottom or bump along as desired. With this rig you can take almost any river fish, from eels to salmon.

A well-balanced spinning rod and reel is the most sensitive outfit for presenting the whole range of spinning type lures such as spinner baits, revolving bar

**Below** *When you use a short, lightweight spinning outfit, whether from a boat or from the bank, playing and landing large fish is a real challenge, and even small fish can put up a good fight.*

spoons or spinners, leadheaded jigs and other lightly weighted lures like attractor bugs.

With the larger spinners and spinner baits (don't forget an antikink vane to stop line twist) use a simple countdown retrieve to explore different water levels, as with spoons. Since most of the attraction comes from the fluttering skirt and vibrating blade, additional rod tip action should be Minimized.

Use basic up-and-down and side-to-side movements and simply vary the retrieve with a pause or total stop every so often, allowing the lure to flutter downwards. Hits will often come the very second you start winding again.

There are two basic ways of attracting bites with leadheaded jigs or bugs on a spinning outfit. They can be jigged vertically up and down in any depth of water from a boat or down beside bridges or piers. Or they can be cast out from the bank or a boat and, after touching bottom, retrieved in an up-and-down nodding action, following the bottom contours or over weedbeds.

As you lift or wind, the jig's head pops upwards and towards the rod. Then as you ease on the retrieve or stop winding, down it goes again. It's this nodding action, plus whatever hairs, feathers or other attractors the jig has for a tail, that makes it so attractive to predatory fish.

You can also use a spinning outfit with small dead fishbaits mounted on special flights, or more simply on two size 8 trebles on a 15 inch swivelled wire trace (snap tackle). The term 'wobbling' perhaps best describes this technique because the bait creates most vibration if it's mounted slightly off line.

For a 5 inch bait, fix the trebles 2 inches apart and work two points of the top treble into the bait's eye sockets, with two points of the lower treble inserted along the flank. In very shallow water, or to work the bait at the surface, no extra weight should be added, but to take the bait down quickly to deeper areas, fix two to four swan shots immediately below the swivel.

Once the bait hits bottom (watch out for bites on the drop), retrieve it in an erratic, sink-and-draw style with plenty of jerks, pauses and twitches. When a fish takes the bait, strike quickly and hard and keep the rod well up so that the hooks go solidly home. Some species, especially pike, are notoriou for throwing the hooks at this stage, so keep plenty of torque on the them.

Because constant casting tends to smash up fish baits, a good supply of fresh deadbaits is necessary. This method will, on occasion, actually out-fish lures or livebaits, particularly in coloured water where visibility is poor.

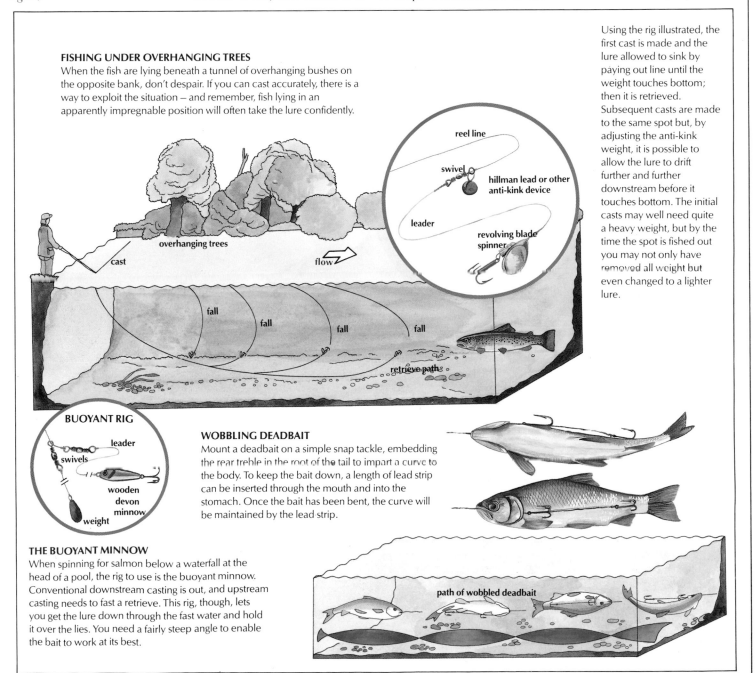

**FISHING UNDER OVERHANGING TREES**
When the fish are lying beneath a tunnel of overhanging bushes on the opposite bank, don't despair. If you can cast accurately, there is a way to exploit the situation — and remember, fish lying in an apparently impregnable position will often take the lure confidently.

Using the rig illustrated, the first cast is made and the lure allowed to sink by paying out line until the weight touches bottom; then it is retrieved. Subsequent casts are made to the same spot but, by adjusting the anti-kink weight, it is possible to allow the lure to drift further and further downstream before it touches bottom. The initial casts may well need quite a heavy weight, but by the time the spot is fished out you may not only have removed all weight but even changed to a lighter lure.

**BUOYANT RIG**

**WOBBLING DEADBAIT**
Mount a deadbait on a simple snap tackle, embedding the rear treble in the root of the tail to impart a curve to the body. To keep the bait down, a length of lead strip can be inserted through the mouth and into the stomach. Once the bait has been bent, the curve will be maintained by the lead strip.

**THE BUOYANT MINNOW**
When spinning for salmon below a waterfall at the head of a pool, the rig to use is the buoyant minnow. Conventional downstream casting is out, and upstream casting needs to fast a retrieve. This rig, though, lets you get the lure down through the fast water and hold it over the lies. You need a fairly steep angle to enable the bait to work at its best.

# SURFCASTING AND SALTWATER SPINNING

A wide variety of species come within the range of the beach angler. Depending on location and time of year, bass, cod, varieties of ray and skate, plaice, dabs, dogfish and mackerel are just some that provide good sport. From dusk to dawn is usually the best time for beach fishing, but gloomy and wet days can also be good.

It is not always necessary to cast a great distance, but the angler with this ability is usually more successful. For example, bass often lurk behind the third line of marching surf and a cast of at least 120 yards may be needed to reach this zone. Fishing for bass can be at its best in the days after a big blow, when a lot of food has been torn out of the bottom by the sea's violence. Cod are also more likely to be taken in a disturbed sea state then in a calm one, and long beaches are often rich in cod during the winter months.

A steeply shelving beach can offer outstanding fishing and is far more likely than a flat one to yield a result. Cod, pollack, coalfish, spurdog, bull huss and conger are likely in very deep water within a 50 yard cast. Tide action often creates a deep gully running along a beach, and this attracts many fish. Its presence can be revealed during the very bottom of a big spring tide.

A a good general set-up for surfcasting is a 12 foot rod with a firm action, capable of casting 5 to 8 ounces of lead plus terminal tackle, with a multiplier or fixed spool reel carrying 18 to 24 pounds test monofilament. A shock leader of 60 pounds test mono should be used between the reel line and the terminal gear to prevent the gear 'cracking off' during casting.

Terminal set-ups are extremely varied and include paternosters with two or three hooks, single hook ledgers, and two-hook pennel rigs. A pennel rig holds soft baits such as peeler or soft crab really well with the assistance of elastic thread, which keeps the offering fully intact during its casting flight. Other successful beach fishing baits include lugworm (which is irresistible to cod), ragworm, razorfish, squid and cuttlefish, and sandeel is an excellent bait for ray. Many bass take these baits, which are often combined in a cocktail.

After the terminal gear has been delivered, place the rod on a sturdy tripod or monopod rod rest and ensure that the angle of the reel line is sufficient to keep it above the first line of breakers. Watch the rod tip intently for signs of bites – sizable bass and cod will pull it down decisively while flatfish species tend to rattle it – and always respond quickly, except when conger are being sought. This species first tests the bait and then takes it down.

Saltwater spinning is very satisfying because you are totally

**Right** *Surfcasting from a shingle beach; the rods in use here are fitted with multiplier reels.*

## THE PENDULUM CAST

This cast is used where rocky ground or the surf make an off-the-ground cast impracticable.

**A.** The starting position is the same as for the off-the-ground cast, but with the rod sloped upwards by 30°. Hang the sinker on a 4-foot leader drop. Using minimum rod movement, swing the weight in a pendulum arc parallel to the line of cast, until the leader is parallel to the ground. Practice this swing to a count of four, with the weight reaching maximum height on the outswing at one and three, and the backswing at two and four. With the weight at maximum height on the backswing (four), begin the cast proper.

**B.** Start the swing, sweeping your left hand smoothly up to eye level. From this point on, the remainder of the cast is similar to the off-the-ground cast which is described below.

## OFF-THE-GROUND CAST

**A.** Stand with your shoulders parallel to an imaginary line out to sea, with your toes touching the line and your feet comfortably apart. Hold the rod level, a foot away from your chest, with your hands at shoulders' width apart. With your left hand at eye level, slope the rod down 30° to the right. The swing your shoulders 45° to the right, and bend at your waist and right knee to dip your right shoulder.

**B.** Keep your arms in position relative to your shoulders, and straighten up and swing your shoulders back parallel to the imaginary line. Continue the swing until your chest faces almost down the line.
**C/D.** As your shoulders parallel the line, push your left hand forward and up, then down to your left hip, punching forward with the right. Stop the rod dead, with no follow through.

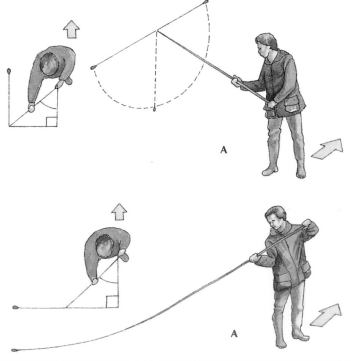

engaged from the moment you cast the lure until you pull it clear of the water at the conclusion of the retrieve. Fast predators such as bass, pollack coalfish and mackerel are the principal species that respond to a spinner, spoon, artificial eel or plug, which to them represents a moving meal.

The lure is best worked in fairly deep water from a rock spit, cliff ledge, jetty, pier, or pontoon. White water is also a good place to work a lure – cast beyond the turmoil and work the lure back through it. Heavy lures have sufficient weight of their own to be cast a good distance, and those that don't can be assisted by a Wye or Jardine weight fastened on the main line, just behind a swivel that connects the lure to it via a 2$^{1}/_{2}$-3 foot trace. After the artificial hits the water allow it to sink to the desired depth before beginning the retrieve. Work the lure with either a steady, even motion or with alternate slow and fast movements. Swinging the rod from side to side makes the lure dart about, which often solicits a take. Keep the retrieve going until the very last

moment: the lure should be virtually under your feet before you lift it from the water. Fish often follow the lure all the way in and strike at the very last moment, so never pluck it out until you have to.

A 7 to 8 foot spinning rod, with a fixed spool reel carrying monofilament of 10 pounds breaking strain, is suitable for most spinning situations. You will also need a selection of lures, including spoons of varying weight, shape and colour, plastic eels and worms, and about half a dozen different plugs.

A 10 foot rod, matched with a small level line multiplier or a fixed spool reel, is a suitable combination for spinning from high cliff ledges through deep water. Use a 3 to 5 ounce weight to carry the lure or bait out. Check the weight as it hits the surface, allow it to take the trace down to about 20 feet, then begin the retrieve. You will need a wide drop net to collect hooked fish from the water.

Working from ledges requires a good head for heights and sure feet in non-slip rubber-soled cliff boots, and your own safety must always be your priority.

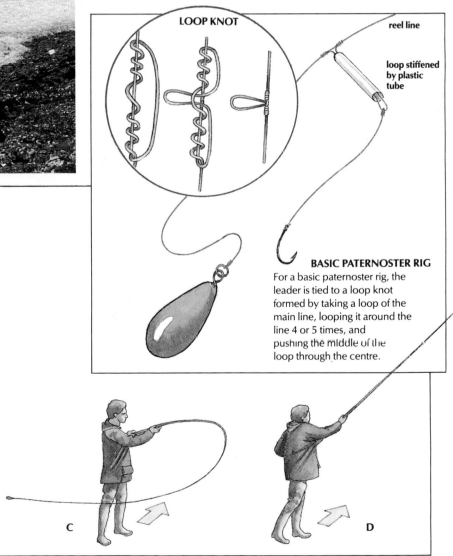

**LOOP KNOT**

reel line

loop stiffened by plastic tube

**BASIC PATERNOSTER RIG**

For a basic paternoster rig, the leader is tied to a loop knot formed by taking a loop of the main line, looping it around the line 4 or 5 times, and pushing the middle of the loop through the centre.

B

B

C

D

# TROLLING—FRESHWATER

Trolling, or trailing as it's sometimes called, is fishing by pulling an artificial lure or mounted fishbait behind a moving boat. As the intention is to give predatory fish the impression that the trolled bait is alive, moving at the right speed, with a suitable lure fished at the correct depth, is the combination which leads to success.

The simplest form of trolling is to trail the lure behind a rowed boat. Where the bottom shelves down deep, you row slowly so the bait can work deeper, and where it shallows you row quickly to bring the bait up, so that it doesn't foul the bottom muck or become stuck in snags or weeds.

If you're trolling alone, use just one or two rods, angled outwards from either side of the boat in rod holders close to the stern. Then when you get a bite, you ship the

oars, possibly drop the anchor, and grab the rod to play the fish.

Some anglers like to trail with a sliding float on the line, set well overdepth beneath a stopknot. The float gives early indication of a predator's attack on deadbaits, and is especially useful with trailed livebaits, a deadly effective method for catching species like pike, muskies or walleye in still water or slow-moving rivers.

Other baits which can be trailed behind a rowboat, with or without a motor, are teams of flies or single large streamer-type flies, fished deep down with a lead-cored line on large lakes or reservoirs.

To troll from a motorboat for trout or pike, use a large-lipped, deep-diving plug with the boat moving at one to three knots. Even heavy spoons can be trolled at depths of several feet on basic

tackle, as long as trolling speed is kept slow to prevent the spoon from surfacing.

Treble hooks should always be kept really sharp, and for all motor trolling use a revolving spool (multiplier) reel which can be put in or out of gear quickly.

Exactly how far behind the boat to troll the lure can never really be defined. A good starting distance would be 50 to 60 feet, but you should try increasing this if you're not getting any bites.

There are various ways of getting a lure down deep and keeping it trolling at that depth. Some anglers use wire-based or lead-covered lines, but others favor heavy, vaned trolling weights fixed well ahead of the lure.

There is, however, nothing to match the simple, effective, all-round control of the downrigger,

which keeps the lure trolling at exactly the depth you want regardless of trolling speed, an impossible feat with all other methods.

Although computerized downriggers with auto winch facilities are widely used, a simple manual downrigger will cover most fishing situations in both still and running waters.

A crank handle centerpin winch, which holds the downrigger cable, clamps to the stern or the side of the boat close to the stern. On top of the winch housing is the tubular rod holder, and protruding from the center is a 24 inch boom with a pulley at the end through which the cable feeds down to the water.

At the end of the cable is the downrigger weight itself, a lead ball weighing 3 pounds or more (depending on trolling depth and

Above *Freshwater trolling can involve simply trailing a lure behind a rowed boat, or, as here, using several lines fished from the stern of a large, powered boat.*

## TROLLING WITH OARS

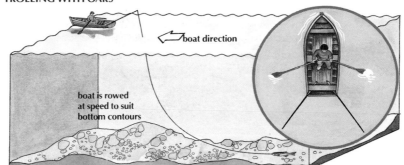

boat direction

boat is rowed at speed to suit bottom contours

When trolling under oars, the rod or rods are wedged beneath the rear thwart. The bait's depth is controlled by the length of line out and the rowing speed of the boat.

## MOTOR TROLLING WITH SONAR

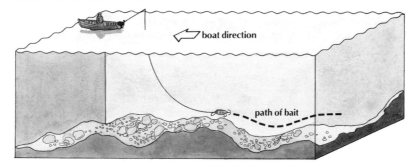

boat direction

path of bait

By skilful use of the motor the fisherman can alter the depth of his trolling bait to closely follow the bottom contours as shown on the sonar readout.

## TROLLING WITH DOWNRIGGER

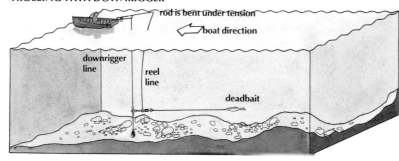

rod is bent under tension

boat direction

downrigger line

reel line

deadbait

As the downrigger line is lowered it takes line from the rod reel against the check. At the desired depth the downrigger is locked as shown. Depth is altered according to the sonar readout.

## THE DOWNRIGGER IN ACTION

Unlike other methods which incorporate additional weight, when a fish takes the bait on a downrigger the breakaway link snaps giving a direct weight-free contact with the fish.

speed). The weight is finned, and a quick release clip which holds the rod line is fixed to it by 4 inches of cable.

The line is clipped in to fish the lure at anywhere from two to a hundred or more feet behind the boat, and the downrigger lowered by the winch to the required depth. Literally any depth can be fished (if the cable and line are long enough), with the lure following horizontally behind the downrigger weight.

The reel is left out of gear, with the ratchet on, for lowering the weight down to trolling depth and for raising or lowering it at any time during the troll. When the lure is set at the trolling depth, the reel is thrown into gear and the preset clutch helps to set the hook and avoid a break when a heavy fish grabs the lure.

The reel line is wound up tight so the rod tip takes on a tight bend. It then quickly straightens and springs up if a fish pulls the line from the quick release clip. With the reel line free of the downrigger, the fish is played in as normal.

Using a downrigger in conjunction with sonar, lures can be trolled up and over obstacles such as submerged treetops, through steep-sided gullies and over shallow bars and weedbeds. Some sonars have color display screens which show what lies beneath the boat – the depth, the bottom contours, obstacles and even the fish.

It's all a far cry from simply walking along the bank, tossing out a lure and cranking it back in. But for trolling on large waters, where the fish could be literally miles away, fitting your boat with equipment that can locate the fish electronically can save you much time and trouble.

# READING THE WATER

Being able to 'read' the water for signs of where a shoal or even an individual fish might be lying is an art that successful anglers use to great effect; others rely more on luck. Luck certainly plays its part in angling, as it does in any other human activity; the ones that get away may do so for reasons completely beyond your control. But an understanding of the habitats preferred by the fish you're after means that you can use a methodical approach which will swing the odds in your favour. At the very least, it'll make it unlikely that you'll waste time fishing a stretch of water when the fish are elsewhere.

This approach applies to all forms of fishing, from creeping up on a wily old brown trout lurking in an awkward run among thick weed, to trolling blue waters for billfish. Being able to read the water and make the most of any opportunity is far more important than owning a rack of expensive rods. Fishermen who produce results – whatever the species and wherever the location – do so through observation, not luck.

They look to see if the water is clear or coloured, and how far into it they can see. This gives them an idea of what kinds of fish might be present, where, how and when they're likely to be feeding, and how close to them the lure or bait must be before they can see it.

Observant anglers also note how fast a river is flowing, and whether it's running at normal height, low, or in full spate. They study the current patterns, not just for a second or two but for several minutes. Then, like the fish which feed on food brought down by the current, they too have an idea of where that food will be deposited – and they know where to put the bait.

If they have time, they study the water at dawn and at dusk, and at other times during the day, watching the feeding and resting habits of the fish. They are constantly aware of the wind direction across still waters, knowing that micro-organisms such as planktons drift with the waves until they come to rest against a shore, when the fish that eat them will gather there, followed by the predators that feed on them in their turn. Observant anglers also watch for tiny, almost imperceptible movements in what is otherwise a totally flat, calm surface, and invariably, except in all but the coldest conditions, they see something which gives them a clue to the location of the fish.

The tools of the trade, apart from keen eyesight, are a pair of good-quality polarized sunglasses to cut through light reflected from the surface, and a good pair of binoculars. The binoculars should be reasonably powerful ($8 \times 30$ is an ideal format) but light enough to hold steady with just one hand, so you won't have to put your rod down when you use them. Binoculars help you to spot distant clues, such as tails or dorsal fins breaking the surface, or the delicate twitches of reed stems when fish move between them, something almost impossible to see with the naked eye at even comparatively short distances like 30 or 40 yards.

When you're fishing at sea, binoculars will help you to see the signs – such as feeding seabirds, a shoal of bait fish being pushed up, changes in water colour, or a fin cutting the surface – that can lead you to a good catch. To find features below the surface, like reefs, dropoffs and wrecks, good charts and a sonar are essential, as they also are on large, deep lakes.

Sea fishing, especially for big game, usually involves a lot more searching than does fishing on all but the largest fresh waters. Out at sea, there's usually very little aquatic vegetation and obviously no bankside trees or shrubs or marginal reeds to guide you to where the fish are likely to be. For the freshwater angler, knowing the various aquatic plants and the depths of water that they grow in, and which fish are attracted to them and why, is an essential part of reading the water.

There are, of course, many other (and far less obvious) signs to watch for in freshwater fish location, so the angler who is constantly on the lookout and who treats observation as a key to success will catch fish, while others waste their time in a barren area, patiently enjoying nothing but the scenery. Patience is a virtue the angler often needs, but successful fishermen are also alert and watchful. They are always watching for indications of fish showing on the surface – fish jumping, snatching flies, creating bubbles or disturbing the vegetation.

Even the appearance of a sudden flat of smooth water on the surface is reason enough for some anglers to head for the spot. It could be simply the result of a 'wind knot', but it could equally well be caused by a big fish turning over just beneath the surface, an action which for a few seconds irons out even quite strong waves.

# ESTUARIES

An estuary is the tidal mouth of a river where it opens into the sea. All estuaries are worth fishing because the inflow of fresh water into the sea attracts and holds the attention of many species of fish.

Some estuaries are created by short, narrow yet strong little rivers that carve their way through steep-sided valleys and high cliffs before passing out into salt water. In deep, narrow estuaries of this kind, the ecological system varies considerably from the upper section of the estuary to the lower section.

The upper section often consists of shallow mud or sandbanks, many of which become exposed at low water. In this section, small ragworms, shrimps and shellfish of the clam type often abound. This natural abundance of small food items is particularly attractive to shoaling mullet and hunting flounder. Bass will also visit the mud banks, but normally confine their activities to the deeper water in the lower section of the estuary.

Where the mud/sand banks finish and the water rapidly deepens, the nature of the bottom changes dramatically. The mud gives way to tiny sand patches and mixed rock and shingle. The higher density of the salt water in this lower section promotes the growth of seaweed, in particular spiral wrack.

This weed, and the natural cover provided by the larger stones, gives ample shelter to colonies of green shore crab, and the sand patches are equally attractive to shoaling sandeel. These food creatures, plus larger worms, in turn attract other, often larger fish, some of which take up semipermanent residence in the lower section of the estuary. Conger, thornback ray and wrasse are typical examples of fish which often become semiresident in deep estuaries, while other fish such as bass and mullet are regular visitors.

Apart from in-running and semiresident sea fish, many estuaries are run by salmon and sea trout, spawning fish on their way inland to shed their eggs in the gravel shallows of the parent river and its tributaries. In some areas, the tiniest inflow of fresh water is enough to attract and hold migratory fish, and sea-run brown trout in particular will stay for long periods of time in the vicinity of such a stream outfall. Fly fishing and spinning on a rising or full tide will often produce excellent catches.

Many anglers overlook the angling potential of estuaries. This is wrong, for estuary fishing is often good and it allows the angler to fish in many different ways. In deepwater estuaries it is often possible to fish from rocks, docks and even roadways as well as from a boat.

Fishing style and baits depend a great deal on the fish you hope to catch. Conger, for example, are often found in the deep marginal areas where they find rich pickings amongst the trash, fish and fish guts dumped there by local fishing boats. For conger, a heavy beachcaster and wire leaders are essential. The bait can be a whole or half fish, cast out only a few yards. Skate and bass may take the same sort of bait, but they are normally found well away from the shore in the deeper gullies. A lighter beachcasting rod, and the ability to cast 80 to 100 yards, are essential if you want to fish for these species.

Further upriver, where the deep water shallows over mudbanks, mullet and flounders are the main angling species. The mullet normally swim and feed in large shoals, which can be attracted by attaching a chunk of stale bread to a length of string and a suitable stone. The length of string depends on the depth of the water at high tide, the idea being to anchor the bread so that it floats on the surface.

With luck, the feeding mullet shoals will find the bread and begin to feed around it. Once you see the fish feeding, you can use a piece of bread, worm, sweetcorn, banana or part-cooked macaroni as hookbait, fished on a freshwater float fishing outfit.

In all estuaries, flounder can be taken on static baits, such as worm or peeler crab, or on a traditional flounder spoon rig. Originally devised by J P Gerrard, the technique of fishing a trailing worm behind a large plastic or metal flounder spoon is still recognised as one of the best ways to catch flounder of all sizes.

The single hook is baited with a ragworm and the spoon and bait are cast out and allowed to touch bottom. Then the spoon is retrieved very slowly so that it ploughs through the top layer of mud and silt. Hunting flounder see and investigate the disturbance, finding what is apparently a small flounder making off with a large, juicy worm. Naturally, the larger fish

tries to steal the worm and gets itself hooked in the process.

The trick to this sort of fishing is to ignore the first few twitching bites and wait for the rod to pull hard over as the taking flounder finally swallows the bait. This technique can also be used from an anchored boat, or by trolling the spoon and bait behind a slowly moving boat.

The mobility of dinghy fishing is a great advantage in estuaries, allowing you to change position quickly and to explore side creeks and saltwater lagoons. Dinghy fishing also scores over shore fishing where the estuary is wide and the river splits into many separate channels running between sand or mudbanks. At low tide, these channels are difficult to reach by boat and too far out to be cast to from the

shore. At this stage of the tide, though, the flow of water through the channels is swift and they contain little natural food to attract fish. It's only during high tide that fish will move into these channels, so as to get to the surrounding mud and sandbanks where they find worms and other foods that live in the slacker water.

At the mouths of these channels, where the fresh water meets the salt water, the flow is slowed and any food being swept down by the freshwater current is deposited there. This can make it a rich feeding ground which attracts many small species, and these in their turn attract larger fish such as flounder, dogfish and bass. Fishing from a dinghy on the seaward side of these channels can be very productive.

In other wide estuaries, the

**Above** *In the lower section of an estuary where the bottom changes from mud or sand of higher up the river to shingle and rock, you can find conger, wrasses, small rays, mullet and other small species.*

**Right** *Fishing from a boat in a large estuary lets you get to the deeper waters, and gives you more mobility than you could hope to get when you're fishing from the shore.*

outflow from the river is gentler and not split into deep, separate channels. The water flow is shallow and gentle, and provides a favourable habitat for many food creatures such as plankton, crabs, shellfish and worms. These create an abundant food supply for flatfish, bass, pollack and mullet, which gives good, productive fishing to both shore and dinghy anglers.

# OFFSHORE WATERS — TEMPERATE

Offshore waters, in this context any water beyond the casting range of shore fishermen, can be fished close-in from a small craft or further out from a large boat.

Small-boat anglers can often find good fishing in the most unlikely places, such as shallow sunk mud or sandbanks. These flats are usually scarred by deep gullies carved out by the prevailing tidal flow, and being deeper than the surrounding flats the gullies act as food traps. Live and dead crabs, worms and small fish all wash across the exposed flats until they reach and drop into a gully.

This plentiful supply of food and the added security of the deep water draws many species of fish into the gullies. Bass, small cod, flatfish, shark and stingray all use gullies as feeding areas, so it pays to learn where these gullies are. The simplest way is to use an echo sounder to locate each natural dropoff. In areas where the mud or sand isn't prone to shifting, once you've found where the gullies are you can use shore marks to guide you to them on future expeditions. In areas subject to exceptional runs of tide, certain places act as natural holding points for fish feeding on small fish and eels trapped in the strong tidal flow. These holding points can normally be located on the downtide side of any projecting rocks or small islands.

As the main flow of the tide races by on either side of the rock, it creates a downtide slack water area practically devoid of movement. Fish use this slack water both as a resting area and as an ambush point. By taking up station a yard or two from the heavy run of water, they can wait in comfort for food to be swept past them in the tide. Then, with a flick of the tail and fins, they shoot out, nail the fish or eel, and dart back into the slack area to wait for the next meal to be swept within range. A bait or lure cast to fall on the edge of the tide run should produce instant results.

In areas where giant common skate are known to exist, you'll often find them in deep water on the downtide side of an island. Another good skate holding point is in between two adjacent islands. Provided the islands are close enough together, they'll act as a natural barrier which funnels the water through the gap between them. This rush of water will scout out a deep hole on the sea bed into which all manner of edible matter will fall, and skate will normally take up permanent residence in this natural food trap

Further offshore, rock pinnacles and submerged rock ledges are well worth investigating. Two distinct types of fish inhabit this sort of ground: true bottom feeders, like conger, and lethargic bull huss live in or on the rock itself, while bass, pollack and coalfish swim above. The bottom dwellers can only be caught by anchoring over the rock pinnacle or ledge and fishing a bait hard on the bottom. The free-swimming fish are better taken on small, trolled lures, livebaits or feathers.

Offshore sandbanks are extremely good places to catch flatfish such as flounder, turbot, brill and plaice, and various members of the ray family. These sandbanks are normally formed by tidal action, and the fish take up feeding positions on the downward slope of the bank. This means that most offshore banks are only fishable at one stage of the tide, some on the ebb, others on the flood, depending on the position of the bank.

Most of the fish present on offshore banks feed almost exclusively on sandeel, and for this reason natural live or dead eels make the best bait, although a simulated eel cut from a fillet of mackerel may also provide good fishing.

The different types of fish on the bank tend to take up distinct feeding positions. Free swimmers like bass normally hang out just below the lip of the bank; flatfish like turbot and brill frequent the middle bank section, while at the base of the bank you're most likely to find skate, ray and monkfish. Additional angling interest is provided by tope and the occasional porbeagle shark, which stage lightning raids in search of small flatfish and the free-swimming mackerel shoals that prey on sandeels.

The best terminal tackle to use for bank fishing is a straightforward running ledger which incorporates an 8 to 10-foot leader. This extra-long leader is essentially an aid to better bait presentation. Sandeels on the move are active fish, so a live, dead or simulated eel must be allowed to move about in the tidal flow. To help the appearance of the bait, use a smaller than normal hook – size 2-0 or 4-0, but

Left *Fishing close-in from a small boat lets you get to spots beyond the reach of the shore angler, and you can find good sport in the gullies between shallow mud or sandbanks, or waters next to small islands and rocky outcrops. Using an echo sounder is a good way to find the gullies when you're fishing sandbanks, especially where the sand is prone to shifting.*

Above *A flock of seabirds, such as gulls, feeding on a shoal of baitfish, often indicates the presence of larger, predatory fish that have chased the baitfish to the surface.*

Below *Sonar and navigational aids essential for safe and successful wreck fishing, along with accurate and up-to-date charts.*

no larger. A big hook may have a better chance of hooking a big-mouthed bass or turbot, but its weight may well cause the bait to work unnaturally.

Always carry a spare rig of heavy tackle in case shark appear. Normally, the first indication of a shark in the area comes when bites abruptly cease or when a hooked fish is chewed up on its way to the boat. Under these circumstances, a bait of one or two fresh mackerel dropped over the lip of the bank will normally get results.

Sunken wrecks can be very productive marks to fish. In many areas the seabed is littered with the casualties of two world wars and thousands of long-forgotten storms. The vast majority of such wrecks are located a long way from land in depths of 150 feet or more, so to locate them and fish them properly you need an electronic navigation system, accurate hydrographic charts showing their positions, and an echo sounder.

A wreck is, in effect, a man-made reef which becomes a haven for many kinds of fish. Within the hull and superstructure of the wreck you will find, for example, conger and often shoals of sea bream. Just above the wreckage live cod and huge ling, and higher still hang the shoals of more active pollack and coalfish.

Wrecks can be fished from an anchored position or by repeatedly drifting over the wreck. When conger are your main target, anchoring is the only practical way to get a bait to the fish, but for all other species, drift fishing with natural baits or artificial lures – or a combination of both – will bring the best results. On a recent wreck which hasn't been heavily fished, catches may run to thousands of pounds in weight, the total bag being made up of mixed fish of a large size. Wreck fishing is a hard-work sport which requires sturdy tackle and equally sturdy anglers, but it almost guarantees large catches of big fish.

# OFFSHORE WATERS — TROPICAL

Offshore fishing in tropical waters is one of the most fascinating forms of angling. The diversity of fish, their size, colours, habits and the methods needed to catch them add immensely to this fascination. Offshore tropical fishing ranges from bonefishing on coral flats to reef fishing in medium depths and fishing the open ocean ranges for giant game fish.

True coral flats are formed of coral sand or marl, and can stretch for miles without the water reaching more than waist deep. Such places hold stocks of bonefish, barracuda, permit, small sharks and rays. The larger species, such as the sharks and rays, are seldom fished for in these waters, but the smaller species make a perfect target for the light-tackle angler.

Most coral flat fishing is done from flat-bottomed boats or by actually wading in the water. It's vital to know where on the flats to find the fish, and for this you need to understand their movements over the apparently featureless coral sand.

An obvious place to find fish is on the very edge of the flats where the shallows cease and the deep water begins. This is a great place to find barracuda, which take advantage of the deep, dark water to lie in ambush for the shoals of bait fish. Barracuda also hunt across the flats, and they can often be found amongst bonefish in ankle-deep water.

Such channels are easy to see, as the normally glass-clear water tends to take on an oily, slightly opaque look as the water deepens. Large permit also follow these deep troughs, although they normally confine their activity to the edge of the gully where they are most likely to find crab or prawn in reasonable numbers.

Any tiny island of sand on the flats is worth investigating, as it usually indicates a stronger than normal tidal flow. Fish use the barrier of sand as a temporary resting and feeding place, lurking in the lee of the island ready to rush anything edible washed past in the tide flow. Bonefish use such places regularly, feeding head-down and giving away their positions by showing their tails above the surface. A bonefish that has its tail up like this is actively feeding and can normally be induced to take a bait.

Reef fishing is very different from coral flat fishing. Reefs may begin in only 25 feet of water,

**Above** Coral flats, which are formed of coral sand or marl, often extend for great distances from the shore before the water reaches more than waist deep. Such flats are prime areas for bonefishing, and/good places to find barracuda, permit and small sharks. Bonefish often betray their presence by 'tailing', feeding nose-down in shallow water with their tails sticking up above the surface.

**Left** Dropoffs, channels and gullies attract predators such as sharks and barracudas, which lurk in the deeper, darker waters and prey on shoals of baitfish and other unlucky victims such as snappers and groupers.

**Above** *Tarpon often gather in small schools to surface feed , and can then be caught by casting to them from an anchored or drifting boat.*

gradually deepening away until they reach depths of over 100 feet. Fishing a tropical reef is one of the greatest of angling experiences; from the moment the bait touches bottom there's the chance of hooking something out of the ordinary.

The places to look for on the shallow parts of the reef are the sunken coral heads. These grow like huge mushrooms and provide all kinds of reef fish with food and protection. Groupers, yellowtail snappers, queen triggerfish and a host of lesser though often equally beautiful fish are the main inhabitants of a coral head. These in turn attract the predatory king mackerel, barracuda and small shark.

Beyond the shallow section of the reef, where it drops away sharply into deep water, the boat can be anchored or allowed to drift. Here, the electronic weaponry of the boat may be used to find the best places to fish. A good echo sounder quickly pinpoints the unseen rock pinnacles

or deep gullies between jagged coral walls.

These are big boat grounds, where fish can weigh up to 100 pounds or more. Giant groupers and huge barracuda are the main species, but such a place can also produce amberjack, shark, and a host of smaller but exotically-marked groupers. This is no place for light tackle fishing, because the instant a fish picks up a bait and feels the drag of the line and rod tip it will bolt for cover – cover that may be less than a yard away.

In this type of fishing, if you hesitate you'll lose. Strike, heave and crank the reel handle all at the same instant, and with luck the fish will swim up into open water; but make a mistake, and it's goodbye fish, goodbye end tackle.

When deepwater fishing for species such as sailfish and blue or white marlin, the 600 foot dropoff line is the place to find, using the boat's echo sounding equipment. Once located, the dropoff should be followed, for it's over this depth of water that billfish like to feed.

Water temperature is another very important factor in marlin fishing. The higher the water

temperature, the more likely you are to find marlin, so the boat should have a digital water temperature gauge giving constantly-updated readouts as the boat covers the likely area. It's surprising how much the water temperature can rise or fall in less than 100 yards. The sea has warm currents that flow through it like rivers; find these, and you'll find the fish.

Floating weed is another place to find billfish, along with dolphin (dorado). After storms, huge rafts of weed will appear on the surface and pack together, forming floating weed islands which on occasions will stretch for mile after ocean mile without a break. This weed becomes a sanctuary for crabs and small fish, which attract the interest of billfish and dolphin. A bait trolled along the edge of a weed raft usually produces a strike very quickly. To see a giant blue marlin burst out of the weed and nail a lure in an explosion of white spray is one of the most thrilling sights in angling.

When dolphin are on the move, it's advisable to use smaller lures, as this species seems to be more attracted to them than to larger

patterns. Dolphin are a very popular sport fish because they strike hard, fight well, and indulge in displays of aerobatic ferocity that have to be seen to be believed.

Dolphin are attracted to just about any sizeable floating object they come across. Many boat skippers put out anchored buoys to attract these fish, and it's worth fishing thoroughly around any flotsam such as an old oil drum or a raft of floating rubbish. If a shoal of dolphin is in residence, sport can be fast and furious. Dealing out newspaper sheets like giant playing cards laid in a row, then returning to number one to fish the line of them, has been known to work, so powerfully are dolphin attracted to shade.

You should always check out any bird activity, as flocks of diving seabirds are a sure indication that bait fish are being harried by some sort of predator.

Even a single bird can lead to fish, if it's a frigate bird. This great, giant-winged bird will nearly always be trailing a big billfish. In the Bahamas, fishermen call it the marlin bird, and watch its every movement intently.

# SHORELINES

The nature of the local shore can vary considerably from one section of coastline to the next. In some areas the shoreline is sandy, in others it's sand mixed with rocks, vast shingle banks, deep rocky gullies or high vertical cliffs.

Shingle beaches are normally found along exposed stretches of coastline, where wave action often heaps the pebbles up to form banks many miles long. Such banks are normally high, shelving sharply down into a good depth of water.

At first glance, a shingle beach looks a dull, uninteresting and rather barren place to fish. Few creatures can live among the constantly moving shingle, so there's little there to interest fish. Further out, though, the water deepens and the environment is normally much richer. The piled pebbles of the bank give way to a fairly level sea bed composed mostly of grit and fine sand, which provides a home for sandeels, crabs and often small fish on which the larger species feed.

Many anglers make the mistake of overcasting when they're fishing a shingle beach. The hotspot areas are normally within 20 to 50 yards of the beach; a cast of 100 yards or more simply places the bait out beyond the main feeding areas. Occasionally, when long periods of winter wind have caused the wave action to scour at the base of the shingle bank, long casting can be effective, but most times a short cast is the best way to put your bait into the major feeding areas.

Most shingle beaches are crescent-shaped, flanked at each end by a headland. This layout forms a natural haven for small, edible creatures and a rich feeding ground for large, predatory fish. At low spring tide it's sometimes possible to locate upthrust sandbanks which are normally covered by water. These usually occur 30 to 75 yards out, and between them and the beach, the wave action often scours out a deep hole which forms a natural bait trap and so this area is usually worth fishing.

Of all the venues open to the shore angler, a rugged, rocky section of coastline is the most fascinating and often the most productive. The places to look for are the deep, sheltered gullies which half-empty on a falling tide. As the tide retreats, many small fish, prawns, crabs and shellfish die from exposure to the air. Later, as the tide begins to flood, these dead and dying creatures are washed out into the deeper water.

This natural groundbait attracts a great many kinds of fish into the mouth of the gully. Some fish, like wrasses and conger, are resident species. Others, including bass, pollack and codling, are marauding visitors. In gullies which have a wide mouth and a sandy bottom, it's often possible to catch flatfish.

From the outer edge of the rocks, the rough grounds may give way to deep water over sand or mixed sand and rock. Long

**Above** *Surf fishing from a sandy Atlantic beach. Surf beaches are at their best in conditions like this, when a strongish inshore wind is pushing the breakers ashore.*
**Left** *Deep rocky gullies below cliffs are good places to find a wide variety of species.*

casting from the rock spurs can produce tope and various types of skate and ray. Places to look for in particular are gullies divided by a sunken ridge of rock, and gullies which are thick with kelp weed. Kelp jungles hold a lot of big fish, while the rock ridges provide cover and feeding areas for the more active incoming predators.

To fish a surf beach on a day when the wind is whipping up the waves to send rollers crashing across the flat sand, is one of the most exciting of all styles of shore fishing. Shallow though the beach may be, the wave action digs out a great deal of food which the more vigorous predators like bass come inshore to feed on.

Most bass anglers like to drop their bait out beyond the third breaker. This is a good ploy, because the inshore section of the beach may hold only crab and shellfish, but out beyond this relatively barren area, free-swimming shoals of bait fish provide the bass with an ample food supply. Even large plaice, flounder and small turbot can be caught from this part of the beach.

A surf beach normally fishes at its best when a strongish inshore wind creates large, powerful breakers. These surge inshore to produce a long, creamy surf, although if there's too much wind the breakers may become too high and ragged to fish. The perfect conditions come one or two days after a period of strong onshore winds, and the leftover ground-swell seems particularly attractive to the fish.

Natural shoreline features such as exposed rocks are worth exploring. The wave action is divided by the rock, and often scours out a deep hole which many incoming fish will visit. On a flood tide, this hole will be on the beach side of the rock; later, when the ebb tide is well established, the inshore hole will fill and a new scour will appear on the seaward side of the rock.

Surf beaches seldom fish well in flat, calm conditions; flounders may be catchable, but little else will. Under such circumstances night fishing is worth trying, and may produce the odd bass.

In areas where the shoreline is made up of sheer or almost-sheer cliffs, the fishing can often be extremely good, and vertical cliffs usually fall directly into deepish water which is an ideal habitat for many species of fish.

In some places, anglers actually fish directly from the clifftops, while in others they scramble down narrow fissures and along rock ledges to reach fishable positions. Good though this fishing may be, great care must be taken to avoid accidents, which all too often prove fatal. Not only is there the danger of falling, there is also the risk of being swept into the sea by a big wave. It's usually safer to fish from an anchored boat below the cliffs.

Piers, sea walls and jetties provide good, safe platforms for anglers wishing to fish into deeper waters. Most of these places provide good mixed fishing for a wide variety of fish. In a sandy area, fishing from a pier or from a sea wall will produce mostly flatfish, small ray or the occasional bass. In more rocky areas, conger, wrasse and mullet, plus the occasional shark or mackerel, will provide the main sport.

Piers can often be extremely good fishing venues. The weed-covered sunken pier supports provide cover for shoals of smelt and similar bait fish, which attract the interest of bass in the summer and cod in winter. The base of a pier support may well become a conger stronghold, so for anglers wanting a big fish, long casting isn't always essential.

# STILL WATERS

Still waters range in size from ponds only a few yards wide to lakes tens or even hundreds of miles across. For the angler, these different waters provide a fascinating and varied range of challenges, and finding out what goes on beneath the surface is interesting in itself as well as being a great help when it comes to catching fish.

A good starting point is to get to know your local ponds, because what happens in ponds also happens in most other still waters, albeit on a much larger scale. Even the largest lakes have shallows around the shore lines, with bays, inlets and coves, where the vegetation and aquatic life can be much the same as in ponds or small lakes.

Whether a pond is deep or shallow, clear and weedy or coloured like a bowl of thick pea soup (as many are), the food chain begins in the bottom silt or detritus. This silt, composed of accumulated rotting vegetation and other organic wastes, is broken down by micro-organisms to form a food supply for tiny creatures, which in turn are eaten by larger ones.

Colonies of small crustaceans,

*Above The rich green colour of many small waters during the warmer months is caused by an abundance of green planktons.*

*Right Water lilies normally grow in depths of between 3 and 6 feet. Waters thickly covered with lilies are usually clear, because their shade prevents sunlight from stimulating plankton growth.*

such as freshwater shrimps, feed through the upper layers of detritus, while further down, in the more mature, finer-particled sediment, are the thread-like annelid worms and the larvae of aquatic insects. These creatures form an important part of the diet of many species of fish, including carp.

Carp feed from the bottom with their heads half-buried in the silt, probing with their barbules to locate their food. They suck in vast quantities of sediment, sift out the food, and blow the sediment out again. This behaviour creates clouds of disturbed sediment, which make it easy to locate feeding carp, especially in normally clear-watered ponds and lakes; it can also cause great damage.

Carp can, and often do, change the entire natural balance of even quite large waters. Their foraging in the sediment digs up beds of soft-rooted plants, and by muddying what was once clear water it cuts off the sunlight that the plants need. By destroying vegetation in this way, carp can make a water unsuitable for many other species of fish.

When bottom-feeding fish are nosing through the detritus, as well as stirring up clouds of silt they release bubbles of natural gas that are trapped in the sediment. During the peak feeding times of early morning and late evening, small groups of bubbles rising to the surface can denote the presence of shoals of fish working the bottom, while straight lines of bubbles usually mean that larger fish are ripping through the layer of rotting vegetation in search of shrimps and other food.

Detritus gas bubbles also rise naturally, without being disturbed by fish, but while such bubbles are rising they usually break the surface at just one point, rather than moving around as they would if released by feeding fish. Another source of static patches of bubbles, which

shouldn't be confused with those caused by fish, are springs which rise through the bed of a pond or lake.

Even a feeding pike can cause bubbles. As it rockets up from the bottom to grab its prey, its powerful tail action can release a great cloud of bubbles from the disturbed sediment.

In general, small waters can be divided into two groups: those with clear water and a lush growth of soft-rooted weeds, and those with coloured water whose vegetation is mainly marginal reeds or sedges. These differences are the result of many factors, including the presence of phosphate and nitrate fertilizer residues washed into the pond from nearby farmland, the amount of sunlight reaching the water through the shade of any bankside shrubs or trees, and the numbers and types of fish present. Depth also plays an important part. Shallow ponds are usually warmer than deep ones, and so the growth of the plants and animals they contain is much quicker.

Sunlight, in conjunction with nutrients such as fertilizer residues, stimulates the growth of the tiny plant organisms known as phytoplanktons. During the warmer months, many waters turn a rich-pea-green colour because of the presence of billions of these single-celled green planktons. These are the staple food of the animal or zooplanktons, such as daphnia (water fleas), and are also eaten by fish during the first few weeks of their lives.

In clear waters, where the numbers of phytoplanktons are kept low by the feeding of zooplanktons, clouds of daphnia can often be seen in the warmer shallows. At first sight, it seems as though the surface of the water has been sprinkled with orange-red brick dust, but closer inspection reveals billions of the upright-swimming water fleas, swimming frantically but drifting helplessly with the wind and water movements.

The balance between phytoplanktons and zooplanktons dictates whether the water is green or clear. A rich variety of aquatic plants, particularly the soft-rooted weeds, also helps to keep the water clear because they consume many of the nutrients which would otherwise be taken up by the phytoplanktons. In addition, where the surface of a pond or small lake is almost covered by plants such as water lilies, the water usually remains quite clear because the sunlight can't penetrate the depths and stimulate phytoplankton growth. However, any water with more than its fair share of carp will be permanently turbid because of the fine silt particles churned up by the fish and held in suspension in the water.

Patches of water lilies and other floating plants are good places to fish during hot, sunny weather, because many species love to rest in the shade they provide. They are also good spots to find predators such as pike, perch and black bass, which lurk among the underwater stems, waiting to rush out and grab any passing food.

Even when the surface is quite thickly covered with lilies or other plants, the stems below will be relatively sparse, enabling slim-bodied fish to pass easily between the stems without touching them. Broad-bodied fish, however, often brush against the stems as they grub about, betraying their presence by causing twitches and knocks in the surface foliage.

Bankside trees and bushes can also create good fish-holding areas. Overhanging branches provide the fish with cover, and food in the form of insects and grubs which fall into the water from them. Underwater roots, and lower branches which actually dip into the water, become covered in algae and attract snails and the larvae of many aquatic insects, so fish gather there to feed, as they do among the stems of marginal reeds.

In many reservoirs, fish are to be found among the submerged trees which grew in the valley before it was flooded. Sometimes these are marked by buoys, or shown on maps of the water, but if not, they can be located by sonar. Where the bed of a reservoir or other still water is virtually featureless, artificial fish-holding areas can be created by anchoring

*Above Dawn is a peak feeding time for many species, which makes it one of the best times of the day for fishing.*

*Right Feeding fish often betray their presence by creating surface disturbances and bubbles.*

*Left Marginal plants are good fish-holding areas. Fish feed on the snails and insect larvae whch live among the plant stems, and on insects, grubs and caterpillars which fall into the water from bankside trees and bushes.*

large rafts of cut trees and branches to the bottom. This is a common practice in North America, where the positions of these brush piles are usually shown by buoys or by shore markers.

If you're going to fish a really large water, it's a good idea to spend some time beforehand studying a map of it. A good map will detail all the obvious hotspots, such as shallows, sunken forests, plateaux, deep-water dropoffs along the marginal shelf, and deep gullies between islands.

Near the shore, the old ideas of always following the wind, or fishing into the wind, can often be very useful. This is because concentrations of plankton, caught in the surface layers, can be blown inshore by the wind. Shoals of bait fish fry are attracted to these buildups of plankton in the shallow waters, .and small predators following the fry shoals attract the interest of large predators such as pike. Before long, a large patch of water which might have been competely empty of fish only the day before, when the wind direction was different, becomes full of life. You can often locate these gatherings of fish by looking out for groups of fish-eating birds, such as gulls, grebes and cormorants, which are usually quick to find them.

Although some predators do roam considerable distances in search of their food, perch and the members of the pike family prefer to find a good source of food, such as a shoal of bait fish, and stay close to it. Good places to find resident bait fish shoals, and their attendant predators, include waters over rough ground, the edges of dropoffs, and the mouths of inflowing rivers.

In contrast, salmon, char and certain species of trout are lovers of deep, open water, and the only really effective way of finding them is by using sonar, preferably in conjunction with a water temperature probe.

Deep waters have three fairly distinct layers: the epilimnion (upper layer), the thermocline (middle layer) and the hypo-limnion (lower layer). During summer and autumn, the thermocline separates the warm epilimnion from the much colder hypolimnion, while in winter the epilimnion is colder than the hypolimnion. The water temperature changes only slowly between the surface and the thermocline, and between the thermocline and the bottom, but it changes rapidly through the comparatively thin thermocline. This rapidly-changing temperature makes the thermocline easy to locate with a temperature probe.

As the epilimnion warms up at the beginning of summer, fish such as lake trout, which prefer cool water, must move deeper, to the thermocline or even below it. To help the angler find these fish, many of today's sonar units are sensitive enough to detect the denser water of the thermocline. There are also temperature probes which can be attached to the downrigger weight, or lowered manually from a drifting boat.

Modern electronics have taken much of the guesswork out of tackling vast, deep waters, and made fishing them far more productive. With the latest equipment it's a matter of reading the display, rather than the water.

# STREAMS AND RIVERS

Apart from those which originate in lakes, most rivers – even the mightiest of them – start their lives as tiny streams, fed by springs or the meltwaters of mountain snows.

The coldwater mountain streams, where small trout rule the roost, are certainly the most picturesque, though because of the low water temperatures they are nowhere near as rich as the lowland streams, and hold far fewer fish. In the upper reaches, invertebrate life is limited to insect larvae and shrimps, which scuttle about among the smooth, worn rocks and stones on the bottom. As a stream widens and matures, it offers a greater variety of habitats, with bottom weeds, marginal plants and bankside trees providing food and shelter for an increasing number of fish species.

Along the course of a high, coldwater river, fish are nearly always found in pools. Not just pools beneath waterfalls, but also the deeper, slower pools carved out of the river bed by water funelling through narrows or between rocks. Pools offer a choice of fast or slow water, where fish like salmon can hold in the slower band just out of the full force of the current, waiting until they're ready to surge upstream over seemingly impossible obstacles to their spawning grounds.

Other species, like trout and grayling, wait in the pools for particles of food brought down by the current, and during the summer months, when insect life is at its most abundant, they need make little effort to secure a meal. In leaner times, they feed from the bottom among the stones, and on grubs and earthworms which are washed into the river during floods.

In lowland streams, an entirely different habitat of lush aquatic vegetation and bankside plants, plus additional general silting of the river bed between runs of sand and gravel, results in a far more complex environment. Food abounds, supporting large numbers of fish of many different species.

Whatever the type of river or stream you're fishing, it pays to know whereabouts the fish are likely to be. For instance, careful study of a boulder-strewn flood river when the water level is low will show you where the fish are likely to lie up when the river returns to its normal level. Look

Left *Pools in rock-strewn upland streams are good places to find brown trout.*
Below left *To catch migratory fish such as salmon, you need to know when to be on the river as well as where to find them.*
Below *Insect larvae and small crustaceans are the main fish foods in gravel-bottomed streams.*

out for large rocks, because the areas of slack water which form behind them are favourite spots for salmon, trout and even pike. Many river keepers actually place large rocks in shallows to create this kind of shelter, and in deeper sections build wooden or steel stagings out from the bank to deflect the current, providing enough slack behind them to accommodate a large fish or two.

Sunken trees and bridge supports also create areas of slower water adjacent to the main flow. Most species like to hole up in slack water, because it's much easier than continually facing the full force of the current, so such areas are always worth exploring when you're fishing a river.

Confluences, where rivers meet, are great hotspots. Where both rivers are fast-flowing, fish rest in the slower water between the two courses, slipping out into the current from time to time to grab some passing food. Close into the bank, among the marginal reeds and rushes where sediment usually builds up, predators like pike will lie in wait.

At a confluence where one river is fast and the other is either much smaller or of a much slower flow, an eddy will form. The swirling water of the eddy will carve out a depression, often quite deep, which is much to the liking of bottom-feeding species. During times of heavy flooding, you can expect to find most species just into the secondary river where the flow is much quieter. Such retreats very often hold both predators and prey, holed up together in even the tiniest of areas because their normal living quarters are under threat.

Islands are also great fish attractors. Predators lurk where trees overhang or the lower branches actually submerge, and any grasses or sedges fringing the island provide fish with cover as well as a large stock of aquatic and terrestrial insects. This food potential, combined with the cover, means that islands are likely to be surrounded by large numbers of fish, so if you're going to fish an unfamiliar river, an island is a good place to begin.

Another place where large numbers of fish are often found is in a weirpool. These pools are perhaps the most interesting and productive of all river features, and a large one might hold practically every species of fish found in the entire river system, from tiny minnows to huge catfish.

Fast water species, such as salmon and trout, will occupy the main white water flow areas where oxygen levels are highest, while in the back eddies, well away from the full current, species like perch, bream, chub and roach will be found. Pike like to lie in wait close to the bank, and in the deepest water, amid the debris which has accumulated over the years, other predators such as eels and catfish will take up residence. Finally, if the river is clean, the very tail end of the pool is a good place to find plentiful stocks of crayfish, one of the deadliest of natural baits for most species.

The presence or absence of crayfish is a good indication of the health of the river, because they have a low tolerance of pollution. When a river becomes contaminated, either by farm chemicals leached in from the land or by industrial pollution, species like crayfish, and the little brook lampreys which cling to the stones with their sucker-like mouths, are the first to suffer.

In really fast, wide sections of river, where the bottom is rocky and uneven, study the surface patterns for a guide to the bottom topography. For instance, huge boils and vortexes on the surface are areas where several currents are merging around a submerged obstacle, usually a particularly large boulder or a high, packed rock outcrop. However, down below, on either side of the obstacle, things are invariably much quieter and fish could be holed up there, so it's worth fishing through the turbulence.

Broken water also occurs over shallow rock plateaux and even, in the case of winter currents, over the remains of the previous summer's reed or bullrush stems. There is nearly always a tiny slack immediately behind these natural barriers where fish shelter from the full force of the current.

Old, well-established millpools and little overshoot pools where water is diverted from the main stream for irrigation are wonderful features to explore. As in the much larger weirpools, trout are to be expected wherever there is a strong pull of white water tumbling over the sill from the river above. Further down, at the tail end where the bottom shelves up to hard gravel and beds of weed, surface feeders will compete with the trout for hatching insects.

Irrigation ditches are usually worth exploring, especially where they've been neglected and become overgrown with a wealth of vegetation, such as lilies, reeds and rushes. In Britain, these ditches are usually the home of rudd, tench and bream, while in North America they are good places to find black bass.

Where irrigation ditches are connected to swampy tropical or subtropical coastal river systems, as they are in Florida, the hard-fighting snook and tarpon may be found. These fish, which occur in the inshore coastal waters, also travel quite far inland, even into fresh waters. The prime hotspots for them, though, are brackish inlets, bayous, creeks and canals where lush and dense vegetation creates a maze of food-rich hideouts for them.

Dams, built across rivers for flood control, hydroelectric power, irrigation systems or to create reservoirs, can also be well worth exploring – not just the stillwaters behind them, but also the often turbulent waters below.

The typical concrete dam wall has a concrete apron over which low-water currents tumble into the huge pool below. When water levels are higher, however, such as in early spring, excess water cascading down from the spillways carves out a very deep hole, called a washout hole, in the bottom of the pool.

Most species can't tolerate this kind of violent water movement, so they seek refuge further down the tailrace, usually behind the wing dams. These are manmade rock piles that jut out from the shoreline and are designed to stop bank erosion by deflecting the current back into the centre of the channel. When the water is really high and fast-running, the

**Below left** *An area of quiet water in an otherwise turbulent river is where fish like to rest.*

**Below** *Reed and rush beds provide many species with shelter and a good supply of insects and other food, but you can't always fish them from the bank.*

**Right** *Chalk streams are excellent trout waters, but a careful and stealthy approach is essential to avoid spooking the fish in the crystal-clear water.*

sheltered water on the downstream side of a wing dam, or any similar patch of slack water, is where you'll find the fish.

When the water returns to its normal, lower level, the fish move back into the mainstream and the pool itself. Though these pools can be massive, they're really only very large versions of the lovely little pools you might find along the course of an upland stream.

Many of the very largest rivers have a deep, often swiftly-flowing main channel which is kept turbid by the high number of boats which use it. This turbidity suits many bottom-dwellers such as eels and catfish, but species which prefer clear water and a roof of aquatic vegetation over their heads will keep to the margins or choose an off-river backwater.

These off-river locations often offer habitats virtually identical to those found in still waters; if so, you should treat them as such. Search areas such as dropoffs, patches of weed, beds of rushes or reeds, around bluffs and in sunken timber, and at cove entrances where fry are gathered.

Another type of location where many river species occur, not always voluntarily, is the oxbow lake. Oxbow lakes are formed in flat country, where the river flows in horseshoe-shaped loops or meanders. The outer banks of a loop are eroded by the current, while silt is deposited along the inner banks. In time, this erosion narrows the neck of the loop so much that the river breaks through it, usually during a flood, cutting a new channel that bypasses the loop.

The ends of the loop become silted up, cutting it off from the river and creating an oxbow lake that still holds some of the species found in the river which formed it. In addition to these species, many oxbows contain others which have been deliberately introduced to create new fisheries.

# CREDITS

**Authors:**
Peter Gathercole
Trevor Housby
Mike Millman
Arthur Oglesby
John Wilson
*Additional material by*
Stuart John
Colin Newman

**Editorial:**
*US Consultant* A. J. McClane
*US Editor* Keith Gardner
*UK Editor* Ian Wood
*Assistant Editors* Nigel Flynn,
Tessa Carias
*Art Director* Steve Leaning
*Designer* Stuart John,
*Computer Consultant* Ray Leaning

**Photography:**
*Main studio photography* Gambit
Graphics
*Additional studio photography*
Theo Bergstrom, Steve Wright
John Darling, Peter Gathercole
*Location photography*
John Darling, Peter Gathercole,
Trevor Housby, Arthur Oglesby,
Graeme Pullen, Mike Millman,
John Wilson, Angling Plus
Magazine

**Artists:**
*Fish species* Colin Newman
*Other artwork* Nigel Bass,
Lyn Cawley

**Acknowledgements:**
For their help in compiling this book, we would like to thank

Shakespeare Company,
PO Box 1,
Broad Ground Road,
Lakeside,
Redditch,
Worcestershire B98 8NQ,
England.

Peter Drennan,
Leopold Street,
Oxford,
England.

John's Tackle Den,
16 Bridewell Alley,
Norwich,
England.

**Detailed credits**
Pages
10-11 *tackle picture* Gambit/Shakespear,
Wright *photo* Wilson
12-13 *tackle picture* Gambit/Shakespear
*photos* Millman (12) Wilson (13)
14-15 *tackle picture* Gambit/Shakespear,
Wright *photo* Wilson
16-17 *tackle picture* Gambit /Shakespear
*photo* Angling Plus
18-19 *tackle picture* Wright *photos* Wilson
20-21 *tackle picture* Gambit/Shakespear
*photo* Gathercole
22-23 *tackle picture* Gambit/Shakespear
*photo* Gathercole
24-25 *tackle picture* Bergstrom
26-27 *tackle picture* Bergstrom *photo*
Wilson
28-29 *tackle picture* Gambit/Shakespear
Bergstom *photo* Wilson
30-31 *tackle picture* Gambit/Shakespear
*photo* Wilson
32-33 *tackle picture* Wright
*photo* Gathercole
34-35 *tackle picture* Wright
*photo* Gathercole
36-37 *tackle picture* Gambit/Sakespear,
Wright, Bergstom *photo* Wilson
38-39 *tackle picture* Gambit/Shakespear
*photo*
40–41: *tackle picture* Bergström, *photo*
Millman
42-43 *tackle picture* Gambit/Shakespear

*photo* Gathercole
44-45 *tackle picture* Bergstrom,Wright
*photo* Millman
46-47 *tackle picture* Gambit/Shakespear
*photo* Gathercole
48-49 *tackle picture* Wright *photo* Wilson
50-51 *tackle picture* Gambit/Shakespear
*photo* Leaning

54–55: *tackle picture* Gathercole;
*illustration* Cawley
56–57: *tackle picture* Gathercole; flies
tied by Gathercole and Steve Parton
(Sparton Fishing Tackle)
58–59: *tackle picture* Gathercole; wet flies
tied by Gathercole and Parton, salmon
flies by Bill Coe
60–63: *tackle pictures* Bergström,
suppliers Abu, Hardy
64–65: *tackle picture* Bergström,
suppliers Abu, Hardy
66–67: *bait picture* Bergström;
*illustration* Cawley
68–69: *bait picture* Bergström
70–71: *tackle picture* Bergström,
suppliers Drennan, Woody's;
*photo* Wilson
72–73: *bait picture* Darling;
*illustration* Cawley
74–75: *photos* Millman

78–127: *all illustrations* Newman

130–131: *illustrations* Bass;
*photo* Gathercole
132–133: *illustrations* Bass
*photos* Gathercole (134), Millman (135)
134–135: *illustrations* Cawley; *photos*
Housby
136–137: *illustrations* Bass;
*photo* Darling
138–139: *illustrations* Cawley;
*photo* Housby
140–141: *illustrations* Bass;
*photo* Gathercole
142–143: *illustrations* Bass;
*photo* Gathercole
144–145: *illustrations* Cawley;
*photo* Oglesby
146–147: *illustrations* Bass, Cawley
(147); *photo* Gathercole
148–149: *illustrations* Bass;
*photo* Pullen
150–151: *illustrations* Cawley;
*photo* Gathercole
152–153: *illustrations* Cawley
154–155: *illustrations* Bass;
*photo* Darling
156–157: *illustrations* Bass;
*photo* Pullen
158–159: *illustrations* Bass;
*photo* Housby
160–161: *illustrations* Bass;
*photo* Darling
162–163: *illustrations* Bass;
*photo* Wilson

164–165: *illustrations* Bass;
*photo* Pullen
166–167: *illustrations* Cawley;
*photo* Darling
168–169: *illustrations* Bass;
*photo* Pullen *inset photo* Wilson

172–173: *photos* Millman
174–175: *photos* Millman (174, 175
bottom), Darling (175 top)
176–177: *photos* Housby (176 top),
Millman (176 bottom, 177)
178–179: *photos* Darling (178), Millman
(179)
180–181: *photos* Millman (180), Wilson
(181)
182–183: *photos* Pullen (182, 183 top),
Darling (183 bottom)
184–185: *photos* Darling (184 top),
Millman (184 bottom), Pullen (185)
186–187: *photos* Pullen (186 left),
Darling (186 right), Housby (187)

you ONLY live ONCE

# JUMP IN!

*Because you only live once...*

IPANEMA BEACH, RIO DE JANEIRO, BRAZIL          Michael Heffernan

'You only live once; but if you do it right, once is enough.'

**Mae West**

you ONLY live ONCE

A LIFETIME OF EXPERIENCES

FOR THE EXPLORER IN ALL OF US

## CONTENTS

## Chapter 03
## A WEEK

*In which we take a week or two to drive the world's most exciting roads, spot the Big Five on safari, hail a helicopter, spend an adventure-packed week on an island and swap houses with someone. Closer to home, a week is time enough to discover delights on your doorstep and learn some dance steps to impress.*

## 148–221

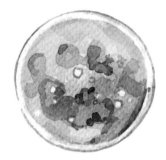

## Chapter 04
## A MONTH

*In which, over a month or more, we venture to the Amazon, travel from one end of a country to the other, train for a marathon and celebrate the seasons. On the water we learn to surf and paddle. We also find time to volunteer and participate in a tradition. And to escape it all, we travel solo and build a log cabin in the wilds.*

## 222–275

## Chapter 05
## A YEAR

*In which we quit the desk job, take flying lessons, ski sweet powder for twelve months, uncover your family's roots, and resolve to learn a new language. Then, consider a sabbatical in the Caribbean or the south of France, or even a round-the-world journey with the perfect travel companion.*

## 276–323

**You Only Live Once**

RO

You Only Live Once

# you ONLY live ONCE

# INTRODUCTION

**L**ife's not a dress rehearsal. 'Carpe Diem.' 'Be happy while you're living for you're a long time dead.' Yes, there are *a lot* of motivational proverbs about living life to the max out there, including the title of this book. But that's probably because it's a big deal.

The average person has a lifespan of threescore years and ten, give or take. And there's a lot to pack in. Some people are born with a knack for sucking the marrow from the bones of life.

Sir Richard Burton, the Victorian explorer, soldier, spy, linguist, writer, ethnologist... we could go on, travelled to India with the British Army at the age of 20, where he learned more than half a dozen local languages, studied Hindu culture and kept a menagerie of monkeys. Later he explored Africa and the Middle East and translated *The Arabian Nights*.

A more contemporary example might be Keith Richards, Rolling Stones guitarist, writer of immortal riffs, and aspiring librarian. As both demonstrate, you can pack a lot into threescore years and ten if you try.

And that's what this book sets out to help you do. It's not just another bucketlist of big-ticket trips We've all heard about Venice and, yes, it is probably worth going to Italy to see its waterways. Instead, hopefully you'll take away something more from this book: a resolve to live life to the fullest, to add a dash of *joie de vivre* to every day.

That doesn't just mean splashing out on exotic holidays but also seeking out and indulging in little pleasures – a new pair of handmade shoes, that simple dish of perfectly dressed pasta. And, while we feature a number of serious challenges – the Appalachian Trail,

# you ONLY live ONCE

---

it's worth noting, doesn't get any easier the older you grow – there are just as many experiences that you can enjoy on your doorstep with a little lateral thinking.

Start by embracing spontaneity; experiences like sleeping under the stars, once in a while, remind you what an amazing privilege it is to be alive, to think and to enjoy the world around us.

And we've tried to suggest opportunities to learn and slake a little of that thirst for knowledge among these pages, with illustrations of how to mix cocktails, identify autumn leaves and train for a marathon with a difference. For hedonists and adventure-lovers we've also mapped once-in-a-lifetime experiences in cities and on islands.

Essentially, **You Only Live Once** is about experiences not places – though we travel to every corner of the planet. It is about those experiences that you will replay in your mind's eye years later; they may not feature the most spectacular destinations, they may even in fact have cost nothing, but they will be the travel experiences that changed you, the ones that still bring a smile to your face.

***So, how does this book work?*** There are five chapters – for an Hour, Day, Week, Month and Year – and in each we suggest experiences that may take about that amount of time. Naturally, these definitions are as elastic as you want them to be. You might wish to spend one hour or several kitesurfing in Greece, you can stretch a day into a weekend, a week into a fortnight. You can spend one month or six working your passage abroad, take a year or more to travel around the world.

But what all these ideas have in common is that they're starting points. They will reignite long-forgotten desires – to learn an instrument or a language – or spark new and unexpected ambitions: why shouldn't you move to Provence for a year?

When you know what's stopping you, you can start working on a solution. Perhaps this book will be as useful in helping you identify obstacles as will be for refining your month's or your year's travel experiences. Then it's time to turn to Lonely Planet's extensive travel resources and begin planning the rest of your life. ●

London 2014

THE DARK HEDGES, COUNTY ANTRM, NORTHERN IRELAND    Brian Glover

# LET'S BEGIN

*'Two roads diverged in a wood and I took the one less traveled by.'*

*Robert Frost*

In which we spend a couple of hours taking care of the little things

**HOUR**

– a shave, a shower, perhaps a cocktail or something to eat –
before tackling the big stuff: sporting events,
extreme feats, life-and-death spectacles,
celestial phenomena and the ever-thought-provoking
rituals of dawn and sunset.

**Chapter**

# 01

# BE AT THE BIRTH

**IT ONLY TAKES A MOMENT OR TWO FOR A NEW LIFE TO BE BORN IN THE AFRICAN BUSH; AND JUST AS LONG FOR IT TO BE OVER. WITNESS THIS AWESOME LIFE-AND-DEATH SPECTACLE IN ZAMBIA'S SOUTH LUANGWA NATIONAL PARK.**

**T**hey euphemistically call it the 'emerald season' – well, it sounds so much better than 'wet season'. But, from December to March, wet is undeniably what it is in Zambia's South Luangwa National Park. And yet, what life amid the water! The snap-crack dry bush and dusty trails are transformed into an almost blinding vivacity of green: trees sport their finest foliage, thickets thicken, grasses seem to grow before your eyes. Amid all that natural profusion – hiding somewhere – an array of African animals is entering the world.

They're clever, these creatures: it makes sense to give birth to your young when food is in abundance. And with the help of a good guide (and a good raincoat), you delve into the bustling jungle to see the circle of life begin. There! A fragile impala wobbles on unsteady legs. Over there! A family of warthogs, antennae-tails pointing skyward, trots down a burrow. In the river! A hefty hippo calf floats next to its massive mother.

There are rarities here too. Wild dogs – often a tough species to spot – have their puppies in the 'green'; at this time, the wide-roaming canines tend to stay closer to their dens, making them easier to find.

The added bonus of being here to see the baby critters is that you're not the only one watching – the predators descend too. For them, it's a succulent pick-n-mix. Hyenas, lions and leopards lurk (the latter particularly prevalent in South Luangwa), looking for an easy lunch as vulnerable newborns enter the world. ●

### Penguins, Antarctic Peninsula
After November's courtships, penguin chicks hatch in December. Cruise to the peninsula's rookeries to see new gentoo, chinstrap, Adélie and emperor parents feeding their newborn chicks.

### Wildebeest, Serengeti, Tanzania
The Great Migration circulates around the Serengeti. Head to the park's south to see a million wildebeest gather to give birth in February; an estimated 400,000 calves are born in one week.

### Grey Whales, Baja California, Mexico
Practically the entire world population of grey whales comes to San Ignacio Lagoon to breed from February to April. Trips in small boats enable you to get close enough to stroke the curious calves.

### Sea Turtles, Rekwa, Sri Lanka
Five turtle species nest on this southern beach from June to August. Contact the local Marine Conservation Society, which monitors when hatchlings will make their dash to the sea.

**An Hour**

# WITNESS THE DAWN

---

**IT'S THE SIMPLE THINGS: TAKE JUST AN HOUR TO STOP AND CONTEMPLATE THE INCREDIBLE BEAUTY OF THE EVERYDAY AND IT'S BOUND TO BE A MORNING TO REMEMBER.**

*Strange things happen in the dead of night.* Worries worsen, trivial troubles assume disastrous proportions and the mind plays tricks. Strange sounds and shadowy flickers morph into ghosts, ghouls and villains. And then the sun comes up; funnily enough, it happens every day, yet always has the power to astonish. It's the combination of slow-burn build-up with sudden illumination – the anticipation with the guaranteed pay-off.

Picture this: you're in the Nepalese Himalaya and up at stupid o'clock to trek through the cold, coal-black night to reach that perfect perch, 3193m up Poon Hill. From here, come first light, the entire Annapurna Range will spread in perfect panorama. You sit and huddle against the altitudinous chill, to wait for nature to do her thing. First the sky's seams seem to tear, a fraying at the edge of the darkness. What was colourless turns off-black, then navy, then paler, paler blue. Purple-pinks begin to warm the horizon, a cheery backdrop for the jagged peaks. All around, rocks, boulders, faces begin to blush in the intensifying glow of pre-dawn. It is the golden hour, when the monsters of the night have slunk away and what lies ahead is enlightenment and fresh possibility.

And then, there it is – the sun itself bursts in. Once it's reared its radiant head, there's no stopping its speedy surge skywards. Golden becomes blazing – wakey, wakey, rise and shine. The world's best alarm clock has rung quite definitively: it's time to start a new day. ●

### Gisborne, New Zealand

The North Island's easternmost city is the first big hub to see the sun rise. It's also within one of the few districts that permits 'freedom camping', so you can wild-camp away from the crowds to watch the new day dawn.

### Mt Sinai, Egypt

Make a pre-dawn pilgrimage up this sacred mountain – where Moses allegedly received the Ten Commandments – to see the sun rise over the biblical landscape.

### Dzibilchaltún, Mexico

At sunrise on the spring and autumn equinoxes, the sun shines directly between the doorposts of Dzibilchaltún's Temple of the Seven Dolls – testament to the architectural mastery of the Maya.

### Longyearbyen, Svalbard

Polar night – when the sun doesn't rise above the horizon – lasts for over four months on this Arctic archipelago. The first time the sun makes an appearance in the capital Longyearbyen (around 8 March) is special indeed.

**An Hour**

You Only Live Once

# OPEN YOUR EARS

**PICK THE RIGHT VENUE AND YOU CAN GET LOST IN BOTH THE MUSIC AND THE MOMENT: A LIVE PERFORMANCE THAT REALLY MAKES YOU FEEL ALIVE.**

**The sense of awe begins well** before the music starts playing. Just entering Verona's ancient Arena takes your breath away. Standing for almost 2000 years in the centre of this northern Italian city, the sheer size of the auditorium is astonishing.

Row after row of seats cling to the time-worn steps that line the inner edges of the Arena. The knowledge that Romans sat on these very steps to watch gruesome gladiatorial battles below is spine-tingling. In the centre, red velvet stalls offer yet more seating. The venue can entertain an immense 15,000 music-lovers in one performance.

As you take your seat, inhaling the mouth-watering aromas wafting over from the bustling restaurants nearby, the lights dim beneath the balmy evening sky. There is yet another surprise to come before the opera starts: first one, then another and soon most members of the audience have lit votive candles in what has become a traditional and incredibly pretty prelude to the performance. Thousands of tiny flickering flames illuminating this historical space is unforgettable.

And then the music starts. Tonight it is Georges Bizet's *Carmen*. All pomp and spectacle, the costumes are incredible and the singers sublime. It goes on for hours, but you don't really mind. It is all part of the experience. Although the sound quality here is less than ideal, especially if you are in the cheap seats up at the top, the visual extravaganza of the performance more than makes up for any imperfections in musical purity. It is an moment that stimulates all the senses. ●

### 1 Sydney Opera House, Sydney, Australia

*Jørn Utzon created an icon when he designed one of the 20th century's greatest buildings. Thankfully what goes on inside is pretty special too. The two main halls are majestic, full of colour and shaped to achieve perfect acoustics.*

### 2 Wilton's Music Hall, London, England

*One of the world's oldest surviving 'Grand Music Halls', this venue is one of London's best-kept secrets. The atmospheric building was left derelict for many years, but was mercifully saved from demolition and is being slowly restored to its former glory. Famous for offbeat and diverse performances, including jazz, cabaret and swing, Wilton's Music Hall is an unsung hero.*

### 3 Concertgebouw, Amsterdam, the Netherlands

*Built in 1888, this Dutch venue is renowned for its incredible acoustics. However, no-one is quite sure how the designer, Dolf van Gendt, managed to create such a perfectly resonant hall, given that the science behind acoustics was relatively unknown at the time. Today it is home to some 900 concerts a year, attracting 700,000 visitors, making it one of the most visited concert halls in the world.*

### 4 The Musikverein, Vienna, Austria

*Famous for the annual New Year concert in its Golden Hall, the Musikverein is widely acknowledged as one of the finest musical venues in the world. The Austrian capital is also home to two other world-class concert halls: the State Opera and the Konzerthaus, making Vienna a must-go destination for classical-music fans.*

## OPEN YOUR EARS

# RODEO!

*So, you've witnessed the running of the bulls in Pamplona, where next? Rodeos take place across the US and Canada, featuring bull and bronco riding, barrel racing (horse races over short circuits) and a lot of denim in one place. If you're inspired to take part, there are growing numbers of bull-riding courses around the continent, such as three-day clinics at Gary Leffew's Bull Riding World. Reassuringly, the veteran rodeo star says 'bull riding is 80 percent mental, 20 percent talent.'*

A BUCKING BRONCO AT A RODEO IN ALBERTA, CANADA   Getty/Robert McGorey

**An Hour**

## ADAM SKOLNICK FINDS SOLACE SWIMMING IN CALIFORNIA'S OPEN OCEAN

**T**he colours soothe me. To be immersed in that aquamarine for more than an hour marinates the mind, opens it up and hushes my restless brain. I'll see JM's bubbles sometimes. The wake of his shallow kicks foaming white on the glassy surface.

Glinting balls of silver sardines swirl as we approach the rock reef just off Point Dume in Malibu, the stones crusted with spiny blue urchins and sprawling lavender starfish. There are striped bass and bright orange garibaldi, and when the sun is high, white bolts bounce off the sandy bottom, forming an underwater sundial.

We explore thick kelp forests, take deep nourishing breaths and follow the billowing light-green foliage to the floor. We slalom the giant stalks that recall a magic-beans fairy tale. Even on bright days, it's dark in the forest, patched together with sandy meadows saturated with turquoise light. I'll strain to make it all the way there and surface to deep breaths of relief, while waves thrash the sandstone cliffs, and the sun glistens gold on the tides.

On winter days we'll emerge on the beach shivering, our hands blue, teeth chattering. In the summer we'll stroll back to our starting point in the sun, warm and alive. We always laugh about something. No matter what else is going on in our lives, when the ocean has done its work, we always smile.

It took years for JM to get me in the water – and I had always previously had an excuse. Then came the summer of 2012. The Mayan apocalypse may never have materialised, but my personal apocalypse arrived right on time. I seriously injured my back and could no longer run. Couldn't even sit. The pain stayed with me for months. I was just 40

# TO THE SEA!

> "I've swum with groups of sea lions 20-strong, with super-pods of dolphins, I've mingled with migrating whales"

years old, and I couldn't move as well as most 70-year-olds. And it wasn't just my back that was wrecked, my marriage was on the verge of collapse. It was as if the emotional weight I was carrying was too much for my physiology and eventually everything blew up at once.

In the midst of the collapse, I met a clever massage therapist from northern Thailand, and she demanded I get in the water. So I found a pool at a nearby community college, and my back started to loosen. My lungs started working again, my body felt strong for the first time in forever. But there was no wild-nature love in the pool. There was never a deeper meaning.

JM called one day. I told him I was swimming and he convinced me to give the ocean a try. It was August. The water was 66°F (19°C) – warm enough to enjoy. The sea was crystal. We counted more than 50 bull rays gliding along the sandy bottom. After the swim, JM started talking about the positive ions, and how they funnel positivity into our cells by osmosis, or something. False or true, I was willing to believe. In those early days, the swim was the only good thing in my life.

Since then I've swum with groups of sea lions 20-strong, with super-pods of dolphins, I've mingled with migrating whales. We'll swim in stormy seas, navigate head-high surf and ride heavy currents sparked by swirling winds that lure in the kitesurfers. Sometimes we'll swim only a metre from one another and not make eye contact for a mile, each of us hidden in the trough of great swells.

We'll swim in soupy fog, we'll swallow bellyfuls of blue water, and watch flocks of pelicans skim the sea in formation. We've made friends with, and occasionally frightened, the lifeguards, who think we're mad. One confessed that he feels scared out by the rock reef: 'I prefer being at the top of the food chain.'

We know great white sharks patrol here, though we've never seen one. Occasionally they cross my mind on murky coldwater days, when we're outfitted like seals in our wetsuits. But usually I swim free and easy.

JM likes to tell a story about the 80-somethings he occasionally swims with at La Jolla Cove. There are a group of about a dozen of these wise, old masters – men and women who gather to swim year-round, without wetsuits. As JM was preparing to go out, one of those ladies came out of the drink with a goofy smile on her face. A bystander sipping coffee approached her and asked how it was.

'Amazing!' she said.

'Was there good visibility?' the bystander asked.

'Oh no, couldn't see anything out there.'

'Was it warm?'

'It was freezing,' said the swimmer. She was towel-drying and shivering by then.

'But you liked it?' asked the confused bystander.

'It was amazing!' she said, beaming gloriously. JM plans to be just like her one day. Me too. ●

GELLERT HOTEL BATHS, BUDAPEST   Getty/Stuart Black

# TAKE A BATH

*Hot or cold, clothed or not, nothing washes away the day like immersing yourself in a bath. Hungarians have long known this and the baths at the Gellert Hotel in Budapest are just one of several grand indoor and outdoor bathing spots in Hungary's capital. In volcanic Japan, steaming hot springs (onsens) are just as much part of the culture. Prefer a cold dip? Head to Finland in winter when 170 ice-holes are open for a post-sauna shock.*

# HARNESS THE WIND

**THE PERFECT DAY: A BOARD, A SAIL AND THE SEA, THE BEACH, THE SUN AND THE WAVES. KITE SURFING WILL BLOW YOU AWAY – LITERALLY.**

**A** *giant, neon-coloured kite* is hovering above as you stand in a restless sea, a board under one arm and waves crashing around your legs. The lines connecting you to this awesome plaything appear to float upwards, powerless. And yet just a tweak of the bar in your hand sends the kite charging one way and then another. The strength of the wind is deceiving.

This is Pounda Beach in Paros, Greece, one of the best kitesurfing locations in Europe, thanks to the long, shallow shoreline and consistently strong winds. The air is sizzling with adrenalin-fuelled excitement.

Kitesurfers are zipping across the choppy water towards you at a frightening speed, seemingly about to crash into the beach. At the last minute they leap into the air and twist around, before speeding off in the other direction. They make it look easy. It is not.

It takes a few hours, and you spend most of your time being lifted violently out of the water and crashing face first into the sea. But eventually you learn how to dip the kite in a figure of eight formation, filling it with just the right amount of power. Suddenly you're up, skimming across the water on your board.

The feeling is one of exhilaration and unlike anything experienced before; as you lean back you're amazed by the force of the wind and the speed at which you're cutting through the waves. You laugh hysterically; you're instantly hooked. ●

# HARNESS THE  WIND

### + 1 Ballooning

To really go where the wind blows, step into a balloon basket. There is no mechanism to steer, so you are literally at the mercy of whatever zephyrs you encounter. Fly over Cappadocia in Turkey, drift above the Serengeti's wildebeest in Tanzania or float above the Australian Outback.

### 2 Windsurfing

If speed is what you're after, then this is the sport for you. Top spots include Bonaire in the Caribbean, Tarifa in Spain and Maui in Hawaii. It can take a few years to master the skill, but its many devotees prove it is well worth the effort.

### 3 Ice sailing

An 18th-century Dutch commercial mode of transport, ice sailing has developed into a fast and exhilarating winter sport. It can be dangerous but this has not deterred people: it is currently practised in over 20 countries worldwide. All you need is a big expanse of thick ice, lots of wind – and no fear.

### 4 Kite flying

By far the easiest way to enjoy wind power is to fly a kite. To take this hobby to the next level, head to one of the many kite festivals around the world. Particularly popular in the East, there are huge, colourful gatherings every year in Japan, China, Indonesia and India.

# TRIAL BY FIRE

FIND OUT WHERE TO TEST YOUR TASTE BUDS' TOLERANCE FOR EXTREME HEAT WITH THIS GUIDE TO THE WORLD'S HOTTEST CHILLIES. BUT CHECK THE HEAT-RATING SCOVILLE SCALE OF EACH FIRST...

**Pure capsaicin**
**16 million units**

**Carolina Reaper**
**2.2 million**

**Pepper spray**
**2 million**

**Naga Bhut Jolokia chilli**
**1 million**

**Habanero chilli**
**350,000**

**Bird Eye chilli**
**100,000**

**Jalapeno chilli**
**10,000**

**Tabasco sauce**
**2500**

### Carolina Reaper
**Heat:** *Hotter than a thousand suns*
**Scoville scale:** *2.2 million*

**More than 400 times hotter than Tabasco sauce, the world's hottest chilli will reduce body-building construction workers to tears. Order seeds from the PuckerButt Pepper Company of South Carolina and bring on the burn!**

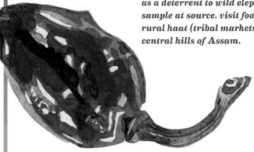

### Naga Bhut Jolokia
**Heat** *Napalm*
**Scoville heat units:** *1,001,300*

**A key ingredient in Assamese curries, stir fries and chutneys, Naga 'ghost chillis' are also smeared over fences as a deterrent to wild elephants. To sample at source, visit food stalls at rural haat (tribal markets) in the central hills of Assam.**

### Trinidad Moruga Scorpion
**Heat:** *Hotter than the gates of hell*
**Scoville heat units:** *2 million*

**The evil-looking Trinidad Moruga Scorpion has a fearsome sting in its tail, despite being knocked off the top spot by the Carolina Reaper. Sample this monster of a chilli pepper as hot sauce on the islands of Trinidad and Tobago.**

### Habanero
**Heat:** *Incendiary*
**Scoville heat units:** *350,000*

**When Mexicans want to turn up the heat, they reach for the habanero, an innocent-looking bell-shaped pepper containing the culinary equivalent of molten lava. Habaneros add pep to the scorching salsa served on the side with most meals in Mexico's Yucatan peninsula.**

### Jalapeño
**Heat:** *Inglenook fireplace*
**Scoville heat units:** *10,000*

**The original 'hot' chilli, this moderate scorcher is still grown in vast quantities in the Veracruz and Chihuahua districts of Mexico. Chipotles (smoked jalapeño peppers) are a key ingredient in Mexico's legendary adobo sauce.**

### Bird Eye Chilli
**Heat:** *Eye-watering*
**Scoville heat units:** *100,000*

**Compared to the record-breaking Carolina Reaper, Thailand's bird eye chilli is as weak as a kitten; try telling that to any traveller who has numbed their tongue on som tam, a fiery Thai salad made from raw bird eye chillies, lime juice and green papaya!**

*An Hour*

You Only Live Once

# TAKE A WATERFALL SHOWER

**DON'T JUST CONTEMPLATE THE VIEW, TAKE THE PLUNGE! A DIP IN A WATERFALL POOL PROVIDES THE ULTIMATE WILD-SWIMMING EXPERIENCE.**

**H**ave **you ever felt quite so refreshed?** It's like being brushed all over with minty toothpaste or lightly slapped by a school of mermaids. You've been in cold water before; over the years, you've even been known to take several showers. But there's something about splashing alfresco beneath the spray of a real, rippling waterfall that makes you feel that bit more revived and alive.

Bursting up and breaking the surface like a model in a shampoo commercial, you survey your surroundings. This is Afu Aau Falls, a tempting water-tumble on Samoa's big island of Savaii. And, because Pacific-stranded Samoa is one of the remoter spots on the planet, there's no one else here. This ideal swim-spot seems to have been created just for you.

Rivulets drip over mossy rocks into the natural basin, and leafy vines drip down from the surrounding trees, as if in competition. Birds chirrup as you dip under, scramble out and leap back in. The pool is chill and clear – it makes your brain zing and your skin tingle. But swimming here isn't simply invigorating; it somehow makes you feel more a part of the place – as though, for a few hours only, you've been invited into Mother Nature's private club.

Of course, you can't just jump into any old waterfall. You don't want to stick your head under the 2832-tonnes-a-second that gushes over Niagara, or the heavy 108m-high splat of Victoria Falls. Plus all that plummeting power creates dangerous currents, froth and tumult at the bottom of a cascade. Some plunge pools are full of gnarly rocks or toothy crocs. But pick the right pool – perhaps a small stream-trickled mountain lake or a hidden gushing gorge (clothing optional) – and there's no finer nor more fun way to wash. ●

 **1**

### Tat Kuang Si Falls, Laos
*These turquoise falls, 30km from Luang Prabang, are popular with locals and travellers alike. You can jump, dive or swing in by rope; a slippery jungle trail leads to the top.*

 **2**

### Lower Ddwli Falls, Brecon Beacons, Wales
*The clue's in the name: more than 20 pools dot a five-mile stretch of river in Waterfall Woods. Lower Ddwli has an arcing cascade, lots of swim space and, with luck, plentiful rainbows.*

 **3**

### Rainbow Falls, Kerikeri, New Zealand
*Walk the riverside trail, via kauri and totara trees, to reach this gorgeous gush, which tumbles over volcanic basalt into a perfect plunge pool.*

 **4**

### Hot Springs Waterfall, Finca el Paraíso, Guatemala
*A short hike leads to this natural spa: the sizzling thermal waters of the Rio Dulce (Sweet River) crash into an ice-cool pool, cloaked in luscious jungle.*

**An Hour**

# PUT IT ALL ON BLACK... NO, RED

*In 2004, Briton Ashley Revell bet the sum total of all his worldy possessions – US$135,000 – on one spin of a roulette wheel in a Las Vegas casino. He put it all on red; the ball fell on no.7... red. But maybe black is the better bet? During a game of roulette at Monte Carlo's casino in 1913 the ball landed on black 26 times in a row. Gamblers lost millions of francs thinking it had to be red next... forgetting that the previous result has no influence on the next spin of the wheel.*

MONTE CARLO CASINO IN MONACO   Getty/Steve Allen

An Hour

# GET A CLOSE SHAVE

**INDIAN BARBERS ARE THE SCOURGE OF FACIAL STUBBLE; SIT BACK AND LET A MAESTRO OF THE RAZOR WORK HIS MAGIC.**

**B**efore the invention of the disposable razor, shaving was an art form. The act of removing facial hair was an elegant dance, involving hogs' hair brushes, lashings of foam, delicate finger-work and a razor of the kind popularised by Sweeney Todd. Fortunately for travellers, this golden era of male grooming lives on in India, where a million backstreet barbers ply their trade with precision.

When sitting down for your first Indian shave, it pays to know the order of business. Step one is preparing the razor – most barbers use a cutthroat razor that takes a fresh disposable blade for every shave. Step two is the lather: shaving soap is whipped into a flurry of bubbles and applied liberally to chin and lip. Then the ballet begins. With gentle tugs and pinches, the barber will pull your facial skin taut and remove soap and stubble with graceful sweeps of the blade. Within minutes, you will make the transition from hairy caveman to well-groomed city gent.

Of course, once the shave begins, you are in the hands of the divine. If you have chosen a barber with homicidal tendencies, your journey ends here. Fortunately, the vast majority of barbers have worked out that slaying clients is a poor business model, and shaves are completed without so much as a nick. Removing stubble is just part of the process. Next comes a quick rub-down with astringent alum, a natural disinfectant that has been used since Vedic times, followed by a splash of cologne and a thorough face and head massage. The whole experience is surprisingly relaxing, if a little surreal. One essential tip – Indian men prefer moustaches so always remind the barber to trim the lip as well as the chin! ●

 **Havana, Cuba**
If you want to live like Hemingway, begin the day with a dry martini and wet shave in a Havana barbers shop. In Cuba, the barber serves the multiple roles of hair-dresser, counsellor, gossip and confidant, and extra atmosphere is provided by whirling ceiling fans and salsa music on a crackling radio.

 **London, England**
To make the most of a shave in London, it pays to have abundant facial hair like a Victorian pastor. Geo F Trumper of Curzon Street in Mayfair has been shaving the faces of well-heeled Londoners since 1875, and it even runs a shaving school where you can learn your own cutthroat technique.

 **Istanbul, Turkey**
Moustaches don't happen all by themselves. They need to be groomed, as any moustachioed gentleman in Istanbul can confirm. A traditional Turkish shave extends to steam treatment with a hot towel, a snip of protruding nasal hair, and removal of offending ear hairs with a taut thread or a lit match.

 **Myanmar**
In Myanmar, shaving has special significance. Enrolling as a Buddhist monk is a rite of passage for Burmese youngsters, and shaving the head is a milestone in that transition. Start your spiritual journey at one of Myanmar's forest monasteries; Pa-Auk has a long tradition of accepting foreign devotees.

*An Hour*

# TAKE AN URBAN HIKE

---

**WHILE AWAY A FEW HOURS ON THE SLOW PATH, AND SEE THE FAMILIAR ON FOOT. IT MAY NEVER LOOK THE SAME AGAIN.**

**N**obody walks in LA. A statement so true it's been immortalised in song. But walking in a city dominated by traffic and defined by freeways can give you a taste of the whole that's impossible at 35mph. Carved into a quilt of individuated neighborhoods, LA has a few connector boulevards that link these patchwork communities, and Sunset Boulevard is its most famous.

This sinuous 26-mile stroll from Union Station to the beach at Pacific Palisades takes about 15 hours to complete. Along the way, you'll skim downtown, and dodge the hipsters, immigrants and long-time locals who mingle in *taquerias* and *pananderías* of Echo Park. You'll glimpse the over-gentrified Silverlake, a hood Beck made famous, and wave at the Scientology complex in Hollywood. You'll be led along the famed Sunset Strip, punctuated by the landmark Château Marmont, all-powerful billboards, and the original House of Blues.

The rolling lawns, stately mansions and wide, empty sidewalks of Beverly Hills fade into paths that snake through the ivy where sidewalks should be. These trails are the exclusive domain of domestic workers as they hike between bus stops and their gigs in nearby Bel Air. Brentwood is next, then Dead Man's Curve, which Jan & Dean sang about in their 1966 tune based on Jan Berry's near-fatal wreck in his Stingray.

You'll climb the hills of the Pacific Palisades, home to folks like Dustin Hoffman and Tom Hanks, and then down you'll stroll toward the beach, stopping for some shade and perhaps a meditation in Paramahansa Yoganada's Lake Shrine, where George Harrison was eulogized in the Windmill Chapel.

In LA all things lead to the beach, and if you time it right, you can make it across town by sunset, where you may find yourself loving a city that you've never seen quite the same way. ●

LOS ANGELES BY NIGHT   Getty/GMG Software

**WALK THIS WAY**

### ① Sydney, Australia

*Australia's largest city has one of the world's most spectacular urban coastlines. And you can walk the entire thing – all 94km of it – if you have a week to spare. The walk begins at Barrenjoey, at the tip of Sydney's northern beaches, and trips a sandy course to Manly before heading inland to the Harbour Bridge and southern shores of Sydney Harbour.*

### ② New York City, USA

*Everyone walks in NYC, and trying to single out a route might cause a fight. Still, we suggest starting at Washington Square Park in Greenwich Village and walking Fifth Ave, north past Bryant Park, into Midtown. Moving Uptown, skirt the perimeter of Central Park then continue to hike north through Marcus Garvey Park in Harlem, where that mythic street ends at the Harlem River.*

### ③ Berlin, Germany

*Best known to cyclists, the Berlin Wall Trail follows the course of the wall that once divided West Berlin from East Germany. Seventeen years after the wall was famously breached (1989), it was transformed into a 160km hiking and cycling path. The trail is signposted and has interpretative boards detailing the 28-year story of the wall and Germany's division, including memorials to those who tried to escape.*

### ④ Hong Kong, China

*The Hong Kong Trail snakes 50km around Hong Kong Island, from Victoria Peak and its cracking views of Victoria Harbour to Tai Long Wan, a beautiful surf beach on the east coast. Take this route and you'll effectively be walking from the island's highest point to its lowest. The trail is divided into eight sections, some of which can be combined to turn the trail into a three- or four-day hike.*

# TOTAL ECLIPSE

NOTHING REMINDS US OF THE CELESTIAL BALLET UNFOLDING AROUND US AS WATCHING AN ECLIPSE OF THE SUN OR MOON. HERE'S WHEN AND WHERE TO SEE UPCOMING ECLIPSES.

## TOTAL SOLAR ECLIPSES

*When* **20 March 2015**
*Where* **Europe, North and East Asia, North and West Africa, West of North America, Arctic**

*When* **8-9 March 2016**
*Where* **South and East Asia, North and East Australia, Pacific and Indian Oceans**

*When* **21 August 2017**
*Where* **West of Europe, North and East Asia, North and West of Africa, North America, North and West of South America, Pacific and Atlantic Oceans**

*When* **2 July 2019**
*Where* **South of North America, South and West of South America, Pacific Ocean**

*When* **4 December 2021**
*Where* **South of Australia, South of Africa, South of South America, Pacific, Atlantic and Indian Oceans, Antarctic**

## TOTAL LUNAR ECLIPSES

*When* **8 October 2014**
*Where* **East of Europe, Asia, Australia, North and South America, Pacific, Atlantic and Indian Oceans, Arctic and Antarctica**

*When* **28 September 2015**
*Where* **Europe, South and East of Asia, Africa, North America, South America, Pacific, Atlantic and Indian Oceans, Arctic and Antarctica**

*When* **31 January 2018**
*Where* **North and East of Europe, Asia, Australia, North and East of Africa, North America, North and West of South America, Pacific, Atlantic and Indian Oceans, Arctic and Antarctica**

*When* **27 July 2018**
*Where* **Europe, South and East of Asia, Australia, Africa, South of North America, South America, Pacific, Atlantic and Indian Oceans, Antarctica**

*When* **21 January 2019**
*Where* **Europe, Asia, North and South America, Pacific and Atlantic Oceans, Arctic**

SUN PICTURES CINEMA, BROOME, AUSTRALIA   Alamy/Hauke Dressler

# STARLIT CINEMA

**KICK BACK FOR A COUPLE OF HOURS AT A THEATRE WHERE THE BACKDROP IS AS DRAMATIC AS THE ACTION ON SCREEN. CHOOSE YOUR SETTING WISELY AND YOU CAN REALLY MAKE IT A MOVIE TO REMEMBER.**

*Every summer, all around the world,* you'll find cities setting up outdoor cinemas. But how many can promise you balmy nights under starry skies with virtually no chance of rain? And of those that can, how many can also deliver an illuminated ancient citadel on a giant rock catching your eye during a performance? Since 1935 the Cine Thisio in Athens, with the Acropolis towering in the background, has been doing just that, wooing tourists and locals alike.

You enter the oldest outdoor theatre in the city through its neon art deco entrance. Family-run since 1980, Cine Thisio shows a mix of classic films and new studio releases, and it takes the decision on what plays very seriously. Rather than distract, the 5th-century-BC Acropolis, and its flagship ruin the Parthenon, only enhance the experience, as does the old-school film projector and the rampant ivy that seems to cover everything except the seats and the screen.

In a world where you constantly view films on planes, phones, and all too often alone, the communal act of movie-watching feels magical, especially somewhere as stunning as this – it gives you goosebumps. You cosy up under your blanket, sup on a homemade sour-cherry drink and savour a freshly baked cheese pie, ready for the action to begin. ●

### Red Rocks Amphitheatre, Colorado, USA
*At 2000m above sea level, the Red Rocks Amphitheatre sits in the shadow of two towering sandstone monoliths, providing both perfect acoustics and an awesome natural backdrop. Completed in 1941 and seating almost 10,000 people, its summer programme includes a mix of '80s, '90s and 2000s cult classics. Recent showings include Point Break, The Blues Brothers and Mean Girls.*

### Sun Pictures, Broome, Australia

*The world's oldest outdoor cinema, Sun Pictures is located in the Chinatown district of Broome, in remotest Western Australia. The tin-fronted building started life as an Asian emporium, switching to showing silent movies in 1916. Now on the State Register of Heritage Places, it screens mainstream and indie movies under the stars. And it'll even provide mosquito repellent if you forget your own.*

### The Galileo, Cape Town, South Africa

*From November to April each year, the super lush lawns of Kirstenbosch, Cape Town's oldest botanical garden, host cinephiles from all over the city. Set against the eastern slopes of Table Mountain, the site has gourmet food trucks or you can bring your own alcohol and pack a picnic.*

### Riviera Maya Film Festival, Mexico

*Since 2012 the Riviera Maya Film Festival has sought to showcase Mayan people and culture with film screenings throughout the Quintana Roo region. These take place in various locations: actual cinemas; makeshift screens on the streets of Cancun and Tulum; and drive-in theatres, though the most enticing are the palm-fringed Caribbean beach screenings at Playa del Carmen, Tulum and Puerto Morelos.*

**An Hour**

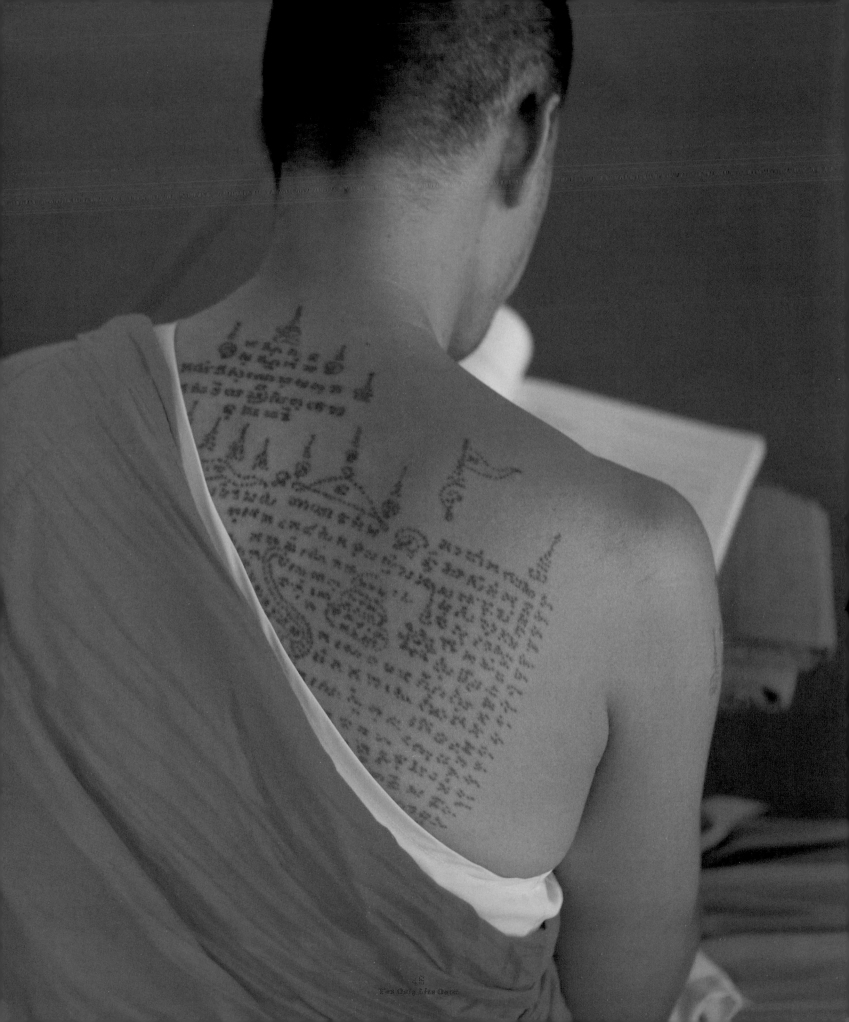

# GET A TATTOO*

---

**HOLIDAY SNAPS FADE, SOUVENIRS ARE THROWN AWAY AND MEMORIES BECOME DISTANT. BUT GET INKED, AND YOU'LL REMEMBER THAT TRIP FOREVER.**

**F**orget handicrafts or Chang Beer T-shirts, a tattoo is the only souvenir of Thailand that will literally last a lifetime. But why waste the opportunity by getting the same tribal armband as every Tom, Dick and Harry on Khao San Road? A tattoo is a commitment, and nothing shows more commitment than joining the queues of devotees at Wat Bang Phra for an intricate Buddhist sak yant tatt, etched by hand with a bamboo or metal spike.

Sak yant is more than just decoration. Every element of the design, from the depictions of tigers and elephants to the reams of blessings in Thai script and the complex grids of numbers and geometric forms, has profound spiritual meaning, designed to protect the bearer from harm. Consider it an amulet for good luck that you can't remove and lose after taking a shower.

The ritual is not for the faint hearted though. In sak yant, the customer is not king, and designs are selected by the monk administering the tattoos, intended as a blessing and a channelling of the divine. You will have to endure excruciating pain as the design is inked in a thousand tiny stabbing motions, and pay for the privilege with a Buddhist offering – either a bundle of incense or some flowers, candles or cigarettes, plus a few hundred baht to support the work of the monastery.

The reward is the feeling of shared human experience, as locals and foreigners, monks and businessmen are all united by the common thread of needle, ink and pain. Whether the tattoo renders you invulnerable to harm, as was believed in the days when Thai warriors were inked before heading into battle, is something only you can find out... ●

### Sailor chic, Hawaii
Long before sleeves and tramp stamps, the tattoo was the mark of a sailor, with its own symbolic language of swallows, dice, snakes, eagles, daggers and damsels. Seek out veteran old-school tattooists on the island of Hawaii, where the legendary 'Sailor Jerry' Collins once practised his art on untold thousands of sailors and marines.

### Samoan spectacular, Samoa
It was the Samoans who came up with the word tattoo – or more correctly 'tatau' – and the traditional art of malofie is still one of the benchmark tests of tattooing endurance. To adorn your body with a hand-tapped pattern of intricate lines from waist to knee, seek out members of the Sulu'ape family, hereditary tattoo masters since pre-colonial times.

### Maori magic, New Zealand
In traditional Maori society, tattoos were the mark of a warrior, and it still takes a warrior's resolve to endure the pain of traditional ta moko, where designs are not so much etched as incised with a hammer and chisel. If that doesn't put you off, seek out trained ta moko artists in Rotorua and Auckland.

### The Full Yakuza, Japan
In Japan, no self-respecting yakuza (gangster) would be seen dead in the steam room without a full-body irezumi tattoo. Applied by hand using a handmade needle brush, irezumi are the ultimate status symbol; a full-body design covering everything apart from the hands, feet and face can cost upwards of US$30,000.

**✳**
*Disclaimer: don't blame us when it's too late to change your mind...*

**An Hour** ⧖

# 69.3

## miles per hour

*speed that the fastest car ferry in the world, running
between Montevideo in Uruguay and Buenos Aires
in Argentina, can travel.*

# 16:20:27

## hours, minutes and seconds

*current speed record for visiting all 270
London Underground stations, set by Geoff Marshall
and Anthony Smith.*

# 16.994

## kilometres

*distance covered in one hour while pulling a wheelie, performed
by German bicycle rider Francesco Wiedemann in 2011.*

# 43

## minutes

*duration that Brazilian surfer Picuruta Salazar spent
riding the Pororoca, a tidal bore that creates a 4m-high
wave that travels 800km inland up the Amazon River.*

# 45

## minutes

*the time it can take venom of the Australian inland taipan to kill
you. The snake grows up to length of 8 ft in length – don't tread on it.*

# 206,864

## number of bounces

*performed on a pogo stick, achieved by James Roumeliotis, who
bounced for 20 hours and 13 minutes in California in 2011.*

# 6

## hours

*amount you need to subtract from international time in order to catch a bus if the timetable has been given to you in Swahili time.*

# 68

## minutes

*the number of minutes you are looking back in time when observing Saturn through an Earth-based telescope.*

# 7:18:55

## hours, minutes and seconds

*time it took Danial Jazaeri to complete the 1990 Prague City Marathon, while she was juggling a football with her feet without letting it touch the ground once.*

# 14

## hours

*decompression stop time required by Jarrod Jablonski and Casey McKinlay after a 7-mile-long, 20-hour, point-to-point cave dive in Wakulla Springs, Florida in 2007.*

# 360

## maximum distance

*in kilometres, you could travel by train in an hour – riding on an AGV Italo train (the Maglevs in China are faster but travel across short distances, taking less than an hour).*

# 42

## minutes

*the time it takes to ski down Alpe d'Huez in France, which, at 16km, is the longest black run in the world.*

# ZIP IT!

*Been bungy jumping? Zip lines should be next on your thrill-list. They're getting bigger and bolder; lines in Wales and Nepal run for more than 1.5km and send you flying at speeds of up to 160kph. But there's only one zip line where a passport is required: LimiteZero's zip line starts in Sanlúcar de Guadiana, Spain, but you'll land on the other side of the River Guadiana in Portugal. The whole experience takes 40 minutes but you'll gain an hour on landing due to Portugal's different time zone.*

CROSSING THE RIVER GUADIANA WITH WWW.LIMITEZERO.COM   RFG Art Photography/R.F. Granada

# COOK SOMETHING YOU CAUGHT

**FORAGED FOOD IS THE ULTIMATE IN LOCAL FOOD. WHAT BETTER WAY IS THERE TO UNDERSTAND A PLACE THAN THROUGH YOUR STOMACH?**

**I***t's the antithesis to the ready meal:* no premixed gloop, no additives (except maybe some soil); 'packaging' courtesy of Mother Nature. Foraging for food, and then magicking it into your own lunch, is simply the most satisfying way to eat. Not only do you get a wholesome feed but a primal reconnection with the earth, a sense that this is how eating used to be. Plus, there's also a cave-person smugness in knowing that, if all the supermarkets disappeared tomorrow, you could fend for yourself.

Autumn is bonanza time for foragers as fruits ripen on trees, berries appear as morsels of sweet delight on bushes – mind the thorns! – and mushrooms sprout from the damp ground. You need only keep your eyes open and a basket at the ready. In the seas and rivers, wild fish such as mackerel and salmon are readily caught.

Sometimes a professional guide will help point you in the right direction but usually asking locals for tips will be enough to get you harvesting the region's specialities for a couple of hours. ●

### Pluck berries, Sweden
*Swedes are serious about foraging. It's even written in their law: allemansrätten (every man's rights) grants permission to hike, camp and berry-pick on another's land, as long as it's done respectfully. Head out into the country's ample empty spaces in summer to find wild food – pick of the crops are sweet strawberries, golden cloudberries, blueberries and lingonberries.*

### Dive for scallops, Nova Scotia
*Clinking masts, bright-painted huts, a salt-whiff on the breeze – the ocean defines Nova Scotia. Its waters are a veritable fish soup and, equipped with a Recreational Scallop Licence, you can dive down and take a portion for yourself. Scallop season runs from Easter to the end of July, and limits are set at 50 a day – quite enough for a magnificent mollusc feast. You can eat them straight from the shell.*

### Pick wild garlic, UK
*Between March and May, many British woodlands start to stink. Wild garlic – or ransoms – grow rampant, their shiny green leaves and cheery white flowers cloaking many an undergrowth, and infusing the air with anti-vampiric fumes. Boot up and hike off with a pair of scissors – the leaves are best snipped carefully at the stem, and more flavoursome before the plants begin to bloom.*

### Funghi, France
*In the great forests of eastern France autumn's seasonal delicacy is the mushroom, piles of which you will see in the town markets. If picking your own it's best to stick to a couple of varieties you can identify with certainty. Start with chanterelles, which are the colour and smell of apricots, and the bulbous cep. And don't be put off by the name of trompettes de la mort (trumpets of death) – they're tasty.*

FRESHLY PICKED SCANDINAVIAN BERRIES   James Bedford

**An Hour**

# WALK

# OF

# LIFE

**NICOLA WILLIAMS RECALLS HER FRENCH WEDDING**

**I**t's fair to say my mother was horrified when I gently suggested, a few days before my marriage, that the groom and I might walk the 2km from church to wedding reception. On the day many guests were shocked too, so inbred is that impulse in our fast-paced lives to jump in the car for the shortest of journeys. Yet when my husband, beneath an exultant shower of rice on the church porch, grabbed my hand and jubilantly cried 'Join us in our first walk of life together!' stilettos, posh frocks and the wheels parked around the corner were momentarily forgotten. Everyone followed.

Two decades later, that slow celebratory walk through sun-baked vineyards in the softly rolling Beaujolais hills in France, remains one of the best walks of my life. Spontaneity and simplicity cast their spell that day, as we walked with best friends from two lives along a bewitching country lane. In a curvaceous sweep our path unfurled from the stone chapel, past a 19th-century marble fountain on the village square and uphill to the resplendent fairy-tale castle of Château de Varennes. Ancient milestones charted our route and the pace was no quicker than snail-slow as the wedding party processed serenely past serried rows of leafy green Gamay vines, pregnant with the promise of autumn's cherry-red wine. The sleek, white pencil dress sculpted to my frame by a Lyonnais designer and the strappy heels purchased a few weeks prior in Paris were *naturellement* as impractical as my mother had feared, but quite frankly, I could have been wearing hiking boots, so certain was my step.

The final curve in the road raised the curtain on a dazzling mirage of thick, gold-stone walls and richly decorated, Renaissance turrets – a fitting climax to a magnificent walk. An interlude between the hypnotic solemnity of the church service and the mad partying until dawn that was to ensue inside those sturdy castle walls, this short Beaujolais walk had been an unwitting celebration of love, life and friendship in glorious slow motion. ●

That slow celebratory walk through sun-baked vineyards in the softly rolling Beaujolais hills remains one of the best walks of my life

**An Hour**

You Only Live Once

# SWIM WITH FISH

**VENTURE BENEATH THE SURFACE OF THE OCEANS TO SEE HOW THE OTHER TWO-THIRDS OF THE PLANET LIVES.**

**E***veryone knows how the Jaws theme goes.* You can guarantee it will be going through your mind as you plunge into the cold, choppy water of South Africa with only an aluminium cage between you and the ocean's apex predator. Diving with great white sharks, while controversial, remains one of the world's great adrenalin rushes and the Gansbaai in the Southern Cape is the ideal place to swim with the big fish. Numerous companies offer dives in Gansbaai's Shark Alley but look for the operators who invest some of their profits back into shark conservation.

Elsewhere in the world, there are sharks with which you can swim without the need for a cage. On either side of the Americas hammerhead sharks go about their business without taking too much notice of humans. Around Bimini in the Bahamas great hammerheads, some up to 6m in length, scour the shallow sea floor for stingrays. On the other side of Central America, lies Cocos Island, described by Jacques Cousteau as the most beautiful island in the world. It's a world-class dive location thanks to the schools of scalloped hammerhead sharks that gather on the edge of the island's seamount. Dive here in December and you'll witness one of the nature's great wonders – but thanks to demand in Asia for their fins, hammerheads are highly threatened by illegal fishing so no-one knows for how much longer they will gather here. ●

### 1
**Whale sharks, Ningaloo Marine Park, Australia**
This World Heritage-listed marine park protects the full 300km length of the exquisite Ningaloo Reef in Western Australia, often just 100m offshore. Over 220 species of coral have been recorded and their spawning attracts the park's biggest drawcard, the whale shark. These gentle giants can reach up to 18m long.

### 2
**Stingrays, Cayman Islands**
Watch a dozen metre-wide rays, each armed with a venomous barb, glide towards you at Stingray City in Grand Cayman's North Sound. With water just 3m deep, visibility is superb; kit up and prepare to feel the rays' sucking kiss. The coolest season is December to April.

### 3
**Tropical fish, Bora Bora**
Strap on a snorkel and fins and you're equipped for one of the world's most colourful wildlife show, just inches beneath the surface of the ocean. Tropical fish, including Sergeant Major fish, and Pacific double-saddle butterfly fish, swarm the fragile coral gardens beneath you.

### 4
**Queensland groupers, Australia**
Off the east coast of Australia, in the protected waters of the Great Barrier Reef, giant groupers up to 3m in length still lurk in dark corners, patrolling the reef for prey. Divers consider them intelligent and inquisitive fish; some are known to hang out at the renowned wreck dive at the SS Yongala, 22km from Alva Beach.

**An Hour**

# LOOK UP!

*You don't have to be standing in Florence's Uffizi gallery to have your mind blown by simply looking up once in a while. We spend most of our time at eye level and a change of perspective opens up a new dimension of marvels: the architectural details of Glasgow, the abstract patterns of a forest canopy and, of course, the urban canyons of New York City.*

PARK AVENUE, NEW YORK    Getty/Lotus Carroll

An Hour

# CLASSIC COCKTAILS

TASTE IS A SHORTCUT TO MEMORY; DON'T JUST TRY AN
ICONIC COCKTAIL IN THE CITY IT WAS INVENTED, TAKE
THE RECIPE HOME FOR WHENEVER YOU WANT TO RETURN.

## NEGRONI, FLORENCE

### THE METHOD

*1 part gin*
*1 part Martini Rosso*
*1 part Campari*
*orange peel for garnish*

*Combine all the ingredients in an ice-filled glass.*
*Add a twist of orange peel to garnish.*

### THE TALE

The story goes that in 1919 Count Camillo
Negroni of Florence asked for a more
potent version of his favourite cocktail, the
Americano. The barman switched soda water
for gin and the lively little Negroni was born.
Florence remains the ideal place to sample
one as an aperitif.

## MOJITO, HAVANA

### THE METHOD

1 part lime juice
2 parts white rum
1 teaspoon of sugar
mint leaves
soda water

Muddle the lime juice, sugar and mint leaves in a glass. Fill the glass two-thirds full of ice and add the rum. Top up with soda water.

### THE TALE

Ernest Hemingway would relieve the heat of Cuba with this refreshingly minty drink. It was a refinement of the mint-sugar-rum-and-lime 'Drake' and first recorded in the 1930s.

*An Hour*

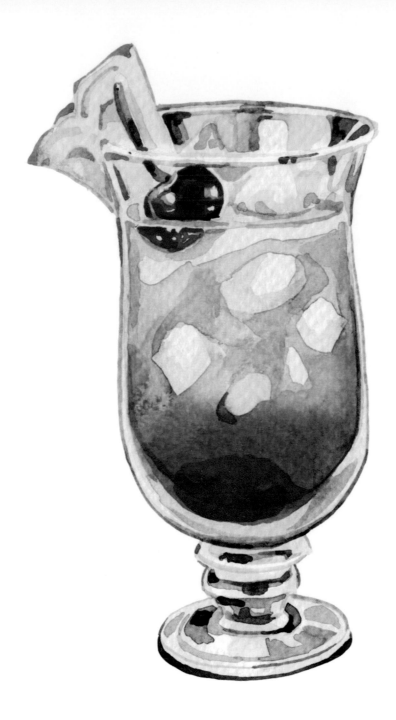

# SINGAPORE SLING, SINGAPORE

**THE METHOD**

*1 part gin*
*1 part cherry brandy*
*1 part Bénédictine*
*1 part fresh lime juice*
*2 parts soda water*
*1 dash of Angostura bitters*
*Mix all the ingredients, except the soda water and*
*bitters, in an ice-filled glass. Stir in the water then*
*add a splash of bitters.*

**THE TALE**

At the Long Bar in Raffles hotel, Singapore,
the gin sling was the perfect antidote to the
steamy climate; then a barman added a dash
of fruitiness to invent the Singapore Sling.

# SIDECAR, PARIS

---

### THE METHOD

*1 part Cointreau*
*1 part lemon juice*
*2 parts cognac*

*Pour all the ingredients into a cocktail shaker filled with ice. Shake well then strain into a chilled cocktail glass.*

### THE TALE

The Ritz Hotel in Paris, France claims the Sidecar as its own creation in the first decade or two of the 20th century. But after a couple of these punchy numbers it's no surprise that memories are hazy. The French School advocates equal parts of the ingredients; the English School prefers a little extra depth. ●

*An Hour*

# PERFECT PARKS FOR PICNICS

**YOU DON'T HAVE TO TRAVEL FAR FROM CITIES FOR GOOD TIMES OUTDOORS – JUST PACK A HEARTY LUNCH.**

**T**o the thousands of Manchester's industrial workers in the early 1930s, a walk in the Peak District was their only chance of getting any fresh air. Every Sunday – the one full day workers had off each week – Manchester London Road (now Piccadilly) railway station was packed full of ramblers excitedly waiting to explore the hills and moors. There was only one problem – they weren't allowed on most of them, least of all Kinder Scout, the highest hill in the Peaks.

What became known as the Kinder Trespass when, on 24 April 1932, 400 ramblers struck out across the fields, evaded Derbyshire's constabulary, and scrambled up the side of Kinder Scout, eventually led to the enshrining of Britain's first national park. And what was once an escape from the cramped, noisy factories below, remains a respite from a city's sound and fury.

Today, the sunlight seems to dance across the peak as it warms your back, picking out flashes of yellow moorland grass and rich green fern for a moment before skitting off to highlight a patch of purple heather. The clouds turn from black to white, before dissipating to reveal a widescreen blue sky, and Kinder turns with it. The dark, brooding moorland menace transforms into a glowing kaleidoscope of colour, beckoning you to clamber to the top. You've packed a pork pie for sustenance; sometimes it's the simple pleasures on your doorstep that are the most memorable. ●

THE PEAK DISTRICT NATIONAL PARK, ENGLAND   Justin Foulkes

An Hour

HIKING IN ABRUZZO NATIONAL PARK, ITALY    Getty/Andrew Bain

# PERFECT PARKS FOR PICNICS

 **Abruzzo National Park, Italy**
*Barely two hours from Rome, these granite peaks and beechwood forests rarely make it onto most people's Italy must-see lists. But they should: this is northern Italy at its most medieval, a wilderness where even short walks offer stupendous views. The main town is Pescasseroli, a jumble of pink stone houses nestled in a valley.*

 **Shenandoah National Park, USA**
*One of the most spectacular national parks in the US, Shenandoah is just 120km west of Washington, DC. In spring and summer the wildflowers explode in a blaze of colour and in autumn the leaves burn a bright red and orange.*

 **Ku-ring-gai Chase National Park, Australia**
*On Sydney's north shore, Ku-ring-gai Chase sits across Pittwater from the narrow peninsula of Palm Beach. On display is that classic Sydney cocktail of bushland, sandstone outcrops and water vistas, plus walking tracks. Aboriginal rock engravings and popular picnic areas.*

**The Black Forest, Germany**
*Between Strasbourg and Stuttgart, the Black Forest region is a vast nature playground featuring peaks and lakes irresistible to hikers, cyclists, bathers and boaters. Day trips are possible but stay for a weekend to explore the Panoramaweg and more scenic picnic spots.*

STAND AT THE BOTTOM OF THE BURJ KHALIFA, THE WORLDS TALLEST SKYSCRAPER, IN DUBAI

SWIM WITH WHALE SHARKS OFF NINGALOO REEF ON THE CORAL COAST OF WESTERN AUSTRALIA

TREK TO EVEREST BASE CAMP AND TAKE IN VIEWS OF THE WORLDS HIGHEST MOUNTAIN

STARGAZE AT GALLOWAY FOREST PARK, SCOTLAND, THE FIRST DARK SKY PARK TO BE CREATED IN BRITAIN

HELP RENOWNED SCULPTOR ED JARRET BUILD A GIANT SANDCASTLE

WALK ALONG THE SOUTH RIM OF THE GRAND CANYON

WATCH THE SURFERS AT NAZAR, PORTUGAL

GO FOR A DRIVE IN THE MIDNIGHT RIDER, THE WORLDS LARGEST LIMOUSINE

SURF THE SAND DUNES OF NAMIBIA ON A TRADITIONAL SWAKOPMUN BOARD

LOSE YOURSELF IN THE DUBAI MALL, UNITED ARAB EMIRATES

EXPLORE THE VAST WILDERNESS OF SPARSELY POPULATED GREENLAND

FOLLOW IN THE FOOTSTEPS OF ERNEST SHACKLETON ON A TRIP TO ANTARCTICA

TAKE A HELICOPTER RIDE OVER FOZ DIGUACU, BRAZIL

DIVE THE GREAT BLUE HOLE, BELIZE, TO SEE THE MARINE STALACTITES

ROAM AMONGST CALIFORNIAS REDWOOD GIANTS

SWIM IN THE TRANSLUCENT WATERS OF AMORGOS, GREECE, WHERE THE BIG BLUE WAS FILMED

GET CLOSE TO ONE OF THE 70,000 KALAHARI ELEPHANTS IN CHOBE NATIONAL PARK, BOTSWANA

SIZE UP THE GIANT VEGETABLES AT THE NATIONAL GARDENING SHOW IN SOMERSET

PLAY A ROUND OF MINI-GOLF IN THE WORLDS LARGEST TENT THE KHAN SHATYR, IN ASTANA, KAZAKHSTAN

SINK YOUR TEETH INTO THE ABSOLUTELY RIDICULOUS BURGER AT MALLIES SPORTS BAR, MICHIGAN, USA

GET LOST IN TRANSLATION IN TOKYO

ENJOY SOME RETAIL THERAPY IN MACYS, NEW YORK

# 50 WAYS TO FEEL SMALL

*By Manfreda Cavazza*

SPLASH OUT ON A VIRGIN GALACTIC SPACE FLIGHT

HEAD TO MONTEREY CANYON, OFF CALIFORNIA, TO SPOT BLUE WHALES

FALL IN LOVE WITH THE MARBLE WALLS, HIGH CEILINGS AND ELABORATE CHANDELIERS OF MOSCOWS IMPRESSIVE TUBE NETWORK

GO HIKING, RAFTING OR MOUNTAINEERING IN SOUTHERN SIBERIA, ONE OF THE LEAST TOURISTED AREAS IN ASIA

FIND THE REPLICA WILLYS WW2 JEEP ON DISPLAY IN THE EMIRATES NATIONAL AUTO MUSEUM

GO ON A CRUISE UP THE RIVER NILE

GO CAMEL TREKKING IN THE SAHARA DESERT

GO ON A TOUR OF BOEINGS EVERETT FACTORY, WASHINGTON, HOME TO THE 777 AND 787 DREAMLINER PRODUCTION LINES

GO PARAGLIDING IN TASMANIA

MARVEL AT THE LITTLE PEOPLE FAR BELOW ON A HOT AIR BALLOON RIDE OVER BAGAN, BURMA

SEARCH FOR DOROTHYS RUBY RED SLIPPERS ALONG THE ENDLESS CORRIDORS OF THE SMITHSONIAN INSTITUTE, WASHINGTON

WATCH THE SUN GO DOWN ON THE MUNDI MUNDI PLAINS IN NEW SOUTH WALES, AUSTRALIA

CLIMB MT KILIMANJARO

SAIL ACROSS THE PACIFIC OCEAN

DRIVE THE PAN-AMERICAN HIGHWAY, FROM PRUDHOE BAY, ALASKA TO USHUAIA, ARGENTINA

FLY OVER THE MUNDI MAN, THE WORLDS LARGEST ARTWORK, IN THE AUSTRALIAN OUTBACK

TAKE IN THE 360 DEGREE VIEWS OF LONDON FROM THE SHARD

SPOT EXOTIC BIRDS IN BRAZILS PANTANAL, THE WORLDS LARGEST (AND MOST COLOURFUL) SWAMP

BOOK A HOLIDAY ON BOARD ALLURE OF THE SEAS, THE BIGGEST CRUISE SHIP EVER BUILT

PAY HOMAGE TO THE SPRING TEMPLE BUDDHA IN HENAN, CHINA

DRIFT DOWN THE AMAZON RIVER ON A CANOE TOUR

MOVE INTO THE SUPERIOR HARBOR SOUTH BREAKWATER LIGHTHOUSE ON LAKE SUPERIOR FREE TO ANYONE WILLING TO LOOK AFTER IT

VISIT SUE, THE SEVEN TONNE T-REX AT THE FIELD MUSEUM IN CHICAGO

DIVE THE GREAT BARRIER REEF, THE WORLDS LARGEST STRUCTURE COMPOSED OF LIVING ENTITIES

CLIMB THE 320 STEPS TO THE TOP OF THE DOME OF ST PETERS IN ROME AND TAKE IN THE VIEWS

LEAVE YOUR MARK ON THE NEW GRAFFITI SECTION OF THE GREAT WALL OF CHINA

HOLIDAY IN HOLLAND, HOME TO THE TALLEST POPULATION IN THE WORLD

EXPLORE THE NEVER-ENDING VINEYARDS OF CALIFORNIAS WINE COUNTRY

**An Hour**

# BUY THOSE BOOTS

**SOMETIMES IT DOESN'T PAY TO DITHER - WHAT MIGHT SEEM LIKE FRIVOLOUS FASHION MAY JUST BE SOMETHING YOU WALK THROUGH YOUR WHOLE LIFE IN.**

***The cowboy boots*** are standing on a shelf at the Boot Barn off I-65, just north of Nashville. They are dove grey with a subtle stitch pattern of curling vines, and they cost US$160, a fortune for you right now. Everything about them feels luxurious and long-lasting, from the cushioned footbed, to the thick rubber heels, to the heavy leather pull-straps.

When you return home, you wear them out to dinner with your new boyfriend, who pronounces them 'totally badass'. A year later, you wear them out to Utah to meet his parents for the first time, returning home with the toes covered in red desert dust. Every time you see your boyfriend's father after that, he asks you where your boots are. A year later, your boyfriend gets a fellowship in Australia, and you pack the boots off to Sydney in his suitcase before following a month later. Boyfriend, boots and you traverse the Sydney Harbour Bridge, circle Uluru, and trek through fields of curious marsupials on Kangaroo Island.

You aren't wearing your boots the night you decide to get married (you and your boyfriend, not you and the boots), but you had them on under your bias-cut silk wedding dress when you wed on a North Carolina goat farm six months later. Less than two years after that, your now-husband takes a job in Hong Kong. There's a photo of you on your first day in your new city, standing at the edge of Victoria Harbour before the splendid and terrifying skyline, wearing your (now-resoled) boots. When US$160 carries you through that much life, it's the definition of money well spent. ●

 **English brogues**
Joseph Cheaney & Sons has been making classic men's shoes since 1886. Its five-eyelet wingcap Oxfords are the definition of timeless good taste, while the Imperial Sandringham wingtips have the same oak-bark leather soles British bankers and barristers have been wearing for nearly a century and a half.

 **Greek sandals**
What better captures the warm weather, devil-may-care spirit of the Mediterranean than a pair of classic leather sandals? At Melissinos Art in Athens, sandals are oiled, shaved, and fitted to your feet on the spot. Just what you need for many years of sure-footed island-hopping.

 **Chinese slippers**
Cheap, satin slippers are ubiquitous in China: you can buy them at any street market. But if you want lasting luxury, the designer Mary Ching offers a collection of slippers with a twist, in materials like cashmere, silk and suede, with embellishments from mink and mother-of-pearl to Swarovski crystal.

 **Australian riding boots**
Founded in 1932 by the legendary bushman Reginald Murray Williams, RM Williams makes boots rough enough for ranch use and sleek enough to wear under a suit. Look for them in ostrich, kangaroo and crocodile, as well as the classic leather.

*An Hour*

# TAKE A SKYWALK

*Walk above the clouds on the latest lofty lookouts. The Grand Canyon Skywalk was one of the first to allow visitors to walk on a glass platform cantilevered over the cliffside. In Jasper National Park, Alberta, Canada, the Glacier Skywalk has views over the Columbia Icefield. Or you can step into the void on Mont Blanc's Aigulle du Midi. Finally, the Aurland Lookout perches above Sognefjord in western Norway.*

AURLAND LOOKOUT BY SAUNDERS ARCHITECTURE IN WESTERN NORWAY · ©Bent René Synnevåg

An Hour

You Only Live Once

LIÈGE-BASTOGNE-LIÈGE RACE, BELGIUM    Alamy/EPA

# FEEL THE PASSION

**BE SWEPT ALONG BY THE WORLD'S MOST COMMITTED SPORTS FANS IN BELGIUM AND BEYOND FOR A COMMUNAL EXPERIENCE TO REMEMBER.**

**A**ll around you there are men and women, young and old, waving the black-on-yellow flag of the Flemish Lion, waiting for the racers of the annual Liège-Bastogne-Liège bike race. You're standing, tight-packed, beside the road up the Cote de Saint-Roch, a short but steep (at 12% gradient) climb in the far east of Belgium. There's a misty drizzle – this is Belgium in April, after all – but the crowd is warmed by frites (potato chips) and beer brewed in the village of Achouffe nearby. The thrum of a helicopter in the distance means that the riders are approaching and the noise builds and the crowd pushes together ever more tightly along the narrow road. Here they come! A car and half a dozen motorbikes force their way through, then the leading riders emerge and are engulfed by the crowd so that it becomes hard to tell rider from fan.

In Belgium, cycling is the national sport, and nowhere are the crowds more numerous or passionate than at the Spring Classics, a series of early-season bike races of which the 250km Liège-Bastogne-Liège, founded in 1892, is the oldest. The heavenly triumvirate of beer, bikes and frites tempts vast numbers of fans; whatever the weather, Belgium's bleak cobbled roads are lined three or four deep with supporters, waving flags and yelling encouragement to their heroes. The Spring Classics, long, tough races over rough roads, favour a hardened breed of cyclist and the same is true of the spectators; this is free, boisterous, street-side entertainment, and it's a credit to cycling's working-class roots that it has been largely unchanged over the decades. ●

ESSENDON FANS ON GRAND FINAL DAY AT THE MCG, MELBOURNE    Getty/Phil Weymouth

# FEEL THE PASSION

 **1**

### Kentucky Derby, USA

'The Most Exciting Two Minutes in Sport' occurs in Louisville, Kentucky, on the first Saturday of May. This horse race – 'decadent and depraved' according to Hunter S Thompson – sees the largest crowds in the infield area, fuelled by mint juleps and consumed by winning and losing on the 2km race.

 **2**

### Australian football, Melbourne

Winter is becoming spring and the Australian Rules footie season is drawing to a close at one of the world's great sporting stadiums, the MCG. It's Grand Final day in the AFL heartland of Victoria and the league's family-friendly vibe continues to the last kick of the season. No matter who you're barracking for, sport is the winner on this day.

 **3**

### Rugby, New Zealand

In the tiny nation of New Zealand rugby rules supreme. Here, 150,000 people lace up boots at the weekend to play, and this grassroots appeal spills out at grounds such as Yarrow Stadium in New Plymouth, Taranaki. Fans are close to the players, making for an intense atmosphere, with Mt Taranaki brooding in the background.

 **4**

### College American football, Georgia, USA

Forget the Superbowl, to find the most passionate American football fans you have to go to college gridiron games – and especially the great rivalry matches such as Georgia's Bulldogs against Florida's Gators – aka the 'World's Largest Outdoor Cocktail Party'.

# FREEFALL!

*What compels a person to jump out of a perfectly serviceable aircraft and fall to earth at 120mph? Skydivers give conflicting answers: it's the adrenalin rush and the sense of peace. It's the freedom and the responsibility. Find out for yourself by making a jump: most nations have a parachuting association that accredits schools.*

SKYDIVING ABOVE UBATUBA BEACH, BRAZIL.   Getty/Rick Neves

**In which we lose ourselves at festivals and carnivals,
dine like kings, party all night in cities and fall asleep**

DAY

in some extraordinary settings.

Then we spend a day or two in the outdoors,

watching wildlife, walking by moonlight

and seeking out the most silent places in the world.

Finally, we face our greatest fears, whatever they may be.

**A Day**

# LOST AND FOUND AT CARNIVAL

**LEAVE YOUR INHIBITIONS AT THE AIRPORT AND CLIMB INTO A DESTINATION'S SKIN. SPEND A DAY WITH THE LOCALS, LEARNING HOW TO REALLY LET YOUR HAIR DOWN.**

**T**o get the most out of **Carnival** in Brazil's northeastern city of Olinda, you shouldn't so much go with the flow, as completely give in to it. Nowhere here will you find the regimented rows of security railings, ticket blockados and spectator seating that defines Carnival in Rio. In Olinda there are no spectators; people, processions, musicians and Carnival freaks all funnel through the town's narrow, cobbled, disorientating streets as one. If you're here, you are Carnival.

So give up on crowd control. Be irresponsible. Dance. Don't sleep. Find friends, then lose them again. Surrender to the insistent, comedic, skipping rhythm of frevo, the musical lifeblood of Olinda's Carnival; a high-speed military two-step-cum-polka (its name taken from the Brazilian word 'to boil'), it will have you flinging your limbs around like your flip-flops are on fire. Follow brass bands led by beaten-up trombones and tarnished trumpets. Bounce over cobbles holding a multicoloured umbrella – the symbol of the region – above your sun-addled head. And wonder not how the thing got into your hands.

Get drawn into a maracatu drumming procession and try, in vain, to shout for directions above the cacophony of cowbells, whistles and hundred-strong battery of *alfaias* (drums). You are lost. Embrace it. Embrace someone. Most people will be: arms and shoulders intertwined, jumping, dancing, losing integral parts of their homemade costumes, noting them being crumpled underfoot with a smile. Encounter everyone from Zorro to Thor during the 'superheroes parade', comprising costumed characters the surreal likes of which never graced the pages of a Marvel magazine. Stroll alongside 'Supermarket Man', riding in a shopping trolley wearing little more than a smile and an oversized papier-mâché carrot, and concede that what it lacks in sophistication, Olinda makes up for in genuine party spirit. ●

REVELLERS AT ATI-ATIHAN, PHILIPPINES    Getty/Bruno Morandi

## LOST AND FOUND AT CARNIVAL

### Lazarim Carnival, Portugal
*14–17 February 2015*
**This pagan-rooted, pre-Lent Carnival pageant, in Portugal's northern interior is characterised not by a parade of semi-clad dancers but macabre hand-carved wooden masks sculpted with devil horns and skull-like faces. The festival's focal point is the ritual burning of male and female effigies and a theatrically read poem of judgement called The Testaments. Deliciously creepy, medieval mayhem.**

### Junkanoo, Bahamas
*26 December & 1 January*
**This Bahamian Carnival–Mardi Gras hybrid, said to date back to plantation-era Christmas parties, sees the nation's streets overrun with merenguing masses, dressed in rainbow costumes and headdresses like towering birds of paradise. Once midnight mass is finished, off roll the floats: musicians drive the crowd wild with goat-skin drums, cowbells, conch-shell horns and whistles.**

### Ati-Atihan, Philippines
*24–30 January 2015*
**This Christo-pagan beaded bacchanal, known as 'the mother of all Philippines festivals', is held on Kalibo, an island in a beach-fringed archipelago only an hour by plane from Manila. Expect tribal dance, fearsome face-paint and parades, all in celebration of Santo Niño (Infant Jesus). And on the last day, a tear-it-up, torchlit dance-off.**

### Bon Om Tuk, Cambodia
*Usually November*
**When the Tonle Sap River does an about-turn and flows in reverse, it signals party season for Cambodia. Honouring this annual hydro happening, coinciding with an auspicious Buddhist full moon, are three days of fireworks, feasting and dragon boat racing; the wildest celebrations are seen along Phnom Penh's Sisowath Quay.**

ROAST ABERDEEN ANGUS BEEF AND YORKSHIRE PUDDING, BRITAINS BEST

FELAFEL, MIDDLE EAST CHICKPEAS

CHURRASCO CON CHIMICHURRI, ARGENTINAS STEAK WITH SPICY SAUCE OVER A FIRE

MIX RICE AND SEAFOOD IN A FLAT PLAN FOR SPANISH PAELLA

WRAP PORK IN LEAVES AND COOK SLOWLY FOR COCHINITA PIBIL IN MEXICO

ENGLANDS LANCASHIRE HOT POT, A WORKING-MANS CASSEROLE OF LAMB, LEEKS AND POTATOES

INDULGE YOUR SWEET TOOTH WITH A SLICE OF SHARLOTKA IN RUSSIA

THE BEST FOR MOMO DUMPLINGS TAKE A TRIP TO TIBET

GOULASH, HUNGARYS PAPRIKA- AND POTATO-RICH MEAT STEW

GET TO GRIPS WITH CONCH, THE BAHAMAS GIANT SNAIL

TAPAS ARE SPAINS BITE-SIZE COMPANIONS TO CHILLED GLASS OF SHERRY

KUAYTIAW, THAILANDS FAST-FOOD NOODLE SOUP

BRIK IS A SAVOURY PASTRY PACKET FROM TUNISIA

**50 DISHES TO TRY BEFORE YOU DIE**

*By Colin Eastwood*

THE BURRITO, MEXICOS STREET-FOOD CLASSIC, IS FOUND AT FOOD TRUCKS AROUND THE WORLD

CHIVITO IS URUGUAYS BASIC BEEFY SANDWICH

BOBOTIE IS SOUTH AFRICAS CUSTARD-TOPPED MEAT CASSEROLE

PIEROGI ARE POLANDS CRESCENT-SHAPED DOUGHY DELIGHTS

FEAST ON FEIJOADA, BRAZILS NATIONAL DISH OF BEANS AND BEEF

FRESH BREAD FROM FRANCES REGAL RICE DISH BAKERS DOESNT DISAPPOINT

BIRYANI IS INDIAS

CULLEN SKINK, A SMOKY, FISHY SOUP FROM SCOTLAND, MADE WITH SMOKED HADDOCK

RICE, CHICKEN AND SHRIMP ARE STIR-FRIEND IN INDONESIA FOR NASI GORENG

AMERICAS HANDHELD CLASSIC, THE HAMBURGER, CAN BE SUBLIME

SINK YOUR TEETH INTO CEVICHE, ZESTY MARINATED FISH FROM PERU

IN VIETNAM ROLL DELICATE BO BIA IN RICE PAPER

CRISPY-SKINNED PEKING DUCK IS CHINAS CULINARY CALLING CARD

BERRIES, BREAD AND SUGAR MAKE ENGLANDS SUMMER PUDDING WORTH THE WAIT

CASSOULET FLAVOUR-PACKED MEAT AND BEANS FROM FRANCE

HANG OUT AT A HANGI BEACH BARBEQUE IN NEW ZEALAND

SWEAT OUT A FIERY CHONGQING HOT POT IN CHINA

RICE, FRESH VEGETABLES AND A SPICY SAUCE FORM SOUTH KOREAS BIBIMBAP

CLAM CHOWDER, SEAFOOD SOUP FROM AMERICAS NORTHEAST SEABOARD

ASHFORD CASTLE, IRELAND   Getty/Peter Zoeller

# SLEEP IN A CASTLE

**OH, WHAT A NIGHT! PLAY OUT ALL YOUR PALACE FANTASIES AND LAY YOUR HEAD ON THE PILLOWS OF KINGS AND QUEENS OF YORE.**

**Y**ou – yes, little old you – are sleeping where Robert the Bruce; Mary, Queen of Scots; Oliver Cromwell; Sir Walter Scott; even Queen Victoria slept. All these luminaries have walked within Dalhousie Castle's thick 13th-century walls in Scotland – and so can you.

The ancestral home of the Ramsay family became a hotel in 1972, as many such piles have had to in these less aristocratically friendly times. However, it still echoes with its illustrious past. The Grey Lady, the spirit of a 16th-century laird's mistress, reputedly haunts the stairs. Fixtures from the original drawbridge can be seen above the door and a Civil War–musket shot is still embedded in the outer walls.

You'll lay on a plush four-poster bed, in a room of 16th-century furnishings, exposed stone walls and a profusion of tartan drapery. There's a fire roaring in the drawing room, a restaurant in the dungeon, and a spa in the old storage vaults. Pose by suits of armour, watch falcons fly across the grounds and listen for a piper striking up Robbie Burns' *Address to a Haggis*. You'll feel like a fleeting part of the castle's story, more so than if you'd just made a day trip. You are living the kitsch-yet-awesome Scottish stereotype, in quite some style. ●

### *Castle Hotel, Schönburg, Germany*
*Teetering on a hilltop beside the Rhine, parts of this bastion date back to the 10th century. It's as romantic as they come; all the rooms are bursting with character – number 22 has a particularly brilliant balcony.*

 **2**

### Ashford Castle, County Mayo, Ireland
This sprawling estate is frequently voted one of the best hotels in the country. As well as wow factor it offers plenty of lordly activities, from falconry and fishing to horse riding and clay pigeon shooting.

 **3**

### Château de Tennessus, Poitou, France
Medieval, moated Tennessus is château perfection. It has original spiral staircases, arrow slits, hoardings, even a working drawbridge. B&B rooms (The Knight's Chamber, The Watch Tower...) start at just €105 a night.

**4**

### Hostel Heemskerk, the Netherlands
The 13th-century Slot Assumburg, easily accessible from Amsterdam, has big towers, venerable stone walls, its own moat – and beds for €23, making regal sleeps a possibility for even budget travellers.

**A Day**

1.
2.
3. CHUCK OUT THE THE CHECKLIST

88
*You Only Live Once*

**S**ome places you pass through, others have an extra gravitational pull. Go for a week, end up staying for months. Or at least that is how it should be. But in a world where we increasingly travel with timetables and checklists, the art of allowing ourselves to be seduced by somewhere, letting a destination derail us – and our schedules – is being lost.

And more's the pity, as these magnetic planetary spots are, often, the last places you imagined you'd end up pausing. And thus the world surprises you, as it should. Take Bali. It's heaving with tourists, tainted with the scars of religious extremism and suffering from a rebranding by way of the blockbuster *Eat, Pray, Love*. But... there's a reason that this mystical Indonesian Island became the 'pray' part of the story. There really is something so soul-stilling about its orderly tiers of rice fields, temple-like mountains and brilliant-white, jungle-fringed beaches.

Do as artists and travellers have done for a century: arrive for those beaches and stay for the grace of the island's interior. The central town of Ubud has been drawing creative types since the 1930s, seducing Europeans with spiritual, decorative and figurative painting, intricate batik and sculpture. In the face of mass tourism, Bali has somehow preserved its rich Hindu culture with dignity and smiles. Temples rise over the crashing ocean like serene gods; handmade Hindu offerings line the street corners, more colourful, even, than the island's myriad endemic butterflies and sudden, Technicolor sunsets.

Bali is the place to master the art of doing nothing, to spend a while in gentle meditation and mindless contemplation. For travellers who let themselves simply 'be', Bali induces a case of eat, love, stay. ●

Do as artists and travellers have done for a century: arrive for Bali's beaches and stay for the grace of the island's interior

**A Day**

# FACE YOUR FEAR

**T**he day starts at Triple B Ranch unapologetically. You're woken by the thunder of a 40-strong herd of horses coming in from the bush for breakfast. If this isn't enough to rouse you, the accompanying neighing, whinnying and snorting will. It's time to get up, boot-up and buckle-up – the day starts here.

Eliminate ignorance and so too goes fear. And being taught to ride by a horse-whispering rancher is arguably the best way to overcome any equine nervousness. Novices and experienced riders alike are drawn to Triple B, a working ranch in the Waterberg Mountains, South Africa's borderlands with Botswana. A wilderness once beloved of Mandela, the Waterberg is home to big game, bigger mountain ranges and hardy herds of Anglo-Arabs, Thoroughbreds and Boerperds. Here, horses are 'tamed' using the round-pen techniques of Shane Dowinton, an expat Brit who applies his natural horsemanship to all species, maintaining there 'are no bad horses, just bad people'.

The day's activities include yoga-in-the-saddle and rounding-up cattle, allowing nervous riders to quickly forget their mount and concentrate on the task in hand. And then there's the game viewing. There's nothing like catching-up with a herd of giraffe to make you forget about your rising trot; staying in the saddle is a means to an end. Horseback safari is an electrifying experience, as you become one with the pack of wildebeest, hartebeest, zebra, impala, kudu, rhino and even hippo.

And at the end of the day, you'll kick back, boots off, with a beer. Storms crackle along mountain ridges, while electric-blue kingfishers flash through trees like forked lightening. If South Africa is, as locals say, God's Country, then Waterberg is His hilltop retreat. ●

### *Walk with wild things, Tanzania*
*Combat a fear of big beasties by putting yourself in the capable hands of the Maasai, on a walking tour through Tanzania. Learn how to forage for bush tucker, track big game and identify mammal calls. Immerse yourself in this ancient, pastoral culture, and learn how beautiful the coexistence of man and beast can be.*

### *A head for heights, Italy*
*Follow in the footsteps of WWI soldiers, trooping across the Vie Ferrate (Iron Ways) of the Alps. This skyscraping series of mountainside cables, metal rungs, rope ladders and chain bridges allows access to some of the most heart-stopping views in Europe.*

### *Public speaking, USA*
*Join Boom Chicago, one of the world's leading improv groups based in the Netherlands, to master acting techniques that will transform your public-speaking presence. Learn about body language, breaking down the wall between speaker and audience, and refine that awe-inspiring finale.*

### *Fear of Flying*
*If there's no greater way to conquer a fear than to face it head-on, aviophobes should consider piloting a plane. Most introductory flying lessons include a 'walk around', where the pilot explains the basics of the instruments, plus the chance to take-off, cruise and sometimes land a dual-control plane.*

**A Day**

# LET THE MUSIC MOVE YOU

**IF LIVE MUSIC IS YOUR PASSION, THERE'S NO BETTER PLACE TO BINGE THAN A FESTIVAL IN SPAIN'S PARTY CITY, IN REMOTE CAPE VERDE OR THE WILDS OF WALES.**

*Y**ou open one eye slowly, tentatively,** and* see from your window that the sun is already high in the sky. Your ears hum with Disclosure's closing tracks from last night and you can still see the dancing lights from Arcade Fire's thrilling set. You stretch lazily, reach for coffee and hope that today will match up to your first day at Barcelona's first-rate festival, Primavera Sound.

You gather your mates and head out the door, deciding to skip the bus and take the beach promenade, sipping a beer as you stroll by the waves. The crowd is already building as you approach the Parc del Fòrum; the sea glints, and the atmosphere builds. You ease your way into the music-filled mayhem by swaying along to Sharon Van Etten, grab a few beers before heading to see SBTRKT, and then throw yourself into the mosh pit for The National. The crowd is immense, and you raise your arms into the air, letting yourself be carried by the momentum of the music.

The tunes keep coming and no-one looks set to stop. You dance in the Boiler Room dome til the sun starts to show, find your friends, and as the tens of thousands of revellers start to depart, you decide that the return walk with the sun rising is probably the perfect way to sober up. ●

***Boi Bumbá, Parintins, Brazil***
*Each June the river island town of Parintins plays host to Brazil's foremost folklore festival, which tells the tale of the death and resurrection of an ox. The story is relayed through the eyes of two competing samba schools – Caprichoso and Garantido – in a typically Brazilian riot of colour, music and lavish carnival.*

### Green Man Festival, Brecon Beacons, Wales
*Set in the beautiful surroundings of Glanusk Park near Abergavenny, this four-day festival hosts over 1500 performers, has an excellent and eclectic musical programme, literature events, comedy and kids' entertainment. Green Man boasts the UK's only 24-hour festival licence, a spectacular site and bountiful distractions so you may never make it back to your tent.*

### Monterey Jazz Festival, USA
*The world's longest-running jazz festival kicked off in 1958 with the simple plan of bringing together 'the best jazz people in the world...having a whole weekend of jazz'. The modern-day festival continues on the original site at the Monterey Fairgrounds, mixing leading live performances with workshops, panel discussions and global food and drink.*

### Salzburg Festival, Austria
*Every summer Salzburg plays host to the world's premier celebration of opera and drama. Held over six weeks during July and August, the festival attracts visitors from around the world to see leading performers and groundbreaking collaborations.*

**A Day**

# THE MEAL OF A LIFETIME

**FIVE HOURS, 12 COURSES, AND BRAGGING RIGHTS THAT WILL LAST A LIFETIME. BLOWING YOUR ANNUAL VACATION BUDGET ON ONE MEAL REALLY IS WORTH IT.**

**Y**ou know it's slightly bonkers to spend a month's salary on a single lunch. Maybe more than slightly. And you know it's crazy to spend eight hours flying each way for one meal. But then you somehow manage to finagle a table at Copenhagen's Noma – one of the world's best restaurants – and you don't think twice.

Now you're not just dressing for dinner, you're packing for it too. And your priority isn't just sharing those Instagram photos with jealous friends, it's to be surprised and delighted by this first-class culinary journey.

And so you show up at Noma slightly before noon, while the northern light is still slanted at the late-morning, industrious angle. But your mission is wholly pleasure. Eleven 'snacks' come out before you decide whether you want the 8- or 12-course tasting menu. You eat them all, and especially love the raw oyster in a cast-iron pot. And then you order the 12-course lunch, with wine pairings – you've come this far, how can you not go all the way now?

Your afternoon unfolds slowly, with course after course brought out and explained by one of René Redzepi's entourage of interns. You can ask them exactly how the juniper foam got that texture, and they know. Or you just talk about German metal bands – the heavy staffing in the kitchen means the cooks have time to socialise.

Lunch is really the way to do this. At Noma you can watch the day unfold, watch the light change over the harbour, the reflections on the buildings change their timbre, and be aware of all the hours you're giving over to pure pleasure. ●

### 1
### El Celler de Can Roca, Girona, Spain
The restaurant that unseated Noma as number one on influential Restaurant magazine's definitive list. The three Roca brothers create culinary masterpieces that combine 'countryside and science'.

### 2
### D.O.M., São Paulo, Brazil
Rock-star chef Alex Atala's palace of gastronomy, where he skillfully employs modernist cooking techniques on traditional Brazilian ingredients.

### 3
### Alinea, Chicago, USA
Wünderkind Grant Achatz pushes theatrical boundaries with his 18-course tasting menus – a recent menu had dessert listed simply as 'balloon: helium, green apple'.

### 4
### Dining Impossible, worldwide
Danish bon vivant and self-proclaimed ambassador of pleasure Kristian Brask Thomsen organizes three-day gastronomic benders for just 18 globetrotting guests at a time. Events are regularly held in Copenhagen, Barcelona, North America and other global destinations.

**A Day**

# DRESS UP FOR A DAY

IF YOU'VE MORE COSTUMES IN YOUR CUPBOARD THAN A YOUNG LIBERACE, TRY ON A COUPLE OF OUR TOP PICKS FOR THE WORLD'S FANCIEST FANCY DRESS OPPORTUNITIES.

## ELVIS EUROPEAN CHAMPIONSHIPS
### BLACKPOOL, ENGLAND

The northern home of 'kiss me quick' hats, illuminated trams and donkey rides along a wind-blown beach gets a dose of Deep South in January, when the impersonator-heavy Elvis European Championships come to Blackpool's Norbreck Castle. Brush up on your hip rotations, dig out your pantsuit, and practise your 'uh-huh-uh-huh's.

## COSPLAY PUBS
### TOKYO, JAPAN

If dressing as a schoolgirl, a manga character or even Hello Kitty is your thing, hit downtown Tokyo for a spot of fancy dress in one of numerous cosplay (short for 'costume play') pubs, where the stars of manga, graphic novels, video games and anime cartoons and storybooks come to life in intricate, elaborately detailed fancy dress costumes.

## JOMSVIKINGS
### EUROPE

The world's largest Viking re-enactment society battles it out in various locations across Europe, offering the perfect opportunity to haul out your warrior regalia. The adventures of the group are based on the doings of the original Jomsvikings, a 10th-century Baltic military brotherhood. Novices can join the scene at festivals on the continent.

## VILLAGE HALLOWEEN PARADE
### NEW YORK CITY, USA

New York City's the place to be come 31 October, when the Village Halloween Parade arrives in a feast of dazzling fancy dress creation, with 50,000 costumed revellers and another 2 million turning out to watch. The pageant was conceived in the mid-'70s by a local puppeteer who lamented the decline in the city's Halloween celebrations.

## DIA DE LOS MUERTES
### PÁTZCUARO, MEXICO

If you find yourself down Mexico way on 2 November, Pátzcuaro provides the perfect place to experience the bright side of Dia de los Muertes (the Day of the Dead). Families gather to pray for deceased loved ones, building private altars and decorating graves with sugar skulls, flowers and the favourite foods of those who've 'passed over'.

**You Only Live Once**

# HIKE TO THE MOON

IF YOU'RE CRAVING AN ALTERED PERSPECTIVE, ESCHEW THE SUN AND TURN YOUR DAY UPSIDE DOWN. SEEING THE WORLD BY THE LIGHT OF THE MOON OFFERS A RENEWED SENSE OF BOTH SERENITY AND EXCITEMENT.

**T**here's something magical about moonlight. The way it bathes everything in a deep, golden glow, looms large then high and lights up the sky so brightly even the stars retreat. And when surrounded by nature, it feels especially profound, making full-moon hikes full of promise and joy. The best ones start late in the evening and high in the mountains, on a trail you know well enough to tackle in the dark hours.

Sandstone Peak in the Santa Monica Mountains makes for a perfect night hike. At around 11pm the glow should be bright enough to reveal the countryside's secrets. You may glimpse an owl peering from the treetops, and grazing deer tracking down a midnight snack. The trail is clear enough to follow through the sagebrush and emerges onto a moonscape plateau between two peaks. The tallest is Sandstone, overlooking the Pacific Ocean, the water white-gold with the moon's reflections. Find a flat rock and take in the scene. Stories are spun, laughter shared – perhaps someone will pass you a bottle of hooch – this moonlit adventure will linger long in the memory. ●

### Rave
*Choose your poison wisely – perhaps a bucket of Red-Bull-throttled rum punch? Grab a bunch of good friends and head to one of several beach bars on Ko Pha Ngan, Thailand, for one of the most famous full-moon parties in the world. Dance, laugh, and howl in the light of the moon, but just make sure you make it home by morning.*

### Paddle
*Paddling takes on a sloshing, calming, quiet in the moonlight. Full-moon whitewater is commonly offered on class II and III river runs, which supercharges the serenity with a safe shot of adrenaline. If it's the ocean for you, know that tides can get wicked during full moons, so check the tidal tables and ask local experts. There's nothing more spectacular than stroking toward the golden patches of a melting moon.*

### Run
*Global urban trend-setters have started to gather in large packs and take on runs through the nighttime streets of New York, LA, Seattle and even towns in Estonia. You get to dodge the hottest part of day and exercise in spaces gloriously empty of their daily traffic.*

### Cycle
*Whether you're biking solo on a beach path, heading into town with pals for a night out or taking part in a community night-ride like Critical Mass, moonlit cycles bring cool breezes, a real sense of freedom and a whole new way to see the landscape.*

**A Day**

# GET LOST & BECOME ONE

CLIMB INTO YOSEMITE OR DIVE BELOW THE OCEAN
TO LOSE YOUR SENSE OF SELF.

**H***ow many valleys are there in the world?* Not a couple of rolling hills leading down to a stream. Not even the kind of valley that sits beneath a couple of alpine mountains. But a flat expanse of land surrounded by granite walls that appear to have risen from the ground. A dramatic announcement that 'this place is not flat'.

You know, maybe there are many. But when you hear of one that does what Yosemite Valley can do – that sense of being subsumed by something infinitely greater and grander than your individual self – make a note of its location and go.

In the half-light of a May morning, the snow on Half Dome glows. Winter barely lets spring have its turn. Among the feelings that the valley inspires – the awe, the insignificance, the First World questions of existence – there is the sensation of revelling in greed. This is all yours.

The place is a shortcut to being humbled by nature. But what you can attain walking solo in the trails is a sense of oneness. True, you're not a billion years old, carved by a glacier, you haven't witnessed dinosaurs and you'll die soon enough while this place lives on and on and on. But all the same, it happens; your thoughts are metered by the beat of your boots on the granite, the resounding anthem draws you in. You are connected here, as an object, no more or less out of place than the stones, the stream, the squirrel or the bear. You start out solo and before you know it your self has disappeared. ●

YOSEMITE VALLEY, CALIFORNIA    Willie Huang

A Day

# GET LOST & BECOME ONE

## 1

### Great Barrier Reef, Australia

When you slip beneath the surface, time as you know it stops. It is another world. And the shock of colour underwater will take your breath away (but try and hold it in!). The sea turns into a confetti-factory explosion of marine life. Colours that shouldn't exist are paraded everywhere you look. Creatures –giant, tiny, fleeting – fall over themselves beneath you. Floating, goggles down, snorkel up, this sensory overload chamber is so numbingly amazing you disappear into it. Only the need for air brings you back.

## 2

### Isle d'Ouessant, France

The island is hammered by the Atlantic waves. The land is bare and wind blown. Créac'h Lighthouse looms above you, a beacon on this most solitary of places. You walk the 8km to the other end of the island, by rocky bluffs above white water and sea foam, and past the occasional sheep, to the Stiff Lighthouse. If this were a country, its chief export would be light. At the island's town, Lampaul, you find the cemetery, a moody view to the past, unknown sailors resting with the roll calls of lost ships. You're taken by the romance of shipwrecks and angry seas, storms and rescue. You're alone and clinging to life, lit by the flashes of light cutting through the gloom. Waiting for salvation.

## 3

### London Underground, England

Wait until it looks full, till it's almost overflowing. Then make your dash and squeeze your way into the carriage. Mind the gap as you go. The press is complete. You've never felt so close to so many people. What is everyone thinking? Why are they just staring like that? And then you realise that they're thinking the same thing. That in every head you see there's a similar chatter of questions and wishes. Your own face is no more animated than theirs, despite the torrent of thoughts running through your mind. All this worry, mirth and bemusement and your claim to being unique fades away, consumed by the crowd. As the train slows for the next station, you join the throng and prepare to exit, a little less sure of your own importance.

## 4

### Death Valley, USA

You head out on the Methuselah Trail, grey and dry underfoot, making your way to the grove. Not a soul disturbs the journey. It's a challenging walk and you imagine life here; it seems all but impossible. But then you meet them, the twisted, gnarled bristlecones. These were growing at the same time the pyramids were being built. They are alive. Still alive. They are timeless. Their driftwood skins and crazed contortions are mesmerising. Time stands still for you. Just for a moment. A tiny, tiny moment.

NICHOLAS HAWKSMOOR'S CHRIST CHURCH IN LONODN    Getty/Stephen Robson

# OPEN HOUSE

*In any city, the urge to peek behind closed doors is almost overwhelming. Whether visitor or resident, there are places forbidden to all but a few – private houses, businesses, institutions. For the incurably curious, the Open House movement offers some respite. On one weekend a year, in an increasing number of cities around the world (London, Dublin, Melbourne, Rome, New York and Chicago) many of those usually closed doors are opened to the public. Guided tours by architects offer a tantalising glimpse of a city's secret layers.*

A Day

# SIGNATURE DISH

**I** *was 18 and in Paris for the first time.*
My father was treating me to a cooking class at the Ritz Escoffier. My imagination was lit up like the Eiffel Tower at night. What would we be learning to cook? Pheasants in chestnut sauce? Foie gras soufflé? A cream-puff tower? Imagine my surprise then, when I arrived in the Ritz's basement classroom and saw what we'd actually be making. Scrambled eggs. Yes, scrambled eggs, that cafeteria-chafing standard, that childhood mum's-too-tired-to-cook weeknight stand-by. A monkey could make scrambled eggs. A chicken could make scrambled eggs.

But as the teacher in his tall white toque began to talk, a hush fell over the classroom and we all focused intently as his slim, elegant hands cracked eggs into a copper bowl. The secret to this simplest of dishes, he said, was to cook the eggs at a very low heat, stirring constantly with a fork in a gentle circular motion to keep the curds soft and delicate. As you stir, slowly add small lumps of butter and drizzles of cream. Most importantly of all, don't rush things.

Finally, he scooped tiny servings of the eggs into paper cups and passed them around the classroom for us to taste. They were – and this is really the only word to describe them – perfect. Like buttery, savoury, daffodil-yellow clouds.

Now, whenever I want to impress a guest or make a loved one feel special, I'll cook them 'my' signature scrambled eggs. Sometimes with chives. Sometimes mushrooms. Sometimes plain.

The lesson is this: there's value in perfecting a simple dish, whether a meticulously prepared cup of Chinese pu-erh tea, a flawlessly crispy grilled cheese sandwich, or a sublime bowl of spaghetti with olive oil and garlic. Perfect it. Make it yours. Then make it for everyone. ●

There's value in perfecting a simple dish, whether a meticulously prepared cup of Chinese pu-erh tea or a sublime bowl of spaghetti

**A Day**

# MEET THE MAKER

---

## WHETHER YOU LOVE WINE, ART, FASHION OR SPORT, THE FINEST LOCAL PRODUCTS ARE MADE BY HAND.

**J**ulien Mareschal, the tall, jazz-playing winemaker at Domaine de la Borde in the Jura town of Pupillon is pouring you a taste of something special. It's *vin de paille*, a traditional blend of local grape varieties. The first grapes on the vine, he explains, are cut and put on boxes to dry for six months (*paille* means straw). The grapes shrivel as the sugars concentrate; then they're slowly pressed. The wine is aged in wood barrels for at least three years, which results in, you discover at Julien's winery, a sweet, green-gold dessert wine that is utterly unique to this understated region of powerful rivers, waterfalls and forested limestone mountains (which lent the name Jurassic to the world) to the east of central France.

Without talking to this young winemaker you would not have been introduced to *vin de paille*; nor would you have understood the Jura's place in winemaking – with land costing less than half of that in Bordeaux, Jura draws adventurous young winemakers. Julien goes on to tell you about another local speciality, *vin jaune*. The Jura might be overshadowed by its neighbour Burgundy but for one weekend of the year, the launch of the region's very own wine variety on the first weekend of February, when 80 winemakers and 40,000 wine lovers converge on the host town, the Jura is the belle of the ball. And when you leave, Julien offers one more tip – the local cheesemaker who produces the very best Comté cheese to accompany a glass of his wine. ●

---

 **Woodblock prints Kyoto, Japan**
In the Japan of 200 years ago, the woodblock print brought art to the masses. The woodblock printing workshop of Takezasa-do in Kyoto, where the fourth and fifth generations of the Takenaka printing family work, is down an alleyway off busy Shijo Avenue.

 **Woollen capes, Madrid, Spain**
Capas Seseña is the only place in Spain that still makes the heavy cloak known as the capa española, a garment traditionally reserved for formal occasions, such as bullfights or nights at the theatre. Pablo Picasso liked his so much he was buried in it.

 **Craft beer, London, England**
South London's 'beer mile' runs beneath Bermondsey's railway arches. Inside the four microbreweries you're likely to be served by the brewer. All four produce pale ales and European styles such as saisons and dubbels.

 **Skis, Colorado, USA**
Telluride, a rootsy haven for snowhounds in southwest Colorado, is home to Wagner Custom, creators of handcrafted made-to-measure skis. Drop in to collect the finished skis and you'll also pick up some tips on the best runs in the steep San Juan Mountains.

 **A Day**

# A NIGHT AT THE MUSEUM

**SLIPPERED FEET PAD DOWN CORRIDORS BURSTING WITH STORIES, AND EXHIBITS SPRING TO LIFE AS YOU OVERNIGHT IN A MUSEUM.**

**T**he grand, high-ceilinged halls are eerily quiet, echoing with only a few light snores – and several millennia of history and innovation. Tonight, you're not just bedding down with your kids and their classmates, you're lying with legends. Under this roof are Ramses and Shiva; Easter Island moai, and Moche warriors; Mayans, Aztecs and Alexander the Great; Hopewell peoples, Minoan warriors and Olmec gods. There is priceless Inca gold, Lachish reliefs and a two-million-year-old stone tool. Oh, Buddha's here too. It's quite a sleepover.

Many museums, galleries and zoos worldwide now offer overnight experiences, a chance to enter after the crowds have left and explore the exhibits in your own sleepy time. These special events usually offer behind-the-scenes opportunities:make your own movie at a media museum; watch laser shows at astronomy centres; play historical dress-up and craft replica artefacts; or watch animals get up to their nocturnal shenanigans on a zoo stay. Having a whole museum as your home is an inspiration, and an invitation to look beyond the usual glass casements. You might be dozing under the belly of a giant blue whale or amid 3000-year-old sculptures from Ancient Egypt.

Many events are themed: London's British Museum runs Viking, Ancient Lives and Ming overnighters; Calgary Zoo offers Penguin, Rainforest and Savannah options, on which you can snooze near different enclosures; and the California Academy of Sciences runs separate Penguins+Pajamas nights for families, and over-21s, so adults get in on the action too.

There are usually snacks and breakfast, as well as fun and games. There may not be a lot of actual sleep, but if you do manage to nod off, imagine the dreams... ●

A BEDTIME BELUGA AT VANCOUVER AQUARIUM   Getty/Peter Timmermans

### Smithsonian, Washington DC, USA
*This venerable institution – setting for 2009 movie Night at the Museum 2 – allows ankle-biters to sleep under Phoenix the whale in the Ocean Hall after an evening of activities.*

 **②**

### Wellington Zoo, New Zealand

*From 7pm to 9.30am the zoo is yours: help feed and look after the animals, bed down overlooking Monkey Island and join in the morning chores, before the doors reopen to the public.*

 **③**

### Golden Hinde, London, England

*Dress up as a Tudor sailor, become part of the crew and learn how to navigate and fire a cannon before laying your head down on the gun deck. In the morning a Tudor-style breakfast awaits.*

 **④**

### Vancouver Aquarium, Canada

*Family Sleepovers get hands-on at the marine lab before you drift off by one of the aquarium's tanks. Hugs & Fishes is for couples, complete with wine, a Sea-fari of Passion (on which you watch marine courtships) and a night serenade from the tuneful belugas.*

**A Day**

# BACK TO NATURE

**WILDLIFE-WATCHING IS NOT ONLY MEDITATIVE BUT IT CAN REAWAKEN SENSES DULLED BY CITY LIFE. TRAVEL TO SCOTLAND TO RECONNECT WITH THE WILD.**

**I**t's *October on the windswept slopes of Scotland's glens* and the air is filled with the sound of rhythmic grunting. On the islands of the Inner Hebrides off the west coast of Scotland, that bellowing can mean only one thing: it's the red deer rut and the islands' stags are staking their claim to the prime territories and duelling with their rivals. While the rest of the island's residents are winding down for the winter, come autumn the islands' deer have only one thing on their mind – making the next generation, and they aren't too bothered who knows about it. These magnificent creatures – stags stand 130cm tall at the shoulder, with antlers that can be 1m in length and have 16 points – inhabit both the Isle of Jura and community-owned Isle of Rum. There are 900 red deer on Rum, most easily seen in the north around Kilmory, where they have been filmed for television shows. In addition to rut-watching, Rum's rangers can offer guided walks and wildlife-viewing, with options ranging from butterflies to eagles.

On larger, wilder Jura, the deer population outnumbers people. They're hard to miss, visiting the foreshore to feed on mineral-rich seaweed and taking over the north of the island for the rut, a spectacular setting for one of nature's great annual rituals. But you don't have to go to Jura to see and hear red stags rutting – in London's Richmond Park they bellow in the bracken from late September to the end of October. Such natural experiences, says writer Patrick Barkham, are a sort of peaceful exhilaration. ●

|  **1** |  **2** |  **3** |  **4** |
|---|---|---|---|
| *Flamingos, France* | *Red-crowned cranes, Japan* | *Howler monkeys, Costa Rica* | *Bower bird, Australia* |
| *The marshlands of the Camargue in southern France are the setting for one of nature's most choreographed courtships. In rhythmic, pink battalions flamingos strut across the Pont de Gau ornithological reserve, which is perhaps the best place to see this performance.* | *Courting cranes dance for each other on Hokkaido in winter, bowing, jumping, strutting and tossing grass and sticks. To the Japanese the cranes symbolise luck and longevity.* | *Like deer, male howler monkeys are judged on the tenor and volume of their calls – which is why the forests of Manuel Antonio National Park on the west coast of Costa Rica are a cacophony of whoops and barks.* | *The male Satin bower bird furnishes his bower (both a stage and nest) with blue objects, from flowers to bottle tops. Drop a flower of any other colour into his bower and he'll remove in an instant. Find the colour-coordinated couples at Lamington National Park in Queensland.* |

*A Day*

# BUILD YOUR LIFE RAFT

**INDULGE YOUR INNER HUCKLEBERRY FINN BY BUILDING AND FLOATING YOUR OWN RAFT IN SWEDEN AND BEYOND.**

**The beaver looks worried** as you clumsily attempt to pull the raft over to the riverbank to moor up for the evening and set up camp. You're on the Klarälven River in Värmland, Sweden, on a wooden raft measuring 6m by 3m, which weighs twice as much as a family car, travels at 2mph and has the turning circle of a barge. No stranger to passing trade – this waterway has been a logging route for generations – perhaps it's your technique the beaver's wary of?

Everyone's a critic. Who cares what the beaver thinks anyway? You haven't worn shoes for the last three days, and you're happily discovering your inner Huckleberry Finn. Yesterday you caught a fish. And cooked and ate it. The kids took a bit of convincing when they realised you were building the raft yourself, out of just logs and rope, but it's held together so far. At the end of the eight-day expedition, you'll simply untie the ropes, let the logs loose, and there will be no sign you've ever been on the river. It's the ultimate eco trip. Zero emissions and maximum engagement with your natural surroundings. And what surroundings they are – pure, pristine Nordic wilderness. ●

 A Day

THE AMAZON INTERNATIONAL RAFT RACE   Rodrigo Kodrich

## BUILD YOUR LIFE RAFT

**1**

### Transylvanian river tramping

*Your sudden shivering fit has nothing to do with the cold water of the Olt River. You've just realised you're exploring Dracula's backyard on a raft constructed from the same timber that Vlad the Impaler (who inspired the garlic-dodging legend) once used to spear his victims on. The first day of this paddling-and-hiking tour of Transylvania was spent building the raft, which you're now sailing from Augustin to Mateias, tackling several rapids en route. Tomorrow you'll paddle to Hoghiz, from where the Carpathians and the Count's castle beckon.*

**2**

### Borneo to be wild

*Racing down rapidly moving rivers on bamboo rafts is a way of life in Malaysian Borneo, and various events in Sarawak encourage visitors to build their own craft and join in, while also experiencing the indigenous rainforest cultures of the region. You overnight in an Iban longhouse during two days of racing in April's Baleh-Kapit Safari River Expedition, while October's 10-hour Baram Whitewater Rafting Challenge passes through remote villages and introduces you to communities such as the Orang Ulu. Both events feature serious rapids.*

**3**

### Fool's gold in the Yukon

*You're an experienced punk rafter – you have the boat-building skills required to lash the right sort of logs together with the correct kind of knots, and the river know-how to take on a wild waterway without having your hand held. The ultra-remote Yukon Territory, where Canada meets Alaska, is your kind of playground. Here you'll follow in the oar strokes of Jack London and the stampede of gold-chasing prospectors who landed in Skagway in the 1890s, climbed the Chilkoot Trail into the Klondike and built homemade rafts to traverse the Yukon River from Whitehorse to Dawson. Just beware the man-eating Five Finger Rapids.*

**4**

### Ride the Amazon

*The shriek of a howler monkey pierces the Peruvian rainforest dawn as you launch your freshly constructed raft onto the planet's greatest river. This is it – 180km of the Amazon lie between you and the finish line in the jungle city of Iquitos. Will your log raft – built of balsawood, like Thor Heyerdahl's Kon-Tiki – survive the next three days? Will you live to tell the tale of the Amazon International Raft Race, the world's longest raft race? Can you beat the locals, who have won every race, bar one, since the event started in 1999?*

DANCING THE SALSA IN HAVANA    Mark Read

# MAKE A DATE
# FOR DANCING

*Where words aren't sufficient, get to know the locals on a dancefloor. Whether you're swinging to Cuban salsa in Havana or waltzing in Vienna, a night out dancing lifts the mood like nothing else. Learn some steps on pages 162-63.*

**A Day**

# SLEEP IN AN ICE HOTEL

*Every winter at Jukkasjärvi, 18km east of Kiruna, the amazing Ice Hotel is built from hundreds of tonnes of ice from the frozen river. This custom-built igloo has a chapel and a bar – where you drink from a glass made of ice . The 50 bedrooms are outfitted with reindeer skins and sleeping bags guaranteed to keep you warm; the hotel promises the rooms never get colder than -8°C...*

# SAVVY WAYS TO SEE THE SUPER-SIGHTS

**IF YOU FIND YOUR BUCKETLIST MATCHES FAR TOO MANY OTHERS',
JUST TRY A LITTLE SIDESTEP. WITH A BIT OF FORESIGHT,
YOU CAN MAKE THE REALITY LIVE UP TO THE DREAM.**

**E**mbarking on the iconic pilgrimage to France's Mont St-Michel in August is, quite frankly, asking for trouble. The incessant, nose-to-tail traffic blocking the final stretch is enough to make you want to dump the car and walk.

Do it! The easy hike across flat sheep pastures is idyllic. The contemplative crown of the mount teases on the horizon and, bar a handful of walkers at the initial roadside stile, you should find yourself alone. Mid-way across the grassy plain dotted white with sheep, break for lunch – a stinky round of gooey Camembert, a baguette and a bottle of local Normandy cider. Apart from having to dodge sheep dung to spread the picnic rug, this is the stuff of French dreams.

And why not defer hitting the concrete causeway linking the mount with the mainland because from then on, it is pure unadulterated August-crowd hell, confirming that savvy-traveller suspicion that the real beauty of Europe's tourism superstars often lies in the seductive mirage they proffer from afar. ●

### Leaning Tower of Pisa, Italy
*Dodge the unromantic scrum of overzealous souvenir sellers, boisterous school groups and photo-posing pandemonium on Piazza dei Miracoli. Amble instead through medieval backstreets east of the piazza to the Museo dell'Opera del Duomo and venerate a miraculous mirage of Italy's greatest icon from its back garden – a beautiful cloistered courtyard to boot.*

### St Peter's Basilica, Vatican City
*There's no reason to endure the inevitable crowds here. Find yourself a room with a view – such as a two-bedroom apartment with a staggering, full-frontal from its 4th-floor perch of one of the most magnificent church domes in the world.*

### The Uffizi, Florence, Italy
*Get in through the back door, literally. The Corridoio Vasariano – an elevated covered passageway built in 1565 for the Medici to meander between riverside Florentine palaces in appropriate secrecy – has priceless art works. It also happens to sneak into Florence's superstar Uffizi art museum in the Third Corridor, moments from High Renaissance maestros Michelangelo and Raphael.*

### St-Tropez, Provence, France
*It was the sensual sweep of burnt-red rooftops and the Italian baroque bell tower seen from the sea that famously seduced the French pointillist painter, Paul Signac, when he sailed into the enigmatic fishing village of St-Tropez in 1892. And arriving by boat (from Ste-Maxime, Port Grimaud or St-Raphaël) remains the only way in high season to understand the sultry beauty of this pouting, Côte d'Azur sexpot.*

**A Day**

# THE NEED FOR ~~SPEED~~ ~~SPES~~ SPEED

**FLOOR IT! TEST YOUR MOTORING METTLE ON A NO-HOLDS-BARRED, HOLD-ONTO-YOUR-HATS DRIVE OF A LIFETIME.**

**Y**ou're about to enter 'Green Hell' – or, to use its more official title, the Nürburgring Nordschleife racetrack. There used to be a big tree and an altar dedicated to St Anthony by the start line, but it was removed in 1935. Shame: some holy protection could come in handy.

You rev your car's engine and you're off; 21km of sinuously snaking, brutally bucking, dipping, cresting, curvaceous tarmac lies ahead. With no speed limit.

This track, built in 1925 and dinted by 73 separate bends, is legendary. It was the most notorious Grand Prix track on the Formula 1 circuit – until Niki Lauda crashed here in 1976 and it was deemed too unsafe to race in modern Formula 1 cars. But its notoriety endures.

On certain days, the public is allowed to tackle the Nordschleife in their own cars – though it's highly recommended to do a few circuits as a passenger first. That way you can start to get the measure of this motor-racing monster, which twists mercilessly and drunkenly though the Eifel Forest. It's essentially a public road, requiring you to adhere to Article 3, Section 1 of the German Highway Code (you must be in full control of your vehicle, whatever speed you're going). But there's no actual restriction on that speed.

As you face section after punishing section – the Schwedenkreuz, Adenauer Forst, Metzgesfeld, Wippermann – your velocity is the very last thing on your mind. Staying on the road and out of the trees is your chief concern. But as you pass under that finishing gantry, feeling like Lewis Hamilton, you can't help but look down at your watch, note your lap time, and be overcome by the urge to do it all again – just a little bit quicker. ●

*YOUR MIG-29 AWAITS* Getty/Anton Balakchiev

### Bobsleigh, Lillehammer, Norway
*Bomb down the 1710m-long Olympic bobsleigh run in one of Norway's oldest winter resorts. Climb into a four-man bob (with a pilot) to reach speeds of 120km/h and face the thrill of 5G.*

 **2**

**Cresta Run, Switzerland**
This historic toboggan course was first carved from the Engadine Valley's ice in 1885. It twists, turns and plunges 157 vertical metres in 1.2km: the record is a terrifying 50.09 seconds.

 **3**

**MiG flight, Nizhny Novgorod, Russia**
Loved Top Gun? Then live it. The MiG-29 Flight Program at Russia's SOKOL airfield sees you take to the sky with a fighter pilot. Break the sound barrier, feel 9G, and complete acrobatic Immelman turns. Epic.

 **4**

**Formula Rossa, Abu Dhabi**
Theme parks are not just for kids. Ferrari World's Formula Rossa is the world's fastest rollercoaster, accelerating to 240km/h in under 5 seconds and chicaning like an F1 car. Safety goggles – and gumption – required.

**A Day**

**You Only Live Once**

# ENJOY

## THE

## SILENCE

---

**THE WORLD'S GETTING LOUDER EVERY DAY. FOR A DAY OF PEACE AND QUIET RETREAT TO A BEACH OR A PARK OR A DESERT.**

**T**he *quietest place on earth* is an anechoic chamber at the Orfield Laboratory in South Minneapolis. The silence inside this room, which is encased in thick concrete and 1m-wide fibreglass wedges, is disorienting. You'll need to sit down and most people can't bear more than 45 minutes. Is an anechoic chamber a practical antidote to the cacophony of our daily lives? No. Instead, try the beach on Benguerra island in the Indian ocean.

Wait until nightfall and then pad down to water's edge and wander along the sand. With just a couple of boutique lodges on the Mozambican island you've got a good chance of avoiding your fellow guests. Wait until you're out of earshot then lie back and feel yourself become absorbed by the warm sand and the stars above as you listen. What you'll notice is, far from the being silent, the island night is full of bird sounds, the soft wash of surf and even the squeak of sand beneath. ●

### Olympic National Park, Washington, USA
Although it's accessed from Hwy 101, Olympic National Park remains one of the least peopled parks in mainland USA. Here, when mountain, forest and ocean meet, you can wander through some of the oldest forests in the country without seeing another soul. Reach the coast and the soundtrack will be the crashing Pacific surf on a wild shore.

### Damaraland, Namibia
In northwest Namibia, where 42% of the country is protected, Damaraland is one of the last refuges of the black rhino. Few people live in this ancient landscape and because it's harder to see megafauna, safari parties head elsewhere. This means that you'll have the place to yourself – just you and the family of elephants noisily sucking up acacia pods like giant vacuum cleaners.

### The Empty Quarter, Arabian Peninsula
Rub al-Khali – the 'abode of silence' – spans a fifth of the Arabian Peninsula, taking in Saudi Arabia, Oman, the United Arab Emirates and Yemen. Imagine a desert larger than France or Texas with dunes 250m tall; on some mornings, when they're cloaked in fog, any sounds are further deadened. The hard part is getting in – and out – on the soft, shifting sands.

### Northumberland National Park, England
With one of the lowest population densities in England, the Northumberland National Park has more than 1000 sq km in which to get away from the hurly-burly. The north is dominated by the Cheviot Hills, once home to Bronze Age people. To the south is Hadrian's Wall.

**A Day**

RUB AL-KHALII, OMAN    Getty/Josef Friedhuber

# 17

## independent countries

*visited within 24 hours by record-breaking team of Yvo Kuhling, Liselott Martynenko Agerlid, Philomena O'Brien and Todd Hepworth in 2012.*

# 290.22

## kilometres

*road distance run in 24 hours by Greek ultra marathoner Yiannis Kouros, known as Pheidippides' Successor, in 1998. He also has the track 24-hour record, which is 303.5km.*

# 2

## days

*time William Allen spent driving around England's circular M25 in 1998, trying to find the turn-off for his daughter's house. (It's possible to do a full lap in one hour 40 minutes.)*

# 13,804

## kilometres

*ground distance covered by Qantas' QF7 service from Sydney to Dallas, Fort Worth in 15 hours 25 minutes. Saudia's SV41 flight from Jeddah to Los Angeles takes longer (16 hours, 55 minutes), but covers less ground (13,409km).*

# 22

## centimetres

*length a tapeworm can grow in your gut in a single day.*

# 2,414

## cups of coffee

*drunk per day, per person in the Netherlands.*

# 70
## miles
*additional daily distance an eastward sailing ship can make while crossing the Atlantic, versus one sailing westward, due to prevailing westerly winds.*

# 20,000
## calories consumed
*per day by Sumo wrestlers, on a diet of Chanko-nabe.*

# 2901.4
## kilometres
*Furthest distance travelled by train in 24 hours, set in Japan by Americans Corey Pedersen and Mike Kim in 2008*

# 238
## miles
*distance travelled by Ben Friberg on a stand-up paddleboard (SUP) in 24 hours, along the Yukon River in Canada in 2012.*

# 45
## average number of climbers
*each day on each of the six routes up Tanzania's Mount Kilimanjaro during 2011–12.*

# 41
## days
*holiday time in Brazil, which has the most generous vacation allowance enshrined in national law.*

# JOIN THE TRIBE

*In the most remote corners of the world, it's possible to meet and even stay with indigenous people. During summer in Mongolia ,tented ger camps on the Gobi's steppes may be open to travellers. On Sarawak in Malaysia, the leader of the local Iban longhouse may offer you shelter from a storm. And then there are the Wigmen of Papua New Guinea's Huli tribe, who grow their hair into a perfectly domed style before it is cut off to become a ceremonial wig, which they're very happy to show off to guests.*

MEET THE HULI TRIBE OF PAPUA NEW GUINEA   Guy Needham

A Day 🕰

# FIND BURIED TREASURE

**THERE'S A SECRET WORLD OF GOODIES BURIED BENEATH THE EARTH'S ROCKS AND WAVES. LOOKING FOR LOOT – FROM PIRATE BOOTY TO SECRET STASHES – IS AN ADVENTURE ALL ITS OWN.**

**S**urrounded on all sides by scorched earth and pounded by the sweltering desert heat, Coober Pedy and its swag of opals lie sparkling in the middle of the South Australian Outback. The heat, dust, flies and harsh sunlight are somewhat of an assault and you immediately realise why most of the action in this town happens... underground. You revel in your cave hotel's cool embrace and marvel at how much the town has managed to squeeze into its subterranean world.

But what you're really looking for down here are gems. Named after the local aboriginal term 'kupa-piti' (meaning 'whitefella in a hole'), this far-flung town is also known as the opal capital of the world. You're itching to strike out and find some stones but there's a good deal to be gleaned at Tom's Working Opal Mine so you take a tour before heading out to 'noodle' – that's fossick to you and me – in the town's many mine dumps. With the sun high overhead, you sweat under a slather of sunscreen, painstakingly sifting through the dusty mullock heaps, until, there! You see a glint among the rocks – a tiny bit of opal! And then another! And you're soon tucking more and more of the tiny pieces into your bag.

Maybe you can't start planning retirement just yet but you can say that you've truly discovered your own buried treasure. ●

### 1
**Wreck diving, Florida, USA**
Thought to be home to more sunken treasure than any other state in the USA, Florida's blue waters may be hiding millions of dollars worth of loot. Check local legalities before you wriggle into your suit, and never dive alone in Florida's oft-treacherous waters: those wrecks are down there for a reason.

### 2
**Arctic amethysts, Kola Peninsula, Russia**
Far above the Arctic Circle, all that glitters is not ice: western Russia's extreme north sparkles with the purple slivers of the prized amethyst. The rugged Kola Peninsula is home to the windswept, Tersky Coast, an ideal hunting ground for this legendary gemstone.

### 3
**Norman Island, British Virgin Islands**
Peg-legs, planks and parrots – if there was a map showing the home of every pirate cliché known to fancy-dressers, Norman Island would be marked with an X. The inspiration behind Robert Louis Stevenson's Treasure Island, it's a haven for snorkellers and nature lovers, but also those convinced there are undiscovered doubloons hidden in its caves.

### 4
**Roman coins, England**
Either togas suffered from a lack of pockets or departing Romans hadn't time to stop at a currency exchange because the English countryside is aglitter with ancient coins. Wielding metal detectors, treasure hunters have been responsible for massive finds; in 2010 a chef uncovered a pot filled with 52,000 coins dated between AD253 and AD293.

**A Day**

# A NIGHT TO REMEMBER

YOU MIGHT NOT REMEMBER THE FINER DETAILS BUT A GREAT NIGHT OUT WITH FRIENDS ALWAYS ADDS UP TO MORE THAN THE SUM OF ITS PARTS. GET THE GANG TOGETHER AND PLAN A BACCHANALIAN BASH WHEREVER YOU ARE. HERE ARE ITINERARIES FOR FIVE OF THE WORLD'S NIGHTLIFE CAPITALS TO GET YOU STARTED.

*Maps by* **Wayne Murphy**

### 1. Dead Rabbit
*Far from dead, this new kid on the cocktail block has wasted no time swagging awards. During the day, hit the sawdust-sprinkled taproom for specialty beers, historic punches and pop-inns (lightly hopped ale spiked with different flavours). Come evening, scurry upstairs to the cosy Parlour for 72 meticulously researched cocktails.*
**deadrabbitnyc.com**

### 2. Balthazar
*Still the king of bistros, bustling (OK, loud) Balthazar is never short of a discriminating mob. That's thanks to three winning details: its location in SoHo's shopping-spree heartland; the uplifting Paris-meets-NYC ambience; and, of course, the stellar something-for-everyone menu. Highlights include the outstanding raw bar, steak frites, salade Niçoise, as well as the roasted beet salad.*
**balthazarny.com**

### 3. Angel's Share
*Show up early and snag a seat at this hidden gem, behind a Japanese restaurant on the same floor. It's quiet and elegant with creative cocktails, but you can't stay if you don't have a table or a seat at the bar, and they tend to go fast.*

### 4. Maison Premiere
*You'll half-expect to see Dorothy Parker stagger into this old-timey place, which features an elegant bar, suspendered bartenders and a jazzy soundtrack to channel the French Quarter New Orleans vibe. The cocktails are serious: the epic list includes more than a dozen absinthe drinks, various juleps, an array of specialty cocktails.*
**maisonpremiere.com**

### 5. Cielo
*This long-running club boasts an attitude-free crowd and an excellent sound system. Join dance lovers on Deep Space Monday when DJ François K spins dub and underground beats. Other nights feature various DJs from Europe.*
**cieloclub.com**

**A Day**

A night in
**HONG KONG**
China

Kowloon Park

East Tsim Sha Tsui Ⓣ

Tsim Sha Tsui
Promenade ○

*Victoria Harbour*

○ Star Ferry

④

Ⓜ Hong Kong Station

③

② Central Station Ⓜ

① 

⑤

*Lung Fu Shan Country Park*

▲ *Victoria Peak*

HONG KONG ISLAND

### 1. Sevva

*If there was a million-dollar view in Hong Kong, it'd be the one from the balcony of ultra-stylish Sevva – skyscrapers so close you can see their arteries of steel, with the harbour and Kowloon in the distance. At night it takes your breath away.*
**sevva.hk**

### 2. Globe

*Besides an impressive list of 150 imported beers, including 13 on tap, the Globe serves T8, the first cask-conditioned ale brewed in Hong Kong. Occupying an enviable 370 sq m, the bar has a huge dining area with long wooden tables and comfortable banquettes.*
**theglobe.com.hk**

### 3. Tim's Kitchen

*This restaurant is considered one of Hong Kong's best – as evidenced by the Michelin honour and the praises lavished by local gourmands. It serves masterfully executed Cantonese fare over two well-illuminated floors, with signature dishes such as crab claw poached with wintermelon. Reservations essential.*
**timskitchen.com.hk**

### 4. Lung King Heen

*The world's first Chinese restaurant to receive three stars from the Michelin people, still retains them. The Cantonese food, when combined with the harbour views and the impeccable service, provides a stellar dining experience. The signature steamed lobster and scallop dumplings sell out early.*

### 5. Drop

*Deluxe lounge action, excellent tunes and potent cocktails keep Drop strong on the scene. It's like walking into Wallpaper\* magazine, but the vibe here is unpretentiously inclusive and the crowd reaches a fever pitch on big nights. The members-only policy after 10pm Thursday to Saturday keeps the dance floor capacity at a manageable 'packed like sardines' level.*
**drophk.com**

### 1. Max und Moritz

*The patina of yesteryear hangs over this ode-to-old-school brewpub named for the cheeky Wilhelm Busch cartoon characters. Since 1902 it has packed hungry diners and drinkers into its rustic tile-and-stucco ornamented rooms for sudsy home brews.*

**maxundmoritzberlin.de**

### 2. Cafe Jacques

*A favourite with off-duty chefs and local foodies. Jacques charms with flattering candlelight, warm decor and fantastic wine. It's the perfect date spot but you only have to be in love with good food to appreciate the French- and North African–inspired blackboard menu. Reservations recommended.*

### 3. Hops & Barley

*Conversation flows as freely as the unfiltered pilsner, malty dunkel (dark) fruity weizen (wheat) and potent cider produced at this congenial microbrewery inside a former butcher's shop. Fellow beer lovers range from skinny-jean hipsters to suits swilling postwork pints among ceramic-tiled walls and shiny copper vats.*

**hopsandbarley.eu**

### 4. Freischwimmer

*In summertime, few places are more idyllic than this rustic 1930s boathouse turned canalside chill zone. The menu draws inspiration from all corners of the world. Also a great spot for Sunday brunch and late-night warm-up drinks before hitting the area's clubs.*

**freischwimmer-berlin.com**

### 5. Berghain

*Only world-class DJs heat up this hedonistic haven inside a labyrinthine former power plant. Upstairs, Panorama Bar pulsates with house and electro, while the factory floor below leans towards hard techno. Arrive after 5am.*

**berghain.de**

A night in
**BERLIN**
Germany

A Day

A night in
# BUENOS AIRES
Argentina

### 1. Manolo
*Honest local cuisine – steaks, salads and a huge menu of Spanish pastas and meat-and-potatoes platters – keep this friendly, family-run corner joint alive and kicking. The budget-friendly prices pull in neighborhood families and groups of hungry boys after fútbol practice. Reserve for dinner.*
**restaurantmanolo.com.ar**

### 2. Doppelgänger
*This cool, emerald-hued corner bar specialises in vermouth cocktails. The atmosphere is calm and the lengthy menu is fascinating: start with the Journalist, a martini with a bitter orange twist, or channel Don Draper and go for the bar's bestseller – an old-fashioned.*
**doppelganger.com.ar**

### 3. Cafe San Juan
*Having studied in Paris and Barcelona, celebrity chef Leandro Cristóbal now runs this renowned San Telmo bistro. Start with tapas, then delve into the grilled octopus, molleja (sweetbreads) cannelloni and the amazing pork bondiola (deliciously tender after 9 hours' roasting).*

### 4. Bar Sur
*Historic Bar Sur is one of the city's most celebrated (and expensive) tango show venues: you'll pay handsomely to sip champagne at one of a dozen tables. Be prepared – the upscale dinner show is often participatory – so avoid it if you're not prepared to try a few tangled steps…*
**bar-sur.com.ar**

### 5. Mitos Argentinos
*This cosy old brick house in San Telmo has hosted rock groups for over a dozen years. It's not too big, with lots of tables, a perfectly sized stage and a small balcony above. Known for its tributes to 'rock nacional' bands.*
**mitosargentinos.com.ar**

## 1. Bermondsey's Beer Mile

Begin your evening early with a Saturday afternoon stroll along the railway arches in South London that have become home to several craft breweries. Kernel Brewery is open until 2pm, Partizan until 5pm.

## 2. Tapas Brindisa

Brindisa attracts a well-heeled, foodie crowd who know good tapas when they taste it. No bookings are accepted, so come early if you want to bag an outside table on Borough Market days.

*brindisa.com*

## 3. Bistrot Bruno Loubet

Overlooking St John's Sq, this is an elegant hotel restaurant with much-lauded chef Bruno Loubet at the helm. High-quality ingredients are transformed into dishes full of gutsy flavour combinations. As you'd expect, there's a well-chosen wine list and the service is impeccable.

*bistrotbrunoloubet.com*

## 4. Book Club

This former Victorian warehouse has been transformed into an innovative temple to good times. Spacious and whitewashed with large windows upstairs and a basement bar below, it hosts a variety of offbeat events, such as spoken word, dance lessons and life drawing, as well as a program of DJ nights.

*wearetbc.com*

## 5. Fabric

This impressive superclub is still the first stop on the London scene for many international clubbers. The crowd is hip and well dressed without overkill, and the music – electro, techno, house, drum and bass and dubstep – is as superb as you'd expect from London's top-rated club.

*fabriclondon.com*

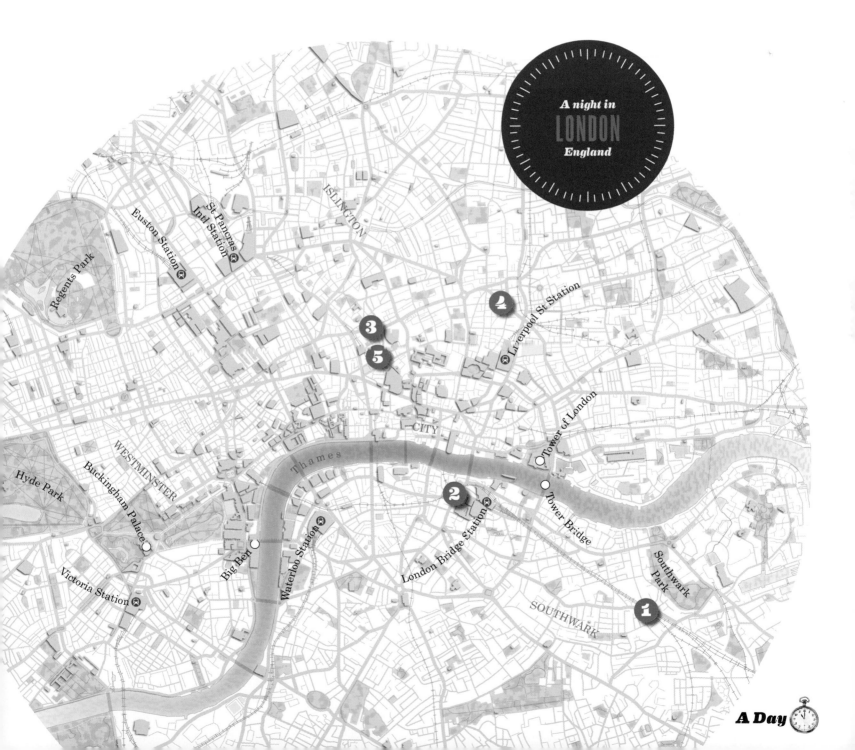

A night in
LONDON
England

A Day

# SEE THE SUNSET

*Put the camera down, there are enough snaps of sunsets in the world already. Instead, sit in stillness and just watch. Reflect on the day that is in the process of becoming yesterday, and what tomorrow will bring. Sunsets are a daily reminder of the passage of time. The average Westerner will see around 30,000, but every now and then, go somewhere spectacular, such as Arches National Park in Utah, and make one count.*

SUNSET AT DELICATE ARCH, ARCHES NATIONAL PARK, UTAH    Getty/Philip Lee Harvey

# SEEK SPIRITUAL ENLIGHTMENT

## ABSINTHE IN PARIS, GIN IN LONDON, WHISKY IN HOBART...
## 'THE ROAD OF EXCESS LEADS TO THE PALACE OF WISDOM', SOMETIMES.

**H**allucinations, fits, madness... all are ailments once said to be induced by drinking absinthe. The green, liquorice-flavoured liqueur had been banned in France since 1915, and was shrouded in mystery. But now the drink also known as the green fairy (*la fée vert* in French) is illegal no more.  The heady drink exploded in popularity in France during the late 19th century, when artists and writers such as Van Gogh, Rimbaud and Wilde savoured its unusual taste, and the effects of drinking it – although most now accept that the influential French wine industry, threatened by the fashionable drink, was behind the ban.

You watch as the bartender begins the ritual, pouring a measure into a small glass, balancing a perforated spoon holding a sugar cube over the glass and then slowly adding water to the spoon, so sweetened water drips into the absinthe. Brewed from a concoction of natural herbs, true absinthe includes three crucial elements: anise, fennel and Artemisia absinthium (grand wormwood, used as a remedy since the time of the ancient Egyptians).  Now you wait expectantly but receive only an agreeably – aniseed-flavoured buzz – perhaps more research is required. ●

 **Whisky, Tasmania**
*Some mistake, surely? Isn't the best whisky from Scotland? It turns out that Tasmania can also deliver some seriously impressive single malts, especially Sullivan's Cove distillery, just outside the state capital Hobart. It must be something to do with wind and rain.*

 **Gin, London**
*London has come a long way since the debauched scenes of Gin Lane in the 18th century. Today, connoisseurs of the gin-and-tonic can tour a new wave of gin distilleries in the city, such as Sipsmith in west London, where you can admire Prudence and Patience, its twin copper stills.*

**Tequila, Mexico**
*Tequila's got a bad reputation for causing many a night out to take a wrong turn. But artisan producers, such as Casa Noble in the Highlands of Jalisco state, are restoring tequila to its rightful place as a drink to be sipped not slammed. Tour Jalisco to taste some fine aged tequilas.*

 **Sake, Akita, Japan**
*In the snowy north of Japan, Akita prefecture is the source of the country's best sake; experts say the cold prolongs the fermentation time. We say sample Akita's premium sake (best served cold) on a tour of the historic kuras or craft breweries and make up your own mind.*

**A Day**

THE JACOBITE STEAMS OVER GLENFINNAN VIADUCT, SCOTLAND   Pete Seaward

# GET STEAMED UP

## TAKE A TRIP BACK IN TIME WITH A DAYTRIP ON A STEAM TRAIN.

**The Jacobite, Scotland's daily steam-hauled service** has achieved a new kind of stardom as the *Hogwarts Express* in the Harry Potter films, in which it steams majestically across the Glenfinnan Viaduct. As you cross the snaking, single-track bridge there's a glimpse of Loch Shiel, and of the monument that marks the spot where Bonnie Prince Charlie first assembled his Jacobite army that nearly did so well for the Scots.

Even without a boyish interest in levers and furnaces, the history and landscape this train passes through is enough to ignite a passion for steam travel.

Beyond Glenfinnan, the train climbs through forests of ash, carpeted in a tartan of bluebells and bracken. The peaks are hung with the fraying rope of streams in spate and the lochs look like slices of sky fallen to the ground. Trailing clouds of steam, the *Jacobite* clatters through this mythical landscape, breathing hard. Then you round a corner and a door is thrown open to the sea. Suddenly, there's a view of islands out across the Sound of Arisaig, where Eigg, Rum and Muck crowd the horizon. Beyond Arisaig lie beaches, and water that's an otherworldly Caribbean blue. And then there's Mallaig, with the Isle of Skye in the distance, and you're standing on the rain-soaked platform at the end of your journey, a foot in the past and the present. ●

**The Watercress Line, England**
*Watercress grown in Hampshire's water meadows was historically delivered to London's markets by steam train; part of the Mid-Hants railway, from Alresford to Alton, has been restored and sees steam trains return regularly to Hampshire's green countryside.*

 **2**

### Durango & Silverton Narrow Gauge Railroad, USA
*On this 70km restored railroad, a 1920s steam engine climbs 3000ft into Colorado's Rockies, over wood bridges and through forests, arriving at the historic mining town of Silverton. It's a breathtaking ride.*

 **3**

### Puffing Billy, Victoria, Australia
*Puffing Billy is just one of around 500 surviving (in various states of repair) steam engines in Australia. The much-loved, little green train puffs 24km daily from Belgrave to Gembrook in the Dandenong Ranges, just outside Melbourne.*

 **4**

### Cass Scenic Railroad, USA
*Short and sweet, this 18km heritage railway in West Virginia's forested mountains was built to service the logging town of Cass. Today it hauls sightseers up to Bald Knob station in open-air carriages; you'll need to wrap up warm.*

You Only Live Once

TAXIS IN BANGKOK, THAILAND  Varsha Arora

# TAKE A CAB

*Nothing beats arriving in a strange new city – by day or night – and taking a taxi from the airport. This is your first sight of your destination. You're still decompressing from the flight, you're absorbing new sounds and smells and you're weighing up your driver. They're often emblematic of their city: forthright in London. Brusque in New York. Is yours a saviour or a shyster? And do you really want to see his cousin's hotel?*

**A Day**

# THE ESCAPE ARTIST

**COLIN EASTWOOD CYCLES ENGLAND'S
SOUTH DOWNS WAY IN A DAY – UK TWO**

**A** **lot of great ideas** are dreamed up in the pub. This one wasn't. It was something we'd talked about for years, maybe a decade. But marriages and kids came along, then I moved abroad. As is the way with these things, other 'stuff' happened and the plan took a backseat to what weekends are usually filled with. Time passed but one summer we could wait no longer: it was on.

The plan was this: on Saturday we'd jump on the early train out of London with our bicycles. An hour later we'd be in Winchester and at the start of the South Downs Way. We'd ride that 160km chalk ridge south towards its end in Eastbourne as far as we could until there was no longer enough light by which to see the ruts and fist-sized rocks of the track. Then we'd find a secluded corner of a wood, break out the bivouac bags, cook a stew over a campfire and settle down for a night under the stars. It was what adventurer Alastair Humphreys (see p307) calls a micro-adventure - a fleeting escape from the daily routine and a communion with nature and the hopefully clement elements.

In common with many of England's long-distance footpaths, such as the

The sun arced over our heads and somewhere between the perpetual motion of the bicycle wheels and the spinning world, there seemed to be harmony

Ridgeway and the Icknield Way, people have been walking the South Downs for about six thousand years of the chalk ridge's sixty million year age. If you know where to look there's evidence of their presence: the climb up Old Winchester Hill, which we reached after a couple of hours of pedalling, passes an Iron Age fort and Bronze Age barrows. From the top of this bowl, as we stood under beech trees a vivid shade of green, the ground sloped steeply downwards, sprinkled with white sheep.

We pressed on past Butser Hill, the highest point on the South Downs, and flew along the farm tracks beyond. The sun arced over our heads and somewhere between the perpetual motion of the bicycle wheels and the spinning world beneath its tyres, there seemed to be harmony. In the golden afternoon light of late spring, low enough that it caught seeds floating in the hazy air, we passed a boy and his younger sister freewheeling the other way as we climbed yet another hill; I think he had a fishing rod strapped to his back. I remember thinking 'treasure days like this, you don't know how precious they are.'

We rode onward, always going up or down, tyres skittering over flints and chunks of chalk. At intervals along the route artist Andy Goldsworthy had carved giant chalk balls, as high as a man, in order that they could weather and shrink under the pressure of time and the elements.

As the sun dipped behind clouds on the horizon to our right, we could hear the soundtrack to the day shift; birds called to each other before roosting and a new nocturnal chorus started. Bats fluttered about our heads as we pulled out the bivvy bags and set up the stove.

We woke early to skylarks above us and a dull ache in our aging backs. But waking at dawn's limpid light had its own compensations; the world looked fresh, the sea in the distance sparkled. Fed and watered, we were ready for the day's ride to Brighton, via Devil's Dyke and the end of the Way in Eastbourne. But each mile we covered also brought us closer to the end of the escape from daily life. As we skirted the city of Brighton, the real world of timetables and traffic returned, and it took all the willpower we had not to turn around. ●

*A Day*

# CLIMB A VOLCANO

**VOLCANOES IGNITE SOMETHING IN ALL OF US. TAKE A DAY TO CONNECT WITH THE DEEPEST REACHES OF OUR LITTLE PLANET.**

**O**ne of the most accessible high-altitude volcano climbs is the ascent of South America's Cotopaxi, a 5897m-high peak that dominates Ecuador's central highlands with its glacier-draped cone, smoking fumerals and imposing stature.

Getting to the top starts in the dark. After a sleepless evening trying to acclimatise at 4800m, you leave the climber's refuge at midnight, stepping out in a headlamp glow across the bizarre moonscape of snow, shadow, rock and ravine. You'll don crampons and ice axe, and rope-up when you hit the glacier proper. From here, it's a six- to eight-hour mission past crevasses and hanging seracs toward the invisible summit.

By the time the sun starts to rise, you're nearly at the top, and a trance-inducing pace of step-breathe-rest, step-breathe-rest has taken over your body. A few more paces and you arrive: the top of the world. Stretching down below you, the volcano's shadow creeps across the high Andean plain. Quiet for now, the perfectly formed crater still smokes, and you pause to take a few more pictures before your descent. ●

CLIMBING COTOPAXI, ECUADOR    Getty/Christian Kober

### Mt Fuji, Japan
*Like many volcanoes around the world, Japan's 3776m Mt Fuji is sacred. Buddhists call it the 'Peak of the White Lotus'. Hundreds of people make it to the summit every day during the July and August climbing season, resting for the night in one of a dozen mountain huts. Find true solitude with a winter ascent.*

### 2
### Kilauea, Hawaii, USA
*Hawaii's Kilauea is arguably the most active volcano in the world; the current eruption has lasted since 1983. With a glorious lava lake at the summit caldera, a visit here, with views of flowing lava and billowing clouds of ash, is truly spectacular.*

### 3
### Mt St Helens, USA
*Part of the Pacific Rim of Fire, Mt St Helens' towering 2549m peak reigns over the lush and precipitous Cascade Mountains in Washington. Most famous for its ruthless explosion in 1980, killing scores of people and raining ash across the world, the beautiful peak can be climbed in a day.*

### 4
### Kilimanjaro, Tanzania
*The famous 'Snows of Kilimanjaro' are predicted by some to disappear in the next 20 years; now's the time to reach the 5895m summit – the highest in Africa – to ensure you see them. Along the way, you'll hike through pristine wilderness and journey with friendly porters and guides who make their livelihood from this natural wonder.*

### A Day

# Chapter
# 03

EEK

In which we take a week or two to drive the world's most exciting roads, spot the **Big Five** on safari, hail a helicopter, spend an adventure-packed week on an island and swap houses with someone. Closer to home, a week is time enough to discover delights on your doorstep and learn some dance steps to impress.

*A Week*

**Chapter**

# 03

## GLASGOW TO OBAN, SCOTLAND
### ASTON MARTIN DB5

**D**ramatic history meets beauty on this drive through Scotland's Highlands to the west coast town of Oban, where a dram of whisky awaits.

Start by leaving gritty Glasgow for the Loch Lomond and the Trossachs National Park, Scotland's first national park but long a favourite weekend getaway with its thickly forested hills and romantic lochs. The Trossach's are Rob Roy country: Robert MacGregor was the outlawed leader of the wildest of Scotland's clans and many Scots see his life as the symbol of the struggle of the common folk – detour east on the A85 to his grave in the small village of Balquhidder.

Get back on the road to Oban, a waterfront town on a delightful bay. Then continue up the coast towards Fort William if you wish to return to Glasgow via the A82 and Glen Coe, scene of the massacre of the MacDonald clan in the 17th century, and more recently driven by James Bond in the *Skyfall* film. **Start?** Glasgow **Finish?** Oban **How far?** 200km **When?** September for autumn hues. ●

# ROAD TRIPS

ROAD TRIPS RULE! DISCOVER THREE CLASSIC ROUTES
– AND THE PERFECT CAR IN WHICH TO DRIVE THEM.

*A Week*

# GRAND STRADA DELLE DOLOMITI, ITALY
## ALFA ROMEO GIULIA

**R**anging across the South Tyrol, Alto Adige and Veneto, the Dolomites are one of the most beautiful mountain ranges in the world. Here, Austrian and Italian influences combine with the local Ladin culture. On this grand road trip your hosts may wear lederhosen, cure ham in their chimneys and use sleighs to travel from village to village.

To start, exit Bolzano on the SS241. As the route climbs towards Parco Naturale Fanes-Sennes-Braies, it passes the spectacular area of Alta Badia; throughout the day the play of shadow and light on the peaks of Pelmo, Civetta and Marmolada is breathtaking.

The high Fanes plateau, with its sculpted ridges and buttress towers of rock, has transfixed artists and poets for centuries; Wordsworth considered it a 'region of the heavens'. The trip ends at the Alpe di Siusi after a staggering 15km drive. There are few more beautiful juxtapositions than the green pastures and the Sciliar mountains.

**Start?** Bolzano **Finish?** Alpe di Siusi **How far?** 195km **When?** June for spring flowers. ●

# BLUE RIDGE PARKWAY, USA
## FORD MUSTANG

**A**merica's *favourite byway curves* through the leafy Appalachians, where it swoops up the East Coast's highest peak and stops by the nation's largest mansion.

The Blue Ridge Parkway stretches from Shenandoah National Park in Virginia to Great Smoky Mountains National Park in North Carolina. Construction of the road began in the Great Depression, harnessing the strength of out-of-work young men. In the Tar Heel State, the road carves a sinuous path through a rugged landscape of craggy peaks, crashing waterfalls, thick forests and charming mountain towns.

Start with a good night's sleep in Valle Crucis, a bucolic village west of Boone. At Grandfather Mountain, stop at the swinging bridge for views of the mountains.

Asheville, North Carolina, is the hippest town in these parts, with plenty of local microbrews to try, and the Blue Ridge Parkway Visitor Center nearby.

**Start?** Valle Crucis **Finish?** Waterrock Knob **How far?** 338km **When?** May to October. ●

# STAY IN A TREEHOUSE

**RELIVE YOUR CHILDHOOD IN A ROOM ABOVE THE FOREST FLOOR. SWEET DREAMS ARE MADE OF THIS.**

**B**uilding a treehouse in childhood was one of those construction projects that, once embarked upon, always went over time and budget. The designer would have to account for fewer branches than anticated. There would need to be extra beams. More planks would have to be bought. And the result would often be lethally unsteady, plagued with splinters, and far from watertight.

But in Swedish Lapland, just outside the village of Harads, 60km south of the Arctic Circle, Britta and Kent Lindvall have done much of the hard work for you, creating the Treehotel. These are no ordinary treehouses; the facilities might be basic but the designs are brilliant. The architectural illusion of the Mirrorcube hides your room for the night among the trees. The Bird's Nest is inspired by a sea eagle's nest, and the UFO is simply out of this world.

These super-stylish and sustainable treehouses still have things in common with the childhood treehouse of your dreams. Sleeping suspended in the forest, you're still closer to the elements, the wind rushing through the branches, the rain pounding on the roof, soft flurries of snow in winter, warm late-night sunshine in the far northern summer, birds both seen and heard. For a few days a year, get back to nature and curl up in one of these treehouses. ●

THE BANGKOK TREEHOUSE, THAILAND  bangkoktreehouse.com

## STAY IN A TREEHOUSE

### 1
### Château dans les Arbes, France
As if a secluded hideaway in the trees wasn't enough of a childhood dream come true, at Châteaux dans les Arbes in the Dordogne, the leafy abodes are also miniature castles. Housed around the former moat of a ruined stronghold, the three creations are the handiwork of veteran treehouse-builder Rémi, who modelled them on nearby châteaux, complete with turrets and spires.

### 2
### Free Spirit Spheres, Canada
The Free Spirit Spheres are suspended in the canopy by a web of ropes in the temperate rainforest of Vancouver Island. The smooth, wooden pods are designed to co-exist with their surroundings, and have minimum impact on the trees and wildlife. Creature comforts, including bathrooms and a sauna, are back on solid ground, while beyond the forest are the wineries and artisan eateries of the Cowichan Valley.

### 3
### Chole Mjini, Tanzania
This cluster of seven treehouses is cradled by baobab trees on Chole, a tropical island east of the Tanzanian coast. Perched amongst vegetation and crumbling ruins, the thatched huts look like the creations of marooned voyagers, and staying in one feels about as removed from urban life as it's possible to be. Beyond the reach of electricity or even roads, they're perfectly placed for guests to appreciate the peace of the island.

### 4
### Bangkok Treehouse, Thailand
Turbocharged Bangkok makes an unexpectedly tranquil location for a treehouse. In the city's southeast is Bang Krachao, a near-island carved by a loop of the Chao Phraya river. It's a place of mangrove, palm and fruit trees, threaded with waterways, semi-rural villages and centuries-old temples hidden in its midst. Presiding over the river are the dozen mid-air hideaways that comprise the eco-conscious Bangkok Treehouse.

# LEARN TO DANCE

**GET YOUR STEPS STRAIGHT IN FOUR OF THE DANCE
CAPITALS OF THE WORLD AND TAKE A NEW SKILL HOME**

**W**hether you're a smooth mover or the clumsy owner of two left feet, nothing can compare to getting to the roots of a dance in its home country. Forget dingy dance halls and robotic instructors, where else can you find an authentic atmosphere but where the people live and breathe the steps invented by their ancestors? You'll learn the history, appreciate the passion and culture and, with any luck, take your newfound expertise home with you – a secret skill you can tap into whenever you please, forever conjuring up memories of that special lesson in that special place. And no-one – no-one can ever tell you that you 'can't dance' when you know you've learnt from the very best in the world! Get set to impress by channelling your inner Astaire or Rogers, once you've swallowed your pride of course. The best bit will be surprising yourself, not just your friends back home.

*Turn over for a tutorial in four dances...*

# LINDY HOP

## NEW YORK CITY, USA

*Evolving in the black communities of Harlem in the 1920s and '30s, the Lindy Hop was considered instrumental in breaking through the race barrier at the Savoy Ballroom, one of few racially integrated dance halls of the era.*
*Considered a fusion of jazz, tap, breakaway and the Charleston, the Lindy Hop's most recognisable steps are the swing-out and the air step, where at least one of the dancing couple has both feet leaving the floor in time to the music. There's no denying its global resurgence in 'swing dancing' clubs but for real authenticity, go back to where it all began at the Harlem Swing Dance Society.*

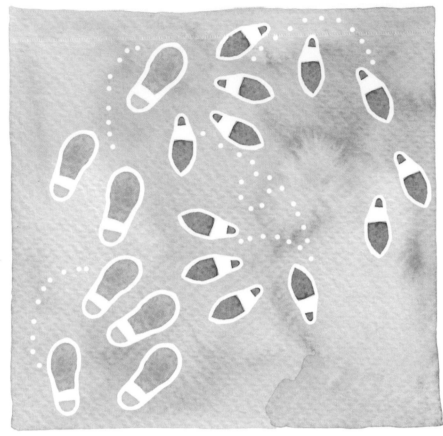

# WALTZ

## VIENNA, AUSTRIA

*The waltz initially caused a stir for its 'dubious morals', given that it – gasp!—required a gentleman to put his arm around a lady and hold her close, unlike less intimate group dancing, previously the fashion in the 1780s. Originating as a folk dance in the Austrian suburbs, the Viennese waltz slightly anticipates the second beat, making it that bit faster than other waltzes.*
*And what better way to glide in ¾ time than by the Danube River to Johann Strauss' Blue Danube Waltz? In fact, ditch Auld Lang Syne and see in the New Year the romantic Austrian way, waltzing to Strauss: the Elmayer Dance School will also teach dance manners and etiquette!*

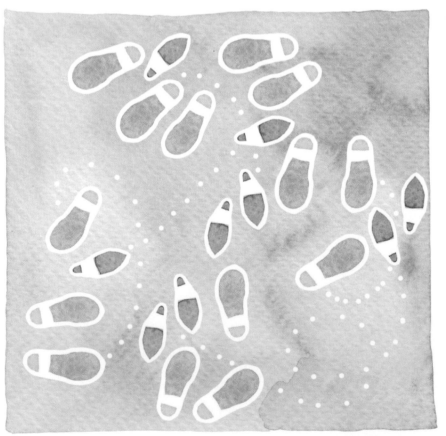

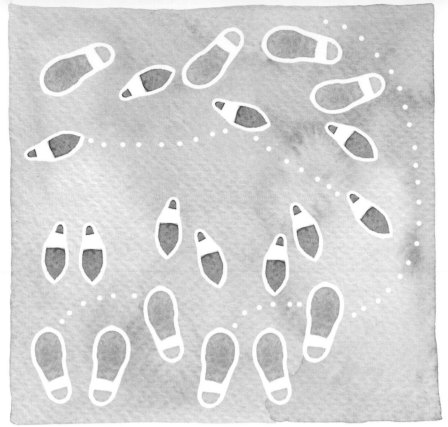

## SALSA
### HAVANA, CUBA

*So you think you can salsa? Then you're in for a surprise in Havana, baby. Cuban salsa (also known as 'Casino') has its origins in sexual flirtation and is a lot more rotational than salsa dances taught elsewhere in the world.*

*Leave your gender equality at the door: male-dominated, Cuban salsa features a strong leader with a push-pull style – ideal for learners! Tradition requires males to be 'macho' and the women 'sexy' and the music needs to be 'felt' rather than necessarily following a beat. Don't be intimidated: it's all part of the cultural experience. Casa del Son in Old Havana is your safe place to start learning.*

## TANGO
### BUENOS AIRES, ARGENTINA

*The tango's history began in the bars and brothels of the city's colourful port area, La Boca. Here, immigrants from all over Europe mingled their own musical traditions with local rhythms like candombe, which arrived a century or so earlier on African slave ships. The rhythm and lyrics combined to symbolise the plaintive cry of the homesick immigrant, the jilted lover's bitter lament and the porteño's hymn to Buenos Aires. Away from the public displays and dinner shows there are milongas (tango dance halls) across the city, from cavernous ballrooms to intimate clubs. Try the Escuela Argentina de Tango for classes and BA Milongas for up-to-date listings.*

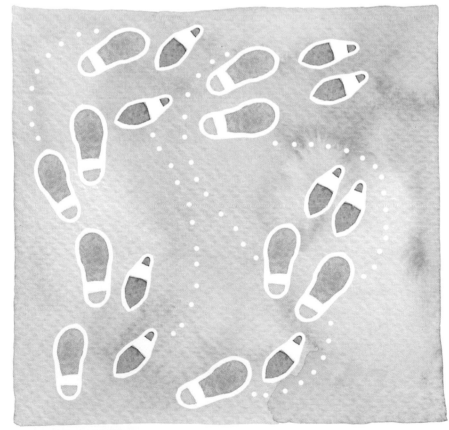

## LEARN TO DANCE

**A Week**

# SEEK OUT SECRET PLACES

*Not every amazing sight will find its way onto the cover of a guidebook. Indeed, some have been forgotten about completely. Websites such as Atlas Obscura are dedicated to rediscovering these alternative attractions. Even in cities there are mysterious places under and above ground. One fertile hunting ground is the former Soviet republics; check out the concrete war memorials built in the 1960s and 1970s in the former Yugoslavia. And what about this strange construction? It's the former Communist headquarters on Mt Buzludzha in Bulgaria, now abandoned.*

STARA ZAGORA, BULGARIA   Matt Munro

A Week

DOORSTEP DISCOVERY

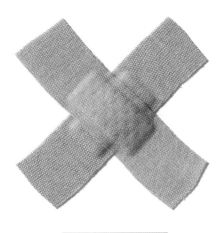

**NICOLA WILLIAMS LEARNS TO LOVE WHAT'S LOCAL**

**A**s the last of the sun's rays blazed across the water before sinking behind the dark mountains beyond, the old-fashioned wooden schooner sliced through its pink reflection. Red sails tangoed in the soft summer breeze and we lazed in their shade, sipping the last of our champagne. And to think this was right on my doorstep, on the southern shore of Lake Geneva.

Several months prior, I'd taken a tumble, broken my back, and was trussed up in a brace for the best part of a year. Travel per se was not prohibited – but planes, trains and automobiles were. If I was to go anywhere, my internal compass required a dramatic reboot.

### Monday

My culinary curiosity was the first to succumb. All too soon my ritual morning stroll wound up at the village *boucherie* where golden roast chickens tantalised on a spit outside, and the line snaked out the door on Sunday mornings. I grilled the butcher for his culinary secrets, smugly leaving with several veal slices and his recipe for *paupiettes de veau* (veal roulades) simmered in local Savoie wine.

### Tuesday

I walked to the neighbouring village to buy fish direct from the fisherman. I'd often watched his boat cross the lake from my kitchen window, a lonesome speck returning home from a pre-dawn

Forget jetting off to Italy to hunt truffles… the sudden grassroots intimacy I was experiencing with my home was revelatory

voyage to empty out crayfish pots and nets swimming with silvery perch and féra. But it took perseverance to find the unpaved lane leading to his house on the shore. The passion with which Madame, deftly filleting the catch, explained how to create the perfect oil, lemon and garlic marinade to douse over her legendary hand-cut *carpaccio de féra* was humbling and overwhelming.

### Wednesday

I started devouring signs. I learnt that the Espace Litorelle, our village hall, which had caused such a rumpus at the time with its radically contemporary facade, was named after *la litorelle* (*Littorella uniflora*), a rare and protected aquatic plant with tiny cream flowers that has grown for centuries on Lake Geneva's shores.

### Thursday

Indulging one's inner child is an essential part of travel – even on one's very own doorstep – hence the day I discovered the Chemin des Douaniers, an overgrown footpath that sneaked from the public beach into thick woods. Ten minutes stumbling over tree roots in the half-dark rewarded with brilliant blue sunshine, a Dolby Surround view of the open lake and a clear footpath that curled as far as the eye could see along the lake's pebbled shore. This secret lakeside path, a voyeur's peephole on the lavish villas bejewelling Lake Geneva, was pure gold.

### Friday

As summer bit the dust and the rains came, I found myself tramping with the local farmer's wife through soggy oak and hornbeam woods in search of wild boletus, golden chanterelles and nutty tasting Trumpets of Death (not deadly, I quickly learnt). Forget jetting off to Italy to hunt truffles or to Japan to chase the sun, the sudden grass-roots intimacy I was experiencing with my home was revelatory.

### Saturday

And so I came to sail La Licorne, a magnificent grand dame of a double-mast schooner that had worked the seas as a fishing vessel in the 1960s, perfectly capping off my local voyage of discovery. ●

*A Week*

# SADDLE UP FOR HORSE PACKING

**GIDDY UP! PICK A STEED, SLIDE INTO THE SADDLE AND SPEND A WEEK IN SOME TOUGH TERRAIN THAT WILL HAVE YOU CONTEMPLATING YOUR EXISTENCE IN NO TIME.**

**A**lways secretly wanted to be the Marlboro Man? Your trip starts in Montana in a small town two hours' drive from anywhere. You overnight in a funky historic hotel, and wait for your guide – an honest-to-goodness cowboy organised by Off The Beaten Path in Bozeman – to collect you in his pick-up. He drives to the trailhead, where a horse trailer is waiting, and while you eat a ham sandwich made by his wife, he saddles-up the horses and packs the gear onto five mules.

And then you set out. The parking lot, such as it was, fades into the distance as the horses ascend the trail into the Beartooth Mountains. All is silent, save for the soft crunch of dry leaves under hooves; there's no expectation of conversation on a long, companionable ride. It's accepted – no, expected – that you'll use the time in the saddle to ponder thorny problems, contemplate your place in the world, let the larger-than-life vistas give you healthy perspective. Your phone won't vibrate, and you won't get a status update, except those from your horse when she's hungry or tired. You'll tune into her as she plods steadily into the wilds. Your back and thighs may get achy, you might feel a bit saddle-sore, and you've certainly earned the right to feel worn out. But you're looking forward to three more days of the same.

Hours later your guide announces it's time to make camp. You could sit your weary bones down on a rock with your book, your thoughts or just that mountain view while he does all the work. But hard, honest labour appeals to you, so you help with the chores: fetching water from the sparkling mountain lake, pitching the tents, feeding the horses, collecting firewood (OK, tinder in your case – there's no question who's doing the real work here). Then you share stories by the campfire, while he grills steaks and you gaze at the riot of stars overhead. ●

RIDING IN THE ROCKY MOUNTAINS   Getty/Cavan Images

### Fazenda Catuçaba, Brazil
This charming farmhouse-turned-boutique-hotel celebrates rural Brazil's equestrian culture, offering rides of varying lengths with charming guides.

### Triple Creek Ranch, USA

Horse riding is a year-round activity at this Montana hideaway. Things ramp up each autumn, when the ranch hosts a women-only 100km trail ride (returning nightly to the comfortable ranch, rather than camping out) called Klicks for Chicks, and donates part of the profits to a local Parkinson's charity.

### Equitours, worldwide

This outfitter has 40 years of experience organising horseback vacations for riders of all abilities in far-flung destinations. Guests might gallop with zebras in Kenya, ride with nomads in Mongolia, drive cattle in Wyoming or saunter through vineyards in France.

### La Morada de Los Andes, Argentina to Chile

Every February this winery and luxury residential community in Mendoza hosts guests on a five-night Gourmet Andes Crossing through the mountains to Santiago. The riding is hard, but the wine flows freely.

# NEW YORK

*There are two places that are truly once-in-a-lifetime musts – and they couldn't be more different. You've got a week, do you spend it in the Big Apple, fast, loud, pulsing with creative energy?*

**Population** *8.3 million*
**Population density** *10,725 / sq km*
**Visitors** *55 million*
**Restaurants** *24,000*
**Most famous landmark** *The Statue of Liberty*

THE HIGH LINE PARK ON THE LOWER WEST SIDE OF MANHATTAN   Matt Munro

# NEW ZEALAND

*Or do you visit the Land of the Long White Cloud, green, serene and pulsing with natural energy? Or – and this is the right answer – somehow do you vow to see both before you die?*

**Population** *4.5 million*
**Population density** *16 / sq km*
**Visitors** *3 million*
**Restaurants** *c.7000*
**Most famous landmark** *The Big Sheep Shearer of te Kuiti*

**A Week**

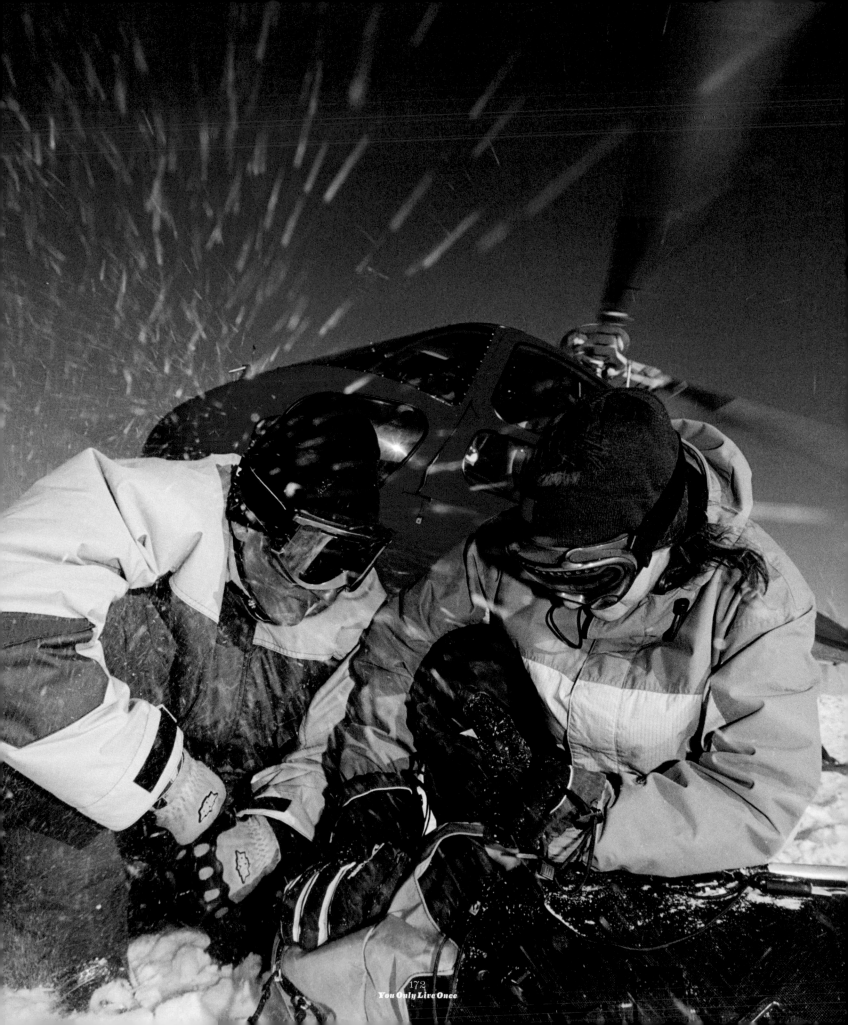

# CHOPPER

# TAKE THE

**IMAGINE SKIING THE BEST RUN OF YOUR LIFE. ON REPEAT. TEN TO I5 TIMES A DAY. FOR A WEEK. ONCE YOU'VE HELI-SKIED, NOTHING ELSE WILL COMPARE.**

**T**his is the kind of descent most people experience once in a lifetime, and only then if perfect weather conditions hit, and they had the good sense to rise at the crack of dawn and make first place in the lift queue.

You're on EA's Last Frontier heli-trip to the Skeena Mountain Range in British Columbia, just 40 miles from the Alaskan border. The terrain at your disposal is 25 times the size of Les Trois Vallées (the largest ski resort in the world), and averages 25m of snow a year, compared to an approximate 5m in Alpine resorts.

In a group of just five, you tackle waist-deep dry cold powder, charging down mountains few people have ever seen, let alone skied. You marvel at the variety of terrain, encompassing steeps, wide-open bowls, seemingly endless glaciers and top-quality tree skiing. With each turn the snow's layer of surface hoar makes its crystals sparkle in the sun, and the experience feels that little bit more magical.

When you can't take any more and your legs start begging for mercy you treat them to a hot tub at the Bell 2 Lodge, home to atmospheric log-wood cabins with cosy fires and mellow vibes. ●

### ① Heli-biking, Wanaka, New Zealand
Circle Mt Cook, New Zealand's highest mountain, and three giant lakes, taking in breathtaking views of snowy peaks before landing at 2200m for the start of the country's highest mountain-bike trail. You'll begin with dual single track undulating along the ridgeline, moving onto rolling hills for the lower section of your ride and finishing up at the region's oldest pub.

### ② Heli-boarding, Kamchatka, Russia
Home to some of the best freeriding on the planet, Kamchatka boasts 29 active volcanoes, many of which you can snowboard down, ending up at the Pacific Ocean. McNab Snowboarding offers heli-trips here for fit and experienced backcountry boarders. McNab, who guides, holds the US Medal of Valor for rescuing a stranded climber – so you're in safe hands.

### ③ Heli-hiking, Pir Panjal Range, the Himalayas
If you want to hike some awesome, untrodden Himalayan terrain and arrive in high spirits rather than with serious journey ennui, try a Himalayan Heli Adventure in the Pir Panjal Range. Aside from quick access to the most pristine rocky meadows with high mountain backdrops, the heli-ride itself is truly stunning.

### ④ Heli-kayaking, Bear Glacier, Alaska
Swoop in above the icebergs and spectacular glacial landscape of the Kenai Fjords National Park, then leave your chopper and kayak right up to Bear Glacier. The trip provides a totally different perspective on this region, plus the chance to get a close-up view of whales, seals, sea lions and puffins.

*A Week*

# SUPER SAFARIS

## WITNESS THE MAJESTY OF MOTHER NATURE'S GREATEST CREATURES IN AFRICA'S FIVE FINEST PARKS.

**W**ith each stroke of the paddle you are stirring a river where giants lurk. And as you glide slowly along the still surface of the Zambezi in your canoe, you quickly get the feeling you are being watched... Eyes pop up here and there, vanishing beneath the surface as swiftly as they appear. You listen to your guide and stick to the shallows, which keeps the onlookers at a distance, something you're grateful for given these eyes belong to creatures who weigh over 1500kg and sport canines that are half a metre long. Hippos are much like icebergs – what looms below is far more impressive than what is visible above the water, and most importantly, you never want to crash into one.

The mighty river's banks in Zambia's Lower Zambezi National Park are no less dramatic – vervet monkeys screech from branches to warn of prowling leopards, hulking elephants tower over sandbanks, and 5m-long Nile crocodiles bask in the sun with their mouths agape and their glistening teeth on display. You might even follow a lion pride from just a few metres away and look each of them in the eye as they stop to slake their thirst.

Yet, despite all the natural theatrics and sense of danger, there are such feelings of peace and absolute wonder. That is what makes a safari so very special. You aren't just seeing the world's most iconic species of wildlife in astoundingly beautiful surroundings, you're witnessing them living their unique lives on their terms. You're a guest in a world that is not yours. And it's never possible to forget that. ●

SAFARI BY CANOE IN THE LOWER ZAMBEZI NATIONAL PARK    Getty/John Warburton-Lee

A Week

A LEOPARD IN THE SERENGETI NATIONAL PARK   Fiona McAnally

# SUPER SAFARIS

### Serengeti National Park, Tanzania
*The Serengeti, which covers 14,763 sq km and is contiguous with Masai Mara National Reserve in Kenya, is Tanzania's most famous park. Wildebeest (and the leopards that ambush them) of which there are over one million, are among the most prominent residents roaming its vast plains and their annual migration is the Serengeti's biggest drawcard.*

### Etosha National Park, Namibia
*Covering an area of more than 20,000 sq km, Etosha National Park is one of the world's great wildlife-watching venues. Its name, which means Great White Place of Dry Water is inspired by a vast flat, saline desert that is converted by rains into a shallow lagoon teeming with animals for a few days a year. The surrounding landscape is home to 114 mammal species and 340 bird species.*

### Kruger National Park, South Africa
*In South Africa's must-see wildlife destination, enough elephants to populate a city wander around, giraffes nibble on acacia trees, hippos wallow in rivers, leopards prowl through the night and a multitude of birds sing, fly and roost. The park has an extensive network of roads but if you prefer to keep it rough there are also 4WD tracks and walking trails. The far north of the Kruger is the wilder side.*

### Moremi Game Reserve, Botswana
*Moremi is the only part of the Okavango Delta that is set aside for the preservation of wildlife. It's a massive oasis, now home to the Big Five (lion, leopard, buffalo, elephant and rhino) and one of the largest populations of African wild dogs. Wildlife concentrations are mind-boggling during the dry season but Moremi is also one of Botswana's most exclusive places to expect to pay for the privilege.*

# 50 WAYS TO UNPLUG

*By Patrick Kinsella*

PLAY A GAME OF CARDS IN A NEW YORK SPEAKEASY

JOIN IN WITH A GAME OF BOULES IN A VILLAGE IN CENTRAL FRANCE

SPEND AN AFTERNOON LAZILY KAYAKING ALONG THE CROATIAN COAST

WATCH THE WEATHER ROLL IN AT VANCOUVER ISLAND

SKIM A STONE ON ONE OF THE GREAT LAKES OF NORTH AMERICA

HAVE A GAME OF STREET FOOTBALL IN LA BOCA, BUENOS AIRES, ARGENTINA

**DO SOME GUERRILLA KNITTING IN CALIFORNIA**

EXPERIENCE AN IMPROMPTU MUSIC SESSION IN A PUB ON THE WEST COAST OF IRELAND

LISTEN TO A VINYL RECORD IN AQUARIUS RECORDS, SAN FRANCISCO

**BUILD A HANGI IN NEW ZEALAND**

TUCK INTO SOME LEGENDARY BANANA BREAD ON A LAKE MALAWI BEACH

**GO SKI TOURING IN LEBANON**

RENT A BIKE AND CYCLE ALONG A CANAL IN AMSTERDAM

CYCLE AROUND THE ANCIENT WALLS OF LUCCA IN TUSCANY, ITALY

**WALK A DOG (OR YOUR FRIENDS DOG)**

EXPERIENCE A GAME OF NON-PROFESSIONAL AUSTRALIAN RULES FOOTBALL IN THE NORTHERN TERRITORY

**BUY A SECOND-HAND BOOK ON CHARING CROSS ROAD, LONDON**

**UPPEVELLI BEACH, SRI LANKA**

VISIT THE OLDEST ORGANISMS ON EARTH, THE STROMATOLITES IN SHARK BAY, AUSTRALIA

CAMP OUT IN A SAFARI TENT IN THE OKAVANGO DELTA, BOTSWANA

GO NIGHT SWIMMING AMONG BIOLUMINESCENT PLANKTON IN MAYA BAY, THAILAND

RIDE A HORSE ALONG THE BEACH IN MONTEGO BAY, JAMAICA

SEE SUNRISE OVER CAPE TOWN FROM THE TOP OF TABLE MOUNTAIN

**VISIT A VINEYARD IN MOLDOVA**

QUAFF A LOCALLY BREWED BEER IN BRUGES, BELGIUM

**WATCH SOME COW WRESTLING IN VALAIS, SWITZERLAND**

PUT DOWN THE IPAD AND PLAY AN AL FRESCO GAME OF CHESS IN ST PETERSBURG

**SOUR IN PERU**

**WALK AROUND THE WALLS OF DERRY IN NORTHERN IRELAND**

**SNOOZE ON** 

**CEREMONY IN JAPAN**

IMMERSE YOURSELF IN AN ONSEN IN RURAL JAPAN

DOZE IN AN APRICOT ORCHARD IN THE ATLAS MOUNTAINS OF MOROCCO

**SHARE A GOURD OF MATE IN BARRA DE VALIZAS, URUGUAY**

OBSERVE A FAMILY OF GRIZZLY BEARS IN KLUANE NATIONAL PARK, YUKON, CANADA

FIND A FOSSIL ON CHESIL BEACH, DORSET, ENGLAND

**PACK A PICNIC FOR THE BEACH**

SEE THE OTHER SIDE OF LAS VEGAS AND GO MOUNTAIN BIKING ON THE NEARBY TRAILS

**DRINK A PISCO**

GET A WET SHAVE IN THE MARKET BARBERS IN SALALAH, OMAN

WATCH A GAME OF VILLAGE RUGBY ON THE YASAWA ISLANDS, FIJI

**STAND NEXT TO THE DIPLODOCUS SKELETON IN LONDONS NATURAL HISTORY MUSEUM**

GO BACK IN TIME AT NEOLITHIC SITES ON ORKNEY, SCOTLAND

**ATTEND A TEA**

WALK THROUGH A WADI IN OMAN AND SLEEP OUT IN THE OPEN UNDER THE DESERT STARS

**EXPLORE THE CATACOMBS IN PARIS**

**DO A SESSION OF LAUGHTER YOGA IN BANGALORE, INDIA**

TRY FREE SOLOING (ROCK CLIMBING OVER WATER) IN HALONG BAY, VIETNAM

LOUNGE AROUND IN A THERMAL POOL UNDER THE MIDNIGHT SUN IN ICELAND

**TAKE A BOAT TO FINGALS CAVE IN SCOTLAND**

EAT A DINOSAUR-SIZED STEAK IN MENDOZA, ARGENTINA

VISIT A GAELTACHT AREA OF IRELAND AND TRY ORDERING A PINT IN IRISH

HIT THE BOOKS AT THE BIBLIOTHÈQUE NATIONALE DE FRANCE

**A Week**

# BECOME A WORLD CHAMPION

---

**WE'VE EACH GOT A UNIQUE GIFT. AND WHERE THERE'S TALENT, THERE'S A TOURNAMENT. TRY YOUR HAND AT AN ARCANE EVENT AND YOU NEVER KNOW WHAT MAD SKILLS YOU MIGHT UNLEASH.**

The buzz of anticipation simmers through freezing Sōbetsu, Hokkaido. You and your six snow-hungry friends are sizing up the 150 teams that make up the competition at this seriously upgraded version of a snowball fight, held annually in northern Japan.

The Showa-Shinzan International Yukigassen (Japanese for 'snow fight') is an icy take on 'capture the flag', with teams of seven players, 90 machine-made snowballs and one mission: to get the opponents' flag or tally points through body hits.

You don helmets, gloves and ready your team flag – and the whistle blows. Blizzards of snowballs rain down but you swing yourself this way, then that, narrowly missing them all. You crouch, crawl, duck, dive and lurch for cover before making a final break for the flag. Success!

But that was just the prelim – your real fight to be champs starts now. ●

### World Beard & Moustache Championship, worldwide
*This superhip, globetrotting event, created in Germany in 1990, will be held in Portland, Oregon (of course) in 2014, and Leogang, Austria the following year. Contestants frequently put as much effort into their outfits (Edwardian suits etc) as the hairy creations on their faces. Nothing beats the unpredictability and wonder of a conceptualised freestyle moustache.*

### Best Baggers Contest, USA
*Grocery bagging is a serious business, with the best baggers able to scientifically fill every cubic inch. Every year, regional competitions culminate with a national Best Baggers Contest, hosted by the National Grocers Association. If you take care to properly distribute the weight, and complete your bagging with lightning speed while maintaining a friendly attitude, you can be number one.*

### Wife Carrying, Finland
*This proud Finnish tradition involves a man negotiating a 253.5m obstacle course while carrying his wife (or the closest he can get), usually upside-down, with her legs wrapped around the man's neck. It's held in July and is governed by the decree that 'everyone must have fun'.*

### World Stone Skimming Championship, Easdale Island, Scotland
*This Scottish tradition involves standing at the shorelines of an old slate-mining island, picking a stone out of a bucket and sliding it across the surface – if it skips at least three times, you're eligible. But it's distance travelled rather than the number of skips that takes the prize in this event.*

MISSISSIPPI
PIPPI
BLUES
PILGRIMAGE

## GARTH CARTWRIGHT GETS THE BLUES
## IN THE DEEP SOUTH

**S**trip back any form of contemporary music and you'll find something that owes a debt of gratitude to the blues. A journey to its birthplace paints an eye-opening historical portrait and is an inspirational pilgrimage for fans of the genre.

Travelling through the Mississippi Delta, you'll spot funky little roadside shacks, often built out of scrap materials and defying all conventional building codes (and don't even think about health and safety). These are the legendary juke joints, the last remaining vestiges of the place where the blues took shape. Once providing a place for African-American sharecroppers to relax after a hard week's labour, juke joints were rowdy places – juke is a West African word meaning 'disorderly' – filled with music

U2 and The Rolling Stones have been known to drop in on an after-hours juke, while Robert Plant has, on occasion, got up and sang

and dancing, and a welcome escape from a crushing existence.

Although now much reduced in number, juke joints are still crowded with locals at weekends, both in urban and rural areas; here they seek out the blues – live, DJed or simply on the jukebox. Juke joints remain the closest a blues fan can get to hearing the music, raw and local.

Paying homage to the likes of Robert Johnson, Muddy Waters and Howling Wolf, blues pilgrims originally tended to be white American music fanatics who risked imprisonment by entering the jukes – until the end of segregation in the late 1960s it was illegal for whites and blacks to socialise together. As blues won a broader international audience, due to the success of British rock bands, Stevie Ray Vaughan and BB King, pilgrims from all across the world began riding Highway 61, which runs through the Mississippi Delta and pulses with blues history. U2 and The Rolling Stones have been known to drop in on an after-hours juke, while Robert Plant has, on occasion, got up and sang.

Mississippi now has a whole host of activities for blues pilgrims. Blues Trail Markers across the state show where famous artists lived, worked, prayed, recorded and died. Clarksdale, 90 minutes' drive south of Memphis, is a mecca for fans; Bessie Smith tragically died here, while Ike Turner and Sam Cooke are famous sons of the run-down cotton town. It's home to the Delta Blues Museum, as well as Cat Head, a fabulous shop specialising in blues and folk art. Ground Zero Blues Club, a live-music bar and restaurant part-owned by Morgan Freeman, is well worth seeking out. Amongst a variety of accommodation there are re-conditioned sharecropper shacks for those who want to experience how the blues singers lived, albeit with 21st-century comforts. And in April the town explodes with the annual Juke Joint Festival, where revellers gorge on beer, barbecue and, of course, plenty of the blues. ●

**A Week**

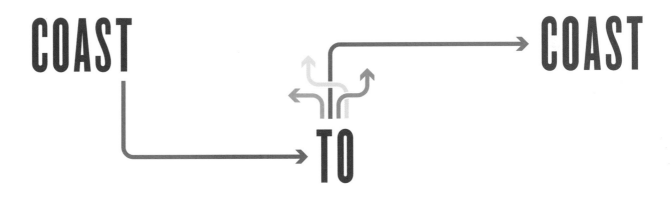

# COAST TO COAST

**FROM SEA TO SHINING SEA: THERE'S MORE THAN ONE WAY TO CROSS A COUNTRY. RIDE A BIKE ACROSS ENGLAND, A HORSE ACROSS COSTA RICA OR HIKE IRELAND.**

**J**ust one more hill... If someone tells you that on the Sea to Sea (C2C) cycle route across northern England, you should be suspicious. For the route crosses some of the more rugged stretches of the country, huffing and puffing its way over the Pennines, England's spine, via the northern Lake District National Park.

For a physical challenge, cycling across a country is as easy or hard as you make it. It's around 550km across Italy, which could easily stretch into a week's ride via idyllic Umbrian and Tuscan towns, fuelled by delicious homemade pasta and Chianti. Then there's the USA, with Adventure Cycling's shortest mapped route being its 4800km Southern Tier tour through California, Arizona, Texas, Louisiana and Florida. This will take more than a week.

But as you pedal up Whinlatter Pass in England's Lake District, before stopping at the 4500-year-old Castlerigg stone circle near Keswick, you may be thankful that this route across England's northern neck is just 225km. Most of the 12,000 cyclists who attempt it annually do so from west to east, hoping for a following wind to push them over the Pennines. And then it's downhill all the way to Newcastle or Sunderland. Mostly. ●

HORSE-RIDING IN COSTA RICA   Getty/Brian Bailey

## COAST TO COAST

### 1 · Ireland by foot
There are almost 10,000 pubs scattered across Ireland and by halfway of your cross-country walk from Dublin to Portmagee on the Atlantic coast, it feels as though you've been inside most of them. Ireland is a country that refuses to be rushed, so take your time on this 622km trail, which stitches together waymarked trails through Wicklow, South Leinster, East Munster, Blackwater and Kerry.

### 2 · Costa Rica on horseback
On each day of this sea-to-ocean odyssey you've faced totally new terrain with your criollo steed, from soft Caribbean sand at the outset to the lushness of the rainforest. The highlands of this astonishingly diverse country will provide the main challenge, as you cross the back of Central America and descend to the Pacific coast.

### 3 · Ski across Spitsbergen, Norway
Few people have done a self-sufficient, coast-to-coast traverse of the largest island in the archipelago of Svalbard, skiing across glaciers and spending each star-spangled night in a mountain tent on the ice. During the four-day west-to-east expedition from the Barents Sea to the Greenland Sea you'll feel like an arctic explorer.

### 4 · Australia's Savannah Way by 4WD
Leaving steamy Cairns and rising through the rainforests to the Tablelands that tower above the Wet Tropics, a long and rough road lies in wait. Driving in the hoofsteps of the old drovers, you've got 3700km to negotiate before reaching Broome in the gorgeous Kimberley. It's incredibly remote driving: mind the saltwater crocs.

## SHOOT A VIDEO

*With the advent of compact and high-quality video cameras there's no reason not to strap on a GoPro and tell the story of your trip from your own point of view. Just remember to cut and edit before you share: nobody wants to see the wobbly out-takes.*

**A Week**

DOG-SLEDDING IN WESTERN GREENLAND    Getty_David Trood

# HUNT A MONSTER

**THEY SEEK HIM HERE! THEY SEEK HIM THERE! TRACK DRACULA IN TRANSYLVANIA, YETIS IN THE HIMALAYA AND LARGE LAKE-DWELLING MONSTERS IN SCOTLAND.**

**S**prawling along the edge of the snowy Carpathians, Europe's last truly wild mountain range, Transylvania is a land that is rich in myths and legends. A region of Romania since 1918 but historically an independent province, Transylvania's history has been shaped by the people that have passed through over the centuries: Saxons, Ottomans, Hungarians, Jews, Serbs and Roma Gypsies. With them came stories collected on their travels: tales of goblins and giants, fairy queens and woodland nymphs, unearthly phantoms, man-eating ogres and predatory ghouls.

Venture out on a moonlit night and you might encounter the *pricolici*, the devilish werewolves said to be the restless spirits of violent men. And then there are the legends of the *strigoi*, or vampires, which fired the imagination of an Irish writer by the name of Bram Stoker, and inspired him to write his Gothic bestseller, *Dracula*, in 1897...

Dracula is everywhere in Transylvania. Every town claims a tenuous link with his real-life counterpart Vlad Țepeș, the warlord who ruled the kingdom of Wallachia intermittently between 1448 and 1476, and who had a predilection for impaling his enemies on stakes. Few places sell their Dracula connections harder than Bran Castle in the Carpathian foothills, about 30km south of the well-preserved medieval town of Brașov. But disentangling truth from tales is more difficult; Vlad's actual castle was 200km north – and many of the more bloodythirsty myths about him were propaganda. ●

 **1**

### Yeti, Himalaya
*Of all the giant ape-man legends, the yeti is the most enduring and documented. This is perhaps because it occupies one of the most remote corners of the world, in the foothills of Nepal and Tibet, where it conveniently leaves an occasional footprint.*

 **2**

### Nessie, Scotland
*Deep, dark and narrow, Loch Ness stretches for 37km between Inverness and Fort Augustus. Its bitterly cold waters have been extensively explored in search of Nessie, the elusive Loch Ness monster first 'sighted' in 1933.*

 **3**

### Bunyip, Australia
*In a land delineated by Aboriginal mythology, tales of the Bunyip are some of the more nightmarish. The beast – consistent descriptions are hard to find – inhabits swamps and rivers. When otherworldy screams are heard in the Outback at night, the Bunyip is blamed.*

**4**

### Bigfoot, USA
*Star of many a blurry Super-8 video, Bigfoot resides in the beautiful forests of the Pacific Northwest. It established itself in popular folklore in the 1950s, round about the time that the regions wild woods were being explored by increasing numbers of hikers.*

**A Week**

# US$100

### weekly budget

*of Graham Hughes, who used buses, taxis, trains to visit 201 countries in the world over 1426 days, finishing in November 2012.*

# 13.7

### shots

*of liquor South Koreans drink per week on average, mostly in the form of soju, a fermented rice spirit.*

# 6

### weeks

*duration of a 1600km record-setting rickshaw ride around Britain by Tim Moss in 2010.*

# 19&2

### weeks and days

*time it took Sean Conway to swim the length of Britain, 900 miles from Land's End to John O'Groats in 2013.*

# 8&1

### weeks and day

*duration of a 2,246.21km roller ski trip taken by Cesar Baena in 2012, starting from Stockholm, Sweden and finishing in Holmenkollen, Norway.*

# 22.4

### minutes

*average time people in France spend shopping every week.*

# 20&2

## weeks and days

length of time Geoff Smith spent buried underground in a 7ft
wooden box in the garden of the Railway Inn, Mansfield, in 1999.

# 560,000

## number of tourists

who flock to the old section of Venice (population: 57,960),
each week during high season.

# 4,4&12

## weeks, days and hours

the longest time it has taken a team to finish the Iditarod
dog-sledding race in Anchorage to Nome in Alaska.

# US$6181

## cost of going glamping

for a week at Sanctuary Swala in Tarangire National Park,
Tanzania, in high season.

# 9

## weeks

average time it will take to walk New Zealand's new
country-spanning trail, the 3000km Te Araroa
(The Long Pathway).

# 8&5

## weeks and day

length of the longest snowmobile journey, a 19,575km
trip completed by Robert G. Davis from the US state of
Maine into Canada in 2008.

# MEND A BROKEN HEART

**WHAT BECOMES OF THE BROKEN-HEARTED? PICK UP THE PIECES WITH THESE TRAVEL IDEAS FOR LIFE AFTER THE EX FACTOR.**

**L***ife goes on.* And it is the little steps that move you forward, quite literally, on the Camino de Santiago. You're on the world's most famous pilgrimage trail, stretching almost 800km through the wilds of northern Spain. Every day eases the heartache and brings new horizons. You can't help but live by your senses as you traverse a 2000m mountain pass in the Pyrenees, battle driving rain on the wave-thrashed Atlantic coast, or hobble to the next *refugio*, blisters throbbing, as day fades to dusk. Forced to let go of the past and embrace the here and now, you become you once again.

Out here on the wide-open trail, there is time to think and space to breathe but no place to hide. Moments of quiet introspection aside, the camino is where friendships are forged and experiences shared – just as they have been for the past 1000 years. Walking side by side with new companions in the shadow of snowcapped peaks, through the undulating vineyards of Rioja and the mist-draped hills of Navarra is refreshing – liberating even. The constant rhythm of footfall on rock is cathartic. The spirit of camaraderie is life-affirming.

Yes, you have been to hell and back in your relationship, but after several weeks on the trail, the fog of depression begins to clear and your spirits soar as you take in the high barren plains of the *meseta* (tableland) and Galicia's ever-changing palette of greens. Like countless pilgrims before you, you rest your weary bones against the ancient pillars of Santiago de Compostela's cathedral, the final resting place of St James the Apostle. Sweet relief floods every fibre of your being; as one journey ends, another begins. ●

NEON-LIT NIGHTLIFE IN NASHVILLE   Myles New

# MEND A BROKEN HEART

 **Sing the blues**

*It's only natural to grieve for lost love, but if you're gonna do it, do it right, yeah? Where better to wallow in the blues than in its rightful home. Follow the Blues Brothers to the dimly lit joints of Chicago or drown your sorrows while dreaming of new tomorrows in Nashville's neon-lit honky-tonks. The ultimate road trip to Bluesville is Highway 61 through Tennessee and Mississippi. It sure beats listening to Van the Man on your iPod.*

 **Spread your wings**

*There's nothing like learning a skill to give you a new focus and lift your spirits, be it a week-long photography course in Morocco, a perfume-making workshop in France or a painting break with like-minded souls in Italy. Always wanted to learn to paraglide or hike the Inca Trail? Now is the time. Physical activity is a great stressbuster and confidence booster, and there's no place like the great outdoors for letting things go.*

 **Trip of a lifetime**

*You're footloose and fancy-free again, and the world really is your oyster. Expense be damned – book that once-in-a-lifetime ticket to Antarctica or the Australian Outback that will give you the vast horizons you need to clear your head. Or perhaps you've always wanted to see the sun rise over the Mongolian steppe on the epic Trans-Siberian. There's never been a better time.*

 **Give back a little**

*Why not turn a negative into a positive? Doing something worthwhile can provide a much-needed switch of focus. A voluntary conservation project in the Ecuadorian jungle, helping orphaned street kids from Mombasa's slums or a deployment with a disaster relief charity will present you with physical and emotional challenges that thrust you into the here and now, leaving you no time to dwell on the past.*

# AUTUMN LEAVES

WHEN AUTUMN LEAVES START TO FALL, TAKE A WEEK TO TOUR THE BRIEF FLURRY OF COLOUR. HERE ARE FIVE OF THE FINEST LOCATIONS AND THE LEAVES TO LOOK OUT FOR.

## MAPLE
### NARA, JAPAN

Autumn in Japan is every bit as stunning as the short-lived *haname* cherry blossom season in spring. *Kouyou*, or autumn leaves, can be seen across the country, starting in the northern island of Hokkaidō and spreading quickly south from the end of September. The ancient capital of Nara, a short train ride from Kyoto, makes a wonderful viewing spot. Its vast park is awash with colour, with sensational views of red, gold and yellow leaves along the paths up to Tamukeyama shrine in its northeast corner.

*A Week*

## BEECH
### FOREST OF DEAN, ENGLAND

This ancient woodland in Gloucestershire was once used as a royal hunting ground; its trees were also used to make Tudor warships. Today, it's the perfect spot for the more prosaic sport of 'leaf peeping'. The mix of oak, beech and sweet chestnut provides a rusty riot of yellow and gold. The Forest of Dean can be easily covered on foot or bike. Just keep an eye out for the wild boar that have called this place home since 2006.

## ASPEN
### COLORADO, USA

It's all about the aspens in Colorado, a tree so ethereally beautiful they named a town and a beer after it. The aspens glow golden in the autumn sun over Kebler Pass, a gravel road out of Crested Butte that passes through Gunnison National Forest in southwest Colorado. September is the best month.

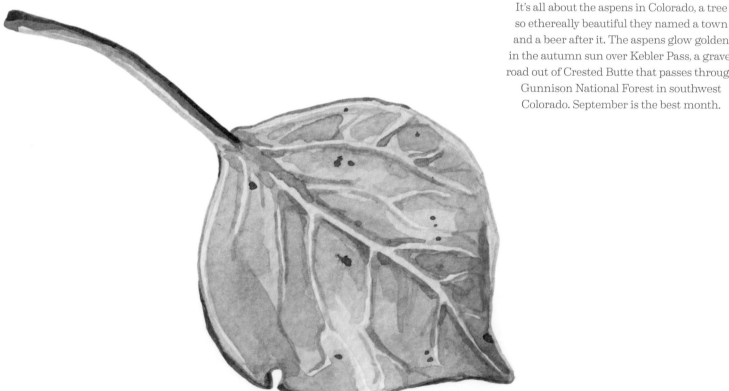

### RED OAK
#### AGAWA CANYON, CANADA

Hop on board the Agawa Canyon Tour Train in autumn and you'll be treated to some of the most beautiful fall foliage on the planet. The ride sets off from Sault Ste Marie on the Canada–USA border, covering 183 km of unspoilt country that looks at its best as the days begin to close in. The views here inspired Tom Thomson and the Group of Seven, Canada's most prominent landscape artists, throughout the early 20th century. You'll need to be quick though, as the leaves peak for a brief period around the end of September and beginning of October.

### ASH
#### WHITE MOUNTAINS, USA

New England is synonymous with 'fall' and picking one must-see spot isn't easy. But New Hampshire's White Mountains are surely one of the best places to see autumn at its most colourful, not just in New England, but the world. Hike through the hills at the start of October and you'll be treated to brilliant red maple leaves. Or drive to Silver Cascade Falls in Carroll County to see the trees glow next to the 76m waterfall.

# HONEYMOON OF A LIFETIME

**MAKE YOUR FIRST HONEYMOON ONE TO REMEMBER WITH THESE FIVE ROMANTIC IDEAS.**

**S**nowflakes fall like delicate confetti in a forest silhouetted against a night sky streaked with stars. You walk together through the hush of a frozen landscape, pausing to gaze in wonder at the Milky Way. Close to the Arctic Circle in northern Norway, the sub-zero temperatures bring you closer to the elements and to each other. Then the magic begins: you stop dead in your tracks, spellbound by the majestic Northern Lights. These swirling bolts of electric green and undulating rays of purple-pink are like being at an enormous disco for Norse Gods – there's nowhere better for your first dance.

It's a myth that a honeymoon has to be somewhere hot. Not when you can spend days kayaking in quiet exhilaration across fjords of molten silver, rimmed by dark mountains. Paddling to islets where it is just the two of you and the vast wilderness, mingling with migratory whales and dolphins, sea eagles wheeling overhead in a bruised sky.

You bounce across Saltstraumen, the world's strongest tidal current, in a rigid-inflatable boat; catch salmon in a river that runs swift and clear, and take a husky-driven sleigh together at twilight. The nights draw in quickly and you gather by an open fire to listen to melodic *yoik* (rhythmic poems) in the cosy shadow of a Sami *lavvu* (tent). The icing on the cake is a stay in the ice-carved bridal suite at Alta's Sorrisniva Igloo Hotel, complete with a four-poster draped in reindeer skins.

Just like with rings, there's no one-size-fits-all when it comes to romance. ●

THE AURORA BOEALIS IN TROMSØ NORTHERN NORWAY   Getty/Antony Spencer

**A Week** JANUARY

A MARRAKECH RIAD  Getty/Paul Harris

# HONEYMOON OF A LIFETIME

 **1**

### It takes two

You're pedalling past the vineyards of the Danube on a tandem bike. You're kayaking in unison along New Zealand's pristine Abel Tasman coastline. You're helping each other traverse the toughest stretches of the Tour du Mont Blanc, where snow-tipped mountains ripple into France, Italy and Switzerland. Or maybe you're learning to make pasta together in Italy. If flopping on the beach is a no-no, a honeymoon that involves shared interests could be just the ticket.

 **2**

### City break

Paris will never lose its touch as the city of amour, but alternatives abound. The hurly-burly of Marrakech's medina soon fades when you step into a rose-petal-strewn riad or onto a roof terrace, open to a star-studded sky. Rome is eternally romantic, but oft-overlooked Italian cities like medieval Lucca, nestled among Tuscan vines, hills and olive groves, have a fresh-faced loveliness all of their own.

 **3**

### Ultimate adventure

Riding high on the buzz of tying the knot, you might want to up the adventure and make that trip of a lifetime you've always talked about. Camel trekking across the Sahara and camping out under the night sky, checking out the grizzlies and geysers in Yellowstone National Park, going on a gorilla safari in Uganda, or gliding over Cappadocia in a hot-air balloon as the golden warmth of sunrise spreads over its fairy chimneys.

 **4**

### Island in the sun

So you want the glossy magazine dream of sunsets, infinity pools, and sugar-white beaches? Go for the castaway experience in Polynesia; the coral atolls and blue waters of the Maldives or the crashing waves and Piton mountains of St Lucia. Paradise doesn't have to cost a mint; from Greece to Thailand and Italy to Indonesia, there are gorgeous beaches with a relaxed vibe and a more affordable price tag.

# ISLANDS OF ADVENTURE

**FORGET FLOPPING ON THE SAND; THESE ISLANDS ARE DESIGNED FOR AN ACTION-PACKED WEEK OF ESCAPADES IN MOUNTAINS, JUNGLES, VOLCANOES AND CROCODILE-INFESTED WATERWAYS.**

*Maps by* **Wayne Murphy**

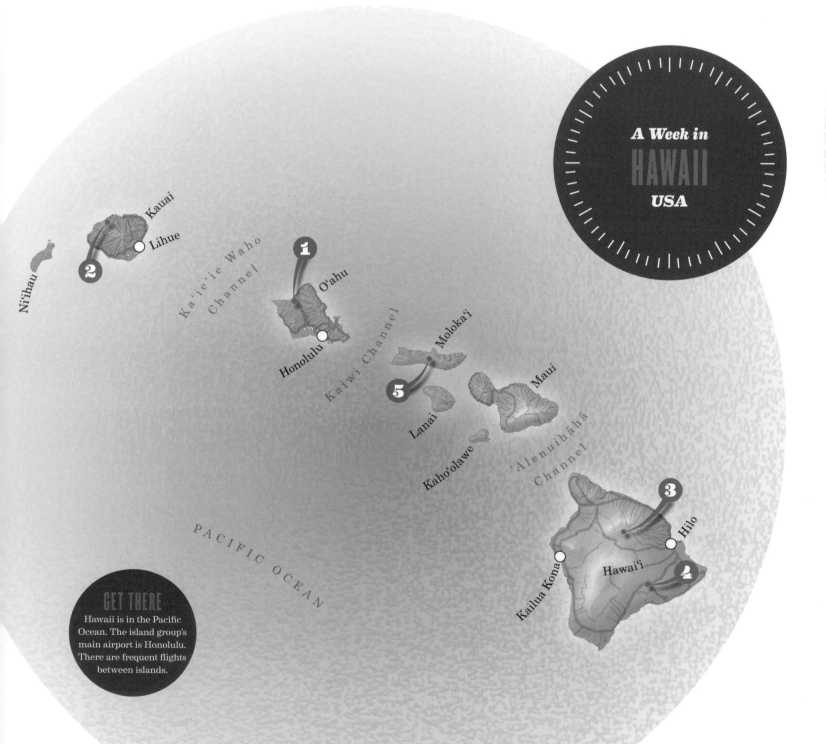

### 1. Oʻahu, North Shore

*Surfing on the North Shore is not for the faint-hearted or inexperienced: giant swells slam into Oʻahu from the deep ocean. As a place to see masters of their craft, though, it's unequalled.*

### 2. Na Pali Coast, Kauai

*Sea kayaks are the best way to access the Na Pali Coast Wilderness Park, which is permitted from May to September, though it's not an excursion for beginners.*

### 3. Mauna Kea, the Big Island

*Star gaze at the Onizuka Center for International Astronomy on top of the dormant volcano of Mauna Kea. Telescopes are available until 10pm.*

### 4. Kilauea, the Big Island

*Hike in the Hawaii Volcanoes National Park: the Crater Rim Trail around the edge of Kilauea, a dormant volcano, features rainforest, desert and volcanic vents.*

### 5. Molokaʻi Island

*Chill out on Molokai, the low-key island with the most native Hawaiians and no high-rise resorts. Take jungle drives or tropical forest walks.*

**A Week in**

**HAWAII**

**USA**

Niʻihau

Kauai

Lihue

Kaʻieʻie Waho Channel

Oʻahu

Honolulu

Kaiwi Channel

Molokaʻi

Lanai

Kahoʻolawe

Maui

ʻAlenuihāhā Channel

PACIFIC OCEAN

Hilo

Hawaiʻi

Kailua Kona

**GET THERE**

Hawaii is in the Pacific Ocean. The island group's main airport is Honolulu. There are frequent flights between islands.

Cap de Formentor

Balearic Sea

Alcúdia

Badia d'Alcúdia

**5**

Sa Dragonera

**2**

Serra de Tramuntana

Inca

**1**

Calvià

Palma de Mallorca

✈ Aeroport de Palma

Manacor

**3**

Badia de Palma

Llucmajor

**4**

Cap de ses Salines

MEDITERRANEAN SEA

Illa de Cabrera

### GET THERE

Mallorca is one of the Balearic Islands. Palma's airport receives frequent flights. Mallorca can also be reached by ferry from mainland Spain.

## A Week in
# MALLORCA
### Spain

### 1. Sa Gubia

*Rock climb at this huge rock amphitheatre west of Bunyola. It's Mallorca's top sport climbing spot and the Spanish limestone is superb.*

### 2. Sóller

*Cycle from Sóller north or south into the heart of the Tramuntana range for some of the best bike-riding routes in Europe. It's easy to put together hilly loops though the mountains: spring and autumn are the prime seasons.*

### 3. Santa Ponsa

*Sail out of the smart and sheltered harbour of Santa Ponsa to join one of Europe's most popular yachting scenes. Charters and courses are available.*

### 4. Parc Natural Mondragó

*Kick back on these secluded beaches near Santanyí after your exertions. They all require a short hike down stony paths.*

### 5. Parc Natural de s'Albufera

*Bird-watch at these wetlands on the north coast, with more than 200 species, residents and visitors, to spot.*

**A Week**

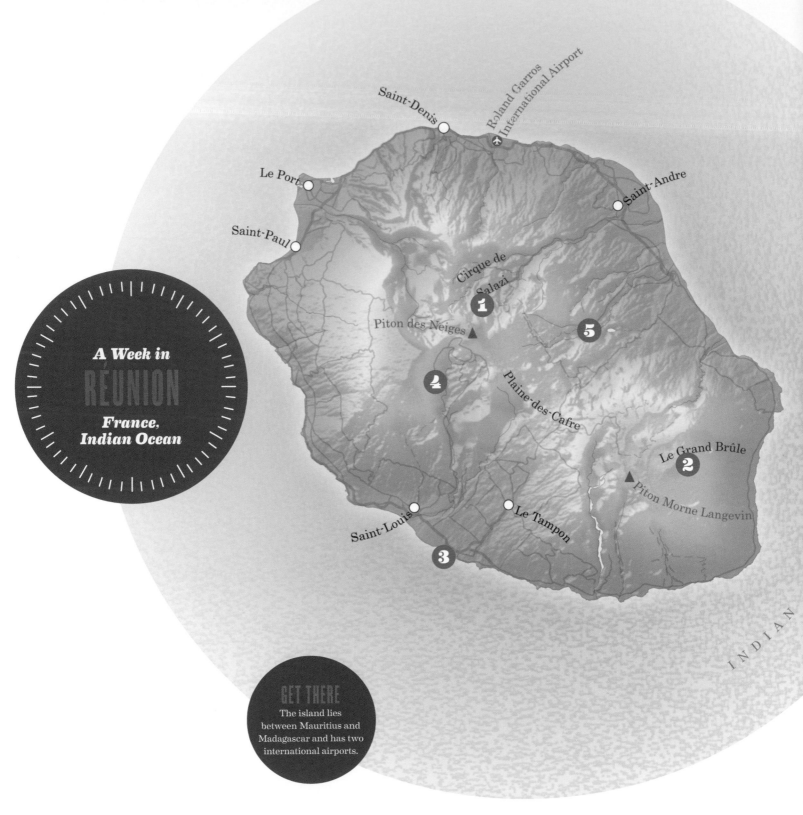

## A Week in RÉUNION
### France, Indian Ocean

Saint-Denis

Roland Garros International Airport

Le Port

Saint-Paul

Saint-André

Cirque de Salazi

**1**

Piton des Neiges ▲

**5**

**4**

Plaine-des-Cafre

Le Grand Brûle

**2**

Piton Morne Langevin ▲

Saint-Louis

Le Tampon

**3**

St Pierre

INDIAN

### GET THERE
The island lies between Mauritius and Madagascar and has two international airports.

### 1. Hell-Bourg
Go Creole in this pretty village on the island's east coast. Savour a cold beer in a shanty bar among Creole musicians.

### 2. Piton de la Fournaise
Climb this active volcano if it's not too lively. The 5hr trek up the loose, sun-scorched slopes is challenging but looking down into the crater and across the Indian Ocean is worth the effort.

### 3. St Pierre
Party in Réunion's third-largest town, in the island's southwest, which pulses with an hedonistic energy after dark.

### 4. Cirque de Cilaos
Hike in the spectacular setting of a steep, volcanic crest. There's a variety of canyoning trips in these snaggle-toothed peaks where you'll be climbing, abseiling and simply sliding down the slopes.

### 5. Grand Étang
Horse ride around the largest lake on Réunion. It's a low-impact way to soak up the drop-dead gorgeous scenery. Horseback trips into the interior can last a few hours or several days.

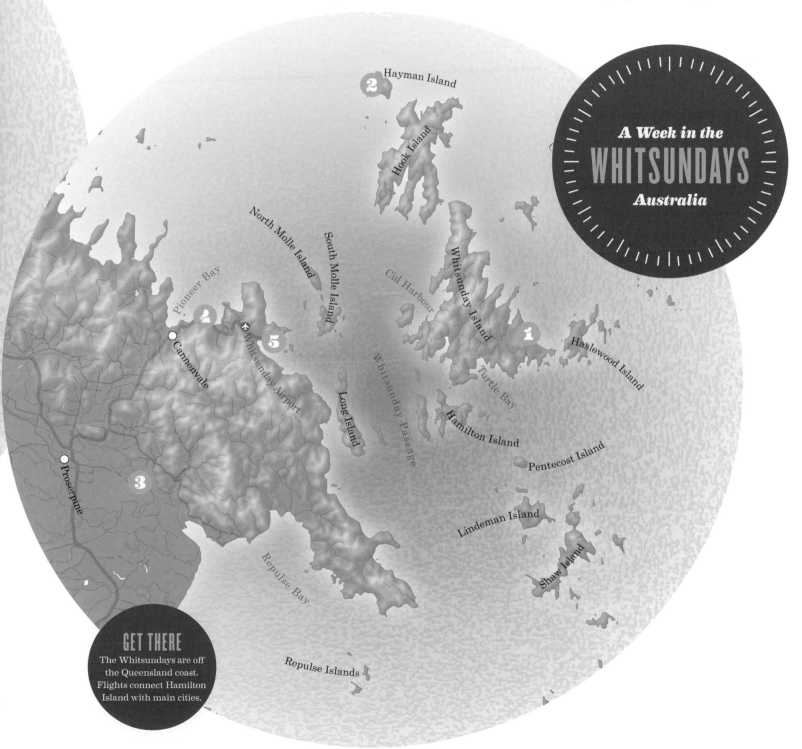

### 1. Whitehaven beach

*Beach comb on what is considered one of the greatest beaches in the world, thanks to its talcum-powder fine sand.*

### 2. Blue Pearl Bay, Hayman Island

*Scuba dive at Hayman Island, one of the 74 islands in the Whitsunday archipelago and a top diving destination.*

### 3. Proserpine River

*Spot saltwater crocs – and other Aussie critters – in these estuaries on a crocodile safari departing from Airlie Beach.*

### 4. Airlie Beach

*Learn to sail a yacht or start a bareboating trip at Airlie Beach, home of the Whitsunday Sailing Club. Sailing is the heart and soul of the Whitsundays.*

### 5. Shute Harbour

*Set out in sea kayaks from Shute Harbour to paddle your way through glassy waters from bay to bay, watching out for whales, dolphins and turtles.*

## A Week in the
# WHITSUNDAYS
### Australia

Hayman Island

Hook Island

North Molle Island

South Molle Island

Pioneer Bay

Whitsunday Island

Cid Harbour

Haslewood Island

Cannonvale

Whitsunday Airport

Turtle Bay

Whitsunday Passage

Long Island

Hamilton Island

Proserpine

Pentecost Island

Lindeman Island

Repulse Bay

Shaw Island

Repulse Islands

### GET THERE

The Whitsundays are off the Queensland coast. Flights connect Hamilton Island with main cities.

# BE BLOWN AWAY BY BIRDS

ARMED WITH CAMERA AND BINOCULARS, SEEK OUT THE CAPTIVATINGLY CURIOUS, THE BOLD, AND THE BEAUTIFUL OF THE BIRD WORLD. TIME IT RIGHT AND YOU'LL SEE FEATHERED SHOWS YOU'LL NEVER FORGET.

**The grit and grind of Papua New Guinea's capital,** Port Moresby, slowly recede as you bump along Sogeri Rd and exalt in a taste of the lush countryside, the sun lazily rising. This isolated archipelago may be a more challenging destination than most, but you're here for the unrivalled natural habitat and enviable array of birdlife. You turn off and head into the rugged Varirata National Park. As soon as you enter, birds call out their greetings and you catch a glimpse of a flycatcher, while a lorikeet flaps through the branches above you and off into the blue sky. You dive further into the park and along a slightly treacherous trail, before spotting the stars of this show – the Raggiana birds of paradise.

You hold your breath as these feathered fornicators begin their unabashed displays of avian affection. Plumes are swept, heart-stopping colours flashed and *amore* professed through a series of leaps, bounds and the spreading of wings, like the opening of ornamental fans.

With the sun now high overhead, you do your best not to crash back through the undergrowth. Taking a moment to pause, you quietly gasp as you spot a dwarf cassowary, its horny casque protruding as it stalks out of the rainforest, heading, it seems, directly for you with its gnarly toes and shimmering black plumage.

You hike on for spectacular views of the surrounding countryside and the Port Moresby area, vowing to return tomorrow for more glimpses of the exotic and the little-seen of the bird world. ●

A BLACK PALM COCKATOO, A NATIVE OF PAPUA NEW GUINEA   Getty/Frans Lanting

RUFOUS-TAILED HUMMINGBIRD, ECUADOR   Jonathan Gregroy

# BE BLOWN AWAY BY BIRDS

### Ecuador
Home to over 1500 species, Ecuador has a huge diversity of birdlife. The rainbow-coloured beaks of treetop-dwelling toucans are often best spotted from boats on the river, where you'll also catch blue and yellow macaws, whose clumsy antics and raucous music provide plenty of entertainment.

### Danube Delta, Romania
This network of channels, lagoons, reed islands, woods and pastures on the Black Sea coast is a natural wonderland, offering an up-close view of thousands of pelicans, herons, ibis, ducks, warblers and white-tailed eagles. Areas of the wetlands are only accessible by kayak or rowboat, from where you can watch the wildlife a mere arm's length away.

### Kruger National Park, South Africa
Better known for the 'big five' of wild animals, Kruger is also the place to spot South Africa's 'big-six' birds – the southern ground hornbill, Pel's fishing-owl, lappet-faced vulture, saddle-billed stork, martial eagle and the kori bustard. Just as thrilling are the ostriches streaking across the savannah.

### Queensland, Australia
Australia's isolation has evolved some unusual birds. The kookaburra sounds like it's laughing, while the lyrebird sounds like any noise it chooses to mimic. Then there's the flightless emu – the world's second largest bird after the ostrich; and an array of brilliantly coloured parrots. One place you're sure to encounter them all is Currumbin Wildlife Sanctuary in Queensland, where flocks of friendly lorikeets are a hallmark attraction.

# HOUSE SWAP

*Whether you'd like to stay in a clapboard house in San Francisco, a cosy stone cottage in England's Cotswolds or an airy French apartment in Paris, specialist home-swap agencies will be able to hook you up with someone who owns one. The advantage of home-swapping, aside from the low cost (typically you pay for travel and living expenses) is that you have an immediate introduction to a neighbourhood and the opportunity to live like a local, if only for a week or two. The downside? You'll have to clean two houses…*

KEEP CLEA

A Week

# Seeing

## is

### believing

**EMILY MATCHAR FINDS TRUTH IS STRANGER THAN FICTION**

**S**o many of the things that capture our childhood imaginations – unicorns, fairies, Santa Claus – sadly don't exist in the real world. But some things we assume to be mythical are in fact quite real.

Remember Glo Friends? Those glow-in-the-dark toys that lived together in the magical forest kingdom of Glo Land. Well Glo Land might not actually exist, but glow-worms really do. In New Zealand (a magical place in its own right) the Waitomo Glowworm Caves feature a large population of Arachnocampa luminosa, which radiate an eerie blue light. Ride a boat through the subterranean grotto, where these curious insects cling to the ceiling, twinkling like strange stars.

Pink dolphins might sounds like they belong firmly in a world of make-believe, but the bubble-gum-hued marine mammals are just as real as the more prosaic grey variety. In the Hong Kong fishing village of Tai O, locals will take you on small boat trips in search of the pink-tinted Chinese white dolphins, which have become increasingly rare in recent years. A surer bet is a visit to the Cambodian town of Kratie, where pink dolphins still frolic in the river.

If you believe hobbits don't exist outside Middle Earth, we understand. But allow us to present *Homo floresiensis*, nicknamed 'the hobbit', an extinct species of hominid whose bones were discovered in Indonesia in 2003. The hobbit was about 1m tall, and may have lived up until only 12,000 years ago.

Certain cities have always had the ring of the mythical about them. Take Troy. You probably read about it at school in *The Iliad*, not realising it was real. To be fair, neither did most historians, until archaeologists located its ruins in the Anatolia region of present-day Turkey in the 1870s. Visit the site to gaze upon the walls of the ruined acropolis that played such a huge part in civilization's founding.

These are just a few examples of the 'mythical' in real life. But the real fun is finding out for yourself. Believe in Atlantis? Visit Bimini in the Bahamas or the Greek island of Santorini, both hypothesized locations of the legendary sunken city. Think Bigfoot might be real? Camp out in the Pacific Northwest with your night-vision goggles and report back. As they say, sometimes truth is stranger than fiction. ●

Certain cities have always had the ring of the mythical about them. Take Troy. You probably read about it at school in *The Iliad,* not realising it was real.

# MARVELLOUS MONASTERIES

**GO BACK TO BASICS AND EXPERIENCE THE SERENITY OF AN AMAZING MONASTERY; SOME YOU CAN STAY IN AND OTHERS WILL EVEN SELL YOU BEER.**

**B**hutan's famous Taktshang Goemba, or Tiger's Nest, monastery was built at the place where Guru Rinpoche – one of the country's favourite religious figures – is said to have arrived on the back of a consort he'd transformed into a flying tigress. Legend tells that he went on to subdue a local demon before spending three months here meditating in a cave.

There are no flying tigers for you, just a stroll up the well-made path from a car park a couple of hours below, or a two-day hike across the craggy spines of the surrounding mountains that follows part of a smuggler's trail that continues to Tibet. The trail passes through cloud forests draped with tendrils of moss, over ridges where trees have been contorted sideways by the prevailing winds and eagles drift far above. At night you'll shelter in tents established by the Uma Paro hotel on a high plateau before setting off for the monastery at first light.

Ahead is the Tiger's Nest, a shimmering monument with golden pinnacles to its rooftops set over stark, whitewashed walls that somehow cling to the cliff face. From the path where pilgrims gather to look on in awe, ropes bearing prayer flags in a rainbow of colours are strung over a deep gorge towards the monastery. It's a sight that will stay with you forever – and the Tiger's Nest isn't the only monastery where you don't have to be a devotee to share in their unique atmosphere. ●

  **1**

### St Sixtus Abbey, Belgium
Here, silent monks of the Trappist order brew Westvleteren 12, a revered beer available in limited quantities only at the abbey itself by prior appointment. That doesn't dissuade beer-loving pilgrims from visiting Belgium's six Trappist breweries.

 **2**

### Santuari de Sant Salvador, Mallorca
On the Spanish island of Mallorca around a dozen monasteries offer accommodation. One of the most sublime, the Santuari de Sant Salvador, sits on a hill outside the southeastern town of Felanitx. It's comfortable, the food is good and you're far from Mallorca's crowds.

 **3**

### Kopan Monastery, Nepal
Kopan, on the outskirts of Kathmandu, is one of the best places in the Himalaya to learn the basics of meditation and Tibetan Buddhism. The seven-day or 10-day courses are usually given by foreign teachers. A popular one-month course is held in November.

 **4**

### San Giorgio Maggiore, Italy
Venice is not known for its tranquillity but that's exactly what you'll find at this 16th-century Benedictine monastery on a secluded island. Accommodation is spartan but how many hotels have Tintorettos? From the bell tower there are beautiful views of St Mark's Basilica.

**A Week**

# WALK THIS WAY

**BREAK LONG-DISTANCE WALKS INTO BITE-SIZE PIECES TO MAKE THEM A WEEK-LONG ENDEAVOUR.**

***Where the land runs out is a wild place,*** where the cliffs are the prows of ships, enduring the battering tides. This is where Wales meets the Celtic Sea and, since 2012, hikers have been able to witness this alchemical transition from solid to liquid along the 1400km-long Wales Coast Path, the first trail to follow a country's entire coastline.

But there's no rule that says you have to walk the whole path in one go. Instead, savour sections at a time and return to forge another link in the chain. Many of the best sections take in the Gower's beautiful beaches, Pembrokeshire's multicoloured cliffs and limestone arches, the remote edges of the Llŷn Peninsula and the ancient vistas of Anglesey.

For a taste, take a ramble along the dramatic Marloes Peninsula in the far southwest of Pembrokeshire just across St Bride's Bay from the diminutive city of St Davids. The Coast Path skirts the yawn of St Bride's Bay in a long curve that runs between fields and the coves, cliffs and beaches, all the way from St David's Head in the north to Skomer Island in the south. So begins one of the most beautiful walks in all Wales; on a clear day, you'll see the whole western tip of Wales.

For the most remote section of the Pembrokeshire coast, continue north to Strumble Head and the path to Cardigan – and don't skip the special section of path on Pen Anglas headland that is designed to be walked barefoot, with soft peat underfoot. ●

THE WALES COAST PATH AT ST BRIDE'S BAY Pete Seaward

A Week

A MOUNTAIN HUT IN THE PYRENEES  Lottie Davies

WALK
THIS
WAY

 **1**

### Appalachian Trail, USA

*The nation's longest footpath is over 3000km long, crosses six national parks and slices through 14 states from Georgia to Maine. Deep woods, alpine peaks, cow-dotted farms, and foraging bears are all part of the landscape. It's estimated that two to three million people trek a portion of the trail every year. Fewer than 600 hikers persevere all the way through, taking around six months: but if Bill Bryson can do it, so can you.*

 **2**

### Via Dinarica, The Balkans

*Three contrasting routes form the newly established Via Dinarica, which splices together historic trails through the Dinaric Alps from Albania to Slovenia. You can go via the coast, hike over the mountains (the 965km-long White Trail) or through forested foothills (for cyclists). It's an ambitious undertaking: the trail passes through Kosovo, Montenegro, Bosnia & Hercegovina, Serbia before arriving at Slovenia's highest peak.*

 **3**

### The Lycian Way, Turkey

*Southern Turkey's coast is outlined by the 530km-long Lycian Way, which follows Greek and Roman roads and aqueducts and traditional herders' trails along cliffs, around coves and through forests of pine and cedar. Lots of the local villages are set up for travellers so it's easy to piece together short hops between them at the outset from Fethiye: it becomes more remote the further you go.*

 **4**

### Pyrenean Haute Route, Spain & France

*This is a walking route between two seas and two countries. It weaves across the high-altitude border between France and Spain, climbing and descending (and climbing again) the steep and sometimes exposed slopes of the Pyrenees; there will be snow on some of the peaks well into summer. But plenty of hospitable villages mean that this 800km trail can be divided into week-long portions.*

# INDULGE IN ART

*Certain cities, even museums, demand more of your time than a rushed afternoon with the hordes. Florence's Uffizi museum, for example, has work by Caravaggio and Leonardo de Vinci hanging in its 16th-century halls. In Madrid's Prado you'll find Bosch, Velásquez and Goya. New York's Metropolitan Museum of Art has an all-encompassing collection ranging from Jackson Pollock to medieval armour. Arrive early on a midweek morning, or just before closing time to appreciate specific works with fewer people in the way; and return to see others at another time.*

THE DUOMO, BASILICA DI SANTA MARIA DEL FIORE, FLORENCE.  Justin Foulkes

**A Week**

A TIGER AT BANDHAVGARH NATIONAL PARK, INDIA    Mark Read

# NOW OR NEVER

**DON'T DELAY! SEE A TIGER OR A RHINO, A RARE FLOWER OR EVEN A GLACIER BEFORE THEY EXIST ONLY IN PHOTOGRAPHS.**

**D**id those grasses just move? And is that a long stripy tail? There's a hush in the jeep as you and the rest of the early-morning tiger-spotters wait to see what if anything emerges from the edge of the forest. Then the owner of an unmistakeable pair of white-furred ears and an enormously long back rises and slinks away into the shadows, vanishing in the bars of light and darkness. Now you see him, now you don't. The group exhales.

You're in Bandhavgarh National Park in Madhya Pradesh, India and what you've just glimpsed is a Bengal tiger, the most numerous of all the tiger species. But when you know that there are just 3000 tigers of all species surviving in the wild across the Asian subcontinent, your elation at having seen one of nature's most majestic creatures will be tempered by sorrow. Bandhavgarh NP is one of the places in India where you are most likely to see a tiger (Pench National Park, also in Madhya Pradesh, is another). But every day India's handful of remaining tigers are at risk from poachers. Elsewhere the situation is worse; there are just 500 Sumatran tigers left.

Tiger-spotting tours are one way of raising awareness and funds for conservation efforts but with demand from China for tiger parts, it's hard to see how they'll thrive again. As Joni Mitchell sang, 'you don't know what you've got 'til it's gone'. ●

### 1
#### Glacier National Park, USA
Of course, Montana's Glacier National Park isn't going anywhere. But its name might need to be changed. Projections suggest that many of the park's glaciers will disappear over the next 20 years, as are many glaciers in the Himalaya and the Andes. It's a slow process that will impact many of the park's species.

### 2
#### Black rhino, Namibia
Of all the animals critically endangered by poaching for body parts, the black rhino is perhaps the most vulnerable. They're short-sighted, easy to track and have a very slow breeding cycle. There are fewer than 5000 left, with Namibia being the species' last, carefully protected stronghold.

### 3
#### Land art, worldwide
Transitory by its nature, land art uses the natural world as a canvas for artworks such as Andy Goldsworthy's sculptures, Robert Smithson's earthworks, which are affected by time and the elements, or Walter de Maria's Lightning Field in New Mexico, which is an array of 400 steel poles over 1.5 sq km.

### 4
#### The ghost orchid, Wales
Orchids, the more elusive the better, would drive plant-hunters to the far corners of the earth. One of the most fleeting sights is the pink bloom of the leafless ghost orchid, which spends most of its life underground. The National Museum of Wales in Cardiff has an extremely precious collection of these flowers.

**A Week**

# REAL LIFE STORY

**FEW EXPERIENCES BRING A BOOK TO LIFE
AS READING IT IN THE PLACE IT IS SET.**

'**In those grand stone buildings** they could bankrupt or hang you as they pleased. They had a courthouse and prison and hospital plus four banks and two breweries and 15 hotels.' So writes Peter Carey, describing the Australian town of Beechworth in the voice of the outlaw Ned Kelly. The book is Carey's award-winning novel *True History of the Kelly Gang*, which follows the fortunes of the lanky 19th-century bushranger as he grows up in the frontier land of Victoria and gets to know every ridge and creek before his demise in Melbourne Gaol at the end of a hangman's rope in 1880.

Beechworth is still a vibrant country town; the prison is being converted into apartments and there's just the one brewery now but it's a good one, serving homemade pizza and beer at weekends. You can sit outside, turning the pages and recognising the places: at Beechworth's Imperial Hotel Kelly boxes Isaiah 'Wild' Wright, he follows the Ovens river south of Beechworth and has his first showdown with police at Stringybark Creek – 'On the ridges the mountain ash gleamed like saints against the massing clouds but down here the crows and currawongs was gloomy their cries dark with murder.' But it's not only the book that is illuminated by its setting; Carey's words help this beautiful corner of Australia live on in the imagination; as Kelly's mentor, Harry Power, says 'If you know the country ... then you will be a wild colonial boy forever.' ●

BEECHWORTH POSTOFFICE, VICTORIA, AUSTRALIA   Getty/Glenn Beanland

**The Snow Leopard, the Himalayas**
*In a remote corner of the Tibetan plateau northwest of Dhaulagiri called Dolpo, Peter Matthiessen seeks to come to terms with nothing less than life and death as he hikes the sheep tracks of these Himalayan ridges and ravines.*

**A River Runs Through It, USA**
*Norman Maclean's short story, set in the 1930s, is about family and love and art and the passing of time itself. The cold, fast-flowing Blackfoot River in western Montana is the backdrop for this soulful American classic.*

**Ulysses, Ireland**
*James Joyce's Ulysses, published in 1922, is set during the passage of a single day in Dublin (16 June, 1904) and that day now sees an annual reenactment of scenes from the epic novel in landmarks across the city, known as Bloomsday, after Joyce's hero, Leopold Bloom.*

**The Beach, Thailand**
*From the backpacker holding bay of Bangkok's Khao San Road to the eponymous beach paradise, via Ko Samui and Ko Pha-Ngan, Alex Garland's mid-1990s novel remains a compelling picture of Thailand.*

**A Week**

# MAKE UP YOUR OWN MIND

*One of the great lessons of travel is that situations evolve, and people and places change. Borders can open as well as close. And sometimes there are difficult decisions to make, such as whether to travel to countries such as Myanmar. The only answer is be informed, to travel responsibly and to make up your own mind.*

SHWEDAGON PAGODA, YANGON, MYANMAR    Matt Munro

**A Week**

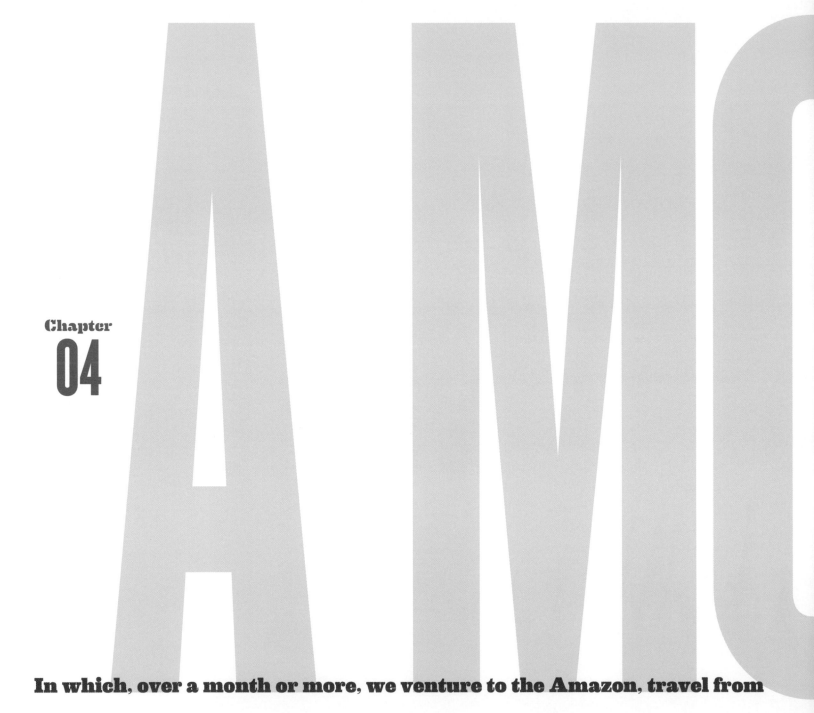

**Chapter**
**04**

In which, over a month or more, we venture to the Amazon, travel from

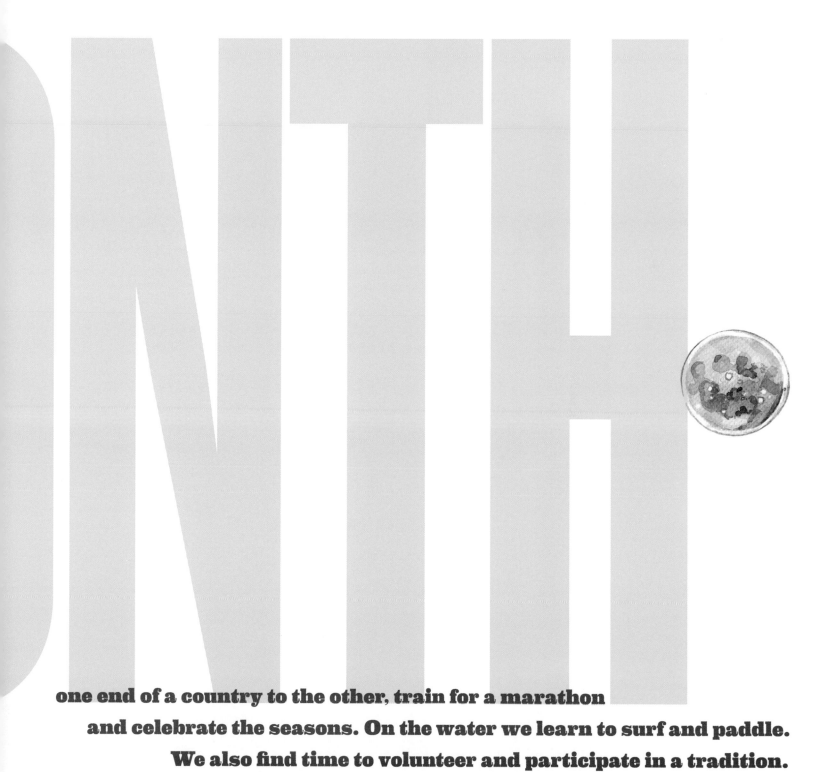

ONTH

one end of a country to the other, train for a marathon
and celebrate the seasons. On the water we learn to surf and paddle.
We also find time to volunteer and participate in a tradition.
And to escape it all, we travel solo and build a log cabin in the wilds.

**A Month**

**Chapter**

# 04

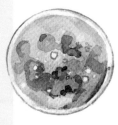

# STOWAWAY ON A SHIP

**NOT ALL CRUISES ARE ABOUT AQUA-AEROBICS AND CABARET. HITCH A RIDE ON A CONTAINER SHIP AND YOU'LL SEE PARTS OF THE WORLD FEW HAVE LAID EYES ON.**

**S**tanding on the deck of the **MV ISA**, watching the chalky coastline of southern England sliding past the tanker's starboard bow, you wonder where this leviathan of a boat is really heading. You're aboard one of the world's last true tramp ships – a vessel whose final destination is unknown, even to its crew, a raggle-taggle bunch who you'll be breaking bread with at the captain's table for the next 30 evenings at least.

You're one of two passengers who joined the boat just before departure from the Dutch port of IJmuiden, but you know as much about where you're going as the sailors who steer her. One thing is sure – you will cross the Atlantic twice. The outbound voyage will take you west from Land's End, across the open ocean until the ship passes between Nova Scotia and Newfoundland and into the embrace of the Gulf of St Lawrence. From here you'll sail along the St Lawrence River, past Québec and Montreal and into the Great Lakes. After skirting the shores of New York State and crossing the inland seas of lakes Ontario, Erie and Huron, you'll finally arrive at Thunder Bay on the banks of Lake Superior, where the tanker will be loaded with a precious cargo of grain from the prairies.

And it is this load that will determine where you end up after making the return trip across the Atlantic. Depending on who flashes the most cash, you might end up in Morocco, or Turkey, Italy, Spain, Norway, Poland or even Russia. For now, though, you're happy to stroll the length of two football pitches along the deck, daydreaming of the adventure to come. ●

**A Month**

CROSSING PANAMA BY CONTAINER SHIP   Getty/Will&Demi McIntyre

# STOWAWAY ON A SHIP

 **1**

### Big-Apple bobbing
*This is how to arrive in the US – sailing past Ellis Island and the Statue of Liberty right into the core of the Big Apple. Maris Freighter Cruises take eight landlubbers on each trip the Hanjin San Diego makes from Europe to the US. You board in the Mediterranean port of La Spezia in Italy, and travel via Genoa, Fos sur Mer (France), Barcelona, Valencia and Algeciras in Spain, before spending 10 days crossing the North Atlantic to arrive in New York.*

**2**

### Panama hat-trick
*Just three passengers get to hop a ride on the Hamburg Süd-operated freighter that leaves Philadelphia and goes to Cartagena, on Colombia's Caribbean coast, before passing through the Panama Canal. From Balboa, you'll experience the agoraphobia-inducing enormity of the South Pacific Ocean before next making landfall in Auckland, New Zealand, some 28 days into the cruise. Next stops are Sydney and then Melbourne, Australia.*

 **3**

### Hunting the Snark
*A tropical freighter-cruise can be had on the Aranui, a mixed-purpose passenger and cargo ship that works the waters of the Pacific Ocean between Tahiti and the Marquesas Islands. The Aranui accommodates 200 people and offers more comfort than your standard freighter, with air-conditioning and a swimming pool, where you sip cocktails as the boat bounces between the islands of the Marquesas, in the wake of Jack London's Snark.*

 **4**

### Suez me
*Sailing out of Southampton in Britain, CMA CGM Cargo Cruises offer limited bunks on its EPIC (Europe Pakistan India Consortium) boats, which head down the coasts of France and Spain, before rounding the Rock of Gibraltar and entering the Mediterranean. At the eastern end of the Med, you pass through the Suez Canal and call at ports in the United Arab Emirates before crossing the Arabian Sea to either India or Pakistan.*

# PLAY MORE!

*It's a happy talent to know how to play.'* Ralph Waldo Emerson

**Play reduces stress, makes us smarter, helps us solve problems and reinforces bonds. So, wherever you may be, at least once a month ensure that you go fly a kite, climb a tree or make a snow angel.**

**A Month**

# BUILD A CABIN OF YOUR OWN

**WE ALL NEED A LITTLE BREATHING SPACE. HEAD TO THE WOODS OF MINNESOTA TO LEARN HOW TO BUILD A RETREAT OF YOUR OWN.**

**F**ew people can have read **Walden** by Henry David Thoreau, who built and lived in a 10 x 15ft cabin in Concord, Massachusetts in 1845, and not contemplated the idea half-seriously: a cabin of one's own in a sunlit glade somewhere far from the asphalt world. (In fact, Thoreau's hut was on the edge of town on land owned by his friend Ralph Waldo Emerson and he was never more than a short walk from a hot bath, or a cold one in Walden Pond.) Thoreau made it look easy; his cabin's frame went up in May and it was ready to be inhabited in July. For more than two years Thoreau came and went from the woods - as he writes 'I wished to live deliberately, to front only the essentials of life'.

For your first log cabin you'd be best advised to gain some professional tuition. The Great Lakes School of Log-Building and Stonemasonry in Minnesota, 2500km west of Massachusetts, has almost 40 years of experience in teaching first-timers how to keep their walls straight and their roofs watertight. You'll learn how to select and prepare logs, level a site, install windows and a door, make a roof truss and use sharp tools safely – don't forget to bring your own Gransfors-Bruks axe. To test your new skills and kick back on your own hand-built porch like a frontiersman or woman you'll need about six months, power tools, a plot of land – and a lot of logs. ●

### 1
### Friggebod, Sweden
Since 1979, Sweden's building code has permitted the construction of buildings of less than 90 sq ft without a permit. These bijoux boxes are called friggebods and typically found on family-owned plots in the wilds, overlooking lakes. Some are available to rent but you're better calling on any Swedish connections you have.

### 2
### Bach, New Zealand
You don't have to go far in New Zealand to escape the crowds and the traditional Kiwi holiday home, known as a 'bach' (pronounced batch), is often near a favourite (secret) beach or a trout-fishing river. Many have a hand-built, hand-me-down look but there are plenty of modern designs available to rent through agencies.

### 3
### Shepherd's hut, France & Spain
Traditional shepherds in the Pyrenees didn't have an easy job, spending weeks alone in the mountains, warding off bears and wolves. But when the weather turned nasty they had cosy stone refuges to retreat into. Known as an orri in the eastern Pyrenees, many still stand and offer shelter to hikers who venture off the beaten track.

### 4
### Bothy, Scotland
Pull on your hiking boots and grab your Gore-Tex to seek out the Scottish interpretation of a mountain hut – the bothy. The Mountain Bothy Association maintains around 100 shelters in the most popular parts of the Highlands but there are many more located in less frequented glens, which are carefully guarded secrets. As the MBA says, you need to be proficient in using a map and compass.

**A Month**

**1**

### Stevenson Trail, France

The 252km Stevenson Trail (or GR70) runs from Monastier-sur-Gazeille to St Jean de Gard, following the path paced by Scottish writer Robert Louis Stevenson and his donkey Modestine in 1878. The countryside of the Auvergne, Cevennes and Languedoc-Roussillon is still magical; taking a mule is optional.

**2**

### Great Railway Bazaar, Asia

In 1975 writer Paul Theroux travelled by train from London to Tokyo and back, a chug that included some epic rails: the Orient Express, Frontier Mail, Khyber Pass Local, Trans-Siberian. He revisited the route in 2008: some tracks are no longer accessible and some areas have opened up, but the journey remains a classic.

**3**

### Priscilla, Australia

The most flamboyant tyre tracks to follow are those of Priscilla, Queen of the Desert. In the eponymous movie, this shiny tour bus transports three drag queens from Sydney to Alice Springs via red, raw and not-entirely-enlightened Outback Australia. Must-stops include Broken Hill, Coober Pedy and plunging King's Canyon.

# FOLLOW IN FAMOUS FOOTSTEPS

**YOU COULD BEAT A NEW PATH, BUT THERE'S MORE ALLURE IN THE PURSUIT OF POETS AND ADVENTURERS. RETRACE A GRAND TOUR TO EXPERIENCE THESE FAMOUS JOURNEYS.**

**Y**ou're setting off from Buenos Aires on a wheezy motorbike – just as Ernesto 'Che' Guevara and his friend Alberto Granado did, in 1952. These are eminent dust trails to follow: it was on this 9-month ride around South America that the charismatic revolutionary learned about his continent and formed many of his beliefs. As you purr southwards across the pampas, warm air buffeting your face, the thrum of the engine beneath, you start to sense how such a journey could change a person. The freedom! The adventure! And, simply, a damn fine ride.

Indeed, the route is epic – from BA, Che crossed Argentina, and then traversed Chile, Peru, Ecuador, Colombia, Venezuela and Panama. His ride linked the sparkling Patagonian lakes and the Inca wonder of Machu Picchu, the communities of the Amazon rainforest and thriving cities such as Lima and Bogotá.

Che did a lot of thinking on his journey – and you find yourself doing the same. On the bike, though moving at speed, you feel a part of the world, in tune with its weather and winds, more able to stop quickly at that Indian village, roadside fruit stall, Andean lookout. And you have the time and clarity to ruminate on all that you see. At night, with a pen in one hand, and a battered copy of Che's *The Motorcycle Diaries* at your side, you may well start to write your own magnum opus. ●

**Patrick Leigh Fermor's Europe**
In 1933, aged just 18, Patrick Leigh Fermor set off to walk from the Hook of Holland to Constantinople, variously staying with shepherds and nobles on his way across the continent. His books about the journey – A Time of Gifts and Between the Woods and the Water – provide inspirational guides.

# CATCH THE SLEEPER TRAIN

**SLOW DOWN AND TAKE THE INDIAN PACIFIC ACROSS AUSTRALIA, ONE OF THE WORLD'S GREAT TRANSCONTINENTAL TRAIN JOURNEYS.**

**The first European to cross the Nullarbor Plain,** was Edward John Eyre in 1841. He described it as 'the sort of place one gets into in bad dreams'. On board the *Indian Pacific* train from Sydney to Perth, via the disconcertingly flat Nullarbor, your dreams will hopefully be happier than Eyre's as you're lulled to sleep by the rhythmic chugging of the train on its three-night journey westward.

After embarking in Sydney's grand sandstone Central Station, the *Indian Pacific* forges a leisurely path over the Blue Mountains, past ancient ochre gorges and rock formations, before descending into the fertile Murray-Darling Basin. You're on the way to Adelaide, South Australia's cultural capital where you can hop off the *Indian Pacific* and explore the wine regions of the Barossa Valley and the Adelaide Hills before rejoining the train for next two-thirds of the trip: the Nullarbor.

Few experiences put Australia's mind-numbing scale into perspective – although the *Indian Pacific* is by no means a fast train, for hour after hour, and all through the night, it trundles through a stunning empty landscape. You'll spot hawks circling above, perhaps kangaroos, but mostly there's just the Outback and your own thoughts. ●

THE INDIAN PACIFIC AT BATHURST STATION, NEW SOUTH WALES   Matt Munro

### California Zephyr, USA
*The Zephyr lives up to its evocative name. Running daily between Chicago and San Francisco, two of the most vibrant cities in the US, this sleeper train crosses the Rockies, slices through hostile deserts and finds a way over the Sierra Nevadas during its 3900km journey. Like the nation's pioneers, travel westward for the best sunset views. The train takes 51 hours but why not stop for a while in Colorado and Utah?*

 **②**

### The Trans-Siberian, Russia, Mongolia & China

*This is the warmly wrapped grandaddy of sleeper trains: a journey on the Trans-Siberian can take in Moscow's Red Square, Beijing's Forbidden City, the Great Wall, icy Lake Baikal and Mongolia's panoramic steppes, depending on the route you select. Most who ride the train hop on and off wherever they fancy along the 9000km route. What better way to arrive in Ulaanbaatar?*

 **③**

### The Blue Train, South Africa

*For 27 hours the endless African veldt rolls effortlessly past your window as your travel in luxury from Pretoria to Cape Town. Yes, the Blue Train is not your average sleeper service; no tired sandwiches and threadbare recliners here: the 84 passengers enjoy the attention of a butler, gold fixtures in the ensuite bathrooms and a wildlife documentary unspooling outside.*

 **④**

### Milan to Palermo, Italy

*Trenitalia's sleeper service from Milan to Palermo, the No.785 service, was recently threatened with closure. This would have been a tragedy: this night route from northern Italy to Sicily is one of the world's classics. Part party-train, part sightseeing tour of Italy's spine, you leave Milan at supper time and arrive in Palermo late the following afternoon.*

**A Month**

你還記得那種什麼都不能理解的感覺嗎？當話語只是噪音，只能憑音調聽出是肯定還是反對；當文字像是鬼畫符，無法明白筆劃的含義；當人們的動作看上去似乎很開心，卻茫然不知緣由。想象一下那種感覺。漠然——是的。無助——也許。但你連自己不知道的是什麼都不知道！

不必害怕這種感覺，解決之道一直都在。你需要去旅行。

首先，列出一串書面語中不使用羅馬字母的國家。然後開始甄選：你要找的是幾乎完全沒有英文或羅馬文字的國家（或地區），比如中國，韓國，俄羅斯，埃塞俄比亞。不要呆在大城市，但也不需要走太遠，離首都一小時車程的地方就很好。然後，就⋯⋯漫步。

走得離你的住處越遠越好。搭一輛巴士。在人群中跌跌撞撞。保持微笑。生命只有一次，但一瞬間你就能變回孩子⋯⋯

**BEN HANDICOTT CROSSES THE
LANGUAGE BARRIER IN CHINA**

**I**t's *New Year's Eve*, you're in a regional city in China. The roads are busy with cars the way department stores are with people at the sales. There's little movement though, just a great deal of noise. You shuffle along the street, a path of neon and people, so many people. Amid the throng, you move as a tide, inevitable and unstoppable. Vendors selling balloons or steamed buns push through, attracting the hungry and annoying the many.

In two hours of shunting along like this, you don't say a word. And you don't understand a word. Everyone is intent on making their way to wherever. No-one gives you a second look. Words fly meaninglessly around you, banners and signs are majestically unreadable. Everything is more or less familiar – people, streets, business, eating, laughter – but the overwhelming sense of confusion, of exclusion, leaves you with no touchstone at all. There's a mild

sense of panic. You can't ask anybody a question. You can't read anything except the occasional brand name on a billboard.

The crowd stirs; something has been communicated. There's a lull and people stop moving. Then a flash and as you look up, a clap like thunder. A booming salvo of fireworks. A noise of equal strength rises from the city as people cheer, then the fireworks retort. Clouds of smoke grow and confetti drifts above you. An hour of strobing light – gold, red and green lacework against the night, and the constant barrage of explosions; it's numbing. And then it stops and the elation of the crowd turns to fatigue. Beneath the orange glow of street lights, through the filtering smoke, colour is leeched from the banners and neon signs; all the brightness turn to sepia and as the crowds disperse, you head back the way you came, and no-one says a word. ●

 Can you remember not understanding anything? When words spoken were just noises, tones of approval (or not); written language just scribbles? Imagine that feeling. Unconcerned – surely. Helpless – maybe, but you don't know what you don't know!

Would it hurt to really tune out, to rediscover a sense of unconcern? Travel can give you this gift.

Make a list of countries that don't use roman script. And then refine it – you want countries (or parts of them) where English is not likely to be spoken at all, such as China. Don't stay in the main cities. You won't need to travel far – an hour from the capital will do it. Then just... wander.

Go as far as you can from your base. Catch a bus. Stumble through transactions. Smile. You might only live once but you can be a child again in a flash. ●

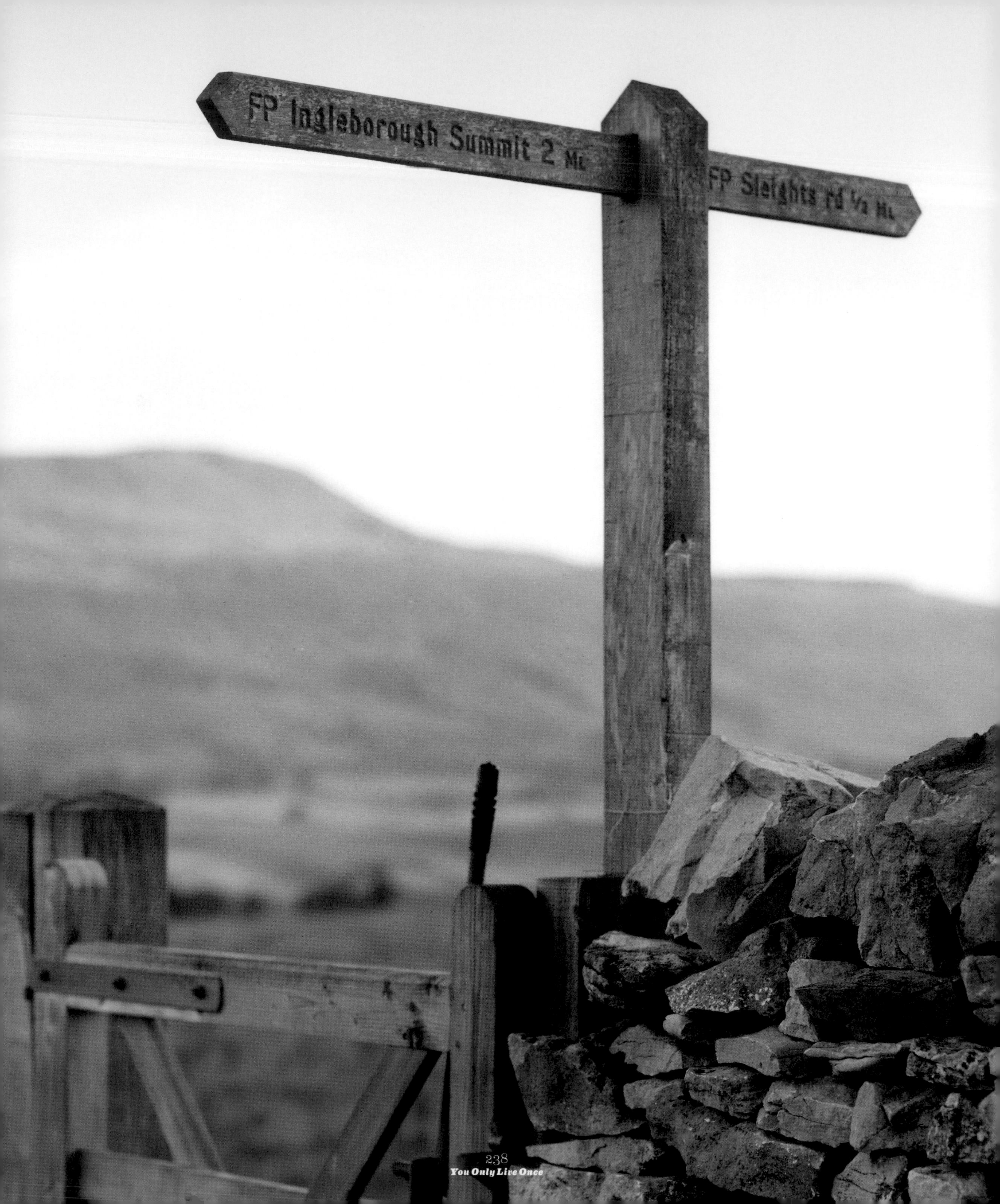
FP Ingleborough Summit 2 Ml
FP Sleights rd 1/2 Ml

# GO END TO END

**STARTING FROM ONE CORNER AND MAKING YOUR WAY TO THE OPPOSITE GUARANTEES A SENSE OF MENTAL, PHYSICAL AND CARTOGRAPHIC SATISFACTION.**

**Y**ou could have taken the short route – but where's the fun in that? Land's End in Cornwall to John O'Groats, in furthest northeast Scotland, is only 970km as the crow flies, or about 1400km by road. But as you're linking Great Britain's mainland extremes on foot, you didn't really fancy walking alongside the M5 motorway.

No, a more interesting top-to-toe journey, a more satisfying way to tackle this challenge, is away from the tarmac. By stringing together national trails, public footpaths and country lanes you have crossed some of the country's most beautiful spots: the wild coast to Exmoor, bits of the Cotswold Way, up the spine of the Pennines, along the Union Canal, through the Great Glen. Despite the fact that roughly 64 million people cluster on this crowded island, it's surprisingly easy to get away from most of them if you chose your route well.

And you've done just that. There are myriad options, but your hike has taken you via the best of British, from smugglers' coves to honey-stone villages, from peaks to lakes, dales to lochs, Wainwrights to Munros. Your limbs feel strong, your mind as free as that golden eagle whirling over the hills.

As you near that final sign that announces Scotland's wind-whipped end of the road, your blistered feet have been pounding for the best part of three months. You've covered around 2000km; you are spent yet have never felt more alive. As is essential, you pose by the post with the other tourists – who've had the cheek to get here by coach! Disappointment starts to bubble – as pilgrimage spots go, John O'Groats is a damp squib, dampened further by all these bus-lazy people. But then you remember that quote – was it TS Eliot? Buddha? Bob Marley?? – 'it's not the arrival that matters, but the joy of the journey'. ●

*A Month*

MOTORBIKING IN HANOI, VIETNAM    Getty/Rieger Bertrand

### Vietnam by Motorbike
*The Ho Chi Minh Trail, used to distribute supplies to the Vietcong during the Vietnam War, has been named 'one of the great achievements of military engineering of the 20th century'. Tackle its 1600km from Hanoi to near Saigon via neighbouring Laos by motorbike, for the ultimate Vietnamese end-to-end experience.*

### Te Araroa, New Zealand
*Opened in 2011, this 3000km hiking trail links Cape Reinga, at the north of the North Island, to Bluff, at the south of the South. Allow 120 days to do the total hike.*

### The Pan-American Highway
*There's around 48,000km of road (and one small blip) between northern Alaska and Argentina's Tierra del Fuego. In short, this is the mother of all road trips; bar a detour to negotiate Panama's Darién Gap, you can drive the entire length of the Americas.*

### Tour d'Afrique, Cairo to Cape Town
*Spend four months cycling through 10 countries to traverse a whole continent. You could do it solo, but more fun is the annual Tour d'Afrique, an epic race for riders of all abilities.*

# COMPLETE A MARATHON

**A CHALLENGE THAT TAKES MONTHS TO TRAIN FOR IS OVER IN A FEW MERCIFULLY SHORT HOURS. MAKE YOUR MARATHON MORE INTERESTING BY TAKING ON THESE FIVE FAR-FROM-ROUTINE RUNNING RACES.**

**Y**ou *don't know whether to high-five,* be sick, collapse or cheer. Big Ben looms ahead, but if it donged you wouldn't hear it over the roaring crowd, or the throbbing in your head. You're LESS THAN A MILE from completing the London Marathon. You're elated! But largely, physically, mentally broken.

And yet, you hobble on. Because, despite the agony, you know you're part of something huge. Humanity has swollen to more than the sum of its parts: the very best of people is on display, spectators and runners both. You round the Mall, see the finish, feel every sinew scream – but on you run. And you know you'll never be quite the same again.

ANY marathon changes you. But select one of these tough scenic races for the ultimate travel challenge. ●

# COMPLETE A
# MARATHON

## 1

### ANTARCTIC ICE MARATHON
#### ANTARCTICA

*The race:* Sub-zero temperatures, katabatic winds, slippy terrain, altitude-thinned air – as if 26.2 miles wasn't testing enough! But running in such pristine wilderness, where the only sound is the crunch of your own (weary) feet, is a privilege indeed.

#### *The stats*

*Coordinates:* 79°47'S, 82°53'W (Union Glacier Camp)
*When:* November
*Participants:* 40
*Profile:* Largely flat, but run at altitude (700m)
*Temperature:* -20°C
*Fee:* €10,500 (US$14,000)
*Distance to South Pole:* 1000km
*Average wind speed:* 10-25 knots
*Daylight:* 24hrs
*Probable calories burned:* 10,000
*Kit list:* Thermal top, fleece, outer windproof shell, long johns, windproof trousers, gloves, mittens, two pairs of woollen socks, neoprene toe covers, balaclava, facemask, hat, neck gaiter, goggles

## 2

### BIG SUR MARATHON
#### CALIFORNIA, USA

*The race:* The 26.2 miles from Big Sur Village to Carmel are prone to landslides, peasoupers and ocean-brewed storms. But they also follow Hwy 1, one of the world's most dramatic drives. Hard work, yes, but drop-dead gorgeous.

#### *The stats*

*Coordinates:* 36°6'N, 121°37'W (Big Sur)
*When:* April
*Participants:* 4500
*Profile:* Hilly, total ascent 300m, 13 hills in last 13 miles
*Temperature:* 10-15°C
*Fee:* US$150
*Porta Potties used:* 385
*Pre-race pasta party comprises:* 250lbs of pasta; 50 gallons of marinara sauce
*Proportion of waste material recycled or composted:* over 91%
*Economic impact of event:* $18 million
*Water supplied:* 1675 gallons at start and finish; 7575 gallons on course

## 3

### THE GREAT WALL MARATHON
#### CHINA

*The race:* Most of this route lies alongside China's beefy barricade, negotiating rice fields and remote villages in the Huangyaguan region. The section on the Wall itself is only 3.5km long but completed twice and malevolently memorable: 5164 punishingly steep steps.

#### *The stats*

*Coordinates:* 40°2'N, 117°23'E (Jixian)
*When:* May
*Participants:* 2000
*Profile:* Hilly, with 5164 steps
*Temperature:* 20-25°C
*Fee:* US$1250 (6-night trip)
*Gradient:* up to 10%
*High-fives given to local children:* 100+
*Oldest runner:* 75
*Bottles of water carried on foot to the Wall on race morning:* 15,000
*Year inaugurated:* 1999
*Hiatus:* cancelled in 2003 due to SARS epidemic

## JUNGFRAU MARATHON
### SWITZERLAND

*The race:* Though it doesn't actually go up the 3454m Jungfrau, this route from Interlaken (560m) to Kleine Scheidegg (2060m) is still a beautiful brute. It turns really vertiginous at the 25km mark, when 500m of ascent squeeze into five zigzagging kilometres, and carries on up from there. Breathtaking in every sense.

### The Stats

**Coordinates:** *46°41'N 7°51'E (Interlaken)*
**When:** *September*
**Participants:** *4000*
**Profile:** *Extremely uphill – total ascent 1830m; max altitude 2205m*
**Temperature:** *10-20°C*
**Fee:** *CHF140 (US$170)*
**Elevation gain:** *1823m*
**Course record:** *2.49:01*
*(Jonathan Wyatt, New Zealand)*
**Time distance takes by train:** *1.15:00*
*(Interlaken-Kleine Scheidegg)*
**Best fuel:** *rösti (fried grated potatoes), birchermüesli, Rivella (milk-whey soft drink)*

---

## LEWA MARATHON
### KENYA

*The race:* Race the world's best long-distance runners AND the wildlife. This dust-track animal-infested 26.2-er crosses Lewa Conservancy, home to rhino, elephant, giraffe and buffalo. All good reasons to keep on moving...

### The stats

**Coordinates:** *0°12'N, 37°25'E*
*(Lewa Wildlife Conservancy)*
**When:** *June*
**Participants:** *1000*
**Profile:** *Undulating, run at altitude (1700m)*
**Temperature:** *20-30°C*
**Fee:** *US$1,500 charitable donation*
**Money raised for charity since inception:** *US$3,800,000*
**Animals potentially seen:** *rhino, lion, leopard, buffalo, elephant, zebra, giraffe, oryx, ostrich and many more*
**Security:** *Armed rangers, Supercub light aircraft, surveillance helicopters*
**Chance of winning:** *0%*
*(past competitors include world-record-holding Kenyan elites)*

---

## FROM 0–26.2 MILES…
### …IN FOUR MONTHS.

Marathon attempts are won or lost in the months before the big day. If you've arrived at the week before your first marathon without having trained, you may have bitten off more than you can chew. For the modestly active person, however, four months of training will be enough to get you across the finish line (though you won't be troubling the Kenyans at the front).

### BASIC TRAINING SCHEDULE

---

#### Weeks 1 to 4
Three rest days per week, not consecutively.

Two days per week with an easy jog, increasing from 20 mins to 50 minutes.

One day per week long run increasing from 40 to 70 minutes.

One day per week gentle recovery run for 30 minutes.

#### Weeks 5 to 8
Three rest days per week, not consecutively.

One day per week steady run for 40-60 minutes

One day per week speed running for 40 minutes

One day per week long run increasing from 80 minutes to ten miles.

One day per week gentle recovery run for 40 minutes.

#### Weeks 9 to 12
Three rest days per week, not consecutively.

One day per week steady run for 40-60 minutes

One day per week speed running for 50 minutes

One day per week long run increasing from 10 miles to 13 miles or a half-marathon race

One day per week gentle recovery run for 40 minutes.

#### Weeks 13 to 16
Three rest days per week, not consecutively

One day per week steady run for 40-60 minutes*

One day per week speed running for 50 minutes*

One day per week long run decreasing from 20 miles to 8 miles*

One day per week gentle recovery run for 40 minutes.

*in the week before the race taper your training and do only 2 x 30 easy runs and a 20 min jog*

You Only Live Once

# RAISING RIPPERS

## IT'S NEVER TOO EARLY TO START ON THE SNOW. GET YOUR KIDS ON THE SLOPES AND YOU'LL BE RESPONSIBLE FOR THE NEXT GENERATION OF TOP-NOTCH BOARDERS.

**Y**ou pause, *look around at your friends*, and suddenly ponder how long you've all been snowboarding. You're nudging close to (whisper it!) middle age, and far from being the spring-chickens who took to their boards with youthful fearlessness aged 18.

There's nothing for it, you're going to have to pass on a love of sliding sideways to your kids. You head to Morzine, where Rude Chalets runs Mini Shred Snowboard Weeks for four- to eight-year-olds in the second half of each snow season, when the weather is more likely to be warm and the snow soft and slushy.

The bright, crisp morning brings 1½ hours of tuition with an instructor. There's no more than two in a group – ratios those at French ski schools can only dream of! The kids love it – learning taking a backseat to an atmosphere of play in a winter wonderland.

The little 'uns are strapped to super-stable snowboards, making it virtually impossible to catch an edge, and pulled on a towing lead, like naughty puppies, while they get used to the sensation of riding.

And when you're not on the slopes, Morzine keeps you all happy. A relatively flat valley town that's easy to get around with buggies, there are indoor swimming pools for bad-weather days, a toy train and merry-go-round, and a slew of tourist-board-organised kids' activities. ●

 **1**

### Woodward at Copper Mountain, Colorado, USA
*If your kids want to shine in the snow park as much as on the piste they should sign up for Freestyle Lessons with Woodward at Copper Mountain. The first half of the day is indoors amid the trampolines and foam pits of the Copper Barn, and in the afternoon they get to put their new gymnastic skills to the test on the award-winning snow parks, where some kickers have air bags to build up the progress slowly.*

 **2**

### Hakuba Heroes, Japan
*Hakuba gets crazy amounts of soft, fluffy snow that makes learning more fun, and is great for building snowmen. It's also warmer than many of the country's other resorts. Hakuba Heroes run group snowboard classes for kids over seven; it can also organise day trips to see the famous snow monkeys in Nagano or snow-mobiling missions for older children.*

 **3**

### The Star Wars Experience, Sierra-at-Tahoe, California, USA
*Children – or should that be Younglings or Padawans – as young as three can learn to snowboard with the help of Jedi Master Yoda and his mind tricks of movement, navigation and control at Sierra-at-Tahoe's snowboard school. The Star Wars Experience includes interactive visuals from the film, and custom wood-carvings of Chewbacca, RD-D2 and C-3PO.*

**4**

### Whistler Adventure Camp, Canada
*If you send your child to a Whistler Adventure Camp don't be alarmed if their instructors appear to be a witch, wizard, or any number of animal cartoon characters – it's all part of the themed snowboard lessons, making learning as fun as possible. Après-ski ice cream is another tactic, and there's a Family Adventure Zone with horse riding, a maze, a luge and bungee trampolining.*

## A Month

HOMELESS VILLAGERS IN POST-QUAKE PAKISTAN, 2006    Alamy/DPA Picture Alliance Archive

# VOLUNTEER!

**LOOKING FOR A MORE MEANINGFUL TRAVEL EXPERIENCE? VOLUNTEERING WILL INTRODUCE YOU TO LOCAL COMMUNITIES AND BUILD YOUR SKILLS.**

'*Time is money.*' How often have you heard that said? Perhaps it came to mind as you spent yet another late night in the office trying to meet a deadline; or perhaps you work in a profession where your time is billed in blocks of 15 minutes. Maybe you've just retired, having worked hard for years in return for an annual salary. Whatever your circumstances, you probably consider your time a precious commodity. So, why give your time for free?

Ask Paul Piaia: 'As I travelled to more and more developing countries I began to appreciate how lucky we are in the West. But as a backpacker travelling through places, there was never enough time to do more than just sightsee. I found out about an Australian medical NGO called Australian Aid International, which strives to make healthcare available in some of the most remote regions of the world. In October of 2005, an earthquake measuring 7.6 on the Richter scale hit northern Pakistan, resulting in three and a half million people being made homeless. AAI were looking for determined individuals to provide logistical support; we were either choppered in or trekked for hours to reach villages cut off by the quake.'

Volunteering is a two-way interaction; people like Paul Piaia share their expertise, or just their time, and in return receive a sense of satisfaction through being exposed to situations far beyond the daily grind. ●

### VSO (Voluntary Service Overseas)
VSO, an international development charity working to alleviate poverty, is the largest independent volunteer agency in the world. VSO sends skilled volunteers who pass on their expertise to local people. It accepts applicants between 20 and 75 from a variety of professional backgrounds. Postings are usually for two years, although shorter placements do exist.

### Peace Corps
Founded in 1961, the organisation is a federal agency of the US Government, and has sent 200,000 people on 27-month development, relief and humanitarian assignments around the world. Even though there was a whiff of Cold War politics behind its founding, these days the Peace Corps' focus is on providing long-term volunteers to needy regions. Any US citizen over 18 can apply.

### Greenpeace
Started as a campaigning organisation in Vancouver, Greenpeace is now an international organisation with offices around the globe. Its mission has remained unchanged: to use non-violent, creative protest to expose global environmental problems. All offices offer plenty of volunteering opportunities, from stuffing envelopes to survival training.

### Willing Workers on Organic Farms (WWOOF)
Well respected and long standing, WWOOF organisations match organic farms with volunteers. Placements usually involve helping out with the farm work but can also include working in an outdoor centre. The programme largely appeals to 'townies' looking for a rural experience and those interested in organic practices.

**A Month**

# PLAY WITH GUITAR GODS

**IF YOU'RE GOING TO PLAY IT, PLAY IT RIGHT. LEARN HOW TO STRUM WITH THE BEST OF THEM IN MEMPHIS ON A CLASSIC GIBSON GUITAR YOU'LL TREASURE FOREVER.**

*Some things in life have to be earned.* You wouldn't play 'Mary Had a Little Lamb' on a Stradivarius, or 'Old MacDonald' on a Gibson Les Paul. Buying a top-of-the-line guitar is a rite of passage, earned by years of bedroom practice and endless repetitions of the riff from 'Mannish Boy'. Only when you've properly mastered all your pentatonics, arpeggios and modes is it time to put away childish strings and raid the college fund for the guitar of your dreams.

Sure, you could buy off the shelf from a local guitar store, but for that once-in-a-lifetime purchase, why not get your Gibson at source, direct from the factory in Memphis, Tennessee? You won't save a dime, but you will have the thrill of testing out your perfect axe just a block from the Beale Street bars where BB King played his first stage shows in the soulful heyday of the blues.

Kick off with a tour of the Memphis factory, where all of Gibson's hollow-body guitars – including the BB King tribute Lucille model – are painstakingly assembled by a team of master luthiers. Then, before you part with your hard-earned bucks, take in a Memphis blues show to see how the masters put a Gibson through its paces; for the real deal, head to Wild Bill's on Vollentine, the last of the old Memphis juke joints.

Having shelled out for the dream guitar, it might be worth stopping off at the junction of Highway 61 and Highway 49 in Clarksdale, 75 miles south of Memphis, where Robert Johnson allegedly sold his soul to the devil for mastery of the blues. Depending on how your own trade goes, you could be ready to join the Memphis Blues Society jam, held every second Sunday at the Blues Hall on Beale Street. ●

CELTIC SONGS BRING PLAYED IN A DUBLIN PUB. IRELAND   Andrew Montgomery

### Seeking a sitar
Buying a sitar is not a purchase, it's a journey. The best concert sitars are made to measure by master makers in Delhi, Kolkata and Benares, and learning to play this multistringed marvel takes almost spiritual devotion. Take your first step on the road under the guidance of a sitar master at the Academy of Indian Classical Music in Benares.

### Game for a gamelan?
OK, so it's not the most portable instrument, but the sound of the gamelan will transport you instantly to the jungles of Indonesia. The Mekar Bhuana Conservancy in Denpasar is devoted to the preservation of Balinese music, with one-on-one training and workshops using antique gamelan sets – perfect prep for buying your own.

### Rock your roots in Ireland
Nothing will help unlock a Celtic soul quite like learning the bodhrán (frame drum) and joining an impromptu Irish music jam, preferably with a freshly pulled pint to hand. Pick up the basics at the Helen McLoughlin Bodhrán School in Wexford, then seek out pub jam sessions at Tig Coili or The Crane in Galway.

### Bang your own drum, Senegal
West Africa was the birthplace of the rhythms that morphed into rock and roll, so this could be the perfect place to discover your inner groove. Sign up for drumming classes in Senegal and Ghana and the first lesson could see you heading into the forest for wood to carve into your own djembe (goblet drum).

A GIANT AMMONITE IN WHITBY, ENGLAND    Andrew Montgomery

# FIND FOSSILS

Some 200 years ago, in the shale cliffs near Lyme Regis, on England's south coast, the teenage Mary Anning uncovered a 5m-long skeleton of an ichthyosaur, a species that last lived 90 million years ago. She was the first person to find an entire skeleton (which is now in the British Museum). There are many places around the world, from the dinosaur fields of Canada and the US, to China and Australia, where fossils, these remarkable links with long-gone ages, can be found. And, no, not all the good stuff has been unearthed yet: in 2014, a bachelor party stumbled upon a 10 million-year-old skull of a stegomastodon at Elephant Butte Lake State Park in New Mexico.

**A Month**

# LEARN TO PADDLE

**A CRASH COURSE ON KAYAKING IN THE SEA OF CORTEZ WILL EQUIP YOU FOR SALTWATER SORTIES ANYWHERE.**

**T***he wind is getting stronger and the waves higher.* Brisk little squalls charge across the surface of the sea; in a boat, this would be fun but in a sea kayak you're not so much on the water as in the water – and this is your second day of sea kayaking ever. Thankfully, you've practised 'wet exits' – the knack of banging on the hull of an upturned kayak then pulling off the sprayskirt to swim out of the cockpit – but, all the same, you're relieved when you surf the warm Pacific waves to the beach where you will camp for the night.

But you're also exhilarated. For this is the first day of a four-day trip up the west coast of Espiritu Santo island just off Baja California in the Sea of Cortez, and travelling by sea kayak means that you're immersed in the environment (if not the ocean). Your guide has explained how and why the safest technique for waves approaching from the side, as they were earlier, is to dig in for a stroke on the oncoming face of the waves because that tilts your body into the waves and resists its inclination to roll the kayak. Then, as the crest passes under (or over) the craft, swing in for a second stroke into the receding backside of the wave, so you're not leaning down the wave. Even in inexperienced hands, however, a sea kayak can handle a lot. And stringing a series of perfect strokes together brings the same joy as surfing.

The Sea of Cortez, the narrow but menacingly deep channel of water between the 1600km-long Baja peninsula and mainland Mexico, was described by Jacques Cousteau as 'the world's aquarium'. It's one of the most diverse marine areas in the world, containing 31 marine mammal species (one third of the world's whale and dolphin species), 500 species of fish and more than 200 bird species. Kayaking allows you to be part of their world without making an impact. ●

PADDLING IN THE SEA OF CORTEZ, BAJA CALIFORNIA, MEXICO  Getty/Steve Bly

KAYAKERS OFF JERSEY IN THE CHANNEL ISLANDS    Michael Heffernan

### Kaikoura
### New Zealand

*Arguably the world capital of wildlife-spotting by kayak, at Kaikoura's kayak school you're likely to be distracted by seals, Dusky and Hector's dolphins and even migrating whales. If you're very lucky, a pod of resident orcas might check out your progress.*

### Channel Islands,
### British Isles

*These slabs of granite, sliced from the French mainland and scattered artfully into the sea, are full of mild adventures and small discoveries. With exquisite coastlines and sheltered coves, they'll keep kayakers entertained for days. There are two large islands, Guernsey and Jersey, and three smaller islets, including car-free Sark.*

### Dalmatian Coast
### Croatia

*Hop from one turquoise-fringed island to the next along Croatia's Dalmatian Coast; the Adriatic is generally warmer and calmer than the Atlantic plus there's the advantage of starting and ending your trip in historic Dubrovnik.*

### Stockholm
### Archipelago
### Sweden

*Stockholm's archipelago, which consists of 25,000 islands, is a remarkable and relaxing place. A good base for sea kayaking is the southerly island of Uto, where your only company on the water will be seals.*

# TRAVEL SOLO

*'To awaken quite alone in a strange town is one of the most pleasant sensations in the world. You are surrounded by adventure.'*
Freya Stark

*There are many benefits to travelling solo from time to time. You will gain in confidence, become comfortable dining at a table for one, and be free to make new friends and wear a string of garlic whenever you please.*

MEETING THE LOCALS IN SERBIA   Matt Munro

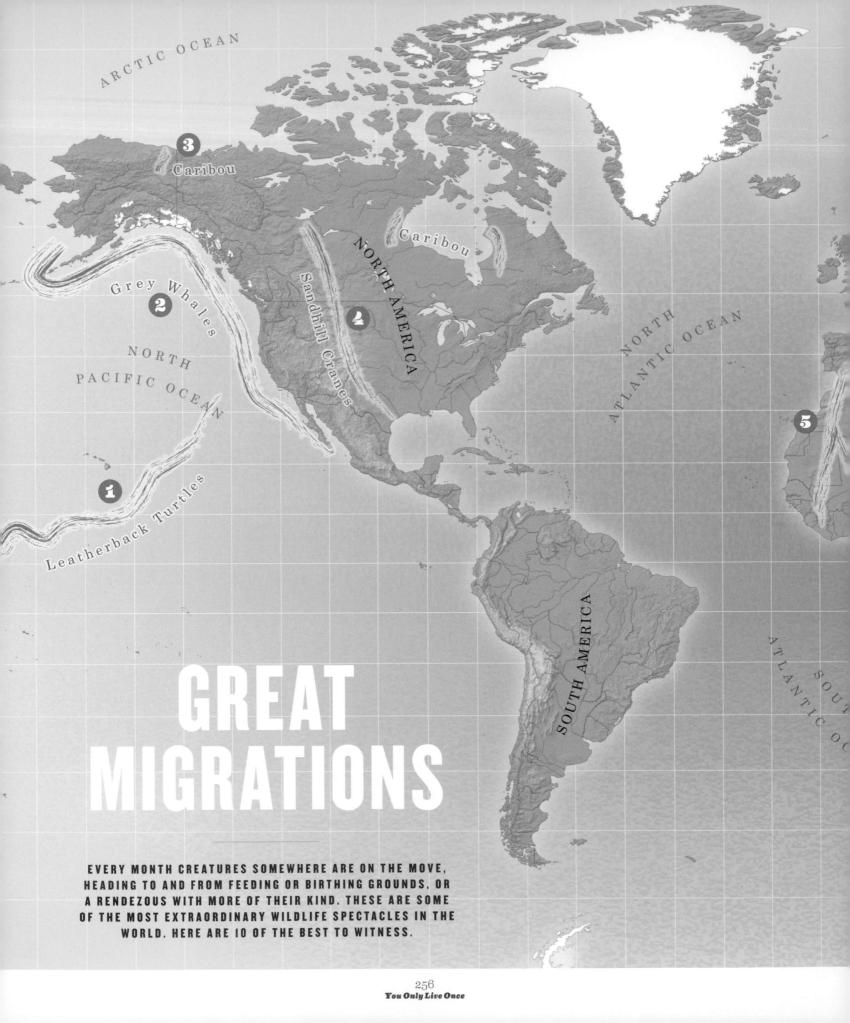

ARCTIC OCEAN

❸ Caribou

Caribou

NORTH AMERICA

Grey Whales

❷

Sandhill Cranes

❹

NORTH

PACIFIC OCEAN

NORTH

ATLANTIC OCEAN

❺

❶

Leatherback Turtles

SOUTH AMERICA

ATLANTIC OC

SOUT

# GREAT MIGRATIONS

EVERY MONTH CREATURES SOMEWHERE ARE ON THE MOVE,
HEADING TO AND FROM FEEDING OR BIRTHING GROUNDS, OR
A RENDEZOUS WITH MORE OF THEIR KIND. THESE ARE SOME
OF THE MOST EXTRAORDINARY WILDLIFE SPECTACLES IN THE
WORLD. HERE ARE 10 OF THE BEST TO WITNESS.

ARCTIC OCEAN

EUROPE

ASIA

**⑥** Common Cranes

**⑨** Bar-Headed Goose

NORTH PACIFIC OCEAN

AFRICA

**⑦** Wildebeest

Giant Fruit Bat

**⑧**

Leatherback Turtles

INDIAN OCEAN

AUSTRALIA

Humpback Whales

**⑩**

**1. Leatherback Turtles**
Pacific Leatherback turtles feed off California but breed around Indonesia: it's one of the longest migrations.

**2. Grey Whales**
Grey whales feed in Arctic waters in the summer and calve off Baja in the winter.

**3. Caribou**
Caribou migrate north to feed and calve in the summer.

**4. Sandhill Cranes**
The cranes winter in southern USA and Mexico, feed in Nebraska from February to April and then nest in the north.

**5. Swallows**
Swallows nest in northern Europe in spring and fly south to Africa at the end of every summer.

**6. Common Cranes**
Common cranes nest in the north and winter in the south every year.

**7. Wildebeest**
From July to October, wildebeest migrate from Tanzania to Kenya to feed (and be fed upon).

**8. Giant Fruit Bat**
Giant fruit bats fly from Democratic Republic of Congo to Zambia to feed from November to January.

**9. Bar-Headed Goose**
The geese winter in India then fly north over the Himalaya to breeding grounds in Mongolia.

**10. Humpback Whales**
Humpbacks feed in Antarctic waters in summer then swim north to calve around Australia.

**A Month** ☽

SURFING THE LONG BREAK AT PUERTO ESCONDIDO, MEXICO   Getty/Michele Falzone

# ENDLESS SUMMER

**LIVE THE DREAM: LEARN TO SURF IN MEXICO AND CATCH WAVES, DAY AFTER ENDLESS DAY.**

**S**ure, you showed up at the beach without a clue about board wax, goofy stance or riptides. It didn't matter. Because after a few days of surf lessons in Puerto Escondido, Mexico, you were doing it—catching waves. Sure, you weren't showing off on the big tubes of the 'Mexican Pipeline,' the famous wave at Zicatela Beach that draws pro surfers from around the globe. You were riding the small and perfect curls nearby, the ones that shot you to the shore in a foaming rush of water and made you crave the next ride like nothing else.

That first day, your instructor pushed you hard. Every time you fell off the board, he made you get right back on. The next day, he didn't have to tell you what to do. You wanted to get on again. The waves seemed limited and the time was now. Every day, surfing felt more intuitive. During week two in the Mexican village, your instincts kicked in and your brain turned off. You felt the swells and communed with the vastness of the ocean.

It wasn't just the surfing that was feeling right. You were always relaxed and hungry, which led to eating plenty of sublime ceviche and taking naps in hammocks. There was the occasional nighttime beach bonfire and yoga class. Every evening, you spent the golden hour on the beach, basking in the glow you'd created by nailing a new sport in just two weeks. ●

### Glitz & glam
*Sure, French royals have made Biarritz a famously posh destination for centuries. But it's the surfers who currently dominate the scene, especially during July's annual surf competition. You seamlessly slip into the stream by taking surf and French lessons rolled into one, which makes for sweet afternoons of forgetting the pain of the subjunctive as you glide toward shore in perfect balance. Toast your accomplishments with a glass of champagne.*

 **2**

### Into the wild
*North of Brisbane on the Sunshine Coast, Noosa Beach reigns as one of Australia's premier surf spots. As part of the National Park, the beaches here feel wild. You may even spot a native koala hanging about in the trees as you carry your board to the break. You'll never forget learning to catch the smooth, glossy waves in the ridiculously turquoise waters.*

 **3**

### Tropical paradise
*You're the kind of newbie surfer who wants to learn within sight of palm fronds – in the tropics. But you like the quiet side of the tropics, a place with surf schools, but where the jungle creeps through every crack. That's why you learn to ride the waves of the crescent-shaped Playa Guiones in Nosara, Costa Rica. There you commune with likeminded surfers from around the world, who totally get your vibe.*

 **4**

### Big appetites
*When you catch a wave in San Sebastian, Spain, you can catch a glimpse of the town's low skyline, a reminder that you're well within the reach of civilization. The Basque town is a serious surf destination, but one that focuses equally on food and nightlife. Enjoy the predictable waves and soft sandy beach during the day, and then head to the city's best pintxo restaurants after the sun sets.*

**A Month**

# 3
## months
*time it takes to make the perfect 1000-year-old egg
(also known as century eggs), much-loved in Asia.*

# 10
## months
*time spent by Britons Paul Archer, Johno Ellison and Leigh
Purnell, driving a London Black Cab for 32,000 miles across 41
countries – the world's longest taxi journey.*

# 9083.33
## tonnes
*of dulce de leche made in Argentina per month.*

# 9.67
## million
*digital train tickets sold by Indian Railways per month.*

# 1,115,680
## number of people
*who pass through Beijing Capital International Airport
in China per month.*

# 316,667
## bikes sold
*per month in Germany in 2013, compared to 245,833 cars.*

## 3.8
### days
*amount of time the average Australian spends a month online.*

## 30
### months
*time it took Briton Joff Summerfield to complete a 22,000-mile cycling circumnavigation of the world on a penny-farthing.*

## 1,127,480
### passports
*number of US passports issued per month in 2013.*

## 1250
### new species of flora and fauna
*discovered per month on average.*

## 22
### months
*combined amount of time Russian cosmonaut Valeri Polyakov has spent in space, including one stay of 437 days 18 hours in 1994–95 on Mir.*

## 196.42
### hours
*the average employee works in South Korea per month.*

LESSONS IN LIVING LIGHTLY

**W**e break camp early: the sun has yet to burn the mist off the treetops. Our campfire is still smouldering despite the insistent humidity that's already made wet rags of my shirt. Segundo, my guide from the local Huitoto tribe, deftly helps me unhook my hammock and mosquito net from the trees, scuffs out the fire, and we step wordlessly out onto a jungle path towards the river. I glance back through the trees to where we'd spent the night, rain tip-tapping on our hammocks' awnings, and Segundo's voice conjuring Huitoto legends of snakes, floods and vengeful gods. Our home for the night in the Colombian Amazon, larger than life under the blanket of darkness, is now untraceable.

Segundo strides out under the dripping forest canopy. I trot sweatily behind. Besides the hammocks he carries nothing. Around his waist, a hip pouch contains not much more than his *mambe* (coca powder) and tobacco. My knapsack of essentials comprises a sarong, a couple of T-shirts, token mozzie spray (the bites continue regardless), some toiletries (rarely used unless near a river), a sleeping bag, water and a camera. Most of my belongings had been dumped in a lock-up in Leticia, the closest Amazon hub town. Mobile phone? There's no reception. Rain mac? What's the point, perspiration will drench you first. Wallet? Banks and shops are far away.

The very first time I trekked and camped in the Amazon, some 15 years previously, it felt as if heading for incarceration. Bound for the densely forested banks of Peru's Tambopata, seven hours up-river from the nearest town, I had handed over keys, phone and wallet to a lock-up, and with them, a significant sense of self. But what I found, in fact, was that this led to liberation rather than confinement. Without these fidgety fixtures of modern identity, I was free to just be.

> I am directed to trees that produce water, twigs that double as toothbrushes; a directory of flora with mystical and medical attributes

Then, as now, my hosts equipped me with all I needed. I am directed to trees that produce water, twigs that double as toothbrushes, a directory of flora with mystical and medical attributes. Within a 3 sq m tract of forest, with the right knowledge, you could treat everything from cuts and abrasions to diarrhoea, arthritis and impotence. What you need here is not technical kit and clothing but know-how. Segundo navigates swiftly through seemingly impenetrable walls of rainforest like a man with an inner GPS, delivering us, suddenly, to a *chacra* – one of the Amazon's small, subsistence farms. It's as if he has just produced a rabbit from a huge, shrub-filled hat.

This formidable knowledge, however, is delivered with an equal dose of humility. Before each journey between *chacras*, Segundo discreetly kneels, inhales *mambe* and blows tobacco smoke low across the ground – a ritual of respect or superstition depending on your perspective. Like most Amazon tribespeople, he believes the forest to be very much alive, a physical and spiritual entity governed by Old Testament–like gods who must be appeased. Become cavalier at your peril; the trees here may take their revenge. Strangler figs and mangroves form gothic cages around you, 'walking' palms block your path, and vines seethe around your ankles, sprouting back minutes after your machete's slash. Everyone, it seems, has a hair-raising tale of a friend missing all night on a route they walked daily.

But this morning, all are present and correct in the *maloca*, the traditional palm-thatch longhouse at the centre of this *chacra*. Abuelo, the community's elder is going about morning chores, frying eggs and corn for breakfast, shadowed by the resident pack of skeletal pups. Tending to crops here must be like pruning a bramble patch with nail clippers, and yet the *chacra* thrives with corn, yam, pineapple and banana. Natural pest control comes by way of the weaver birds and caciques that prey on insects, nesting in one or two strategically planted trees.

Here is a wild world made manageable – not tamed but tacitly understood. I settle down between the vast roots of a kapok tree and watch one of the boys deftly weaving palm leaves for the *maloca's* roof, efficient against the rains for years to come. It's an age-old process, simple yet skilled and completely sustainable – a metaphor for a life lived lightly. ●

# KEEP IT TRAD

SPRING, SUMMER, WINTER OR AUTUMN, WHATEVER THE MONTH THERE
WILL BE A TRADITIONAL RITUAL SOMEWHERE AROUND THE WORLD – SOME
STRANGER THAN OTHERS – WITH WHICH YOU CAN JOIN IN.

**W**hen the locals in a Stockholm bar invited you to come and celebrate Midsommarfirande with them, you were thrilled – how better to experience Sweden's Midsummer Festival than by getting out of the city and seeing how it's traditionally done?

But a few nerves began to jangle when they started telling you the stories – about washing a smörgåsbord of raw herring varieties down with silly sounding amounts of brännvin – and showing you videos of last year's shindig on their smartphones.

That maypole really did look a touch risqué from that angle. And what kind of jig were those people doing? Oh, that's right, the famous frog dance. Of course. Still, there looked to be plenty of hilarity and high spirits. More than you've ever seen before, now you think about it, here in this friendly but slightly tightly buckled country.

Midsommarfirande is a celebration of the summer solstice – a happy time this far north, when the sun-starved Swedes savour every bit of daylight they can get their skin under. In a modern interpretation of a tradition that goes back to pagan times, many evacuate urban areas and seek out al fresco parties, as fresh-air festivities kick off all across the countryside, on islands and yachts, and in lakeside cabins.

Overdosing on vitamin D, gravadlax, smoked salmon, and *nubbe* (Swedish snaps), people let their hair down, don garlands of flowers and indulge in some solar-powered flirting.

And then there's the *Små Grodorna* of course – the frog song – the moves to which you've been practising in mirror like Kermit going gangnam style. What do those words mean again? 'Little frogs are funny to look at / They don't have ears or tails'. Maybe something gets lost in translation, but there's no denying it – this place is hopping. ●

BEARING A BLAZING BARREL IN DEVON, ENGLAND    Pat Kinsella

KEEP
IT
TRAD

**1**

### Sourtoe cocktails in the snow, Canada

'Bottoms up!' yells Captain Dick, who pours the 'special' measures in Dawson City's Downtown Hotel. You grit your teeth, and drink. The 80-proof whisky burns your throat, but the alcohol content of the Sourtoe Cocktail isn't what worries you. The real challenge is letting the dead person's toe touch your lips, as tradition demands in this curious corner of the planet, where 'strange things done 'neath the midnight sun', as the Yukon's bard Robert Service observed. To earn themselves bragging rights, drinkers have been sipping Sourtoes – drinks with a preserved human toe floating in them – since 1973.

**2**

### Penis envy in spring, Japan

Carving a penis from a giant radish – of course, what else would you be doing on the first Sunday in April? If you're anywhere near the Kanayama Shrine in Kawasaki, Japan, you're bound to be doing something relating to the male member, as is traditional during the Shinto Kanamara Matsuri. The occasion is marked by thousands of people – families included – who walk around eating various phallic food items, buying penis-shaped candles and generally celebrating gentlemen's genitals.

**3**

### Barefoot climbing in summer, Ireland

The Irish summer's finally arrived and now you're sweating, even 700m above the Atlantic, on the flanks of Croagh Patrick in the wild-west county of Mayo. The sharp scree near the summit of Ireland's holiest mountain is tricky enough in walking boots, but the people ahead of you are battling it barefoot – no wonder there are injuries every year. This is Domhnach na Cruaiche, or Reek Sunday. Reek is the locals' name for the peak, not the aroma of pilgrim's feet as they dispense with footwear to follow a 1500-year-old tradition. In 441, St Patrick apparently spent 40 days fasting on this mountain, but the climbing ritual goes back further, to pagan times when the Celts celebrated the harvest festival of Lughnasadh.

**4**

### Blazing barrels in autumn, England

Your eyelashes curl in the heat as a man sprints past, carrying a barrel billowing with furious fire at head height. You're in Ottery St Mary, a sleepy English hamlet that explodes into fiery action every 5 November, as locals observe a 400-year-old tradition. The exact origins of Ottery's Flaming Tar Barrels are lost in the smoke of time, but it harks back to the 1605 Gunpowder Plot. The Devon village's pubs sponsor tar-lined barrels, which are ceremoniously set on fire and hoisted onto the shoulders of participants, who then run up and down the increasingly busy streets – the object being to keep the barrel burning for as long as possible. As the evening wears on, the crowd swells, the cider drinking gets faster and the competition heats up.

# TAILOR MADE

*When the explorer David Livingstone finally met Henry Stanley on the shores of Lake Tanganyika, Livingstone was wearing a suit tailored by Gieves of Savile Row, London, and Stanley one by Henry Poole, also of Savile Row. A well-cut suit is clearly not just for dandies. But it is an investment in time as well as money; expect a waiting time of a couple of months. Unless you're in India, Hong Kong or Singapore, where the turnaround time is far more speedy.*

**A Month**

A SEAMSTRESS IN SPAIN   Mark Read

**I**ndiana Jones – with an umbrella. That's the aesthetic. The scene is pure *Raiders*; you may as well be wearing a sable fedora and belt whip, such is the cinematic jumble of exotic ruins encroached by jungle, such is the sense of adventure. But it ain't half wet.

The rain is falling with military fury. It's not droplets; this is ammunition-made-aqua, a soggying salvo of water-bullets firing from a gunmetal sky. It's the sort of storm that could maim, rain so forceful it leaves a mark on the skin, a sting on the cheek.

But this onslaught is awesome. Watching Mother Nature's rage, witnessing her hurl her worst, adds to the general drama. The scouring thump of water on sandstone is like watching erosion in action. The forest seems to be growing at visible speed. The smack of water on broad leaves and ornate edifice is near-deafening.

Cambodia – specifically, Angkor – in the monsoon is damp, yes, but offers thrills of the highest Indiana order. The jungle that threatens to (and occasionally succeeds in)

> Rice terraces glow in the rudest of health; cities are spring-cleaned of their usual dust; and waterfalls are in their fullest, most fabulous flows

reclaim the sprawl of Khmer temples is vivid green, the finery of the trees is fresh-washed and never more profuse. Plus the moats that enclose some of the ancient complexes are authentically full to bursting.

The best thing though – as with heading to any destination in the off season – is the paucity of other people. Of course, you're never completely alone; there are always other diehards braving the adverse climatic conditions. But queues are shorter, viewpoints less busy, and any crowds that do amass are so much easier to lose. There's even, you fancy, a moist camaraderie. When a deluge hits and you find yourself cowering under a 10th-century cloister with a similarly wet-through traveller, you can strike up a conversation about the weather, and shelter in your shared resilience. You can also feel smug about the price tag: airfares, hotel rooms, taxi rides, even watermelon shakes, all cost less in the low season.

But it's not all plain sailing. There are distinct downsides to the wet – not least of all, the wetness. As dramatic as a storm can be, it would be nice to see a sunny sky, and to leave the brolly in your room. That said, a monsoon is not a constant drenching. Rain comes in bursts – an hour's shower here, an afternoon's torrent there; some days there is no rain at all. It's arguably better for your psyche this way. If you visit any destination in its dry season and get some unfortunate freak downpours, you'll be cross that your trip is a washout; visit in the wet, fully prepared for precipitation, and any dry days you have will seem like gifts from the gods. It's all a case of perspective.

Of course, getting around can be a bit trickier during the monsoon. Roads across much of Southeast Asia have improved in recent years, particularly in Thailand and Vietnam, but some backwaters remain tough to reach when the weather turns motorways to mulch. This is a downer; you must accept that some places may be off limits, unless you are tenacious, or have webbed feet.

But overall you're on to a winner: rice terraces glow in the rudest of health; cities are spring-cleaned of their usual dust; and cooling waterfalls, are in their fullest, most fabulous flows. Glowering skies might seem to dull your snapshots but actually they enliven them. Unmitigated sunshine washes out photos, while brooding clouds, and rays bursting through them, bring a landscape to life.

Rainy season? Nah, let's call it the brainy season. ●

# WORK YOUR WAY

## NO CASH? NO PROBLEM. BEG, BORROW OR STEAL THE AIRFARE AND MONTHS OF WORK AND PLAY AWAIT.

**Ah, la France...** Morning lifts a curtain on a scene straight out of a Monet painting. You're in Le Breui, in beautiful Beaujolais. Vines march up rolling hills cloaked in mist, interspersed with proud stands of pine and oak. As you trudge through the mud breathing in the dewy dawn air, the first light spills like warm honey across patchwork fields of russet and gold, lighting up a stone village cupped in the valley below.

Allez! You set to work, secateurs in hand, slowing getting into the groove of clipping bunches of grapes and filling buckets. Before you know it, you are singing along to *vendange* (grape harvest) ditties with bonhomie and gusto. Or perhaps, if you are built like an ox, you'll be chosen as a porteur, where the backbreaking work of lugging a 50kg basket of grapes up and down a steep slope is eased by copious amounts of wine at the tractor from dawn to dusk.

While some aspects of the grape harvest in France are undeniably idyllic, you might not want to put on those rose–tinted spectacles just yet. It is hard graft, with early starts, long hours – typically 10 to 12 a day – no day off, and rock-bottom wages of around €50 a day. Oh, and a downpour can delay the harvest for days.

But hey, who cares? This is still living the dream. You get your bed and board thrown in, the scenery is gorgeous and you meet new friends from all over the world – trading stories and drinking deep of free wine under the stars. They tell you, through the grapevine, about other harvest work, from olives in Provence to oysters in Arcachon Bay. After a couple of hazy September weeks, you return home with better French, a healthy glow to your cheeks and a lifetime of memories. And you'll never look at a bottle of wine in the supermarket in the same way again. ●

HARVESTING GRAPES IN BURGUNDY, FRANCE   Getty/Ian Shaw

HANDS UP IN A CLASSROOM IN CHINA Getty/Oktay Ortakcioglu

### Working holiday in Oz

*Working visa? Check. Return flights? Check. Sense of adventure? Check. A job? No worries, mate. Whether you dream of Sydney Harbour at sunset or swimming with whale sharks in Western Australia, travels here can easily be combined with casual jobs. Do your homework before setting off or just rock up and see what you can find as a fruit picker, bar tender, hostel worker, tour guide, even jackaroo.*

### Au pair in the USA

*Stop California dreamin' and go see it for yourself. Or perhaps it's Manhattan's skyline or Colorado's rugged wilderness that make you swoon. Provided you have a knack with kids, common sense, a driving licence and clean bill of health, you could earn a decent crust slipping into Mary Poppins' shoes and staying with a host family pretty much anywhere in the States.*

### Ski season in the Alps

*Skiing in the Alps is expensive, so working here for a winter season is a great way to pound powder for a few months, fund your lift pass and fondue dinners, and brush up your French, Italian or German. Think chalet maid, hotel and bar work, or, if you're a whizz on the slopes, ski or snowboard instructor.*

### Teaching in Asia

*A TEFL (teaching English as a foreign language) qualification is your golden ticket to a decently paid teaching job in Asia. Not only will this throw you into the deep end of the culture and help you hone your language skills, you'll often gain much kudos from the local community. And you can use that pay cheque to see the temples of Burma, the teahouses of Japan or the beaches of Thailand.*

PLAY A GAME OF CONKERS IN THE ENGLISH AUTUMN ● GET YOUR KICKS WITH A STORM-CHASING TOUR ON THE GREAT PLAINS OF AMERICA IN MAY, TORNADO HIGH SEASON ● TREK ALONG HIMALAYAN TRAILS COVERED IN BLOSSOMING RHODODENDRONS IN SPRING ● CATCH A DISPLAY OF THE AURORA BOREALIS IN TROMS, NORWAY, WHICH HOSTS THE NORTHERN LIGHTS FESTIVAL IN JANUARY FEBRUARY ● DIVE WITH LEVIATHAN MANTA RAYS FOLLOWING THE TRADEWINDS THROUGH THE MIIL CHANNEL IN YAP, A CLUSTER OF ISLANDS IN MICRONESIA, NOVEMBER MAY ● GO BLACK TRUFFLE HUNTING WITH A RABASSIER IN THE DORDOGNE, FRANCE, DURING JANUARY AND FEBRUARY, WHEN THE DIAMONDS OF PRIGORD ARE AT THEIR BEST ● TAKE UP VIZ MIGGING (VISIBLE MIGRATION), A FORM OF TWITCHING, WHERE BIRD ENTHUSIASTS WATCH MASS ARRIVALS AND DEPARTURES OF MIGRATORY SPECIES ● WATCH WHALES GO PAST AS YOU SURF ON WORLD-CLASS BEACHES IN ALBANY, WESTERN AUSTRALIA, MAY TO DECEMBER ● SEE THE RISING WINTER SOLSTICE SUN ILLUMINATE THE STONE AGE PASSAGE TOMB AT NEWGRANGE IN THE BOYNE VALLEY, IRELAND ● IN THE ENGLISH SPRING, WALK THROUGH VALLEYS OF BLUEBELLS AROUND HARDCASTLE CRAGS, YORKSHIRE ● GET YOUR GLOVES ON AND EXPERIENCE THE WINTER ICE-SCULPTURE FESTIVAL IN HARBIN, CHINA ● WATCH SURFERS DURING HAWAIIS WINTER BIG WAVE SEASON (NOVEMBER MARCH) ● SCARE YOURSELF SILLY ON KRAMPUSNACHT (6 DECEMBER) IN AUSTRIA AND GERMANY, WHEN THE ANTI-SANTA SORTS THE NAUGHTY FROM THE NICE KIDS ● SURF THE BEST BORE WAVES UP SEVERN ESTUARY BETWEEN ENGLAND AND WALES IN MARCH, SEPTEMBER AND OCTOBER ● BUILD A SNOWMAN IN CENTRAL PARK, NEW YORK ● BEHOLD THE PHANTOM FALLS OF THE BLUE MOUNTAINS IN NEW SOUTH WALES, AUSTRALIA, AN OPTICAL ILLUSION THAT TAKES PLACE IN THE SOUTHERN AUTUMN AND SPRING ● BETWEEN JULY AND OCTOBER, DRIVE SOUTH AFRICAS NAMAQUALAND FLOWER ROUTE ● ICE SKATE ACROSS THE FROZEN SEA BETWEEN ISLANDS IN THE STOCKHOLM ARCHIPELAGO IN SWEDEN ● GET INTO THE HEAD OF JAMES JOYCE AND WANDER AROUND DUBLIN UNDER THE LUKEWARM IRISH SUN ON BLOOMSDAY ● CHECK OUT THE STAIRCASE TO THE MOON IN ROEBUCK BAY, WESTERN AUSTRALIA, A PHENOMENON THAT TAKES PLACE ON CLEAR NIGHTS WITH A FULL MOON, MARCH OCTOBER ● HIKE THROUGH NEW ENGLANDS FORESTS AS THE LEAVES TURN INTO A KALEIDOSCOPE OF COLOURS ● EXPLORE KENYAS MAASAI MARA NATIONAL RESERVE FROM JULY FOR THE GREAT MIGRATION ● DO A WINTER OVERNIGHT STAY IN NORTH RONALDSAY LIGHTHOUSE IN ORKNEY, SCOTLAND, FOR THE ULTIMATE STORM-WATCHING EXPERIENCE ● WATCH GRIZZLY BEARS CATCHING SALMON AT BROOKS FALLS IN KATMAI NATIONAL PARK,

# 50 WAYS TO CELEBRATE THE SEASONS

*By Patrick Kinsella*

ALASKA, IN JULY ● PAINT YOUR WORLD PINK WITH CHERRY BLOSSOMS IN JAPAN ● GET YOUR CHRISTMAS SHOPPING DONE AT THE WINTER MARKETS IN PRAGUE ● CATCH THE BLOOMING OF THE TISZA, WHEN MILLIONS OF MAYFLIES EMERGE IN CLOUDS FROM HUNGARYS TISZA RIVER IN LATE SPRING ● LAY BACK ON A CLEAR MOONLESS AUGUST NIGHT ATOP SUGAR LOAF MOUNTAIN IN BRECON BEACONS NATIONAL PARK, WALES, AND CONTEMPLATE YOUR PLACE IN THE UNIVERSE ● JOIN A WILD-MUSHROOM FORAGING TOUR IN THE LUBUSZ LAKE DISTRICT, WESTERN POLAND ● SLEEP IN A SNOWHOLE IN THE CAIRNGORMS, SCOTLAND, IN THE MIDDLE OF WINTER ● DANGLE A FISHING LINE THOUGH A HOLE IN A FROZEN LAKE AT THE HWACHEON SANCHEONEO ICE FESTIVAL IN GANGWON-DO PROVINCE, KOREA ● TAKE A BOAT TRIP THROUGH BANGLADESH, ONE OF THE PLANETS LEAST-VISITED COUNTRIES, DURING THE COOL SEASON OCTOBER FEBRUARY ● OBSERVE MASS CORAL SPAWNING ON NINGALOO REEF IN WESTERN AUSTRALIA, TWO WEEKS AFTER THE MARCH OR APRIL FULL MOON ● GET YOUR GHOUL ON AND CELEBRATE DA DE MUERTOS (DAY OF THE DEAD) IN MEXICO IN EARLY NOVEMBER ● GO TIGER SPOTTING IN BANDHAVGARH NATIONAL PARK IN INDIAS SUMMER, WHEN THE ELUSIVE ANIMALS LOOK FOR WATER ● PACK A PICNIC AND WITNESS THE GREENING OF THE SOUTHERN TIP OF THE ARABIAN PENINSULA DURING THE KHAREEF, JUNE SEPTEMBER ● CUT LOOSE DURING FEBRUARYS FESTIVAL SEASON IN BRAZIL AND CHECK OUT THE ACTION AT THE CARNAVAL OF SALVADOR DA BAHIA ● CELEBRATE THE BOND BETWEEN MAN AND REPTILE AT THE SEPIK RIVER CROCODILE FESTIVAL IN PAPUA NEW GUINEA IN EARLY AUGUST ● SEE EVIL SPIRITS OFF AND EMBRACE A NEW YEAR AT THE COMRIE FLAMBEAUX, A PAGAN HOGMANAY FESTIVAL IN THE SOUTHERN HIGHLANDS OF SCOTLAND ● VISIT PUNTA NORTE, ON PENINSULA VALDES IN PATAGONIA, ARGENTINA DURING ORCA SEASON, LATE FEBRUARY-LATE APRIL, WHEN KILLER WHALES HUNT SEA LIONS ● GET A TEAM TOGETHER AND DO A 24HR-MOUNTAIN BIKE RACE UNDER THE MIDSUMMER MIDNIGHT SUN IN WHITEHORSE, YUKON ● LOAD YOUR WATER-RIFLE AND JOIN IN THE CHAOS SURROUNDING SONGKRAN IN APRIL, AS ASIA WELCOMES MONSOON SEASON ● CELEBRATE THE IMMINENT ARRIVAL OF SUMMER WITH THE OBBY OSS FESTIVAL IN PADSTOW, CORNWALL, ON MAY DAY ● AVOID THE CROWDS AND VISIT VENICE IN THE MIDST OF WINTER ● SEIZE A SUMMER DAY IN MILFORD SOUND IN NEW ZEALANDS FJORDLAND, AND DO A DIVE THROUGH 10M OF FRESH WATER BEFORE HITTING THE SALTY STUFF ● VISIT THE SERENGETI NATIONAL PARK IN TANZANIA TO WITNESS WILDEBEEST CALVING ● PUT YOUR PLAYING-OUT CLOTHES ON AND GET AMONGST IT DURING LA TOMATINA FOOD FIGHT IN THE VALENCIA TOWN OF BUOL ● SEE AUSTRALIA IN A NEW LIGHT DURING JULY AND AUGUST WHEN THE ALPINE AREAS OF VICTORIA AND NEW SOUTH WALES ARE CLOAKED IN SNOW ● GO KAYAKING AT THE BOTTOM OF THE PLANET DURING A SUMMER BOAT CRUISE TO ANTARCTICA ● TAKE A 4WD ACROSS BOLIVIAS SALAR DE UYUNI DURING WET SEASON WHEN THE REFLECTION MAKES IT SEEM AS THOUGH YOURE DRIVING THROUGH THE SKY ●

**A Month**

# TO THE SOURCE

*In 2010 Ed Stafford became the first person to walk the entire length of the Amazon, after an epic journey that lasted 28 months. But you don't have to pick one of the world's gnarliest rivers to follow to the source: even a minor river will usher you through enthralling landscapes. Many rivers make it easy: both the Danube and the Rhine can be cycled from source to sea or you can copy Jerome K. Jerome and take a boat up the River Thames. But Ed Stafford has some comforting words if you select a more remote river: 'I washed in the same river that I caught piranhas from every day, with no problems. I never got bitten by snakes either – I always saw them at the last minute, just as they were rearing up to strike.' So that's OK.*

**A Month**

# Chapter
# 05

**A Y**

**In which you quit your cubicle, take flying lessons,
ski sweet powder for twelve months,**

**EAR**

uncover your family's roots, and resolve to learn a new language. Then, consider a sabbatical in the Caribbean or the south of France, or even a round-the-world journey with the perfect travel companion.

**A Year**

**Chapter**

# 05

# LEARN TO FLY

**TAKE THE CONTROLS AND FEEL THE THRILL
OF BEING IN CHARGE OF YOUR AIRBORNE DESTINY.
BUT DON'T GET TOO DISTRACTED BY THAT VIEW.**

**I**t's your first time on safari in Africa. You're riding shotgun on a 12-seat charter plane when the young bush pilot asks if you want to fly. There's only one answer to that question. He explains that the U-shaped steering column works like the wheel of a car and points out which gauges to watch, then takes his hands off his steering column as you grasp yours. The plane rocks a bit as you find an equilibrium. And then – it's smooth and steady. You're doing it. You're flying!

You start paying less attention to the gauges and peek up over the dashboard to make sure the horizon remains horizontal and you're on course. Puffy cumulous clouds drift by gracefully below, and farther down, the majestic animals of Africa appear as specks on the dry savannah. If you turn too sharply, your fellow passengers suck in their breath, but you soon figure out how sensitive the steering is. You're disappointed when you have to hand over control so the pilot can land.

You come home from Africa raving not about the lions and elephants but about piloting the Cessna. You start joking that your plan-B career will be becoming an African bush pilot. People tell you about local flight schools, but you're not quite ready to commit to the many hours and considerable expense needed to quality as a fully fledged pilot.

And then someone who knows you well gives you the best gift ever: a combination scenic aerial tour and intro-to-flying lesson at a nearby flight academy. It turns out many schools offer these to entice would-be students; they're also able to feed a post-safari appetite for more. Most Western schools are more by-the-book than the average bush pilot, so your instructor asks you to demonstrate more fluency with the instruments and is more cautious about handing over the controls. No worries – once you feel the plane tilting in response to your touch and become aware that you're holding yourself aloft, the magic returns. ●

REFUELLING THE CESSNA IN THE SERENGETI   Alamy/National Geographic

*Heritage Flight Academy, USA*
*During the intro flight at this Long Island school, the instructor steers you over the Atlantic and up the Hudson River, with Manhattan's skyscrapers sparkling at eye level. When you get to the less-crowded airspace north of the city, you fly over the Long Island Sound.*

### Austrian Flight Academy, California, USA

*The one-hour flight at this LA-area school has you and an instructor – and two friends, if you want – over Long Beach, Palos Verdes and California's stunning coastline and beaches.*

### IcelandAirclub, Iceland

*Based at Reykjavik airport, this club offers piloted sightseeing trips over Iceland's fjords, glaciers, waterfalls and black-sand beaches, as well as arranging one-hour intro flights for anyone who wants a taste of the air.*

### Basair Aviation College, Australia

*Australia's largest flight school, in a Sydney suburb, offers hour-long scenic trial instructional flights over the city in a Cessna 152. Students may even take off and land (with assistance from the instructor).*

A Year

# SAY
# YES

**DAVID CORNTHWAITE IS THE 'YES' MAN**

**A**fter an incredible 156 days and a sole-searing 5823km, I finally rolled into Brisbane, smashing two world records in the process. I'd traversed the whole of Australia, from Perth on the west coast, across the never-ending Nullarbor Plain, to the eastern shore. On... a skateboard.

Following my graduation from university, I had found a job fast, accepted it without thinking and lapsed into a disenchanted life of ennui and materialism. After 18 months I awoke with a feeling of moderate anger, something that drove me to a buy long skateboard – with the original intention of improving my snowboarding skills.

After two weeks of skating around town, I started to see my familiar world from a different perspective and I developed an urge to explore. I skated to work, put the keys on the desk, quit my job and promised myself that I'd skate further than anyone else ever had.

One year later I became the first person to skate the length of Britain. And within two

I have fallen in love with the simple process of trying to make my life memorable. Not to others, just to me

years, I was setting off for Australia. Shortly after I arrived in Brisbane, my phone rang – and I was asked to write a book. I said yes.

And from there, I set about saying yes, a lot. I created Expedition1000, a project of 25 journeys of 1000 miles (1609km) or more, each using a different form of non-motorised transport. Among other endeavours, I said yes to paddling from source to sea down the Murray River, riding a tandem bike 2253km between Vancouver and Vegas, paddle-boarding over 3862km along the length of the Mississippi, swimming down the Missouri River, sailing across the Pacific on a 22m yacht, and riding an elliptical bicycle 3219km across Europe.

But adventure doesn't necessarily mean painfully long and difficult journeys. Saying yes doesn't mean you have to quit your job or sell your house or buy a tent. It's just a very effective means of slowing time, by weighing it down with experiences we really want to have, rather than those we feel we should. ●

**A Year**

# 507
## years
*age of an ocean quahog (Icelandic clam) called Ming, discovered when scientists killed it by prising it open to see how old it was.*

# 4.2
## years
*length of time it takes light leaving Proxima Centauri (Earth's nearest star, beyond the sun) to reach your telescope.*

# 21
## years
*length of time Horace Burgess has spent building a treehouse in Crossville, Tennessee.*

# 3&12
## years and days
*length of time Bob Hanley spent pushing a wheelbarrow 14,500km around Australia between April 1975 and May 1978.*

# 7
## years
*length of time it took Oskar Speck to paddle a folding kayak from Germany to Australia. He arrived in 1939, just in time to be interned for the duration of WWII.*

# 50%
## extent of decline
*in performance level in crucial muscles after two years spent in a weightless environment, such as the space station.*

# 8000
## international tourists
who annually arrive in Moldova, Europe's
least-visited country.

# 6.961
## pounds
of tea consumed per person per year in Turkey.

# 17
## years
average time British people will spend on the sofa over
their lifetime, according to a 2008 study.

# 359
## years
length of time the Rocky Hill to Glastonbury public ferry in
Connecticut has been continually running.

# 88
## years
length of time a photography project has been documenting
ponderosa pine trees in Montana's Bitterroot National Forest.

# 93,363
## passports
number of Irish passports issued by Irish embassies and
consulates in foreign countries in 2012 (when the in-country
population was 4.58 million).

# FOOD FOR THOUGHT

## GIVE THE DESK JOB THE SACK AND STEER YOUR CAREER OUTDOORS.

**T***he hours are terrible, they said.* And the conditions horrific. You'll never have time for yourself and you'll end up as fat as a butcher's dog – always snacking and eating leftovers. Friends were full of negatives when you quit your office job to go to catering college. But they weren't privy to your master plan. You never had any intention of working sadistic split-shifts in a sweaty restaurant kitchen or hellish hotel. Those that paid attention might have noticed that you'd also signed up to do a PADI openwater Scuba-diving course, and that should have given them a clue. Now, as you prepare a tasty seafood lunch for the divers beneath the luxury live-aboard boat – who will soon surface with happy, hungry and appreciative looks in their mask-ringed eyes – your mind wanders to later this afternoon. That's when you'll get a couple of hours off to hook up with one of the trainee dive instructors and go for your own daily dive. You're above Osprey Reef today – north of the Great Barrier Reef and several days' sailing time from mainland Australia – one of the best diving spots on this big blue planet. Yesterday a minke whale surfaced not 20m from the galley window while you were chopping onions. There's no way you could ever have afforded a trip like this, but here you are getting paid. The clients were up early doing a dawn dive, with a bit of luck you'll fit a night dive in later too – every hour underwater takes you a bit closer to the second part of the plan: to finish your divemaster course.

Live-aboard dive boats operate in Australia, Egypt, the US – they're always looking for gregarious and skilled crewmembers, from cooks and hosts through to diving instructors and boat handlers. ●

### *Cool callings*

*'Don't forget your bobble hat!' said the farewell card from your co-workers. You're not going to see those guys for some time – not where you're going. Telecommunications never felt like the sexiest of careers – until you saw an ad for a communications officer, in Antarctica. You passed the aptitude test and convinced them that you wouldn't crack up spending 6 months in a research station. The work is challenging, the pay is great, and where else can you go snow kiting in your lunch break?  Monitor websites such as usap.gov and antarctica.ac.uk.*

### *Career highs*

*Stopping for lunch you have a clear view of the pub on the corner, but there's no chance of sneaking off for a pint. Beer's not a great idea when you're working 23 storeys up. You're roped and harnessed, but this isn't the place to make mistakes. Can't beat the view though – you can even see the awful place where you used to work, before you turned the skills you'd acquired rock climbing into a new career as a high access specialist. Now, where's that Kit Kat gone? Visit irata.org for details.*

### *Going with the flow*

*You push off from the bank, with a raft full of excited clients clutching paddles in their hands. The river still has more than a hint of winter about it and the levels are high, swollen by the ice melting up on the hills. You've been waiting for this moment since getting your RAJ (Japan River Guide Association) qualification, to go along with your IRF (International Rafting Federation) Award. You thought you'd be teaching English in Japan, but the only classroom you've been in has been the great outdoors. See internationalrafting.com.*

### *On your bike*

*It wasn't easy watching your friends go to university while you were 'considering your options'.  But kicking back in a bar in the French Alps, you think you chose wisely. You've always loved cycling, but it wasn't until a buddy scored a bike mechanic's job in Moab that you realised your passion could take you somewhere. After getting qualified, you picked up a gig here – with free accommodation and access to some of the best trails in world.  Bike guides in Europe need to complete an International Mountain Leader award.*

A Year

# A YEAR IN PROVENCE

*You wind down the car window
and the scent of lavender wafts
through on a gust of dry heat. Few
places are as blessed with food,
wine, sunshine and scenery as
Provence in the south of France,
and spending more than a couple of
weeks here will help you get under
the skin of the place.*

*It's been about a quarter of a
century since Peter Mayle's A Year
in Provence was published. Mayle's
best-selling memoir spawned a
terrible TV series, a dire film
and inumerable imitations. But
despite all that, the idea remains as
brilliant as ever.*

THE HILLTOP VILLAGE OF ÉZE IN PROVENCE, FRANCE  Lottie Davies

A Year

# THE UNQUENCHABLE

FIRST

Getty/Westphalia

**PATRICK KINSELLA EXPLAINS HOW TO LIVE FOREVER**

**H**ow to achieve immortality? It's an age-old question. You could try setting a world record, but records can always be broken. If you nail your name to a world first – that's yours for keeps.

Now you might moan that you've been born a hundred years too late and all the biggies have already been bagged. And in some senses you'd be right: it's been a busy century, with flags stabbed into most of our poor planet's extremities. But sometimes you have to think outside the square.

Roald Amundsen may have reached the South Pole in 1911, with a team of four men who had to eat their dogs as they went, but in 2013 Maria Leijerstam achieved a first by pedalling to the Pole on her own, without so much as nibbling her bicycle. And while Edmund Hillary and Tenzing Norgay were the first people to stand on top of the world on 29 May 1953, they did so fully clothed – not like 24-year-old Lakpa Tharke Sherpa, who straddled Everest's peak in the buff for three minutes in 2006.

Not everyone attempting a first is motivated by vanity. Consider Annie Taylor, a widowed schoolteacher who, on her 63rd birthday in 1901, became the first person to survive going over Niagara Falls in a barrel. Virtually destitute, Annie decided that risking death by taking the plunge (and hoping for fame and fortune in the process) was preferable to life in the poorhouse. Sadly the money never materialised, but her name has gone down in history. That is more than can be said for Robert Overcracker, who in 1995 died in his attempt to become the first person to ride a jet-ski over Niagara.

And therein lies a cautionary tale: you tread a thin line between becoming immortalised by achieving a 'first' and being remembered as a winner of a Darwin Award (annual anti-plaudits dedicated to people who die in stunningly stupid ways).

Some firsts are achieved by accident. In November 2013, when Sean Conway staggered ashore at John O'Groats as the first person to swim the length of Great

You only get one life, but there are ways to ensure your name lives on after you depart this mortal coil

Britain, his support kayaker Emily Bell discovered she'd inadvertently become the first woman to paddle the length of the island – albeit very slowly.

Achieving a first, even multiple firsts, doesn't guarantee fame, though. In the 1930s, German drifter Oskar Speck spectacularly kayaked from his home country to Australia. En route he knocked off the first paddling circumnavigation of Sri Lanka, but few people know about his efforts.

One last note of warning: if you do score a first, even a big one, the goalposts can change. In 2012, kayaking guide James 'Rocky' Contos was using Google maps to scout virgin river trips in Peru, when he discovered a 'new' source of the Amazon River, the Mantaro River tributary. His claim cast doubt over previous source-to-sea descents of the world's biggest river, which had all started on the Apurimac tributary, including the original 1985-86 expedition by Polish kayaker Piotr Chmielinski and American journalist Joe Kane, and British explorer Ed Stafford's epic Amazon walk completed in 2010. It also opened up a new opportunity to achieve one of earth's greatest firsts, a challenge which Contos bitterly fought with American paddler West Hansen, who he narrowly beat to the Atlantic by using motorised transport.

*If you want to bag a first, here are a few that remain unclaimed:*

- Scale Gangkhar Puensum – at 7570m, this is the world's highest unclimbed peak
- Do a source-to-sea paddle along the Seine River in France
- Reach the real bottom of the Mulu Caves, deep in Sarawak's Gunung Mulu National Park on Borneo
- Swim the length of Lake Tanganyika (677km), the longest freshwater lake in the world
- Run the newly opened John Muir Way, which stretches 215km across Scotland, from Helensburgh to Dunbar.
- Unicycle the length of Ireland, 555km from Malin Head to Mizen Head
- Canoe the Tigil River on Russia's Kamchatka Peninsula
- Skateboard from Deadhorse, Alaska to Ushuaia in southern Argentina
- Paddle around Jamaica ●

# ENDLESS WINTER

*(calendar wheel: January, February, March, April, May, June, July, August, September, October, November, December)*

RECKON YOU CAN ONLY SKI FOR FOUR MONTHS A YEAR? THINK AGAIN. EVERY WEEK OFFERS THE POWDER-HUNGRY A CHANCE TO SATE THEIR APPETITE SOMEWHERE IN THE WORLD. YOU CAN BASE YOURSELF IN THE HOTEL FROM THE SHINING, BOUNCE DOWN MOROCCAN SLOPES, SKI UNDER SWEDEN'S MIDNIGHT SUN AND SCOFF OCTOPUS SUSHI IN JAPAN: THESE DESTINATIONS OFFER UP CULTURAL ADVENTURES AS WELL AS SKI- AND BOARD-BASED THRILLS.

## OUKAÏMEDEN, MOROCCO
### JANUARY

There are more places to ski in Africa than you might think: Algeria, Lesotho and South Africa have pistes of varying quality. Oukaïmeden, which tops out at 3243m, is possible as a day trip from Marrakesh and offers one chair, several drags and bracing but skiable pistes. Donkeys also transport skiers and kit, although investment in a more automated system is planned.

## SHIGA KŌGEN, JAPAN
### FEBRUARY

Japan's highest resort offers varied terrain and – rarely for Japan – the chance to explore interlinked villages. The snow here is set off by Siberian winds and can be spectacular, but there's plenty more to enjoy: with saunas, slopeside sushi and Japan's famous snow monkeys to keep you occupied, Western visitors will find this an experience as well as a ski trip.

## VALDEZ, UNITED STATES
### MARCH

Alaska's Chugach Mountains get heaps of sticky snow – 25m a year falls here, and because of the salt water that blows off the sea, it results in precipitously steep slopes. Heli-skiing and snowmobiles are the only way to access the terrain. Packages don't come cheap, but if you want to rocket down the steepest off-piste in the world, this is where to do it.

## BĚIDÀHÚ, CHINA
### APRIL

Fuelled by China's rising prosperity, skiing in the country is growing rapidly, and Běidàhú, in Jílín province, northeastern China, is attempting to add 10km of trails every year. Most of the runs are appealingly tree lined, and the vertical drop is around 900m, with lodgings (many of them built for the Asian Winter Games) at the bottom of the mountain.

## RIKSGRÄNSEN, SWEDEN
### MAY

Riksgränsen is 300km inside the Arctic Circle in northern Sweden – it's so far north that the resort doesn't bother opening till February due to lack of daylight. By May, lifts stay open to catch the midnight sun and the snow is still plentiful. There's only a limited number of pisted runs, but for the experienced, there's a vast amount of off-piste to explore.

## BLACKCOMB, CANADA
### JUNE

Come June much of Blackcomb, Whistler's sister resort, is as green as you'd expect – and temperatures down by the lakes can be positively balmy. But the Horstman Glacier is open for around four hours a day, and has a substantial snow park served by two T-bars – perfect for honing those tricks in your sunnies.

## ZERMATT, SWITZERLAND
### JULY

A few high-altitude glaciers in the Alps offer skiing through the summer – meaning you can ride in your t-shirt in the morning and soak up the sun further down the mountain in the afternoon. The towering Theodul glacier in Zermatt offers surprisingly extensive skiing on blue and red runs throughout the summer, with views of the nearby Matterhorn.

## PERISHER, AUSTRALIA
### AUGUST

The Southern hemisphere's largest ski resort, south of Canberra, has its best snow depths in August and plenty of snow-making equipment (useful, since snowfall has been patchy in recent years). There are 47 lifts and there's varied terrain on offer, with alpine and cross-country runs, plus bowls to cruise through.

## VALLE NEVADO, CHILE
### SEPTEMBER

It's only 60km from Santiago, Chile's capital, but Valle Nevado is linked to two other resorts – La Parva and El Colorado – and offers the largest ski area in South America. Ski-in/ski-out accommodation, 45km of runs, a snow park and heli-skiing complete the high-altitude Andean picture.

## NORTH ISLAND, NEW ZEALAND
### OCTOBER

By October, the skiing is winding down in New Zealand, but the twin resorts of Whakapapa and Turoa, on either side of Mt Ruapehu on North Island, offer the country's largest ski area and one of its longest seasons. Expect precious few tree-lined runs, but well-priced skiing and relaxed après-ski – if you get some fresh powder, you'll find it hangs around for days.

## TIMBERLINE LODGE, UNITED STATES
### NOVEMBER

Timberline Lodge famously stood in for Jack Nicholson's haunted hotel in *The Shining*. Almost as freaky is the fact that you can ski at this Oregon resort twelve months a year – national teams train here in the summer, but the seven lifts and 700m of descent are open to anyone. It's only 100km from Portland.

## VAL THORENS, FRANCE
### DECEMBER

Europe's highest ski resort sits at 2,300m, with lifts heading up to 3,200m – making it a great place for guaranteed early-season snow. The functional town centre won't win any architecture awards, but with steep runs, vast stretches of off-piste, a lively bar scene and access to the immense Three Valleys area, you probably won't be worrying too much about the lack of dainty timber chalets.

**A Year**

# START TICKING OFF A LIST

*In 2014, Botswana's Okavango Delta became the 1000th addition to Unesco's list of World Heritage sites. In order to be selected for the list, sites must be considered of outstanding universal value. It is as good a measure of human genius or exceptional natural beauty as any. With stone circles, coral reefs, entire cities and precious wildernesses, there is, as the expression goes, something for everyone.*

A Year

# LEARN A LANGUAGE

**BREAK DOWN BARRIERS AND CONNECT WITH A CULTURE LIKE NEVER BEFORE. A LITTLE LANGUAGE-LEARNING GOES A VERY LONG WAY.**

**Y**ou *studied Spanish in school* for years, but never managed to learn the difference between 'ser' and 'estar.' What's more, you didn't really care. It wasn't until you spent a semester in a small, dusy desert town – San Martin in Argentina – at the age of 17 that the language took root in your brain and began to blossom. Because learning a language isn't just about conjugating verbs. It's also about drinking maté tea with new friends and dancing at the discoteca, and chatting with the bakery ladies as you buy your dulce de leche pastries.

There are so many reasons to learn a new language. It unlocks new cultures and new experiences. It keeps your brain youthful and active. It even opens up professional opportunities: those who speak Mandarin as a second language, for example, now find themselves in high demand.

Snoozed your way through high-school Spanish class? Make up for it with a Spanish immersion in the handsome colonial city of Oaxaca in southern Mexico. The Intituto Cultural Oaxaca (ICO) offers Spanish classes, homestays with local families, and cultural courses on topics from cooking to salsa dancing to piñata making. ●

OAXACA'S CENTRAL ZÓCALO   Getty/Darryl Leniuk

### Cantonese
*Sure, Mandarin may be the dominant Chinese dialect, but Cantonese has better curse words! Plus, you can watch Bruce Lee movies without the subtitles. The Hong Kong Language School, in Hong Kong's neon-lit Wan Chai neighborhood, has classes ranging in duration between two and 16 weeks.*

### Danish
*Want to read Kierkegaard in the original? Study Danish at Studieskolen in the heart of Copenhagen. It's got the royal seal of approval – the Crown Princess of Denmark, an Aussie who met her husband in a Sydney pub, learned Danish here. New courses start every six weeks.*

### Hindi
*A great place to learn the world's 4th most widely spoken language is Language Must in Delhi, where native speakers will guide you through basic conversation skills. After just a few lessons, you'll be ordering your jalebis (syrup-soaked fried pastries) and chole bhature (spicy fried chick-peas with bread) like a local.*

### Swahili
*Commonly used throughout southeast Africa, Swahili is considered relatively straightforward to learn. Find out whether or not this is true with a Swahili homestay in Kenya through Kenya Xperience. Spend the morning studying, and take the afternoon to roam Nairobi putting your skills to the test.*

**A Year**

**CASS GILBERT PEDALS
PERU'S BACKROADS**

**I**t had been one of those days. The kind that drag you out of your comfort zone, flip you upside down, prod you this way and that, and spit you out where you least expect. Our road had turned to quagmire. Gore Tex jackets had long soaked through. And my fingers clawed numbly at the brake levers of my bicycle. A tag team of electrical storms barrelled across the sky, chasing us 'like a pack of hungry grey wolves,' as my riding companion Kurt had put it.

In the distance, the outline of a corrugated shack signalled a blip of hope on this empty, unforgiving Peruvian plateau. We approached it with mounting excitement. It was unlocked and empty. Like prospective home-owners, we peered in, admiring the quality of its dry dirt floor and noting the rusty nails: perfect for hanging sodden clothes. Wasting no time in firing up our stoves, we were soon smiling contentedly, congratulating ourselves on our good fortune, hands cupped around warming brews like they were hard-earned trophies.

Some time later, after we'd made ourselves fully at home and the sprawl of our belongings marked our territory, voices could be heard carrying in the wind. Our luxury shack's owners had returned. Two young shepherd girls gingerly called to us from a distance, wondering what these strange, bicycle-riding gringos could want. When we brokered a deal to stay the night, they headed back to their family home across the plains. The following morning they returned, and when I asked if I could take their photo, they shyly brandished a documenting device of their own: a pink Chinese mobile phone, with which they video'd us waving hello, introducing ourselves and smiling sheepishly. Welcome to the road less travelled, where surprises lie around every corner.

Over the last few years, I've sought to follow this road whenever I can. It's taken me to a place where destinations cease to become the goal of a journey, displaced by the space that lies between A and B. In this case,

**FINDING** **ROAD**

**YOUR**

> Part of the landscape, at one with the environment, these roads are the lifeblood of a country and they remind me of the reason I choose to travel

two weeks of riding Peru's remote mining roads, tracing a path along the faint veins and capillaries that course through its mountains, had revealed a succession of rugged Andean peaks and valleys of unfathomable beauty. Within, lay the most minuscule of *pueblecitos*, where women wore fresh flowers in the brims of their sombreros, as if in defiance

of the harsh reality of their surroundings. On these roads less travelled, our path was roughly chiselled into bare, impregnable rock. It wound its way up and over one mountain pass after another. Sometimes it unravelled slowly and graciously, in long and looping bows, as if tying one valley to next. At others times it marched forward with an unrelenting sense of purpose, grit and determination, like the mines that burrowed into the hillsides and pillaged from the earth, in this stark and buckled landscape.

For a thousand kilometres, Kurt and I pedalled our way onwards, passed herds of alpaca bred for meat and wool, to a land where condors glide and swoop. We dug deep within our reserves and conquered climbs that unfurled for over 2000m at a time. The forlorn and forgotten mountain villages, upon which we descended with such anticipation, felt undiluted and real, and we valued them for what they were. They weren't destinations I'd necessarily

recommend people visit. Rather, their appeal lay in their normality, and the context within which we discovered them.

And when we occasionally chanced upon larger settlements, promising bowls of hot soup, grizzled meat and all, or simply mounds of rice and fried eggs – the Peruvian mountain staple – then our lives felt complete. 'Entra gringitos,' said one restaurant owner with a smile. Come in, little gringos. Her words seemed all the warmer given our need to stoop through the doorway, and the way our lanky frames towered over all the local mine workers around. Like a favourite aunt, she invited us to platters of food and cups of steaming tea. When the time came to head back out onto the bumpy jeep roads of the sierras, she refused any notion of payment, bidding us instead a warm and heartfelt 'feliz viaje'.

But why go to all this trouble? After all, aren't there highways fashioned to save us hours on the road and deposit us neatly at our chosen destination? Why make life harder than it is? With every passing mile, with every experience and encounter, I've become increasingly convinced that it's these roads – and the connecting horse tracks, mule trails and footpaths – that reveal the essence of the land. Away from the brash whoosh of traffic and the sound of metal bluntly cutting through the air, they feel peaceful, organic and natural: worn gently and subtly into the earth from lifetimes of travel, like the stone steps of an old church that are grooved and polished by time. Part of the landscape, at one with the environment, these roads are the real lifeblood of a country, and they remind me of the very reason I choose to travel.

And they're everywhere. It's as easy as loading up your bicycle, and joining the dotted lines on your map. As sticking out your thumb, and engaging with the people around you. As choosing a bus because it's headed beyond the index of your guidebook. Next time you head out, pick the route that takes twice the time to reach the exact same place. Journey to villages that lie at dead ends. Investigate names that resonate.

Step out of your comfort zone, with the belief that it will all work out, and it will. Find your road less travelled. The experiences you'll earn will be unlike anywhere else you've been. ●

# TRAVELLED

# LESS

# GET ON YOUR BIKE

*'It is by riding a bicycle that you
learn the contours of a country
best, since you have to sweat up
the hills and coast down them.
Thus you remember them as they
actually are...'*
Ernest Hemingway

DEEP IN PERU   Cass Gilbert

A Year

friends

with

# Travelling

**A**lone I would never consider hitchhiking into the wild blue yonder. But give me a like-minded travel companion and suddenly the doors to adventure fling wide open. And so I find myself at the entrance to Khao Yai National Park in Thailand, on the edge of a track that slithers into a green haze of impenetrable monsoon forest. Hitchhiking Thai-style means waving with your palm down. Get it right and you're almost guaranteed a lift, we are told. We start waving like crazy, aware that time is ticking, with just a couple of hours of daylight left and the nearest campsite miles away.

Our chariot arrives after just five minutes: a battered Mitsubishi pick-up that grinds to a halt in a cloud of dust, its driver beaming at us with a toothless, whisky fuelled grin. We climb into the back, where three women in skimpy shorts and with heavily lipsticked smiles welcome us like long-lost relatives. Between the peanuts and prawns they are shelling from 10-kilo-heavy sacks and broken conversation, we decipher that they are prostitutes, abandoning the red lights of Phuket for a night of national park wildlife-spotting. The driver, it would seem, is their pimp.

We pelt along the road, past mist-wreathed jungle and savannah alive with cackles and hoots, muffled growls and squeals. Every so often we stop for the obligatory thumbs-up snapshots at staggeringly beautiful waterfalls, my friend and I descending into fits of giggles at the randomness of it all.

Then it happens. We've read about the resident tigers, leopards, bears, gibbons and elephants. But on paper they seemed unreal, like fictional characters in a Rudyard Kipling story. But the three tons of muscle and flapping ears that is blocking the road now seems very real indeed. Instead of backing away or letting the elephant pass, the driver slams his foot down. The now angry adolescent elephant begins to trumpet and charge. It is close. Very close. And we are ridiculously exposed. My friend and I desperately cling on to the truck, as adrenaline, fear and excitement cartwheel through our bodies. It all happens so quickly.

The friend who stopped you drowning in New Zealand's rapids, or made you laugh when you had Delhi Belly will be a friend for life

We arrive in one piece at the campsite, a blood orange sunset creeping over the canopy as we pitch our two-person tent, listening to creatures move in the dusky shadows and laughing about a shared once-in-a-lifetime moment that neither of us will ever forget.

It is would-you-believe-it moments like these that make travelling with friends so special. Choose your travel buddy and your itinerary wisely and you'll strengthen the bond that already exists. The friend who stopped you drowning in the rapids in New Zealand, made you laugh when your insides were on fire with Delhi Belly, or called for oxygen when altitude sickness struck on the Bolivian altiplano will be a friend for life. Beyond the practical, friends can provide the sense of humour needed to overcome what would otherwise be a hellish experience if you were on your lonesome.

And whether it's to be a Thelma and Louise-style road trip through the USA or a multi-day trek in the Himalaya, sharing the experience with a good friend makes it that much more real. Get it right and you'll be the perfect double act – trading tips and suggestions, sharing stories and pooling your travel skills – haggling, map reading, getting to grips with the local lingo, you name it.

Of course, the bubble can burst, so it makes sense to test the water with a short break to make sure you are a good match before heading off together on a round-the-world trip. Common interests are key for successfully travelling with friends. After all, you don't want to venture to the other side of the globe only to find out that your travel buddy would rather watch *Lord of the Rings* at the hostel than tramp the Milford Track; that their budget means fine dining whereas yours allows for street food; or their idea of seeing Mexico is from the comfort of a hammock, Corona in hand, while yours is touring Mayan ruins. That irritating personality trait? It is going to be magnified when you spent 24 hours a day with someone, which is why breathing space and respect for personal space is so important when you travel as a duo.

'I have found out that there ain't no surer way to find out whether you like people or hate them than to travel with them,' Mark Twain once quipped. How right he was. ●

# BREAK DOWN WALLS

*We're good at putting up walls. All over the world you'll find them: in China, the Middle East, the Southwest USA, the UK, Germany. But history shows us that walls don't stay standing forever. This is Hadrian's Wall in northern England. Building began in AD 122 and it probably seemed like a good idea at the time. Today, it's an even better spot for watching the sun set over Northumberland.*

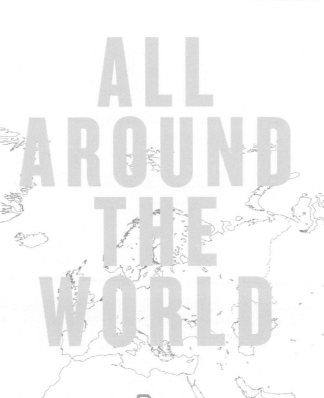

# ALL AROUND THE WORLD

FROM THE TIME OF FERDINAND MAGELLAN IN THE EARLY 16TH CENTURY, CIRCUMNAVIGATIONS HAVE INSPIRED MANY TO SET OUT FROM THEIR FRONT DOOR TO SEE THE WORLD. OVER THE PAGE, DISCOVER HOW SOME HAVE SUCCEEDED (OR NOT) BY BOAT, PLANE OR BICYCLE. BUT YOU DON'T HAVE TO BE A GRIZZLED ADVENTURER TO JOIN THE GANG: ROUND-THE-WORLD PLANE TICKETS ARE EXCEPTIONAL VALUE. AND YOU CAN ALWAYS WARM UP WITH SOMETHING SMALLER THAN THE GLOBE; AN ISLAND LIKE ICELAND FOR EXAMPLE.

# AROUND THE WORLD IN 80 DAYS
## PHILEAS FOGG

**N**ot all laps of the world actually happened. The popularity of Jules Verne's story, featuring globetrotter Phileas Fogg and his French valet Passepartout, is partly down to the rollicking good quality of the tale, but it's also attributable to brilliant timing. The novel was published in 1873, just after transcontinental railways had been completed in India and America, and the Suez Canal had opened: suddenly the world had become a much smaller place. This captured Verne's imagination and the French author's portrayal of an Englishman betting £20,000 (£1.5 million in modern terms) that he could circle the globe in 80 days was a winner with armchair adventurers. In the tale, Fogg and Passepartout travel mostly via train and boat. Fogg never existed but in 1889 an intrepid American journalist called Nellie Bly did a circumnavigation of the planet in 72 days (seven days faster than Michael Palin managed 100 years later) using the same methods of transport. ●

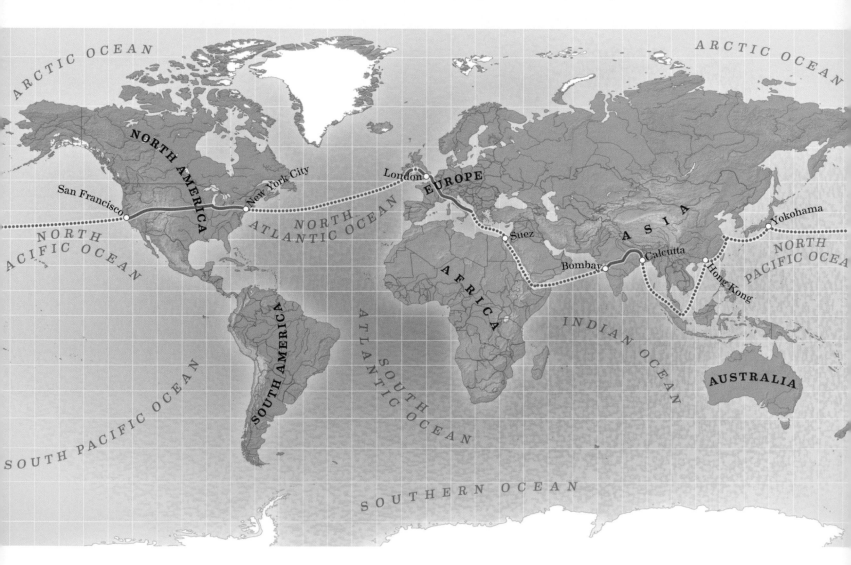

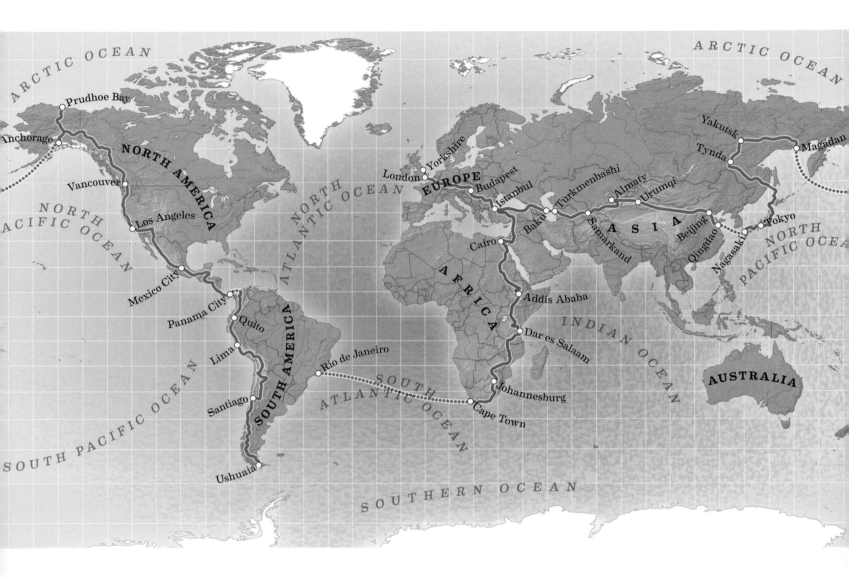

# BY BICYCLE
## ALASTAIR HUMPHREYS' TWO-WHEELED TRIP

**B**efore he got into micro-adventures, British explorer Alastair Humphreys took on some major macro-missions, the first of which was a mammoth circumnavigation of the planet by bicycle. Starting from his back door in Yorkshire in 2001, he pedalled 74,000 km through 60 countries, traversing five continents to arrive back home in time for tea, just over four years later. His route was designed to take in countries that interested him, rather than to set any sort of speed record, as the map shows. He left his watch behind, rose with the sun and frequently collapsed into slumber in a wild camping spot at dusk. Humphreys made a point of having conversations with locals wherever he went, and along the way ate a sheep's head, guinea pig, bear, sea urchin, horse, fried worms and scorpions. He rode with a granny-style basket on the front of his bike, discovered that car drivers are far more dangerous than both lions and bandits, and picked up enough language skills to convince Japanese police not to arrest him for cycling naked. Mission successful. ●

A Year

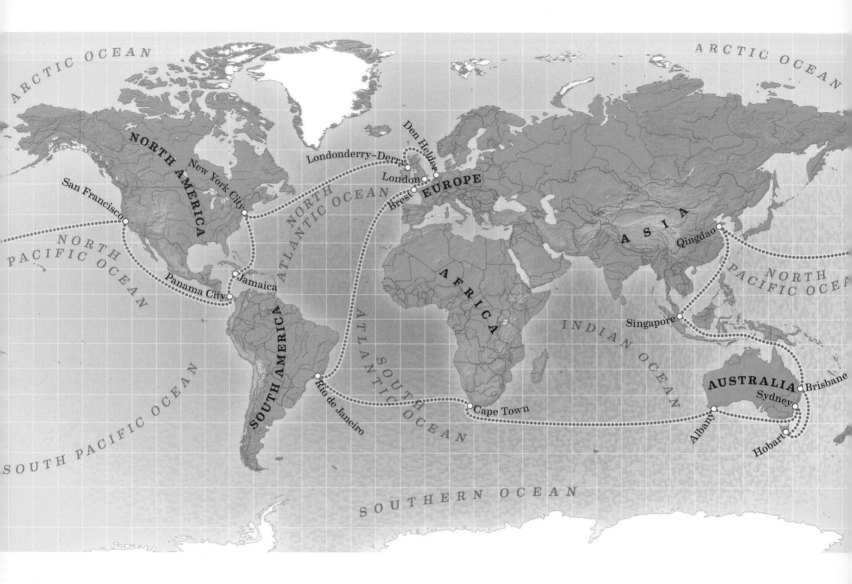

# BY BOAT
## CLIPPER ROUND-THE-WORLD RACE

**For others it's about speed.** In the Clipper Race, teams of amateur sailors go head-to-head in an epic 64,000km contest. Sailing identical yachts, the fleet departs from London's St Katharine's Docks and follows a set route back to Britain. The race was dreamt up in 1995 by Sir Robin Knox-Johnston, winner of the Jules Verne Trophy for being the first person to single-handedly sail around the planet without stopping. Competitors in the modern race are allowed to stop, and the last challenge (2013–14), saw 12 boats duke it out on a course that sent them to France, Brazil, South Africa, Australia, Singapore, China, the US, Panama, Jamaica, Northern Ireland and the Netherlands. En route there was drama aplenty; one sailor had a brush with death, falling overboard in heavy weather and floundering in the Pacific for 90 minutes. The threat of piracy plagued them on some stretches, while icebergs menaced in others, but all made it home. ●

# BY PLANE
## AMELIA EARHART'S LAST FLIGHT

**S**ome circumnavigations don't succeed. On 2 July 1937, Amelia Earhart was two thirds of the way around the planet on a pioneering small-plane flight. As Earhart rolled her twin-engine Lockheed Electra down a jungle runway in Lae, New Guinea, the Americas were in her rear-view mirror, along with Africa, the Middle East and Australia. Next to her sat Fred Noonan, a specialist in celestial navigation, but the weather was dire and ahead lay 7000 miles of Pacific Ocean, punctuated only by slivers of terra firma. A smudge of land called Howland Island was their target. Three ships nearby were burning their lights to aid with navigation. One of these, the *Itasca*, had been receiving messages from Earhart for hours, but couldn't reply. At 7.42am they heard Earhart say, 'We must be on you, but we cannot see you. Fuel is running low.' An hour later, one more message: 'We are running north and south.' Then silence. The aviatrix disappeared without trace. ●

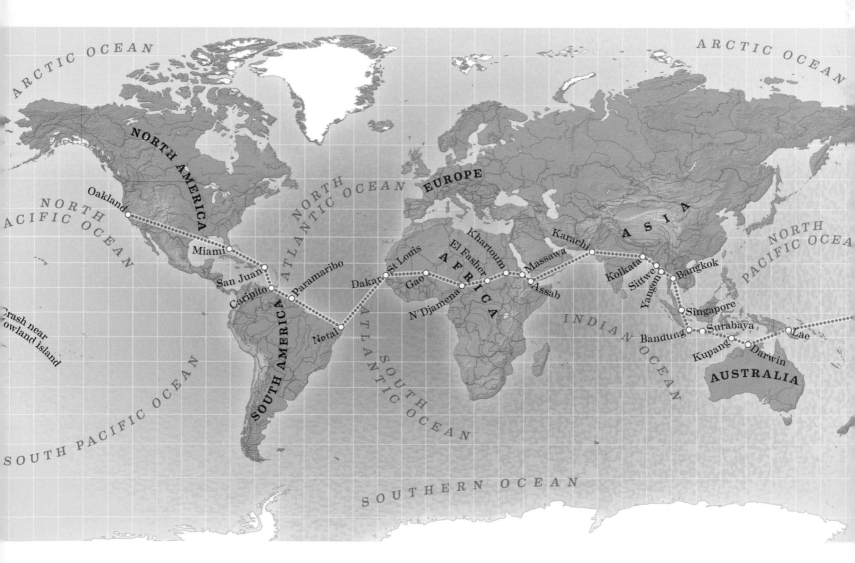

all photos © Tom Robinson

# TAKE A PHOTO A DAY

*Chronicle your year and all your adventures – far and near – by taking a photo a day and saving them in one place (several online communities allow this). For enthusiastic photographers it's a good discipline to observe. And at the end of the year, when you look back through the shots, expect to laugh, cry and be surprised at the memories attached to them.*

## CLOVER STROUD WRANGLES ON A RANCH IN TEXAS

**W**henever I'm feeling confined – by domesticity, or penned in with deadlines – there is a place I journey to, in my mind's eye, to find my very own source of spiritual oxygen. That place is west Texas. England might be my home, but Texas is the place that remains in my heart.

The journey that took me to Texas propelled me far from my home in Oxford, to the arid, epic, legendary ranch-lands I'd dreamed of since I was a child. It was a journey that changed me. I only need to close my eyes, and I'm straight back there, surrounded by the bleached-out denim of a cowboy's shirt, the jingle of spurs on a bunk-house porch and the distant, lonely howl of a coyote under a starless sky. Texas is a part of me as much as the dense, wet,

green landscape of the southern England of my youth.

I was 22 and had spent much of the previous three years in the dusty, and occasionally very dull libraries of Oxford, studying for a degree in English literature. But after pursuing a life of the mind, I craved a tough physical challenge, somewhere far from home.

It was the late 1990s, and the dot-com bubble had yet to burst. While my friends from university all headed east to London, to pursue shiny dreams in air-conditioned offices, I packed a rucksack with three pairs of jeans, two T-shirts , my battered leather riding boots, and flew to America.

My unconventional parents had raised me on a diet of country music and a lot of western

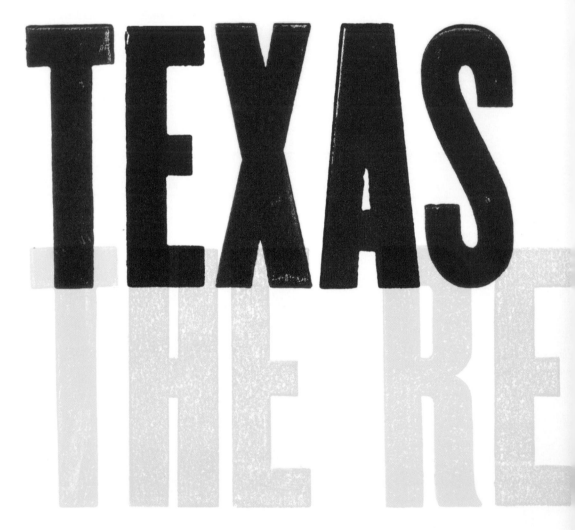

> For a year and a half, a log cabin was my home, the cook house my kitchen and the back of a horse my place of work

movies. I was looking for big skies and an empty landscape with herds of horses, spikey green cactus and, hopefully, real live cowboys in leather chaps.

I first worked as a groom for a millionaire on a dude ranch somewhere near Denver. But I was looking for grit rather than glamour. Wasting time in a junk shop, I found a red t-shirt with TEXAS IS THE REASON printed across it in tiny gold letters, and knew I'd found my direction. I caught the next bus to Dallas, hired a car, and headed out to west Texas.

But I was soon to find out that dreaming is one thing and doing is another. I was young and fearless, unaware how ridiculous the idea of an English cowgirl was on a Texas ranch, where life is deeply traditional and very patriarchal. A woman's place here is in the home, barefoot and pregnant, making beans and babies, not out under the huge blue skies of the range.

Finding a ranch to take me on was part of the journey I now value so much. I was laughed off more ranches than I can remember, and I might have given up if I hadn't met a cowboy called Lonnie at a rodeo near Amarillo. He kept a bottle of whiskey among old copies of *Playboy* under his pick-up seat, and drove me out onto the plains to give me my first lesson in roping. When his truck broke down, we slept in the pick-up, sheltering in the cab when an electric storm crackled through the dark blue sky.

He said I had cajones, and because he liked my spirit, he pointed me in the direction of a ranch in the Panhandle of Texas, where he thought I might be given a start. The cowboys I met there still laughed at me, but because I could handle a horse, and was willing to work very hard, for very little, I was offered a job.

For a year and a half a log cabin was my home, the cook house my kitchen, and the back of a horse my place of work. We branded cattle in searing temperatures in high summer, and fixed fences when an ice storm in darkest winter threatened to cut the power to the ranch. Big hearted and intensely practical, the cowboys taught me much more than simply how to throw a rope around a cow's neck, ride a bucking horse in a rodeo ring, or fix a barbed wire fence. Today I feel an intense gratitude for the fortitude, tenacity and bravery that my life beneath those huge Texan skies gave me.

But after almost two years, I understood that my fate didn't lie in Texas; I loved the place and the people, but England would always truly be my home. After I came home I got married and had two children in quick succession. By the age of 27, I was a single mother, facing a future supporting a toddler and baby entirely alone. The road that lay ahead of me was steep and rocky, but Texas had taught me how to cowboy-up. Today my home is Oxford but Texas is still, and will always be, the reason. ●

# LEARN TO FREEDIVE

*If skydiving is about the adrenalin rush of freefall, then freediving is the opposite: it's about finding and focusing on an inner kernel of serenity that comes through controlling your breathing and your emotions. This is one of the world's fastest growing sports, in part because of that feeling of empowerment that comes from defying human physiology. For many people, freediving is a lifelong obsession; not surprising if you can practise your skills swimming with manta rays in the Maldives.*

# CRUISE THE CARIBBEAN

**RAISE THE ANCHOR AND GIVE THE KIDS AN EDUCATION ON THE OPEN WAVES, ISLAND-HOPPING IN THE CARIBBEAN.**

'**D**olphins! Look! At the bow!' Your children groan. 'Not again. We're busy,' they reply. They have seen this marvel of nature countless times. Nonetheless, they drag themselves away from their games down below and climb into the cockpit. The lure of seeing these playful creatures is clearly just too great.

You are in the Caribbean on your own yacht with your family. You haven't worked for months. The sun is dazzling. Dolphins are dipping and diving through the translucent waves at the bow, darting this way and that, occasionally looking up to make sure their antics are being watched. The children laugh. It is difficult not to.

This may sound like a dream, but taking extended time out to cruise the Caribbean is easier than you think. Especially with little people in tow.

The benefits of travelling from the comfort of your own (floating) home are obvious: no lugging heavy bags across busy airports, no faceless hotels and plenty of space to stash all your possessions.

Sailing is an environmentally friendly way to get around, as long as the wind blows. Between December and April, outside hurricane season, trade winds in the Caribbean blow consistently from the east, taking you from one stunning island to the next.

You don't need to be experienced or break the bank to go cruising. Those new to sailing can master the art relatively easy on a course and the secondhand boat market will have something for any budget. Anchoring is free (and there hundreds of sheltered bays where you can drop the hook). If you can handle a fishing rod, your dinner could be free too.

There are literally thousands of islands to explore and all are surprisingly varied. If you're after stunning beaches and turquoise water, the Caribbean will certainly not disappoint. But there are also jungles to hike in Dominica, waterfalls to marvel at in Guadeloupe, a chocolate factory to explore in Grenada and history to learn in Nelson's Dockyard, Antigua.

Sailing these waters is safe, the scenery spectacular and the sun (pretty much) always shines. It is a lifetime experience you would be mad to miss out on. ●

**1**

**Dominica, Roseau**
*Unspoilt, mountainous, jungle-covered island where locals greet you like old friends. The waterfalls are breathtaking and the snorkelling superb.*

**2**

**Union Island, Chatham Bay**
*Drop anchor in this picturesque forest-lined bay and you will struggle to find a reason to pull it up again. Pelicans dive into the sea, tuna jump out of it and turtles bob sleepily on the surface.*

**3**

**Bequia, Admiralty Bay**
*A yachty hangout and understandably so. This bay has shelter, markets to shop in, plenty of bars and restaurants along the water's edge, as well as an idyllic beach.*

**4**

**St Barth, Gustavia**
*Boasting the best croissants in the Caribbean, this French island is also a magnet for super-yachts. You will need your credit card but it is worth the trip for the relaxed, laissez-faire atmosphere alone.*

**A Year**

# CLIMB EVERY MOUNTAIN

**START SUMMITING SCOTLAND'S MUNROS AND YOU MIGHT FIND IT A HARD HABIT TO KICK.**

**I**t's eight o'clock in the morning and your breakfast of eggs, bacon, mushrooms, tomato and a thick slice of black pudding is already finished. You're at Sligachan Hotel on the Isle of Skye and the reason for the rush is that you've got a Munro to bag and when the Scottish weather is favourable, it pays not to waste time.

A Munro is any hill in Scotland that is more than 914m (3000ft) high; they're not a single range but rather a collection named after a list kept by Sir Hugh Munro in the 19th century. There are rather a lot of them but the one with your name on today is Sgurr nan Gillean, Skye's most recognisable peak. This will be your first and if the hike goes well, perhaps it won't be your last.

Striking out from the hotel with a daypack filled with waterproofs food and water, a compass, a map and the wherewithal to use them, you head up to Coire Rhiabhach, the curved head of the valley. The 12km walk gets tougher now, becoming more of scramble then a balancing act along a snow-crusted ridge. Up here the views of wild Skye are staggering. And so is the wind. You hug the rock at the summit limpet-like before turning round, exhilarated.

For many, collecting Munros becomes an obsession; people compete to climb them all as quickly as possible (the quickest 'round' took less than 40 days). For you, perhaps it will just be something to do when you're next in Scotland. One down, 282 to go. ●

SGURR NAN GILLEAN ON THE ISLE OF SKYE   Getty/Chris Hepburn

### Corbetts, Scotland
*Daunted by the number and altitude of the Munros? Then perhaps start peak-bagging with the Corbetts, which is the collective name for Scottish hills from 2500 to 3000 ft in height. There are just 221 of them.*

 **2**

### Fourteeners, USA
*Colorado and California are home to most of the peaks in the US higher than 14,000ft (4270m), though the highest is Mt McKinley in Alaska. Ticking off Colorado's 53 Fourteeners is a popular pastime for climbers.*

 **3**

### The Aussie 8, Australia
*To scale the highest peak in each of Australia's eight states you won't be climbing higher than 2228m (that's Mt Kosciuszko in New South Wales' Snowy Mountains) but you will be journeying vast distances between them.*

 **4**

### Eight Thousanders, Nepal, China, Pakistan & India
*Of the 14 peaks higher than 8000m on earth, the most famed is Mt Everest: the others are also in the Himalaya and the Karakoram. Summit all 14 and you'll join an exclusive club of 30 climbers, led by the legendary Reinhold Messner.*

**A Year**

**W**e humans are restless. More than a billion international travellers cross borders annually, while over 200 million of us are migrants, living outside our country of origin. The urge to migrate seems embedded in our collective DNA. With so much frenetic motion, 'home' can just as easily signify the cloud where we store our Instagrams as it can a physical address or country of origin.

I'm a 4th-generation American. My great-grandfather, Peter Pearson, left the village of Tvååker, Sweden, in 1883, to start a new life in the mining and logging boom town of Tower, Minnesota. Legend has it that the Norway pines were so tall on this frozen frontier that they blocked the sun.

In the spring of 1909 my great-grandfather, his wife Josephine, also a Swedish immigrant, and their nine children moved into a farmhouse, 10 miles south of Tower. The house was 6m by 8m, a storey

Northern Minnesota is the antithesis of progressive or exotic, but it is the place where I still feel a tangible link to my family's past

and a half, and built on wooden blocks, with a kitchen, dining room, and living room downstairs, and one low-ceilinged giant bedroom upstairs.

'On the cold winter nights to keep from freezing it was necessary to sleep in our long woollen underwear, plus German socks which extended over one's knees.' my Great Uncle Morrie wrote in his diary. 'There was no ceiling upstairs and the roof was not insulated, the rafters were visible and white with frost. When the temperature got down to -40°F, the jack-pine logs in the walls boomed like a rifle shot as they cracked open.'

The summer was short, but the giant garden would still sprout potatoes, cabbage, lettuce, carrots, cabbage, squash and raspberries. In late June the field to the east would bloom with thousands of daisies, buttercups, and Indian paintbrushes.

'On nice, warm sunny Sundays,' Morrie wrote 'the family would pack a picnic basket and follow a narrow path to the crest of the hill where we would sit on the ground and enjoy the most delicious food ever served, listening to the birds and the wind playing a tune through the needles of the pine trees. Their pungent fragrance added to the taste of the food.'

More than a century later, I live 1500 miles south in Santa Fe, New Mexico. But my parents still spend summers on a lake 30 miles from the homestead. When I return in late June, I ride my bike to the farmhouse. It's a wreck. Falling in on itself and infested with mice, it's been condemned as a fire hazard. But if I time my visit correctly, the blooming buttercups, daisies, and Indian paintbrushes still overtake the adjoining field.

I often dream of tearing down the farmhouse, erecting a modern, light-filled cabin, and re-rooting the Pearson name to this place. It's an irrational impulse. The farm was never my own home and I visited my Great Uncle Arnold, who took it over from my great-grandfather, only a few times a year as a child. Northern Minnesota is the antithesis of progressive or exotic, but it is the place where I still feel a tangible link to my family's past. And, for me, that makes it one of the most desirable destinations in this wide, restless world. ●

# SOW SOME SEEDS

*By taking part in one of the many tree-planting schemes worldwide or purchasing your very own parcel of Amazonian rainforest you can sow seeds literally. But metaphorically, this is about the adage 'you get out of life what you put into it'. As they say in Australia, from little things big things grow.*

ANCIENT MYRTLE TREE, TASMANIA   Getty/Rob Blakers

A Year

Index

# OPEN DOORS

*The Peacock Gate in Jaipur's City Palce is perhaps the most beautiful doorway in the world.*

THE PEACOCK GATE, JAIPUR, INDIA    Matt Munro

# APPRECIATE THE DETAILS

*Azulejo has been a form of decorative ceramic tilework in Portugal for 500 years. The overall effect, as seen on many of Lisbon's buildings is mesmerising but look closer to appreciate the beautiful details of the tradition.*

PORTUGUESE TILES IN LISBON    Getty/Holger Leue

# LIFE GOES ON

*Even in Death Valley, one of the most inhospitable places on earth, with extreme heat and drought, life persists. Occasional rainstorms cause wildflowers to bloom across the Mojave Desert, for as far as the eye can see.*

JOSHUA TREES UNDER THE MILKY WAY IN DEATH VALLEY NATIONAL PARK, USA   Getty/Marc Adamus

# ACKNOWLEDGEMENTS

## PUBLISHED BY LONELY PLANET GLOBAL LIMITED

Publishing Director
**Piers Pickard**

Commissioning Editor
**Robin Barton**

Art Director
**Daniel Tucker**

Editors
**Sally Schafer, Karyn Noble,
Jessica Crouch**

Illustrator
**Holly Exley**

Cartographer
**Wayne Murphy**

Authors
**Ann Abel, Sarah Barrell, Sarah Baxter,
Greg Benchwick, Lucy Burningham,
Garth Cartwright, David Cornthwaite,
Cass Gilbert, Sam Haddad, Ben Handicott,
Patrick Kinsella, Emily Matchar, Karyn
Noble, Stephanie Pearson, Manfreda
Penfold, Adam Skolnick, Nicola Williams**

Pre-Press Production
**Tag Publishing**

Print Production
**Larissa Frost**

Published October 2014

ABN 36 005 607 983
ISBN 978 1 74360 164 8
PRINTED IN CHINA
10 9 8 7 6 5

AUSTRALIA
The Malt Store, Level 3, 551 Swanston
St, Carlton, Victoria 3053
T: 03 8379 8000

USA
124 Linden St, Oakland, CA 94607
T: 510 250 6400

IRELAND
Unit E, Digital Court, The Digital Hub,
Rainsford St, Dublin 8

UNITED KINGDOM
240 Blackfriars Rd, London SE1 8NW
T: 020 3771 5100

STAY IN TOUCH
lonelyplanet.com/contact

Paper in this book is certified against the
Forest Stewardship Council™ standards.
FSC™ promotes environmentally responsible,
socially beneficial and economically viable
management of the world's forests.